THE FUTURE OF BIBLICAL ARCHAEOLOGY

D1234171

The Future of Biblical Archaeology

REASSESSING METHODOLOGIES AND ASSUMPTIONS

The Proceedings of a Symposium
August 12-14, 2001
at Trinity International University

Edited by

James K. Hoffmeier *&* Alan Millard

WILLIAM B. EERDMANS PUBLISHING COMPANY
GRAND RAPIDS, MICHIGAN / CAMBRIDGE, U.K.

Wm. B. Eerdmans Publishing Co.
255 Jefferson Ave. S.E., Grand Rapids, Michigan 49503 /
P.O. Box 163, Cambridge CB3 9PU U.K.

Printed in the United States of America

08 07 06 05 04   7 6 5 4 3 2 1

Library of Congress Cataloging-in-Publication Data

The future of biblical archaeology: reassessing methodologies and assumptions:
  the proceedings of a symposium, August 12-14, 2001 at
  Trinity International University / edited by James K. Hoffmeier & Alan Millard.
        p.   cm.
    Includes bibliographical references.
    ISBN 0-8028-2173-1 (pbk.: alk. paper)
    1. Bible — Antiquities — Congresses.   I. Hoffmeier, James Karl, 1951-
    II. Millard, A. R. (Alan Ralph)

  BS621.F88   2004
  220.9'3 — dc22

                                                        2004047168

www.eerdmans.com

To Harvey L. and Janice Miller
in appreciation for their support
for biblical archaeology.
Because of their generosity
the future of biblical archaeology looks bright.

Contents

CONTENTS

Preface

Biblical archaeology has gone through some turbulent times in the past several decades. In the late 1970s and into the 1980s, William Dever ignited a fruitful and legitimate discussion about the appropriateness of the discipline of biblical archaeology, especially as it had been practiced mainly by biblical scholars and theologians who had a religiously-inspired agenda and were not trained as field archaeologists. There have been many positive results from the ensuing debate, especially the concern for greater methodological precision, and many scholars are now less inclined to jump to unwarranted conclusions regarding the correlation of archaeological data with the Bible. On the other hand, there have also been many negative consequences from the debate of the past 15 years, the main one being whether biblical archaeology should even continue as a discipline. In 1999 the venerable American Schools of Oriental Research jettisoned the name of its semipopular journal *Biblical Archaeologist* after 60 years, replacing it with the bland title *Near Eastern Archaeology*. This move was undertaken over the objection of the majority of the membership. This expunging of the title *Biblical Archaeologist* was undoubtedly undertaken to provide ASOR with an inoffensive or academically correct title. Interestingly, Dever still is not sure what expression to use for what has traditionally been called biblical archaeology (cf. William G. Dever, "Whatchmacallit: Why It's So Hard to Name Our Field," *BAR* 29/4 [2003]: 56-61).

This name shift illustrates that the field of biblical archaeology has been dealt a blow from within its ranks. A second line of attack against biblical archaeology has been under way for the past two decades from outside the discipline. Here the assault has come from biblical scholars often known as historical minimalists, who have been inspired by postmodern literary approaches and tend to trivialize, ignore, or misuse archaeological data. Their extreme views, and the philosophical assumptions of these advocates, have been addressed in a compelling manner by Dever himself (cf. *What Did the Biblical Writers Know and When Did They Know It?* [Grand Rapids: Wm. B. Eerdmans, 2001]). Some of the papers in this volume will also serve as a response to the threat minimalism poses to biblical history.

In a climate of growing skepticism towards biblical archaeology and the historical worth of the Bible's narratives, the North Sinai Archaeological Project organized a colloquium in August 2001, hosted by Trinity International University (Trinity Evangelical Divinity School) in Deerfield, Illinois. It was titled, "The Future of Biblical Archaeology: Reassessing Methods and Assumptions." The scholars, whose papers appear in this volume, met along with others to discuss the crisis in biblical archaeology. They believe that it is too early to write the obituary of biblical archaeology, and that there is a bright future ahead for integrating archaeological materials with the study of the Bible. The participants, attenders, and presenters came from universities, such as Chicago, Wisconsin, Pennsylvania, Miami (Ohio), Harvard, Johns Hopkins, Andrews, and Liverpool; liberal arts colleges, such as Gustavus Adolphus, Wheaton, Regent (Canada); and seminaries, including Southern Baptist (Louisville), New Orleans Baptist, Denver, Hebrew Union, and Trinity. The disciplines represented in this group included Syro-Palestinian archaeology, Egyptology, Assyriology, Hittitology, Sumerology, North-West Semitic languages, Hebrew studies, historical geography, geology, history, and biblical studies. The unifying feature of this diverse group was an interest in biblical archaeology.

We maintain that biblical archaeology has been misunderstood by some as the archaeology of Palestine with a religious bias. The latter embraces every vestige of human activity from Palaeolithic flint tools to 20th-century rifles, but biblical archaeology is not concerned with either of those. Biblical archaeology is interdisciplinary in nature, and thus is not Syro-Palestinian archaeology, nor Assyriology, nor a branch of such fields. Rather, its focus is on the times and places, the physical remains and written documents from across the Near East that relate to the biblical text either as background and context or by more direct contact. More than a century of intensive exploration and research has produced enough discoveries, theories, hypotheses, and speculations for another century to consider! Yet new discoveries continue to be made, some strengthening existing evidence, some challenging earlier conclusions, all spawning fresh ideas. The contributors to this book believe that biblical archaeology still has much to offer, and if these papers stimulate advances in it their authors will be gratified.

The North Sinai Archeological Project, which organized this colloquium, is supported by the Harvey L. Miller Family Foundation. It was also the generosity of Harvey and Janice Miller, to whom this book is dedicated, that made both the colloquium and this monograph possible. The papers in this volume were prepared for that meeting and have been revised in the light of discussion there. The participants, religious or nonobservant, were invited on the basis that they held a positive attitude to the Hebrew Bible or Old Testament and would examine aspects of it, or parts of it, in the light of archaeological data from the ancient Near East. Some of the papers address methodological and philosophical questions surrounding the biblical archaeology debate, and others illustrate how their authors believe archeology and the Bible should be carefully and critically used.

This volume appears at the dawn of a new century and the third millennium. We hope that it sheds light on the recent debate and charts a positive course for the future of biblical archaeology.

JAMES HOFFMEIER
and
ALAN MILLARD

Abbreviations

AAR	American Academy of Religion
AASOR	Annual of the American Schools of Oriental Research
AB	Anchor Bible
ABC	*Assyrian and Babylonian Chronicles,* ed. A. Kirk Grayson
ABD	*The Anchor Bible Dictionary,* ed. David Noel Freedman
ABRL	Anchor Bible Reference Library
ABW	*Archaeology in the Biblical World*
ACOR	American Center of Oriental Research
ADD	*Assyrian Deeds and Documents,* ed. C. H. W. Johns
AfO	*Archiv für Orientforschung*
AHw	*Akkadisches Handwörterbuch,* ed. Wolfram von Soden
AJA	*American Journal of Archaeology*
AJS	Association for Jewish Studies
AJSL	*American Journal of Semitic Languages and Literature*
AkkGE	*Akkadische Götterepitheta,* ed. Knut Leonard Tallqvist
ALASP	Abhandlungen zur Literatur Alt-Syrien-Palästinas und Mesopotamiens
AnBib	Analecta biblica
ANET	*Ancient Near Eastern Texts,* ed. James B. Pritchard
AnOr	Analecta orientalia
AOAT	Alter Orient und Altes Testament
ARAB	*Ancient Records of Assyria and Babylonia,* ed. D. D. Luckenbill
ARM	*Archives royales de Mari*
ASAE	*Annales du service des antiquités de l'Egypte*
ASOR	American Schools of Oriental Research
ASORDS	American Schools of Oriental Research Dissertation Series
AUSS	*Andrews University Seminary Studies*

AV	Authorized Version
BA	*Biblical Archaeologist*
BaM	*Baghdader Mitteilungen*
BAR	*Biblical Archaeology Review*
BASOR	*Bulletin of the American Schools of Oriental Research*
BBR	*Bulletin for Biblical Research*
BETL	Bibliotheca ephemeridum theologicarum lovaniensium
BH	*Biblia Hebraica*
BHS	*Biblia Hebraica Stuttgartensia*
Bib	*Biblica*
BICS	*Bulletin of the Institute of Classical Studies of the University of London*
BIFAO	*Bulletin de l'Institut français d'archéologie orientale*
BiOr	*Bibliotheca orientalis*
BJS	Brown Judaic Studies
BM	British Museum
BMes	Bibliotheca mesopotamica
BN	*Biblische Notizen*
BoSt	Boghazköi-Studien
BRev	*Bible Review*
BZAW	Beihefte zur Zeitschrift für die alttestamentliche Wissenschaft
CAD	*Chicago Assyrian Dictionary*, ed. A. Leo Oppenheim et al.
CahRB	Cahiers de la Revue Biblique
CANE	*Civilizations of the Ancient Near East*, ed. Jack M. Sasson
CBET	Contributions to Biblical Exegesis and Theology
CBQ	*Catholic Biblical Quarterly*
COS	*The Context of Scripture*, ed. William W. Hallo and K. Lawson Younger
CRIPEL	*Cahier de recherches de l'Institut de papyrologie et d'égyptologie de Lille*
CRRAI	Compte rendu, Rencontre assyriologique internationale
CSSR	The Council of Societies for the Study of Religion
CT	*Cuneiform Texts from Babylonian Tablets in the British Museum*
CTH	*Catalogue des textes hittites*, ed. Emmanuel Laroche
DDD	*Dictionary of Deities and Demons in the Bible*, ed. Karel van der Toorn, Bob Becking, and Pieter W. van der Horst
DJD	Discoveries in the Judaean Desert
DMOA	Documenta et monumenta Orientis antiqui
DN	Deity name
DNWSI	*Dictionary of the North-West Semitic Inscriptions*, ed. J. Hoftijzer and K. Jongeling
EA	El-Amarna tablet
EBib	Etudes bibliques
EHAT	Exegetisches Handbuch zum Alten Testament
ErIsr	*Eretz-Israel*
FM	*Florilegium marianum*

FRLANT	Forschungen zur Religion und Literatur des Alten und Neuen Testaments
HAL	*Hebrew and Aramaic Lexicon of the Old Testament*, ed. Ludwig Koehler and Walter Baumgartner
Herm	Hermeneia
HNT	Handbuch zum Neuen Testament
HO	Handbuch der Orientalistik
HSM	Harvard Semitic Monographs
HSS	Harvard Semitic Studies
HTR	*Harvard Theological Review*
HUCA	*Hebrew Union College Annual*
ICC	International Critical Commentary
IDBSup	*Interpreter's Dictionary of the Bible: Supplementary Volume*, ed. Keith Crim
IEJ	*Israel Exploration Journal*
Int	*Interpretation*
IRT	Issues in Religion and Theology
JANES	*Journal of the Ancient Near Eastern Society*
JAOS	*Journal of the American Oriental Society*
JARCE	*Journal of the American Research Center in Egypt*
JBL	*Journal of Biblical Literature*
JCS	*Journal of Cuneiform Studies*
JEA	*Journal of Egyptian Archaeology*
JEOL	*Jaarbericht van het Vooraziatisch-Egyptisch Genootschap: Ex oriente lux*
JHS	*Journal of Hellenic Studies*
JNES	*Journal of Near Eastern Studies*
JPS	Jewish Publication Society
JRS	*Journal of Roman Studies*
JSOT	*Journal for the Study of the Old Testament*
JSOTSup	Journal for the Study of the Old Testament: Supplement Series
JSS	*Journal of Semitic Studies*
JSSSup	Journal of Semitic Studies: Supplement Series
JTS	*Journal of Theological Studies*
K	Tablets in the Kouyunjik collection of the British Museum
KAI	*Kanaanäische und aramäische Inschriften*, ed. Herbert Donner and Wolfgang Röllig
KBo	*Keilschrifttexte aus Boghazköi*
KTU	*Die keilalphabetischen Texte aus Ugarit*, ed. Manfried Dietrich, Oswald Loretz, and Joaquin Sanmartín
KUB	*Keilschrifturkunden aus Boghazköi*
LÄ	*Lexikon der Ägyptologie*, ed. Wolfgang Helck, Otto Eberhard, and Wolfhart Westendorf
LAPO	Littératures anciennes du Proche-Orient

MANE	Monographs on the Ancient Near East
MARI	Mari: Annales de recherches interdisciplinaires
MDOG	Mitteilungen der Deutschen Orient-Gesellschaft
MPP	Madeba Plains Project
MR	Map Reference
MSL	Materialien zum sumerischen Lexikon, ed. Benno Landsberger
MT	Masoretic Text
NABI	National Association of Bible Instructors
NABU	Nouvelles assyriologiques brèves et utilitaires
NAC	New American Commentary
NEA	Near Eastern Archaeology
NEAEHL	The New Encyclopedia of Archaeological Excavations in the Holy Land, ed. Ephraim Stern
NEASB	Near Eastern Archaeological Society Bulletin
NICOT	New International Commentary on the Old Testament
NIV	New International Version
NJPSV	New Jewish Publication Society Version (Tanakh)
NRSV	New Revised Standard Version
NSAP	North Sinai Archaeological Project
OBO	Orbis biblicus et orientalis
OBT	Overtures to Biblical Theology
OIP	Oriental Institute Publications
OLA	Orientalia lovaniensia analecta
OLZ	Orientalistische Literaturzeitung
Or	Orientalia
OrSuec	Orientalia suecana
OTL	Old Testament Library
PEFQS	Palestine Exploration Fund Quarterly Statement
PEQ	Palestine Exploration Quarterly
PIASH	Proceedings of the Israel Academy of the Sciences and Humanities
PIOL	Publications de l'Institut Orientaliste de Louvain
PJ	Palästina-Jahrbuch
PNA	The Prosopography of the Neo-Assyrian Empire, ed. Simo Parpola, K. Radner et al.
PRU	Le Palais royal d'Ugarit, ed. Claude F. A. Schaeffer and Jean Nougayrol
RA	Revue d'assyriologie et d'archéologie orientale
RB	Revue biblique
RHA	Revue hittite et asianique
RHPR	Revue d'histoire et de philosophie religieuses
RIMA	Royal Inscriptions of Mesopotamia, Assyrian Periods
RIME	Royal Inscriptions of Mesopotamia, Early Periods
RLA	Reallexikon der Assyriologie und vorderasiatischen Archäologie, ed. Erich Ebeling et al.

RS	Ras Shamra text
RSO	*Revista degli studi orientali*
RSV	Revised Standard Version
SAA	State Archives of Assyria
SAAS	State Archives of Assyria Studies
SAOC	Studies in Ancient Oriental Civilizations
SBL	Society of Biblical Literature
SBLABS	Society of Biblical Literature Archaeology and Biblical Studies
SBLDS	Society of Biblical Literature Dissertation Series
SBLRBS	Society of Biblical Literature Resources for Biblical Study
SBLSBS	Society of Biblical Literature Sources for Biblical Study
SBLWAW	Society of Biblical Literature Writings from the Ancient World
SBT	Studies in Biblical Theology
SCA	Supreme Council for Antiquities
SEL	*Studi epigrafici e linguistici sul Vicino Oriente antico*
Sem	*Semitica*
SHANE	Studies in the History and Culture of the Ancient Near East
SIC	Scripture in Context
SSI	*Textbook of Syrian Semitic Inscriptions,* ed. J C. L. Gibson
StBoT	Studien zu den Boğazköy-Texten
STT	*The Sultantepe Tablets,* ed. O. R. Gurney, J. J. Finkelstein, and P. Hulin
TA	*Tel Aviv*
TAD	*Textbook of Aramaic Documents from Ancient Egypt,* ed. Bezalel Porten and Ada Yardeni
TOTC	Tyndale Old Testament Commentaries
TynBul	*Tyndale Bulletin*
UF	*Ugarit-Forschungen*
VT	*Vetus Testamentum*
VTS	Supplements to Vetus Testamentum
WBC	Word Biblical Commentary
WMANT	Wissenschaftliche Monographien zum Alten und Neuen Testament
WO	*Die Welt des Orients*
WW	*Word and World*
WZKM	*Wiener Zeitschrift für die Kunde des Morgenlandes*
YBC	Tablets in the Babylonian Collection, Yale University Library
YNER	Yale Near Eastern Researches
YOS	Yale Oriental Series, Texts
ZA	*Zeitschrift für Assyriologie*
ZAH	*Zeitschrift für Althebräistik*
ZAW	*Zeitschrift für die alttestamentlichen Wissenschaft*
ZDMG	*Zeitschrift der deutschen morgenländischen Gesellschaft*
ZDPV	*Zeitschrift des deutschen Palästina-Vereins*

Contributors

RICHARD E. AVERBECK *Trinity International University–Divinity School*

THOMAS W. DAVIS *Cyprus American Archaeological Research Institute*

DANIEL E. FLEMING *New York University*

WILLIAM W. HALLO *Yale University*

RICHARD S. HESS *Denver Seminary*

JAMES K. HOFFMEIER *Trinity International University–Divinity School*

HARRY A. HOFFNER, JR. *The Oriental Institute, University of Chicago*

DAVID MERLING *Andrews University*

ALAN MILLARD *Liverpool University*

CYNTHIA L. MILLER *University of Wisconsin-Madison*

JOHN M. MONSON *Wheaton College*

STEVEN M. ORTIZ *New Orleans Baptist Theological Seminary*

BENJAMIN EDIDIN SCOLNIC *North Sinai Archaeological Project*

ANDREW G. VAUGHN *Gustavus Adolphus College*

DAVID B. WEISBERG *Hebrew Union College, Cincinnati*

EDWIN YAMAUCHI *Miami University*

K. LAWSON YOUNGER, JR. *Trinity International University–Divinity School*

RANDALL W. YOUNKER *Institute of Archaeology, Andrews University*

ZIONY ZEVIT *University of Judaism*

Biblical Archaeology:
The Recent Debate
and Future Prospects

The Biblical Archaeology versus Syro-Palestinian Archaeology Debate in Its American Institutional and Intellectual Contexts

ZIONY ZEVIT

The debate on which I intend to focus was provoked by a suggestion of William G. Dever in the 1970s. He proposed that what was then termed "biblical archaeology" should be labeled more accurately by a properly descriptive term: "Syro-Palestinian Archaeology." Presented initially in various lectures, his suggestion first appeared in print in the "Introduction" to *Biblical Archaeology*, a volume co-edited with Shalom M. Paul in 1973. There he stated that the term was intended to present a particular branch of archaeology as an "independent, secular discipline . . . pursued by cultural historians for its own sake." The second and the most usually cited reference to his proposal was in a lecture delivered at a theological seminary, published in 1974 as *Archaeology and Biblical Studies: Retrospects and Prospects*.[1]

Frank M. Cross presented a negative response to the suggestion in a small *Biblical Archaeologist* article published in 1973. Cross argued that the term "biblical archaeology" should be maintained because it best reflected William F. Albright's vision of the discipline. His article represented an attempt to maintain the *status quo* on the basis of Albright's authority.[2]

---

1. William G. Dever and Shalom M. Paul, *Biblical Archaeology* (Jerusalem: Keter, 1973). Dever, *Archaeology and Biblical Studies: Retrospects and Prospects* (Evanston: Seabury-Western Theological Seminary, 1974), 17-25, 34-43; "Syro-Palestinian and Biblical Archaeology," in *The Hebrew Bible and Its Modern Interpreters*, ed. Douglas A. Knight and Gene M. Tucker (Philadelphia: Fortress, 1985), 31-74. The adjective then cropped up regularly in many of his published studies.

2. Frank M. Cross, "W. F. Albright's View of Biblical Archaeology and Its Methodology," *BA* 36 (1973): 2-5.

Cross's views were countered and rebutted almost immediately in the next issue of the same journal. D. L. Holland argued that the terminology should reflect the actual discipline as practiced in the 1970s and as understood by its practitioners. Consequently, Albright's views from earlier decades, despite their prestige, were not relevant to the point at issue.[3]

The debate achieved a higher academic profile at an ASOR symposium held at the national joint meeting of SBL-AAR-ASOR in 1978. In a standing-room only session, biblicists and religiologists, many unfamiliar with the archaeological debate, learned of its existence and became aware of how the issues underlying it might affect their own research and perceptions of their research. Between 1978 and 1982, when the proceedings were finally published, Dever, a gifted and much-sought-after lecturer, continued to promote the change before many academic and popular audiences. From that point on, all interested scholars were able to engage the issues raised, pro and con, through the clearly written presentations.[4] Dever's paper "Retrospects and Prospects in Biblical and Syro-Palestinian Archaeology," in which he addressed himself to both biblicists and archaeologists, set the agenda for subsequent discussions.

Most important to the history of the debate is the fact that in 1981 Hershel Shanks presented a version of Dever's views in *Biblical Archaeology Review.* This was abstracted from Dever's writings and his statements in different symposiums, lectures, and private conversations between 1973 and 1980.[5] Shanks's short article in his widely-read magazine dumped what had been essentially an in-house, academic debate onto a very public platform.[6] Whereas only a few thousand people, academicians and their advanced students, may have been aware of the debate prior to Shanks's article, after its publication well over 100,000 people from all walks of life — a minimal guess

3. D. L. Holland, "'Biblical Archaeology': An Onomastic Perplexity," *BA* 37/1 (1974): 19-23.

4. They were published in *BA* 45/2 (1982) with an introductory letter by the then editor, Edward F. Campbell. Particularly relevant to this discussion is H. Darrell Lance, "American Biblical Archaeology in Perspective," *BA* 45 (1982): 97-101; and William G. Dever, "Retrospects and Prospects in Biblical and Syro-Palestinian Archaeology," *BA* 45 (1982): 103-7.

5. Hershel Shanks, "Should the Term 'Biblical Archaeology' Be Abandoned?" *BAR* 7/3 (1981): 54-57. In a letter to the editor, Dever reacted negatively to what he felt were improper representations and dismissals of his views; cf. *BAR* 7/5 (1981): 12.

6. *BAR* 7/5 (1981), the same issue that published Dever's reaction, carried pro and con letters.

Intimations of the tones that the debate would take were already present in a letter written by Harvey Weiss of Yale in which "biblical archaeology" was used as a derogative (*BAR* 5/5 [1979]: 15-16); and cf. J. Edward Barrett, "Piety and Patriotism — Secularism and Skepticism: The Dual Problem of Archaeological Bias," *BAR* 7/1 (1981): 54-55.

at the readership of the magazine assuming one reader per subscribed copy — were aware. The significance of the new platform provides the background against which the following analysis is to be understood.

Good reasons were elicited in favor of the change for which Dever called, and it had much support among professional archaeologists and archaeological cognoscenti.

1. Archaeologists generally use adjectives referring to a period (e.g., Chalcolithic, Middle Bronze) and/or geographical region (e.g., Babylonian, Egyptian) and/or culture (e.g., Hittite, Roman) to describe the focus of their work — never an adjectivized book title. There is neither "Beowulf Archaeology" nor "Iliadic Archaeology." In archaeological parlance, "biblical" was a vacuous word.

2. Individuals employing the expression intended "biblical" to refer primarily to the historical periods during which personages mentioned in the Bible lived in the "biblical world." This latter term became widely used in American scholarship under the influence of Albright. As Albright used "biblical archaeology," it encompassed all countries and cultures of the Middle East mentioned in the Bible or relevant to events portrayed there. Excavations in Spain and Syria, Tunisia and Arabia could be classified under its rubric. Used this way, "biblical" blanketed too much territory and was, as a result, not informative.

3. "Biblical" refers to nothing that archaeologists do as archaeologists, i.e., as experts in excavating, cataloguing finds, tracing the development and evolution of material culture.

4. In addition to describing the profession accurately for all of the time periods within its purview, from Palaeolithic through Modern Arab, "Syro-Palestinian" could serve as a catchy yet distinguished cachet, a plus for scholars applying to scientific and government organizations for excavation funding. This was no small matter. In American federal organizations and agencies where the appearance of impropriety vis-à-vis church-state issues sufficed to frighten bureaucrats, the new term could open doors where the traditional, parochial-sounding one could slam them shut.

Considering these sound reasons, it is difficult to comprehend why Dever's reasonable proposition encountered so much hostility and opposition a quarter century ago, why it failed to carry the day, and why it precipitated a debate. The remove of a quarter century helps clarify these matters by providing perspective. Additionally, archaeologists and biblicists have grown aware of how concerns not considered part of a proper academic agenda can and do influence scholarly work.

I group objections to Dever's proposal loosely under three rubrics: *institutional,* reflecting enlightened self-interest; *semantic,* reflecting language change as well as certain types of hermeneutics; and *theological.*

The following analyses of these objections are easier to comprehend if two relevant historical and sociological data are borne in mind:

1. American involvement in the excavation of sites mentioned in the Bible since its inception has been an overwhelmingly successful Protestant undertaking. The pioneers, William F. Albright, Ovid Sellers, William F. Badé, and James Kelso were Methodists and Presbyterians, and all, aside from Albright, were associated with seminaries. The post–World War II generation of archaeologists, many of whom are retired or senior scholars today, were also primarily associated with denominational seminaries or were graduates of such seminaries (as was Dever himself). They were Dever's archaeological colleagues.[7]
2. The overwhelming majority of *BAR* readers are Protestant. In 1979, 60 percent identified themselves as conservative and/or fundamentalist — some identified themselves in more than one category — whereas 41 percent self-identified as theologically liberal.[8]

More traditional readers of the journal, laypeople as well as clergy, were sufficiently versed by what they read to begin to ask questions within their own faith communities. Informed and partially-informed individuals knew to ask their ministers and professors of Bible and/or archaeology about *their* views on the debate. More zealous congregants and students also knew what responses they wanted. And what is more, professors and ministers were aware of this.

This convergence of demography, religious anthropology, and popularly presented information made it impossible to contain the discussion with its corollary issues within the confines of academic journals and meetings. A knowledgeable lay readership had turned it into a public issue.

7. Cf. an unsigned article, "In America, Biblical Archaeology Was — and Still Is — Largely a Protestant Affair," *BAR* 8/3 (1982): 54-56. The article reports on a paper by Gus Van Beek of the Smithsonian Institution.

8. Cf. *BAR* 5/3 (1979): 5 and the advertising throughout the years.

Institutional Objections

Most full-time archaeologists from the United States and virtually all from Europe and Israel were inclined to favor Dever's suggestion; biblicists and theologians — some archaeologists, and many others regular or sometime participants in excavations — were divided. The overwhelming majority of excavators interested in biblical periods who were working in Israel and Jordan were not full-time archaeologists. Most were employed at seminaries or denominational institutions teaching Bible or biblical theology and the like. They were reluctant to adopt and promote terminology suggesting or giving the appearance that archaeology was irrelevant to their work as biblicists.

Furthermore, the terminology proposed by Dever might have fostered perceptions of archaeology counter-productive to procuring assistance and release time from their own denominational institutions or financial support from generous patrons and private granting institutions, and may have been thought to be a disincentive when recruiting individual student and adult volunteers for digs. After all, excavating a biblical city simply has more panache than excavating a Syro-Palestinian one.[9]

Semantic Objections I

Among those who recognized the essential validity of Dever's concerns were people who wished to maintain the term "biblical archaeology." They argued on Albrightian grounds that it was both useful and meaningful when referring to Iron Age archaeology in Israel and Jordan. "Biblical archaeology" was appropriate because, although it alluded to canonical Scripture, the collocation was commonly understood as referring to a particular people in a particular place and time: Israelites in the Land of Israel from the Iron Age until the days of Ezra and Nehemiah in the Persian period, i.e., ca. 1200-332 B.C.E. (when the referent of "biblical" was the Hebrew Bible). It could even cover Jesus, Paul, and the early church (when the referent was the New Testament).[10]

---

9. As recently as summer 2001, archaeologists from denominational institutions indicated to me that they would procure neither private nor denominational institutional financial support unless they could make significant connections between their site and the Bible. Electing to excavate Iron Age levels of an identified biblical city was the safest route to financial support.

10. As "New Testament archaeology" increasingly gains favor because it is an unambiguous, marked term, "biblical archaeology" may evolve a more restricted sense of "Old Testament archaeology."

With this sense, it resembled terms such as "Roman" or "Greek" when used as branches of classical archaeology. Consequently, the debate was just so much semantic quibbling. The meaning of the expression was to be sought in how it was used, not its etymology.

This position reflected a way of maintaining intellectual and professional integrity while providing a reasonable way for individuals to function within the constraints of institutional pressures. It enabled individuals to be "biblical archaeologists" in the U.S.A. even as they understood that when in the field, working up data and publishing reports they were "Syro-Palestinian archaeologists."

Semantic Objections II

Complicating this delicate situation was the fact, generally unknown to people who came of age after the 1950s, that "biblical archaeology" was an old term, well established in biblical studies since the early 19th century, whose general sense was transparent to all. For example, in 1839, an English edition of Johann Jahn's *Biblical Archaeology* began providing generations of American seminarians and clergy the following definition adopted from Greek sources as diverse as Plato, Dionysius of Halicarnassus, and Josephus:

> Archaeology . . . considered subjectively . . . is the knowledge of whatever in antiquity is worthy of remembrance, but *objectively* is that knowledge reduced to a system. . . . In a limited sense [archaeology] has special reference to religious and civil institutions, to opinions, manners and customs, and the like.[11]

Jahn's book assumed this archaeological agenda and illustrated what it could accomplish using the Bible itself as its primary source and resource, but also ancient monuments, coins, the writings of Philo, Josephus, Rabbinic and some Patristic literature, and travel journals. For Jahn, archaeology could be done in the scholar's study.

---

11. Johann Jahn published an original five-volume *Biblische Archäologie* in German starting in 1802. In 1814, he published a one-volume abridgment in Latin, *Archaeologia biblica,* which was translated into English by the American poet and translator Thomas C. Upham in 1823. Upham's translation was reprinted with additions and corrections and a change in title after "Jahn" became a recognized name, until 1853. The quotation is from an 1839 edition published in New York by Gould, Newman, and Saxton.

Carl F. Keil noted the sources of Jahn's definition; cf. *Handbuch der biblischen Archäologie* (Frankfurt: Hender & Zimmer, 1858), 2.

In 1858, Carl F. Keil, a scholar whose exegetical works are still used in conservative circles, adopted a slightly different definition and understanding of the term for his own *Handbuch der biblischen Archäologie:* "We call by the name of *Biblical Archaeology,* or *Knowledge of [Biblical] Antiquity,* the scientific representation of the forms which life assumed among the people of Israel as that nation of antiquity which God had selected to be the bearer of the revelations recorded in the Bible." This knowledge, according to Keil, excluded history *per se,* but included physical geography; religious institutions such as places of worship, personnel, rituals, and calendar; social institutions such as houses, food, clothing; family institutions and organizations and concerns; and civil organizations such as law, courts, and army. The significance of this archaeology was to set forth the objective distinctiveness of Israel as a witness to revelation, but "the method of description must be historical in keeping with the historical character of biblical revelation."[12]

The differences between Jahn and Keil are explained by advances in the field that expanded the meaning of "archaeology." In 1801, Edward Clark set out to travel in the Holy Land in order to discover ancient cities and holy sites. He was followed by Ulrich Jasper Seetzen in 1802, Johann L. Burckhardt in 1809, and a host of others. The most famous of these, Edward Robinson, Professor of Bible at Union Theological Seminary in New York, first traveled there in 1839 with his former student, Eli Smith, an Arabic-speaking missionary. Robinson's literate, engaging three-volume book published in 1841, *Biblical Researches in Palestine, the Sinai, Petraea and Adjacent Regions,* laid the ground for a historical geography of the Bible. It became a best seller and was widely read.[13] Robinson demonstrated the possibility of identifying many of the sites mentioned in the Bible and, by implication, the accuracy and trustworthiness of the Bible. His work was taken as indicating that scientific research could verify biblical facts.

Progress in research did not stop with the publication of Keil's book in 1858. Jerusalem was explored and excavated from 1864 to 1867. According to the *Oxford English Dictionary,* "archaeology," referring unmistakably to dirt archaeology, is first attested in the *magnum opus* of the pioneering ethnographer E. B. Tylor, *Ancient Cultures,* published in 1871: "Archaeology displays old

12. Keil, 1-5.

13. Philip J. King, *American Archaeology in the Mideast: A History of the American Schools of Oriental Research* (Philadelphia: ASOR, 1983), 3-4; C. C. Lamberg-Karlovsky, *Beyond the Tigris and Euphrates* (Beersheba: Ben-Gurion University of the Negev Press, 1996), 26-29. Indeed, most of the travelers published either popular or scientific accounts of their travels, so that information about the Holy Land and the Bible was widely circulated in English, French, and German.

structures and buried relics of the remote past." The second German edition of Keil's book was translated into English as *Manual of Biblical Archaeology* in 1887.[14] In 1890, Flinders Petrie launched the first scientific excavation in the Holy Land at Tell el-Hesi. In 1892, excavations were undertaken at Gezer, a city given by an Egyptian king to Solomon. New excavations in Jerusalem were undertaken in 1894.

In 1896, J. G. Lansing published *Outlines of the Archaeology of the Old Testament,* in which he listed archaeology as a branch of exegetical theology: "Biblical Archaeology is the science of sacred *things* as over against sacred words" [emphasis in the original]. The "things" included the same subjects treated by Keil along with the antiquities of other nations "so far as these have any direct bearing on any passage of Scripture."[15] This volume emphasized the direct connection between "thing" and exegesis and, as in Keil's work, left history somewhat aside.

In 1906, excavations were initiated at Megiddo, a city fortified by Solomon and the site of Armageddon; in 1907, at Jericho, where Joshua's spies spent a night and where the "walls came atumbling down"; in 1908, at Samaria, the capital city of the northern kingdom built by Omri; in 1913, at Shechem, one of the first cities that Abraham encountered in the land and the city whose prince raped Jacob's daughter.

Between 1870 and the 1930s, after Heinrich Schliemann excavated Troy and claimed, with a publicist's sure sense of audience, to have authenticated Homer's stories, an excited popular audience expected reasonably that archaeology would provide physical substantiations of known past events as well as new information about unknown events and personages in the past.[16] Great discoveries from Greece, Egypt, and Mesopotamia, reported in the press and presented in museums, held promise for what Palestine might produce that was relevant to the Bible.

This attitude is reflected in a telling letter written by Archibald H. Sayce,

---

14. *Manual of Biblical Archaeology* (Edinburgh: T. & T. Clark, 1887-88).

15. John G. Lansing, *Outlines of the Archaeology of the Old Testament* (New Brunswick: N. Heidingsfeld, 1896), 4-5.

16. For example, the *Illustrated London News* carried major stories about the following discoveries: the Nimrud Sculptures (June 26, 1847; Dec. 16, 1848; March 31, 1849; March 2, July 27, Oct. 26, Dec. 21 and 28, 1850; May 29, 1852); Nineveh (Nov. 3, 1855); Halicarnassus (Oct. 24, 1857; Jan. 22, 1859; Oct. 19, 1861); Pompeii (Dec. 31, 1864); Wilson's Jerusalem explorations (April 24, 1869); Mycenae (Dec. 9, 1876; Feb. 3 and 24, March 24 and 31, 1877); Troy (Dec. 29, 1877; Jan. 5 and 12, 1878), Tell el-Mashkutah (sic!) and the Exodus (Aug. 4, 1883); Tahpanhes (Sept. 11, 1886) etc. Cf. Edward Bacon, ed., *The Great Archaeologists* (Indianapolis: Bobbs-Merrill, 1976); stories and illustrations covering events from 1842 to 1969 are reproduced in this volume.

Professor of Assyriology at Oxford. Sayce, committed to the assumptions and methods of higher criticism in his youth, had become impressed by the implications of archaeological discoveries in the ancient Near East. In 1898 he wrote:

> . . . Just as the archaeological discoveries in the Mediterranean had given a death-blow to critical theories about Homer . . . so similar discoveries were now giving the same death-blow to theories about the Old Testament and its contents which had been imported from Germany. *Subjective fantasies must make way for the solid facts of science which were at last being recovered.* [emphasis added][17]

Sayce's private comment points to an interesting leitmotiv that began cropping up in the writings of others: archaeology was set in opposition to higher criticism. I assume that this is because higher critics tended to date the authorship of biblical historiographic compositions to the postexilic and Hellenistic periods and to question the historicity of the underlying events.

In perusing books and booklets with titles approximating "biblical archaeology" written from the late 19th through the early 20th century, I noticed how their contents differed from Jahn's, reflecting a semantic drift in the term "archaeology" over 50 years.[18] "Newer" works were characterized more by the incorporation of travel reports about topography and sites, local peoples and their crafts and customs, and information about scientific and not-so-scientific excavations as it became available. In these, the difference between "archaeology" and "history" seems to have been that "history" referred to knowledge of past political events — in accord with the Rankian program for history writing that evolved in Germany ca. 1825-1850 — while "archaeology" referred more to the *realia* and processes of daily life.[19] Knowledge gained from dirt archaeology was included with the *realia*. It produced information that clarified philological archaeology and was applied likewise to illustrate and provide background for biblical historical narratives, all of which were considered accurate descriptions. To the extent that I am able to discern,

17. Cited in a short, published essay by David E. Hart-Davies, *Biblical History in the Light of Archaeological Discovery Since A.D. 1900* (London: Victory Institute, 1935).

18. I observed what was available in the stacks of the library at Princeton Theological Seminary in August and November 2000. Due to a shortage of books with the required two words, I included books whose titles indicated that they were dealing with similar types of data.

19. Cf. Edmund Kalt's *Biblische Archäologie* (Freiburg: Herder, 1924), a short volume focusing on political, religious, and social institutions in their geographical setting. Although written more than 60 years after Keil — it could be considered an updated abridgement of the earlier work — it did not refer to any dirt archaeology.

the 25 or so books examined were all written by biblicists, individuals involved in the study, exegesis, and theological explication of Scripture.

What changed over 170 years, from the time that Jahn published his first German volume until the emergence of the debate, was the content of the term "archaeology." The new meaning replaced the old in popular parlance *but continued to coexist with it in denominational settings* in the frozen term "biblical archaeology" along with the understanding of how such "biblical archaeology" was to be used properly in Bible study.[20]

Although it was not noted in scholarly literature and in public discussions, some of Dever's critics were simply unwilling to ignore part of the semantic field of "archaeology." Considering "biblical archaeology" a perfectly good term with a long tradition in biblical studies, ministerial training, and Christian education, they were not particularly bothered by issues raised by Dever and may have considered his call for change much ado about little.[21]

Theological Objections I

By the 1950s, under the influence of Albright, "biblical archaeology" had come to include under its rubric studies of the Ugaritic literary texts as well as the newly discovered Dead Sea Scrolls among which were the oldest known biblical manuscripts. These two discoveries from the chronological limits of

20. Forty-five years after Sayce, Siegfried H. Horn, an archaeologist with many years of field experience, echoed the exact same sensibilities in a popular volume that appeared both in English and German: *The Spade Confirms the Book,* rev. ed. (Washington: Review & Herald, 1980). Individual chapters, originally short articles in church magazines, featured titles such as "Discoveries in Nimrud Support the Bible," "Nineveh Confirms Bible Prophecies," "Where Was the Tower of Babel?" Horn, for example, writes that consideration of the Amarna letters "has given us . . . documentary material that had great influence in the later part of the nineteenth century in defeating Bible critics and in clarifying important parts of ancient history, especially during the period when such important issues for God's people were at stake" (109). The Amarna letters were also discussed by Hart-Davies.

For both Sayce and Horn, archaeological data, properly interpreted, trumped historical reconstructions of text-based scholars when they altered the presentation of history in the Bible itself.

21. About one-half of all institutions of higher education in the United States are church-sponsored or church-related. In many, if not most, of these schools, confessional doctrine and traditional theology determined the parameters of academic freedom whenever the content of instruction impinged on religious matters. The situation began to change in some of the more liberal denominational institutions beginning in the 1960s.

To the best of my knowledge, Dever never addressed himself to the institutional settings and environments within which his call for change would have to be implemented.

the biblical period shed crucial light on the cultural background and literary history of ancient Israel and on the textual history of the Bible; consequently, they were thought to illustrate the Bible's historical accuracy in some vague, undefined way. Similarly, the physical presence of excavated objects, such as small altars similar to the tabernacle altar described in the Bible, figurines taken to be examples of images outlawed by biblical legislation, and material evidence for sequences of events such as the destruction of a Canaanite city at the beginning of the Iron Age, were taken as mute testimony to the accuracy of what was written about them in biblical books.

Conservative scholars in particular, but liberal scholars as well, assumed that if archaeology could demonstrate that something might have occurred, that was proof sufficient that it had occurred if the Bible so indicated.[22] The halo effect of such thinking in combination with the conception of "biblical archaeology" as a handmaiden of exegesis continued to extend the authenticating implications of dirt archaeology from particular details about *realia* to features of nonmaterial culture such as history, historiography, and theology.[23]

This testimony became grist for the mills of the liberal, positivistic "biblical theology" movement that achieved great popularity starting in the 1950s and has had a profound influence on what has been taught subsequently in both Christian and non-Orthodox Jewish settings since.

Distinguishing this movement from more conservative approaches was its ability to discern a difference between the reliability and accuracy of the Bible's historical descriptions as tested by archaeological investigations and the theological predications of the text.[24] Predications were raised to

---

22. Cf. King, 83, regarding the approach of Melvin Kyle, a conservative biblicist long associated with Albright and American archaeology in the Holy Land.

Historically, the American Schools of Oriental Research, an umbrella organization coordinating and encouraging American excavations in the Holy Land, but not only there, was founded primarily by large universities, not seminaries, and major excavations were undertaken primarily by universities (cf. King, 27). Although universities tended to attract the more liberal scholars, many ending up there came from seminary backgrounds and sometimes from seminary careers. Thus, those lining up on different sides of this debate cannot be distinguished easily by their academic affiliation. Finally, I think it erroneous to assume that only individuals concerned with inerrancy aligned themselves with a positivistic agenda or adopted some form of the "Bible is true" attitude.

23. See James C. Moyer and Victor H. Matthews, "The Use and Abuse of Archaeology in Current Bible Handbooks," *BA* 48 (1985): 149-59; "The Use and Abuse of Archaeology in Current One-volume Bible Dictionaries," *BA* 48 (1985): 222-37. Many of the abuses sighted and cited by these authors address the older, traditional use of archaeological material in denominational settings.

24. This description is borrowed from Walter P. Weaver, who used it to suggest how the

prominence as "proclamation," while events tested and not found wanting were esteemed as witnesses to the proclamation. Events found wanting, such as the enslavement of Israelites in Egypt, were defined as "myth," their lack of historicity ignored, and they were milked for their kerygmatic predications alone.

Among this movement's more influential leaders were George Ernest Wright, a noted archaeologist and theologian who published *God Who Acts: Biblical Theology as Recital* in 1952, and John Bright, known primarily as author of the well-written and highly regarded *A History of Israel,* first published in 1959.[25] Both Wright and Bright followed tendencies well developed in some publications of their own teacher Albright, who, concerned about the diminished role of the Bible in the church, expressed his desire to increase its influence through his own work.[26] Indeed, in 1967 Bright argued that the authority to interpret Scripture had passed from professional theologians to those who were masters of the philological-historical method of studying Scripture developed during the 20th century, a method that included control of data from excavations.[27] Bright's history, with its potent mix of history and

---

historical impasse caused by archaeology might be addressed theologically in the 1990s. Cf. Walter P. Weaver, "The Archaeology of Palestine and the Archaeology of Faith: Between a Rock and a Hard Place," in *What Has Archaeology to Do with Faith?* ed. James H. Charlesworth and Weaver (Philadelphia: Trinity Press International, 1992), 75-111, esp. the section entitled "The Failure of Archaeology as an Apologetic Strategy," 89-105.

25. George Ernest Wright, *God Who Acts: Biblical Theology as Recital.* SBT 8 (London: SCM, 1952); John Bright, *A History of Israel* (Philadelphia: Westminster, 1959). Although Wright's book was less popular than Bright's, the phrase "God who acts" remains current in discussions of biblical thinking and theology. In liberal Jewish thought, it fit nicely with late-19th-century notions and slogans of "revelation through/in history" that remain current.

Wright's book, heavily influenced by Gerhard von Rad's notions of cultic recitation, appeared more interested in the verisimilitude of events crucial to the ancient and contemporary faith communities and less interested in actual occurrences; Bright's reversed the emphases. Cf. also William G. Dever, "Biblical Theology and Biblical Archaeology: An Appreciation of G. Ernest Wright," *HTR* 73 (1980): 1-15, esp. 1-7. Cf. Burke O. Long, *Planting and Reaping Albright: Politics, Ideology, and Interpreting the Bible* (University Park: Pennsylvania State University Press, 1997), 15-70.

American "biblical theology" was independent of the similar movement in England almost 30 years earlier. Both, however, were similar responses to similarly perceived problems. Cf. Robert C. Dentan, *Preface to Old Testament Theology,* rev. ed. (New York: Seabury, 1963); James Barr, *The Concept of Biblical Theology: An Old Testament Perspective* (London: SCM, 1999), 27-52, 312-29, 497-60.

26. William F. Albright, "Archaeology Confronts Biblical Criticism," *American Scholar* 7 (1938): 176-88, esp. 182-88; Long, 111-48.

27. John Bright, *The Authority of the Old Testament* (Nashville: Abingdon, 1967), 42.

theology, is still required reading in some institutions training ministers and rabbis.[28]

To the extent that theologians were bound to the constructive, upbeat positivism of "biblical theology," they could not function without "biblical archaeology." In adopting Dever's proposal, much might be lost and nothing perceptible gained.

Theological Objections II

Although Dever framed his proposal in the secular language of the academy, his audiences at the joint annual meetings of the Society for Biblical Literature and American Academy of Religion consisted of men and women teaching primarily in denominational institutions.

It is useful to recall that what has been called the AAR since 1963 was formerly called NABI, the National Association of Bible Instructors, whose *Journal of Bible and Religion* had the following slogan: "To Foster Religion in Education."[29] This journal continued to function until replaced by *Journal of the American Academy of Religion* in 1967. Although the name-change from NABI to AAR reflects the significant shift in the understanding of what is meant by religion and of the connection between religion and the Bible, a large conservative element remained within the AAR when Dever broached his proposal. Additionally, many AAR members then, as now, were also members of SBL. Consequently, the majority of his audience was most likely sensitive to currents running through American religion at the time. It was a rough period for many denominations.

Between 1964 and 1984, years of rapid growth in the population of the U.S., the percentage of Catholics in the American population dropped from 47 to 30 percent and of Protestants from 57 to 53 percent.[30] The period was

28. Although deceased, Bright continues to influence seminarians through the 4th edition of *A History of Ancient Israel* (Louisville: Westminster John Knox, 2000).

29. NABI itself was an evolved form of the Association of Biblical Instructors in American Colleges and Secondary Schools (1909-1922). Cf. Jonathan Z. Smith, "Bible and Religion," *CSSR Bulletin* 29/4 (2000): 87-93. This essay was delivered originally as a plenary address to the annual SBL meeting in 1999.

30. Cf. Andrew M. Greeley, *Religious Change in America* (Cambridge, Mass.: Harvard University Press, 1989), 18-19 and fig. 2.1.

From 1960 through 1973, the U.S. population grew by about 35 million, from 175 million to 210,410,000. Although the population of both Catholic and Protestant churches grew with the population, their rate of growth lagged significantly behind the general growth curve. Jew-

one in which people moved between churches and denominations, and in which people moved out of churches completely. Conservatives were becoming liberal, liberals conservative, and many nonaffiliated. Much of this change was due to the theological pluralism that exists within churches but not always within individual congregations or parishes. The movement between denominations may be explained also as due to the maturation of the baby-boomers and to what religiologists consider a function of youthful religion.[31]

As a consequence of this movement, there were gainers and losers among the large Protestant groups. Those that gained membership were Assemblies of God, Seventh Day Adventists, and Southern Baptists; those that lost were Episcopalians, Presbyterian U.S. and United Presbyterian, United Church of Christ, and United Methodists.[32] The drift was clearly toward conservative churches committed to literal interpretations of the Bible and toward churches staunch in maintaining traditional religious convictions despite new ideas and less willing to accommodate their views when challenged by new ideas. Similar movements were afoot in Catholicism and Judaism, but neither of these diverse faith communities were so vested in and committed to literal interpretations as were some Protestant ones.[33]

---

ish population remained flat. Cf. Jackson W. Carrell, "Continuity and Change: The Shape of Religious Life in the United States, 1950 to the Present," in *Religion in America, 1950 to the Present,* ed. Carrell, Douglas W. Johnson, and Martin E. Marty (San Francisco: Harper & Row, 1979), 12 fig. 1.

31. Greeley, 21.

32. Carrell, 13-14.

33. The scholastic traditions in Catholicism and Judaism provided intellectual space and tolerance for new ideas and interpretations emerging from 19th- and 20th-century research in Bible and archaeology. Paragraphs 35-36 of the papal encyclical *Divino Afflante Spiritu* issued in 1943 stated that the literal sense of a passage in the ancient writings is not always obvious and that it needs to be established with the aid of history, archaeology, ethnology, and other sciences. This document officially freed Catholic biblical scholars to go their own way, unhindered by dogmatic theology.

For Judaism, the rabbinic notion that the Torah has "70 faces" and the tradition of printing one or more conflicting interpretations of the literal meaning of any text (i.e., *peshat*) on the same page made for the tolerance of many "literal" interpretations. If a given individual did not like a particular "modern" interpretation, he could dismiss it as an unfounded *derash* (i.e., a homiletic or fanciful interpretation).

Among conservative Protestants, a key passage invoked in discussions was 2 Tim. 3:16. It could be interpreted in a manner that allowed scholars to propose a range of interpretations of biblical texts that included archaeological considerations. Some explained that the usefulness of Scripture — all of which was inspired and held to be without error, for teaching, reproof, correction, and training — depended on its meaning, which had to be established on the basis of the original languages and texts.

To the extent that biblical dirt archaeology as presented by Bright and interpreted by biblical theologians had emphasized the positive connectedness between archaeological results and depictions in narratives, and because it performed a useful exegetical and educational function, there was no reason for conservatives to relinquish a productive term, and no reason for liberals to estrange their own members over what may have been perceived as a nonissue.

In proposing the term "Syro-Palestinian archaeology," Dever, a former student of Cross and Wright at Harvard, declared that he had given up on the old term with its associative links to exegesis and theological explication. He may have been perceived as attacking religion. He certainly was perceived — and correctly so — as attacking those arguing from denominationally normative (and/or biblical) theology to archaeological interpretation.[34] But, to the best of my knowledge, he did not raise this as a general issue in public presentations. Those discerning the implications of his case were capable of drawing conclusions on their own.

Dever lost the debate. It was almost inevitable. There are many more teachers of Bible in the world than there are archaeologists working in the Iron Age period, and the overwhelming majority of these teachers work in denominational settings with explicit and implicit theological programs that are *a priori* to whatever archaeologists might discover. The call for a change in terminology was intended to sever the connection between the archaeological and the theological, to disallow any claims that archaeology of the physical had implications for the metaphysical, to "academize" archaeology completely and distance it from "unacademizable" theology, and to delegitimize any interpretative authority that theologically-driven biblicists might claim over archaeological data.

Writing in 1979, James D. Smart, from the "liberal" Union Theological Seminary in New York, expressed concern about the negative influence of American university standards on what he termed the "science" of biblical theology: "An empire of invisible forces operates within the educational realm to move university study of religion toward a minimizing of what to

---

34. I recall sitting with an Israeli colleague at the 1978 ASOR symposium, mentioned above, attended by a few hundred people anticipating fireworks after Dever's presentation. The hue and cry raised by his lecture were incomprehensible to him. He asked, "Why is everybody so troubled by what he says? What's the difference? Biblical archaeology, Syro-Palestinian, or Eretz Israel archaeology, it's all the same." He was deaf to the theological resonance of "biblical archaeology," considering it an adequately descriptive term. *"Archaeologiya miqra'it,"* a direct translation of the English expression, is a widely-used term in Modern Hebrew but lacks any theological overtones. It is simply what some Iron Age archaeologists do.

the church is primary and an ignoring as irrelevant of any claims for biblical revelation or authority."[35] I take Smart's statement to be a kind formulation of the mindset that may be described charitably as inhospitable to Dever's suggestion.

Understandably, Dever's call for a change in terminology remained unanswered, at the time. By the late 1980s, after the decline of biblical theology as a dynamic and aggressive movement, the situation sorted itself out in the following manner: "Syro-Palestinian" archaeology became a broadly-accepted term referring to a discipline that usually requires either a combination of postgraduate training and a few seasons of field and lab experience or many seasons of field and lab experience and relevant publications. It remains restricted to professional circles and has become the term of preference in departments of archaeology, anthropology and history. "Biblical archaeology" evolved into a term used primarily in popular culture, in titles of public lectures, magazine articles, books, and undergraduate or seminary courses. The term came to signal that both textual and archaeological matters would be dealt with in presentations with this title, but not the proportion of archaeology to text and not the professional orientation of the author or lecturer. Considering that all Syro-Palestinian archaeologists working in certain historical periods must needs exploit information in the Bible when interpreting some of their finds, they are *ipso facto* biblical archaeologists; but not all biblicists using archaeological information who may fashion themselves biblical archaeologists can claim to be Syro-Palestinian archaeologists. Even Dever made an uneasy peace with this situation.[36]

As imperceptible as it was in the 1970s and 1980s, the debate had precipitated permanent conceptual changes. It disseminated the message that the Albrightian synthesis of biblical studies and archaeology no longer maintained its integrity: archaeologists and biblicists could part company.[37] In bib-

---

35. James D. Smart, *The Past, Present, and Future of Biblical Theology* (Philadelphia: Westminster, 1979), 153. The quotation, from a chapter entitled "The Uncertain Future," builds on a concern of Paul S. Minear about what would happen to theology in America by the year 2000 when, Minear predicted, all respectable theology would be done in university departments.

36. William G. Dever, "What Archaeology Can Contribute to an Understanding of the Bible," *BAR* 7/5 (1981): 40-41; "Archaeology and the Bible: Understanding Their Special Relationship," *BAR* 16/3 (1990): 52-58, 62. In an article, "Marginalia," published in *Current Research: Biblical Studies* 8 (2000), the terminological tension remains. He wrote: "We also agree that biblical archaeology (although I wouldn't call it that) ought to 'attempt to uncover the cultural context of the biblical authors'" (130).

37. By the middle of the 1980s Ugaritologists no longer determined research agendas with biblical exegesis in mind. In many institutions, Ugaritic was no longer viewed as related somehow to "biblical archaeology," a perspective leading to a declining interest in the study of the

lical studies there was a turning away from historical studies towards analyses informed by currents in literary theory; in Iron Age archaeology, a turning away from historical interpretations of excavation data based on biblical historiography towards political-economic ones based on social-anthropological models and theory.[38]

---

language and its texts other than the few famous parallels to biblical passages. As Ph.D. programs relaxed Ugaritic requirements, fewer people training in the U.S. studied the language and it became increasingly difficult to put together sessions on Ugaritic at annual meetings of the SBL.

Dead Sea Scrolls studies, aside from lower-critical matters, came to be recognized as having to do with postbiblical Judaism exclusively and as being increasingly irrelevant to the study of the Hebrew Bible *per se.*

38. Cf. Ziony Zevit, "Three Debates about Bible and Archaeology," *Biblica* 83 (2002): 2-9; "Anatomy of an Impending Divorce," *AJS Perspectives* (Fall/Winter, 2002): 5-8.

Theory and Method in Biblical Archaeology

THOMAS W. DAVIS

"Though this be madness, yet there is method in it." Polonius's shrewd observation of the seemingly mad Hamlet could equally apply to the tangled tale of biblical archaeology. Though our field sometimes appears to be madness incarnate, we too are bound by our methods.

One of the goals of this symposium is to try to articulate a reasoned interfaith response to the minimalist approach in biblical archaeology. By necessity, such a response must deal with theory and method in Near Eastern archaeology. I am a professional archaeologist, so it is to the archaeology side of the issue that I will address my remarks. Let me make clear my definitions. In current terms, I follow a "Dever-ian" view of "biblical archaeology" meaning by the term the place where archaeology and biblical studies interact. Historically, I refer to the specific endeavor exemplified at its height by William F. Albright and G. Ernest Wright. The term classical biblical archaeology for this endeavor is not inappropriate. For "theory and method," theory frames the questions and methodology explains how we will answer them, or simply put, "why we dig and how we dig."

Historical View

Self-awareness has come late to biblical archaeology. Albright and Wright did not articulate a clear theoretical and methodological framework for classic biblical archaeology. If you asked Albright what his theory was, he might have said that he was a positivist about archaeology and history. Wright would have answered that he dug to find the hand of God in history, at least in his early years. However, a careful study of the field expeditions and writings of the practitioners of biblical archaeology can allow a fairly clear picture to emerge of the movement's theory and method.

Classical biblical archaeology was, in simplest terms, a search for *realia*. In this context, realia is data gained by explicitly scientific methods; the results of rigorous experimentation, upon which sound and enduring conclusions can be built. It was an attempt to ground the historical witness of the Bible in demonstrable historical reality. Only when the archaeological data themselves became recognized as dependent on interpretation for their meaning (in other words, no longer seen as purely objective data) did biblical archaeology lose its foundation and collapse.

The theoretical base for the archaeology lay in the field of theology. The practitioners of biblical archaeology believed, albeit in different ways, that biblical faith, both Christianity and Judaism, depends on the historical reality of the events that displayed the hand of God. If the events, which the Bible interprets as the intervention of the divine, have no basis in reality, then there is no basis for believing in the biblical witness. Thus, any evidence that might help to buttress the hope of faith is welcome.

William F. Albright

Stephen Jay Gould writes that "The most creative theories are often imaginative visions imposed upon facts; the source of imagination is also strongly evolutionary."[1] William F. Albright's theory and method was an evolutionary growth out of his own exposure to Palestinian archaeology in the 1920s. His goal was to discover in the dirt the support for the biblical narrative. He saw the recovery of the world of the patriarchs as particularly important because this was the starting point of higher criticism.[2]

Albright saw ceramics as the key to dating the tells of Palestine and thereby documenting the presence/absence of sites mentioned in the biblical record. Albright was tutored in the ceramics of Palestine by Père Louis Hugues Vincent (whom Albright considered a "scholarly genius"),[3] W. J. Phythian-Adams, and Clarence S. Fisher. With that ability, Albright could an-

1. *The Mismeasure of Man* (New York: W. W. Norton, 1996).
2. William F. Albright, *The Archaeology of Palestine and the Bible* (New York: Fleming H. Revell, 1932).
3. *The Excavations of Tell Beit Mirsim, I: The Pottery of the First Three Campaigns.* AASOR 12 (New Haven: ASOR, 1932): xiv.

swer the questions of biblical history that became increasingly more important to him. In the study of pottery, the rational, mathematical mind of Albright found its archaeological niche. G. Ernest Wright explained the Albright approach in a review of a French treatment of archaeology and the Bible. According to Wright, the goal of the Albright method was to be able to date a "homogeneous locus" to within a quarter century on ceramic typology alone.[4]

The desire to date pottery with the precision demanded by the Albright method caused anomalies to be overlooked. The idea of a "homogeneous locus" is key to the issue. A locus was determined to be "homogeneous" on typological grounds, not stratigraphic ones. Albright lacked the necessary stratigraphic understanding, and the accompanying field techniques, to make a stratigraphic determination of a "clean" locus. Therefore, a locus was "clean" if its pottery assemblage contained only forms that on comparative grounds did not conflict chronologically. Such a "clean" locus could then be used to test other material. This could become a circular trap, simply reinforcing preconceived ideas about pottery groups. Pottery forms are assumed to be chronological markers, not cultural ones. The Albright method prevented stratigraphic experimentation, leading to methodological stagnation in Palestine. There was no need to develop field techniques that could expose and clarify micro-stratigraphy, since pottery typology held the promise of pinpointing intrusive material.

Wright, Albright's student, explicitly combined theology and archaeology in his approach to biblical archaeology. William G. Dever[5] has labeled Wright's career "schizophrenic" in the way Wright appeared to oscillate between the two fields. In reality, Wright's theology and his archaeology interacted throughout his professional life, and results in one field often had an effect in the other. Unlike Albright, Wright was an ordained clergyman who remained a churchman his entire life. Wright followed Albright's lead and studied Palestinian ceramics.

In a 1947 article, Wright first defined his view of biblical archaeology. He saw it as "a special 'armchair' variety of general archaeology which studies the discoveries of excavators and gleans from them every fact which throws a direct, indirect or even diffused light upon the Bible."[6] At the same time when Wright was formulating his views on biblical archaeology, he was making a

---

4. G. Ernest Wright, "Review of Barrois, *Manuel d'archéologie biblique*," *AJA* 44 (1940): 401.

5. William G. Dever, "Biblical Theology and Biblical Archaeology: An Appreciation of G. Ernest Wright," *HTR* 73 (1980): 1.

6. "Biblical Archaeology Today," *BA* 10 (1947): 7.

reputation for himself in theological circles. Wright was recognized as a spokesman for the movement known as "biblical theology." The most important aspect of his theology from the perspective of his archaeology is his focus on revelation in history. This theme received its classic treatment in *God Who Acts*. (It is important to remember that this work came out before Wright began to excavate at Shechem.) In the preface to the book, Wright says, "Biblical Theology is the confessional recital of the redemptive acts of God in a particular history, because history is the chief medium of revelation."[7] This then is the justification for Wright's archaeology — to better understand the "Mighty Acts" of God.

Wright approached archaeology in general as a historian, albeit a biblically-oriented one. "Archaeology is a branch of the humanities," he wrote. "Its aim is the interpretation of life and culture of ancient civilizations in the perspective of the whole history of man."[8] In the popular book Wright wrote on Shechem, the site of his major excavations, he elaborated on the connection of history and archaeology. "Archaeology is not an independent or isolated discipline; it is the research arm of the historian, and the discipline suffers when it is not treated as such."[9]

Nelson Glueck was another major figure in biblical archaeology, and his views on the reliability of the Bible helped give the Albright/Wright school an aura of fundamentalism. Glueck was an ordained rabbi, and a biblical orientation is never far below the surface in his archaeology. He held a very positive view of the historicity of Scripture, and from that standpoint he issued a famous (or infamous) statement: "It may be stated categorically that no archaeological discovery has ever controverted a Biblical reference."[10]

In a Festschrift for Nelson Glueck, Roland de Vaux, one of the deans of Palestinian archaeology, wrote a quiet paper that was devastating in its insight into biblical archaeology.[11] De Vaux accepted Wright's belief that the faith of Israel was founded upon the interventions of God in history, but pointed out that archaeology can only validate the event upon which the biblical writer has placed his interpretation, and part of that interpretation is

---

7. G. Ernest Wright, *God Who Acts: Biblical Theology as Recital.* SBT 8 (London: SCM, 1952), 15.

8. Wright, *BA* 10 (1947): 8.

9. G. Ernest Wright, *Shechem: The Biography of a Biblical City* (London: Gerald Duckworth, 1965), 36.

10. *Rivers in the Desert: A History of the Negev* (New York: Farrar, Straus, and Cudahy, 1959), 31.

11. "On Right and Wrong Uses of Archaeology," in *Near Eastern Archaeology in the Twentieth Century*, ed. James A. Sanders (Garden City: Doubleday, 1970), 64-80.

seeing an event as the act of God. De Vaux was at heart a man of faith, and he was willing to assume the veracity of a biblical account: "Lack of archaeological evidence would not be sufficient in itself to cast doubt on the affirmations of the written witnesses";[12] even if the footprints of the Divine were harder to find, they were no less valid. Placing himself in the middle between biblical archaeology and biblical criticism, de Vaux believed that compromise was possible: "There should be no conflict between a well established archaeological fact and a critically examined text."[13] The key was his definitions of "well established" and "critically examined," which allowed him to escape current or potential areas of conflict. In general, de Vaux believed that biblical archaeology had done very well in establishing the first part of the equation; it was the lack of a critical examination of the biblical text that de Vaux discerned in Wright and biblical archaeology. A major problem in biblical archaeology that de Vaux dwelt upon was the confusion of correlation between cause and effect. He used the example of Joshua's conquest. Clearly, many sites in Palestine were destroyed at the end of the Bronze Age, the time at which the Albright/Wright reconstruction placed the conquest. De Vaux pointed out the weakness in the reconstruction: that we have no clue archaeologically as to the perpetrators of the destructions claimed to be the work of the Hebrews.[14]

Wright's immersion in the field at Shechem started a process of profound change in Wright. He decided to use the methodology of Kathleen Kenyon, and this decision forced him to pay close attention to stratigraphy. Through this analytical process, Wright began to think that data and interpretation were more closely linked than he had previously been willing to accept. If this were true, then archaeological data were not the objective *realia* called for by biblical archaeology. In the 1968 Sprunt lectures at Union Theological Seminary, Wright addressed the question of revelation in history: "In the end, we can never measure this Biblical reality with Reality itself, whether we attempt this measurement in the field of value or in the field of fact. . . . God has not committed his truth to respond adequately to our tests."[15] In his Anchor Bible commentary on Joshua, Wright makes clear his realization that archaeology is not always an external, objective source for biblical study:[16] "With regard to biblical events, however, it cannot be overstressed that ar-

12. De Vaux, 70.

13. De Vaux, 70.

14. De Vaux, 75.

15. G. Ernest Wright, *The Old Testament and Theology* (New York: Harper & Row, 1969), 184-85.

16. Robert C. Boling and G. Ernest Wright, *Joshua.* AB 6 (Garden City: Doubleday, 1982).

chaeological data are ambiguous."[17] In short, Wright has disavowed a fundamental premise of biblical archaeology; *realia* could no longer be found in the dirt.

A student of Wright's, William Dever, followed the lead of de Vaux to its ultimate end, challenging the whole idea of a discipline entitled biblical archaeology. His main target was Wright's *de facto* equivalency of biblical archaeology and Palestinian archaeology. Dever found at Gezer that archaeological data speak only in response to a question, and that biblical archaeology was unacceptable as the dominant mode in Palestinian archaeology because it asked only very limited questions.

According to Dever, the new staff needed for excavation in Palestine would not ask the questions posed by biblical archaeology, but those raised by anthropological archaeology as practiced in North America. No longer would archaeology in Palestine be a subfield of biblical studies, relying on the Bible for its agenda. Syro-Palestinian archaeology (as Dever christened it, adopting a term of Albright's) would be treated as a field of general archaeology, subject to the same concerns and using the same methods. In his new enthusiasm, Dever, like any other evangelist, overlooked some of the problems of the new Syro-Palestinian archaeology. In the Winslow lectures, he made it clear that he thought that objectivity was a problem only for theologians, not archaeologists. Dever has since admitted that all scholars have this problem, and that Wright was not overly biased in his archaeology.[18]

Dever turned to anthropology for a theoretical base, finding it in the "new archaeology" (or processual archaeology) of Lewis R. Binford.[19] Ironically, processual archaeology is very positivist in its approach to the archaeological record. Dever embraced the new paradigm not because it included a more nuanced appreciation for the archaeological record, but because it was *abiblical*. As he became more versed in the argumentation, Dever did see some of the flaws associated with processual archaeology.[20]

---

17. Boling and Wright, 76.

18. *Archaeology and Biblical Studies: Retrospects and Prospects* (Evanston: Seabury-Western Theological Seminary, 1974).

19. William G. Dever, "The Impact of the 'New Archaeology' on Syro-Palestinian Archaeology," *BASOR* 242 (1981): 15-29.

20. William G. Dever, *What Did the Biblical Writers Know and When Did They Know It?* (Grand Rapids: Wm. B. Eerdmans, 2001).

THOMAS W. DAVIS

So Where Are We Today?

When all the rhetoric is stripped away, both sides in the maximalist/minimalist debate essentially share the same theoretical and methodological approach to the archaeological record: i.e., a somewhat modified processualist/semi-positivist approach. This is clear in *The Bible Unearthed,* by Israel Finkelstein and Neil Silberman.[21] Where the combatants disagree is on the value placed on the biblical record. I believe this uniform archaeological methodology is part of the problem.

I suggest that we need to break out of this dated new archaeology processual paradigm and enter the postprocessual world. Allow me to present guidelines for the archaeology side of the issue that may help us find a way out of the impasse.

1. *Biblical archaeology deals with two texts* (and I don't mean the Hebrew Bible and the New Testament). Ian Hodder has argued for years that material culture is a meaningfully constructed text.[22] Just like the Bible, the archaeological record can be highly fluid in its meaning and interpretation. Perhaps we can modify de Vaux to say "there should be no conflict between a critically examined archaeological text and a critically examined biblical text." Some have taken Hodder to mean that there is no correct or incorrect interpretation of such a work of literature. This takes the analogy too far. What Hodder means is that material remains are ordered according to a logic held by past peoples.

2. *Do not be "temprocentric."* We do *not* know what meanings a specific object or even a site carried in its own lifetime. What we may see as primary in an artifact's importance may have been unknown to the original users. When I was a graduate student, the question came up in a seminar regarding the contents of a specific structure discussed in an excavation report. When I questioned the interpretation placed upon it by the report, one of my fellow students said that "We are anthropologists; we ignore the idiosyncratic!" Too often this is the case in interpretation. We seek patterns, a legacy of our processual approach to archaeology, even when they are not there. Sometimes we even create them ourselves, then trumpet the "discovery" of them in the record. We must remember that we do not dig the "type" site. We excavate the remains of individuals. In fact, the idiosyncratic artifact or site may be more in-

21. *The Bible Unearthed* (New York: Free Press, 2001).
22. Ian Hodder, *Theory and Practice in Archaeology* (London: Routledge, 1992).

sightful than the patterned one. For example: Why should there be fired brick at Tell el-Borg? What does the discovery of jars stamped with cartouches of Smenkhkare and Tutankhamun at a small Sinai site mean? Wright was right when he warned the "pure scientists" that archaeology deals with human beings and thus must remain a humanistic discipline.[23]

3. *Archaeology is NOT an exact science.* Fundamentally, no archaeologist can repeat his experiment in the ground. My square from Tell el-Borg can never be re-excavated. Admittedly, my notes and records should be of a high quality that allows any other archaeologist to re-create, as closely as humanly possible, the sequence of excavation and the findspots of the material, but that is not a repeat of the excavation. We use many attributes of the true sciences in archaeology, but there is a danger in this. It can give a veneer of accuracy that belies reality. The use of radiocarbon dating is an example. A date given as 880 B.C.E. ±60 means an *equally valid* date range from 940 B.C.E. to 820 B.C.E.. Finkelstein and Silberman[24] do not seem aware of this in their discussion about David and Solomon. The dates from Megiddo need to be seen in this light. An average means nothing, but an overlap range does have meaning.

4. *An excavation is a dialogue, not a monologue.* One of the basic aspects of any archaeological endeavor is a research design. No excavation will enter the field without one. We all agree that data speak only in response to a question and that the question we seek to answer shapes our field methods. However, remember the military stricture that no plan of battle survives contact with the enemy unchanged. An archaeologist must approach a site with a question, but should not seek a specific answer. The danger comes when we try to dictate what the answer should be. We need to remain flexible and respond to the site formation processes and to the material recovered from the site. We must be especially wary when we apparently find what we seek.

5. *People do not live in square holes in the ground.* This is the answer to the question often asked in my everyday life as a CRM archaeologist when people visit a site: "Why did those Indians live in square holes in the ground?" Archaeologists are arrogant souls. We claim to know a site and interpret it from a very small window, often less than 10 percent of a site. We miss so much, and yet this does not prevent us from drawing

23. G. Ernest Wright, "The 'New' Archaeology," *BA* 38 (1975): 104-15.
24. *The Bible Unearthed.*

sweeping conclusions from our tiny windows. We can be dominated by our adherence to a very specific and time-tested field methodology to the exclusion of the real message of a site. We need to be willing to try new techniques such as the many varieties of remote sensing equipment that have appeared in the last decade.

6. *Complexity is complex; simple answers are too simple.* The current interest in complexity theory underlines an important guideline for archaeologists. The world of the Bible was a complex, multifaceted society. Archaeologists like to follow Occam's Razor and find the simplest solution to a question. An example of the dangers of too simplistic an answer is the current re-evaluation of Mayan history in light of the newly-developed ability to read some of the texts. We know now that the cause of the classic Mayan collapse was much more complex than environmental failure alone.

7. *The flaws of a model are not fatal to the source.* Too often, the biblical narrative has been forced to conform to an archaeological model. A glaring historical example is the Albright/Wright conquest model, an archaeological construct, being equated with the biblical record.

Dostoevsky, in *Notes from the Underground,* said: "Man has such a predilection for systems and abstract deductions that he is ready to distort the truth intentionally; he is ready to deny the evidence of his senses in order to justify his logic." We must look inside ourselves, approach archaeology with humility and not with arrogance, and be constantly alert to our own subjectivity. When we do that, we may indeed see the Mighty Works of God.

The Relationship between Archaeology and the Bible: Expectations and Reality[1]

DAVID MERLING

An American Perspective

Between the 1930s and the 1950s, those who believed that the Bible was generally reliable as a source for history had much to cheer.[2] Not only were William F. Albright and G. Ernest Wright, the most prominent American Syro-Palestinian archaeologists, proponents of the conquest theory, but a number of astounding archaeological discoveries had all but "proved" the historical nature of the Bible. The Amarna letters pictured the *hapiru,* which almost all scholars saw as, at a minimum, somehow related to the Israelites, pilfering Canaan in a way not too removed from the descriptions of the book of Judges. John Garstang had riveted the biblical world by his discovery of Joshua's walls at Jericho. And numerous archaeological sites had been excavated, all of which seemed to lend credence to the biblical account of the Israelite conquest.[3] The picture of the conquest was not the only area that had been illuminated. Connections had been made between the patriarchs and the Nuzi tablets; the Hittite treaties and biblical covenants; the Gilgamesh

---

1. This paper deals with issues similar to "The Book of Joshua, Part II: Expectations of Archaeology," *AUSS* (2001): 209-21. Cf. David Merling, Sr., *The Book of Joshua: Its Theme and Role in Archaeological Discussions.* Andrews University Seminary Doctoral Dissertation Series 23 (Berrien Springs: Andrews University Press, 1997), 238-62.

2. I use the dates 1930s-1950s in the broadest generic sense, knowing that one could criticize both the dates I have used and the generalities that I have drawn from this time period.

3. Cf. G. Ernest Wright, "Epic of Conquest," *BA* 3 (1940): 25-40.

Epic and the biblical flood — all of which seemed to underscore the reliability and reality of the biblical narratives.

In short, in too many minds the relationship between archaeology and the Bible was straightforward. While it was acknowledged that archaeology could not "prove" the Bible, that is what archaeology was: the physical re-incarnation of the biblical stories.

As we begin the 21st century, many of our colleagues would suggest that the relationship between archaeology and the Bible is estranged. Almost no point of the conquest theory is still accepted as reliable. The sites once connected with the biblical stories are seldom associated with those stories today. The most recent literature regarding the *hapiru* suggests no ancient connections between them and the Hebrews of the Bible. It has long been realized that Garstang mistook walls hundreds of years too old for Joshua's Late Bronze Age walls. Questions about the Nuzi tablets, Hittite treaties, Mesopotamian flood stories, and the Bible all produce more questions than affirmations.[4] What has caused this change in perception? That question is the focus of this article.

In William G. Dever's recent book, *What Did the Biblical Writers Know and When Did They Know It?*, he writes about the demise of biblical archaeology.[5] The poignant connection he makes is that biblical theology and biblical archaeology died at the same moment. What killed both of them was their dependence on the historicity of the biblical stories. Dever quotes G. Ernest Wright to say that "everything depends upon whether the central events actually occurred."[6] In the 1960s and 1970s, when Wright's own students — Dever being one of them — demonstrated that those "central events" did not occur, in Dever's view biblical archaeology and theology died. Dever writes, "Many of the 'central events' as narrated in the Hebrew Bible turn out not to be historically verifiable (i.e., not 'true') at all."[7] In short, the biblical text has been proven to be unreliable thereby killing both biblical archaeology and theology.

To make this point as concrete as possible and the issues of this essay clear, I will let J. Maxwell Miller frame the question using the situation of Ai/et-Tell. Furthermore, since Miller writes so well and speaks for so many others, I will allow the following quote to be a foil for much of this essay.

That biblical Ai is to be equated with present-day et-Tell is an obvious conclusion, therefore, and one which scholars were agreed upon before

---

4. For the sake of this paper I will focus on the issues of the Israelite conquest.
5. (Grand Rapids: Wm. B. Eerdmans, 2001), 57-59, 83-84.
6. Dever, 21; G. Ernest Wright, *God Who Acts*. SBT 8 (London: SCM, 1952), 127.
7. Dever, 21.

any excavations were undertaken at the site. According to Josh. 7-8, Ai was a fortified city at the time of the Israelite invasion (this is implied by the description of Joshua's military tactics and confirmed by the reference to the city gate in 7.5); it was conquered and burned by Joshua; and it remained "forever a heap of ruins" (*tel 'ôlam*, 8.28) from that day onward. However, archaeological excavations at et-Tell have indicated rather conclusively that the site was virtually unoccupied following c. 2000 B.C.E. except for a small unfortified village which stood on the old ruins c. 1200-1050 B.C.E. (Marquet-Krause, Callaway). Thus, if the conquest occurred at any time during MB or LB, Ai/et-Tell would have been nothing more than a desolate ruin.[8]

What conclusions have some scholars reached regarding Ai and the biblical story? "The archaeological situation at et-Tell cannot be squared with the biblical claims,"[9] and "what archaeology does not confirm, indeed, what archaeology denies, is the explanation provided by the narrative as to how the ruins came to be."[10]

While Dever and Miller are often on opposite sides of issues regarding the relationship of archaeology and the Bible, on this point they agree; the early biblical stories are not historically reliable. Again, repeating, Dever writes, "Many of the 'central events' as narrated in the Hebrew Bible turn out not to be historically verifiable (i.e., not 'true') at all."[11] While I do not want to make the dilemma more strident that it is, I do not believe it accidental that both Dever and Miller have acknowledged their evangelical roots and the loss of those beliefs within the context of this dilemma.[12] I am sure that in all paradigm shifts there are many factors that bring about such a change, but since both Dever and Miller have introduced the issue within this topic, I do not think their paradigm shifts are completely outside this arena. My point is, the change in perception about the Bible that has occurred from "archaeology demonstrates the reliability of the Bible" to "the archaeological facts are at odds with the Bible" is so severe that it has encouraged some to make the most major of paradigm shifts, from faith to loss of faith.

8. J. Maxwell Miller, "Archaeology and the Israelite Conquest of Canaan: Some Methodological Observations," *PEQ* 109 (1977): 88-89. I greatly admire Miller, and my extended use of this quotation only emphasizes how significant he is to biblical-archaeological discussions.

9. Miller, 89.

10. Miller, 89.

11. Dever, 21.

12. Dever, ix-x; J. Maxwell Miller, "Reflections on the Study of Israelite History," *What Has Archaeology to Do with Faith?*, ed. James H. Charlesworth and Walter P. Weaver (Philadelphia: Trinity Press International, 1992), 66-67.

Dever's definition of not "historically verifiable" as meaning "not 'true'" is a disappointing repetition of the illogic that I believe has created the presumed divorce between archaeology and the Bible.[13] Of course, we all know that neither the work of Judith Marquet-Krause nor the excavations of Joseph Callaway found any evidence of Late Bronze Age Israelites, neither their conquest nor habitation. Where scholarship has failed, however, is by not engaging in more discussion as to the why, or even more damning, in failing to continue to expose the nature of archaeology and the Bible and how they interact. The too-ready conclusion that has been reached is that the biblical stories do not contain reliable history.

The essence of that conclusion lies in the chasm between Dever's not "historically verifiable" and the "not true." This essay suggests that the present dilemma that many see surrounding archaeology and the Bible is a false construct based on false expectations. These false expectations of archaeology and the Bible were assumed to be facts by some scholars. Those same expectations have continued to drive research into wrong directions. For the sake of my own interest, this essay will focus on issues related to the book of Joshua.

Can Archaeology Prove the Bible?

One of these false expectations is that archaeology can prove the Bible. In my first class in archaeology I was taught that archaeology cannot prove the Bible, and I believe that there has been a general agreement that archaeology cannot prove the Bible. What I mean is that if we polled 100 Syro-Palestinian archaeologists as to whether or not archaeology could prove the Bible, I think we would find a clear majority that would reply, "No." Even Sir Frederic Kenyon, the father of Dame Kathleen Kenyon, writing in 1940 acknowledges that archaeological discoveries seldom bear directly or immediately on the biblical text.[14]

If archaeological finds seldom impose on the biblical stories, how is it then that some have concluded that those stories are in error, based on the archaeological data? I would suggest that the logic of Miller, as exhibited in his comments about et-Tell/Ai, contains within it a subtle acknowledgment of his belief that archaeology can prove the Bible. Miller's logic: archaeologists

13. Dever's critique of the text is focused on the earlier narratives. He finds historical materials in Iron Age biblical stories, which are the main focus of his book.

14. Frederic Kenyon, *The Bible and Archaeology* (New York: Harper & Brothers, 1940), 17.

did not find evidence of the biblical events of Ai at et-Tell; therefore, the Bible account has been disproved. The logic and corollary to this logic would be: the truthfulness of the biblical text has been disproved by archaeology; therefore, it is also possible that archaeology could have proved the truthfulness of the Bible. If this is not so, then the Bible suffers from double indemnity, damned if it does and damned if it does not. In short, whether Miller and Dever are willing to admit it or not, their acceptance that the Bible has been disproved is evidence that they believe that archaeology can prove the Bible.[15] Those who think that archaeology has disproved the Bible have used a false concept of what constitutes evidence and have fallen victims to poor assumptions/expectations.

No Evidence Is Nothing

One of the curious features of archaeological theory is the use of nonevidence as supporting data. Such nonevidence is used as though it had the status of true data, even though it is what does not exist. I have recently written on what I call "nonevidence," so I will not expand on that topic here.[16] On the other hand, it will be helpful to define nonevidence. Miller and Dever would point to the lack of evidence at et-Tell for the biblical story of Ai and count that lack as evidence. In sum, Callaway found nothing of the Israelites at et-Tell, so that is the evidence against the biblical story. It may be a trite response, but I believe nothing is nothing. Nothing is not evidence; it is nothing, or what I call, to give it some importance, nonevidence.

Almost 30 years ago David Hackett Fischer collated a list of the false assumptions used by historians.[17] One of those false assumptions was what he called the "Fallacy of the negative proof." Wrote Fischer, "*The fallacy of the negative proof* is an attempt to sustain a factual proposition merely by negative evidence. It occurs whenever a historian declares that 'there is no evi-

---

15. Linking Miller and Dever together in this article is no accident. Miller represents textual scholars who believe their interpretation of the Bible should be of greater value than archaeology, while Dever represents archaeologists who view archaeological discoveries as more neutral and, therefore, more valuable for interpreting the text. Together their views cover a broad spectrum of biblical scholars and archaeologists.

16. David Merling, "The Book of Joshua, Part I: Its Evaluation by Nonevidence," *AUSS* 39 (2001): 61-72.

17. I am thankful to James K. Hoffmeier, *Israel in Egypt: The Evidence for the Authenticity of the Exodus Tradition* (Oxford: Oxford University Press, 1997), 10-11, for alerting me to Fischer's book.

dence that X is the case,' and then proceeds to affirm or assume that not-X is the case."[18]

According to Fischer's dictum, to assume that one has disproved a specific point of an ancient literary account because one does not know of, or cannot find any evidence of, its historicity is a historical fallacy. To admit that one has found nothing is only proof that one has found nothing. Again, Fischer summarizes: "A good many scholars would prefer not to know that some things exist. But not knowing that a thing exists is different from knowing that it does not exist. The former is never sound proof of the latter. Not knowing that something exists is simply not knowing."[19]

Miller has used the nonevidence of the archaeological excavations at et-Tell to conclude that the biblical story is erroneous.[20] Miller's use of nonevidence is methodologically unsound and, therefore, says more about the nature of much of archaeological interpretation than it does about any biblical story. The lack of evidence cannot support or deny the reliability of a biblical story because it says nothing about why that lack of data occurred. Other explanations may abound. One cannot arbitrarily choose one of several possibilities and conclude that is the only answer.

The et-Tell/Ai Connection

There are also some methodological problems with the easy assumption that et-Tell is Ai. While I too assume that et-Tell is Ai, I am less sure than Miller. Consider how Miller reached his conclusion. He uses Gen. 12:8 as proof-text to locate the Ai of the book of Joshua.[21] I am surprised by Miller's connection of Gen. 12:8 with the book of Joshua, given the complexity he assumes for the text in general.[22] In one sense, it is Miller's unquestioning acceptance of the helpfulness of Gen. 12:8 that provides a basis for his disallowance of Joshua 8 as a historical account. There are many reasons why directions provided in Genesis may not be applicable to the book of Joshua.[23] However, Miller is safe

18. David Hackett Fischer, *Historians' Fallacies: Toward a Logic of Historical Thought* (New York: Harper & Row, 1970), 47.

19. Fischer, 48.

20. Merling, *AUSS* 39 (2001): 61-72.

21. Miller, *PEQ* 109 (1977): 88.

22. J. Maxwell Miller, "The Israelite Occupation of Canaan," in *Israelite and Judaean History*, ed. John H. Hayes and Miller (Philadelphia: Westminster Press, 1977), 213-84; *A History of Ancient Israel and Judah*, ed. Miller and Hayes (Philadelphia: Westminster, 1986), 76-79.

23. For example, later editors amended the text to fit a later relationship between two cit-

in his conclusions because there is no way to check the accuracy of Gen. 12:8, so he can assume by default that the Genesis location for the Ai of Joshua 7-8 is correct. With site identification, archaeologists and biblical scholars assume much more than the evidence dictates.[24]

The relationship between archaeology and the book of Joshua is less clear than many assume. The locations of most sites mentioned in the Bible are not so clearly identified as supposed, yet these assumptions are the absolutes from which archaeologists begin their investigations of the book of Joshua. Miller assumes the connection must be true, simply because archaeologists agreed beforehand that Ai and et-Tell are one and the same.[25] On the other hand, the main connection between these two sites is an untested expectation.

Was Ai a Fortified City?

Another expectation of the text is that some archaeologists believe that they are able to determine beforehand the nature of the settlements based on the biblical stories.[26] What fosters this judgment in the account of Ai is the reference to the "gate" in Josh. 7:5. Since the text mentions "gate," Miller, for example, concludes Ai was a "fortified city." While this is one possible conclusion, it is not a necessary one. At Megiddo (Stratum IX), a seemingly free-standing gate has been found in Late Bronze Age strata. Writes Rivka Gonen, "Free-standing gates, though not a common phenomenon, are not inconceivable, for gates served more than a defensive function. The gate was the ceremonial entrance, the town showpiece, and the focus of trade, public gatherings, litigation, news reports, and even cult."[27] It is also possible that Late Bronze Age Hazor had a gate without a connecting wall.[28] If the book of Joshua's stories reflects Late Bronze Age realities, when city walls may possibly have been pro-

---

ies, assuming they were the ones mentioned in Genesis; the geographical relationship was confused when manuscripts were copied. Consider that Gen. 12:8 does not provide directions to either city, only the relationship between the two cities. Would we recommend the use of a map of unknown date to a present-day driver trying to get from Philadelphia to New York City?

24. H. J. Franken, "The Problem of Identification in Biblical Archaeology," *PEQ* 108 (1976): 6-7.

25. Franken, *PEQ* 108 (1976): 6-7.

26. Miller, *PEQ* 109 (1977): 88.

27. Rivka Gonen, "The Late Bronze Age," in *The Archaeology of Ancient Israel*, ed. Amnon Ben-Tor (New Haven: Yale University Press, 1992), 219.

28. Rivka Gonen, "Urban Canaan in the Late Bronze Period," in *The Archaeology of Ancient Israel*, ed. Ben-Tor, 69, 70.

hibited by the Egyptians for military reasons, ceremonial gates could still be expected.[29] One could even argue that a ceremonial gate is implied in the story of Ai, since at the end of the story the gate itself is used for illustrative purposes (Josh. 8:29).

That there were ceremonial gates during the Late Bronze Age not associated with fortifications (i.e., walls) does not, however, necessarily suggest that the Ai of Joshua 7 and 8 had only a ceremonial gate. The Late Bronze Age Megiddo and Hazor gates emphasize only the possibility of a trap into which scholars, using unsupportable assumptions/expectations about the Bible and the finds of archaeology, can fall. One cannot, by the information provided in the story of Ai, conclude anything about the gate itself, whether large and imposing or small and tenuous. All that the biblical story tells us is that biblical Ai had a gate. What we know from archaeology is that at et-Tell no Late Bronze Age gate or city was found. What one concludes about the difference between biblical Ai and the so-far-discovered archaeological data uncovered at et-Tell is more theology than evidence.

Was Ai a City?

Just because Jericho (or Ai, etc.) is identified as a "city" does not imply more than what the *ancient* people called a city. Those of us who are part of Western civilization cannot help but interpret the word "city" with certain assumptions. Note how Gabriel Barkay places the emphasis on *our* (meaning modern readers) interpretation of city: "We tend to define cities as large sites, well fortified, where the building density is greater than in sites termed villages. In biblical times, however, any place built by royal initiative or housing a representative of the central authority, even a small site or isolated fort, was called a city *('ir)*."[30] Although Barkay has reference to the Iron II-III periods, his words seem even more applicable for earlier, less politically-structured periods, when a regional power was not in control. A city (or king) was what the ancients considered a city/king, not what modern readers interpret.

Consider that Shishak referred to the Arad fortress as a "city" or "town" in his list of "cities" conquered,[31] while the Iron Age fortress at Arad was

29. Gonen, "The Late Bronze Age," 219.

30. Gabriel Barkay, "The Iron Age II-III," in *The Archaeology of Ancient Israel,* ed. Ben-Tor, 329.

31. James Henry Breasted, *Ancient Records of Egypt* (Chicago: University of Chicago Press, 1906-7; repr. London: Histories & Mysteries of Man, 1988), 711, 716.

never larger than 50 × 55 m.[32] Unless we can re-create with exactitude the meaning of the biblical writers' words, it is safe to allow only the widest possibility of meaning to the few details of the stories of the book of Joshua. Otherwise, we may be transposing 20th-century-c.e. expectations while thinking we are interpreting the book of Joshua.[33]

Archaeology and Ancient Events

If anything, excavations of the past tell us that the one area where archaeology is least helpful is with events. Events are usually short-lived and, when described in the Bible, too little detail is provided to be of much help to the archaeologist.[34] Some might question this conclusion due to the many destructions that are clearly identifiable among archaeological strata found at MB IIC and LB IIC sites. In the same way, if literary texts are accurate, should we not expect to find LB destruction layers at sites, where destructions are suggested by those texts (e.g., the book of Joshua)? My answer to this question is that, again, we do not know anything substantive about the nature of the MB IIC or LB IIC destructions. Were MB IIC and LB IIC destructions caused by one-day events, as the book of Joshua suggests of its battles, or were they produced by prolonged sieges or repeated attacks, which indeed reduced each city to absolute ruin? While the evidence of MB IIC and LB IIC destructions may seem compelling, remember, archaeologists cannot agree on who or what caused these destructions, even though we have excavated dozens of sites that have provided numerous parallel destruction layers. If archaeology cannot conclusively answer the simple question of who caused the MB IIC and LB IIC destructions, how can we imagine that it can answer the complex questions we are asking it about the book of Joshua?

Does it not sound a little conceited for those of us who live thousands of years after an event to believe that we can read a story about that event, written by those who had absolutely no interest in, or intention of, providing clues of discovery of that event, and clearly predict what kind and amount of

32. Miriam Aharoni, "Arad: The Israelite Citadels," *NEAEHL* 1:82.

33. Consider Table 1, which lists the book of Joshua's statements about each conquered site. Note the lack of details. Should not so few specifics give pause to expectations of archaeologists excavating sites they think are mentioned in the book of Joshua?

34. Lawrence T. Geraty, "Heshbon: The First Casualty in the Israelite Quest for the Kingdom of God," in *The Quest for the Kingdom of God: Studies in Honor of George E. Mendenhall*, ed. Herbert B. Huffmon, Frank A. Spina, and Alberto R. W. Green (Winona Lake: Eisenbrauns, 1983), 245.

DAVID MERLING

Cities Destroyed according to the Book of Joshua
with Details of Their Destruction[1]

Site	Reference	Description
Jericho	6:20	wall fell in its place (וַתִּפֹּל הַחוֹמָה תַּחְתֶּיהָ)
	6:24	burned the city with fire (וְהָעִיר שָׂרְפוּ בָאֵשׁ)
Ai	8:19	set the city on fire (וַיַּצִּיתוּ אֶת־הָעִיר)
	8:28	Joshua burned Ai; made it a heap forever (וַיִּשְׂרֹף יְהוֹשֻׁעַ אֶת־הָעָי וַיְשִׂימֶהָ תֵּל־עוֹלָם)
Makkedah	10:28	utterly destroyed it (them) (הֶחֱרִם אוֹתָם)
Libnah	10:30	nothing specific about city destruction[2]
Lachish	10:32	nothing specific about city destruction[2]
Eglon	10:35	nothing specific about city destruction[2]
Hebron	10:37	he utterly destroyed it (וַיַּחֲרֵם אוֹתָהּ)
Debir	10:39	nothing specific about city destruction[2]
Hazor	11:11	he burned Hazor with fire (וְאֶת־חָצוֹר שָׂרַף בָּאֵשׁ)

---

1. Madon, Shimron, and Achshaph (Josh. 11:1) could conceivably be added to this list. It seems, however, that the pronoun "them" (Heb. אוֹתָם) of הֶחֱרִים אוֹתָם (11:12) does not refer to these cities, but to the kings, since "kings" is the closest antecedent to this pronoun and the pronoun has the masculine form. In any case, nothing specific in the text is said about the destruction of Madon, Shimron, and Achshaph.

2. Josh. 10:37, 39 could be seen as implying the total destruction of Libnah, Lachish, Eglon, and Debir, but there is no specific statement in the text that describes the destruction of these cities.

38

artifactual data will be recovered and, by which, we will then affirm or disprove the truthfulness of that account? At the same time, it should not be forgotten that the ancient event for which evidence is sought is not of some major architectural feature that took years to build, but, as in the case of Ai (Joshua 8), is an event that is presented as occurring in one day, and of what specific deed done we have little knowledge.

As to events, the biblical writers chose not only those they deemed helpful for their message; they also limited their recording of the events to those parts that met their objective. The entire episode of the actual destruction of Ai is presented in three Hebrew words: וַיִּשְׂרֹף יְהוֹשֻׁעַ אֶת־הָעָי ("And Joshua burned Ai," Josh. 8:28). This story does not tell us that the gate was destroyed. It does not tell us how much of the site was burned. It does not tell us that any specific building on the site was destroyed. It does not even inform us that there was a building on the site. For all we know, those living at Ai were living among the ruins of the previous Middle Bronze Age city, and the fire set burned the grass that covered its surface. After all, its name "the ruin" might have been a literal description.

There Is a Better Approach

To conceive of only one scenario from either the biblical story or the archaeological data is the result of little reflection. Frederic Brandfon has perceived the dynamic possibility of archaeology.

> It is just as likely that a sequence of events, such as the invasion of Canaan first by Israelites and then by Philistines, would leave many different traces in the stratigraphic record all over the country. It is also possible that a sequence of historical events may leave no traces in the stratigraphic record at all. Or it may be the case that the stratigraphic traces which were originally left behind by events have been eroded by natural forces or destroyed by later stratigraphic processes. It seems most likely that, in excavating strata of the land of Israel at the time of the Conquest or Settlement, all of these possibilities will be found as each site yields its own stratigraphic sequence. The archaeologist must therefore contend with the fact that the inference of historical events — the invasion of Canaan first by Israelites, then by Philistines, for example — is far from self-evident or self-explanatory from a stratigraphic standpoint. Again, the archaeological evidence does not *dictate* the historical "story" that can be told from it.[35]

35. Fredric Brandfon, "The Limits of Evidence: Archaeology and Objectivity," *Maarav* 4 (1987): 27-28.

The real dilemma, when archaeology and a Bible story do not seem to support each other, is that the archaeological evidence found, as interpreted, does not mesh with the biblical account, as interpreted.[36] Miller wanted to conclude that the book of Joshua is wrong in its story of Ai, and for one to suggest that either or both sets of data be altered is to introduce a "looseness in objective controls."[37] Miller's conclusions are reasonable, but not necessarily correct. The problem is that there is a gap between the text and the archaeological data.[38] This gap is what Franken called the missing "straight link" between the two.[39]

As Brandfon described the situation, scholars have misunderstood the nature of archaeological data, falsely assuming that archaeology is somehow more scientific than biblical studies. This misunderstanding is based on the correspondence theory, which supposes that there is no difference between what is found and the description of what is found.[40] When one comprehends that the description of the archaeological data is a theory, then the dilemma between the book of Joshua and archaeology is not so severe. The correspondence theory confuses theory with fact and, thus, confuses itself with "truthfulness." An alternative to the correspondence theory is the coherence theory, which "defines truth not as the relationship of statements to facts but as the relationship of statements to each other. . . . The criterion for truth becomes intelligibility and not verifiability through external checkpoints."[41] Such a change in philosophy puts the archaeological and biblical data in a better defined relationship.

All evidence of archaeology and the Bible (and other ancient texts) must be coalesced to arrive at any proximity of understanding of the past. To allow archaeology to rule over the biblical stories or textual criticism to rule over archaeology, or for either of them to ignore the thematic purposes of the biblical writers, is to talk long and miss much (none of which are new problems).[42]

Archaeology is a tool that can greatly help the biblical scholar better understand the background of the Bible stories.[43] It can, on occasion, provide

36. Roland de Vaux, "On Right and Wrong Uses of Archaeology," in *Near Eastern Archaeology in the Twentieth Century,* ed. James A. Sanders (Garden City: Doubleday, 1970), 70.

37. Miller, "The Israelite Occupation of Canaan."

38. Larry G. Herr, "What Archaeology Can and Cannot Do," *Ministry,* February 1983, 28.

39. Franken, 4.

40. Brandfon, 31.

41. Brandfon, 35.

42. Kenyon, 17.

43. Trude Dothan, *The Philistines and Their Material Culture* (New Haven: Yale University Press, 1982).

external evidence of individuals (e.g., Baruch, Mesha, David).[44] And archaeology can provide houses and temples and cities (including their defensive features) where biblical characters can live.[45] Yet, archaeology has limits as well. As Miller himself has suggested, archaeologists think archaeology can do more than it really can.[46]

Archaeology and the Bible

What archaeology often suggests is that the Sunday School picture of the Bible events might be wrong. Biblical scholars can be thankful to archaeology that they have been and are continuing to be forced to re-evaluate their interpretation of the text. An assumed picture of the Israelite conquest on the scale of modern military invasions, against cities the size of New York or Tokyo, must be modified. Dever rightly called this process of archaeology bringing the Bible to the real world of the past.[47] On the other hand, disproving any or all of one's preconceived ideas about the stories of the book of Joshua does not hint at that book's reliability.

Archaeology cannot determine the trustworthiness of theology or, as again Dever has written, "create or destroy faith."[48] De Vaux made the same point this way: "This spiritual truth can neither be proven nor contradicted, nor can it be confirmed or invalidated by the material discoveries of archaeology."[49] It is precisely at this level where those who think archaeology has disproved the Bible live in a Sunday School world.[50] Where the problem arises is in trying to separate faith from history. While some believe that is possible,

---

44. Baruch: Nahman Avigad, *Hebrew Bullae from the Time of Jeremiah* (Jerusalem: Israel Exploration Society, 1986), 28, 29; Mesha: *ANET*, 320, 321; David: Avraham Biran and Joseph Naveh, "An Aramaic Stele Fragment from Tel Dan," *IEJ* 43 (1993): 93.

45. Avraham Biran, ed., *Temples and High Places in Biblical Times* (Jerusalem: The Nelson Glueck School of Biblical Archaeology of Hebrew Union College — Jewish Institute of Religion, 1981); Aharon Kempinski and Ronny Reich, eds., *The Architecture of Ancient Israel* (Jerusalem: Israel Exploration Society, 1992).

46. J. Maxwell Miller, "The Israelite Journey through (around) Moab and Moabite Toponymy," *JBL* 108 (1989): 154; Cf. Franken, 10.

47. William G. Dever, *Archaeology and Biblical Studies: Retrospects and Prospects* (Evanston: Seabury-Western Theological Seminary, 1974), 28.

48. Dever, *Archaeology and Biblical Studies*, 42.

49. De Vaux, 68.

50. J. Maxwell Miller, "Is It Possible to Write a History of Israel without Relying on the Hebrew Bible?" in *The Fabric of History*, ed. Diana Vikander Edelman. JSOTSup 17 (Sheffield: JSOT, 1991), 96.

the presence of those who say the Bible has been disproved belies that separation.

Dever has placed the debate about the relationship of archaeology and the Bible in its proper perspective and has also spoken to the heart of the point I make here: "The failure was that of those biblical scholars and historians who were asking the wrong questions of archaeology."[51] To ask archaeology the wrong questions (i.e., to prove or disprove events mentioned in the Bible) forces it to provide answers about the text that it cannot possibly provide. Neither archaeology nor the Bible is specific enough to provide answers about the questions that speak to the historical reliability of the Bible. Unfortunately, I think that Dever himself has fallen into the trap of proving/disproving the Bible he so clearly sees.

Summary and Conclusion

In the past, readers of the Bible have expected too much from archaeology and too much from the biblical record. Archaeology is the scattered collection of what has been found, while the Bible is the scattered record of what would have fit the biblical writers' theological purposes. Rarely should one expect that these two agendas would intersect. When they do, scholars and the general public might applaud, but such intersections should not be expected and only cautiously accepted.

Those who discount the Bible stories because of archaeological data are working in outdated "prove the Bible mode," along the lines of correspondence theories. They likewise have not realized that archaeology and the Bible provide different information, which is largely incapable of being compared and, most often, elusive. Information from the Bible and archaeology is parallel, not perpendicular; it supplements/complements, but rarely intersects. For true understanding to emerge, we must look beyond a "prove the Bible" (or "disprove") synthesis and draw on a coherence theory model.

In the end, the relationship between the Bible and archaeology is fluid, not static. Both can help us better understand the other, but neither can, nor should, be used as a critique of the other. They must live separately and be blended and amended together cautiously.

---

51. William G. Dever, "'Will the Real Israel Please Stand Up?' Archaeology and Israelite Historiography: Part I," *BASOR* 297 (1995): 63.

Integrating Faith, the Bible, and Archaeology:
A Review of the "Andrews University Way"
of Doing Archaeology

RANDALL W. YOUNKER

In late 1995 I received a phone call from journalist Gordon Govier. He had just read an article by William Dever in *Biblical Archaeology Review*[1] entitled "The Death of a Discipline," in which Dever decried the decline of support for Syro-Palestinian archaeology, or what others have called "biblical archaeology." In this article, Dever charged that top-level secular academic institutions such as Arizona, Chicago, UCLA, and Harvard, among others, had failed to keep their programs fully operational. One of the few projects that Dever has anything favorable to comment on was the Madaba Plains Project (MPP), a long-standing excavation in Jordan supported by a consortium of Seventh-day Adventist colleges and universities, led by Andrews University. Wrote Dever,

> The major American project is the Madaba Plains Project, which has been running for nearly 25 years under the direction of a consortium of Seventh Day Adventist schools. I am full of admiration for the very progressive and productive project. I have supported it strongly from the beginning, and many of my graduate students are involved there (so much for Dever the "anti-Biblical archaeologist"). Yet the fact remains that this is an "atypical" American project whose success gives us little reason to be hopeful about the future of the field in general. Adventists have not only contributed generously to field work out of their devotion to the Bible, but as a group they have been remarkably astute and single-minded in

1. *BAR* 21/5 (1995): 50-55, 70.

43

training and placing young people in their own network of educational institutions. Unless other American institutions and organizations — theological seminaries, church-related colleges and other groups — learn a lesson from Seventh Day Adventists about seriousness of intent and necessity of support, the effect of their success will be lost on the rest of us.[2]

Naturally, those of us involved in the Madaba Plains Project were flattered by Dever's remarks. Since I had been listed in the article as a leader of the project and a student of Dever's, Govier wanted to know why Andrews had been singled out for such positive recognition by a leading Syro-Palestinian archaeologist not known for doling out praise easily. Govier also wanted to know how a relatively small university from a small denomination could mount such a major excavation project. The answer I gave was similar to the one I gave Dever while I was studying under him at the University of Arizona. At the time, Dever was in the midst of his campaign to change the name of our discipline from biblical archaeology to the more neutral Syro-Palestinian archaeology. One of the reasons he gave us (his students) for this name change was his hope that the more neutral name would attract more government grants and provide archaeology with a firmer financial foundation. As that dream failed to materialize, Dever became increasingly interested in why Andrews University was successful. I told him that the reason for Andrews' success in the area of archaeology is simply that Adventism had traditionally taken the Bible very seriously and, because of that, has been willing to invest heavily in a line of research that is felt to be essential to the healthy maintenance and growth of its denomination. That seriousness and respect for the Bible are derived, in part, from the fact that Adventism's theological system is founded on a view that takes the *history* of the Bible seriously. This is not to say that Adventists believe archaeology can prove the Bible — generally they don't believe faith needs to be based upon the verification of science. Nevertheless, because they believe history is an important component in the foundation of theology, biblical history is important to them. This means they are willing to invest considerable time and energy investigating both the historical claims that the Bible appears to make and the claims that modern historians make about biblical history. Because of the importance of biblical history to their belief system, early Adventists quickly saw the importance and value of archaeology to biblical research and, early on, began to incorporate archaeological findings into their research and writing. This also meant they were willing to invest in the training of competent archaeologists and to incorporate archaeology as an important part of the curriculum in their seminaries.

2. Dever, 53.

I will not say that the "Andrews experience" was the sole cause, but since his interaction with our team, I noticed that Dever began to soften his anti-biblical archaeology crusade and began to talk about a "new biblical archaeology." Dever began to realize that if biblical archaeology is to survive in the United States, churches, synagogues, and other entities that have a natural interest in and love for the Bible are going to have to take a lead in providing support. Of course, it was those very groups Dever had originally wanted to move away from. For Dever, these groups were the very ones who would send out untrained, Bible-pounding amateurs whose only research objective was to "prove" the Bible true, no matter what. To avoid the simplistic and parochial "prove-the-Bible" approach that typifies many faith-based institutions would require Dever to endorse an approach that Andrews had already pursued on its own — encourage these institutions to invest in top professional training and learn to use archaeology in an informed and responsible way.

I would like to trace briefly the development of Adventist involvement in archaeology, showing how the "Andrews Way," as some of our friends have called it, came about. In this brief review, I will follow only those scholars who contributed most directly to the trajectory that led to Andrews' major involvement in archaeological fieldwork. The history of this trajectory can generally be traced in a doctoral dissertation written by Lloyd Willis. This dissertation, which was chaired by Lawrence Geraty, was published in 1982 by Andrews University and provides a comprehensive study of Adventists' usage of archaeology in their research and writing from 1937 to 1980.[3] In this dissertation, Willis notes that Adventist use of archaeology in writings evolved through four phases. During the earliest phase in the early part of the last century, various Adventist writers tended to employ archaeology in an uncritical fashion in the service of apologetics. Because of the importance of history to Adventist theological understanding, there was a definite tendency to use archaeology to "prove" the Bible. For the most part, these early writers were ministers, untrained in archaeology.

This situation began to change when the seminary acquired its first academically-trained scholar in ancient Near Eastern history and archaeology. This person was Lynn Harper Wood (1887-1976). In 1934, Wood obtained a leave of absence from his duties as president of Emmanuel Missionary College (forerunner of Andrews University) to study archaeology and Old Testament at the University of Chicago. His M.A. thesis, entitled "Oriental Influences on Hebrew Religious Architecture," was completed in June 1935. He

---

3. Lloyd A. Willis, *Usage of Archaeological Data in North American Seventh-day Adventist Literature, 1937-1980*, 2 vols. (Berrien Springs: Andrews University, 1982).

immediately continued on with his doctoral studies. While pursuing his doctoral degree, Wood spent seven months in Jerusalem as a Jastrow Fellow at the American School in Jerusalem. During this time, he studied under Nelson Glueck and participated in the Tell el-Kheleifeh and Khirbet et-Tannur excavations. He functioned as expedition surveyor and draftsman (he had previously obtained a degree in architecture from the University of Michigan in 1909). His Ph.D. dissertation, "The Evolution of Systems of Defense in Palestine," was completed in 1937.

Immediately after completing his doctorate, Wood was asked to teach at the Seventh-day Adventist Theological Seminary in Washington, D.C. (the seminary moved to Berrien Springs to become part of Andrews University many years later). Wood taught archaeology and Old Testament background courses in the Religious History department from 1937 to 1941. In 1941 he played a role in the establishment of the new Archaeology and History of Antiquity department, of which he was the sole professor. The department grew, and Wood became chair from 1944 until his retirement in 1951.

Wood maintained his conservative convictions even after completing his formal training at the University of Chicago. In his writings for church publications, which tended to be apologetic, he reacted strongly against and rejected most, if not all, of the historical-critical reconstructions of Israel's history. Thus, it is not surprising that Wood responded favorably to much of William F. Albright's work and often quoted Albright in a favorable light — especially Albright's evaluations and dating of the Dead Sea Scrolls. As Willis notes,[4] Wood focused his writing energies on popular Adventist periodicals, so that his thinking did not reach many members of the Albright school. In the few scholarly, non-Adventist articles he published, Wood avoided his apologetic tone and his anti–historical-critical polemic, which was considerably stronger than Albright's. It probably would not have mattered to Albright, who seemed oblivious to the strict, faith-based conservative views of some of his friends and associates, such as Melvin G. Kyle. Albright was more interested in solid scholarship, and in this arena Wood was able to impress Albright with his chronological work on the Kahun papyri, published in *BASOR* in 1945. Indeed, Albright used Wood's suggested dates for the 12th Dynasty in his own article, noting that the closing dates for that dynasty were "now apparently fixed by Wood."[5]

Willis notes that, in spite of his major interest in apologetics, Lynn

4. Willis, 535.
5. William F. Albright, "An Indirect Synchronism between Egypt and Mesopotamia, cir. 1730 B.C., *BASOR* 99 (1945): 15.

Wood encouraged a more responsible use of archaeology in Adventist research and writing. He discouraged the sensationalism and inaccuracy that were exhibited in reports such as those that touted the discovery of Noah's ark. The responsible use of archaeological finds, in relationship to the study of Old Testament history in Adventist research and writing, was greatly enhanced by Wood's contributions. Nevertheless, there was a tendency to use archaeology to "prove" the historicity of the Bible. Wood believed that, if accurate archaeological information were disseminated to ministers and teachers, the result would be an increase in faith.[6] Wood's interaction with the scholarly world outside his denomination was minimal; instead, he focused his energies on the church.

The second major figure in Adventist archaeology is Edwin Richard Thiele (1895-1984). Like Wood, Thiele was a church employee who went back for further education at the University of Chicago. Early during his course work for the M.A., one of Thiele's professors, William Irwin, made some remarks impugning the accuracy and historical value of the chronological data that the Bible provides for the Hebrew kings. Thiele asked permission to examine this issue for his M.A. thesis, but was refused. Instead, he completed his M.A. in 1937 with a thesis entitled "The Beginnings of Land Transportation in Mesopotamia." However, Thiele persisted in working on the problems of the chronologies of the Hebrew kings on his own until he worked out a plausible model that appeared to successfully synchronize most of the Bible's chronological data with both itself and extrabiblical sources. The model showed enough potential that, in spite of their skepticism, both Irwin and Thiele's major professor, George C. Cameron, agreed to allow Thiele to tackle this issue for his Ph.D. dissertation. The result impressed both professors and ultimately led to the publication of Thiele's *The Mysterious Numbers of the Hebrew Kings.*[7] By discerning a number of ancient practices in counting the regnal years of kings and by recognizing that two different calendars were used in the northern and southern kingdoms, Thiele was able to propose a model that synchronized the chronological data in Kings and Chronicles that not only fit the internal biblical data, but also locked Israel's history into that of Assyria and Babylon. The history of the divided monarchy was placed on a firm chronological foundation. While some scholars have proposed variations or alternatives to Thiele's work (including Albright), many scholars such as Anson Rainey still insist that Thiele's work is the best on the subject.

Thiele's success in the venture was in part the result of his insistence on

6. Willis, 534.

7. (Chicago: University of Chicago Press, 1951; 3rd ed. repr. Grand Rapids: Kregel, 1994).

taking the biblical data seriously on their own terms. Thiele thus advanced Adventist use of archaeology by applying its findings carefully to the biblical text and by showing that the chronological data in the Bible, particularly those recorded in Kings and Chronicles (the Iron Age), were rooted in history and that the history of this period should be taken seriously. In contrast to his predecessor, however, he more actively engaged the scholarly community with his work and thus made a larger impact in the fields of biblical history and archaeology.

The third major figure in Adventist archaeology is Siegfried H. Horn (1908-1993). Horn was born in Germany, the son of conservative Adventist parents. His father, an aviation pioneer, was killed in an airplane crash when Horn was still a child. Although a Christian, Horn as a boy attended a Jewish primary school, where he learned Hebrew and developed a lifelong interest in the history of the Old Testament. Just prior to World War II, Horn was sent as a missionary to the Dutch West Indies. When the war broke out, Horn was interred as a prisoner of war by the Dutch authorities for six years. While this would have been a devastating experience for most, Horn, who was able to eventually build up a library in prison, used this as an opportunity to further his ancient Near Eastern language skills, study ancient history and archaeology, and write several books — in longhand! In essence, Horn treated his internment as an extended sabbatical — every scholar's dream!

After the war, Horn made his way to the United States, where he studied for a year with Albright at Johns Hopkins. However, thanks in part to his prison sabbatical, Horn's mastery of Syro-Palestinian archaeology was such that Albright indicated that there was nothing more he could teach Horn, and suggested that he expand his field of knowledge in Egyptology at the University of Chicago. Horn thus went to Chicago and completed his Ph.D. in Egyptology at that institution in 1951.

After completing his doctorate, Horn was immediately hired by what would become Andrews University as Professor of Archaeology and History of Antiquity to replace the retiring Lynn Wood. In 1953, Horn made his first extensive tour of the Holy Land, visiting virtually all the major excavations and their directors. In subsequent years, he worked as a volunteer at the excavations of (1) Max Mallowan at Nimrud, Iraq; (2) Yohanan Aharoni at Ramat Rahel, Israel; and (3) Claude Schaeffer at Ugarit, Syria. He was then appointed as a square supervisor at G. Ernest Wright's excavations at Shechem in Israel (ironically, William Dever was a young student volunteer under Horn at Shechem — I remember when Dever took me to Shechem in 1990 and showed me the first square he ever excavated under Horn's supervision).

After several seasons of working under Wright at Shechem, Horn determined to direct an excavation of his own under the sponsorship of his own university. After raising the necessary funds and securing the approval of the Andrews University board, Horn approached his friend Wright, who was then president of the American Schools of Oriental Research, and asked about ASOR affiliation for an Andrews University project. Wright assured Horn that if he acquired a competent field archaeologist to ensure the quality of the excavations, ASOR would be happy to approve and even cosponsor the dig. Roger Boraas was secured as the field archaeologist for the project. As for the site, Horn solicited the opinion of a number of leading scholars of the day who were more than happy to provide advice. Among the scholars who gave Horn suggestions were Albright, Martin Noth, Roland de Vaux, and, of course, Wright. Horn noted that the one site that appeared on everyone's list was Hesban, whose Arabic name appeared to be clearly derived from the Hebrew Heshbon. The universal interest in this site was not hard to understand. During the 1960s, the Albright school was in dominance, including its preference for supporting the conquest model for Israel's origins in Palestine. Jericho's results under Kathleen Kenyon were contradictory and disappointing at worst, and inconclusive at best. Several leading scholars thought that, if Hesban equaled the Heshbon of Numbers, then it might provide the evidence for the conquest that Jericho had failed to produce. However, the excavations found no evidence for any Late Bronze Age occupation — the time when Sihon should have been living there. Although disappointed, Horn and his team quickly and accurately published the results. Horn's honesty in dealing with results that were contrary to what he was hoping for gained important credibility for Adventist archaeologists, who because of their conservative Christian profession were viewed with suspicion in some quarters.

Another factor that helped the Hesban project to gain respect was the fact that it was the first major project in Jordan — indeed one of the first throughout the Middle East — to pioneer what would be known as a multidisciplinary approach in excavation. Beyond the usual stratigrapher, draftsperson, architect, and ceramicist, the Hesban project employed a variety of other specialists in areas such as geology, anthropology, paleobotany, and zooarchaeology. Much of the credit for this goes to Øystein LaBianca, who as a graduate student in anthropology was attuned to some of the new trends of what would become known as the "new archaeology." LaBianca was particularly interested in faunal remains (primarily bones) and the information they would provide about various aspects of ancient societies — especially their food systems. To Horn's credit, he allowed LaBianca and others to collect and analyze these materials. It must be noted that this was at a time when most excavations typically just threw out their bones and seeds.

In a sense, the innovative multidisciplinary approach provided the research team with some compensation for the failure of the excavations to shed any light on the historical question that was the principal motivation for Horn's selection of Hesban as an excavation site — the question of Israel's conquest of Canaan.

Another important result of the Hesban project is that it spawned a new generation of field archaeologists. Andrews University no longer just taught archaeology in the classroom, but was actually conducting its own accredited field project. This hands-on experience motivated a number of students to consider going into field archaeology for themselves. Some of Horn's more outstanding students included Larry Herr and, of course, Larry Geraty. Both would eventually go to Harvard — Geraty to study under Wright and Herr under Frank Cross.

The Horn period led to an important transition in Adventist usage of archaeology. While the project was largely motivated during its initial phases by a desire to nail down evidence for a biblical-historical event (the conquest and the date of the exodus), its failure to recover the hoped-for evidence led the team to examine other ways in which the data they *had* recovered could profitably be used to illuminate biblical history. This led to the great emphasis on a multidisciplinary approach that would illuminate the environment, social organization, trade, economy, food systems, and other aspects of this region during the Bronze and Iron Ages. If archaeology could not produce much in the way of direct evidence about the people and events of biblical history, it could at least reconstruct the background and context in which this history took place.

The next phase of Adventist archaeology is marked by the career of Lawrence T. Geraty. Geraty, the son of missionary parents, grew up in Burma, China, Hong Kong, and Lebanon. He received his B.A. from Pacific Union College, an M.A. from Andrews University in 1963, and a B.D. from that same institution in 1965. In 1972, Geraty received a Ph.D. in Old Testament and Syro-Palestinian archaeology, with distinction, from Harvard University.

Geraty, who joined the faculty at Andrews University, succeeded Horn as director of the Hesban project. Geraty then became the senior project director of the Madaba Plains Project, which succeeded the original Hesban project. The original team of directors included Herr from Canadian Union College and LaBianca from Andrews University. When Geraty left Andrews University for administrative duties elsewhere, Randall Younker was appointed the new director of the Institute of Archaeology, and joined Geraty, Herr, and LaBianca as codirector of the project. Douglas Clark from Walla Walla College also joined the team.

Geraty, supported by LaBianca, continued to move the project towards a multidisciplinary research design. While historical questions still remained, the experience at Hesban taught the MPP team that such questions are not so easily answered, and that broader research questions, including nonhistorical ones, offered a more promising result. During the next 16 years, MPP would undertake several extensive and intensive hinterland surveys, numerous excavations of hinterland sites, as well as the excavation of the major tell sites of al-'Umayri and Jalul. LaBianca has commenced additional work at Hesban. The al-'Umayri excavation is now directed by Herr and Clark, while Jalul is under the direction of David Merling and Younker.

In terms of Adventist contribution to archaeology, Geraty's period of leadership greatly accelerated the elements started by Horn. The multidisciplinary approach blossomed even more under Geraty than it had under Horn. Hinterland surveys not only documented archaeological sites. Rather, specialists whose work initially tended to be restricted at or immediately around the main tell now employed aggressive research strategies focused more on the hinterland. Botanists, geologists, zoologists, and ethnographers conducted research far into the hinterland to expand our knowledge of the context in which the ancient tells flourished. The survey and excavation at the prehistoric site at Azrak is one example of this new expansion. Geraty even more aggressively encouraged the growth of young scholars, going out of his way to make opportunities for professional growth and advancement.

Geraty's leadership of MPP led to the spawning of numerous other projects. Graduate students and senior staff members started a number of projects on their own under the umbrella of MPP, which currently has three major overseas tell excavations and numerous hinterland excavations and surveys. Projects such as Michele Daviau's excavations at Tell Jawa and Wadi Themed and Tim Harrison's work at the town of Madaba can be seen as extensions of MPP. MPP staff have also more than ever insisted on interacting with mainstream scholarship. ASOR's Committee on Archaeological Policy (CAP) approves our projects. We present our results at annual professional meetings and publish them in standard journals. And all of the senior staff are heavily involved in scholarly societies: Geraty is Vice President of the American Center of Oriental Research (ACOR) in Amman; Herr is co-editor for *BASOR;* LaBianca is on the boards of both ACOR and ASOR; Clark is chair of ASOR's annual program committee; and Younker serves on the ASOR board and chairs the nominations committee. Most recently Larry Geraty was elected President of ASOR — sounds like an Adventist mafia!

If I were to summarize what I have seen evolve as the "Andrews Way" of doing archaeology:

1. Be forthright with findings. Do not minimize problems or stretch interpretations of data to explain things away.
2. Do not make claims beyond what the data can support.
3. Be quick and complete in publishing results.
4. Engage and work within mainstream scholarship.
5. Include a diversity of people and specialists.
6. Take the history of the Bible seriously, but do not place upon archaeology the burden of "proving" the Bible.

Taken altogether, I believe these six guidelines are what lie behind the success of the "Andrews Way" of doing archaeology.

The North Sinai Archaeological Project's Excavations at Tell el-Borg (Sinai): An Example of the "New" Biblical Archaeology?[1]

JAMES K. HOFFMEIER

The Current State of "Biblical Archaeology"

The discipline of biblical archaeology has recently fallen on hard times. Beginning in the mid-1970s, Thomas L. Thompson[2] and John Van Seters[3] penned books that for many dealt a mortal blow to the historicity of the Hebrew patriarchs of Genesis. Thus began the slide down a slippery slope to historical minimalism that has dominated biblical scholarship for the past 25 years. Radical changes in the field of biblical studies were also unfolding. Hebrew historiography began to be redefined, and new literary approaches replaced older ones. The Bible was considered by some, like Thompson, Neils Peter Lemche, Giovanni Garbini, Philip Davies, and Gösta Åhlström, to be made up of prose fiction, legends, folk tales, theological treatises, and novellas, and thus devoid of history.[4]

About this time, William Dever, arguably the most influential voice in biblical archaeology since George Ernest Wright, began his campaign to reform traditional "biblical archaeology," separating it from "Syro-Palestinian" archaeology.[5] To make matters worse, biblical archaeology had not delivered

---

1. While this paper was presented on 12 August 2001, a few points have been added that reflect the 2002 season at Tell el-Borg.

2. *The Historicity of the Patriarchal Narratives*. BZAW 133 (Berlin: de Gruyter, 1974).

3. *Abraham in History and Tradition* (New Haven: Yale University Press, 1975).

4. For a review of this development and the views of these particular scholars, see James K. Hoffmeier, *Israel in Egypt* (Oxford: Oxford University Press, 1997), chs. 1 and 2.

5. Cf. "The Impact of the 'New Archaeology' on Syro-Palestinian Archaeology," *BASOR*

the evidence the Albright-Wright school thought it would in support of the historical claims of the Bible, especially regarding Israel's origins, a point not missed by historical minimalists.

Thus in just over 20 years time, the Bible's credibility as a source for Israel's early history had diminished, leading many scholars to reject the historicity of the sojourn-exodus tradition, the Sinai period, the military conquest of Canaan, the period of the judges, and most recently, the existence of the united monarchy of Saul, David, and Solomon. Needless to say, the relationship between archaeology and biblical studies had become seriously strained in the 1990s. This "falling out" is best symbolized by the American Schools of Oriental Research decision to separate its annual meeting from that of the Society for Biblical Literature and to change the name of its semipopular journal *Biblical Archaeologist* to *Near Eastern Archaeology* over the objection of a majority of its membership.

While skepticism dominates the field of biblical scholarship, it hardly represents the majority view of biblical scholars and archaeologists. But historical minimalists have certainly had a disproportionate amount of influence in the field, and they have managed to control the agenda. One result has been that those who approached the Bible more positively have been put on the defensive and have struggled to know how to operate. Whether working with texts or in the field of archaeology, one needs to think carefully about how to undertake serious biblical scholarship in the current climate that is, regrettably, characterized by inflamed rhetoric and *ad hominem* attacks. In part, one can understand why the tone of the debate has been so harsh — much is at stake, be it religion, tradition, theology, or even politics. Everyone realizes this reality but is reluctant to acknowledge it for fearing to appear to be unacademic, anti-intellectual, or worse yet, to be called a "fundamentalist" (a favorite label of the minimalists).

One of the aims of this colloquium is to address some of the issues that confront those of us who still think it is intellectually viable to integrate archaeological materials with the Bible. The outcome, I hope, will be to enrich each other and advance our discipline. This initial session provides the opportunity for some team members of the North Sinai Archaeological Project to present its goals, methods, and discoveries in order to receive the feedback, criticism, and advice of colloquium participants.[6] It is our goal to do "biblical

---

242 (1981): 15-29; "Retrospects and Prospects in Biblical and Syro-Palestinian Archaeology," *BA* 45 (1982): 103-7; "Archaeology, Syro-Palestinian and Biblical," *ABD* 1:354-67.

6. Thomas Davis, Benjamin Scolnic, and Stephen Moshier presented papers at the conference. The first two are published in this volume. Moshier's paper will be published in *Tell el-Borg* I (forthcoming).

archaeology" in a responsible and convincing way. Together, we can hopefully begin writing a new chapter in the field of "biblical archaeology" for the new century.

The Beginnings of the North Sinai Archaeological Project (NSAP)[7]

The roots of the North Sinai Archaeological Project go back a decade to the early 1990s when the Egyptian Antiquities Organization — now the Supreme Council for Antiquities (SCA) — announced that archaeological sites in North Sinai were endangered because of an irrigation project that was designed to transform the desert of the region into farm land. Realizing the importance of this frontier region to understanding ancient Egypt's military and economic history, not to mention the connections with the Levant and possibly to biblical history, I visited the Qantara region in 1994 after having been encouraged to work there in 1988 by Dr. Mohamed Abd el-Maksoud of the SCA, and in 1992 by one of my graduate school professors, Donald Redford. In 1995 and 1998, other visits were made to conduct archaeological and geological survey work with the aim to identify a New Kingdom site that might help answer questions about the so-called "Ways of Horus." Tell el-Borg was brought to my attention in 1998 as a recently identified site by the SCA that was threatened by the As-Salam irrigation project.

A small team visited Tell el-Borg in 1999 to learn more about it and assess the feasibility of excavating the site.[8] From our initial surface survey of the tell, we concluded that it indeed was a New Kingdom site, thanks to the presence of sherds of blue-painted "Amarna ware," Cypriote "milk bowls," as well as some diagnostic LB II Canaanite wares such as pilgrim flasks. With encouragement of Abd el-Maksoud, it was decided to return for excavations, despite the fact that the site did not look promising because it had served as a military base for both Israeli and Egyptian armies that did considerable damage and in recent years the canal project had destroyed significant areas of the site.[9] Thus the NSAP was born.

We immediately had to wrestle with how we would operate. Well aware

---

7. North Sinai Archaeological Project is the name used of our project when speaking to general audiences; however, in Egyptological circles we are the East Frontier Archaeological Project.

8. The team included Harvey Miller, Scolnic, Moshier, Lyla Brock, and James Hoffmeier.

9. See my brief report in "Tell el-Borg in North Sinai," *Egyptian Archaeology* 18 (Spring 2002): 18-20.

of the climate of skepticism towards the historicity of the Bible and the growing antipathy towards biblical archaeology, we were determined to attempt to
conduct our work with precision and academic integrity. The result of that
intention is laid our in the following section in which our approach is presented.

The Goals and Methods of the NSAP

Vision Statement of NSAP

To conduct all aspects of this project with excellence and the highest professional standards. Our team will consist of professionals, experts, and students
that enjoy working together towards the project's goals.

Project's Goals

- To provide a comprehensive picture of the paleo-environment and geo-
  morphology of the eastern delta, North Sinai, and the Isthmus of Suez.
- To learn about the archaeological history of this region, particularly
  during the New Kingdom period, and to investigate Tell el-Borg's role
  in the region and relationship to other New Kingdom sites.
- To reconstruct Egypt's frontier defense system during the New Kingdom, including ongoing investigation of the East Frontier canal.
- To lead towards identifying archaeological, geographical, and historical
  material that might shed light on the geography and toponymy in the
  biblical exodus tradition.

How Are We Accomplishing These Goals?

1. We take seriously Dever's call for an interdisciplinary approach; that goes
without saying. A team of experienced specialists and professionals make up
our staff, including geologists, Egyptologists, biblical scholars, Syro-
Palestinian archaeologists, an architect-draftsman, a physical anthropologist,
conservators, computer data managers, ceramicists, photographers, and
paleo-zoologists. Each discipline is vital to our investigation, and each member's contribution is valued. Having such an interdisciplinary team working
together — and having lots of fun in the process — allows us to have the kind

of dialogue between artifacts, ancient texts, and the Bible that Dever rightly noted had been missing in the "biblical archaeology" of earlier days.

2. We are not, however, driven by a particular theory about the exodus, nor do we have a predetermined "route" that we are trying to prove, and no firm exodus date (e.g., early or late) we are trying to substantiate (although the New Kingdom is the most likely time period). We are committed to going where the evidence leads us.

3. We welcome staff members with differing views on the Bible, as well as those who have no particular interest in the Bible whatsoever. For example, Benjamin Scolnic and I entered the project with differing views about the geography described in Exodus. However, in the course of our work we have both adjusted our views in the light of new evidence and thoroughly hearing each other's ideas. Simply put, people are free to challenge and question each other. Having key team members who have no particular interest in the current debates in biblical archaeology, and no predisposition towards or bias against the Bible, is perhaps the best way of keeping honest those of us who might prematurely assign biblical significance that is unwarranted.

4. We welcome collaboration and consultation with other scholars who are experts in our field of study. From the beginning, Kenneth Kitchen has served as an advisor and consultant with us on all the textual materials we discovered. During the 2000 and 2001 seasons, Manfred Beitak, the director of the University of Vienna's work at Tell el-Dabʿa, visited our site and has been most helpful. In addition, his ceramicists, David Aston, Irmgard Hein, and Perla Fuscaldo, consulted with our pottery team. Domonique Valbelle and Charles Bonnet, our neighbors who work at Tell el-Herr and Tel Maghzan, visited our excavations and offered their expertise. We are also in touch with Eliezer Oren, who has graciously advised us and shared useful information. Marcus Müller, of Potsdam University and excavating at Tell Basta, is an expert in New Kingdom battle scenes and is assisting us with identifying our military reliefs. Dietrich Klemm of Munich University offered his specialization as a petrologist with these blocks. In April 2002, at our instigation, William Dever visited Tell el-Borg to help the analysis of our Levantine and Aegean pottery and to offer a comprehensive assessment of the project.

5. To a degree, I am sympathetic with those who want to disassociate "biblical archaeology" from "Syro-Palestinian." Because I am an Egyptologist, I do not want to be known as a "biblical Egyptologist," that is, one who studies Egyptology purely as a tool for answering biblical questions and disregards other periods and areas that might not have any direct bearing on the Bible. Egyptology, like Syro-Palestinian archaeology, must operate as an inde-

pendent discipline. However, when these disciplines, be it Egyptology or Syro-Palestininan archaeology, converge with the Hebrew Scriptures, then "biblical archaeology" comes into play. Biblical archaeology must be viewed as an interdisciplinary science that integrates biblical studies with all facets of the archaeology of the ancient Near East (not just that of ancient Israel). In my view, for biblical archaeology to work effectively and receive the respect it deserves in the 21st century, it will require teams of experts working together to investigate all the dimensions of the subject under study. Rigorous archaeological investigation techniques must be pursued along with study of the paleo-environment of the area. The concerns raised by sociology and anthropology must be considered, and all pertinent texts must be seriously and critically evaluated and used where appropriate.

Earlier generations of Egyptologists such as W. M. Flinders Petrie, Archibald H. Sayce, Edouard Naville, and Alan Gardiner were scholars who worked in Egypt and were interested in investigating problems of biblical history. In the past 30-40 years, Egyptology has developed as an independent discipline resulting in Egyptologists having little or no interest whatsoever in biblical literature, even when it relates to Egypt.[10] Egyptologists interested in integrating their discipline with biblical studies are few in number.

I was trained as an Egyptologist at the University of Toronto[11] and in the field with the Akhenaten Temple Project at East Karnak with Donald Redford. I value Egyptology for its own sake. I am an active member of the International Association of Egyptologists, and have presented papers at the last six congresses over the past 20 years, and hold memberships in other Egyptological organizations (e.g., Egypt Exploration Society, Society for the Study of Egyptian Antiquities, and the American Research Center in Egypt). At the same time, I have an abiding interest in the Old Testament, so I studied Hebrew and biblical studies in graduate school, am a member of the Society of Biblical Literature and the Institute for Biblical Research, and have taught a wide range of Hebrew Bible courses over the past 25 years.

I believe strongly that Egyptology ought to be studied as a cognate discipline along with biblical studies. Ronald Williams, my *doktorvater,* was a first-rate Egyptologist who also worked in the fields of Assyriology and Bibli-

---

10. At the SBL annual meeting in November 2002, I presented a paper entitled "Egyptologists and the Exodus" which traces the history of the use of the Bible by Egyptologists. Part of the research for this paper entails a survey of over 125 Egyptologists designed to get a picture of the attitude of Egyptologists towards the Bible. The early returns show that the vast majority of Egyptologists today are simply not interested in biblical studies.

11. My dissertation, *"Sacred" in the Vocabulary of Ancient Egypt,* was published in *Orbis Biblicus et Orientalis* 59 (Freiburg: Universitätsverlag, 1985).

cal Hebrew. He modeled for me how an Egyptologist should integrate Egyptology and biblical studies in a responsible manner.

Consequently, I believe it is imperative for the NSAP to operate on two tracks, first as a project working with Egyptological goals (namely, understanding Egypt's east frontier defense system during the New Kingdom). Personally, I am delighted that our discoveries have already contributed new information about "the Ways of Horus," Egypt's military road of the New Kingdom. For over 75 years, Egyptologists have pondered the exact route of this road, and after three seasons of excavations we have made a significant contribution, in fact, forcing me to change my own views published as recently as 1999.[12]

The second track brings the biblical record to the Egyptian archaeological and textual data, treating them as one would other ancient Near Eastern written sources. Consequently, I maintain that if Exodus 13 and 14 and Numbers 33 provide real information about the route traveled by the Israelites, then one might expect that Hebrew toponymy in some way to be reflected in the archaeology and topography of the region of the eastern Delta and North Sinai. As a consequence of this two-track approach, Egyptologists and biblical scholars can work together with both disciplines reaping the benefits.

6. How do we read ancient texts? Since texts, be they Hebrew or Egyptian, play such a key role in our work, our approach to them must be disclosed. We fully agree with William Hallo's maxim to "treat the ancient sources critically but without condescension."[13] Careful reading of texts and consideration of genre and form are essential. Texts that appear to be making factual statements or historical observations should be treated as innocent until proven guilty, or accurate until proven erroneous. What historical minimalists have done over the past 25 years is to shift the burden of proof from their provocative views to the text. This approach constitutes a methodological fallacy. It is what historian David Hackett Fischer calls "the fallacy of presumptive proof" that "consists of advancing a proposition and shifting the burden of proof or disproof to others."[14]

After leading the discipline of biblical archaeology through a period of

---

12. See Hoffmeier, *Israel in Egypt*, ch. 8, where I suggested that the military highway followed the coastal ridge east of Hebua I. Our investigation, both geological and archaeological, shows that an ancient lagoon or lake located east of Hebua I and Tell el-Borg could not have been crossed on foot as the coastal ridge had too many large openings where lagoon and sea water met.

13. "The Limits of Skepticism," *JAOS* 110 (1990): 189.

14. *Historians' Fallacies: Toward a Logic of Historical Thought* (New York: Harper & Row, 1970), 48.

self-introspection, William Dever's recent writings strike a greater balance between tell and text. Dever's diatribe against the excesses of the historical minimalists is powerfully presented in his book *What Did the Biblical Writers Know and When Did They Know It?* I believe that textless archaeology, or unbiblical Syro-Palestinian archaeology, has had a direct bearing on the very historical minimalism that he is now combating. Dever's recent works have offered some helpful methodological guidelines for integrating the Hebrew texts of the Bible with archaeological data that will serve as a corrective to the "unbiblical" archaeology of the historical minimalists. After a critical assessment of both sources of information, Dever looks for convergences between the two, rather than forcing the data to fit a preconceived theory (cf. ch. 4, "Getting at the 'History behind the History'"). In a section of the book, Dever offers a "Defense of Ancient Texts". Here he suggests seven useful points on how ancient texts should be interpreted over against new literary readings of the postmodern hermeneutic.[15] For Dever the historical and social context and authorial intent are paramount, and he rejects a reader-response hermeneutic. We fully concur with the hermeneutic Dever espouses.

Our approach to texts, then, be they Hebrew or Egyptian, is to treat them with equal respect rather than with condescension. Furthermore, we assume that when they offer what appear to be factual data, such as toponyms, trace routes, and describe geographical features, archaeological and paleo-environmental research may uncover evidence that corresponds to the textual materials. When this happens, we have a convergence, to use Dever's term,[16] of biblical and archaeological data.

These are some of the methodological concerns that guide the North Sinai Archaeological Project's work. Now we turn to look at our investigation in North Sinai, starting with an overview of the history of explorations in the region and how this region may play a role in the identification of toponyms recorded in Exod. 13:17–14:2 and Numbers 33.

A Century of Archaeological Investigations in North Sinai: 1887 to 1987

The military road connecting Egypt to the Levant that ran across North Sinai

---

15. *What Did the Biblical Writers Know and When Did They Know It? What Archaeology Can Tell Us about the Reality of Ancient Israel* (Grand Rapids: Wm. B. Eerdmans, 2001), 16-17.

16. Dever, 82ff.

has been the subject of scholarly investigation since the early part of the 20th century.[17] Sir Alan Gardiner made the first systematic attempt at identifying this route by linking the sequence of toponyms on the so-called "Ways of Horus" from the battle reliefs of Seti I at Karnak and the itinerary outlined by the scribe in Papyrus Anastasi I with the known tells in North Sinai.[18] Gardiner proposed that Tjaru, the key frontier town and fort of Egypt, was Tell Abu Sefêh (ca. 3 km. E of Qantara East), that the Dwelling of the Lion (or Sese) was possibly Tell Habwe[19] (not Tell Hebua located 7 km. NNE of Tell Abu Sefêh), and that the Migdol of Menmaatre (Seti I) was Tell el-Herr (Figure 1). The use of the Semitic loanword Migdol, meaning "tower" or "watchtower,"[20] is significant because it is not widely found in Egyptian texts and might be equated with Migdol of the exodus itinerary (Exod. 14:2). In fact, it was Gardiner who suggested that "there is good enough reason for believing, despite the doubts of some scholars, that it corresponds to the Migdol of the Old Testament and the Magdolo of Greco-Roman times."[21] He believed that Migdol of Exod. 14:2 and the Numbers 33 itinerary is the same as Migdol mentioned as being Egypt's frontier town in Jer. 44:1; 46:14 and Ezek. 29:10; 30:6. We believe that Gardiner's proposed association of Migdol of Egyptian texts with Migdol of the exodus narratives is a reasonable one, and thus accept it as our working hypothesis.

In 1887, F. Ll. Griffith discovered some inscribed blocks of Seti I and Ramesses II at Tell Abu Sefêh that contributed to the belief that it was Sile (Tjaru).[22] He also reported of having dug a few trenches which revealed only Roman period remains,[23] a factor that unfortunately was not taken seriously by subsequent generations of scholars when seeking to identify this site. The

---

17. Cf. Carl Küthmann, *Die Ostgrenze Ägyptens* (Leipzig: J. C. Hinrichs, 1911).

18. "The Ancient Military Road between Egypt and Palestine," *JEA* 6 (1920): 99-116. For a recent study of this travel route during the Ptolemaic through Byzantine periods, see Pau Figuera, *From Gaza to Pelusium: Materials for the Historical Geography of North Sinai and Southwestern Palestine (332 BCE–640 CE)* (Beersheba: Ben Gurion University Press, 2000).

19. This site is likely Tell el-Ahmar as named by the Egyptian Antiquities Organization; "Projet de sauvetage des sites antiques du Nord-Sinaï," *Discussions in Egyptology* 24 (1992): 7-12. Cf. W. M. Flinders Petrie, *Tanis II, Nebesheh (Am), and Defenneh (Tahpanhes)* (London: Egypt Exploration Fund, 1888), 97-108.

20. Ludwig Koehler and Walter Baumgartner, *Lexicon in Veteris Testamenti Libros,* 2nd ed. (1958; repr. Leiden: Brill, 1985), 492-93.

21. *JEA* 20 (1920): 107.

22. Petrie, 97-108. The inscriptions are available in Kenneth A. Kitchen, *Ramesside Inscriptions* 1:105-7 and 2:402-3 (Oxford: Blackwell, 1976-78); and commented upon in Kitchen, *Ramesside Inscriptions: Translated and Annotated* (Oxford: Blackwell, 1993), 1:13-14.

23. Petrie, 97-98.

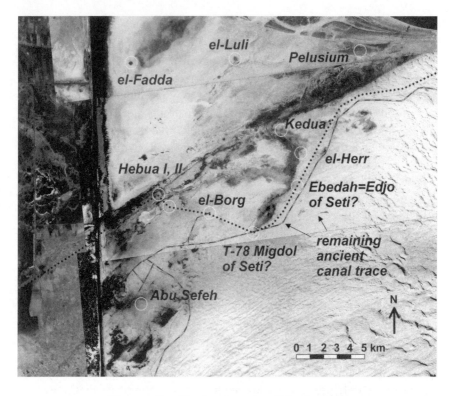

Figure 1. Satellite image map of North Sinai

inscribed Ramesside blocks found on the surface were enough to convince Gardiner and many scholars since that Tell Abu Sefêh was Egypt's New Kingdom frontier town and fort, Tjaru (Sile). Beyond this brief investigation, few archaeological excavations were conducted in this area in the following decades, due largely to the military activity in Sinai from the 1940s to the early 1980s. Over that period, Gardiner's route was widely accepted, but not confirmed, nor investigated until recently.

During the Israeli military occupation of Sinai after the 1967 war, a comprehensive archaeological survey was conducted by Eliezer Oren between 1972 and 1982. He identified more than 150 New Kingdom sites of varying sizes between the Suez canal and Gaza.[24] His excavations of New Kingdom sites were primarily focused in the el-Arish area, namely Bir el-ʿAbd (site BEA

---

24. Eliezer D. Oren, "The 'Ways of Horus' in North Sinai," in *Egypt, Israel, Sinai: Archaeological and Historical Relationships in the Biblical Period,* ed. Anson F. Rainey (Tel Aviv: Tel Aviv University Press, 1987), 76; "Northern Sinai," *NEAEHL* 4:1388.

10) to the west of el-Arish and Haruba (sites A-289 and A-345) to its east.[25] One site briefly excavated by Oren in the Qantara-Baluza region was Tell Qedua (T 21), which has produced only 7th- and 6th-century B.C.E. remains. This led him to suggest that T-21 was the Migdol of Jer. 44:1 and Ezek. 29:10; 30:6, spoken of as Egypt's frontier town, but in the absence of New Kingdom remains could not be the Migdol of 19th-Dynasty references that is mentioned in Exod. 14:2 and Num. 33:7.[26] Oren also visited Tell Abu Sefêh, where he collected pottery from the surface and made some soundings. The earliest materials encountered were Persian and "a few specimens of the Saite period" (7th century B.C.E.).[27] His recent investigations of these important sites raised doubts about locating Tjaru at Tell Abu Sefêh and New Kingdom Migdol at Tell Qedua. Writing in 1984, Oren concluded: "Therefore the location of New Kingdom Thel [Tjaru], like that of Migdol, remains hypothetical and must await further study."[28]

While Oren's survey of this region identified some New Kingdom sites, none were excavated. Therefore, not until the excavations of Mohamed Abd el-Maksoud of the Egyptian Supreme Council for Antiquities at Hebua I in the mid-1980s was the first New Kingdom site discovered in the Qantara-Baluza region. Its massive fortification system from the New Kingdom is thought to have covered an area 800 m. by 400 m.[29] This site can now be certainly identified with the long-sought Tjaru (Sile), the starting point of the military road to Canaan as recorded in Papyrus Anastasi I.[30] This identification is now certain, thanks to the discovery in May 1999 of a 19th-Dynasty votive statue with the name Tjaru inscribed upon it. I had the privilege of inspecting the statue with Abd el-Maksoud only a few hours after it had been uncovered.[31] We clearly could read Tjaru on it.

25. Oren, "The 'Ways of Horus' in North Sinai," 77-112.

26. Eliezer D. Oren, "Migdol: A New Fortress on the Edge of the Eastern Nile Delta," *BASOR* 256 (1984): 7-44. Donald Redford has excavated a few seasons at Kedua during the 1990s; cf. "Report on the 1993 and 1997 Seasons at Tell Qedwa," *JARCE* 35 (1998): 45-57.

27. Oren, "The 'Ways of Horus' in North Sinai," 113, n. 3.

28. *BASOR* 256 (1984): 35.

29. Mohamed Abd el-Maksoud, "Une nouvelle fortresse sur la route d'Horus: Tell Heboua 1986 (Nord-Sinaï)," *CRIPEL* 9 (1987): 13-16.

30. Mohamed Abd el-Maksoud, *Tell Heboua (1981-1991): Enquête archéologique sur la Deuxième Période Intermédiaire et le Nouvel Empire à l'extrémité orientale du Delta* (Paris: Éditions Recherche sur les Civilisations, 1998). Initially, Abd el-Maksoud thought that Hebua was the second fort in the Seti sequence, "the Dwelling of the Lion"; cf. *Abstracts of the Fifth International Congress of Egyptology, October 29–November 3, 1988*, 4-5.

31. Publication of this important text is in preparation and is scheduled for a future issue of *Mémoires de l'institut français d'archéologie Orientale.*

Now that Tjaru's location has at long last been established, the direction of the route from Hebua I eastwards can more accurately be traced.[32] In my 1997 book, I proposed that it continued east along the ancient dune ridge. I am happy in the light of new evidence to revise my earlier hypothesis. Also during the 1990s, Tell Abu Sefêh and Tell el-Herr were excavated, and work at these sites is ongoing. They have revealed no New Kingdom remains.[33] Consequently, Tell Abu Sefêh cannot be associated with Tjaru, and Tell el-Herr is not New Kingdom Migdol. Commenting recently on the results of the excavations at Tell Qedua and Tell el-Herr, Kitchen, the NSAP epigrapher, has observed, "The New Kingdom 'Migdol' of Sethos I is identical with neither of these sites, but remains to be discovered somewhere in the vicinity."

The recent excavations at Tell el-Borg, we believe, shed light on the location of the military road of the New Kingdom, and possibly the location of the Dwelling of the Lion and Migdol of Men-maat-re (Seti I). During the first season, March-April 2000, we discovered inscribed blocks of a temple of Ramesses II and walls measuring 3.8 m. in width that belonged to a 19th-Dynasty fort. Subsequently we determined that there were two building phases to this fort, which in turn was constructed over a moat of an even earlier fort that we have provisionally dated to the 18th Dynasty. On the basis of work from the 2002 season which revealed the NE corner of the second fort, we calculate that this fort occupied 5600 square meters. Thus regardless of when in the New Kingdom one may want to date the exodus, this fort, like Tjaru to its north, was occupied from ca. 1450 to 1200 B.C.E..

A preliminary report of the first two seasons' excavations at Tell el-Borg is now available.[34] There I have tentatively proposed that Tell el-Borg is the second stop on the New Kingdom itinerary, the Dwelling of the Lion, although I have not ruled out its being the Migdol of Men-maat-re, the third stop in the sequence. The key to answering the uncertainty possibly lies in

32. In 1997 I had proposed that the route ran due east along the dune ridge on which Hebua I is situated; *Israel in Egypt*, Figure 2. Now, in the light of our work at Tell el-Borg, our regional study of the paleo-lagoon to its east, and the dune ridge to the north, it is clear for archaeological and geological reasons that the military road did not follow the dune ridge.

33. For Tell el-Herr, see Dominique Valbelle and Giorgio Nogara, "La fortresse du IVe siècle avant J.-C. à Tell el-Herr (Nord-Sinaï)," *CRIPEL* 21 (2000): 53-66; Valbelle, "A First Persian Period Fortress at Tell el-Herr," *Egyptian Archaeology* 18 (2001): 12-14. Publication of the finds at Tell Abu Sefêh are in progress, but I have received firsthand briefings on the site by its various excavators between 1995 and 2001. Mohamed Abd el-Maksoud, Mohamed Kamal, and Abdul Rahman al-Aydi of the SCA were kind enough to share with me the preliminary results of their work, and only Greco-Roman period remains have been documented.

34. *Egyptian Archaeology* 20 (2002): 18-21; James K. Hoffmeier, *JEA* 89 (2004).

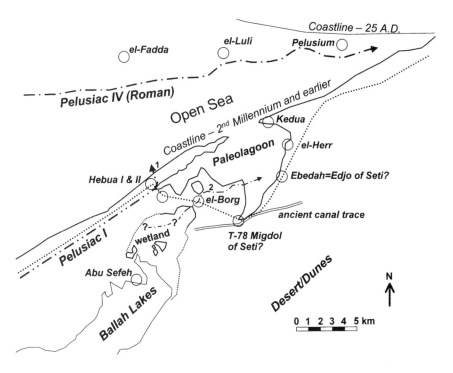

Figure 2. North Sinai

further excavations at Hebua II, which lies between Hebua I and Tell el-Borg. It has only been excavated briefly in 1999 and produced 19th-Dynasty remains. The next site on the road to Asia after Tell el-Borg was probably located on the southern side of the eastern lagoon, but may have been destroyed in the past decade during the massive irrigation project work in that area. Oren's T-78 is a candidate for the Migdol of Men-maat-re. Thus far we have been unable to locate this site. On the eastern side of the lagoon, and about 2 km. south of Tell el-Herr, is Oren's T-116, called Tell Ebedah by the local bedouin. In April 2002 several of our team reconnoitered at this site. We were able to identify New Kingdom sherds on the surface of this small tell. This too is another site that could be the Migdol of Men-maat-re.

If Tell el-Borg turns out to be the Dwelling of the Lion, then the site of the Migdol of Men-maat-re, and possibly Migdol of the exodus, cannot be too far away. The work of our geologists has shown that Tell el-Borg was surrounded by ancient lakes and lagoons (Figure 2). This means that a region that today is desert was largely covered with water in ancient times. This picture accords well with Egyptian data which suggests that *p3 ṯwfy, yām sûp* of the Bible, was located near Tjaru.[35] A more detailed study of the geography of the exodus and how the biblical references might relate to our investigation in North Sinai is taken up in more detail in another chapter in this volume by Benjamin E. Scolnic.

35. See discussion of these Egyptian and Hebrew terms in Hoffmeier, *Israel in Egypt*, ch. 9; and see full discussion in James K. Hoffmeier, *Ancient Israel in Sinai* (Oxford: Oxford University Press, forthcoming), ch. 5. The Onomastica of Amenemope records in its geographical list the names of sites, moving from south to north. It places Tjaru and *p3 ṯwfy* as the last two toponyms in the NE frontier; cf. Alan H. Gardiner, *Ancient Egyptian Onomastica* (Oxford: Oxford University Press, 1947), 2:201*-2*.

Archaeology: Approaches and Application

Homer and Archaeology: Minimalists and Maximalists in Classical Context

EDWIN YAMAUCHI

Introduction

In William Dever's vigorous denunciation of the so-called biblical minimalists, he makes a very important observation:

> I cannot resist pointing out that here, once again, the revisionists reveal how scarcely innovative they are, indeed how out of touch with developments in many allied fields. For instance, "biblical" archaeology's attempts to deal with the question of the historicity of the Hebrew Bible have often been compared with Classical archaeology's struggle with the "Homeric legends." A generation ago, even a decade ago, Classicists and ancient historians would have dismissed Homer as a mythical figure and would have argued that the tales of the Trojan Wars were mainly "invented" by much later Greek writers. (Sound familiar?) . . . It is now thought that those stories of warfare do not simply reflect the situation of Greece in the 8th-7th centuries, but go much farther back to a genuine historical situation of the 13th-12th centuries, that is, to the period of the movements of the various "Sea Peoples" across the Mediterranean (including the biblical "Philistines"). Thus, it is now argued, a long oral tradition, preserving many authentic details of earlier Greek history, persisted down until about the 8th century, at which time these traditions were finally reduced to writing.[1]

---

1. William G. Dever, *What Did the Biblical Writers Know and When Did They Know It?* (Grand Rapids: Wm. B. Eerdmans, 2001), 278-79.

Though Dever does not provide specific details, he does call attention to a *Festschrift* for Emily T. Vermeule as an example of recent confirmations of Homeric traditions.[2]

As someone who has taught both ancient Near Eastern and ancient Greek history, and as a student of Cyrus H. Gordon, who emphasized links between the Bible and Homer,[3] I have long been interested in parallel developments in both biblical and classical studies.[4] In the following essay I would like to expand an earlier article on Homer and archaeology, following the lead of Professor Dever's insight.[5]

Aegean Archaeology

Just over a century ago Heinrich Schliemann inaugurated Aegean archaeology in a spectacular fashion by his excavations at Troy in 1870, followed by his work at Mycenae in 1876.[6] Before this most scholars began Greek history with the First Olympiad in 776 B.C. Homer's story of a war with Troy in the Heroic Age was simply a tale without historical foundation. According to Carl W. Blegen:

> Professional Homeric scholarship in the nineteenth century was to a great extent marked by a deep skepticism; the poems were ripped to shreds, the subject matter was regarded as fiction or fancy inspired by mi-

2. Jane B. Carter and Sarah P. Morris, eds., *The Ages of Homer* (Austin: University of Texas Press, 1995).

3. Cyrus H. Gordon, "Homer and the Bible," *HUCA* 26 (1955): 43-108; *Before the Bible: The Common Background of Greek and Hebrew Civilizations* (New York: Harper & Row, 1962); *Homer and the Bible: The Origin and Character of East Mediterranean Literature* (Ventnor, N.J.: Ventnor, 1967). See Louis H. Feldman, "Homer and the Near East: The Rise of the Greek Genius," *BA* 59 (1996): 13-21; Howard Marblestone, "A 'Mediterranean Synthesis': Professor Cyrus H. Gordon's Contributions to the Classics," *BA* 59 (1996): 22-30.

4. See Edwin M. Yamauchi, *Composition and Corroboration in Classical and Biblical Studies* (Philadelphia: Presbyterian & Reformed, 1966); "The Archaeological Confirmation of Suspect Elements in the Classical and the Biblical Traditions," in *The Law and the Prophets,* ed. J. Skilton et al. (Nutley, N.J.: Presbyterian & Reformed, 1974), 54-70.

5. Edwin Yamauchi, "Homer, History and Archaeology," *NEASB* 3 (1973): 21-42.

6. For the fascinating story of Schliemann's career, see Leonard Cottrell, *Realms of Gold* (Greenwich: New York Graphic Society, 1963); and William A. McDonald, *Progress into the Past* (New York: Macmillan, 1967). A little-known facet of his fabled life is that Schliemann came to Indianapolis in 1869 and purchased property there in order to divorce his Russian wife under Indiana law. Cf. Eli Lilly, ed., *Schliemann in Indianapolis* (Indianapolis: Indianapolis Historical Society, 1961).

nor episodes and raids, transferred by the poet or poets from various other places to Troy, and the possibility that there was any substratum of historical truth was brushed aside.[7]

In his naive and boundless enthusiasm, Schliemann leaped to conclusions which were quite erroneous. He identified the gold jewelry from Troy II as "Priam's Treasure," and sent a cable to King George of Greece with the message that he had beheld the face of Agamemnon on a gold mask from Mycenae. But Troy II, the level where the treasure was found, was a city which flourished over a millennium before Priam, and the shaft grave from Grave Circle A, where the mask was found, dated from three centuries before the time of Agamemnon.

In the light of subsequent discoveries and developments, including the decipherment of Linear B,[8] scholars have come to recognize that Homer, who lived in the 8th century, has preserved some memories of the Mycenaean epoch (14th-13th centuries). What is a matter of dispute is whether the *Iliad* has preserved a minimal number of garbled recollections and primarily reflects conditions of Homer's Geometric Age or whether it has conserved accurate and substantial traditions.[9]

Ancient historians in both biblical and classical studies have three sources for their reconstructions: (1) traditional and literary sources, which have been passed down in oral and written form for centuries, (2) contemporary inscriptions and texts, and (3) material remains. In her classic work, *Greece in the Bronze Age*,[10] Vermeule compiled some very interesting lists of objects as they are attested in Homer, Linear B inscriptions, and material remains from excavations. From an examination of possible overlapping circles of these sources of evidences, one can see that theoretically there are seven possible relationships: (1) a maximum scenario where all three sources overlap, (2)-(4) cases where there is a double overlap, and (5)-(7) cases where an object is attested only by one source.[11] For example, (1) linen is attested in all

---

7. Carl W. Blegen, "The Mycenaean Age," in *Lectures in Memory of Louise Taft Semple*, ed. D. W. Bradeen et al. (Princeton: Princeton University Press, 1967), 16-17.

8. Cf. Leonard Cottrell, "Michael Ventris and His Achievement," *Antioch Review* 25 (1965): 13-14; John Chadwick, *The Decipherment of Linear B* (Cambridge: Cambridge University Press, 1958).

9. Some have sought to establish the geographical background of the *Odyssey*. Cf. Lewis Pocock, *Reality and Allegory in the Odyssey* (Amsterdam: Adolf M. Hakkert, 1959); Ernle Bradford, *Ulysses Found* (New York: Harcourt Brace, 1962). Such attempts are quite subjective.

10. (Chicago: University of Chicago Press, 1964).

11. Edwin Yamauchi, *The Stones and the Scriptures* (Philadelphia: Lippincott, 1972), 158-59.

three sources, (2) the pear by both Homer and excavations, (3) the cypress by both Homer and Linear B, (4) the coriander by both Linear B and excavations, (5) the apple by Homer alone, (6) the mint by Linear B only, and (7) the almond by excavations only. Given the fragmentary nature of inscriptional and material evidences, there will always remain gaps in our evidences so that there will always be room for skepticism. But scholars who insist upon external corroboration of items in the traditional materials have not reckoned with the fragmentary and random nature of the archaeological and inscriptional evidences.

Despite a large residue of unconfirmed materials, the striking confirmation of some elements does raise the possibility that Late Bronze information could be accurately transmitted over the divide of centuries to later eras. This was the conviction of Vermeule: "We say in justification that large parts of the poems incorporate Mycenaean traditions, that the five hundred years separating the fall of Troy VIIA from the Homeric version of its fall have wrought only minor innovations, a few misunderstandings of the past and adaptations to more modern experience."[12]

Homer

The literary criticism of Homer reached a new level of sophistication with the publication in 1795 of F. A. Wolf's *Prolegomena ad Homerum*. Later critics known as "analysts" or "separatists" dissected the poems into various lays, which had supposedly been combined by anonymous compilers. The 20th century has been a return to a positive appreciation for the personality of Homer and for the unity of the Homeric poems, particularly after the publication in 1921 of John A. Scott's *The Unity of Homer*. The greatest advance in Homeric studies was the demonstration in 1928 by Milman Parry that the Homeric epics were oral compositions. Parry and his disciples have illustrated their thesis by recording poems composed orally by Yugoslav bards. A lively controversy has raged over the relationship between the oral composition of the epics and the alphabet, which was adopted from the Phoenicians by the Greeks about the same time that Homer lived.[13]

12. Vermeule, x.

13. G. S. Kirk, *The Songs of Homer* (Cambridge: Cambridge University Press, 1962); J. B. Hainsworth, *Homer* (Oxford: Clarendon, 1969); Adam Parry, ed., *The Making of Homer* (Oxford: Clarendon, 1971). The earliest Greek texts in the alphabet borrowed from the Phoenicians date to the 8th century B.C.E. Some scholars, arguing from the shape of the letters, have argued for even earlier dates for the adoption of the alphabet by the Greeks. See Martin Bernal,

Inasmuch as after the collapse of the Mycenaean civilization writing seems to have disappeared in the Greek world, except in Cyprus,[14] any memories that were transmitted must have been conveyed by word of mouth for over 400 years through the Greek Dark Ages.[15] In view of such a long span of time during which great changes took place, we are compelled to wonder whether it is really possible that historical memories of the Mycenaean Age have been preserved in the Homeric epics.

Historical Memories?

To the question of whether the epics can be used as a source for reconstructing the Mycenaean Age, some historians have given an emphatically negative answer. Moses Finley, a distinguished American expatriate who taught at Cambridge University, was a most critical skeptic of the Homeric traditions. In a BBC lecture given in 1963, Professor Finley criticized the interpretation of Carl Blegen of the University of Cincinnati, who re-excavated Troy from 1932 to 1938. Of the latter's view that the ruins of Troy VIIA represent the city destroyed by the Achaeans, Finley asserted: "However, they have found nothing, not a scrap, which points to an Achaean coalition or to a 'king whose overlordship was recognised' or to Trojan allies; nothing which hints at *who* destroyed Troy."[16] As an alternative Finley proposed that Troy VIIA may have been destroyed by some unknown and unnamed northern barbarians.[17]

In an earlier article published in 1957, after pointing out the discrepancies between Homer's heroic society and the bureaucracy of the Linear B texts, Professor Finley concluded: "The Homeric world was altogether post-

---

Cadmean Letters (Winona Lake: Eisenbrauns, 1990); P. Kyle McCarter, "The Early Diffusion of the Alphabet," *BA* 37 (1974): 54-68; Alan R. Millard, "The Uses of the Early Alphabets," in *Phoinikeia Grammata,* ed. Claude Baurain et al. (Namur: Société des études classiques, 1991), 101-14; Joseph Naveh, *Early History of the Alphabet* (Leiden: Brill, 1982).

14. Cf. J. F. Daniel, "Prolegomena to the Cypro-Minoan Script," *AJA* 45 (1941): 249-82.

15. Cf. V. R. d'A. Desborough, *The Greek Dark Ages* (New York: St. Martin's, 1972).

16. Moses I. Finley, "The Trojan War," *JHS* 84 (1964): 1-9; the same issue (9-20) contains responses to Finley's skepticism by John L. Caskey, G. S. Kirk, and Denys Page. Sinclair Hood, "The Bronze Age Context of Homer," in Carter and Morris, 25-32, now suggests that Troy VIIB may be the level which should be associated with the Trojan War.

17. Of a similar alternative to the traditional view, Denys Page, *History and the Homeric Iliad* (Berkeley: University of California Press, 1959), 57, remarks: "I do not see how this suggestion could be positively refuted. It enjoys a status well known in academic circles and doubtless elsewhere, — that of the Remotely Conceivable Alternative, contrary to the obvious implication of the facts, incapable of proof or disproof."

Mycenaean, and the so-called reminiscences and survivals are rare, isolated, and garbled. Hence Homer is not only not a reliable guide to the Mycenaean tablets: he is no guide at all."[18]

Over a decade later Finley conceded that there are a number of Mycenaean objects which are faithfully described in the epics, but he continued to emphasize the inadequacy of the epics as a source for Mycenaean history or institutions.[19] His own reconstruction would view Homer's society as essentially a reflection of the 10th-9th centuries of the Dark Ages.[20]

G. S. Kirk also emphasized the difficulty of extracting historical data from the epics.[21] Influenced by Finley, Professor Kirk confesses: "In particular I remain sceptical about the current tendency, sharply accentuated by the decipherment of Linear B, to find Mycenaean elements everywhere in the poems."[22]

The historian's reluctance to accept Homeric traditions which lack corroboration from either inscriptions or archaeology is understandable. On the other hand, such skepticism may be based upon a failure to appreciate how fragmentary is the archaeological evidence which is available for comparison. We may chart the progress of Homeric archaeology by noting especially the discoveries made in the decades since the publication of Hilda Lockhart Lorimer's magisterial work, *Homer and the Monuments*.[23] Elements that were not attested by archaeological evidence were rejected by Lorimer as anachronisms retrojected into the Heroic Age from Homer's own Geometric Age.

Classical Archaeology

Objects

One of the few items which Rhys Carpenter was willing to concede as authentic in 1946 was the boar's tusk helmet.[24] Actual remains of such helmets, as

18. Moses I. Finley, "Homer and Mycenae: Property and Tenure," *Historia* 6 (1957): 159.

19. Moses I. Finley, *Early Greece: The Bronze and Archaic Ages* (New York: W. W. Norton, 1970), 82-84.

20. Moses I. Finley, *The World of Odysseus* (New York: Viking, 1965).

21. G. S. Kirk, *The Homeric Poems as History* (Cambridge: University Press, 1964).

22. G. S. Kirk, ed., *The Language and Background of Homer* (Cambridge: Heffer, 1964), xi.

23. (London: Macmillan, 1950). There was, of course, no archaeological activity during World War II, so Lorimer's work is basically a summary of information gathered before 1940.

24. *Folk Tale, Fiction and Saga in the Homeric Epics* (Berkeley: University of California Press, 1946).

described in the *Iliad* 10.261-65, have been found in a number of Mycenaean tombs. In the 13th century it was already an antique element; inasmuch as 30 to 40 boars were needed for a single helmet, these animals rapidly became scarce. Homer correctly describes the boar's tusk helmet as an heirloom which is loaned by Meriones to Odysseus.[25]

Lorimer held that ivory, derived from Syria and Phoenicia, was barely known in Greece before 750.[26] Today we have a rich collection of ivories found in Greece dating from Mycenaean times.[27] In addition, since the decipherment of Linear B in 1952 we have detailed descriptions of furniture inlaid in ivory, ebony, etc. to illustrate such objects as Penelope's chair (*Odyssey* 19.55).[28]

Homer's treatment of metals in general corresponds with the state of metallurgy in the Late Bronze Age rather than in the Early Iron Age. The former epoch was characterized by a wealth of goldwork, bronze weapons, and decoration with niello that was not true of the later period.[29] Homer mentions only bronze swords and spearheads but no iron examples. Anthony M. Snodgrass, who holds that much of Homer reflects the Dark Age period, concedes:

> His exclusive use of bronze, for every sword and every spearhead mentioned in both poems, is the point of greatest significance; for these are the two supreme weapons of the Epic. There is no period of Greek history or prehistory, later than the first half of the eleventh century B.C., of which such a picture would be representative.[30]

Actual remains from the 11th to the 8th centuries include four bronze swords but over 50 iron swords, 13 bronze spearheads but over 50 iron spearheads.[31] It is true that among the 48 times iron is mentioned in the epics some iron weapons such as axes and maces are included. But in many cases, such as at *Il-*

25. A miniature papyrus, which was discovered at Amarna in 1936, but which only came to light in 1991 after its purchase by the British Museum, displays what appear to be Mycenaeans, wearing boar's tusk helmets, fighting with Egyptians against Libyans. See Vronwy Hankey and David Aston, "Mycenaean Pottery at Saqqara," in Carter and Morris, 71.

26. Lorimer, 507 and *passim*.

27. H. Kantor, "Ivory Carving in the Mycenaean Period," *Archaeology* 13 (1960): 14-25.

28. E. Laroche, "Sur le nom grecque de l'Ivoire," *Revue de Philologie* 39 (1965): 56-59.

29. R. J. Forbes, *Bergbau, Steinbruchtätigkeit und Hüttenwesen*. Archaeologia Homerica 2/K (Göttingen: Vandenhoeck & Ruprecht, 1967), 17.

30. Anthony M. Snodgrass, "An Historical Homeric Society?" *JHS* 94 (1974): 122.

31. Anthony M. Snodgrass, *Early Greek Armour and Weapons* (Edinburgh: Edinburgh University Press, 1964), 174.

iad 6.48 and *Odyssey* 14.324, iron is treated as a precious metal that was not yet common.[32]

In 1950 Lorimer reported: "No metal greaves of Bronze Age date have occurred in Greece."[33] The only early example came from Enkomi, Cyprus. She therefore held that the epithet *euknēmides,* which is used of the Achaeans some 36 times in the epics, was late and intrusive. The epithet "well-greaved" does not require that the Achaean greaves be metallic; only in *Iliad* 7.41 is the word *chalkoknēmides* "bronze-greaved" used. In any case, we now have no reason to view these terms as anachronisms, as a pair of Late Helladic III greaves was found in Achaea in 1953 and a pair of Late Helladic II greaves at Dendra in 1960. C. M. Bowra therefore asserts:

> We may, then, conclude that in Mycenaean times bronze greaves were worn at least by superior warriors. . . . It is true that no word or ideogram for "greave" has been found in Linear B texts, but, since the same is true of "shield," nothing can be deduced from it. On the other hand no late Mycenaean representation of warriors shows them without greaves. . . . There is thus no inherent difficulty in the epithet εὐκνήμιδες going back to Mycenaean times.[34]

In a similar fashion, Lorimer regarded the epithet *chalkochitōnes* as an anachronistic reference to the bronze corslet of the Greek hoplite soldiers from after 700. In 1960 a Greco-Swedish excavation uncovered a chamber tomb at Dendra that yielded a complete bronze cuirass of Late Helladic III date (ca. 1400). Its several pieces match the ideograms in Linear B texts from Pylos and Knossos. Vermeule notes: "Many details of its construction agree with formulas in Homeric poetry which used to be thought of as post-Mycenaean innovations."[35] In 1963 a second Mycenaean bronze corslet was found at Thebes in Boeotia.[36]

---

32. Iron was not superior to bronze, unless it could be carbonized as steel. See Edwin Yamauchi, "Metal Sources and Metallurgy in the Biblical World," *Perspectives on Science and Christian Faith* 45 (1993): 252-59. The substitution of iron for bronze probably had more to do with the disruptions caused by the dislocations ca. 1200 B.C.E., which disrupted access to the rare metal tin, which was necessary to form the alloy bronze with the more abundant copper. See John DeFelice, "Tin and Trade: An Archaeometallurgical Approach to Dating the Exodus," M.A. thesis (Oxford: Miami University, 1994).

33. Lorimer, 250.

34. C. M. Bowra, *On Greek Margins* (Oxford: Clarendon, 1970), 21.

35. Vermeule, 135. Cf. C. King, "The Homeric Corslet," *AJA* 74 (1970): 294-96.

36. N. Platon and E. Stassinopoulou-Touloupa, "Ivories and Linear-B from Thebes," *Illustrated London News* (5 December 1964), 896-97.

A hunting spear called by Homer an *aiganeē* (e.g., *Odyssey* 9.154ff.) has hitherto been thought to be an anachronism because vase paintings do not show this kind of spear in use until about the 7th century. Attention has now been drawn to a fragment of a Mycenaean vase in the National Museum at Athens that shows just such a spear with a hook for propulsion. The sherd dates to the middle of the 13th century.[37]

Customs

Lorimer questioned the use of perfume in the epics and considered the few references to be allusions to later practice.[38] But the Linear B texts indicate that in Mycenaean times the manufacture of perfume, using ingredients such as coriander and cypress imported from the Near East, was one of the chief industries at Pylos.[39] Homeric references to shining and fragrant garments, as in the case of Helen's robe (*Iliad* 3.141, 385, 419), are confirmed by the Linear B texts as is the custom to use oil in tannage. According to Cynthia W. Shelmerdine, "This Bronze Age information, then, provides a real-life analogy to explain Homeric references to fragrant and shining cloth, just as oil tannage, accurately described at *Iliad* 17.389-393, is reflected in the Mycenaean allocation of oil to tanners (Fh 5428, 5435) and for hides (Fh 353, 5432) at Knossos."[40]

A suspect practice mentioned in Homer was the custom of the giving of baths to men by women servants as at Pylos. That this was an ancient practice is confirmed by a terra cotta object from a Mycenaean tomb in Cyprus that shows a young woman bathing a man in a bath tub.[41] Moreover, Linear B tablets from Pylos list 37 women who are called "bath-pourers," confirming the antiquity of the Homeric word *loetrochoos*, which had been considered by some scholars as an interpolation.[42]

That the slaying of horses at the funeral of Patroclus was an ancient cus-

37. Hans-Günter Buchholz and Vassos Karageorghis, "Homeric aiganeē," *Athens Annals of Archaeology* 3 (1970): 386-91.

38. Lorimer, 383-84.

39. Pylos Un08. See Michael Ventris and John Chadwick, *Documents in Mycenaean Greek* (Cambridge: Cambridge University Press, 1956), 103ff.; Leonard R. Palmer, *The Interpretation of Mycenaean Greek Texts* (Oxford: Clarendon, 1963), 268.

40. Cynthia W. Shelmerdine, "Shining and Fragrant Cloth in Homeric Epic," in Carter and Morris, 103.

41. Albert Severyns, "Homère et l'histoire," *L'Antiquité classique* 33 (1964): 332.

42. Cf. Pylos Tn 996 in Ventris and Chadwick, 238.

tom has been confirmed by the discovery of two horse skeletons in the dromos of a 15th-century tomb at Marathon. Additional evidence has been found at a Mycenaean tomb at Argos and a Minoan tomb at Arkhanes.[43] The sacrifice of horses was not continued in Greece, but was still practiced in Cyprus until the 8th-7th centuries.[44]

Buildings

Nineteenth-century critics assumed that ancient houses were never more than one story high, and that men and women occupied separate quarters. This assumption was not based on any evidence and disregarded Homer's references to staircases. Even after Schliemann's excavations at Tiryns in 1884, which revealed clear evidence of staircases and basements, critics continued to maintain their skepticism. According to A. J. B. Wace, "Even modern writers like Miss Lorimer have not been able to cast off the shackles of old assumptions and have failed to take advantage of the information derived from the House of Columns at Mycenae."[45] The latter structure fully illustrates the type of building depicted in the *Odyssey*.[46] O. T. P. K. Dickinson, who is otherwise quite skeptical, concedes, "it is undeniable that what is described in the *Odyssey* is more complex than any Dark Age building so far discovered, but seems to have many features in common with Mycenaean palaces."[47]

Blegen's discovery of a Mycenaean palace at Pylos, similar to palaces at Mycenae and Tiryns, has provided further archaeological evidence for the Homeric megarons. The Mycenaean palaces with their hearths, four-column bases, and thrones aptly fit the description of the megaron of Nausicaa's father (*Odyssey* 6.303-9):

> As soon as you are safe inside, cross over and go straight through into the megaron to find my mother. She'll be there in firelight before a col-

43. J. Sakellarakis, "Minoan Cemeteries at Arkhanes," *Archaeology* 20 (1967): 276ff.

44. Vassos Karageorghis, "Horse Burials on the Island of Cyprus," *Archaeology* 18 (1965): 282-90.

45. "Houses and Palaces," in A. J. B. Wace and Frank H. Stubbings, eds., *A Companion to Homer* (New York: Macmillan, 1962), 490.

46. Excavations have revealed that the House of Columns was actually the central unit of the east wing of the palace. Cf. George E. Mylonas, *Mycenae's Last Century of Greatness* (Sydney: Sydney University Press, 1968), 19ff.

47. O. T. P. K. Dickinson, "Homer, the Poet of the Dark Age," *Greece and Rome* 33 (1986): 29.

umn. . . . My father's great chair faces the fire, too; there like a god he sits and takes his wine.[48]

Homer's references to temples (e.g., *Iliad* 1.39) were long considered glaring anachronisms.[49] In a work published in 1962, the earliest temples that could be cited by Paul MacKendrick were 9th-century structures found at Perachora and Sparta.[50] In that very year Professor John L. Caskey of the University of Cincinnati published a report of a Mycenaean temple he had discovered on the island of Keos off the coast of Attica in 1961.[51] The temple, which was established by settlers in the Middle Bronze Age and later remodeled in the Late Helladic period, provides a convincing example of religious continuity:

> There is one particularly striking illustration of this remarkable religious conservatism which emerges from a history of the Greek votive terracottas: in the Bronze Age sanctuary at Hagia Eirene in Keos, where cult endured through the Dark Age, the head from a sixteenth century statue was fixed on a makeshift base and still served as a cult image in the eighth century.[52]

Then in 1968-69 at Mycenae itself Lord William Taylour discovered a second Mycenaean temple and some unique cultic objects, including a clay snake with a movable tongue. All told, there were originally 17 serpentine objects.[53] Snodgrass concludes:

> There are now free-standing religious buildings, worthy of the name νηός and conforming to the Homeric references, known from Bronze Age Greece. I would cite the structure found by Professor Caskey at Ayia Irini on Keos, and the temples of Mycenaean date at Kition in Cyprus which Dr. Karageorghis has recently excavated. There is also the smaller shrine which Lord William Taylour has uncovered at Mycenae.[54]

---

48. Translation by Robert Fitzgerald (Garden City: Doubleday, 1963), 107-8.

49. Cf. D. Gray, "Homer and the Archaeologists," in *Fifty Years (and Twelve) of Classical Scholarship,* ed. Maurice Platnauer (New York: Barnes & Noble, 1968), 22, also 46; cf. Kirk, *The Homeric Poems as History,* 28.

50. *The Greek Stones Speak* (New York: St. Martin's, 1962), 140-47.

51. John L. Caskey, "Excavations in Keos 1960-1961," *Hesperia* 31 (1962): 263-83.

52. Bernard C. Dietrich, "Some Evidence of Religious Continuity in the Greek Dark Age," *BICS* 17 (1970): 22. The original torso was recovered from the floor below the level where the head was later reused.

53. William Taylour, "Mycenae's First Temple," *Illustrated London News* (27 December 1969), 24-25; "New Light on Mycenaean Religion," *Antiquity* 44 (1970): 270-79.

54. Snodgrass, *JHS* 94 (1974): 123.

Places

The Homeric Catalogue of Ships in the second book of the *Iliad* is a document that demonstrates the accuracy of oral traditions. Of the 164 places listed, 96 can be identified; Mycenaean occupation can be demonstrated for three-fourths of the latter. Many of these Mycenaean sites were abandoned, some so completely that they were forgotten by the later Greeks. Accurate epithets are recorded for 50 of the sites.[55]

The results of on-the-site investigations of places mentioned in the Catalogue by R. Hope Simpson and J. F. Lazenby, conducted from 1958 to 1961, were published in 1970. These scholars concluded:

> . . . there is not a single place mentioned in the Catalogue which can be shown *not* to have been inhabited in the Mycenaean period . . . of those which have been *excavated*, none has so far failed to produce evidence of Mycenaean occupation.

It may also be argued that the Catalogue betrays its Mycenaean origins in its failure to mention some of the important towns of historical Greece.[56] Conversely it may be argued that the comparatively insignificant kingdoms assigned to Achilles and Odysseus are not the likely creations of a later poet.[57]

The prominence of Mycenae with 100 ships and Pylos with 90 ships accords with the archaeological evidence of these sites, as well as the moderate figure of 50 ships credited to Athens (*Iliad* 2.546-56).[58] Skepticism about the prominence of Boeotia in the Catalogue has been proven to be unjustified, as it can be shown that Boeotia was densely populated in the late Mycenaean period.[59]

In spite of the fact that Homer's poetic license in describing Troy creates for us the vision of a far more magnificent city than that which flourished in the 13th century, some of Homer's epithets reflect an accurate memory of the Late Bronze Age Troy. Bowra suggests:

55. Page, 118-77.

56. R. Hope Simpson and J. F. Lazenby, *The Catalogue of the Ships in Homer's* Iliad (Oxford: Clarendon, 1970), 154.

57. Simpson and Lazenby, 156. J. K. Anderson, "The Geometric Catalogue of Ships," in Carter and Morris, 181-91, is not convinced of the antiquity of the catalogue. As an alternative he suggests the rather unlikely hypothesis that a Boeotian poet went around the various sites associated with the Homeric heroes and created the list as he sang for his supper.

58. For Mycenaean Athens, see MacKendrick, 118-52.

59. George L. Huxley, "Mycenaean Decline and the Homeric Catalogue of Ships," *BICS* 3 (1956): 22.

It is no accident that the faulty structure of the western fortifications of Troy, which has been revealed by excavation, was known to Homer's Andromache: (Iliad VI.433-34) . . . or that the batter of the walls, which . . . provides an easy climb up to the angle, . . . where the perpendicular battlements on top of them begin, was enshrined in Patroclus' attempts to scale them: (Iliad XVI.702-03).[60]

The ruins of Hissarlik in Homer's day could hardly have inspired the poet's conception of the Trojan citadel.

As is well known, the ruins of Troy do provide a fitting archaeological background for the city besieged by the Greeks in the Trojan War. In the words of the excavator, Carl Blegen:

> Almost every house was sooner or later equipped with large storage jars, evidently for wine and oil and food supplies. . . . This was surely a precautionary measure laying up supplies to withstand a siege. This town had lasted probably no more than one generation when it was destroyed in a devastating fire. Scattered about in the wreckage of houses and streets were recovered a few fragments of human bones, indicating that the destruction was accompanied by violence. The Cincinnati Expedition therefore concluded that Troy VIIa must be recognized as the ill-fated city that was besieged, captured, sacked and burned by the Achaean invaders.[61]

Peoples and Persons

Quite a number of the Linear B names may be interpreted as the equivalents of Homeric names: e.g., *ai-wa*, "Aias"; *a-ki-re-u*, "Achilles"; *de-u-ka-ri-yo*, "Deukalion"; *e-ko-to*, "Hektor"; *ka-ra-u-ko*, "Glaukos"; *o-re-ta*, "Orestes"; *pa$_2$-da-ro*, "Pandaros"; *ta-ta-ro*, "Tantalos"; *te-se-u*, "Theseus"; *to-ro-o*, "Tros"; *wi-ro*, "Ilos."[62] What is even more significant than the presence of Mycenaean names in Homer is their occurrence in certain clusters as in the Pylos cycle, the Thessalian cycle, etc. As D. H. F. Gray concludes: "But the association of the names with families and relationships shows that it was not bare names only

---

60. Bowra, 10.

61. Blegen, "The Mycenaean Age," 18; *Troy and the Trojans* (New York: Praeger, 1963).

62. Ventris and Chadwick (104-5) believed that they could identify 58 such Homeric names. For the spelling rules governing the rendering of Linear B, see E. Vilborg, *A Tentative Grammar of Mycenaean Greek* (Göteborg: Elanders Boktryckerei, 1960).

that were handed down, and this is confirmed by the Mycenaean names connected with episodes not found elsewhere in the poems."[63]

When the Hittite documents discovered in 1907 were first published, a heated controversy arose over the possibility of identifying the *Ahhiyawa* with the Achaeans, and more particularly of identifying specific individuals. On the one hand, Emil Forrer in 1924 claimed that he had identified Atreus, Eteocles, etc. On the other hand, Ferdinand Sommer argued in 1932 that such equations were simple fantasy. Most scholars today follow the position articulated by Fritz Schachermeyr in 1935, which rejects the specific identifications of Forrer but accepts the identification of the Hittite *Ahhiyawa* with the Mycenaean Achaeans. The Hittite texts that indicate contact with the *Ahhiyawa* for 150 years prior to the sack of Troy VIIa provide the historical background for the Trojan War.[64]

Recent developments, which include the publication of the Hittite hieroglyphic inscription of Tudhaliya IV from Yalburt and of his cuneiform treaty on a bronze tablet and the decipherment of the Hittite hieroglyphic rock relief from Karabel (inland from Izmir), have enabled J. D. Hawkins to clarify the situation of western Anatolia in the Late Bronze Age.[65] Hawkins notes that after Mursili II, the Hittite king, crushed the rebellious state of Arzawa in southwestern Anatolia, a rump state of Mira, with its capital at Apasa (Ephesus), continued under three generations of kings attested by inscriptions. The cumulative evidence confirms earlier identifications of Millawanda with Miletos and Wilusa with Ilium, i.e., the region of the Troad. Hawkins concludes, "I have to declare my opinion that the evidence offered in this article strongly supports the view that Ahhiyawa does represent the Mycenaean Greeks, whether on the Aegean islands or on the Greek mainland."[66]

Homeric references to the Phoenicians, particularly in the *Odyssey*, have been considered to be allusions to contacts with the Phoenicians of the 8th century.[67] There has been a long and torrid controversy over the date of the westward expansion of the Phoenicians in the Mediterranean.[68] Many classi-

63. D. H. F. Gray, "Mycenaean Names in Homer," *JHS* 78 (1958): 47.

64. Page, chs. I and III; cf. George L. Huxley, *Achaeans and Hittites* (Belfast: Queen's University Press, 1960).

65. J. D. Hawkins, "Tarkasnawa King of Mira 'Tarkondemos', Bogazköy Sealings and Karabel," *Anatolian Studies* 48 (1998): 1-31. I thank Alan R. Millard for calling this important article to my attention.

66. Hawkins, 30.

67. Lorimer, 78-80.

68. Cf. A. G. Horon, "Canaan and the Aegean Sea: Greco-Phoenician Origins Reviewed," *Diogenes* 58 (1967): 37-61.

cal scholars, following Julius Beloch, had held that Phoenician expansion did not antedate Greek colonization in the 8th century.[69] The discovery of early Phoenician inscriptions at Nora, Sardinia, has helped confirm the traditional date for a western expansion of the Phoenicians before the Greeks. The dates of the so-called Nora inscription and the Nora fragment are disputed. Frank M. Cross has argued for an 11th-century date for the Nora fragment,[70] but other scholars would date this to the beginning of the 9th century.[71]

The presence of the words *ponikiya, ponike,* and the gentilics *Aradayo, Perita,* and *Turiyo* (referring to men from Arad, Beirut, and Tyre) in the Linear B texts,[72] as well as imported objects at both ends of the Aegean-Phoenician trade route, may be taken to confirm Homer's references to early contacts between the Greeks and traders from the Levant.[73] The discovery and the recovery of a Phoenician ship, dated to 1200, shipwrecked off Cape Gelidonya in southwestern Anatolia, has provided vivid evidence of the carriers of such trade.[74] George F. Bass, the excavator of the shipwreck, concludes:

> Further study is necessary, but our findings support the recent statement by Stubbings that "there is no anachronism in Homer's Phoenicians; his picture of the heroic age would indeed be less true without them."[75]

The Phoenician Cadmus was the legendary founder of Thebes in Boeotia. A spectacular confirmation of the early relations between Thebes and the Near East came in the course of building operations in 1963. A cache of 36 cylinder seals of lapis lazuli, 14 with cuneiform inscriptions, was uncovered. Lapis lazuli is a prized blue stone that was mined in eastern Afghanistan. One of these seals bears the name of an official of Burraburriash II (1367-

69. Rhys Carpenter, "Phoenicians in the West," *AJA* 62 (1958): 35-53; James D. Muhly, "Homer and the Phoenicians," *Berytus* 19 (1970): 19-64.

70. Frank Moore Cross, "Early Alphabetic Scripts," in *Symposia Celebrating the Seventy-Fifth Anniversary of the Founding of the American Schools of Oriental Research (1900-1975),* ed. Cross (Cambridge, Mass.: ASOR, 1979), 103-5.

71. See Benjamin F. Sass, *The Genesis of the Alphabet and Its Development in the Second Millennium B.C.* (Wiesbaden: Harrassowitz, 1988), 91-93. I owe this reference to Millard.

72. Cf. Michael C. Astour, "Second Millennium B.C. Cypriot and Cretan Onomastica Reconsidered," *JAOS* 84 (1964): 240-54.

73. Cf. Edwin Yamauchi, *Greece and Babylon: Early Contacts between the Aegean and the Near East* (Grand Rapids: Baker, 1967).

74. Cf. Jack M. Sasson, "Canaanite Maritime Involvement in the Second Millennium B.C.," *JAOS* 86 (1966): 126-38.

75. George F. Bass, *Cape Gelidonya: A Bronze Age Shipwreck* (Philadelphia: American Philosophical Society, 1967), 167, citing Wace and Stubbings, 543.

1346), a Kassite king of Mesopotamia.[76] According to Edith Porada, "The eleven Kassite cylinder seals from Thebes include the finest and largest known among original seals and impressions on tablets."[77] The seals come from various dates but must have been brought to Thebes no later than 1120. Porada hypothesizes that the cache of seals captured from Babylon ca. 1225 by Tukulti-Ninurta I was sent by the Assyrian king as a gift of lapis lazuli to the Mycenaean king at Thebes.[78]

The *Odyssey* was but one of a number of tales about the *nostoi* or returns of the Achaeans from the expedition to Troy. One Greek story concerns Mopsus, a seer of Colophon, who at the time of the Trojan War led some followers to Pamphylia and then to Cilicia in southeastern Anatolia. The discovery of a bilingual inscription of King Azitawanda of Karatepe in Cilicia has provided a dramatic confirmation of this tale. Azitawanda claims descent from *Mukshush* (Hittite), *M-p-sh* (Phoenician). According to R. D. Barnett, H. T. Bossert's 1943 discoveries at Karatepe transformed Mopsus into an undeniable historical figure.[79]

The singular reference to writing on a folded tablet, given to Bellerophon, to carry with him to Lycia on the southwest coast of Anatolia (*Iliad* 6.168-69), illustrates Homer's accurate traditions about this area and this practice as dramatically confirmed by the discovery of the Ulu-burun shipwreck off the coast of Lycia.[80] As Machteld J. Mellink comments, "The first tablet of this kind excavated in Anatolia, ironically or poignantly, came to the surface in Lycian waters, near the shore where Bellerophon landed."[81]

---

76. N. Platon and E. Stassinopoulou, "Oriental Seals from the Palace of Cadmus . . . ," *Illustrated London News* (28 November 1964), 860; cf. Michael C. Astour, *Hellenosemitica*, 2nd ed. (Leiden: Brill, 1967), 391-92. See Edwin Yamauchi, "Kassites," in *The New International Dictionary of Biblical Archaeology*, ed. Edwin M. Blaiklock and Roland K. Harrison (Grand Rapids: Zondervan, 1983), 276-78.

77. Edith Porada, "The Cylinder Seals Found at Thebes in Boeotia," *AfO* 28 (1981): 66. I owe this reference to Millard.

78. Porada, 70.

79. R. D. Barnett, "Mopsos," *JHS* 73 (1953): 140-43. On the details of the various traditions about Mopsus, see J. D. Hawkins, "Muksas," *RLA* 8/5-6: 413. I owe this reference to Millard.

80. George F. Bass, "Oldest Known Shipwreck Reveals Bronze Age Splendors," *National Geographic* 172 (1987): 692-733. For details see: Robert Payton, "The Ulu Burun Writing-Board Set," *Anatolian Studies* 41 (1991): 99-110. I owe this reference to A. R. Millard.

81. Machteld J. Mellink, "Homer, Lycia, and Lukka," in Carter and Morris, 41.

Discrepancies

After one has examined the increasing number of elements which have been confirmed as authentic, there still remain other elements which either lack archaeological confirmation or which stand in apparent conflict with the evidence. As examples of discontinuity in the Homeric traditions, Kirk lists throwing spears, the peculiar use of chariots, and the bureaucracy of the Linear B tablets, which is not reflected in the epics.[82]

It is clear that the clothing and jewelry in Homer seem to reflect much that is known only from the Geometric Age.[83] Shields with central bosses (*Iliad* 7.267) have not yet been found in Late Bronze strata from Greece, though bronze-faced shields are common in Anatolia and the Near East.[84] Likewise, a shield decorated with the face of the Gorgon (*Iliad* 1.36) is not attested before the 8th century.

On the other hand, not all scholars agree that other alleged discrepancies are insuperable problems. The contradiction, for example, between the Homeric throwing spears and the Mycenaean thrusting spears may be more apparent than real.[85]

It has often been noted that except for Nestor's reminiscences (*Iliad* 4.303-9), chariots in the epics are not used for chariot charges as in the Near East but merely to taxi individual warriors to the battlefield. But this may be due to the construction of the chariots and the unsuitable terrain of the lands bordering the Aegean. Robert Manuel Cook suggests:

> The Mycenaeans seem to have used chariots in war, unsuitable though the Greek terrain is for fast wheeled traffic; perhaps Homer was not misunderstanding tradition when he made his heroes drive up to battle and then dismount to fight.[86]

Vermeule comments that anyone driving a chariot off the road would have been liable for a spill within 10 yards.[87]

82. Kirk, *The Homeric Poems as History*, 21-33. For generally skeptical recent treatments of the issue, see John Bennet, "Homer and the Bronze Age"; and Ian Morris, "Homer and the Iron Age," in *A New Companion to Homer*, ed. Morris and Barry Powell (Leiden: Brill, 1997), 511-33, and 534-59.

83. Spyridon Marinatos, *Kleidung, Haar- und Barttracht*. Archaeologica Homerica 1/A (Göttingen: Vandenhoeck & Ruprecht, 1967), 51-53; Erwin Bielefeld, *Schmuck*. Archaeologica Homerica 1/C (Göttingen: Vandenhoeck & Ruprecht, 1968), 67-68.

84. Snodgrass, *Early Greek Armour and Weapons*, 169ff.

85. Snodgrass, *Early Greek Armour and Weapons*, 174; Simpson and Lazenby, 3-4.

86. Robert Manuel Cook, *The Greeks until Alexander* (New York: Praeger, 1962), 29.

87. Vermeule, 263.

One glaring contradiction seems to be the contrast between the cremation of Homeric heroes and the inhumation of the dead, which seems to have been the almost universal practice in Greece until ca. 1200. Cremation is introduced at the end of the Mycenaean era and becomes dominant from the Protogeometric Age to the end of the 9th century.[88] Increased evidence, though still sporadic, of cremations prior to 1200 have been found at Rhodes, Naxos, Argos, Pylos, Leucas, Attica, and Troy VI.[89] The most extensive of Mycenaean cemeteries in the 13th century is that at Perati in eastern Attica, where seven cremation burials were uncovered. Simpson and Lazenby have argued that the peculiar circumstances of cremations in the epics need not be explained as anachronisms:

> But, as Kirk points out, most of the references to cremation in Homer concern the practice of soldiers serving in a foreign land: can we be sure that, in such circumstances, the Mycenaeans buried their dead? Would they not have been afraid that the tombs would be insulted and rifled when they withdrew, just as Agamemnon feared that the Trojans would insult the tomb of his brother (*Il.* 4:174-7)? Furthermore, it may not merely be a coincidence that one people with whom the Mycenaeans were in contact and who certainly practised cremation were precisely the people of Troy VI-VIIa. Thus we cannot really be sure that the practising of cremation by the heroes does reflect post-Mycenaean custom.[90]

Scholars such as Finley and Kirk have stressed the disparity between the social institutions as we find them depicted in the epics and as represented in the Linear B texts. We find almost nothing in the epics of the bureaucracy and specialization that we have in the Linear B texts. But this may simply be due to a different point of view as Simpson and Lazenby comment:

> The fact that the poems betray little if any knowledge of the quasi-feudal bureaucracy of the tablets may not be so much due to the disappearance of the system as to the fact that it was something quite alien to the poetic tradition, and therefore failed to impinge upon it, however fundamental it may have been to real life.[91]

---

88. Manolis Andronikos, *Totenkult.* Archaeologica Homerica 2/W (Göttingen: Vandenhoeck & Ruprecht, 1968), 129-30.

89. Vermeule, 302-3; Dietrich, 19.

90. Simpson and Lazenby, 5-6.

91. Simpson and Lazenby, 7. T. B. L. Webster, *From Mycenae to Homer* (New York: Praeger, 1959), maintains that the epics and the Linear B evidence can be harmonized.

Indeed, it would be rather captious for critics living three millennia hence — such is the distance in time which separates us from the Mycenaean Age — to object that the writings of a Norman Mailer do not present an authentic picture of 20th-century society because they bear little resemblance to stock quotations or inventories from the Department of Agriculture!

Post-Mycenaean Traditions

Archaeological discoveries, especially in recent decades, have provided some dramatic confirmations of post-Mycenaean traditions as well. The tradition of Dorian attacks against Mycenaean centers has often been questioned. In a symposium on the subject published in 1948, J. F. Daniel argued:

> It is significant that these defensive moves seem to have been made on a purely individual basis. . . . There seems to have been no concerted plan for a unified defense of Greece. No block-houses have been discovered in the passes and no fortifications at the Isthmus.[92]

In 1957 Oscar Broneer found long stretches of a cyclopean wall near Isthmia on the Isthmus of Corinth. The wall faced north and was designed to protect the Peloponnese against invaders. It is dated to the transitional period between Late Helladic IIIB and IIIC (ca. 1230). According to Broneer, "The known Mycenaean settlements in the Corinthia are too small to have been capable of such an undertaking, and we are justified in concluding that the wall was erected by concerted efforts of the kings and chieftains in the thickly populated Argolid."[93]

According to tradition, migrations of the Greeks to Ionia in western Anatolia took place after the Dorian attacks on the Mycenaeans. Many classical scholars doubted that any migrations to Ionia had taken place as early as the 11th or 10th centuries. In a comprehensive survey of the evidence published in 1948, G. M. A. Hanfmann asserted: ". . . the traditional dates for the foundation of Ionian cities are in complete disagreement with archaeological facts. . . . But not until 800 B.C. did the historic Greeks coming from the islands begin to wrest the towns of Ionia from the Anatolians."[94] In an article written less than two decades later, which does not refer to his previous de-

92. John Franklin Daniel, "The Dorian Invasion: The Setting," *AJA* 52 (1948): 109.

93. Oscar Broneer, "The Cyclopean Wall on the Isthmus of Corinth and Its Bearing on Late Bronze Age Chronology," *Hesperia* 35 (1966): 357.

94. G. M. A. Hanfmann, "Archaeology in Homeric Asia Minor," *AJA* 52 (1948): 146.

nial, Professor Hanfmann acknowledged that discovery of Protogeometric pottery at Miletus, Smyrna, Phocaea, and Teos had confirmed the traditional date for the Ionian migrations:

> It looks as if two or three generations after the fall of Miletus the Greeks returned to the western coast of Asia Minor, but now in sufficient strength to make their settlements permanent. The time of their arrival at Miletus would be close to the date that ancient Greek chronographers conjectured — 1044 B.C.[95]

Conclusions

I think that it should be apparent that too often negative criticisms of the traditions are based upon arguments from silence and therefore represent not so much the inaccuracy of the traditions as the inadequacy of our archaeological data.

In the first place, with the exception of the University of Minnesota surveys in Messenia in the southwest Peloponnese, many areas of the Aegean have not been subjected to thorough, systematic surveys. Alan E. Samuel estimates that "All in all, well over three hundred Mycenaean sites are known, and it is probable that this number would be quadrupled if all Greece were carefully explored for evidence."[96]

At Ephesus the Austrians since 1894 have found vast remains of the later periods. But nothing of the Bronze Age was found until Turkish engineers building a parking lot in 1963 found a Mycenaean burial. For decades nothing of the Bronze Age was found at Halicarnassus until in 1962 George Bass saw a man walking the street carrying a Mycenaean jar from a nearby village.[97]

It is my expectation that increased archaeological discoveries will but add to the list of confirmations which we have seen in recent years. A. J. Graham, in words that can be applied, *mutatis mutandis*, to the Homeric traditions, writes:

> One of the results of the possession of the new evidence from archaeology has been a tendency to be unwilling to trust the literary evidence

---

95. G. M. A. Hanfmann, "Archaeology and the Origins of Greek Culture: Notes on Recent Work in Asia Minor," *Antioch Review* 25 (1965): 52.

96. Alan E. Samuel, *The Mycenaeans in History* (Englewood Cliffs: Prentice-Hall, 1966), 101.

97. Hanfmann, *Antioch Review* 25 (1965): 42-53.

when it stands unconfirmed by archaeological discoveries. . . . Such an attitude is no doubt from an ideal point of view perfectly correct. We must all look forward to the day when the literary evidence can all be evaluated against a background of adequate archaeological exploration. But it seems to me that the outstanding general result from all the archaeological discoveries about Greek colonisation has been that the literary record is on the whole thoroughly trustworthy.[98]

In conclusion, the extreme skepticism of minimalists like Finley is not warranted, as it underestimates the range of possibly authentic elements which have been preserved in Homer. On the other hand, the extreme optimism of maximalists like Vermeule does not adequately account for the many (some would say majority of) materials in Homer that betray a Dark Age or even early Geometric origin.

E. S. Sherratt, in a comprehensive analysis of the question of the relationship between Homer, history, and archaeology, offers a persuasive explanation of the growth of the amalgam of an originally ancient core of traditions, which over the centuries of oral transmission necessarily added new elements to make the story comprehensible to later audiences. He identifies those elements that were least susceptible to change (episodes, formulaic scenes, necessary description or detail, formulaic lines, formulaic endings, retrospectives, major characters) and those that were most susceptible to change (episodic links, speeches, incidental description or detail, similes, nonformulaic scenes, catalogues, minor characters).[99] His programmatic approach can offer a helpful paradigm for biblical scholars as well.

Though new developments both in archaeological interpretation and the analysis of texts have raised questions about a consensus reached in the 1960s about the historical correlations of the Homeric traditions, John K. Davies, after listing nine criteria for testing oral tradition, concludes, "Such as they are, however, their combined application seems to me on balance to encourage the hypothesis that in our *Iliad* we are dealing with a literary creation which reflects an orally transmitted tradition of an historical Trojan War."[100]

---

98. A. J. Graham, "Patterns in Early Greek Colonisation," *JHS* 91 (1971): 38.

99. E. S. Sherratt, " 'Reading the Texts': Archaeology and the Homeric Question," *Antiquity* 64 (1990): 807-24.

100. John K. Davies, "The Reliability of the Oral Tradition," in *The Trojan War: Its Historicity and Context,* ed. L. Foxhall and Davies (Bristol: Bristol Classical, 1984), 101. I owe this reference to Millard. Eric H. Cline, "Achilles in Anatolia: Myth, History and the Assuwa Rebellion," in *Crossing Boundaries and Linking Horizons,* ed. Gordon D. Young, Mark W. Chavalas, and Richard E. Averbeck (Bethesda: CDL, 1997), 202-3, suggests that the aid of the Ahhiyawans

The implications of these positive archaeological confirmations of the Homeric texts should not be missed by biblical scholars. As Dever concludes, "The parallels with the early history of Israel and the growth of biblical tradition and literature are clear, even extending to the chronology of events," adding, "If Homer can in a sense be 'historical,' why not the Hebrew Bible?"[101]

(Mycenaeans) in Assuwa's revolt against the Hittites may be reflected in the *Iliad*'s account (e.g., 5.640-43) of earlier expeditions in the Troad.

101. Dever, 279.

A New Working Hypothesis for the Identification of Migdol

BENJAMIN EDIDIN SCOLNIC

Encyclopedias and dictionaries make it seem that site identifications are definitive and certain, where there really is only confusion and difficulty. And yet, a central dilemma of biblical archaeology remains balancing the need to identify the geographical contexts of biblical events with the standards of evidence required by modern archaeology. The truth is that there are very few sites indeed that yield the kind of evidence required to make the site identifications that we, especially we who are openly interested in religion, yearn to make. And so many of us make speculative identifications, only to watch the reputation of biblical accuracy rise and fall on the fortunes of our speculations.

Let me state my own prejudices from the outset: If utilizing the information provided by the Bible as data to be considered in the identification of ancient sites means that one is a maximalist, then I am a maximalist. But I do not think of myself this way. I take every bit of geographical data in the Bible seriously. But I also take extrabiblical texts and archaeological evidence seriously. I ignore and dismiss nothing.

Here is a simple program that all responsible students might use for site identification of biblical toponyms:

1. The biblical data — what the Bible says happened at the site and any information about where the site is;
2. Relevant extrabiblical texts about the toponym;
3. Possibly relevant archaeological data; that is, evidence from sites that may be the place in question; and

4. An explicitly tentative conclusion, which might very well be a purposeful refraining from concluding anything for the present.

If, for instance, I were studying the problem of the identification of biblical Hormah or Arad, I would need to study the biblical texts intensely, even though they may conflict with each other. Indeed, the more I would study the biblical data, the more I would realize how complex it is. I would, in order to complete this first step, have to divide texts of Israelite victory from texts of Israelite defeat. I would have to make a tentative conclusion about the time period of that defeat and/or victory. With that tentative conclusion, I would then bring any relevant extrabiblical documents or inscriptions, such as a reference from an Egyptian Execration text, which would attest the existence of a place with that name in 1900 B.C.E. Third, I would study every possibly relevant archaeological excavation in that area of the Negev in a search for possible sites of Arad and Hormah. Fourth and last, I would then decide whether the various pieces of evidence relate to each other in order to reconstruct the historical realities involved. It would be my hope, but certainly not my expectation, that I could put the pieces together. On the contrary, my assumption would be that, unless I surprised myself by fitting some edges together that others have not, I would not have enough pieces of the puzzle to make anything work. If I did not surprise myself, I would not jump to the conclusion that the Bible has been "proved" or "disproved." I would wait for new data to emerge in the future.

That particular cluster of problems is not a bad model for the more famous and religiously more important set of problems that we are dealing with here, the route of the exodus and the site of the miracle at the Sea. I do not need to trot out all of the bibliography of the 19th-century travelers and the amateur speculators who, interestingly, often have theories that are the same as those who are professional scholars and archaeologists. We know that there are those who would deny the enslavement in Egypt and the historicity of the exodus, not to mention the miracle at the Sea. There are those who would say that the whole thing is a metaphor. There are those who see it as a kind of historicization of the myth of the combat with the sea-god.[1] There are those who would employ source-critical tools on the narratives, only to find their approach unfruitful.[2]

1. Norman H. Snaith, "ים־סוף: The Sea of Reeds: The Red Sea," *VT* 15 (1965): 395-98; Bernard F. Batto, "The Reed Sea: *Requiescat in Pace*," *JBL* 102 (1983): 30-33; Frank Moore Cross, *Canaanite Myth and Hebrew Epic* (Cambridge, Mass.: Harvard University Press, 1973), 112-44; Frank E. Eakin Jr., "The Reed Sea and Baalism," *JBL* 86 (1967): 378-84; Brevard S. Childs, "A Traditio-historical Study of the Reed Sea Tradition," *VT* 20 (1970): 412-14.

2. The confusion of this narrative makes it important grist for the source-critical mill.

I would say, I think without prejudice, that there is such a thing as making an assumption in order to create the opportunity to prove that assumption. If we simply deny the historicity of these events, we will never try to demonstrate their historicity and we will certainly not find the necessary evidence. It is only the assumption of their historicity, at least as a working hypothesis, that sends us forward in our search.

Now let me turn to the matter at hand. There is no more crucial site than that of the crossing of the Sea, hence the preponderance of theories. There are those, like Beke and some modern adventurers involved in a best-selling pot-boiler called *The Gold of Exodus*,[3] who say that the Israelites crossed the Gulf of Aqaba, one arm of the Red Sea, into Arabia and went to a Mount Sinai in that area. There are those who would say that the Israelites

---

The source-critical approach follows each source's account independently and then compares the various versions of the story that are now incorporated in the present text. Brevard S. Childs makes a fine presentation of these versions: *The Book of Exodus*. OTL (Philadelphia: Westminster, 1974), 218ff. In E, we have the problematic Exod. 13:17-19; the people may become afraid if they see war, so God leads them "roundabout, by way of the wilderness at the Sea of Reeds." The Egyptians pursue the Israelites (14:5a, 7) and are defeated by God (14:19a, 25a). In J, the Egyptians chase their former slaves (14:5b, 6, 9a); the Israelites are afraid (10b, 11-14). God protects them (19b, 21a, 24, 25b, 27a, 30, 31) and the Egyptians are defeated. P's account has the Israelites travel from Succoth to "Etham at the edge of the wilderness" (13:20). The Israelites are told "to turn back and encamp before Pi-hahiroth, between Migdol and the sea, before Baal-zephon" (14:1-4). When we turn to Num. 33:5-11, we see the Israelites move to the edge of the wilderness at Etham as in the P account of Exod. 13:20.

They then turned about toward Pi-hahiroth, which faces Baal-zephon, and they encamped before Migdol. They set out from Pene-hahiroth and passed through the sea into the wilderness (Num. 33:7-8a).

Before the Israelites actually enter the wilderness, it seems, they turn back towards the sea, which they then pass through in order to reach the wilderness. It is interesting that Num. 33:7-8 does not mention *yām sûp*, and that the P passages in Exod. 13-15 do not refer to the sea by this name either. Since, in Exod. 14:2 and 9, P attempts to locate the site of the miracle with unusual precision, the absence of the name given to the sea in E (13:18) and J (15:22) seems somewhat strange. The Egyptians chase the Israelites because God has hardened Pharaoh's heart to do so (14:8a). The Israelites are "departing defiantly, boldly" (14:8b) and are overtaken by the Egyptians "after having encamped by the sea, near Pi-hahiroth, before Baal-zephon" (14:9). The Egyptians are defeated and the Israelites are saved (14:15-18, 21-23, 26, 27a, 28-29).

For my immediate purposes, source-criticism does not help much, which is instructive in itself. The accounts are basically the same, at least in outline. One difference from the other two sources may be that P makes the Israelites turn back (they have left Egypt in 12:41ff.) in 14:2 and that it is P that is interested in the specific toponyms.

3. Howard Blum, *The Gold of Exodus: The Discovery of the True Mount Sinai* (New York: Simon & Schuster, 1998).

crossed the Gulf of Suez, the other arm of the Red Sea, or a connected lake or tributary, and went into the Sinai Peninsula and a Mount Sinai in the southern part of that region. There are those, like Colonel C. S. Jarvis, Otto Eissfeldt, William Foxwell Albright, and Eliezer Oren, who prefer a northern route, speaking of Lake Bardawil, the Gulf of Serbonis, as the site of the great miracle. (Figure 1)

Before the North Sinai Archaeological Project was created, I was an adherent of the northern route. I was long past the problem of the Red/Reed Sea. Since Numbers 33 distinguishes between the sea of the miracle and the Red Sea,[4] the other sea in the area must be the Mediterranean. Indeed, to call the Mediterranean "the Sea" makes perfect sense; it was *the* sea in the biblical world. I was also consumed, as I still am, with the fact that God instructs Moses to *šûḇ*, to have the Israelites "turn back." The Israelites, moving south, heading away from the Nile Delta and Mediterranean, are now told to turn

---

4. Notice carefully that the sea through which the Israelites pass is a different sea from the Sea of Reeds and is separated by at least a number of days and several stages of the Israelites' journey. The Red Sea is too far away from the places in Egypt from which the Israelites escaped to be the scene of the event. The sea of the event is the Reed Sea and is one of the lakes or bodies of water east of the Nile Delta or may even be a body of water that no longer exists. Some translations, including NJPSV (the Tanakh), have followed this logic and have replaced "Red Sea" with "Sea of Reeds."

The name of the sea in question, *yām sûp*, does not literally mean "Red Sea" but "Sea of Reeds" or "reedy sea." *Yām sûp* does mean "Red Sea" in other biblical texts; this had led to great confusion. Biblical parallelism demands that the poet use a poetic variant with the word "sea." "Pharaoh's chariots and his army" has its parallel in "the pick of his officers." "Cast" has its parallel in "are drowned." "Sea" finds its parallel in "reedy sea." When, later, the Red Sea and its arms became known as the *yām sûp*, the traditions grew that the miracle of the Sea had happened at the Red Sea.

It is important to emphasize that in the prose account of Exodus 14 the place of the famous crossing is not the *yām sûp* but simply "the sea." Exodus 13:18 states that the Israelites were led in a roundabout way "by the way of the wilderness *yām sûp*." The syntax is terrible here; there is no preposition stating "to the *yām sûp*" or "at the *yām sûp*." The phrase seems to have been added by a later glossator.

Even if we do take *yām sûp* here as "Red Sea," it could merely mean that the original route was to go on the highway south to the Red Sea. Indeed, those who have studied the names of ancient roads in the Sinai have found that if you were on a road going north, you would call it one name. If you were going south on the same road, you would call it by the name of a southern destination. So the Israelites were on a wilderness road going south.

> Pharaoh's chariots and his army
> He has cast into the sea;
> And the pick of his officers
> Are drowned in the *yām sûp*. (Exod. 15:4)

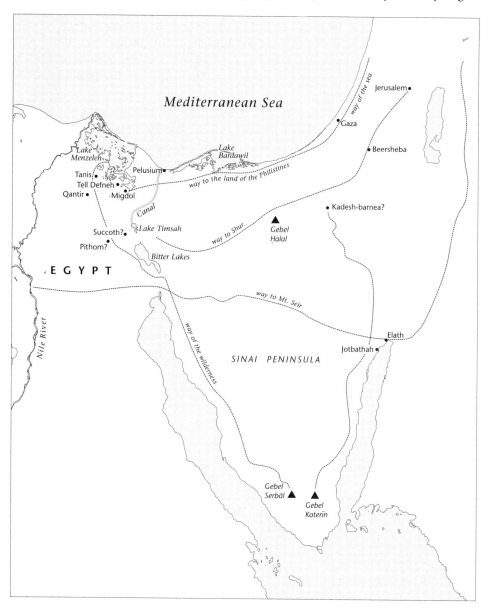

Figure 1. Routes of the Exodus

around, that is, to come back north, to the Yām, the Mediterranean. After a trip to Egypt more than 50 years ago (1948), Albright stated: "In any case, the new discoveries prove conclusively that we must give up the now traditional southern crossing and separate the Red Sea completely from the Reed Sea in Exodus."[5]

I accepted this. To me, Lake Bardawil was just perfect for the spinning of a theory about the miracle at the Sea. Lake Bardawil is a vast lake on the Mediterranean coast between Port Said and el-Arish. It is a place where armies get swallowed up, an area that changes from land to sea and back to land because of periodic flooding. At certain points on the shores of this lake, there are big areas of rushes. If Lake Bardawil is the "Sea of Reeds," then add the Mount of Lawgiving (Gebel Hellal), the quails and manna that could be found only in the north, the area with provisions for a large host; and so, the northern Sinai became, for me, a plausible context for the Israelites' wanderings. These various elements, Jarvis said, "fit into each other like the parts of a jig-saw puzzle."[6] And I agreed.

Certain elements in the argument, however, began to bother me. I became unsure that the so-called new discoveries, such as the speculation about Mount Casius as Baal-zephon, had proven anything. I really stopped believing in the northern theory when I started going to Egypt and saw the distances involved. I knew the biblical story too well to think that the Israelites would have gone that far before the Egyptians pursued and caught up to them. But most of all, I wondered if the Mediterranean had come much further south than Albright and the other northern proponents had thought. I kept asking, "What about the Big Biblical Picture? What did the map look like?" To trace the route of the exodus based on modern-day maps is incredibly unscientific. It is common knowledge that coastlines change, whether we are speaking of the site of ancient Troy, the harbor of Alexandria, or the beach in New Haven, Connecticut. A map of the ancient Sinai was required so that we could know what the possibilities for the route of the exodus were. In thinking about the area of the site of the miracle at the Sea, I became a man without a region.

Now, thanks to the work of the project's geologist, Steve Moshier, and his collaborator from the Geological Survey of Egypt, we have a better picture of the paleo-environment of North Sinai going back to 3300 years ago. While there are still some modifications to make, we basically know the map of the part of the Sinai relevant to the first stages of the exodus. (Figure 1)

As one who believed in the northern theory, I now admit that it was

5. "Baal-zephon," in *Festschrift Alfred Bertholet*, ed. Walter Baumgartner et al. (Tübingen: J. C. B. Mohr, 1950), 13.

6. C. S. Jarvis, *Yesterday, Today and Tomorrow in Sinai* (Edinburgh: Blackwood, 1936), 155.

quite simply impossible to begin with. Frankly, some people, like James Hoffmeier, knew this before Moshier did his work. Bruno Marcolongo had presented an interesting reconstruction of the route of the Pelusiac branch of the Nile, showing that 2000 years ago the coastline of the Mediterranean was further south than it is today.[7] In 1978, Israeli geologists had reported that the mound and lake of Sabakhat Bardawil rose up only in the 8th century.[8] In Oren's archaeological excavations at 20 sites in the northern Sinai, no evidence was found before the 6th century, the Persian era.[9] And yet even Oren still backed Lake Bardawil as the site of the great event.[10] Why? Because it is hard to change the map in one's head. Still, that is exactly what we need to do. Using the new map, we must focus on one possible route out of Egypt, the strip of land between the Mediterranean and this southern body of water (Figure 1).

The Biblical Passage

Let us consider the key biblical passage in order to try to understand the relationship between the key toponyms involved in the great event:

> The Lord said to Moses: Tell the Israelites to turn back and encamp before Pi-hahiroth, between Migdol and the sea, before Baal-zephon; you shall encamp facing it, by the sea. Pharaoh will say of the Israelites, "They are astray in the land; the wilderness has closed in on them." Then I will stiffen Pharaoh's heart, and he will pursue them, that I may gain glory through Pharaoh and all his host; and the Egyptians shall know that I am the Lord. And they did so. (Exod. 14:1-4)

7. Bruno Marcolongo, "Evolution du paleo-environnement dans la partie orientale du Delta du Nil depuis la transgression flandrienne (8,000 B.P.) par rapport aux modèles de peuplement anciens," *CRIPEL* 14 (1992): 23-31 and fig. 1.

8. David Neev and Gerald M. Friedman, "Late Holocene Tectonic Activity Along the Margins of Sinai Subplate," *Science* 202 (1978): 427-29.

9. Eliezer D. Oren, "Migdol: A New Fortress on the Edge of the Eastern Nile Delta," *BASOR* 256 (1984): 7-44; "An Egyptian Fortress on the Military Road between Egypt and Canaan," *Qadmoniot* 6 (1973): 101-3 (Heb.); "Military Architecture along the 'Ways of Horus': Egyptian Reliefs and Archaeological Evidence," *ErIsr* 20 (1989): 8-22; 21 (1990): 6-22; "Northern Sinai," *NEAEHL* 4:1386-96; "The Overland Route between Egypt and Canaan in the Early Bronze Age," *IEJ* 23 (1973): 198-205; "The 'Ways of Horus' in North Sinai," in *Egypt, Israel, Sinai: Archaeological and Historical Relationships in the Biblical Period*, ed. Anson F. Rainey (Tel Aviv: Tel Aviv University, 1987), 69-119.

10. Eliezer D. Oren, "How Not to Create a History of the Exodus — A Critique of Professor Goedicke's Theories," *BAR* 7/6 (1981): 46-53.

The very specific geographical information makes it clear that the biblical text is attempting to provide a precise set of referents. The unusually detailed identification, "before Pi-hahiroth, between Migdol and the sea, before Baal-zephon," makes the sentence somewhat awkward. Awkwardness may mean a gloss, but it may be an attempt to ensure identification. While, for instance, the biblical writers do not have any interest in telling us where Mount Sinai is, they are particularly interested in telling us where the miracle occurred. An articulate summation of this point comes from Joseph H. Hertz:

> The landmarks mentioned in this verse (Exod. 14:2) have long ago disappeared, and cannot be identified with certainty. The precision, however, with which they are designated, guarantees that the spots were once well known. No portion of the world outside of Palestine was more familiar to the Israelites than the western border of Egypt; and no event in Bible history more perennially popular than the story of the Deliverance from Egypt.[11]

It is the challenge of the modern scholar and archaeologist to find a place that was known to the ancient readers of the Bible, the scene of the greatest event in biblical history.

After considerable reflection on Exod. 14:2, I agree with Hertz that the Bible wants us to know where the great event occurred. We are given four referents. The Israelites are to *šûb*, to turn back. As we know from Josh. 19:12, *šûb* in biblical geography means to turn in the opposite direction. After the Israelites *šûb*, they are to encamp before Pi-hahiroth, the first coordinate, between Migdol (the second) and the sea (the third), before Baal-zephon (the fourth). They are to encamp facing Pi-hahiroth, by the sea. If the sea is *the* sea, the Mediterranean, then we need to know how far south the sea came. If Pi-hahiroth is indeed the mouth of the diggings and is a reference to a site connected with the Eastern Frontier Canal (as I will discuss below),[12] then we have two referents. If we could know, obviously, where either Migdol or Baal-zephon is, we could know the location of the most famous miracle of them all.

What can we glean from the details of the verse? One point is that Pi-hahiroth is by the sea and another is that there is enough land between Migdol and the sea for a sizable — and I do not wish to go into how sizable — encampment. It would be helpful to have some idea how large an area is

11. Joseph H. Hertz, ed., *The Pentateuch and Haftorahs* (London: Soncino, 1967), 266.

12. James K. Hoffmeier, *Israel in Egypt* (Oxford: Oxford University Press, 1997), 169-71, 182-91.

formed by these four landmarks. In other words, do we need to think about the three place names as being in tight geographical proximity? It is possible that the four coordinates create a large area. But I will suggest that the verse describes a very precise and narrow area.

Here is the key verse in its forms in Exodus 14 and Numbers 33.

> Tell the Israelites to turn back and encamp before Pi-hahiroth, between Migdol and the sea, before Baal-zephon; you shall encamp facing it, by the sea. (Exod. 14:2)

> They set out from Etham and turned about toward Pi-hahiroth, which faces Baal-zephon, and they encamped before Migdol. They set out from Pene-hahiroth and passed through the sea into the wilderness. (Num. 33:7-8)

Lipnê occurs 634 times in the Bible. The most common usage is *lipnê Adonai*, "before God," "in the presence of God," which occurs literally hundreds of times. Other common usages are *lipnê hamizbēah*, "in front of the altar," or *lipnê ha-miškan*, "in front of the tabernacle," or *lipnê 'ohel mô'ēd*, "in front of the tent of meeting." In all of these cases, *lipnê* means immediately in front of or near the place, which brings one into the presence of God. *Lipnê* rarely comes to describe a physical relationship to a place. I will note the few occurrences of this usage. Abraham buys the cave of Machpelah that is before or in the immediate vicinity of Hebron, where the transaction is taking place. According to Num. 33:47, the Israelites encamp in the hills of Abarim, *lipnê* Nebo, "in the hills," "in the shadow of," "in view of," or perhaps "to the east of," Mount Nebo.[13] *Lipnê* used in this way means "in sight of," "in the face of," as in our American colloquial phrase "in your face." We should think about the Israelites' encampment as being within sight of Pi-hahiroth and Baal-zephon. If one can see both of these places from the encampment, and if that encampment were between Migdol and the sea, then all of these places are in a narrow, prescribed area. I even wonder if the Num. 33:8 usage, *penê hahirōt*, is not somehow related to this emphasis on *lipnê*, "towards," "before," "before the face of."

If *lipnê* is an indicator that the places are close to each other, we have a very helpful clue for the site identification of at least one of the relevant place names. I will return to this below.

---

13. In the account of the battle of Ai in Joshua 8, the enemy rushes out to the descent *lipnê* the Arabah to engage in battle.

Migdol

Of the three place names, Migdol, Pi-hahiroth and Baal-zephon, my emphasis will be on Migdol. In *The Archaeological Encyclopedia of the Holy Land,* we find the following entry for "Migdol":

> One of the halts on the route of the Exodus (Exod. 14:2), before the crossing of the Red Sea. Identified with the Migdol fortress of Sethos I and of Merneptah at Tell el-Heir, 13 miles northwest of Qantarah.[14]

This simple paragraph obscures the mystery and the importance of this site. As will be discussed later on, Tell el-Her does not have any evidence of occupation before the Persian period. The sentence is thus misleading and makes it seem that there was a Migdol fortress of Sethos I and of Merneptah at Tell el-Her. Based on the archaeological evidence, Tell el-Her cannot be the Migdol of the Exodus, or the fortress of Migdol mentioned in Egyptian documents in the New Kingdom era.

The fact is that there should not be a consensus about the location of Migdol. And yet the equation of biblical Migdol with Tell el-Her, in Oren's words, "has become a primary datum for Egyptologists and Bible students, as a glance at almost any biblical atlas or historical map of the region will demonstrate."[15]

One of the most complicating factors in the identification of Migdol is that it was used as a toponym, a component of a toponym, and a simple noun. The term *migdōl* comes from Northwest Semitic and means "tower" or "fortress."[16] Migdol is a place name found in the Bible (Jer. 44:1; 46:14; Ezek. 29:10; 30:6). Jeremiah 44:1 talks about Migdol in the same breath with Tahpanhes and Noph (Memphis):

> The word that came to Jeremiah for all the Judeans who live in the land of Egypt, who live at Migdol, and at Tahpanhes, and at Noph, and in the land of Pathros.

What we may have here is a series of Jewish garrisons or settlements in an or-

---

14. *Archaeological Encyclopedia of the Holy Land,* ed. Abraham Negev, 3rd ed. (New York: Prentice-Hall, 1990), 262.

15. Oren, *BASOR* 256 (1984): 34. See for instance Herbert G. May, ed., *Oxford Bible Atlas* (London: Oxford University Press, 1962), 135.

16. Raphael Giveon, *LÄ* 4 (1982): 124-25; Hoffmeier, 189; James E. Hoch, *Semitic Words in Egyptian Texts of the New Kingdom and Third Intermediate Period* (Princeton: Princeton University Press, 1994), 169-70.

der going northeast to south, with Migdol the most easterly and the land of Pathros, which is Upper Egypt (Egyp. *P3 t3 rsy*), at the southernmost side of Egypt. In Jer. 46:14, Migdol is listed first before Tahpanhes and Noph. Ezekiel 29:10 and 30:6 state: *mimigdōl sᵉwēnēh*, "from Migdol to Aswan," from the northeast frontier settlement to its southern counterpart.

There are several other biblical and rabbinic texts with the place component Migdol/Migdal but which are not related to the Migdol in the northwest Sinai.[17] The Migdol of the Pentateuch (Exod. 14:2; Num. 33:7), in theory, could be the Migdol of Jeremiah and Ezekiel. We will have to see the data provided by extrabiblical texts and archaeology, however, to see if we have a site that yields evidence from both periods.

Extrabiblical Data

When we turn our attention to Migdol in extrabiblical documents, we find the name Migdol appearing in Egyptian documents for the first time in the 18th Dynasty. The use of this Semitic term in naming an Egyptian locality is interesting in itself. Since the Egyptians, and not just the Bible, called places by this name, the use of the Semitic term probably reflects Semitic influence in this part of Egypt, as common sense would suggest. Migdol, Oren[18] states and most would agree, is a direct borrowing into Egyptian as a common noun meaning fortress and as a proper name for different settlements and stations. Ellen Fowles Morris has shown that the term Migdol "is useful in distinguishing compact, self-contained forts from walled fortress-towns."[19]

---

17. Examples are: (1) Migdal-eder, "The Tower of Eder" or "The Fold-Tower," in the vicinity of Jerusalem on the road to Bethlehem, where Jacob lived after Rachel's death and where Reuben slept with Bilhah, his father's concubine (Gen. 35:21; Mic. 4:8; also mentioned in *b. Qidd.* 55a); (2) Migdal-el in Josh. 19:38, a stronghold of Naphtali; (3) Migdal-gad in Josh. 15:37, a stronghold in Judah (perhaps Kh. el-Mejdeleh, east of Ashkelon; MR 140105). In addition, we find these Migdals in rabbinic literature: (1) Migdal Dyo (cf. *Gen. Rab.* 98:11), a town in northern Israel, apparently in the Galilee or southern Lebanon; (2) Migdal Gedor (cf. *Ta'an.* 100); (3) Migdal Nunia, near Tiberias (*Pesaḥ.* 46a). We find the term *migdal* as a tower (in Gen. 11:5; Judges 8-9; 2 Sam. 22:51). It is found in religious poetry (the figure of God is a tower in Ps. 61:3 and Prov. 18:10). Migdal is also found in romantic biblical poetry (a beautiful neck is like the tower of David in Song 4:4; an ivory tower is found in Song 7:4; and breasts are like towers in Song 8:10). Special towers are found in Lebanon in Song 7:4; at Penuel (Judg. 8:17), at Shechem (Judg. 9:46, 47, 49), and at Jerusalem (Song 4:4).

18. Oren, *BASOR* 256 (1984): 7-44; *Qadmoniot* 6 (1973): 101-3 (Heb.).

19. Ellen Fowles Morris, *The Architecture of Imperialism: An Investigation into the Role of*

According to H. Y. Bar-Deroma,[20] there are 25 settlements called Migdol in Israel and Lebanon dating from the First and Second Temple periods, in addition to many ruins. Some scholars feel that the name is found in Egypt only where a Semitic settlement existed. They say that the Semitic name Migdol (Gk. *Magdōlon*) is given as either a proper name or a common noun to various localities where foreign mercenaries were posted. I am not at all sure that this hypothesis can be sustained, but it is suggestive and interesting to think that the toponym Migdol was used only where Semites lived.

Egyptian References to Migdol

On the Karnak reliefs of Seti I, Migdol is one of the first forts on the Ways of Horus.[21] The third station on the Ways of Horus, after "the Fortress of Sile" and "the Dwelling of the Lion," is "the Migdol of Menma're," the Migdol of Seti I. This Migdol has often been equated with the Migdol of Exod. 14:2 and Num. 33:7.[22] It remains to be seen if this equation is plausible.

Migdol is mentioned in important Egyptian papyri as a border fortress that monitored on the movement of men through the net of forts along the desert border (the Bible calls these forts "the wall of Egypt"). In Papyrus Anastasi V 19:18ff., "the Chief of Bowmen of Tjeku, Ka-kem-wer" describes how he is looking for two slaves who have fled from what seems to be Pi-ramesses and slipped through the network of forts and escaped. In the spring, around the year 1200 (the reign of Seti II), Ka-kem-wer had left the palace on

---

Fortresses and Administrative Headquarters in New Kingdom Foreign Policy (Ph.D. diss., University of Pennsylvania, 2001), 512.

20. H. Y. Bar-Deroma, *The Negev* (Jerusalem, 1935), 517 (Heb.).

21. The Epigraphic Survey, *The Battle Reliefs of King Sety I*. Reliefs and Inscriptions at Karnak 4 (Chicago: Oriental Institute, 1986), pl. 6. For convenience's sake, and after Alan Gardiner and Yohanan Aharoni, we can list the stations between Sile and Gaza in the two important sources:

Karnak reliefs of Seti I	Papyrus Anastasi I
1. The dividing waters	
2. The fortress of Sile	"The ways of Horus"
3. The dwelling of the lion	The dwelling of Ramsses
4. The Migdol of Menma're (Seti I)	
5. The well of *ḥ-p-n*	*ḥ-t-y-n*

22. Alan H. Gardiner, "The Ancient Military Road between Egypt and Palestine," *JEA* 6 (1920): 108; "The Geography of the Exodus," in *Recueil d'Études Égyptologiques dédiées à la Mémoire de Jean-François Champollion* (Paris: E. Champion, 1922), 212; Oren, *BASOR* 256 (1984): 31.

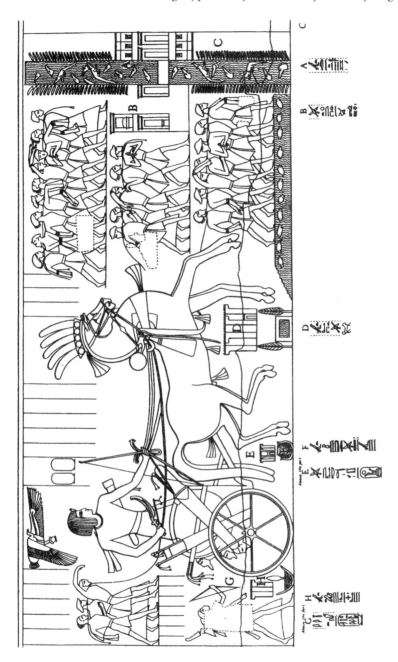

Figure 2. Seti I relief from Karnak temple

the ninth day of the third month of the third season and reached "the enclosure-wall *(sgr)* of Tjeku"[23] by the next day. When he reaches "the fortress" (probably the chief frontier post Sile), he is told that the fugitives had gone north, up to the Migdol of Seti I.[24] This Migdol is east of Tjeku, either the area or the place. If it is the place, we can identify it with Succoth and Tell el-Maskhuta, as will be argued below.

There is no reason not to connect the Migdol of Seti I on the Karnak reliefs with the Migdol of Seti I in Papyrus Anastasi V,[25] and there is no reason not to allow for the possibility that the Migdol of the exodus is the same place.

The third Egyptian reference to Migdol is in the Amarna Letters 234.[26] In this letter written in the time of Akhenaten, Satatna, ruler of Akka, explains his actions concerning a deserter named Zirdamyašda:

> Akka is like Magdalu in Egypt, and has the king, [*my lord*], not [h]eard *that Šuta is turned* against me? May the king, my lord, [sen]d his [com]missioner to fet[ch] him.[27]

23. Gardiner, *JEA* 6 (1920): 109.

24. *ANET*, 259 (BM 19244 xix 2-xx 6). The text is a model letter used in the instruction of schoolboys. It is from the end of the 13th century; the copy of the letter is probably from Memphis.

25. In his forthcoming book, *Ancient Israel in Sinai* (Oxford: Oxford University Press), James K. Hoffmeier argues that Migdol in Pap. Anastasi V is one and the same as Migdol in the Seti I relief at Karnak.

26. William L. Moran, *The Amarna Letters* (Baltimore: Johns Hopkins University Press, 1992), 292; VAT 1641; Copies WA 95; VS 11, 134; Translation: William F. Albright, *ANET*, 484-85.

27. The full text of the letter is as follows:

> To the king, m[y] lord, the Sun from the sky: Message of Satatna, the ruler of Akka, your servant, the servant of the king, and the dirt at his feet, the ground on which he treads. [I] prostrate myself at the feet of the king, my lord, the Sun from the sky, 7 times and 7 times, both on the stomach and on the back.
>
> May the king, my lord, heed the word of his servant. [Zir]damyašda des[er]ted [B]iryawaza. He w[as] with Šuta, a ... [...] of the king, in the *gar[rison]* city. He said [n]ot[hi]ng [t]o him. Out came the troops of the king, my lord. He w[as] with them in Magidd[a]. Nothing was said to hi[m]. Then he deserted to me, and Šuta has just written to me, "Hand over Zirdamyašda to Biryawaza." But I have not agreed to hand him over. Akka is like Magdalu in Egypt, and has the king, [*my lord*], not [h]eard *that Šuta is turned* against me? May the king, my lord, [sen]d his [com]missioner to fet[ch] him.

Zirdamyašda seems to have been quite an active fellow. He had been with Biryawaza, the prince of Damascus under Egyptian suzerainty. Then Zirdamyašda left the service of Biryawaza and was under Šuta, who may have been the great-grandfather of Rameses II. Šuta was an Egyptian officer who may have been the commander of a garrison city. Although Satatna did nothing to

What is important for us is the identification of the Migdol referred to here and the meaning of the phrase "Akka is like Magdalu in Egypt." Albright, who was certain that the Migdol here is the Migdol of the Bible, translates that "Acco is (as Egyptian)" as the Migdol in Egypt. Notice that Satatna does not modify the place name Migdol as the Migdol of a particular pharaoh. It would seem that though there may have been a few Migdols in Egypt, there was one that was quite famous, famous enough to be used rather casually in this protestation of loyalty to Egypt. Both the sender and the receiver of this letter do not have to sift between possible Migdols to establish which place is being mentioned. This is why Satatna can be quite confident that he will be understood. The point is that there was a famous Migdol in Egypt in the New Kingdom period. It may be that the letter implies that Semites of unquestioning loyalty to the pharaoh inhabited Migdol.

All of this is especially instructive because there were Magdalus in several other Amarna letters as well as other Egyptian sources, both early[28] and late.[29]

---

win him over to his service, Zirdamyašda came over to him. Now Šuta has demanded that Satatna should turn Zirdamyašda back to Biryawaza. I cannot quite make out Šuta's relationship to Biryawaza. On the one hand, Zirdamyašda is with Šuta after he left Biryawaza. Šuta does not do anything about it. Now, on the other hand, Šuta is demanding that Satatna should return Zirdamyašda to Biryawaza. Perhaps Šuta's loyalties have changed in the political games between Egyptian vassals. Maybe he's just trying to make Satatna look bad.

28. There is a Magdalu near Tripoli in EA 69 and 70. There is also a Magdalu in Amqu (modern Lebanon) in EA 185 and 186. Even a quick glance at the contexts and personal and place names will show that the Migdol in the northwest Sinai cannot be indicated.

In EA 256, there is a list of cities in Garu that are hostile to the writer of the letter, Mut-ba'lu: Udumu, Aduru, Araru, Meshqu, Magdalu, Eni-anabu, and Zarqu. Mut-ba'lu is a prince of Pella in the northern Jordan Valley, opposite Beth-shan. He is opposed by Ayab, prince of Ashtartu, which is familiar to biblical students as Ashtaroth in Bashan. The land of Garu was in the southern Golan between the two principalities of Pella and Ashtartu. So this is a clear example of a Magdalu in the Amarna Letters that is not the Migdol of the northwestern Sinai.

See William F. Albright, "Two Little Understood Amarna Letters from the Middle Jordan Valley," *BASOR* 89 (1943): 7-17.

The Memphis and Karnak Stelae of Amen-hotep II (ca. 1428) list a Migdal-yen(et) in the Sharon Plain: "His majesty went forth by chariot at dawn, against the town of Iteren, as well as Migdol-yen" (*ANET*, 247). It is interesting that even in an Israelite area, there are place names that we would not be aware of without Egyptian sources.

29. In the Cairo Demotic Papyrus 31169, there are four places called Migdol in the eastern Delta; cf. Wilhelm Spiegelberg, *Die demotischen Papyrus* 273 and 278. There is a reference to a Migdal in Shishak's long topographical list preserved in the Amon temple in Karnak. Migdol is listed as a place in the Jordan Valley near Tirzah, Adamah, and Penuel. This Magdalu is different from the Migdol in or near Egypt; Yohanan Aharoni, *The Land of the Bible*, 2nd ed. (Philadelphia: Westminster. 1979), 323ff.; Nadav Na'aman, "Sennacherib's 'Letter to God' on His Campaign to Judah," *BASOR* 214 (1974): 25-39.

In the reliefs of Ramesses III at Medinet Habu,[30] there is a reference to "Migdol of Ramesses-Prince-of-Heliopolis." The texts concerning the sea battle and the nearby scenes say that "the peoples who had come from their islands in the midst of the sea were advancing against Egypt" and that they had "entered the river-mouths," a word used only for the estuaries of the Nile. The enemy may have attacked the Pelusiac branch of the Nile. (It is hard for me to see "river-mouths" and not wonder about a connection to Pi-hahiroth.) Ramesses III may have moved back to the fort of Migdol nearby. From Migdol, he might have moved out again after the victory was won to congratulate his successful army and to be given a hand, or actually the many cut-off hands of his defeated enemies. The word Migdol here does not have the definite article and is determined by the sign for town. While Alan H. Gardiner believes that this Migdol must be the Migdol that he locates at Tell el-Her,[31] we can say for now that it is possible to connect this Migdol to the Migdol of Seti I.

In an Aramaic papyrus, probably from 5th-century Elephantine,[32] a father in the Migdol garrison writes to his son in Elephantine who has made the journey between the two points, vividly illustrating Ezekiel's two geographical landmarks.

> . . . since the day when you left (Lower) Egypt (Misrayim) salary has not been given to us. And when we lodged a complaint with the governor *(phwt')* about your salary here in Migdol we were told thus: "About this (matter) complain to the scribe and it will be given to you.[33]

It would seem that father and son are soldiers in garrisons at either end of Egypt. This letter gives us a Migdol in the northeast at a much later date than the other extrabiblical texts but brings us close to the time period of the prophets Jeremiah and Ezekiel.

---

30. Jean-François Champollion, *Monuments de l'Égypte et de la Nubie* (Paris: Didot frères, 1845), pls. 222-25; Ippolito Rosellini, *I Monumenti dell' Egito e della Nubia*, 1: *Monumenti storici* (Pisa: N. Capurro, 1832), pls. 131-33. Trans. in James H. Breasted, *Ancient Records of Egypt* 4 (Chicago: University of Chicago Press, 1907), 74-77; and Gardiner, *JEA* 6 (1920): 110. It should be noted that there is another Magdalu to be found in these reliefs but that this is one of the Syro-Palestinian examples; see Gardiner, *JEA* 6 (1920): 109.

31. Gardiner, *JEA* 6 (1920): 113.

32. The papyrus is now in the Museo Civico of Padova. See Edda Bresciani, "Papyri aramaici egiziani de epoca persiana presso il Museo Civico de Padova," *RSO* 35 (1960): 11-24; Joseph A. Fitzmyer, "The Padua Aramaic Papyrus Letters," *JNES* 21 (1962): 15-24; Joseph Naveh, "Early Aramaic Inscriptions," *Leshonenu* 29 (1965): 183-97; Bezalel Porten, *Archives from Elephantine: The Life of an Ancient Jewish Military Colony* (Berkeley: University of California Press, 1968), 42.

33. Oren, *BASOR* 256 (1984): 33; Porten, 42.

Herodotus[34]

The great Greek historian writes:

> King Necos . . . then turned his attention to war; he had triremes built,
> some on the Mediterranean coast, others on the Arabian Gulf, where the
> docks are still to be seen, and made use of the new fleets as occasion arose;
> and in addition he attacked the Syrians by land and defeated them at
> Magdolus, afterwards taking Gaza, a large town in Syria. (Herodotus, *Histories* 2:159)[35]

Necho, in alliance with Assyria and concerned about the emergence of Babylon as a major power, conducted a military campaign against the latter. Students of the Bible are familiar with this campaign because Josiah, in alliance with Babylon, took on Necho at what the Bible calls Megiddo (2 Kgs. 23:29-30; 2 Chr. 35:20-24). Many say that we can disregard this reference to Migdol. The Magdolus where Josiah lost his fatal battle against Pharaoh is usually understood as what Gardiner called "a blunder for Megiddo." They say that this is Megiddo and not Migdol. I had always assumed this to be true; after all, the Bible is clear enough in calling the place of the battle Megiddo, which became the name over time of Armageddon.

Oren's excellent article on what we now know as Tel Kedua, however, makes an interesting case in the other direction. Oren claims that the scene of the battle was the Migdol of Ezekiel and Jeremiah, not Megiddo. In this reckoning, Josiah tried to stop Necho *before* he began his campaign. As soon as Necho left Egypt, Josiah met him at the beginning of the ancient road between Egypt and Canaan. After this battle, Necho conquered Gaza at the other end of the road.

Oren has a point: For Necho to defeat Josiah at Megiddo and *backtrack* to Gaza really does not make any sense.[36] So what we have in Herodotus may indeed be a reference to the Migdol of the prophets and the Aramaic letter.

---

34. Abraham Malamat, "Josiah's Bid for Armageddon: The Background of the Judean-Egyptian Encounter in 609 b.c.," *JANES* 5 (1973): 267-79; W. W. How & J. Wells, *A Commentary on Herodotus* (1912; repr. Oxford: Oxford University Press, 1991); J. Gwyn Griffiths, "Three Notes on Herodotus Book II," *ASAE* 53 (1955): 139-52.

35. Herodotus, *The Histories,* trans. Aubrey De Sélincourt (London: Penguin, 1996), 145.

36. L. Elliott Binns, "The Syrian Campaign of Necho II," *JTS* 18 (1917): 36-47, esp. 40; Yigael Yadin, *The Art of Warfare in Biblical Lands* (Jerusalem: International, 1963), 2:375-76.

The Antonine Itinerary[37]

This important Roman period source locates Magdolum between Pelusium and Sile. Scholars often mention the exact relationship between Migdol and these sites: Migdol was supposed to be 12 Roman mi. from each place.[38] This Migdol, however, would have been the classical Migdol and not necessarily the Migdol of New Kingdom times.

My modest conclusion from this survey is this: For all of the Migdols in different places and different times, there was a Migdol in the northwestern Sinai in the New Kingdom era, the period of the Exodus. There was also at least one Migdol, in the same area but not necessarily on the same site, in the 6th-4th centuries. Biblical references to Migdol, both early and late, should not be dismissed, and biblical data on this subject should be respected and used.

Scholarly Reconstructions of the Location of Migdol

Even before the advent of serious archaeological excavation in the area, scholars were more than happy to make claims about the identification of Migdol. H. Clay Trumbull, in 1844, stated there were three Migdols along the Great Wall of Shur and along the three routes leading out of Egypt. Trumbull said that the Migdol of Seti I was Tel es-Samut (Tell Hebua I), south of Pelusium along the Way of the Land of the Philistines.[39] According to Trumbull, then, Tel Hebua is Migdol.

Gardiner followed Trumbull, but added another Migdol to the three. All four Migdols were to the east of the Delta.[40] He said that it was possible that they were all somehow connected to the main routes leading to the land of Canaan, Edom, and Midian, on the hilltops or "the Walls of Shur" that stood

---

37. *Itineraria Romana* 1, ed. Otto Cuntz (Leipzig: J. C. Hinrichs, 1929).

38. Oren, *BASOR* 256 (1984): 33-35.

39. H. Clay Trumbull, *Kadesh Barnea* (New York: Scribner's, 1844), 371. Beside the Way of Shur is a well called Bir Makdal that is situated to the east of El-jiser (Trumbull, 374). Along the Way of the Red Sea in northwest Suez is a fortress called Qal'at 'Ajrood, which served as a stopping-place for Moslem pilgrims on their way from Cairo to Aqaba. There is also a pass called el-Maktal that is an observation point overlooking all movement into Egypt from the east (Trumbull, 377). According to Trumbull, there are no cities on the route of the Israelites. There are only stopping-places, encampments, fortresses, and topographical items. Etham is a wall; Migdol is a fortress; Succoth and Rameses are districts.

40. Gardiner, *JEA* 6 (1920): 108-9.

out above the lakes. These Migdols were built to guard against foreign enemies and to watch over the Semitic tribes who came to procure provisions.

J. J. Simons thought that the Migdol of Seti I and Ramesses II was Jebel abu-Hassah.[41] He said that there was a ford, directly opposite Migdol and 8 km. to its east, which was in use until the construction of the Suez Canal. The miracle was that the Israelites crossed the ford at the right time. Yohanan Aharoni stated that the names of the first stations and incidents could be "all located in the northeastern part of the Nile delta."[42] Migdol was the Migdol of Egyptian lists, by the Mediterranean. Baal-zephon, following Eissfeldt, was a temple for mariners located on a piece of land jutting into the sea. The "Reed Sea" was the Gulf of Serbonitis. This northern theory, as we have seen, can no longer be sustained.

Possibly Relevant Archaeological Sites

I now turn to those archaeological sites in the area of the northern Sinai that may be relevant.

Tell el-Her[43]

As mentioned earlier, most scholars assume that Tell el-Her is Migdol. The identification with Tell el-Her, south of Pelusium near the Mediterranean coast, is based on what we may call circumstantial geographical evidence: it happens to be in the area where people are looking for Migdol. Tell el-Her is 10 km. south of Tell Farama (ancient Pelusium) and 15 km. northeast of Tell Abu-sefeh. Tell el-Her, however, has a date (based on its earliest remains) of the Persian period in the 5th century. Tell el-Her was a site that was inhabited too late to be the Migdol of New Kingdom sources and the exodus. It was even too late to be the Migdol of Jeremiah and Ezekiel.

And yet Gardiner thought that for Migdol "the only location possible

---

41. J. J. Simons, *The Geographical and Topographical Texts of the Old Testament* (Leiden: Brill, 1959), no. 423.

42. Aharoni, 196.

43. Brigette Gratien and Daniel Soulié, "La céramique de Tell el-Herr, campagnes 1986 et 1987. Etude préliminaire," *CRIPEL* 10 (1988): 23-55; Gratien and Etienne Louis, "Tell el-Herr: Premières observations sur l'agglomération antique," *CRIPEL* 12 (1990): 71-83; Mohamed Abd el-Maksoud, "Fouilles récentes au Nord Sinai, sur le site de Tell el-Herr: Première saison, 1984-85," *CRIPEL* 8 (1986): 15-16.

seems to be at Tell el-Her." In this, he followed Greville Chester[44] and others. Here is what he says about Tell el-Her:

> Tell el-Her stands on the south side of a spit of sand running westward into the bed of a lake; it is conspicuous for a high medieval fortress of red brick, but besides there are traces of a town of large size, where innumerable sherds of pottery, fragments of ancient glass, and Ptolemaic coins are still found scattered over the surface of the mound.

Gardiner admits that Tell el-Her does not fit the description of the Itinerary since it is much closer to Pelusium, about 7 Roman miles, than it is to Sile, 12 Roman miles. But then he says that these distances are all probably exaggerated anyway. This is all that Gardiner offered as evidence. Consequently, it is amazing that scholarship followed him on so little evidence.

Tell Kedua (T. 21, Oren's Migdol)[45]

The next site that has gained popularity as a biblical Migdol is Tell Kedua, Oren's T. 21. Tell Kedua, enclosed by a wall 15-20 meters wide, has a center occupied by a massive fortified compound measuring 200 by 200 meters. Small cellular compartments were constructed at fixed intervals inside the wall, and structures and installations densely covered the central area. Egyptian, Phoenician, Greek, and Cypriot classes represent its large ceramic corpus; there are also many metal objects, copper ores, and slags. The fortress was destroyed by fire in the late 6th century.

Oren thinks that this site, which is just 1 km. north of Tell el-Her, was replaced by Tell el-Her as Migdol. This site has close affinities with other Egyptian sites of the Saite period in the Nile Delta region. The military architecture, pottery, metallurgic industry, and dates all are related. Oren says that Tell el-Her seems to have replaced Tell Kedua as the major frontier garrison in the eastern Delta. The idea is that Cambyses destroyed Tell Kedua in 525 and that the name Migdol was eventually transferred to the nearby site of Tell el-Her.

44. Greville Chester, "A Journey to the Biblical Sites in Lower Egypt . . . ," *PEFQS* (July 1880), 148.

45. Oren, *BASOR* 256 (1984): 7-44; *Qadmoniot* 6 (1973): 101-3 (Heb.); "The Fort of Migdol in North-western Sinai," *Qadmoniot* 10 (1977): 71-76 (Heb.); "Landbridge between Asia and Africa: Archaeology of Northern Sinai up to the Classical Period," in *Sinai: Pharaohs, Miners, Pilgrims and Soldiers,* ed. Benno Rothenberg and Helfried Weyer (Washington: Joseph Binns, 1979); *ErIsr* 20 (1989): 8-22; 21 (1990): 6-22; *NEAEHL* 4:1386-96; *IEJ* 23 (1973): 198-205; "The 'Ways of Horus' in North Sinai," 69-119.

Donald B. Redford conducted two seasons of excavations at Tell Kedua in the 1990s. He has concluded, like Oren before him, that the site was occupied from the late 7th century and into the 5th century.[46]

These sites need not be measured stops that are a certain distance from each other. After all, it was Tell el-Borg's location in relation to Hebua I that led us to excavate what was at first a quite unpromising site. Once we know everything we need to know about the topography of the area, we may find that the Egyptians had military bases and way stations at every possible important point. That is, topography, and not distance, may have dictated the location of the stations and garrisons. Also, the biblical *lipnê* might imply that there were several places in a small area, which would fit what we are finding in the area of Tell-Hebua (I-IV) and Tell el-Borg. More on this presently.

We are not willing to consider Tell Kedua for the exodus/New Kingdom picture without any evidence that it existed during the 14th through 13th centuries. Oren explicitly states that this site has nothing to do with the period of the New Kingdom and biblical texts about the Exodus. His claim that Tell Kedua is Ezekiel's Migdol is certainly plausible. But I would have to agree with Kenneth Kitchen's assessment of the identification of Tell el-Her and Tell Kedua: "The New Kingdom Migdol of Sethos I is identical with neither of these sites, but remains to be discovered somewhere in the vicinity."[47]

Tell Abu Sefeh[48]

As people who have lived at the edge of Tell Abu Sefeh at the North Sinai Archaeological Center, anyone in our project will confirm that it is an impressive site. Two Ramesside-period inscriptions were found on the surface at the end of the 19th century.[49] It is small wonder that Carl Küthmann[50] and, following him, Gardiner thought that it was the major fort in the area, Tjaru.[51]

---

46. Donald B. Redford, "Report on the 1993 and 1997 Seasons at Tell Qedwa," *JARCE* 35 (1998): 45-49.

47. Kenneth A. Kitchen, ed., *Ramesside Inscriptions: Translated and Annotated: Notes and Comments* (Oxford: Blackwell, 1993), 1:14.

48. Oren, *BASOR* 256 (1984): 35.

49. Kitchen, 1:13-14.

50. Carl Küthmann, *Die Ostgrenze Ägyptens* (Leipzig: J. C. Hinrichs, 1911). I have been unable to see this work for myself.

51. Ricardo Augusto Caminos, *Late-Egyptian Miscellanies* (Oxford: Oxford University Press, 1954), 73; Hermann Kees, *Ancient Egypt* (Chicago: University of Chicago Press, 1961), 190; Nahum Sarna, *Exploring Exodus* (New York: Schocken, 1986), 105.

Located 3 mi. east of modern Qantara, Abu Sefeh would fit the geographical criterion of being near water and of being the major departure point for Egyptians crossing into the Sinai or an important intake-point for Asiatics on their way to Egypt.

But something unexpected came to light. First Oren and then the Egyptian Director of Antiquities for the North Sinai, Dr. Mohamed Abd el-Maksoud, excavated Tell Abu Sefeh, and neither found anything relating to the New Kingdom. The earliest evidence seems to be from Persian times.

Tell Abu Sefeh is an impressive mound, and it may be that there is earlier evidence buried further down. The trenches that have been dug, however, indicate otherwise. This site seems to be the Sile of the classical period. It may be that changing topography dictated the move from Tell Hebua I to Tell Abu Sefeh.

Tel Hebua[52]

Tell Hebua is made up of four sites in some combination. It is Tell Hebua I that interests us here. Abd el-Maksoud has found New Kingdom pottery and parts of a huge fortress. An important find is an inscription from King Nehsy in the Second Intermediate Period[53] that demonstrates that the site goes back to the 17th century.

Though it is still in press, Abd el-Maksoud found a votive statue at Hebua I in 1999 with an inscription that mentions Tjaru. Thus the long search for this key frontier town is over. Tjaru was the first of the forts on the Ways of Horus, the frontier fort on the Karnak reliefs. This is the Archimedean point of this discussion. Tjaru was a crucial point on the Ways of Horus, so crucial that it was sometimes called the Ways of Horus itself.[54] The identi-

52. Abd el-Maksoud, *CRIPEL* 8 (1986): 15-16; "Une nouvelle fortresse sur la route d'Horus: Tell Heboua 1986 (Nord Sinaï)," *CRIPEL* 9 (1987): 13-16; "Tjarou porte de l'Orient" in *Le Sinaï durant l'antiquité et le Moyen-Age*, ed. Dominique Valbelle and Charles Bonnet (Paris: Errance, 1998), 61-65; *Tell Heboua (1981-1991): Enquête archéologique sur la Deuxième Période Intermédiare et le Nouvel Empire à l'extrémité orientale du Delta* (Paris: Éditions Recherche sur les Civilisations, 1998).

53. Mohamed Abd el-Maksoud, *ASAE* 69 (1988): 1-3.

54. Gardiner was the first to suggest that "the Ways of Horus" was a town with a garrison by the period of a 10th-century Herakleopolitan king; *JEA* 6 (1920): 99. He cites the "Instruction of King Akhthoy" (King Khety Nebkaure providing instruction to his son Merikare) where the monarch states: "I drove in my (?) mooring-post in a region that I made to the east of the boundaries of *hbn*(?) at Way(s)-of-Horus, equipped with townsmen, and filled with people of the best of the entire land, in order to repel the arms of. . . ." When Sinuhe came back from Ca-

fication of Tjaru gives us a legitimate right to claim that the Dwelling of the Lion and Migdol must be nearby to the east, following the order of the Karnak reliefs.

My purpose in discussing the various Migdols was to establish the plausible connection between the Migdol of the New Kingdom Pharaohs and the Migdol of the exodus. So if we look near Tel Hebua for the Dwelling of the Lion and Migdol, what are our possibilities?

First, our new map limits the possibilities (see above, p. 62, Figure 1, and p. 65, Figure 2). The map indicates a relatively narrow strip of land between the Mediterranean and the southern body of water, which may, for all we know, have been the *Yām sûp*. Perhaps our confusion about the Red/Reed Sea problem is that the Bible actually refers to both bodies of water. Perhaps the event involved the strip between them. Perhaps there was flooding at just the right point to inundate the Egyptians whereas the Israelites made it through.

Second, the archaeological evidence limits the possibilities. Tell el-Her, Tell Kedua, and Tell Abu Sefeh cannot be part of this discussion unless we want to speculate about the Migdol of the prophets and classical times. What is important to remember about these sites is that there is not a shred or a sherd of evidence that indicates anything about Migdol, even the Migdol of the later period. These identifications are made on the basis of circumstantial geographical evidence.

With the identity of Tjaru now assured, we can move on to try to follow this important route by finding the Dwelling of the Lion and Migdol. I believe that we have found one of these sites.

Tell el-Borg

In 1999, we began to investigate Tell el-Borg, "the Mound of the Tower" (see above, p. 62, Figure 1, and p. 65, Figure 2). Using the method applied by such archaeologists as Aharoni, it is legitimate to ask this question: Since Migdol meant "tower," could Borg simply be the Arabic translation of Migdol? The earliest documentation for Tell el-Borg we have been able to find is in Jean

---

naan after the death of Amenemhet, he stopped at a frontier town at the end of what was considered to be Egypt proper and the beginning of the road to the east. This town is referred to as "the Ways of Horus." See a translation of the relevant passage in Hoffmeier, *Israel in Egypt*, 167. See also Dominique Valbelle, "La (Les) Route(s)-D'Horus," in *Hommages à Jean Leclant* 4. Bibliothèque de l'école des Hautes études 106 (Cairo: Institut français d'archéologie orientale, 1994): 379-86, where she offers the theory that "the Ways of Horus" is a region of the northern Sinai.

Clédat's notes from his visit to North Sinai in 1909.[55] We know that just this type of evidence often creates an identification of a site.[56]

We have discovered inscriptions from Ramesses II, the likely pharaoh of the exodus, and other pharaohs as well.[57] This place had been occupied, the inscriptions indicate, for at least 200 and perhaps 300 years. We have found evidence of a fort, a temple, tombs, and perhaps of a settlement there.

Let me review what we have so far:

1. Both Egyptian texts and the Bible tell us that there was a place called Migdol in the eastern Delta/northwest Sinai;

2. The Egyptian reliefs place it as one of the western forts on the Ways of Horus;

3. We have used geology to show that Tell el-Borg was on the Ways of Horus;

4. We know what and where the first fort was: Tjaru, now called Tel Hebua; Tel Hebua is 5 km. northwest of Tell el-Borg;

5. It was definitely inhabited at the time of the exodus: We have New Kingdom pottery;

6. It was a fort with walls (3.8 m. wide) that were built and re-fortified. The walls present two different forts, the second of which is represented by two building stages. The earlier fort, thus far survived only by a large fosse (D), we tentatively date to the time of Thutmose III or Amenhotep II. The second fort was constructed over the fosse, possibly in the late 18th Dynasty,

55. Dominique Valbelle and Françoise le Saout, "Les Archives Clédat sur le Nord-Sinai," *CRIPEL* 20 (1999): 71-73; Jean Clédat, "Fouilles à Khirbet el-Flousiyeh," *ASAE* 16 (1916): 6-32; "Notes sur l'isthme de Suez," *BIFAO* 16 (1919): 201-28.

56. Aharoni; Clinton Bailey, "Bedouin Place-Names in Sinai: Towards Understanding a Desert Map," *PEQ* 116 (1984): 42-57; Wilhelm Borée, *Die alten Ortsnamen Palästinas*, 2 vols. (Hildesheim: G. Olms, 1968); B. S. J. Isserlin, "Place Name Provinces in the Semitic-speaking ANE," *Proceedings of the Leeds Philosophical and Literary Society* A8/2 (1956): 83-110; Ernst Axel Knauf, "Toponymy of the Kerak Plateau," in *Archaeological Survey of the Kerak Plateau*, ed. J. Maxwell Miller (Atlanta: Scholars, 1991), 281-90; Miller, "Site Identification: A Problem Area in Contemporary Biblical Scholarship," *ZDPV* 99 (1983): 119-29; Avraham Negev, "Permanence et disparition d'anciens toponymes du negev central," *RB* 83 (1976): 545-57; Anson F. Rainey, "The Toponymics of Eretz-Israel," *BASOR* 231 (1978): 1-17; Baruch Rosen, "Early Israelite Cultic Centres in the Hill Country," *VT* 38 (1988): 114-17; Thomas L. Thompson, Francolino C. Gonçalves, and Jean-Marie Van Cangh, *Toponymie Palestinienne*. PIOL 37 (Louvain-la-Neuve: Institut orientaliste de Louvain, 1988); Ran Zadok, "Notes on Modern Palestinian Toponymy," *ZDPV* 101 (1985): 156-61.

57. Other pharaohs whose names have been documented at Tell el-Borg include: Thutmose III, Amenhotep II, Smenkhkare, and Tutankhamun; Queen Tiye was added to the list of royals in 2002. For a preliminary report on the excavations, see "Tell el-Borg in North Sinai," *Egyptian Archaeology* 20 (Spring 2002): 18-20.

and continued in use throughout the 13th century. TBO X 27, an inscription from the Weapon-bearer Kha of the Company of Amun, is a nameplate for a military company (Figure 3). This company was part of the army division of Amun, probably based at or near Tell el-Borg. A company was made up of 200-250 men.[58] The nameplate may have been set near the gate or door of the barracks-compound.

The point here is that there was a garrison at a fort. This would fit the idea of a series of forts on the Ways of Horus in the New Kingdom period. It would also fit what I would like to call "the concept of Migdol" in its two or three manifestations, a garrison fort standing as a guardian-post at the entrance to Egypt.

7. This fort, like other Egyptian forts, had a temple. Our site has a temple with granite blocks brought all the way from Aswan in the south. If they were shipped around 800 km., it was for a very important reason such as the construction or rebuilding of an important temple in a significant fort.[59] This reality is a vivid illustration of the prophetic verses and the Migdol letter from Elephantine.

Kitchen, the foremost Ramesside scholar in the world today, in one of the most interesting intellectual exercises I've ever seen has provisionally reconstructed the temple at Tell el-Borg (Figure 4). Kitchen takes the fragments of blocks and inscriptions and performs the archaeological equivalent of building a model of a dinosaur from a few bones. I do not know what is more exciting about it: the staggering knowledge of parallels or the ability to recreate the very size of the original blocks. Kitchen predicted that we would find a temple of 80-by-30 or 35 ft., and that it would have plinths for cult images. We have found what we think is that temple, very close to the huge granite block. So far, it is a little smaller than the reconstruction, but we may have

58. R. O. Faulkner, "Egyptian Military Organization," *JEA* 39 (1953): 32-47; "Egyptian Military Standards," *JEA* 27 (1941): 17-18; Alan Richard Schulman, *Military Rank, Title and Organization in the Egyptian New Kingdom*. Munchner Ägyptologischen Studien 6 (Berlin: B. Hessling, 1964), 26-30.

59. TBO I 2A seems to be evidence of a small shrine in a border-fort in the time of Thutmose III, a king who reigned some 200 years before Ramesses II. Since Thutmose III waged many campaigns in Syria and Canaan, a fort like Tell el-Borg would have been an important post for staging a campaign. This shrine might have been rebuilt during the Amarna Period. Akhenaten (1353-1333) curbed the powerful cult of Amun and promoted the worship of the Aten solar disc; Aten was to supersede all other deities. The temples of other gods were closed and the scars of their desecration remained visible even after they were re-established. After "the heresy" ended, thousands of images and names of Amun and other gods had to be re-cut into the very temple walls from which they had been erased. The Ramesside period that followed was characterized by great growth and building. Ramesses II (1290-1224) built more temples than any other pharaoh.

Figure 3. Hieroglyphic text from Tell el-Borg,
name plate of the weapon's bearer, Kha

found three plinths for the idols.[60] Nearby we have found a small statue of a pharaoh and inscriptions from Ramesses II and other pharaohs going back to the Amarna period.

In comparing the reconstructed triumph scene at Tell el-Borg with the scenes from Tell el-Retaba, the one at our site is twice as big.[61] In short, this was a sizable temple. Only a few Egyptian temples are known from the Sinai

60. Ramesses II would have used any available stonework in building his temple. An additional note is that we have found animals buried in a pit right next to what may be the temple.

61. W. M. Flinders Petrie, *Hyksos and Israelite Cities* (London: British School of Archaeology, 1906), pls. 29/30, 31 left.

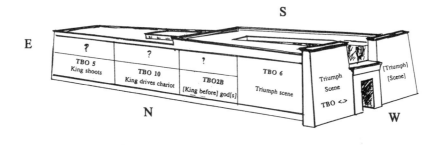

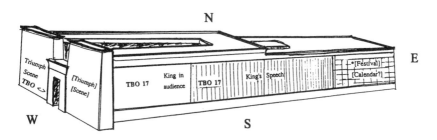

Figure 4. Reconstruction of Temple, Tell el Borg
(Kenneth A. Kitchen)

in the New Kingdom period. (The best-known temple is found at Serabit el-Khadim.[62]) Since it was at least unusual to have a large temple in the Sinai, our site becomes even more noteworthy and all the more likely to be known to the people of the biblical period.[63]

8. Since what I am calling "the concept of Migdol" may have the dimension of a sizable Semitic population, a natural question is if we have any evidence of Semites at Tell el-Borg. In a sense, yes. In comparing the number of examples of Base Ring I and II juglets with Cypriote White Slip II vessels, we see that the proportion of White Slip II to Base Ring I and II reflects the proportions found at sites in Israel rather than in Egypt. In Nile

62. "Egyptian Temples in Canaan and Sinai," in Sarah Israelit-Groll, ed., *Studies in Egyptology Presented to Miriam Lichtheim* (Jerusalem: Magnes, 1990). For New Kingdom temples, see Peter J. Brand, *The Monuments of Seti I and Their Historical Significance: Epigraphic, Art Historical and Historical Analyses* (Leiden: Brill, 2000); Karol Mysliwiec, *Eighteenth Dynasty Before the Amarna Period*. Iconography of Religions 16. Egypt 5 (Leiden: Brill, 1985).

63. In 2001 and 2002, excavations at Hebua I have revealed new Pharaonic period temples, but these are completely made of brick.

Valley sites, Base Ring I and II will be found in double the amount found from the Levant.[64] White Slip II bowls became popular in the period ca. 1425-1320.

Most of the pottery at Tell el-Borg has been dated to the late 18th Dynasty and 19th Dynasty and is characteristic of the New Kingdom. While I do not know of any evidence of pieces from later dates, there are at least two sherds that seem to be earlier, from the early 18th Dynasty. The imported pottery dates from the Late Bronze II A/B period in the Levant. The Mycenaean pottery from Greece and the many Cypriot pottery fragments fit with this date.[65] In addition to the inference from the proportions of imported pottery that this is a site reflective of Semitic usage, there is also the direct evidence of Canaanite wares datable to the LB IIA period, the Amarna Age.

If we are hoping to identify Tell el-Borg as the Migdol of the Amarna Letters, the pottery fits the period of occupation we are looking for.

If we are looking for evidence of Semitic occupation, the pottery fits this conclusion. At the very least, we must agree with Rexine Hummel's judicious statement:

> The fact that imported wares found at this Egyptian site should be more closely comparable to Palestinian excavated materials of the same period than to Nilotic sites is interesting. This raises questions about trade and settlement patterns which invite more investigation.[66]

Two important stamped jar handles were discovered. One is stamped with the prenomen of Tutankhamun.[67] The other stamped jar handle has the

---

64. Rexine Hummel, "Tell el Borg Pottery: Preliminary Report March 2000," *Tell el-Borg Reports 2001* (unpublished).

65. The commercial trade between Cyprus and Egypt and the Near East during the Late Bronze Age is a familiar fact. An interesting point for us is that the trade with Cyprus reached its apex during the Amarna Age in Egypt and LB IIA in Canaan. Barry M. Gittlen has shown that at sites in Israel the amount of Late Cypriot pottery declined during LB IIB, the reigns of Seti I and Ramesses II, which are of such crucial importance for us. In particular, White Slip II pottery and White Shaved pottery peaked and ended during LB IIA. Cypriot White Shaved Ware appears often in excavations in Israel and the North Sinai during LB IIA and B but is rarely found in Egypt. Barry M. Gittlen, "The Cultural and Chronological Implications of the Cypro-Palestinian Trade During the Late Bronze Age," *BASOR* 241 (1981): 49-59; Celia J. Bergoflin, "Overland Trade in Northern Sinai: The Evidence of the Late Cypriot Pottery," *BASOR* 284 (1991): 59-79.

66. *Tell el-Borg Reports 2001*.

67. Maksoud has found another jar stamp from this famous king in the area.

name Smenkhkare on it, the successor and coregent of Akhenaten.[68] The only other extent stamp with his name was found at Tell Jerishe in Canaan.[69] Lyla Brock concludes that the two stamps suggest a connection between the North Sinai and Canaan and trade of the commodities in the vessels between these two areas. She also reminds us that the Amarna pharaohs had vineyards in the Sinai.[70]

Earlier, I asked if the Migdol of the Pentateuch (Exod. 14:2; Num. 33:7) could be the Migdol of Jeremiah and Ezekiel. In terms of archaeological evidence, the Migdol of the two different sets of texts cannot be the same if the later Migdol is Tell el-Her, nor if it is Tell Kedua, nor if it is Tell el-Borg. If Tell el-Borg is Migdol, it could not be the Migdol of Jeremiah and/or Ezekiel because it is New Kingdom and not Saite like Tel Kedua, Oren's candidate for the later Migdol[71] — unless, of course, we have just not found the part of the settlement that provides us with evidence of this later period.

Tell el-Borg would fit the geographical requirements of the Roman documents such as the Antonine Itinerary that speak of Magdolum, which is between Pelusium and Sile. But if we need to conform to the idea that Migdol is exactly equidistant between Sile and Pelusium, it is too close to Sile and too far to the west.

Either Tell el-Her or Tell Kedua or both may be the later Migdol(s). Just as the name Sile/Tjaru may have moved from Tell Hebua I to Tell Abu Sefeh, there may have been a succession of Migdols. But if so, Tell el-Borg, rather than Tell el-Her, was the Migdol of the New Kingdom and the exodus story, and Tell Hebua, not Tell Abu Sefeh, was Tjaru.

---

68. His dates as sole pharaoh are 1336-1334; Alan H. Gardiner, "The Grafitto from the Tomb of Pere," *JEA* 14 (1928): 10-11. At his tomb in the Necropolis at Thebes, a third regnal year is indicated. Smenkhkare means "Vigorous is the Soul of Re." He is probably buried in a tomb in the Valley of the Kings. There is the possibility that he was preparing to return Egypt to the old orthodoxy and had left Akhenaten. Akhenaten died ca. 1334. Smenkhkare's sister-in-law married Tutankhamun.

69. Orly Goldwasser, "A Cartouche of Semenkhare from Canaan," *Göttingen Miszellen* 115 (1990): 29-32.

70. Lyla Brock, "Report on the Objects Found at Tel Borg, March-April, 2000 Season," *Tell el-Borg Reports 2001* (unpublished).

71. Steve Moshier has taken a survey of New Kingdom sites by Oren and superimposed them on our developing map. When the Israelis had the Sinai, Oren had plotted a large number of sites between Egypt and Israel that were inhabited in the New Kingdom period, the era of the exodus. At least two, and perhaps three or four of what he thought were different sites, are all parts of our site, Tell el-Borg.

BENJAMIN EDIDIN SCOLNIC

The Dwelling of the Lion[72]

I must admit to thinking that Tell el-Borg is not Migdol but the second fort on the Ways of Horus, called "the Dwelling of the Lion" in the Karnak reliefs and "the Dwelling of Sese" in Papyrus Anastasi I. The Lion refers to the reigning pharaoh, Seti I; this epithet was replaced by Sese (i.e., Ramesses II). In Papyrus Anastasi V 23-7-25, 2 the name becomes "the-Dwelling-of-Ramesses-Beloved-of-Amun":

> Look, we passed the fortress of Ramesses-miamun which is at Tharu in regnal-year 33, second month of Shomu, day 23, and we shall go to empty the ships at "The-Dwelling-of-Ramesses-mi-Amun." . . .[73]

The Dwelling of Ramesses, according to Gardiner, was the farthest point one could go by sea along the route to Canaan.[74] The passage speaks of three stelae with triumphal inscriptions designed to impress the beholder with the might of the pharaoh. Since (1) we have found inscriptions from Ramesses II, and we know that the site was inhabited in earlier times, and (2) we have even found granite blocks, and (3) Tell el-Borg was clearly near water, it is conceivable that Tell el-Borg was "the Dwelling of the Lion" and then "the Dwelling of Sese."

If Tell el-Borg is the Dwelling of the Lion, it would not give our site a direct biblical correlation, but would mean that we are in the right neighborhood and that Migdol could be located 3-5 km. to the southeast.

72. Jean Clédat identified the Dwelling of the Lion with el-Flusiyeh, Ostracine at the eastern end of Lake Sirbonis; cf. *ASAE* 16 (1916): 6-32; *BIFAO* 16 (1919): 201-28. We now see that this is impossible, geologically. He did not have any evidence to support this contention, anyway.

73. Alan H. Gardiner, *Late-Egyptian Miscellanies* (Brussels: Édition de la Fondation égyptologique Reine Élisabeth, 1937), 69-70.

74. Gardiner, *JEA* 6 (1920): 107.

120

Deconstructing and Reconstructing the United Monarchy: House of David or Tent of David (Current Trends in Iron Age Chronology)

STEVEN M. ORTIZ

Introduction

The text of the archaeologist is the potsherd. From this small piece of material culture we derive interpretations, models, and historical reconstructions of the past. Pottery continues to be one of the basic building blocks for the archaeologists. Therefore, the future of biblical archaeology is rooted in its past — ceramic analysis.

Current deconstructionist trends in biblical studies are focusing on the nature of the Israelite monarchy. Most of the models proposed have either ignored or misused the archaeological data.[1] It appears that these trends have now been adopted by Israel Finkelstein, who has proposed a new interpretation of the Iron Age cultural horizon. He proposes a drastic redating of the Iron Age ceramic corpus by proposing that the current traditional dating should be lowered by almost 100 years. He has termed this the "Low Chronology."

---

1. Niels Peter Lemche, *Ancient Israel: A New History of Israelite Society* (Sheffield: JSOT, 1988); Philip R. Davies, *In Search of "Ancient Israel"* (Sheffield: JSOT, 1992); Thomas L. Thompson, *Early History of the Israelite People from the Written and Archaeological Sources* (Leiden: E. J. Brill, 1992); *The Mythic Past: Biblical Archaeology and the Myth of Israel* (New York: Basic Books, 1999). William G. Dever is one of the few archaeologists to address the misuse of the archaeological record in light of these new paradigms and label these trends as deconstructionist; "'Will the Real Israel Please Stand Up?' Archaeology and Israelite Historiography: Part 1," *BASOR* 297 (1994): 61-80; "Ceramics, Ethnicity, and the Question of Israel's Origins," *BA* 58 (1995): 200-13; "Archaeology, Ideology, and the Quest for an 'Ancient' or 'Biblical' Israel," *NEA* 61 (1998): 39-52.

The result of this major ceramic reappraisal is to move all archaeological evidence for state development into the 9th century B.C.E.. The 10th-century void is filled with the villages of the Iron Age I cultural horizon, leading Finkelstein to conclude that David was not the king of an emerging secondary state, but only a small bedouin tribal chief.

Crisis in Methodology

The goal of this conference is to reassess the methods and assumptions of the discipline of biblical archaeology, particularly the interpretation of the archaeological record. The underlying question of current trends in Iron Age research is whether the current ceramic typology has been established, or if there is still the possibility for major chronological shifts. The advances made in ceramic chronologies in the southern Levant are discredited if different scholars can use the same assemblages to support their individual ceramic typologies and chronologies.

Several questions must be asked. Is the archaeological record so fragile that major shifts can still be proposed in the cultural horizon of the Levant? Can we miss the state by 100 years? Have we been relying on the biblical text so much that we have created the archaeological record in the image of the text? Is Finkelstein right and everybody else wrong?

The goal of this essay is to present an overview of the major tenets and issues of the debate and provide a critique of the Low Chronology based on the ceramic data. I propose that the basic theoretical problem is a positivistic approach that assumes ceramic change was consistent and homogeneous throughout the southern Levant.[2] It will be demonstrated that the tenets of the Low Chronology are incorrect and that the traditional Iron Age ceramic horizon should be retained. Hence, recent proposals to associate the house of David with a tribal chiefdom are not supported by the archaeological record.

2. For example, see John S. Holladay, Jr., "Red Slip, Burnish, and the Solomonic Gateway at Gezer," *BASOR* 277/278 (1990): 23-70; Israel Finkelstein, "Pots and People Revisited: Ethnic Boundaries in the Iron Age I," in *The Archaeology of Israel: Constructing the Past/Interpreting the Present*, ed. Neil A. Silberman and David B. Small (Sheffield: Sheffield Academic, 1997), 216-37; David Ussishkin, "Notes on Megiddo, Gezer, Ashdod, and Tel Batash in the Tenth to Ninth Centuries B.C.," *BASOR* 277/278 (1990): 71-91; and Bryant G. Wood, *The Sociology of Pottery in Ancient Palestine: The Ceramic Industry and the Diffusion of Ceramic Styles in the Bronze and Iron Ages* (Sheffield: JSOT, 1990).

History of Research: Iron Age Pottery

The most dramatic change evident in the Iron Age II ceramic horizon was the introduction of red slip and burnished decoration on the tableware. William F. Albright was the first to acknowledge this as a diagnostic feature and noted that the changes in this decorative technique would be important for establishing the chronology of the 10th and 9th centuries.[3] Albright's conclusions became the standard for Syro-Palestinian ceramic chronologies — so much so that one scholar refers to David and Solomon as the red-slip-and-burnish kings.[4]

In the 1960s, Kathleen M. Kenyon challenged Albright's chronology. On the basis of her excavation of Samaria, Kenyon dated the appearance of the red slip pottery to the 9th century and attempted to lower the Megiddo and Hazor stratigraphy. One of the issues pertinent to the debate was whether sherds within the fill beneath the floor were contemporary with the surface. G. Ernest Wright addressed the issue, and a stratigraphical methodological debate between Kenyon and Wright ensued.[5]

The association between the 10th century and the appearance of the red slip decorative technique came into question in the 1980s. It was publicly known as the "debate over David and Solomon."[6] This debate about the historicity of David and Solomon was focused on the archaeological data attributed to the 10th century, and an attempt to define the nature of state development in the southern Levant during the Iron Age ensued.

In the following decade the Iron Age I horizon became the target of these reevaluations, particularly the Philistine ceramic corpus.[7] One of the outcomes of these major ceramic reappraisals was the proposal of a new

---

3. William F. Albright, *The Excavation of Tell Beit Mirsim I: The Pottery of the First Three Campaigns.* AASOR 12 (New Haven: ASOR, 1932), 85.

4. John S. Holladay, "The Kingdoms of Israel and Judah: Political and Economic Centralization in the Iron II A-B (ca. 1000-750)," in *The Archaeology of Society in the Holy Land,* ed. Thomas E. Levy (London: Facts on File, 1995), 368, 370.

5. Kathleen M. Kenyon, "Megiddo, Hazor, Samaria and Chronology," *Bulletin of the Institute of Archaeology* 4 (1964): 143-56; G. Ernest Wright, "Archaeological Fills and Strata," *BA* 25 (1962): 34-40.

6. The principal scholars and the issues were defined in a special issue dedicated to this debate in *BASOR* 277/278 (1990).

7. Shlomo Bunimovitz, "Problems in the 'Ethnic' Identification of the Philistine Material Culture," *TA* 17 (1990): 210-22; Israel Finkelstein, "The Date of the Settlement of the Philistines in Canaan," *TA* 22 (1995): 213-39; "Pots and People Revisited"; Ussishkin, *BASOR* 277/278 (1990): 71-91.

chronology of the Iron Age in Syro-Palestinian archaeology — the Low Chronology.[8]

Basically, there are three tenets underlying all the arguments and various points of the Low Chronology. There are two crucial ceramic corpora — Lachish and Jezreel — and one theoretical ceramic distribution postulate. The theoretical assumption is that ceramic forms must always be the same in adjoining regions — the principle of homogeneity of ceramic assemblages.

The Current Debate: The Low Chronology

The term "Low Chronology" was first defined by Israel Finkelstein in his 1995 article, "The Date of the Settlement of the Philistines in Canaan."[9] In this article, he proposed lowering the currently accepted dates of the initial Philistine occupation in southern Canaan from the 12th to the 11th century. He based this proposal on two assumptions. First, the Egyptians ruled over the southern coastal plain and the Shephelah (Ashkelon-Lachish line) in the first half of the 12th century until the middle of the 11th. Second, sites in close proximity to each other must have similar ceramic assemblages. Finkelstein assumes that if the Philistines were in sites in the southern coastal plain during Iron Age IA (ca. 1200-1150/30) as evidenced by locally-made monochrome pottery (Myc IIIC:1b), this pottery should also be found at nearby sites controlled by Egyptians. Since these sites (e.g., Lachish VI and Tel Sera' X) do not have monochrome pottery, the initial Philistine presence must postdate these levels. This article introduced the first two tenets of the Low Chronology.

Tenet #1: Lachish and Philistine Monochrome Pottery

The first tenet of Finkelstein's Low Chronology proposal is to date the appearance of Philistine Monochrome pottery (Myc IIIC:1b) after Lachish VI. He assumes that if Lachish VI is contemporary with Philistine Monochrome

---

8. Israel Finkelstein, "The Archaeology of the United Monarchy: An Alternative View," *Levant* 28 (1996): 177-87; "The Stratigraphy and Chronology of Megiddo and Beth-shan in the 12th-11th Centuries B.C.E.," *TA* 23 (1996): 170-84.

9. *TA* 22 (1995): 213-39. Proposals to redate Iron Age stratigraphy were already presented in the literature by David Ussishkin, "Levels VII and VI at Tel Lachish and the End of the Late Bronze Age in Canaan," in *Palestine in the Bronze and Iron Ages,* ed. Jonathan N. Tubb (London: Institute of Archaeology, 1985), 213-30; and G. J. Wightman, "The Myth of Solomon," *BASOR* 277/278 (1990): 5-22.

sites (e.g. Tel Miqne, Ashkelon, Ashdod), it should contain this type of pottery. Since Lachish VI does not contain Philistine Monochrome pottery, this pottery must postdate the Iron Age IA. The result is that all strata with Philistine Monochrome pottery must be lowered nearly 100 years to the end of the 12th century or beginning of the 11th century. This creates a domino effect lowering all Iron Age strata of the Philistine coast. An artificial phase is created (Finkelstein's Phase 3, Table 1) adding 70-100 years to the Iron Age cultural horizon. The result is a cultural horizon in the southern Levant that is represented by major abandonment of several sites (see Table 1). Finkelstein briefly acknowledges these gaps but does not attempt to explain such a drastic demographic change in the archaeological record.[10]

Tenet #2: *Principle of Homogeneity of Assemblages*

The reliance on the Lachish ceramic corpus to lower the Iron Age horizons is also based on an underlying theoretical ceramic distribution model. The Low Chronology model purports that all contemporary sites must exhibit the same ceramic patterning. For example, if Site A has Pot C then Site B across the valley must also have Pot C. As stated earlier, one of the basic assumptions is that Lachish VI must contain Philistine Monochrome pottery if it is contemporary with other sites that have this pottery (e.g., Miqne VII).

The nature of Finkelstein's argument is illustrated by his reply to Amihai Mazar:

> The only way out of this equation [lack of Monochrome pottery in Egyptian strongholds, and lack of Egyptian pottery in Monochrome strata] is to argue for a complete segregation between the two neighboring communities: the gates of the Philistine cities were closed to Egyptian finds, including the popular Egyptian pottery, with not one find or one vessel penetrating through the "iron curtain." At the same time, not one Monochrome vessel crossed the lines and found its way to the Egyptian strongholds or to Canaanite cities influenced by Egyptian culture. The reader should be reminded that we are dealing with sites located only several kilometers away from each other, and with a period praised for its dynamic trade and cultural mélange.[11]

---

10. *TA* 22 (1995): 231-32.

11. Israel Finkelstein, "Bible Archaeology or Archaeology of Palestine in the Iron Age? A Rejoinder," *Levant* 30 (1998): 168.

Table 1. Five Phases of Finkelstein's Low Chronology
(adapted from Finkelstein 1995; * = destruction)

late 13th–early 12th c. B.C.E.	early 12th– ca. 1130 B.C.E.	late 12th–beg. of 11th c. B.C.E.	11th c. B.C.E., poss. early 10th	10th c. B.C.E.
LB II	Post Myc IIIB; Pre-Monochrome	Monochrome	Philistine Bichrome	
Aphek X12*	X11	GAP	(X10, X9)	
Jaffa	"Lion Temple"	GAP		
Tel Mor 7	Mor 6-5	GAP	4	3*
Ashdod XIV*	GAP	XIIIb	XII	XI*
Gezer XV	XIV	XIII	XII	XI X I IX*
T. Beit Mirsim C	B3	GAP	B2	B1
Lachish VII	Lachish VI*	GAP	GAP	V*
Tel Sera'	IX*	GAP	VIII	
Tel Miqne	VIIIA*	VII	(VI-V)	IV*
Ashkelon	GAP	Occupied		
Tel Masos			(II, II)	I
T. el-Farah	Cemetery 900	GAP		*
Tel Haror	B6-5	GAP	(B4-2)	
Beersheba	——	——	IX VIII	VII
Arad	——	——		XII
T. el-Jarisheh	GAP			*
T. Zippor III	GAP	GAP	II	
Tel Batash VI	GAP	GAP	V	
Halif VIII	GAP	GAP	VII→	
Tell Jemmeh	GAP	GAP		*
Deir el-Balah		GAP		
Megiddo	VIIA	GAP	(VIIB)	VIA* VB
Beth-Shean	Lower VI (S3)	GAP	GAP	S2*
Hazor	GAP	GAP	GAP	XII XI X
Jokneam	GAP	GAP	XVIII	XVII

The next stage of Finkelstein's Low Chronology proposal came a year later with the publication of his article, "The Archaeology of the United Monarchy: An Alternative View."[12] In this article, Finkelstein states that the current dating of the rise of the Israelite state to the 10th century is wrong. Finkelstein's arguments are based on a correlation between the stratigraphy of Megiddo and Jezreel.

Tenet #3: Jezreel Is the Key

The third tenet of Finkelstein's absolute dating is based on the dating of the Jezreel enclosure to the 9th century.[13] In spite of the polemics on the use of archaeology and the biblical text, most archaeologists accept the association between the Jezreel enclosure and its founding by either Omri or Ahab. The pottery of the enclosure is similar to ceramic assemblages that are currently dated to the 10th century.[14] Three reconstructions are possible:

1. Ceramic forms are similar between the 10th and 9th century (currently held position);
2. 10th-century horizons have been incorrectly dated and should be changed (this is Finkelstein's position);
3. Most of the surfaces of the site of Jezreel have been disturbed, and it is possible that the pottery reflects an earlier occupation. This is similar to the stratigraphic debate between Kenyon and Wright (Amnon Ben-Tor holds to this position).

Finkelstein concluded that with the lowering of Iron Age strata ca. 100 years, all the evidence of state development that was originally dated to the 10th century (e.g., monumental architecture, gate systems, palaces, city planning) should now be dated to the 9th century. Thus, biblical references to the

---

12. *Levant* 28 (1996): 177-87.

13. Ironically, one of the major polemics in Finkelstein's publications, particularly in his response to Mazar (*Levant* 30 [1998]: 172), is the "accusation" that biblical archaeologists are basing Iron Age chronology solely on the biblical record. This double standard of Finkelstein accusing his opponents of relying on textual records while his key site is solely based on the biblical account was forcibly illustrated by Amnon Ben-Tor's response to the Low Chronology; "Hazor and the Chronology of Northern Israel: A Reply to Israel Finkelstein," *BASOR* 317 (2000): 9-15.

14. Orna Zimhoni, "The Iron Age Pottery from Tel Jezreel — An Interim Report," *TA* 19 (1992): 57-70.

Davidic and Solomonic kingdoms are a later "glorification of the past" by the biblical editors. Finkelstein does not abandon David and Solomon. He proposes that they were nothing more than leaders of major chiefdoms.

As the archaeological horizons are reinterpreted under Finkelstein's Low Chronology, the smaller village sites of the 11th century now belong to David and Solomon. The monumental architecture of the 10th century now belongs to the 9th century. Therefore, the rise of states in the Iron Age is shifted to the 9th century. David and Solomon's kingdom becomes the small villages currently associated with the Iron Age I horizon.

Response to the Low Chronology

Currently, Finkelstein is the only outspoken proponent of the Low Chronology.[15] All archaeologists agree to the relative dating among all the assemblages of the Iron Age ceramic horizon. The point of contention is the absolute dating of the horizon. The underlying premises of the Low Chronology were quickly challenged. Mazar published an immediate response to Finkelstein's article that proposed redating the united monarchy.[16] Mazar concluded that Finkelstein's suggestion to push the date of the Philistine Monochrome pottery beyond the end of the Egyptian presence in Canaan is based on a debatable assumption (Tenet #2). Mazar also introduced two additional critical variables into the debate. First, he introduced several important northern assemblages that contradict the redating proposal of the Low Chronology. Second are examples of other ceramic horizons that exhibit regional patterning, such as the Khirbet Kerak Ware distribution of the Early Bronze III period and the Bichrome pottery of Middle Bronze III/Late Bronze I horizon.

A second article criticizing the Low Chronology was published by Anabel Zarzeki-Peleg.[17] She also focused on the Iron Age stratigraphy of northern assemblages. Zarzeki-Peleg presented a ceramic typological study of three important northern sites (Megiddo, Jokneam, and Hazor) and concluded that the stratigraphical redating of the Low Chronology is not possible.

Finkelstein promptly responded to both of these criticisms of the Low Chronology with the publication of three articles. The first was the polemical

---

15. Ussishkin and Wrightman, who first published views that belong to the Low Chronology, have not published or openly supported Finkelstein in the literature.

16. "Iron Age Chronology: A Reply to I. Finkelstein," *Levant* 29 (1997): 157-67.

17. "Hazor, Jokneam and Megiddo in the Tenth Century B.C.E.," *TA* 24 (1997): 258-88.

response to Mazar's criticism,[18] and the next two[19] presented reinterpretations of Iron Age stratigraphy of northern assemblages. One article redated the Taanach Iron Age stratigraphy,[20] and the second redated the Hazor stratigraphy.[21] Finkelstein acknowledged that Zarzeki-Peleg's conclusions regarding the relative stratigraphy are accurate and notes that she does not provide any data regarding the absolute chronology. He attempts to address this by stating that the pottery of the Jezreel enclosure is similar to that of the Hazor citadel in Area B. Since the Jezreel enclosure can be dated, based on the biblical account, to the 9th century, then Hazor Stratum X and Megiddo VA-IVB must also be redated to the 9th century.

A second set of responses to Finkelstein's Low Chronology came in a 2000 issue of *BASOR*.[22] First, Nadav Na'aman challenged Finkelstein's redating of the Philistine Monochrome pottery using Trojan Grey Ware from Lachish and Tel Miqne-Ekron.[23] Na'aman noted that the Philistine Monochrome pottery appears directly above sites with Trojan Grey Ware and therefore Finkelstein's "post Mycenaean IIIB–pre Monochrome phase" (Phase 2) is an unsubstantiated creation. A second article by Ben-Tor addressed Finkelstein's redating of the northern sites, particularly Hazor.[24] He addressed two methodological issues: the validity of treating Jezreel as a key site for Iron Age chronology in Israel, and the relationship between the archaeological record and the biblical data. Ben-Tor posits that to use the Jezreel enclosure assemblage as the type site to lower the date of all other assemblages is the methodological flaw in Finkelstein's argument because the loci cannot be associated with secure floor levels and are probably earlier fills.[25]

18. *Levant* 30 (1998): 167-74.

19. "Notes on the Stratigraphy and Chronology of Iron Age Ta'anach," *TA* 25 (1998): 208-218. "Hazor and the North in the Iron Age: A Low Chronology Perspective." *BASOR* 314 (1999): 55-70.

20. *TA* 25 (1998): 208-218.

21. *BASOR* 314 (1999): 55-70.

22. *BASOR* 317 (2000).

23. Nadav Na'aman, "The Contribution of the Trojan Grey Ware from Lachish and Tel Miqne-Ekron to the Chronology of the Philistine Monochrome Pottery," *BASOR* 317 (2000): 1-7.

24. *BASOR* 317 (2000): 9-15.

25. This methodological problem is similar to the critique of Kenyon's dating of the Samaria stratigraphy. For a complete discussion of the Samaria dating issue. see Ron E. Tappy, *The Archeology of Israelite Samaria*, 1: *Early Iron Age through the Ninth Century B.C.E.* HSS 44 (Atlanta: Scholars, 1992).

A Case Study: Homogeneity of Ceramic Assemblages

Introduction

The important theoretical issue that needs to be addressed in the Low Chronology debate is the principle of homogeneity of ceramic assemblages. One of the major theoretical developments in the discipline of Syro-Palestinian archaeology is the development of ceramic typologies for chronological comparisons. Relative chronology is based on the degree of uniformity between ceramic assemblages. Almost all dating and chronological correlations of Iron Age sites are based on comparisons between ceramic assemblages. Some of these comparisons are based on a particular ceramic type, in this case, Philistine Monochrome pottery.

Several attempts have been made to demonstrate that some contemporary sites can exhibit marked differences in ceramic distribution. As stated earlier, Mazar uses the Khirbet Kerak Ware of the Early Bronze III and the Middle Bronze III/Late Bronze I Bichrome pottery as examples. Finkelstein dismisses these case studies by showing that they refer to sites in different regions several kilometers away, not nearby as in the case of the Philistine coastal sites and Lachish.[26] Recently, Shlomo Bunimovitz and Avraham Faust used ethnographic data to demonstrate that the material culture between neighboring sites can exhibit marked differences, contradicting the basic tenet of the Low Chronology.[27]

Aijalon Valley Region

The principle of homogeneity of ceramic assemblages can easily be tested by a comprehensive ceramic analysis of an individual region. I recently analyzed the Tel Miqne Stratum IV ceramic assemblage and the Aijalon Valley Region during the 11/10th century transition.[28] The Aijalon Valley Region extends from the Yarkon River to the Sorek River. Although there are similarities between all the assemblages in the region, there are also individual vessel types that appear at only one site or within one subregion. For example, of the nine major bowl types of the Aijalon Valley Region (see Table 2, Plate 1; these and

---

26. *Levant* 30 (1998): 167-74.

27. "Chronological Separation, Geographical Segregation, or Ethnic Demarcation? Ethnography and the Iron Age Low Chronology," *BASOR* 322 (2001): 1-10.

28. Steven M. Ortiz, *The 11/10th Century* B.C.E. Transition in the Aijalon Valley Region: New Evidence from Tel Miqne-Ekron Stratum IV (diss., University of Arizona, 2000; Oxford: Archaeopress, forthcoming).

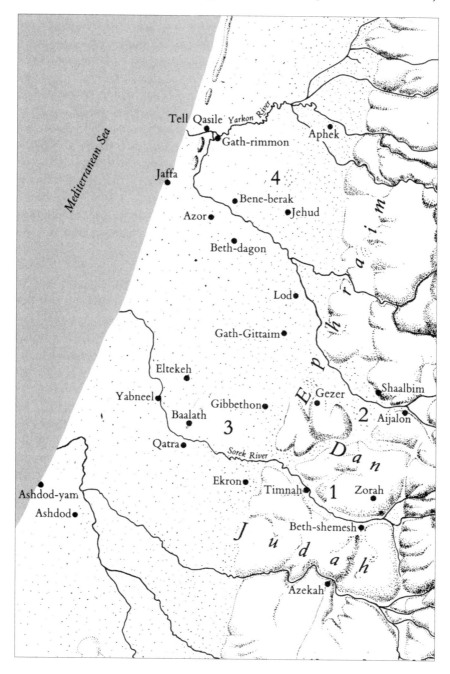

Figure 1. The Aijalon Valley Region
(Benjamin Mazar, *IEJ* 10 [1960])

subsequently cited tables and plates appear at the end of the chapter, on pp. 140ff.), only three types are found in all sites: round simple-rim (Plate 1:1-9), cyma-profiled bowls (Plate 1:10-14), and bell-shaped bowls (Plate 1:15-23).

There are five major cooking pots (Table 3, Plate 2). Only three are found at all sites: triangular-profiled (Plate 2:1-6), flanged-tongued rim (Plate 2:7-11), plain simple-rim (Plate 2:16-19). Triangular-profiled cooking pots are remnants of the Canaanite Late Bronze Age and are found only at those sites adjacent to the Western Highlands (e.g., Tel Gezer, 'Izbet Ṣarṭah, and Beth-shemesh), while cooking jugs are common only at sites on the coast (e.g., Tell Qasile, Tel Ashdod, and Tel Miqne).[29] The Western Highlands and Sharon Plain also contained cooking jugs in the 10th century. Based on this patterning, it is clear that the cooking jug started in the Philistine coastal sites in Iron Age I and eventually dispersed up the coast to the Sharon Plain and into the Western Highlands.

Intrasite variation is also found among juglets and storage jars (Plates 3 and 4). Dipper juglets and piriform juglets are found at Beth-shemesh and Tel Miqne but not at nearby Gezer. Large collared-rim pithoi are found at 'Izbet Ṣarṭah, Gezer, and Beth-shemesh (Plate 4:2-5, 8, 9) but not at the coastal sites of Tel Miqne or Ashdod. They are found at Tell Qasile (Plate 4:1, 6), which is on the coast. Gezer has "knob"-rim and molded-rim storage jars. Beth-shemesh is the only other site within the region that also has "knob"-rim storage jars. In the 10th century, Khirbet ed-Dawwara has molded-rim storage jars (Plate 4:20).

The inconsistency of the assumptions of the Low Chronology can be illustrated with any one of the above examples. If we were to interpret the Aijalon Valley Region on the basis of the assumptions of Finkelstein's homogeneity of assemblages principle, then all the sites in the study will have to post- or predate Gezer because of the absence of molded-rim storage jars (Plate 4:21, 22). Or perhaps we would have to lower the Gezer assemblage to the 10th century or raise the Khirbet ed-Dawwara assemblage to the 11th. A more plausible interpretation is that Gezer, as a Canaanite enclave, incorporated molded storage jar rims earlier than those sites on the coastal plain. As the Khirbet ed-Dawwara assemblage shows, these storage jars became popular in the 10th century in the Western Highlands.

When Finkelstein's principle of homogeneity of assemblages is actually applied to the archaeological record, it is shown to be too simplistic a principle for the development of ceramic distribution models. The 11/10th-century Aijalon Valley Region ceramic typology demonstrates that within one cul-

---

29. The notable exception is Gezer, which also contains a cooking jug.

tural horizon within a specific region it is possible for assemblages of neighboring sites to exhibit some heterogeneity in the ceramic assemblages. When other regional assemblages are analyzed as intensely as the Aijalon Valley Region, they will probably also confirm this pattern. Ceramic distribution patterns are more complex than the simplistic typologies of the earlier period of biblical archaeology. The irony is that Finkelstein is the one who is practicing the biblical archaeology of the earlier generations, and his critics are reconstructing the past based on more sophisticated approaches to the archaeological record.

Lachish V and Gezer X

A second test of the validity of the Low Chronology can easily be applied to a ceramic comparison of Finkelstein's Phase 5. It is important to note that in all of the articles Finkelstein has written in support of the Low Chronology, he does not produce any ceramic comparisons between Lachish and post-Philistine Bichrome strata (Finkelstein's Phase 5).

Finkelstein's Low Chronology can be tested by a comparison between the Lachish V assemblage and all the other assemblages that are lowered to the 10th century. In 1997, Orna Zimhoni's ceramic analysis of Lachish Strata V and IV[30] was published posthumously. She analyzed three ceramic forms: bowls, cooking pots, and storage jars.[31] A quick perusal of the ceramic typology of Lachish V[32] shows that almost all the major vessel types of proposed related strata are missing! Lachish V does not contain any cyma-profiled, bell-shaped, hemispherical, or round- and simple-rim bowls of the Iron Age I. Of the cooking pots, there are no triangular-profiled or flanged-rim cooking pots. The Lachish V assemblage does contain cooking jugs and plain- and simple-rim cooking pots, but these cooking pots clearly show later developments than the Aijalon Valley Regional types (cooking jug). Among the storage jars, Lachish V lacks the large collared-rim pithoi found in almost all 11th-century sites. Most of the Lachish V storage jars have an oval body typical of the Iron Age II tradition. In the 11/10th-century Aijalon Valley Region corpus, storage jars still maintain the elongated body common in Iron Age I storage jars reminiscent of the Late Bronze Age tradition.

---

30. *Studies in the Iron Age Pottery of Israel: Typological, Archaeological, and Chronological Aspects* (Tel Aviv: Institute of Archaeology, 1997).

31. In Zimhoni's typology, there are 27 bowl and krater types, 7 cooking pot types, and 8 storage jar types (in Stratum V there are only 24 bowls, 3-5 cooking pots, and 5 storage jars).

32. Zimhoni, *Studies in the Iron Age Pottery of Israel*, 72-156.

Finkelstein is correct to note that Lachish VI does not contain the Philistine Monochrome pottery of the Philistine coast, but to move the Iron Age stratigraphy down does not provide a better fit of the homogeneity of these assemblages. A systematic study of the stratigraphy by the author demonstrates that there is actually less homogeneity between Lachish V (10th century) and assemblages that are currently dated to the end of the 11th century (e.g., Gezer X, Miqne IV, Qasile X).[33]

An alternate and more plausible explanation for the abandonment of Lachish during the later Iron Age I was offered by Raphael Greenberg.[34] He examined the Tell Beit Mirsim material and offered a forceful proposition that the Iron Age I inhabitants of Lachish relocated up the valley to Tel Beit Mirsim.

Conclusion

The proposal of the Low Chronology to redate current Iron Age ceramic horizons based solely on isolated ceramic assemblages or individual ceramic types is found to be based on theoretical assumptions that cannot be supported by the archaeological record. The 11/10th-century Aijalon Valley Region ceramic typology demonstrates that, although there are chronological patterns distinguishable in the ceramic record, ceramic variation is evident in contemporary assemblages of neighboring sites. Any archaeological or historical interpretation must account for this variability of the archaeological record. Finkelstein's assumption that sites contemporary with Philistine Monochrome pottery must also contain this type of pottery is wrong. A comparison of the assemblages between his type-site of Lachish V and the Aijalon Valley Region sites shows that these sites are not contemporary. A critical evaluation of other assemblages, particularly from sites in the north, will also show that Finkelstein's redating proposals are wrong.

The results of the study provide important data for future Iron Age research. First, the study validates current research that shows there are regional variations in the material culture during the Iron Age, particularly the Iron Age I. In addition to the Aijalon Valley Region ceramic typology, other intensive regional ceramic typologies should be developed to produce a more ac-

33. Steven M. Ortiz, "Does the Low Chronology Work? A Case Study of Qasile X, Gezer X, and Lachish V," in I Will Speak the Riddles of Ancient Times (Ablah Chidot Minei-Kedem — Ps 78:2b): Archaeological and Historical Studies in Honor of Amihai Mazar, ed. Aren M. Maeir and Pierre de Miroschedji (forthcoming).

34. "New Light on the Early Iron Age at Tell Beit Mirsim," BASOR 265 (1987): 55-80.

curate model of ceramic chronological change. These types of studies will allow future research to define production and distribution patterns of ceramics in order to isolate political and ethnic boundaries. The present study also validates the current trends to view the Iron Age I period as a time of intense ethnic and regional diversity.[35] Although ethnicity is difficult to isolate in the archaeological record, recent trends in state formation studies are emphasizing the importance of ethnic identification and group boundaries in state development.

A lot of archaeological and biblical research has focused on defining the Davidic and Solomonic state. Recent trends in biblical studies have de-emphasized historical criticism of the biblical text and have adopted emphases that focus on the literary structures. Recent trends to redate the Iron Age ceramic horizons probably arise from the trends in biblical studies instead of the archaeological data. Even though Syro-Palestinian archaeology and biblical studies must integrate their research strategies, archaeologists must refrain from letting theoretical trends in biblical studies dominate the interpretation of the archaeological record. The archaeological record still demonstrates that the house of David can correlate with the rise of the state in the Western Highlands from the Iron Age I to the Iron Age II, during the 10th century. Although archaeologists have a lot of work to define the nature of the kingdom, we know that it was not a small tribal chiefdom.

Additional Resources

Aharoni, Yohanan, and Ruth Amiran. "A New Scheme for the Sub-division of the Iron Age in Palestine." *IEJ* 8 (1958): 171-84.

Davies, Philip R. "'House of David' Built on Sand: The Sins of the Biblical Maximizers." *BAR* 20/4 (1994): 54-55.

Dever, William G. "Monumental Architecture in Ancient Israel in the Period of the United Monarchy." In *Studies in the Period of David and Solomon and Other Essays*, ed. Tomoo Ishida, 269-306. Winona Lake: Eisenbrauns, 1982.

Finkelstein, Israel. *The Archaeology of the Israelite Settlement.* Jerusalem: Israel Exploration Society, 1988.

————. "Excavations at Khirbet ed-Dawwara: An Iron Age Site Northeast of Jerusalem." *TA* 17 (1990): 163-208.

————. *Izbet Sartah: An Early Iron Age Site near Rosh Ha'ayin, Israel.* Oxford: British Archaeological Reports, 1986.

35. Elizabeth Bloch-Smith and Beth Albert Nakhai, "A Landscape Comes to Life: The Iron Age I," *NEA* 62 (2000): 62-92, 101-27.

Herr, Larry G. "The Iron Age II Period: Emerging Nations." *BA* 60 (1997): 114-83.

Holladay, John S. "The Use of Pottery and Other Diagnostic Criteria, from the Solomonic Era to the Divided Kingdom." In *Biblical Archaeology Today, 1990*, ed. Avraham Biran and Joseph Aviram, 86-101. Jerusalem: Israel Exploration Society, 1993.

Mazar, Amihai. "The 11th Century B.C.E. in Palestine." In *Proceedings of the International Colloquium: Cyprus in the 11th Century B.C.*, ed. V. Karageorghis, 39-58. Nicosia: University of Cyprus, 1994.

————. "The Emergence of the Philistine Material Culture." *IEJ* 35 (1985): 95-107.

————. *Excavations at Tell Qasile, Part One: The Philistine Sanctuary: Architecture and Cult Objects*. Jerusalem: Hebrew University, Institute of Archaeology, 1980.

————. *Excavations at Tell Qasile, Part Two: The Philistine Sanctuary: Various Finds, The Pottery, Conclusions, Appendixes*. Jerusalem: Hebrew University, Institute of Archaeology, 1985.

————. "The Iron Age I." In *The Archaeology of Ancient Israel*, ed. Amnon Ben-Tor, 258-301. New Haven: Yale University Press, 1992.

————. "The Northern Shephelah in the Iron Age: Some Issues in Biblical History and Archaeology." In *Scripture and Other Artifacts: Essays on the Bible and Archaeology in Honor of Philip J. King*, ed. Michael D. Coogan, J. Cheryl Exum, and Lawrence E. Stager, 247-67. Louisville: Westminster John Knox, 1994.

Timnah (Tel Batash) I: Stratigraphy and Architecture. Jerusalem: Hebrew University, Institute of Archaeology, 1997.

Thompson, Thomas L. "Historiography of Ancient Palestine and Early Jewish Historiography: W. G. Dever and the Not So New Biblical Archaeology." In *The Origins of the Israelite States*, ed. Volkmar Fritz and Philip R. Davies, 26-43. Sheffield: Sheffield Academic, 1996.

Wright, G. Ernest. "Israelite Samaria and Iron Age Chronology." *BASOR* 155 (1959): 13-29.

Zimhoni, Orna. "The Iron Age Pottery of Tel 'Eton and its Relation to the Lachish, Tell Beit Mirsim and Arad Assemblages." *TA* 12 (1985): 63-90.

Table 2. Aijalon Valley Region — Bowls 11/10th-cent. CERAMIC HORIZON

Bowl Types:	Qasile	'Izbet Sartah	Gezer	Beth-shemesh	Ashdod	Tel Miqne	Kh. ed Dawwara
	type numbers						
Round, simple rim	1-4	5, 8	1	1	1	5, 6	1
Cyma profile	8	3, 6	2	2	2	15	
Bell-shaped bowls	16	28	4	4	5a/b	14	
Hemispherical	(11)		3			12, 13	
Carinated-shallow incurved						1, 4	
Straight-sided				6		2-3	4
Everted-grooved rim	5				4	8, 9, 19	
Round-thin walled	12		8		(4)	7, 10, 11	
Flat bowls	14-15						
Large bowls round-thick rim	(1) 7		6, 7	(1) 5	6, 7/b	16-17 18	2
round-everted rim	6		5	3			
carinated	11				3a/b	20-22	
Misc. Bowls	9, 10, 13, 17, 18			7		23	
Decoration: burnishing	*		*	*	*	*	*
red slip	*		*	*	*	*	5
bar handles	*		6		*	*	3
horizontal handles	*		*	*	*	*	
appliqués	*		*	*	6	*	

Table 3. Aijalon Valley Region — Cooking Pots 11/10th cent.

Cooking Pot Type	Tel Qasile	'Izbet Ṣarṭah	Tel Gezer	Beth-shemesh	Tel Ashdod	Tel Miqne	Western Highlands	Sharon Plain
Triangular-profiled		3	6	3			√	
Flanged-tongued				3	2	1	√	√
erect	7	17						
slanted		20						
elongated, concave	18		10					
Plain/simple-rim (vertical, inverted)	7	12	8	9	1	8	√	√
Ridged-rim		28	4	4	3		√	√
w/ inverted-rim		36	2			1		
Cooking Jug	1		1		1	2	√	√
Other (unknown)	1			1	1	3		
Total	34	116	31	20	8	15	—	—

Western Highlands includes Shiloh, Giloh, and Khirbet ed-Dawwara
Sharon Plain includes Tel Mevorakh, Tel Michal, Tel Poleg
√ = present

Table 4. Aijalon Valley Region — Juglets 11/10th century

Juglet Type	Tell Qasile	'Izbet Ṣarṭah	Gezer	Beth-shemesh	Ashdod	Tel Michal	Tel Mevorakh	Total
Dipper juglets								
elliptical body	8	1						9
oval body	5							5
sack-shaped body	4						4	8
cylindrical body	8			1	2	6	6	23
Piriform juglets	1	1		7	6		2	17
Hybrid: Piriform/dipper					4			4
Specialized juglets			1		4			5
Small black juglet				1		2		3
Cypriote — black on red						4	2	6
Other						1		1
Unknown		1						1
Totals	26	3	1	9	16	13	14	82

Table 5. Aijalon Valley Region — Storage Jar Types 11/10th cent.

Storage Jar Type	Qasile	'Izbet Ṣarṭah	Gezer	Beth-shemesh	Ashdod	Tel Miqne	Kh. ed-Dawwara	Total
Pithoi collared-rim neckless	6 (2)	21 (13)	5 (1)	1 (6)	—	—	16 (24) 17 (6)	52
LB Tradition	2 (0)	20 (0)			2 (1)			1
Canaanite commercial	3 (1)				3 (1)			2
Elongated egg-shaped, short vertical thick-rim	1 (137)	22 (11)	2 (8)	2 (4)	1 (8)		18 (4)	235
Plain-rim, short-neck		23 (53)			4 (1)	1 & 2 (5)		
Narrow-rim, long-neck				3 (9)				9
"Knob"-rim			1 (17)	4 (5)				22
Hole-mouth					6 & 7 (3)			3
Molded-rim (ridged/grooved)			3, 4 (12)				19 (10)	22
Hippo jar	—	—	?	—	—	—	—	
Other	5 (2)			5 (1)	5 (1)			4
Total	142	77	38	25	15	5	44	350

Note: Vessel type number is in bold; total vessel count is in parentheses.

Plate 1: Aijalon Valley bowls

Site   Reference

Simple Bowls

1.	Ashdod	*Ashdod II/III* Plate 4.2
2.	Qasile	*Qasile* Plate 39:12
3.	Gezer	*Gezer IV* Plate 45:19
4.	'Izbet Sartah	*'Izbet Sartah* Plate 20.2
5.	Beth Shemesh	*'Ain Shems IV* LXII.22
6.	Beth Shemesh	*'Ain Shems IV* LXII.19
7.	Qasile	*Qasile* Plate 33:13
8.	'Izbet Sartah	*'Izbet Sartah* Plate 20.15
9.	Gezer	*Gezer IV* Plate 42:20

Cyma Profiled Bowls

10.	Gezer	*Gezer IV* Plate 41:18
11.	Beth Shemesh	*'Ain Shems IV* LIX.14
12.	Gezer	*Gezer IV* Plate 41:10
13.	Qasile	*Qasile* Plate 39:21
14.	'Izbet Sartah	*'Izbet Sartah* 21.14

Bell-Shaped Bowls

15.	'Izbet Sartah	*'Izbet Sartah* Plate 20.1
16.	Qasile	*Qasile* Plate 34:7
17.	Qasile	*Qasile* Plate 46:5
18.	Ashod	*Ashod IV* Plate 1.15
19.	Beth Shemesh	*'Ain Shems IV* LXIII.11
20.	Beth Shemesh	*'Ain Shems IV* LXII.4
21.	Gezer	*Gezer IV* Plate 41:14
22.	Gezer	*Gezer IV* Plate 41:13
23.	Ashod	*Ashod V* Plate 43.1

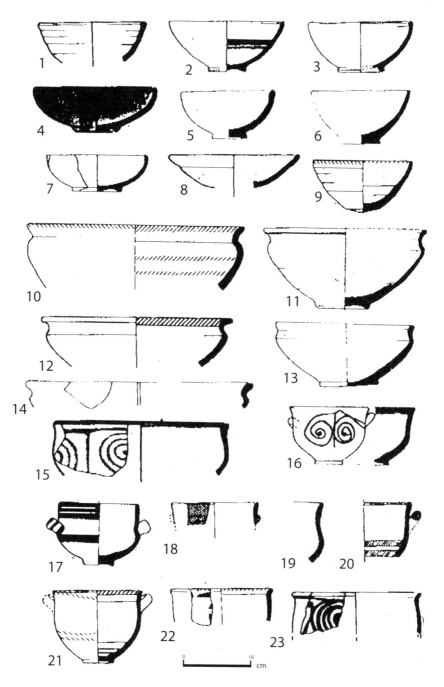

Plate 1: Aijalon Valley bowls

Plate 2: Aijalon Valley cooking pots

Site	Reference

Triangular-shaped Rim Cooking Pots

1.	Gezer	*Gezer IV* Plate 46:1
2.	Beth Shemesh	*'Ain Shems IV* LXIII:32
3.	Gezer	*Gezer I* Plate 35:21
4.	Beth Shemesh	*'Ain Shems IV* LXII:33
5.	Qasile	*Qasile* Plate 47:6
6.	Beth Shemesh	*'Ain Shems IV* LXII:30

Flanged-Rim Cooking Pots

7.	Ashdod	*Ashdod II-III* 74:10
8.	Beth Shemesh	*'Ain Shems* LXII:27
9.	'Izbet Sartah	*'Izbet Sartah* Plate 22.1
10.	Gezer	*Gezer IV* Plate 44:21
11.	Gezer	*Gezer IV* Plate 37:18

Simple-Rim Cooking Pots

12.	Qasile	*Qasile* Plate 45:22
13.	'Izbet Sartah	*'Izbet Sartah* Plate 22.3
14.	Beth Shemesh	*'Ain Shems IV* LXII:31
15.	'Izbet Sartah	*'Izbet Sartah* 24.8

Cooking Jugs

16.	Gezer	*Gezer IV* Plate 37:12
17.	Ashdod	*Ashdod II-III* 74:11
18.	Qasile	*Qasile* Plate 41:1
19.	'Izbet Sartah	*'Izbet Sartah* Plate 24.15

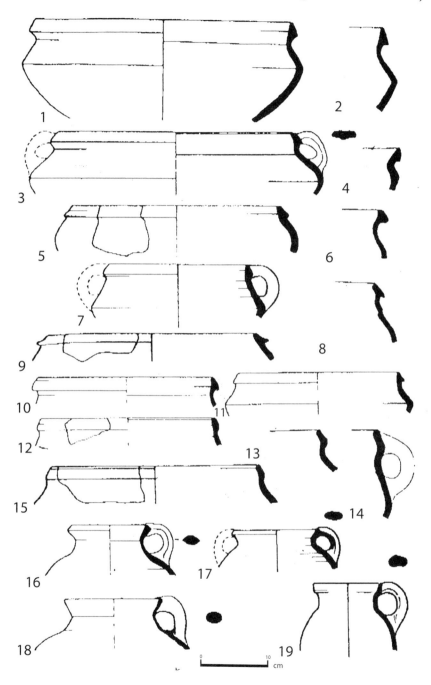

Plate 2: Aijalon Valley cooking pots

Plate 3: Aijalon Valley juglets

Site	Reference

Dipper Juglets

Site	Reference
1. Ashdod	*Ashdod V* 46:3
2. Ashdod	*Ashdod IV* 3:9
3. Qasile	*Qasile* Plate 42:2
4. Qasile	*Qasile* Plate 42:1
5. Qasile	*Qasile* Plate 36:4
6. Qasile	*Qasile* Plate 42:4
7. Qasile	*Qasile* Plate 36:5
8. Qasile	*Qasile* Plate 50:4
9. Beth Shemesh	*'Ain Shems IV* LXIV:42
10. Beth Shemesh	*'Ain Shems IV* LXI:39
11. 'Izbet Sartah	*'Izbet Sartah* 21:9

Piriform Juglets

Site	Reference
12. Qasile	*Qasile* Plate 50:5
13. Beth Shemesh	*'Ain Shems IV* LXI:35
14. Ashdod	*Ashdod II-III* 74:12
15. 'Izbet Sartah	*'Izbet Sartah* 21:10
16. Ashdod	*Ashdod IV* Plate 8:5
17. Ashdod	*Ashdod V* Plate 46:2
18. Gezer	*Gezer IV* Plate 44:8
19. Ashdod	*Ashdod IV* Plate 3:6
20. Beth Shemesh	*'Ain Shems IV* LXI:39
21. Beth Shemesh	*'Ain Shems IV* LXI:36

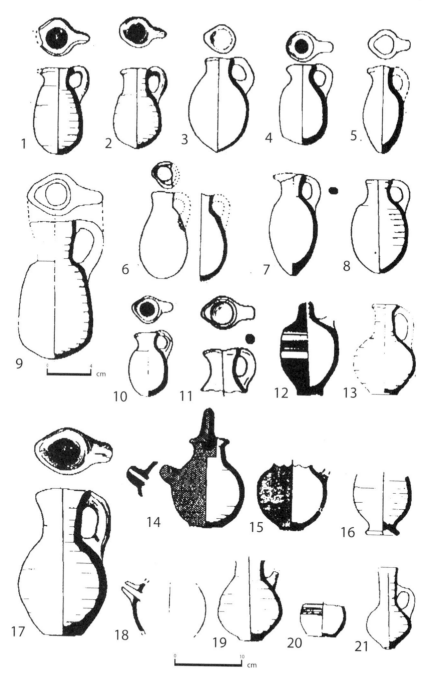

Plate 3: Aijalon Valley juglets

Plate 4: Aijalon Valley storage jars

Site	Reference

Collared-Rim and Large Pithoi

1.	Qasile	*Qasile* 34:18
2.	'Izbet Sartah	*'Izbet Sartah* 22:12
3.	Beth Shemesh	*'Ain Shems IV* LXI:1
4.	Beth Shemesh	*'Ain Shems IV* LXI:2
5.	Beth Shemesh	*'Ain Shems IV* LXI:21
6.	Qasile	*Qasile* 45:16
7.	Kh. ed-Dawarra	*ed-Dawarra* 16:8
8.	'Izbet Sartah	*'Ain Shems IV* 23:18
9.	'Izbet Sartah	*'Izbet Sartah* 20:7
10.	Kh. ed-Dawarra	*ed-Dawarra* 16:7
11.	Ashdod	*Ashdod V* 47:6

Knob-Rim Storage Jars

12.	Beth Shemesh	*'Ain Shems IV* LXI:22
13.	Beth Shemesh	*'Ain Shems IV* LXI:23
14.	Beth Shemesh	*'Ain Shems IV* LXI:25
15.	Gezer	*Gezer IV* 42:15
16.	Gezer	*Gezer IV* 42:12
17.	Kh. ed-Dawarra	*ed-Dawarra* 15:10
18.	Gezer	*Gezer IV* 42:7
19.	Gezer	*Gezer IV* 42:7

Molded-Rim Jars

20.	Kh. ed-Dawarra	*ed-Dawarra* 15:11
21.	Gezer	*Gezer IV* 42:8
22.	Gezer	*Gezer IV* 42:14

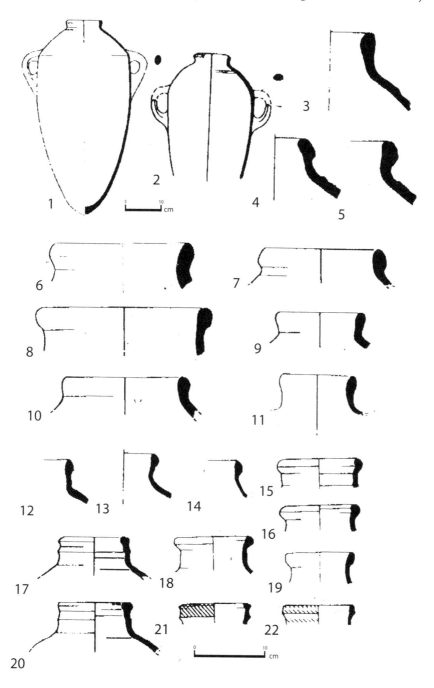

Plate 4: Aijalon Valley storage jars

Amorites and Israelites: Invisible Invaders — Modern Expectation and Ancient Reality

ALAN MILLARD

About 1900 B.C.E. in Babylonia, Ishmael the scribe decided to write a memoir for his son. He would describe the turbulent times he had seen. It was those dreadful wandering foreigners that were the trouble. People had known about them for years. Quite a few had come into the land and settled peacefully, but whole tribes had been living in the outback, moving about with no settled address, not behaving in the way decent people do. Now they had overrun the country. City after city had fallen. One tribe took this one; another tribe took that, each with their own leader. Some of the people were killed, but most survived and adapted to their new masters. But when his son grew up, what would he know about it? The invaders had not just taken control; they had taken over the whole culture. Why, he was writing their letters for them, drawing up their house sales in the style he had always done, in the same language and the same characters. They were living in the same sort of houses as everyone always had done, using the same shaped pots and pans, the same tools and weapons. The only differences anyone could easily notice were in the dialect they spoke and the names they bore. Ishmael could see that his son might never know there was any difference between the old families and the newcomers.

Seven hundred years later in Canaan, another Ishmael the scribe decided to write a memoir for his son. He would describe the turbulent times he had seen. It was those dreadful wandering foreigners that were the trouble. People had known about them for some time. They had been living in the outback. It was said they had fled from Egypt. Now they had swept across the land in lightning attacks. Cities had been taken, their kings killed. Then the invaders had come back, tribe by tribe, and eventually won control of many places. Some of the people were killed, but many survived and adapted to their new masters and neighbors, mixing with them in every aspect of life. The invaders had not just taken control; they had taken over the whole culture. Why, he was writing their letters for them, drawing up their house sales in the style he had always done, in the same language and the same characters. They were living in the same sort of houses as everyone always had done, using the same shaped pots and pans, the same tools and weapons. The only differences anyone could easily notice were in the dialect they spoke, the names they bore, and the particular god they worshipped. Ishmael could see that his son might never know there was any difference between the old families and the newcomers.

Amorites in Babylonia

Our first scenario imagines a situation in Babylonia after the fall of the Third Dynasty of Ur, ca. 2000, when "Amorite" invaders divided the land into numerous small states, each with its own king. They grouped in alliances that easily shifted from one leader to another, often fighting each other. For a while Isin was the most powerful place; then Larsa and eventually Hammurabi took Babylon to dominance. His line of kings was known as "the dynasty of Amurru."[1] Amorites had been entering Babylonia during the last centuries of the 3rd millennium. When they were perceived as a threat to the land, the kings of Ur built a wall, or line of forts, in the north of their realm, between the Tigris and the Euphrates, to try to keep them out, but that failed. Perhaps drought, drying up the pastures the Amorite herdsmen needed, had driven them in large numbers into the well-watered Babylonian plains.

Early in the 2nd millennium many of the small kingdoms in Babylonia were ruled by men with Amorite names. Although the rulers of Isin do not do so, others reflected their origins in their titles: *rabiān Amurrim*, "chieftain of Amurru," was quite common.[2] At Babylon, Hammurabi was "king of all the Amorites" as was Ammi-ditana.[3] A slightly different title was "father of the

---

1. According to the text published by J. J. Finkelstein as "The Genealogy of the Hammurabi Dynasty," *JCS* 20 (1966): 95-118; *COS* 1:462.

2. The texts are found in Douglas Frayne, *RIME* 4: *Old Babylonian Period (2003-1595 B.C.)* (Toronto: University of Toronto Press, 1990): Arim-Lim of Me-Turran, 700; Zabaya and Abisare of Larsa (1941-1933, 1905-1895), 112, 122, 128; Itur-Sharrum and Sîn-gamil of Diniktum, 683, 685; Ushashum son of Abda-il, *rabiān Amurrim*, was given a seal by Nur-Ahum of Eshnunna in the time of Ishbi-Erra (ca. 2017-1985), 486.

3. *RIME* 4:343-46, 411-12; *COS* 2:258-59.

Amorite land" borne by Kudur-mabuk of Larsa, who had an Elamite name, according to inscriptions of his son Warad-Sin (ca. 1834-1823).[4] That these epithets referred to the western incomers as a whole becomes clear from the use of "Amorites" beside Akkadians to designate the citizens of Babylonia under the rule of, probably, Samsu-iluna (ca. 1749-1712) and of Ammi-saduqa (ca. 1646-1626), according to the royal edicts.[5]

Several epithets referred to tribal groups within the overall designation: Kudur-mabuk was also titled "father of Emutbal"; Itur-Shamash of Kisurra was *rabiān Rababi;* Simu-Shamash of Shadlash in the Diyala region was *rabiān Amnan ša Šadlaš.*[6] The Amnanum tribe was widespread, being also at Uruk (Sîn-kashid was "king of Amnanum," as was Sîn-gamil),[7] and a letter from Anam of Uruk to Sin-muballit of Babylon tells of forces of Amnan-yahrur joining with those of Uruk and Emutbal.[8] From other documents it is clear there were Amorite tribespeople inhabiting or camped around various cities. Sippar had two sections, one named after the Amnanum tribe, one after the Yahrurum. There were Uprabum near Larsa and Sutu people around Ur and in other places.[9]

The name Amurru was shared by a god who was known in Babylonia from the latter part of the 3rd millennium onwards, appearing as an element in personal names and also revered in the cult.[10] On cylinder seals he is identified with the figure holding a short crook. He was, however, a foreigner, at home in the "mountain' or "steppe," whom the Babylonian theologians had to fit into their pantheon. They made him son of Anu, the chief god, some supplying as his mother Ninhursag, the mother-goddess, whose name is literally "lady of the mountain." The copper figure of Hammurabi kneeling in worship, now in the Louvre, was dedicated to

---

4. *RIME* 4:206-16, 219-22; *COS* 2:251-52.

5. F. R. Kraus, *Königliche Verfügungen in altbabylonischer Zeit* (Leiden: E. J. Brill, 1984), 160, 168-83; *COS* 2:362-64.

6. *RIME* 4:226-267, 273, 275; 697; 651.

7. *RIME* 4:441-63; cf. *COS* 2:255; *RIME* 4:466.

8. Adam Falkenstein, "Inschriftenfunde Uruk-Warka 1960-61," *Baghdader Mitteilungen* 2 (1963): 1-82; see 56-71.

9. Jean-Robert Kupper, *Les nomades en Mésopotamie au temps des rois de Mari* (Paris: Les belles lettres, 1957), 51, 52, 76-90; Rivkah Harris, *Ancient Sippar* (Leiden: Nederlands Historisch-Archaeologisch Instituut te Istanbul, 1975), 10-14; W. Yuhong and Stephanie Dalley, "The Origins of the Manana Dynasty at Kish, and the Assyrian King List," *Iraq* 52 (1990): 159-65. Some other references to Amorites as distinct groups are noted by J. N. Postgate, *Ancient Mesopotamia* (London: Routledge, 1992), 81, 244.

10. See Michael P. Streck, *Das amurritische Onomastikon der altbabylonische Zeit* 1. *AOAT* 271/1 (Münster: Ugarit-Verlag, 2000): 68-72.

Amurru.[11] Various minor goddesses are listed as his wives, one being Ashratum, who was known in the Levant as Asherah. She occurs more often outside the god lists, with Amurru on cylinder seals, in a dedication for the life of Hammurabi, "king of the Amorites," and in a hymn to Amurru.[12] Clearly Amurru had western associations for the Babylonians, yet, curiously, the personal names of people labeled "Amorite" in antiquity or classed as Amorite today do not have Amurru as a component. He was popular, on the other hand, in Babylonian personal names, both Sumerian and Akkadian, from Old Akkadian times onwards. A variety of deities is praised or invoked in Amorite names, both Babylonian and western, but there is no trace of a specifically Amorite religion in the written or material remains of Babylonia.

The texts attest the advent of the Amorites to dominate Babylonia. However, nothing among the material remains from the first half of the 2nd millennium in Babylonia discloses any evidence of cultural changes that might point to the presence of such newcomers in society. In architecture the monumental buildings usually adhere to old plans, and kings proudly proclaimed their restoration of old temples. Their work shows little difference from their predecessors of the Third Dynasty of Ur. Where they built new structures, there is no distinctively non-Babylonian element in them. Houses of the wealthier classes followed the pattern current in previous centuries, and that pattern was continued into the subsequent Kassite period.[13] Pottery fashions, too, display development but no major changes. So almost 40 years ago, Donald Hansen could write,

> In the areas of TA and TB at Nippur, there are some forty different pottery types covering the period from the Third Dynasty of Ur to the end of the First Dynasty of Babylon. These pottery types present a continually

---

11. *RIME* 4:360; *COS* 2:257.

12. Dedication: *RIME* 4:359-60; *COS* 2:257-58. See Jean-Robert Kupper, *L'Iconographie du Dieu Amurru dans la glyptique de la Ire dynastie babylonienne* (Brussels: Académie royale de Belgique, 1961); D. O. Edzard, "Martu," *RLA* 7/5-6 (1989): 433-38; William W. Hallo, "Two Letter-Prayers to Amurru," in *Boundaries of the Ancient World. A Tribute to Cyrus Gordon*, ed. Meir Lubetski, Claire Gottlieb, and Sharon Keller. JSOTSup 273 (Sheffield: Sheffield Academic, 1998), 397-410; Douglas Frayne, *COS* 2:253-54; O. R. Gurney, *Literary and Miscellaneous Texts in the Ashmolean Museum*. Oxford Editions of Cuneiform Texts 11 (Oxford: Clarendon, 1989), no. 1; Jacob Klein, "The God Martu in Sumerian Literature," in *Sumerian Gods and Their Representations*, ed. M. J. Geller and I. L. Finkel (Groningen: Styx, 1998), 99-116; Steve A. Wiggins, *A Reassessment of "Asherah."* AOAT 235 (Neukirchen-Vluyn: Neukirchener, 1993): 132-50.

13. E.g., at Ur, Leonard Woolley and Max Mallowan, *Ur Excavations VII: The Old Babylonian Periods*, ed. T. C. Mitchell (London: British Museum Press, 1976), xvi, 4, 5; Woolley, *Ur Excavations VIII: The Kassite Period and the Period of the Assyrian Kings* (London: British Museum Press, 1965), 1.

evolving series; there are no sharp breaks until the end of the First Dynasty of Babylon. The fact that there is no sharp break in the pottery sequence implies that it is difficult to define this time range from the Ur III through the Old Babylonian Period in precise cultural phases on the basis of the pottery, a fact worthy to be noted.[14]

More recently he remarked,

Pottery from Ur III to the end of the Old Babylonian period shows a large number of types which increase and decrease within the period without sharply determined breaks at the beginning or the end. . . . 32 types can be traced from before Ur III down to the end of the Old Babylonian period. . . . Of . . . 52 identified as first appearing in the Ur III period, 35 continue into the Old Babylonian period, 17 of which last into Kassite times. . . . Within each type . . . small changes and developments [occur] over time, representing a gradual evolution.[15]

Only the texts prove the presence of Amorites in Babylonia. Two features of Babylonian culture attributed to them by many scholars are, again, known only from written sources: the *lex talionis* seen in Hammurabi's Laws but not in earlier collections, and the combat between a deity and the unruly sea, famously described in the Babylonian Creation Poem, *Enuma Elish*.[16] If the Amorites brought material changes to the culture, they are not preserved, or have not yet been recognized; none of the technological innovations of the 2nd millennium, such as glass-making, horse training, or iron-working, can be noted as their achievements.

Israelites in Canaan

The absence of the Amorites from the archaeology of Babylonia affords a fruitful analogy, I submit, to the invisibility of the Israelites in the archaeol-

14. Donald P. Hansen, "Relative Chronology of Mesopotamia, Part II," in *Chronologies in Old World Archaeology,* ed. Robert W. Ehrich, 2nd ed. (Chicago: University of Chicago Press, 1965), 201-13; see 210.

15. Hansen in Ehrich, 3rd ed. (Chicago: University of Chicago Press, 1992), 118, drawing upon S. A. S. Ayoub, *Die Keramik in Mesopotamien und in den Nachbargebieten von der Ur III-Zeit bis zum Ende der kassitischen Periode* (Mittenwald: Mäander Kunstverlag, 1982).

16. See W. G. Lambert, "A New Look at the Babylonian Background of Genesis, Postscript, Second Postscript (September 1994)," in *I Studied Inscriptions from before the Flood*, ed. Richard S. Hess and David Toshio Tsumura (Winona Lake: Eisenbrauns, 1994), 94-113.

ogy of Canaan between ca. 1200 and 1000. Obvious differences demand attention before we proceed. First, the Amorite presence in Babylonia is established by means of many contemporary documents as well as being reflected
in later tradition, whereas a single contemporaneous text attests Israel's presence in Canaan (Merneptah's "Israel Stele" of 1209)[17] and no manuscripts
containing the narratives of her occupation exist closer than a thousand years
to the time of the events they are supposed to describe. That is probably the
result of accidents of survival and discovery, although some would disagree.
There is really no ground for supposing that accounts of events could not be
handed down accurately over many centuries and be known to us now only
from copies made late in the process, as demonstrated previously.[18] The hypothesis that all biblical texts written in the so-called "Deuteronomistic style"
were new compositions in the late 7th century, or thereafter, has a strangle-
hold on the study of early Israel that should be broken. In other ancient Near
Eastern cultures a style of writing could be used continuously for several centuries; there is no good reason to assume that it was only after the discovery of
the Book of the Law in King Josiah's reign that the style became a standard. If
we allow that the narratives of Joshua-Judges may relate events that occurred
at the end of the Late Bronze Age and the start of the Iron Age, what do we
find? Israel entered Canaan from the east under Joshua, who led a series of
lightning raids to break the back of local opposition, then following generations gradually spread across the land, taking over some places, mostly set-
tling alongside the Canaanites in existing towns and colonizing the country-
side. It is in that process that we learn of particular tribes in particular areas,
which were called by their names, while they were known collectively as Israel. The tribes are portrayed warring with the indigenous peoples and, occasionally, with each other, under leaders who arose in different tribes and acted
for some or all of the tribal grouping.

The impotence of archaeology to demonstrate ethnic differences in
many situations has to be recognized. Without the cuneiform texts, no Akkadian, Ur III, or Kassite periods could be distinguished in Babylonian history,
only phases of a continuing culture. In the same way, without the Hebrew Bible, the Iron Age in Palestine would be simply a sequence of archaeological

---

17. Recent translation of the relevant lines by James K. Hoffmeier, "The (Israel) Stela of
Merneptah," in *COS* 2:40-41; see also the discussion in his *Israel in Egypt* (Oxford: Oxford University Press, 1997), 27-30.

18. Alan Millard, "How Reliable Is Exodus ?" *BAR* 26/4 (July-August, 2000): 50-57; "History and Legend in Early Babylonia," in *Windows into Old Testament History: Evidence, Argument and the Crisis of "Biblical Israel,"* ed. V. Philips Long, David W. Baker, and Gordon J.
Wenham (Grand Rapids: Wm. B. Eerdmans, 2002), 103-10.

periods, perhaps with subdivisions, until external sources become sufficient to name kingdoms there. The intensely debated, constantly raised problem of how to recognize the presence of the early Israelites from archaeological remains that continues to be the focus of intense debate should be viewed in this light, for both the Hebrew narratives and the Amorite analogy make the attempt far more questionable than is usually allowed. (Of course, if the biblical texts are dismissed wholesale or only parts of them accepted on *a priori* grounds, then almost any scenario can be conjured up to agree with the interpreter's presuppositions or other information.)

Surveys of the central hill country of Canaan have plotted scores of small villages, often on hilltops, dated by potsherds to Iron Age I. The correlations made with the tribal territories allocated by Joshua have led to the conclusion that these are Israelite settlements. That has to be recognized as a conclusion drawn from the biblical texts, for there is no other source to give such an identification. To establish any material remains of Iron Age I as specifically Israelite is impossible at present. It is worth noting that the surface surveys on which views about the Israelites occupying the hills rest are limited in what they can reveal and are never final. On the basis of survey work, the area of Judah is said to be poorly occupied at this time, yet rescue work unexpectedly uncovered one more site,[19] and we may suppose more await discovery or have been obliterated by later farming activities.

In architecture, Early Iron Age I sees the prevalence of the "four room house" or "Iron Age house" at numerous small sites in the hill country. Here there is a difference from the occupations of the previous Late Bronze Age II period, both in design and in location. Yet there is no way one can say these houses were exclusively occupied by Israelites, nor that they were invented by them. They occur in Jordan as well as in Israel, so it is misleading to apply the term "Israelite" at this juncture.[20]

The pottery of the Early Iron Age I is clearly derived from the pottery of Late Bronze Age II. In her standard work, *Ancient Pottery of the Holy Land,* Ruth Amiran wrote, "The continuity between the Canaanite pottery culture of the Late Bronze and the Iron Age pottery culture . . . is clearly ap-

---

19. David Amit, "Jebel el-Habun (Alon Shevut)," *Excavations and Surveys in Israel* 20 (2000): 115*-17*, a single stratum site on top of a ridge south of Giloh, very eroded and heavily cultivated. See also the comments by Shimon Gibson, "Agricultural Terraces and Settlement Expansion in the Highlands of Early Iron Age Palestine: Is There any Correlation between the Two?" in *Studies in the Archaeology of the Iron Age in Israel and Jordan,* ed. Amihai Mazar. JSOTSup 331 (Sheffield: Sheffield Academic, 2001), 112-45, esp. 122-23.

20. Chang-Ho C. Ji, "A Note on the Iron Age Four-room House in Palestine," *Or* 66 (1997): 387-413, esp. 399, 409-10.

parent. . . . Almost every pottery type can be traced back to its origins in the Bronze Age."[21] More recently, William G. Dever stated, "The common early Israelite pottery [i.e. Early Iron Age I] turns out to be nearly identical to that of the late 13th century B.C.E.; it comes right out of the Late Bronze Age urban Canaanite repertoire. . . . Based on the pottery evidence, we would not even suspect that the people living in these hill-country sites were newcomers at all. . . . This early Iron Age I (ca. 1200 B.C.E.) pottery goes back eight or ten centuries in a long Middle-Late Bronze Age tradition."[22] Amihai Mazar, similarly, asserted the continuity of Late Bronze Age forms into the Iron Age, beside some new fashions.[23] In particular, it is essential to recognize that examples of the "collared-rim" jar, commonly held to be an "Israelite" vessel following William F. Albright's lead,[24] have been discovered in Late Bronze Age strata. For example, one lay on the ground floor of the "Egyptian Governor's Residence" at Aphek, beside typical "Canaanite" storage jars, and a number of others were uncovered at various sites in the coastal and valley regions, including Megiddo.[25] This type of jar can no longer be used as a means of distinguishing Israelite occupation from Canaanite.[26]

While there was clearly a new pattern of simple farming settlement in the hills, characterized by four-room houses whose inhabitants used many collared-rim jars, there is nothing in the material remains to enable an ethnic distinction to be made between those people and the urban centers of the val-

21. (New Brunswick: Rutgers University Press, 1970), 192.

22. "How To Tell a Canaanite from an Israelite," in *The Rise of Ancient Israel*, ed. Hershel Shanks (Washington: Biblical Archaeology Society, 1992), 27-56, see 40; cf. "Cultural Continuity, Ethnicity in the Archaeological Record and the Question of Israelite Origins," *ErIsr* 24 (1993): 22*-33*; "Ceramics, Ethnicity, and the Question of Israel's Origins," *BA* 58 (1995): 200-13.

23. "Jerusalem and Its Vicinity in Iron Age I," in *From Nomadism to Monarchy*, ed. Israel Finkelstein and Nadav Na'aman (Jerusalem: Israel Exploration Society, 1994), 70-91; see 87-88 and note the presence of a bronze dagger described as "Canaanite" at the Iron Age I site of Giloh, with Mazar's observation: "all weapons discovered in these sites [i.e. supposedly Israelite settlements] are of Canaanite types" (88-89).

24. "Further Light on the History of Israel from Lachish and Megiddo," *BASOR* 68 (1937): 22-26, esp. 25.

25. Pirhiya Beck, Moshe Kochavi, "A Dated Assemblage of the Late 13th Century BCE from the Egyptian Residency at Aphek," *Tel Aviv* 12 (1985): 29-42, see 34; cf. Beck, "Pottery Vessels" in *Aphek in Canaan: The Egyptian Governor's Residence and Its Finds*, ed. Kochavi (Jerusalem: Israel Museum, 1990), xx, 19; Douglas L. Esse, "The Collared Pithos at Megiddo: Ceramic Distribution and Ethnicity," *JNES* 51 (1992): 81-103.

26. See D. Wengrow, "Egyptian Taskmasters and Heavy Burdens: Highland Exploitation and the Collared-Rim Pithos of the Bronze/Iron Age Levant," *Oxford Journal of Archaeology* 15 (1996): 307-26.

leys and coastal plain with their richer repertoires of architecture, pottery, and metalwork.[27]

One significant distinction between the Late Bronze Age II and Early Iron Age I levels is the desertion or destruction of shrines. In 1987 Dever listed "at least twenty" Late Bronze Age shrines excavated in Canaan. Clear examples are at Beth-shan, Hazor, and Lachish, to which Tel Mevorakh is a good addition.[28] Whereas Amorite rulers in Babylonia restored long-established shrines and their rites (e.g., Nur-Adad of Larsa, ca. 1865-1860), rebuilding the temple of Enki at Eridu[29] and acknowledging Babylonian deities with their titles (e.g., Itur-Shamash of Kisura, chief of the Rababu, "beloved of Shamash and Anunitum"[30]), shrines of Late Bronze Age Canaan evidently did not remain as centers of worship in the Iron Age. At Shechem, excavators concluded that a building in Field IX "with what may be an altar and what is certainly a *maṣṣeba*" of Late Bronze Age IB-II was rebuilt in Iron Age I, but the altar and masseba were buried under the floor, "suggesting its nullification as a shrine."[31] The nature of the reuse of the "migdal" temple at Shechem in the Early Iron Age is uncertain.[32] Neither the identity of any deity worshipped there nor of the worshippers can be determined. All alleged Iron Age cult places seem to be new foundations. There are the "Bull Site" on a hill near Dothan, the Mount Ebal "altar" site, and the "cult place" in Stratum XI at Hazor where a pot contained the most hideous of the bronze "Baal" figures.[33]

27. This conclusion finds support in a detailed analysis limited to 10 sites in the hills north and south of Jerusalem made by Uta Zwingenberger, *Dorfkultur der frühen Eisenzeit in Mittelpalästina.* OBO 180 (Freiburg: Universitätsverlag, 2001).

28. William G. Dever, "The Contribution of Archaeology to the Study of Canaanite and Early Israelite Religion," in *Ancient Israelite Religion: Essays in Honor of Frank Moore Cross,* ed. Patrick D. Miller, Paul D. Hanson, S. Dean McBride (Philadelphia: Fortress, 1987), 209-47; see 223.

29. *RIME* 4:144-45.

30. *RIME* 4:697.

31. Edward F. Campbell, "Shechem: Tell Balâtah," *NEAEHL* 4:1345-54; see 1352. See L. E. Stager, "The Fortress-Temple at Shechem and the 'Heart of El, Lord of the Covenant,'" in *Realia dei: Essays in Biblical Archaeology and Interpretation in Honor of Edward F. Campbell,* ed. P. H. Williams, T. Hiebert (Atlanta: Scholars, 1999), 228-49. I am indebted to Larry Stager for drawing this study to my attention and for other helpful comments.

32. G. Ernest Wright, *Shechem: The Biography of a Biblical City* (London: Duckworth, 1965), 123-38.

33. Amihai Mazar, "The 'Bull Site' — An Iron Age I Open Cult Place," *BASOR* 247 (1982): 27-42; Adam Zertal, "An Early Iron Age Cult Site on Mount Ebal: Excavation Seasons 1982-1987, Preliminary Report," *Tel Aviv* 13-14 (1986-87): 105-65; Yigael Yadin, *Hazor III-IV* (London: Oxford University Press, 1972), 132-34, pls. XXIV, XXXVII-XXXIX. Israel Finkelstein has articulated a long-held view that the pot contained a hoard of scrap-metal; "Hazor XII-XI with an Adden-

[In passing it may be noted that the animal bones found at the Mount Ebal site — mainly of sheep, goat, cattle, and fallow deer — are comparable to those from the Late Bronze Age "Fosse Temple" at Lachish — sheep, goat, cattle, and ibex or gazelle, but at Lachish "practically all of the identifiable bones are metacarpals of the right foreleg" (the portion that biblical law required to be offered to the priest; Lev. 7:32), whereas at Mount Ebal there was a variety of bones.[34]] Even at Tell Far'ah (North), where the excavator claimed an Iron Age shrine stood on the site of earlier ones, at best this indicates recollection of the sanctuary at the place, not necessarily continuity of worship.[35] Nothing in the form of these sanctuaries, nor anything found in them permits anyone to state that they were created by Israelites rather than Canaanites. Either is possible; the common appellation "Israelite" begs the question. The reports in the book of Judges of the Israelites intermingling with the Canaanites and the ready involvement of Israelites in Canaanite religious practices described in that book equally allow these sites to be either Canaanite or Israelite; without inscriptions, no distinction can be made.[36] This analogy between Amorites and Israelites does not prove anything, yet it should warn against superficial interpretation of written sources and expectations about archaeological discoveries.

Some archaeologists, accepting the hypothesis that the relevant Hebrew texts were produced so long after the supposed events that they can be discounted, currently assert that the lack of major change in the material remains demonstrates that there was no Israelite invasion or conquest of Canaan. Observing the continuity of pottery styles in particular, Dever has written on the "overwhelming archaeological evidence today of largely indigenous origins for early Israel."[37] Yet that is to step beyond the permissible limits of archaeological interpretation. Instead, the question should be asked,

---

dum on Ben-Tor's dating of Hazor X-VII," *Tel Aviv* 27 (2000): 231-47; see 233. It is worth observing that the production of such bronze figurines ceased throughout the Levant at the end of the Late Bronze Age.

34. See D. M. S. Watson, in *Lachish II (Tell ed-Duweir): The Fosse Temple,* ed. Olga Tufnell, C. H. Inge, and G. Lankester Harding (London: Oxford University Press, 1940), 93; L. K. Horwitz, "Faunal Remains from the Early Iron Age Site on Mount Ebal," *Tel Aviv* 13/14 (1986-87): 173-89.

35. Mervyn D. Fowler has argued that the structure was not a sanctuary at all; "Cultic Continuity at Tirzah? A Re-examination of the Archaeological Evidence," *PEQ* 113 (1981): 27-31.

36. Cf. Lawrence E. Stager in "Forging an Identity: The Emergence of Ancient Israel," in *The Oxford History of the Biblical World,* ed. Michael D. Coogan (Oxford: Oxford University Press, 1998), 123-75: "Without clear indications from texts, it is doubtful that archaeologists can distinguish one highland group from another" (136).

37. *What Did the Biblical Writers Know and When Did They Know It?* (Grand Rapids: Wm. B. Eerdmans, 2001), 99.

What archaeological evidence for the Israelite conquest may be expected? Usually it is supposed that Late Bronze Age towns will end in destruction levels followed by a new style of occupation that can be attributed to the Israelites. The first criterion for making "a persuasive archaeological case for the mass migration of peoples from one homeland to another," according to Lawrence E. Stager, is that "the implanted culture must be distinguishable from the indigenous cultures in the new zones of settlement, if the intrusive group launches an invasion (as proponents of the Israelite 'conquest' postulate), then there should be synchronous discontinuities, such as destruction layers separating the previous 'Canaanite' cultures from the newly established 'Israelite' cultures."[38] Whether an invasion would leave such visible traces, or not, can be questioned. In a valuable essay, B. S. J. Isserlin compared archaeological evidence for the Saxon and Norman invasions of Britain and the Arab invasion of Palestine with that for the Israelite invasion of Canaan. On the basis of the first three, he showed that major cultural change need not be expected to appear in the material remains immediately after the arrival of a new group of people reported in written records.[39] The Amorite analogy offered here seems to be a closer and more forceful one; Babylonia makes clear how one people could adopt the material culture of another without leaving any lasting physical trace of their presence. This analogy makes a strong case for ceasing to seek distinct Israelite features following Late Bronze Age strata at sites in Canaan. It indicates that there may be little material sign of a change in population, so complementing the biblical narrative, notably Judges 1, which repeatedly reports the continued existence of Canaanites in the land, often sharing places with the Israelites, exactly as the Akkadians did with the Amorites. In fact, the changes that can be seen in the 12th century — the decline of large towns, the surge of small settlements in the hill country, the disappearance of painted pottery, the spread of the "four room" house and the wholesale abandonment of established shrines — might be the consequence of a new element dominating the population, but that cannot be proved from these changes.[40]

While this study has concentrated upon the limits of archaeological interpretation, it should be made clear that there are dangers in interpreting

38. Stager, 129 n. 36.

39. "The Israelite Conquest of Canaan: A Comparative Review of the Arguments Applicable," *PEQ* 115 (1983): 85-94.

40. For a recent discussion of ethnic identity, migration and cultural change, see Thomas E. Levy, A. F. C. Holl, "Migrations, Ethnogenesis, and Settlement Dynamics: Israelites in Iron Age Canaan and Shuwa-Arabs in the Chad Basin," *Journal of Anthropological Archaeology* 21 (2002): 83-118.

texts, too. Wooden literalism is to be avoided. Our translations often carry nuances that exceed the intention of the ancient writers. The word "city," for example, is widely used for the Akkadian *ālum* and for Hebrew *ʿîr* when a small town is meant — Jericho was not a city like London, Liverpool, New York, or Chicago, but more like one of the small mediaeval walled towns of Tuscany or the Near East. When an enemy conquered a place, destruction did not automatically follow. Killing citizens did not mean that no one was left alive. The words for "all" *(kl)* rarely imply 100 percent, signifying rather "a lot," perhaps "most," or "the majority," or "those that mattered," as K. Lawson Younger has pointed out.[41] The concept of widespread destruction by the Israelites as they occupied Canaan is an unhappy example of misinterpretation. Thus the list of kings "whom Joshua and the Israelites defeated on the west side of the Jordan," given in Josh. 12:7-24, summarizes the actions of the previous three chapters, embodied in the names of the leaders defeated. The list should not be treated as a list of towns that were captured and destroyed, for the texts concerning each place specify that it was the inhabitants who were put to the sword, many being "put under the ban," while the towns themselves were not burned, "except Hazor" (Josh. 11:13). This distinction is important. Entering the land after a transhumant life, the Israelites expected to settle in towns and villages. Destroying the Canaanites' houses would have been wasteful; the intention was that the Israelites should take them over, just as they took over the harvest (Josh. 5:11, 12). Expecting to find destruction levels that might be associated with the arrival of the Israelites is, accordingly, to chase a chimera. Destructions did occur, Judges 1 reports, but at a later stage, not simultaneously — indeed, probably spread over several decades. Careful attention to the biblical texts should produce a clearer understanding of the situation that would avoid misleading assumptions about destructions that continue to be made. Thus in a table listing "Biblical references and archaeological evidence concerning Canaanite sites claimed to have been taken by the Israelites (Late Bronze–early Iron I)," Dever included Bethel as "destroyed," citing Josh. 8:17; Judg. 1:22-28 [read 25], yet both passages speak only of the slaughter of the inhabitants of Bethel, and that is true for Libnah, Lachish, Debir, Makkedah. and Eglon in the same list.[42] To search for signs of destruc-

41. *Ancient Conquest Accounts: A Study in Ancient Near Eastern and Biblical History Writing.* JSOTSup 98 (Sheffield: Sheffield Academic, 1990), esp. 241-49.

42. *Recent Archaeological Discoveries and Biblical Research* (Seattle: University of Washington Press, 1990), 57-58. Equally misleading is the notation "not destroyed" for several towns in Table 2 (59), for the texts specifically report that the inhabitants were not driven out, destruction was not intended. Regrettably, a similar misrepresentation is present in Stager, "Forging an Identity," 129 n. 36, 132-33.

tion at the sites of those places, where identifiable, is to search for traces of something that no ancient source attests.

What is the attitude behind this study? Why take the trouble to set up an alternative to the currently fashionable views? On the scientific level it is as proper to argue that the reports ancient documents give should be credited unless there is conclusive, indisputable evidence against them, or very strong statements indeed for which no alternatives can be found. Interpretation of ancient texts has to be made within their own parameters; imposing solely modern concepts of consistency, chronological order, or comprehensiveness is unacceptable. Emending ancient texts or attributing parts to different sources to suit modern theories is, it should be acknowledged, totally unscientific, as it is, in effect, altering the evidence.

For anyone holding the Bible to be divinely inspired, its records of past events will be true, if correctly interpreted, taking account of the authors' standpoints. Accordingly, it is appropriate to try to find alternatives to those views that deny the affirmations of the scriptural texts or treat them as sources of little worth (see, for example, the demonstration of the feasibility of the descriptions of King Solomon's wealth as opposed to their characterization as fables in the style of the Arabian Nights, or the contradiction of the allegation that Sennacherib took Hezekiah's Jerusalem[43]). Admittedly, this faith affects the direction of research, but so do the beliefs of those who give little credence to the biblical texts. In any case, the results of all studies should rest on facts known about the biblical world and interpretations that are consistent with current knowledge of that world.

43. See Alan R. Millard, "King Solomon in His Ancient Context," in *The Age of Solomon: Scholarship at the Turn of the Millennium*, ed. Lowell K. Handy. Studies in the History and Culture of the Ancient Near East 11 (Leiden: Brill, 1997), 25-29, 30-53, esp. 31-42; "Sennacherib's Attack on Hezekiah," *TynBul* 36 (1985): 61-77.

Using Texts in Biblical Archaeology

Sumer and the Bible: A Matter of Proportion[1]

WILLIAM W. HALLO

The reviewers of the first two volumes of *The Context of Scripture* have been almost unanimously generous in their assessments of the project, its intentions, its scope, and its execution. But one point on which many of them have taken a more critical stance is the *title* of the work, and with it the notion that the (Hebrew) Bible should play so central a role in determining the selection of texts from five cultures that, in their own terms, existed quite independently of the culture that produced the Bible. The following sample is representative of the opinions on this score as expressed in the reviews.

> Can we in good conscience regard the ancient Near East as primarily "the context of Scripture"? . . . it seems a little ethnocentric to describe the ancient Near East as primarily a context for a different book.[2]

This and similar critiques call for a response. They are reminiscent of the campaign to free Assyriology of its role as handmaiden of biblical studies and to recognize the *Eigenbegrifflichkeit* of ancient Mesopotamian culture.

---

1. This is a slightly expanded version of remarks prepared for delivery to the colloquium on "The Future of Biblical Archaeology: Reassessing Methods and Assumptions" held at the Divinity School of Trinity International University, Deerfield, IL, 12-14 August 2001. The original version of my remarks appears as part of the introduction to *The Context of Scripture III: Archival Documents from the Biblical World*, ed. William W. Hallo and K. Lawson Younger, Jr. (Leiden: Brill, 2002), and is reproduced here in modified form with the kind permission of the publisher.
2. Ronald S. Hendel, *BRev* 14/4 (August 1998): 16.

That campaign was launched 75 years ago, in 1926, by the late great Benno Landsberger. It insisted on studying the ancient cultures in their own terms. It was not enough to compile dictionaries of lexical equivalents to our modern languages, let alone cognates to other ancient (Semitic) languages. Rather, the very different semantic systems of the ancient languages had to be approached first of all through the discovery of a system of "autonomous grammatical concepts."[3] Only then could one move on to other manifestations of the ancient systems, such as their apprehension of space, or law and commerce. In the event, Landsberger practiced what he preached: he identified the basic grammatical categories of Akkadian and Sumerian that were then elaborated and justified by his students while he himself devoted the bulk of his own research to lexicography.

Landsberger laid out his *programme* in his inaugural lecture at the University of Leipzig, and then published it in a volume of the University's own new journal, *Islamica,* in a special issue dedicated to the Arabist August Fischer — all indications of the importance Landsberger attached to his remarks. The term *"Eigenbegrifflichkeit"* was presumably his own coinage; one looks in vain for it in German dictionaries and despairs of translating it.[4] I suggested "conceptual autonomy" in an article of 1973,[5] and this was adopted by the team of translators when the original essay appeared in English in 1976.[6] The concept, if not the term, also informed Landsberger's three seminal essays on the Sumerians that were published in Turkish and German during the 13 years when he found refuge in Ankara (1935-1948).[7] In 1948, Landsberger received a call to the Oriental Institute of the University of Chicago, where I had the personal privilege of studying under him for five years (1951-56). I learned to heed his strictures on the conceptual autonomy of each

3. Benno Landsberger (below, n. 4), 3. Cf. also the interesting quotation from an unpublished paper by Landsberger incorporated in his obituary by A. Leo Oppenheim, *Or* 37 (1968): 368.

4. "Die Eigenbegrifflichkeit der babylonischen Welt," *Islamica* 2 (1926): 355-372; repr. as vol. 142* of the series *Libelli* (Darmstadt: Wissenschaftliche Buchgesellschaft, 1965), 1-18, together with a short *"Nachwort"* by the author (19); and Wolfram von Soden, "Leistung und Grenze sumerischer und babylonischer Wissenschaft," 21-133.

5. William W. Hallo, "Problems in Sumerian Hermeneutics," *Perspectives in Jewish Learning* 5 (1973): 1.

6. "The Conceptual Autonomy of the Babylonian World," trans. T. Jacobsen, B. Foster and H. von Siebenthal, *MANE* 1/4 (1976): 59-71. Erica Reiner prefers to translate it by "singularity"; see her *An Adventure of Great Dimension: The Launching of the Chicago Assyrian Dictionary.* Transactions of the American Philosophical Society 92/3 (Philadelphia: American Philosophical Society, 2002), 5, 7.

7. "Three Essays on the Sumerians," trans. Maria deJ. Ellis, *MANE* 1/2 (1974): 23-40.

of the principal ancient Near Eastern cultures.[8] I even became the first of a line of assistants who aided him in his later years. But I chose to write my dissertation under another of my Chicago teachers — a decision he never forgave me. I agreed with what he liked to call the "phenomenological" component of his approach: the desirability of identifying and assessing the phenomena of antiquity according to native conceptions, i.e., in the languages of ancient Mesopotamia themselves. It was this aspect of Landsberger's approach that explained and justified his lifelong preoccupation with lexicography. But I shared the reservations about this approach expressed most recently and most explicitly by Karel van der Toorn, when he said,

> We cannot understand cultures different from our own unless we appropriate them by an effort of translation. Scrupulous adherence to the rule of *Eigenbegrifflichkeit* would condemn us to incomprehension.[9]

And I parted company with those who, in the name of *"Eigenbegrifflichkeit,"* went beyond merely ridding ancient Near Eastern studies of excessive or even exclusive preoccupation with their relevance for biblical studies and began to imply the irrelevance of the one for the other, throwing out the biblical baby with the Babylonian bath, so to speak.[10] My own career over the 50 years since I first entered Landsberger's classroom demonstrates that. This personal jubilee is then a golden opportunity to answer Landsberger and to make the case for "Sumer and the Bible."

Let me begin on the most obvious level, the case of literary borrowings or what in recent terminology is sometimes referred to as intertextuality. Here a case in point is the Preacher's saying that "the three-ply cord is not easily cut" (Eccl. 4:12). As first shown by Samuel Noah Kramer, the biblical use of this saying was anticipated by a passage in the Sumerian tale of Gilgamesh and Huwawa.[11] And lest it be said that the Sumerian text could not have been known to the biblical author, we can point to the subsequent discovery of the missing links, so to speak, in both space and time: the publication in 1959 of a

---

8. Cf. William W. Hallo, "New Moons and Sabbaths: A Case-Study in the Contrastive Approach," *HUCA* 48 (1977): 1-18, esp. 2.

9. Karel van der Toorn, *Family Religion in Babylonia, Syria and Israel: Continuity and Change in the Forms of Religious Life.* SHANE 7 (Leiden: Brill, 1996), 7.

10. Cf., e.g., A. Leo Oppenheim, *Ancient Mesopotamia: Portrait of a Dead Civilization* (Chicago: University of Chicago Press, 1964), 21: "There are scholars who are inextricably entangled in attempts to relate Assyriological data to the Old Testament in some acceptable way...."

11. Samuel Noah Kramer, *JCS* 1 (1947): 40 *ad* line 107.

fragment of the Akkadian counterpart of the story of Gilgamesh and Huwawa found at Megiddo, and in 1965 of a fragment of the Akkadian Gilgamesh Epic which includes the very same passage and relieves the translation of the earlier Sumerian version of any doubt that it is indeed talking about a cord as in the Hebrew and not a garment,[12] though I will admit D. O. Edzard's new translation of the Sumerian reverts to the garment.[13]

Moving upward on the literary scale, we can proceed from the isolated topos or (common) place to the level of whole compositions. Here, by way of illustration, we may cite another contribution by Kramer, the indefatigable recoverer and reconstructor of Sumerian literature. In 1955 he published a composition to which he gave the title "Man and his God," and the subtitle "a Sumerian version on the 'Job' motif."[14] And indeed it anticipates the biblical book of Job in content, raising as it does the perennial question of theodicy, the justice of God, and doing so by the example of the just sufferer or what, if that seems to beg the question of whether the suffering was or was not justified, can perhaps better be called the pious sufferer.[15] A number of Akkadian compositions take up the same theme; they are not simply translations or even adaptations of the Sumerian composition, but they fill the chronological interim, being attested for Old Babylonian, Middle Babylonian, and Neo-Assyrian times.[16] Some of them, notably the "Babylonian Theodicy," introduce the dialogue structure characteristic of the biblical treatment of the theme.

The next logical step in the literary progression is the genre, something to which the Sumerians were notably sensitive. Though they had no word for the concept as such, they did have a rich terminology of separate genres and were careful to indicate generic classification in the rubrics and colophons of individual compositions and in the literary catalogues that, often enough,

12. Aaron Shaffer, "New Information on the Origin of the 'Three-fold Cord'," *ErIsr* 9 (1969): 159-60 (Hebrew).

13. D. O. Edzard, *ZA* 81 (1991): 202; followed by Douglas Frayne and Benjamin R. Foster, *The Epic of Gilgamesh* (New York: W. W. Norton, 2001), 109, 131: "cloth"; but note that Andrew George, *The Epic of Gilgamesh* (New York: Barnes & Noble, 1999), 154-55, restores the rope. Note also J. V. Kinnier Wilson's translation of a line in the Middle Assyrian version of Etana (*The Legend of Etana* [Warminster: Aris & Phillips, 1985], 63 line 4) as "If treble-twisted (the thread), the cloth [will not tear]" (ref. courtesy Benjamin R. Foster), though it may be questioned whether *e-ṣíp-ma* A.RÁ.III *er-su-ú* [. . .] can bear this translation.

14. See *COS* 1:179 for the latest translation and bibliography.

15. Gerald L. Mattingly, "The Pious Sufferer: Mesopotamia's Traditional Theodicy and Job's Counselors," in *The Bible in the Light of Cuneiform Literature,* ed. William W. Hallo, Bruce W. Jones, and Mattingly. SIC 3 (Lewiston, NY: Edwin Mellen, 1990), 305-48.

16. See *COS* 1:151-54.

grouped numbers of compositions by genre. I can again illustrate the point by appeal to proverbs, and will combine these here with the genre or subgenre of riddles. Both proverbs and riddles are, of course, well-nigh universal genres, and often endure for millennia and across linguistic boundaries in either oral or written form. The Sumerian examples of both genres are the oldest known anywhere and have a special connection to their biblical counterparts. I have already illustrated this for proverbs by an instance, not from the book of Proverbs, but from Ecclesiastes. For riddles the Bible has only isolated examples, the most famous being the riddle posed by Samson to the Philistines. In his narrative, Samson even provides the name of the genre: *ḥida* (Judg. 14:12-19). This is cognate with Akkadian *ḥittu,* and that in turn is the equivalent of Sumerian I.BI.LU.(DU₁₁.GA). The existence of the Sumerian genre-designation, and of examples of the genre so labeled, goes some way toward explaining the occurrence of a corresponding genre within biblical narrative.

A further example is provided by the letter-prayer. This genre, first recognized among Sumerian examples to be dated to the 20th and 19th century B.C.E., continues with bilingual (Sumero-Akkadian) examples from the later 2nd and early 1st millennium. It thus provides a possible precedent for the prayer of Hezekiah in Isaiah 38, there described as a "letter" (literally, a writing).[17]

We can go yet one step further in literary taxonomy and speak of coherent *groups* of genres. Here even our own terminology fails us and perhaps the term supergenre can be suggested — on the analogy of subgenre — to cover the phenomenon. For when genres as diverse as myths, epics, and songs of praise are all labeled as "hymns" (ZÀ.MÍ) in Sumerian, we realize that such hymns are more than a simple genre. Or to take the more familiar case of the genres I have already delineated: proverbs, riddles, and "just sufferer" compositions are readily recognized as forming a supergenre of "wisdom literature." This term, borrowed from the language of biblical criticism where it has long been serviceable in linking the rather diverse genres represented by the books of Proverbs, Job, and Ecclesiastes, reminds us that the relevance of Sumerian and biblical studies is a two-way street. Sumerian, however, adds other genres to the mix: fables, disputations, debates, and diatribes, to mention only the most obvious.[18] And their rediscovery has led in turn to the recognition of comparable phenomena within the biblical corpus, albeit not in the form of discrete compositions let alone whole books. I refer here to such pericopes as the fable of the trees and the thornbush (Judg. 9:8-15) or of the thistle and the

17. See *COS* 1:164-65 and literature cited there.
18. See *COS* 1:178, 180-86 for examples.

cedar of Lebanon (2 Kgs. 14:9; 2 Chr. 25:18). And long ago, it was pointed out that the book of Job not only reflects the debate format in its poetic portions, but that its prose-frame too ends in the manner typical of some of the Sumerian literary debates. When the "friends of Job" acknowledge his rhetorical triumph, they do so by each presenting him with a gold ring and a $q^e \acute{s} \hat{\imath} \hat{t} \hat{a}$ (Job 42:11) — and whether that is a coin or some other token gift can be debated, but it provides an interesting parallel to the gold and silver which Summer gives to Winter at the end of their disputation.[19]

The ultimate level of literary classification is the totality of subgenres, genres, and supergenres, or what I have long ventured to call the canon. That term had already been used by Landsberger at least as long ago as the *"Eigenbegrifflichkeit"* article of 1926, and at intervals thereafter.[20] In 1945 he spoke specifically of "the literary canon established in the Kassite period." The term was borrowed *not* from *biblical* criticism but from *general* literary criticism. In other words, it was not a matter of investing the term with the overtones of the sacred and authoritative that adhere to the concept of the biblical canon, but of using it as literary critics do when they speak of, e.g., the Chaucer canon to refer to all those compositions that careful study attributes to Chaucer.

Of course, there are other differences between the biblical canon and the cuneiform canons. I summarized these a decade ago.[21] But despite these and other disclaimers,[22] the subtitle of volume 1 of *The Context of Scripture*, "Canonical Compositions from the Biblical World," exercised the critics almost as often as the main title. Here again, one example may serve for many:

> . . . the titles of the book are misleading. "Scripture" and "biblical" refer to the Old Testament alone, and "canonical" is not used in the normal sense as when referring to the Bible.[23]

---

19. Cf. *COS* 1:183, 313.

20. *Islamica* 2 (1926-27): 355 = English 61; *ZA* 41 (1933): 184; *Die Serie* ana itti-šu. MSL 1 (Rome: Pontifical Biblical Institute, 1937): iii; "Die Sumerer" (1943), 99 (above, n. 7) = English 27; "Die geistigen Leistungen . . ." (1945), 155 (above, n. 7) = English 38.

21. William W. Hallo, "The Concept of Canonicity in Cuneiform and Biblical Literature: A Comparative Appraisal," 1-19, in *The Biblical Canon in Comparative Perspective*, ed. K. Lawson Younger, Jr., Hallo, and Bernard F. Batto. SIC 4 (Lewiston, NY: Edwin Mellen, 1991), esp. 10-11.

22. See now also my introduction to *COS* 2, xxi-xxii.

23. W. G. Lambert, review of *The Context of Scripture* 1, *JTS* 49 (1998): 210. For views more in accord with mine, see Victor Avigdor Hurowitz, "Canon and Canonization in Mesopotamia — Assyriological Models or Ancient Realities?" in *The Bible and Its World*, ed. Ron Margolin. Proceedings of the Twelfth World Congress of Jewish Studies . . . Division A (Jerusa-

Such cavils notwithstanding, I maintain that there was a Sumerian canon or rather, over the millennia of the existence of the language, a succession of three Sumerian canons. I have identified these as the Old Sumerian, the Neo-Sumerian, and the post-Sumerian canon respectively.[24] Without repeating the details of their history, suffice it to say that each in turn formed the core of the curriculum of scribal schools wherever Sumerian was taught — often far from Sumer and ultimately long after the demise of Sumerian as a living language. The persistence of Sumerian compositions, sometimes with translations into Akkadian and other languages, at scribal schools in Syria — places like Emar on the Euphrates and Ugarit on the Mediterranean coast — to the very end of the Bronze Age in or about 1200 (and beyond) provides the technical basis for at least their potential transmission into Canaan in the Iron Age and for the survival of Sumerian topoi, pericopes, compositions, and genres in alphabetic scripts.[25]

But the contextual approach is not confined to the literary sphere. If it were, then *The Context of Scripture* could have ended with volume 1. True, the soil of the Holy Land is singularly poor in monumental inscriptions from the biblical period; the possible reasons for this are discussed in the introduction to volume 2. But there are ample biblical reflexes of the monumental category as defined in my taxonomy of documentation, i.e., inscriptions on stone, metal, or other media designed to last into the future, or produced in multiple copies to the same end, or copied from such inscriptions. This definition, admittedly broad, makes room for such genres as law codes, known as inscribed on stone stelae since the discovery of the Laws of Hammurapi on the great stela in Susa (along with fragments of two others) at the beginning of the 20th century C.E. It also includes treaties, long familiar as carved on the walls of temples in Egypt but more recently seen to have been inscribed on bronze plaques deposited in temples among the Hittites. Both genres have reflexes in the Bible.

Specifically, the casuistic legislation of Exodus and Deuteronomy includes startling parallels with the Laws of Hammurapi, sometimes explained as evidence that these laws, which survived to later periods as models of both Akkadian style and legal acumen, became known to the Israelites during the Babylonian captivity. But Hammurapi was preceded by and drew on earlier

lem: World Union of Jewish Studies, 1999), 1*-12*; Nili Shupale, "'Canon' and 'Canonization' in Ancient Egypt," *BiOr* 58 (2001): 535-47.

24. William W. Hallo, "Toward a History of Sumerian Literature," *Sumerological Studies in Honor of Thorkild Jacobsen* (Chicago: University of Chicago Press, 1975), 181-203.

25. William W. Hallo, "The Syrian Contribution to Cuneiform Literature and Learning," in *New Horizons in the Study of Ancient Syria,* ed. Mark W. Chavalas and John L. Hayes. BMes 25 (Malibui: Undena, 1992), 69-88.

compilations, and these did not survive their immediate period of composition. When therefore we find closer parallels than with the Laws of Hammurapi between biblical legislation and the Laws of Eshnunna, as in the case of the goring ox, we can no longer content ourselves with the hypothesis of a 6th-century date of transmission. Rather, we may have to operate with the concept of an oral body of legal wisdom shared widely across the "Fertile Crescent" in the 19th century B.C.E. — much as is bedouin law in poetic form in the identical geographical parameters to this day.[26]

But the ultimate origins — or at least the first attested examples — of precedent law are, once more, to be sought in Sumer. While the Reforms of Uruinimgina (Urukagina) in the 24th century cannot claim to be casuistic or conditional in formulation, the laws attributed to Ur-Nammu (or Shulgi) in the 21st and Lipit-Ishtar in the 20th definitely can. It remains for future investigation to trace the chain of transmission by which Sumerian precedents passed via Akkadian, Amorite, and Canaanite intermediaries to their Hebrew reformulation, but the connection is apparent.

In the meantime, one can point to the transcendent justification for the legislation — "that the strong not oppress the weak" — as a common thread running from one end of the continuum to the other. It occurs in one formulation or another in the Reforms of Uruinimgina of Lagash, in the laws of Ur-Nammu of Ur, in the hymns of his son Shulgi and of Ishme-Dagan and Lipit-Ishtar of Isin, in the laws of Hammurapi of Babylon, and in the inscriptions of Sargon II and Assurbanipal of Assyria, and of Darius I of Persia. This whole long record, assembled in 1990,[27] can already be augmented from the inscriptions of Gudea of Lagash, as noted long ago by Adam Falkenstein,[28] by Shalom M. Paul,[29] and by an Old Babylonian letter as I noted myself in 1991.[30] The last example, moreover, was cited in connection with the levitical legislation regarding the biblical Jubilee (Lev. 25), which, though it does not verbally echo the ancient formulations, aspires to put them into practice.

26. See for now William W. Hallo, *Origins. SHANE* 6 (Leiden: Brill, 1996), 245.

27. William W. Hallo, "Proverbs Quoted in Epic," in *Lingering over Words: Studies in Ancient Near Eastern Literature in Honor of William L. Moran,* ed. Tzvi Abusch, John Huehnergard, and Piotr Steinkeller. HSM 37 (Atlanta: Scholars, 1990), 203-17, esp. 205-6.

28. Adam Falkenstein, *Die Inschriften Gudeas von Lagaš.* AnOr 30 (Rome: Pontifical Biblical Institute, 1966), 187 n. 1.

29. Shalom M. Paul, *Studies in the Book of the Covenant in the Light of Cuneiform and Biblical Law.* VTS 18 (1970): 18-19, which also assembles several of the other examples noted above, as Paul kindly reminded me by letter of 12 December 1990.

30. William W. Hallo, *The Book of the People.* BJS 225 (Atlanta: Scholars, 1991), 149-50, selection 38 and n. 149.

The chain is shorter for treaties. The "net-cylinders" of Enmetena (Entemena) have long been recognized as a sort of vassal treaty imposed by a victorious Lagash on its defeated neighbor state of Umma. More recently, the treaty of Ebla with a state variously read as A.BAR.SILA4, Apishal, or even, but improbably, Assur has been found to represent the earliest known parity treaty. But neither of these 3rd-millennium documents served as models for their respective genres known from the late 2nd and early 1st millennia. It is these that influenced biblical formulations, for example in the introduction and conclusion to the "book of the covenant" in Exodus or the curse formulas of Deuteronomy.[31]

What then of archival documents, the titular topic of the last volume of *COS*? Long ago, there was recognition of "archival data in the Book of Kings" by James A. Montgomery, and "the descriptive ritual texts in the Pentateuch" by Baruch A. Levine.[32] More importantly, however, Sumerian archival texts reveal *institutions* that have biblical echoes. Take the case of the "Sumerian amphictyony." Forty years ago, I used a Greek concept to characterize a Sumerian institution, leaving it to others to draw the logical implications for biblical history.[33] This was done most equitably, in my opinion, by H. E. Chambers in 1983.[34] Among Sumerologists, some like T. Maeda have generally supported the theory,[35] others like M. Tanret[36] have questioned aspects of it. The main challenge has come from Piotr Steinkeller and his student Tonia M. Sharlach, who have gone beyond the BALA of the provincial governors in particular to the BALA in general and have reinterpreted that as a redistribution system for agricultural products rather than as a specific means of channeling livestock to the cult.[37] The basic link between the calendar and

---

31. See *COS* 2:17-18, 127-29 and references there.

32. James A. Montgomery, "Archival Data in the Book of Kings," *JBL* 53 (1934): 46-52; Baruch A. Levine, "The Descriptive Tabernacle Texts of the Pentateuch," *JAOS* 85 (1965): 307-18.

33. William W. Hallo, "A Sumerian Amphictyony," *JCS* 14 (1960): 88-114; cf. esp. 96 n. 72a.

34. H. E. Chambers, "Ancient Amphictyonies, *Sic et Non*," in *More Essays on the Comparative Method*, ed. William W. Hallo, James C. Moyer, and Leo G. Perdue. SIC 2 (Winona Lake: Eisenbrauns, 1983), 39-59.

35. T. Maeda, "Bal-ensi in the Drehem texts," *Acta Sumerologica* 16 (1994): 115-64. See also Ze'ev Weisman, "Israel's Ancient Amphictyony — History or Utopia?" in *Cult and Ritual in the Ancient Near East*, ed. H. I. H. Prince Takahito Mikasa. Bulletin of the Middle Eastern Culture Center in Japan 6 (Wiesbaden: Harrassowitz, 1992), 108-19.

36. Michel Tanret, "Nouvelles données à propos de l'amphictyonie néo-sumérienne," *Akkadica* 13 (1979): 28-45.

37. Piotr Steinkeller, "The Administrative and Economic Organization of the Ur III State: The Core and the Periphery," in *The Organization of Power: Aspects of Bureaucracy in the Ancient Near East*, ed. McGuire Gibson and Robert D. Biggs. SAOC 46 (Chicago: Oriental Institute,

the provincial contribution known as BALA ("turn") remains unchallenged, and with it the potential link to Solomon's taxation system and its congeners.

Another example can be drawn from the sacrificial cult. Here the abundant Sumerian archival material helps to explain the comparable biblical institutions not so much by comparison as by contrast. Both cultures featured deities and temples, but while Israelite religion developed into monotheism with a single deity and, eventually, a single sanctuary, the polytheistic cults of Mesopotamia generated ever more deities and temples, 5580 of the former by one count[38] and 1439 of the latter by another.[39] The fundamental focus of the Sumerian cult was the cult statue of the deity, while the Israelite cult was fundamentally aniconic or even anti-iconic. The Mesopotamian cult involved first and foremost the "care and feeding of the gods" in the guise of their cult statues, as attested by thousands of archival account tablets best described as "descriptive rituals," i.e., after-the-fact accounts that describe in detail the expenditures incurred in cultic exercises against the possibility of future accounting by higher authority. In the process they provide an invaluable objective account of what actually transpired as against the idealized and subjective instructions, not necessarily carried out, which characterize the canonical texts best described as "prescriptive ritual texts." We gain a better understanding of the actual procedures of the Israelite sacrificial cult in light of the archival texts from Sumer even where the canonical literature of both cultures assigns it somewhat comparable origins. In Mesopotamia, the sacrificial animal was first stripped of its entrails, including intestines, lungs, and especially the liver. All these were evidently considered unfit for consumption but instead became the basis for an elaborate system of divination by means of the *exta* (entrails) or "extispicy" and more especially by means of the liver or "hepatoscopy." The rest of the meat offerings were offered in their entirety, ostensibly to the deity — but in actuality to the statue of the deity, which consumed nothing, leaving the meat thus sanctified to the priesthood and worshippers to enjoy. In Israel, the meat offering was divided in advance among deity, priest, and worshipper, and the portion assigned to the deity was truly consumed entirely by fire, whose smoke went up to produce the "pleasant savor" for divine enjoyment; hence the meat sacrifice was called *ʿōlâ* in Hebrew

---

1987), 19-41; Tonia M. Sharlach, *Bala: Economic Exchange between Center and Provinces in the Ur III State* (diss., Harvard, 1999); rev. ed. *Provincial Taxation in the Ur III State.* Cuneiform Monographs 26 (Leiden: Brill, 2003).

38. William W. Hallo, "Albright and the Gods of Mesopotamia," *BA* 56 (1993): 18-24, esp. 21.

39. Andrew George, *House Most High: The Temples of Ancient Mesopotamia.* Mesopotamian Civilizations 5 (Winona Lake: Eisenbrauns, 1993), 171.

(something which *goes up*) and holocaust in the Greek translation (something wholly consumed, i.e., by fire).[40]

The foregoing has done no more than illustrate the proposition that, just as Sumer is relevant for the Bible, so too the biblical debt to, reaction against, and amplification of the themes struck by the Sumerian documentation help to illuminate the latter in crucial ways. "Conceptual autonomy" cannot, in other words, mean cultural isolation. The ancient Near East was a geographical unit; then as now, developments in one part spread rapidly and enduringly to other parts. The five linguistic cultures included in the *Context of Scripture* were inextricably linked with each other; the indices in volume 3 help to make this clear. But they were also linked with biblical culture, which it is the special purpose of the middle column of each page of *COS* to demonstrate. Cultural interdependence is not primarily a function of proximity, whether in space or time; it is rather a function of the degree to which the channels of communication are open across the frontiers of both space and time.

My personal response to Landsberger's "conceptual autonomy" is the "contextual approach," which I have defined in various venues as being made up in equal parts of comparison and contrast,[41] and setting the biblical evidence both in its vertical dimension as the product of historical kinship with precedents, or intertextuality, and in its horizontal dimension as an expression of the geographical context in which it is set. But even this broad basis does not exhaust the possible analogies that can usefully be drawn from the evidence.

In his essay of 1926, Landsberger had used mathematical formulas to express the scope and limits of comparison. The English version of 1976 put it this way:

> All understanding consists first of all in establishing some link between the alien world and our own. In the initial stage this is expressed by a number of simple equations, which are compiled in grammar and lexicon, e.g. ending -*um* [=] nominative singular, root *halak* [=] "to go"; but such full equations are possible only to a limited extent; most often we have to content ourselves with partial equations of the type: part of Babylonian concept x corresponds with part of our concept y. All these equations are correct in so far as both a and b are beyond any doubt.[42]

---

40. Hallo, *Origins*, 212-21.
41. For the latter, see Hallo, *HUCA* 48 (1977): 1-18.
42. Landsberger, *MANE* 1/4 (1976): 62. The confusion between x and y, a and b is in the original.

Landsberger was talking about comparisons between Babylonian and modern (actually: German) concepts, but the same strictures would apply to comparisons with biblical evidence. A year later, though not necessarily with reference to Landsberger, I extended his resort to mathematical formulas to argue that if A is the biblical text or phenomenon and B the Babylonian one, their relationship can often be expressed mathematically as $A = B$, or $A \sim B$, or $A < B$ or $A > B$ or even $A \neq B$.[43] But even these more variegated equations do not exhaust the possibilities, limited as all of them are to two terms. Sometimes the analogy involves a relationship among four terms, e.g., between A and A2 on the one hand and between B and B2 on the other, or again between developments from A to A2 in the one culture and from B to B2 in the other. In such cases the analogy of the relationships or of the development can best be expressed by four terms in proportion: $A:A2 = B:B2$.

A first example of this sort that I came up with was drawn from Akkadian rather than Sumerian evidence. It involved the relationship between the Laws of Hammurapi and the Edicts of his successors on the one hand, and between the biblical laws of the Sabbatical and the postbiblical institution of the *prosbol* on the other.[44]

Other examples could be cited to illustrate the inherent potential of this "proportionate technique." In terms of Sumerian, one can support the concept of a Sumerian amphictyony[45] by appeal to more recent history. Its calendaric basis is paralleled by the Greek institution, by the Solomonic administrative system (of the northern tribes), and by a contemporary Egyptian system. But beyond its purely fiscal aspect, the Solomonic system also pursued a political agenda. It served to break up the old tribal boundaries and therewith attempted to strike a blow at old tribal loyalties. It may have represented a clever attempt — ultimately unsuccessful — to centralize royal power in Jerusalem by using the outward form of a traditional intertribal cultic institution to mitigate the real threat to tribal identity implied in the old borders. I have always thought of it as an analogy to the French Revolution, which sought — more successfully — to destroy old provincial boundaries and loyalties by creating smaller and more numerous *départements* on a purely mechanical basis. (Among the proposals put forward in the Constitutional Assembly of 1789-90, there was even one to subdivide France into

43. See Hallo, *HUCA* 48 (1977): 1-18.

44. William W. Hallo, "Slave Release in the Biblical World in Light of a New Text," in *Solving Riddles and Untying Knots: Biblical, Epigraphic, and Semitic Studies in Honor of Jonas C. Greenfield*, ed. Ziony Zevit, Seymour Gitin, and Michael Sokoloff (Winona Lake: Eisenbrauns, 1995), 79-93; cf. *COS* 2:134 and references there.

45. See above, nn. 33-37.

"eighty rectangular departments, each with a half-diagonal of eleven to twelve leagues, [which] would permit travelers from any point to reach the administrative center in a day's journey.")[46] We could thus set up a proportion:

premonarchic tribal lands : Solomonic administrative districts = prerevolutionary French provinces : French *départements.*

The proportion lends support to the older theories of a premonarchic tribal league, now not much in favor. But it does not stand or fall with these theories.

Moving beyond the Sumerian evidence, we can cite the debate on history and tradition. To my knowledge, this began with Donald B. Redford's study of the Hyksos.[47] It was taken up with enthusiasm by John Van Seters, whose dissertation dealt with the Hyksos, but who applied the concept more particularly to patriarchal traditions.[48] I resisted this approach to the extent that Mesopotamian historiography seemed at the time exempt from it. That has since ceased to be the case, notably with respect to the traditions about Sargon of Akkad and the rest of the Old Akkadian period, an expansion of the concept to which I have taken exception more recently.[49] But whatever one's stand, it is possible to set up another proportion, according to which, arguably,

Sargonic history: Sargonic tradition =
patriarchal history : patriarchal tradition =
Hyksos history : Hyksos tradition.

If the premises of the proportionate technique are granted, then it furnishes a further avenue for overcoming the problems of distance in time and space and for breathing new life into the contextual approach.

46. Ted W. Margadant, *Urban Rivalries in the French Revolution* (Princeton: Princeton University Press, 1992), 103. My thanks to my colleague John M. Merriman for referring me to Margadant.

47. Donald B. Redford, "The Hyksos Invasion in History and Tradition," *Or* 39 (1970): 1-51.

48. John Van Seters, *Abraham in History and Tradition* (New Haven: Yale University Press, 1975).

49. William W. Hallo, "New Directions in Historiography (Mesopotamia and Israel)," in *Dubsar anta-men: Studien zur Altorientalistik. Festschrift für Willem H. Ph. Römer zur Vollendung seines 70. Lebensjahres.* AOAT 253 (Münster: Ugarit-Verlag, 1998), 109-28; "Polymnia and Clio," in *Historiography in the Cuneiform World. Proceedings of the XLVe Rencontre Assyriologique Internationale,* ed. Tzvi Abusch, Paul-Alain Beaulieu, John Huehnergard, Peter Machinist, and Piotr Steinkeller (Bethseda: CDL, 2001), 195-209.

Ancient Israel's Literary Heritage
Compared with Hittite Textual Data

HARRY A. HOFFNER, JR.

There is a certain irony in the fact that we owe our knowledge of the civilization of the Hittites to the curiosity of biblical scholars, since the intensity of
interest of those early days has cooled over the intervening century.[1] As I
noted in a recent article, few Hittitologists today show a significant interest in
the bearing of their materials on the interpretation of the Bible. There are
several reasons for this. The principal reason is that most people are under
the impression that very little if any of the historical information offered in
the pages of the Bible is in fact historical. There is a very influential point of
view that only what the Bible says about the period following the return of
Jewish exiles from Babylonia under Zerubbabel can be considered relatively
reliable. Most else is mere tribal traditions or stories invented from scratch by
late scribes. If the Bible cannot be trusted to recount actual historical events,
it can safely be ignored not only by Egyptologists, Assyriologists, and
Hittitologists, but even by historians of Palestine during the Bronze and Iron
Ages.

Because of this attitude toward the Bible, and in our case specifically the
Hebrew Bible (or Old Testament), it is to a certain extent understandable that
specialists in ancient Near East studies today, unlike their predecessors a century ago, have relatively little familiarity with biblical studies as a discipline or

---

1. Symptomatic is the small number of Hittitologists (as compared to the biblical schol-
ars) represented in the excellent volume *Religionsgeschichtliche Beziehungen zwischen
Kleinasien, Nordsyrien und dem Alten Testament. Internationales Symposion Hamburg 17-21.
März 1990*, ed. Bernd Janowski, Klaus Koch, and Gernot Wilhelm. OBO 129 (Göttingen:
Vandenhoeck & Ruprecht, 1993), which was devoted to the subject at hand.

even with the contents of the Bible as might be known by a well-read user of the English Bible. In their publications today's Hittitologists rarely note or point out matters of interest to biblical scholars. Furthermore, the fact that the Hittite capital was located in central Asia Minor seems to many Hittitologists as well as biblical scholars ample reason to assume that there would be little chance of a direct contact between Hittites and their contemporaries living in Palestine. Certainly there is no indication in Hittite texts of a direct contact. Hittite armies campaigned as far south as the northern reaches of Damascus, but no farther. There is then the question of the age of the biblical written materials. Many assume that most if not all biblical texts originated much later than the fall of Hatti in 1190 B.C.E., and they assume that the meager returns for biblical study do not justify the time and effort necessary to learn the Hittite language and investigate Hittite and Luwian sources.

Happily, a few scholars in both fields have attempted to evaluate mutually relevant materials. And although very few comprehensive surveys have been attempted, quite a number of individual items in Hittite texts have been compared in print to biblical materials. Obviously, volumes like *ANET* and the *Context of Scripture* volumes[2] — like their German counterparts (the older Bousset-Gressmann,[3] and the newer series *Texte aus der Umwelt des Alten Testaments*[4]) — are making translations of important ancient Near Eastern texts available to a broader public. And the Society of Biblical Literature series entitled *Writings from the Ancient World* has produced around 12 volumes of translated documents from the ancient Near East, including three consisting entirely of Hittite texts.[5]

2. William W. Hallo and K. Lawson Younger, Jr., 3 vols. (Leiden: Brill, 1997-2002).

3. Wilhelm Bousset, *Die Religion des Judentums im späthellenistischen Zeitalter,* 3rd ed. by Hugo Gressmann. HNT 21 (Tübingen: Mohr, 1926).

4. Ed. Otto Kaiser: Einar von Schuler, "Die hethitischen Gesetze" in *Rechtsbücher* (Gütersloh: Gerd Mohn, 1982), 96-123; Elmar Edel, "Der Vertrag zwischen Pharao Ramses II. und Hattusili III. von Hatti," in *Rechtsbücher* (Gütersloh: Gerd Mohn, 1983); Hans Martin Kümmel, "Hethitische historisch-chronologische Texte" in *Rechts- und Wirtschaftsurkunden, Historisch-chronologische Texte* (Gütersloh: Gerd Mohn, 1985), 455-95; "Rituale in hethitischer Sprache," in *Rituale und Beschwörungen I* (Gütersloh: Gerd Mohn, 1987), 282-92; Ahmet Ünal, "Hethitische Hymnen und Gebete," in *Lieder und Gebete* 2 (Gütersloh: Gerd Mohn, 1991), 791-817; "Hethitische Mythen und Epen," in *Mythen und Epen* (Gütersloh: Gerd Mohn, 1994), 802-65.

5. Harry A. Hoffner, Jr., *Hittite Myths,* 2nd ed. SBLWAW 2 (Atlanta: Scholars, 1998); Martha Tobi Roth, *Law Collections from Mesopotamia and Asia Minor,* 2nd ed. SBLWAW 6 (Atlanta: Scholars, 1997) (which contains my translation of the Hittite laws); Gary M. Beckman, *Hittite Diplomatic Texts,* 2nd ed. SBLWAW 7 (Atlanta: Scholars, 1999); Itamar Singer, *Hittite Prayers.* SBLWAW 11 (Atlanta: SBL, 2002).

The history of the discovery of the Hittites has been often traced. O. R. Gurney's *The Hittites* is the most easily accessible to the general public.[6] In a fascinating essay entitled "Resurrecting the Hittites," the eminent scholar Hans Gustav Güterbock told the story from the viewpoint of a participant.[7] An entire volume devoted to that subject, lavishly illustrated with rare photos and containing retrospective essays by the students of Güterbock, Sedat Alp, Kurt Bittel, H. T. Bossert, Tahsin Özgüç and others of the earlier generation, is *From Boğazköy to Karatepe: Hittitology and the Discovery of the Hittite World,* edited by Münevver Eminoğlu for the Yapi ve Kredi Bankasi of Istanbul.[8] Most recently it has been capably recapitulated by Itamar Singer.[9]

As for the subject of Hittite parallels to the Old Testament materials, historical, legal, and religious, there are not many studies that attempt to survey that subject comprehensively. Early surveys, when little was known from the Hittite texts themselves, focused on how the Hittites described in the Bible could be related to the newly-discovered materials from the Hittite capital in Turkey. But already they also tried to bring Anatolian Hittite evidence — both archaeological and textual — to bear upon the biblical content. The earliest was a theory of J. A. Knudtzon, who had anticipated Bedřich Hrozný in the identification of the language of the so-called Arzawa letters from Tell el-Amarna as a previously unknown ancient Indo-European language, but later gave up his claim.[10] Misreading the name *Kal-ba-ya* in the Arzawa letter as *Lab-ba-ya* and identifying him with the well-known Lab'ayu of Shechem, he supposed that the kingdom of Arzawa from where the letter was sent to Egypt was in Transjordan, and that the Arzawans were the "Hittites" of the early parts of the Old Testament.

The real breakthrough came when Hugo Winckler and Theodor Makridi excavated the huge mound near the Turkish village of Boğazköy,

---

6. 2nd ed. (Baltimore: Penguin, 1961), 1-11.

7. In *CANE* (New York: Scribner's, 1995), 4:2765-77.

8. (English title); *Boğazköy'den Karatepe'ye: Hititbilim ve Hitit Dünyasinin Kerfi* (Istanbul: Yapi kredi Cultural Activities, Arts and Publishing, 2001).

9. Itamar Singer, "The Hittites and the Bible Revisited," in *"I will speak the riddles of ancient times" (Abiah chidot minei-kedem — Ps 72:8b): Archaeological and Historical Studies in Honor of Amihai Mazar on the Occasion of His Sixtieth Birthday,* ed. Aren M. Maeir and P. de Miroschedji (Winona Lake: Eisenbrauns, forthcoming 2004).

10. The initial claim was published in J. A. Knudtzon, Sophus Bugge, and Alf Torp, *Die zwei Arzawa-Briefe, die ältesten Urkunden in indogermanischer Sprache* (Leipzig: J. C. Hinrichs, 1902), based upon noun case endings, possessive pronouns, and the imperative form *estu* "let it be," all occurring in the Arzawa letters. Knudtzon was quoted as giving up his claim in vol. 2 of his *Die El-Amarna Tafeln: Anmerkungen und Register,* ed. Otto Weber and Erich Ebeling (Leipzig: J. C. Hinrichs, 1915), 1074.

finding thousands of tablets and clear evidence that this was the capital of the Hittites. The outlines of Hittite history could very soon be drawn based upon documents from the palace archives written in the Akkadian language. The bulk of the tablets, written in the same language as the Arzawa letters from Tell el-Amarna, were accessible after Hrozný deciphered the language in 1915.[11] As the texts in the Hittite language were translated and studied, there was a much broader basis for tackling the question of the relationship of this people to the land of Palestine and to the Bible. The first competent attempt was by the Swiss Assyriologist Emil Forrer, who had also been working on the decipherment at the same time as Hrozný and later wrote one of the first lengthy grammatical sketches of the Hittite language after Hrozný's decipherment.[12] Forrer's study appearing in two installments established the basic parameters of a classification of references to "Hittites" in the Bible and in 2nd- and 1st-millennium written sources outside the Bible.[13] Forrer believed that one or more groups of people living in the greater Hittite Empire had migrated southward through Syria into Palestine, and constituted the group known there as the "Hittites" *(ḥittîm)* or the "sons of Heth" *(benê ḥēt)*. Another very early publication was a 1928 article by Archibald Henry Sayce, entitled "Hittite and Mitannian Elements in the Old Testament."[14] Forrer in 1940 saw in the ubiquitous references in Hittite cult texts to "drinking" various

---

11. Initial announcement in Hrozný ("Die Lösung des hethitischen Problems," *MDOG* 56 [1915]: 17-50) was followed by a fuller treatment in his *Die Sprache der Hethiter*, vols. 1-2, ed. Otto Weber. *BoSt* (Leipzig: J. C. Hinrichs, 1917).

12. Emil Forrer, "Die Inschriften und Sprachen des Hatti-Reiches," *ZDMG* 76 (1922): 174-269.

13. Emil Forrer, "The Hittites in Palestine I," *PEQ* 68 (1936): 190-203; "The Hittites in Palestine II," *PEQ* 69 (1937): 100-15. In its main lines this classification is still accepted by many today; e.g., Hans G. Güterbock, "Towards a definition of the term 'Hittite'," *Oriens* 10 (1959): 233-39. A different view is held by this writer. I expressed myself most fully on the issue in the 1968 Tyndale Archaeology Lecture (published in *TynBul* 20 [1969]: 27-55), proposing to see no connection with the so-called Hittites or sons of Heth in the premonarchic period, but a connection through the North Syrian Neo-Hittite realms in the references in Israel's premonarchic period. This view has been followed by Gregory McMahon ("The History of the Hittites," *BA* 52 (1989): 62-77; "Hittites in the OT," *ABW* 3 (1992): 231-33. Mordecai Cogan ("Locating *māt Ḫatti* in Neo-Assyrian Inscriptions" in *Aharon Kempinski Memorial Volume: Studies in Archaeology and Related Disciplines*, ed. Eliezer D. Oren and Shmuel Ahituv [Beer Sheva: Ben Gurion University, 2002]) is right that the description of "all the land of the Hittites" in Josh. 1:4 corresponds to North Syria and Southern Anatolia, but it is incorrect to say that this description fits only the Neo-Assyrian inscriptions of the 1st millennium. It is equally, perhaps even better, fitted to the political situation in the late 2nd millennium immediately after the fall of Ḫattuša ca. 1190 B.C.E.

14. *JTS* 29 (1928): 401-6.

gods a forerunner of the Christian Eucharist.[15] Another early survey, which was largely confined to the question of how "Hittites" are described in the Bible, was the 1947 Tyndale Archaeology Lecture given by the New Testament scholar F. F. Bruce.[16]

Twenty-two years later, in 1969, I gave the annual Tyndale Archaeology Lecture on "Some Contributions of Hittitology to Old Testament Study,"[17] in which I sought to update the summary of both what was known about Hittites in Palestine and about Hittite materials that could elucidate the Old Testament. I concluded from the onomastics and customs of persons called "Hittites" in the premonarchic period that these had no clear connection to the 2nd-millennium Hittites of Anatolia and were probably a separate group the biconsonantal root of whose name h-t was early conflated with the name $Hatti$.[18] Their personal names are all easily derivable from common Semitic roots and observe the common name structure appropriate to Semitic names of that period.[19] Monarchic references to Hittites I considered to pertain to the so-called Neo-Hittite kingdoms of Syria. Aharon Kempinski[20] and James C. Moyer[21] did not share my conviction that the premonarchic "Hittites" of the Bible were not Hittites of the Anatolian type. They cited archaeological evidence for Hittite — or at least Anatolian — influence in Bronze Age Palestine from Amarna texts and artifacts excavated in Israel. A similar point of view was held by Nahum M. Sarna in

15. Emil Forrer, "Das Abendmahl im Hatti-Reiche," in *Actes du XXe Congrès Internationale des Orientalistes (Bruxelles, 5-10 septembre 1938)* (Louvain: Bureaux du Museon, 1940), 124-28.

16. F. F. Bruce, *The Hittites and the Old Testament.* Tyndale Archaeology Lecture 1947 (London: Tyndale, 1947).

17. *TynBul* 20 (1969): 27-55.

18. Singer ("The Hittites and the Bible Revisited," n. 18) cited the case of Sayce, whose claim for a Hittite presence in Canaan in an early 12th-Dynasty Egyptian inscription was refuted by James H. Breasted, "When Did the Hittites Enter Palestine?" *AJSL* 21 (1904): 153-58.

19. See Hoffner, *TynBul* 20 (1969): 27-55, and repeated more briefly in "The Hittites and Hurrians," in *Peoples of Old Testament Times*, ed. Donald J. Wiseman (Oxford: Oxford University Press, 1973), 197-228. George E. Mendenhall (*The Tenth Generation* [Baltimore: Johns Hopkins University Press, 1973], 162) thought he could detect "a clustering of Anatolian names in the regions of Benjamin, Bethlehem-Hebron, and the upper Jordan Valley and Transjordan," using what Singer ("The Hittites and the Bible Revisited," n. 133) called "farfetched etymologies" such as *Kenaz* < Luwian Kunz, Ruth < Luwian Ruwanda, Eglon < Cappadocian Ḫaḫḫaluwan, Tirʿatim < Tarhunti-mu(wa), Lewî < Luwi, etc.

20. "Hittites in the Bible: What Does Archaeology Say?" *BAR* 5/5 (1979): 20-45.

21. "Hittite and Israelite Cultic Practices: A Selected Comparison," in *More Essays on the Comparative Method*, ed. William W. Hallo, Moyer, and Leo G. Perdue. SIC 2 (Winona Lake: Eisenbrauns, 1983), 19-38.

his JPS commentary on Genesis,[22] citing the non-Semitic names ÌR-Hepa[23] and Šuwardata of Amarna period rulers in Palestine alongside of Hittite pottery types and hieroglyphic Luwian seals found in Late Bronze sites in Israel. In a forthcoming article,[24] Singer gives a very thorough review of the proposed archaeological evidence for Hittite presence in Palestine, including Hittite seal impressions from Aphek, Megiddo, Tel Nami, and Tell el-Farʿah, which he judges to be "stray finds related to the Egyptian-Hittite diplomatic contacts and do not represent any lasting Hittite presence in Israel. . . . none of these Hittite seals was found in the central highland where the biblical Hittites are said to have lived." According to Singer, the silver scrap hoard from Shiloh and the Hittite ivory panel from Megiddo are also products of the Egyptian administration of Canaan and do not prove a Hittite presence there. A final type of evidence that would be compelling, were it to be established, is burial practices. For as Singer notes, the cremation burial is "a distinctive Hittite mortuary practice which may indeed serve as a lead in the search for Hittite migrations." This clearly spread from Anatolia southeastward to Alalakh and Carchemish, and the 11th-century grave at Azor near Jaffa, which the excavator calls "Danite,"[25] but which Singer challenges. Singer's conclusion that we have no evidence for this distinctive Hittite form of burial in Israel does not, he cautions, exclude the possibility of a Hittite presence, since the Hittites also practiced other forms of burial, but it weighs heavily against it.

Since no finds of Hittite or Hurrian *texts* have been made in these regions, Sarna argued that these Hittites or Hurrians in Hebron and the Judean hill country were culturally "Hittite" but no longer linguistically so. Hence, in the Bible too they used the same Semitic language as the patriarchs. A further attempt to see Anatolian Hittite influence on the sale of the cave of Machpelah was made by Raymond Westbrook.[26]

Meanwhile, regardless of whether they believe that premonarchic "Hit-

---

22. *Genesis.* JPS Torah Commentary (Philadelphia: Jewish Publication Society, 1989).

23. The first component of this name is usually read with West Semitic ʿAbdi rather than Akkadian *Warad.* This can *only* be a Semitic name pattern, since no such pattern ("servant" + DN in that sequence) exists either in Hurrian or Hittite onomastics (see Gernot Wilhelm, "Name, Namengebung. D. Bei den Hurritern," *RLA* 9 (Berlin: Walter de Gruyter, 1998): 121-27; and Harry A. Hoffner, Jr., "Name, Namengebung. C. Bei den Hethitern," *RLA* 9:116-21.

24. "The Hittites and the Bible Revisited."

25. Moshe Dothan, "A Cremation Burial at Azor — A Danite City," *ErIsr* 20 (1989): 164-74 (Hebrew), *200 (English abstract).

26. "Purchase of the Cave of Machpelah," in *Property and the Family in Biblical Law.* JSOTSup 113 (Sheffield: JSOT, 1991), 32-34.

tites" in the Bible were really Anatolian Hittites, scholars have continued to mine Hittite texts for material to elucidate the Old Testament.

Fifteen years after my Tyndale Archaeology Lecture, James C. Moyer, in volume 2 of the four-volume set *Scripture in Context*,[27] reviewed many suggested parallels that I had already adduced in 1968, but also summarized and evaluated proposals made by others in the intervening years. No other book or article that I am aware of has appeared since Moyer's that has attempted to review systematically all proposals of Hittite or Hurro-Hittite materials having a bearing on Old Testament interpretation. But an international symposium was held in March of 1990 in Hamburg that addressed the subject of "History of Religions Connections between Anatolia, North Syria, and the Old Testament."[28] A paper delivered by Moshe Weinfeld at that symposium approximates the general coverage achieved by Moyer, but without its critical evaluations.[29]

No reasonably complete bibliography of the subject has been published. A start was made by Moyer in 1983.[30] A somewhat larger, but still only partial bibliography of publications on this subject through 1995 was published in 1996 by the late Vladimir Souček and his wife Jana Siegelová.[31] The footnotes of Singer yield a harvest of additional bibliography.[32]

The area that has drawn the most attention among biblical scholars is the question of the origin of the covenantal forms found in the Bible. It was George E. Mendenhall who in 1955 first posited a connection between the Israelite covenantal forms and the international treaties of the late 2nd millennium, focusing almost exclusively on Hittite vassal treaties of the 14th and 13th centuries.[33] Since that time scholars have lined up — pro and con — on whether the Hittite material has significant relevance to the central biblical formulations of the Sinai covenant. Many have claimed an equal similarity between the Israelite covenant forms and 1st-millennium Assyrian ones.[34] Kenneth Kitchen surveyed the forms of all known international treaties from

27. Moyer, 19-38.

28. Janowski, Koch, and Wilhelm (see above, n. 1).

29. "Traces of Hittite Cult in Shiloh, Bethel and in Jerusalem," in Janowski, Koch, and Wilhelm, 455-72.

30. Moyer, 19-38.

31. *Systematische Bibliographie der Hethitologie 1915-1995*. 3 vols. HO (Prague: Národní Muzeum, 1996).

32. Singer, "The Hittites and the Bible Revisited."

33. *Law and Covenant in Israel and the Ancient Near East* (Pittsburgh: Biblical Colloquium, 1955).

34. This subject is reviewed also by Singer, "The Hittites and the Bible Revisited," §4.2.

Egypt, Mesopotamia, Syria, and Anatolia in the 2nd and 1st millennia, and concluded that those most closely resembling the biblical form were dated in the mid-2nd millennium, the period in which tradition places Moses. In addition, central covenant vocabulary — such as the verbs "love" (*'āhab*) and "know" (*yāda'*)[35] — have been compared to the usage of Hittite treaty terminology. Singer, in a forthcoming study, also notes the importance of the Hittite border descriptions in their treaties (for example, those in the Tarhuntassa treaties) with biblical border descriptions. As he says, this is particularly important, since the 1st-millennium Assyrian treaties, often considered to be the true source of the biblical covenant form, do not as a rule include border descriptions.

Although I participated with A. Kirk Grayson, John Van Seters, Donald B. Redford, and others in a Symposium on Ancient Historiography held in the late 1970s at the University of Toronto,[36] which had the potential of linking ancient Near Eastern historiographies, the first systematic attempt to show similarity between Israelite and Hittite historiography was made in 1976 by Hubert Cancik of Tübingen in his excellent book *Grundzüge der hethitischen und alttestamentlichen Geschichtsschreibung*.[37] Four years later, in 1980, P. Kyle McCarter, Jr. was able to build upon Hittite historical materials that were first compared to the stories of Saul and David by Herbert M. Wolf and me[38] in order to construct his own analysis of what he called "the Apology of David."[39]

Another area within Hittitology that provides cultural data comparable to biblical texts has been less widely discussed among biblical scholars.[40] That is the legal formulations found in the Hittite "code." Although in 1953 Manfred R. Lehmann, somewhat unconvincingly, claimed that Hittite law

---

35. William Moran, "The Ancient Near Eastern Background of the Love of God in Deuteronomy," *CBQ* 25 (1963): 77-87; Herbert B. Huffmon, "The Treaty Background of Hebrew *Yāda'*," *BASOR* 181 (1966): 31-37; Huffmon and Simon B. Parker, "A Further Note on the Treaty Background of Hebrew *Yāda'*," *BASOR* 184 (1966): 36-38.

36. Grayson's and my contributions were published in the same issue of *Orientalia* N.S. 49: see Harry A. Hoffner, Jr., "Histories and Historians of the Ancient Near East: The Hittites," *Or* 49 (1980): 283-332.

37. (Wiesbaden: Harrassowitz, 1976).

38. Herbert M. Wolf, *The Apology of Hattusilis Compared with Other Political Self-justifications of the Ancient Near East* (diss., Brandeis); Harry A. Hoffner, Jr., "A Hittite Analogue to the David and Goliath Contest of Champions?" *CBQ* 30 (1968): 220-25.

39. P. Kyle McCarter, Jr., "The Apology of David," *JBL* 99 (1980): 489-504.

40. But see Eckart Otto ("Körperverletzung im hethitischen und israelitischen Recht," in Janowski, Koch, and Wilhelm, 391-426), who makes good use of Hittite law on bodily injuries to elucidate the corresponding laws in the Pentateuch.

(specifically laws §§46-47) explained the conditions of property transfer between Abraham and "Ephron the Hittite" (Genesis 23),[41] more cogent examples of Hittite laws bearing a resemblance to laws in the Pentateuch have appeared in publications not usually consulted by biblical scholars.[42] Among the topics worthwhile exploring are: levirate marriage (§192-193), the case of the unknown manslayer (§6 and §IV), laws about sexual relations with animals (§187, §199), and compensation for bodily injuries (§§7-16).[43] Many of the possible parallels between Hittite and Israelite laws are cited in the center column of my translation of the laws in COS 2:106ff.

Other areas of interest, many briefly surveyed by Moyer, are: (1) necromancy,[44] (2) rites of gender transformation,[45] (3) purity regulations concerning contact with unclean animals,[46] (4) ritual elimination of impurity by

41. Manfred R. Lehmann, "Abraham's Purchase of Machpelah and Hittite Law," BASOR 129 (1953): 15-18. Better discussions of the legal aspects of this sale are the articles by H. Petschow and G. M. Tucker cited by Kenneth A. Kitchen, Ancient Orient and Old Testament (Chicago: Inter-Varsity, 1966); and Westbrook, "Purchase of the Cave of Machpelah." See the latter two for listing of the literature on the subject.

42. Ephraim Neufeld, The Hittite Laws (London: Luzac, 1951); Harry A. Hoffner, Jr., The Laws of the Hittites (diss., Brandeis, 1963); "Incest, Sodomy and Bestiality in the Ancient Near East," in Orient and Occident. AOAT 22 (Neukirchen-Vluyn: Neukirchener, 1973), 81-90; Moyer, "Hittite and Israelite Cultic Practices"; Raymond Westbrook, Studies in Biblical and Cuneiform Law. CahRB 26 (Paris: Gabalda, 1988); Otto.

Richard Haase, "Deuteronomium und hethitisches Recht: Über einige Ähnlichkeiten in rechtshistorischer Hinsicht," WO 25 (1994): 71-77; Harry A. Hoffner, Jr., "Agricultural Perspectives on Hittite Laws §167-169," in Acts of the IIIrd International Congress of Hittitology, Çorum, September 16-22, 1996, ed. Sedat Alp and Aygül Süel (Ankara: Grafik, Teknik Hazirlik Uyum Ajans, 1998), 319-30; The Laws of the Hittites: A Critical Edition. DMOA 23 (Leiden: Brill, 1997); "On Homicide in Hittite Law," in Crossing Boundaries and Linking Horizons, ed. Richard Averbeck, Mark W. Chavalas, and Gordon D. Young (Bethesda: CDL, 1997), 293-314.

43. See Otto; and the commentary in Hoffner, The Laws of the Hittites.

44. Esp. the use of the Israelite 'ōb and the Hurro-Hittite ābi; cf. Harry A. Hoffner, Jr., "Second Millennium Antecedents to the Hebrew 'ōb," JBL 86 (1967): 385-401. This connection is denied by Oswald Loretz ("Nekromantie und Totenevokation in Mesopotamien, Ugarit und Israel," in Janowski, Koch, and Wilhelm, 285-318), who notes that in no instance does the Hurro-Hittite ābi serve to evoke the dead. But he overlooks my theory that the models of ladders or stairways lowered into the ābi obviously served symbolically to allow spirits or deities to ascend from the netherworld. When this is compared with the Witch of En-Dor's remark upon seeing the spirit of the dead Samuel ("I see 'elōhîm coming up from the earth"), Loretz's objection loses its force. It is true, however, that no text so far known uses the term akkanza (or Sumerogram GIDIM) "dead person" to describe those approached through the ābi.

45. See Harry A. Hoffner, Jr., "Symbols for Masculinity and Femininity: Their Use in Ancient Near Eastern Sympathetic Magic Rituals," JBL 85 (1966): 326-34.

46. On the pig in diet and ritual, see Billie Jean Collins, The Representation of Wild Ani-

scapegoats, (5) regulations regarding the duties and responsibilities of priests and temple officials, (6) rituals for the summoning of a departed deity, (7) drink ordeals to determine perjury, which cause the forswearing person to swell up,[47] (8) the symbolism of cult gestures,[48] (9) the occasional use of the contest of champions in warfare,[49] and (10) the characteristics of texts employed to legitimize royal usurpers (the so-called apologies).[50] In addition, there is the interesting area of shared lexical items, words that need not have been loanwords from Hittite to Hebrew or vice versa, but that appear to be common to both Hittite or Anatolian Hurrian and Biblical Hebrew. Chaim Rabin surveyed this field some 40 years ago, but new evidence has accrued.[51]

In his 1993 article entitled "Traces of Hittite Cult in Shiloh, Bethel and Jerusalem," delivered orally at the 1990 Hamburg symposium,[52] Moshe Weinfeld listed a large number of examples of Hittite influences in the biblical description of the Israelite cult. Some are more convincing than others.

1. He claims that "The quantity of festival offerings in the Bible equal the quantity of the offerings in the Hittite festival calendars" (455-56). But he has arbitrarily selected one Israelite festival (Num. 29:2-6, 8-11, 13-16) to compare with one Hittite festival (the festival at Karaḫna[53]), where the distribution of victims happens to be the same but without demonstrating the need to associate particularly these two. The correlation would not work if one selected a different Israelite or Hittite festival. Even more serious, Weinfeld has mistranslated the primary data. The Hittite passage does not read "one bull, seven lambs . . . one goat . . . ," but "one fattened ox, seven sheep, two lambs, . . . one goat . . . ," and the passage in Num. 29:2-6, etc. has "one bull of the herd, one ram (*not* "goat"), and seven yearling lambs" (JPS). Even with the two chosen festivals to be compared, the numbers do not coincide!

---

mals in Hittite Texts (diss., Yale, 1989), 284-85. On impurity among the Hittites and its sources, see James C. Moyer, *The Concept of Ritual Purity among the Hittites* (diss., Brandeis, 1969).

47. See *COS* 1:166 §11 with n. 12 and center-column reference "c" to Num. 5:16-28.

48. See David P. Wright, "The Gesture of Hand Placement in the Hebrew Bible and in Hittite Literature," *JAOS* 106 (1986): 433-46.

49. See Hoffner, *CBQ* 30 (1968): 220-25.

50. See Wolf, *The Apology of Hattusilis;* Harry A. Hoffner, Jr., "Propaganda and Political Justification in Hittite Historiography," in *Unity and Diversity: Essays in the History, Literature, and Religion of the Ancient Near East*, ed. Hans Goedicke and J. J. M. Roberts (Baltimore: Johns Hopkins University Press, 1975), 49-62; McCarter, *JBL* 99 (1980): 489-504.

51. Harry A. Hoffner, Jr., "Hittites," in *Peoples of the Old Testament World*, ed. A. J. Hoerth, Gerald L. Mattingly, and Edwin M. Yamauchi (Grand Rapids: Baker, 1994), 127-56.

52. Weinfeld, "Traces of Hittite Cult," 45-72.

53. He cites this from the edition of Ali Dinçol and Muhibbe Darga, "Die Feste von Karahna," *Anatolica* 3 (1970): 99-118.

2. In rituals for the purification of a childbearing woman, a distinction is made between cases in which the child is male or female, but the offerings at the end of the purification period are identical in both cultures: one lamb and one bird (Lev. 12:6, compared with a passage in a Hittite birth ritual) (Weinfeld, 456).[54] This is a valid observation, but one wonders if in *all* Hittite or Hurrian birth rituals the same offerings were used. It was not uncommon in Hurrian type rituals from Kizzuwatna — and not just purification or birth rituals — to offer a single lamb and a single bird. Usually the species of bird is not given, but occasionally it is a MUŠEN.GAL. In Lev. 12 it is a pigeon *(tôr)* or a turtledove *(ben yônâ)*.

3. Weinfeld mentions the ceremonies for purification of a house (456), which according to him employ two birds, cedar, and crimson. Lev. 14:49ff. is the biblical example he cites, which also involves hyssop. It is true that cedar and red wool are used together in some Hittite rituals of Kizzuwatnean origin (e.g., CTH 477.1 and CTH 483), but not together with two birds, nor to my knowledge does this occur in a ritual to purify a house (CTH 446).[55] Weinfeld refers to data in an earlier article.[56]

4. The scapegoat ritual of Leviticus 16, according to Weinfeld, is "very close to the substitution ritual among the Hittites." Here the fundamental studies were by van Brock, Kümmel, Gurney, Moyer, Wright, and Janowski and Wilhelm.[57] It should be noted that in the Hittite examples the animal carrier of the impurity is not always a domestic animal like a bull, sheep, or goat. In one case it is a mouse.[58] Wright and Weinfeld claim that one difference between the Hittite and biblical examples is that in Hittite the scapegoat is intended both to appease an angry deity and to remove the impurity. But not all Hittite examples of its use entail appeasement of a deity. Nor in all ex-

---

54. Gary M. Beckman, *Hittite Birth Rituals,* 2nd ed. Studien zu den Bogaskoy-Texten 29 (Wiesbaden: Harrassowitz, 1983), 206-7 i 10'-12'.

55. See the edition in Heinrich Otten, "Eine Beschwörung der Unterirdischen aus Bogazköy," *ZA* 54 (1961): 114-57; translation and discussion by Volkert Haas in *Geschichte der hethitischen Religion.* HO 1/15 (Leiden: Brill, 1994), 283ff.; and translation in *COS* 1:168ff.

56. Moshe Weinfeld, "Social and Cultic Institutions in the Priestly Source against Their Ancient Near Eastern Background," in *Eighth World Congress of Jewish Studies. Panel Sessions, Bible Studies and Hebrew Language* (Jerusalem, 1983), 101.

57. Nadia van Brock, "Substitution rituelle," *RHA* 17/65 (1959): 117-46; Hans Martin Kümmel, "Ersatzkönig und Sündenbock," *ZAW* 80 (1968): 289-318; O. R. Gurney, *Some Aspects of Hittite Religion* (London: Oxford Univ. Press, 1977); Moyer, "Hittite and Israelite Cultic Practices"; Weinfeld, "Traces of Hittite Cult"; David P. Wright, *The Disposal of Impurity: Elimination Rites in the Bible and in Hittite and Mesopotamian Literature.* SBLDS 101 (Atlanta: Scholars, 1987); Janowski and Wilhelm.

58. CTH 391.1; KUB 27.67 i 37ff.; cf. Gurney, *Some Aspects of Hittite Religion,* 50.

amples is the animal a substitute for a person who has offended the gods. It has been noticed that the Hittite carrier is sent, not into the desolate wilderness or desert, but to an enemy country. It would seem that the "scapegoat" in Hittite religion was not a unified concept. Some aspects of its employment concur with the Leviticus scapegoat and others do not.

Scholars have so far concentrated on the parallel of these Hittite scapegoat rituals with Leviticus 16. But equally relevant in this discussion is the account in 1 Samuel 5–6 of the sojourn of the ark of the covenant in Philistine territory. To be sure, the ark, which is eventually sent back into Israel with gifts to pacify Yahweh is not a scapegoat, but a propitiatory gift, what in Hittite would be called a *maškan* or a *zankilatar*. The occasion of the sending is a plague of tumors upon the Philistines by Yahweh. And the ark is sent back by allowing the oxen that draw the cart on which it sits to go where the god wishes them to. The "guilt offering" (Heb. *ʾāšām*) that is sent to Yahweh with the ark consists of gold images of the mice and tumors that ravaged the Philistine cities (1 Sam. 6:4-18). The ark is sent to the enemy land, which is the land of the offended deity, not to transfer the evils to that land, but to return the cult object to its owner. To be compared here is the Middle Hittite ritual of the city of Šamuha (CTH 480, KUB 29.7 + KBo 21.41), translated by Albrecht Goetze in *ANET*, 346, and reproduced in part with discussion by Gurney.[59] The carrier in this case is inanimate, but capable of transporting propitiatory gifts: it is a boat. Into this boat they place little silver and gold representations of the oaths and curses that have oppressed them. The boat is floated downstream to a river and by the river to the sea. The Philistine gold mice and tumors compare well with the gold and silver images of the curses. And since both are made of precious metals, they should not be thought of as impurities to be removed, but as propitiatory gifts in the shape of the calamities, sent to the deities who sent those calamities.

In the Leviticus 16 ritual a crux has always been the term *ʿăzāʾzēl*, rendered in the Septuagint and Vulgate by "as a scapegoat" (followed by the English AV), but replaced in more recent English translations by "for Azazel," sometimes thought to denote a wilderness demon. Appealing to scapegoat rites in the Hurrian language from the Hittite archives, Janowski and Wilhelm would derive the biblical term from a Hurrian offering term, *azazhiya*.[60] This is particularly appealing to me. There were two goats used in the Leviticus 16 ritual. One is designated for Yahweh as a "sin offering" (Heb. *ḥaṭṭaʾt*; LXX Gk. *peri hamartias*) (16:9), and the other is "for Azazel," but is presented

59. Gurney, *Some Aspects of Hittite Religion*, 51-52.
60. Janowski, Koch, and Wilhelm, *Religionsgeschichtliche Beziehungen*.

alive before Yahweh to make atonement, and is sent away into the wilderness "to/for Azazel." The contrast could either be (1) Yahweh versus Azazel or (2) sin offering versus Azazel. If one adopts the first, Azazel seems to be a divine being or demon, who must be appeased. But if one adopts the second as primary, the word *ʿăzāʾzēl* represents the goal of the action. In the system of Hurrian offering terms to which Wilhelm's *azazḫiya* belongs, the terms represent either a benefit that is sought by the offering (e.g., *keldiya* "for well-being; cf. Heb. *šelāmîm*) or the central element offered (e.g., *zurgiya* "blood"). If Janowski and Wilhelm's theory is correct, the Hebrew term would not denote a demon as recipient of the goat, but some benefit desired (e.g., removal of the sins and impurities) or the primary method of the offering (e.g., the banishment of the goat).

5. Weinfeld also notes (458) a similarity between Hittite and Israelite cultic rules that exclude physically injured or deformed persons from full access to the cella. He traces its origin in the Bible to 2 Sam 5:6-8, where David is told that he may not enter Jerusalem unless he removes the blind and the lame. This would mean that Weinfeld considers this aspect of Israelite cultic law to be a Davidic innovation, almost two centuries after the fall of Hattuša. Yet he confidently ascribes it to Hittite influence.[61] I do not doubt that there is a similarity. But I wonder if this kind of attitude toward physically maimed persons in the cult is not so widespread as to be a trivial comparison. Certainly it was widespread that sacrificial animals had to be without defect.

David P. Wright's treatment of the Hittite evidence is of a higher quality. He has also called attention to the similarity in the use of a hand placement gesture in Israelite (Heb. *sāmak yādô*) and Hittite ritual *(kiššaran dāi-)*, noting that in each it has the same two possible implications: (1) conferring authorization on another to act (usually in a ceremony) on behalf of the gesturing person, and (2) attributing the offering material to the one performing the hand placement.[62] The fact that both cultures preserve the same two functions is significant. But Weinfeld goes a step further, claiming that in both it is a two-handed placement for the first significance and a one-handed one for the second. There is good evidence in the Bible for this distinction, but in Hittite texts there is no evidence for it: rather, in both significances the texts read "he places the hand (singular!)."

Other parallels cited by Weinfeld are too general to constitute anything

---

61. The passage, KUB 5.7 obv. 27, 36, was translated by Goetze in *ANET*, 497. The terms used for these people, *kuiššanteš* and *iškallanteš*, are garbled in Weinfeld's discussion (458).

62. Wright, *JAOS* 106 (1986): 433-46.

specifically Anatolian and are sometimes garbled in their details.[63] For example, that ritual slaughter was accomplished by cutting the throat of the animal is extremely widespread. Weinfeld misunderstood Cord Kühne's key article on the Hittite practice.[64] Weinfeld claims the Hittite slaughterer cut the "windpipe" of the victim, whereas Kühne's proposal for the difficult term *auli-* was "neck artery."[65] Nor is the prohibition of persons with physical disabilities from entering the sacred temple precincts something exclusively Hittite or Israelite.[66] His attempt to compare the description in 1 Samuel 3 of Eli and Samuel sleeping just outside the temple of Yahweh with KUB 31.113 also suffers from enormous misunderstandings and mistranslations of the Hittite text.

But there are a few new sources not mentioned by Moyer or Weinfeld. A fairly recently-published source of great relevance to this question is the 15th-century Hurro-Hittite bilingual literary text called the "Song of Release," the edition of which was published in 1996.[67] A substantial portion of this text contains parables or fables illustrating with stories involving animals or inanimate objects certain kinds of undesirable or foolish human behavior. One is about a coppersmith who makes a beautiful cup, only to have it curse him, so that he in turn pronounces a curse on the cup. The Hurro-Hittite text compares this behavior to that of an ungrateful son, who by his refusal to care for his weak and aged parent earns his father's curse. This is obviously an early source of the biblical *topos* about the potter and his clay creation, used both by the prophets Isaiah (29:16; 45:9) and Jeremiah (18:6) and by St. Paul (Rom. 9:20-21). But the main part of the story concerns the demand made by Teššub, the god of the city of Ebla, that its citizens free the men of the town Ikakali, who are currently their slaves. It is still unclear if they are also debt slaves. When the citizens resist this demand, the god threatens to destroy the city. Volkert Haas and Ilse Wegner have suggested that the intention of this com-

---

63. Weinfeld, "Traces of Hittite Cult."

64. Cord Kühne, "Hethitisch *auli-* und einige Aspekte altanatolischer Opferpraxis," *ZA* 76 (1986): 85-117.

65. The Hittite word for "windpipe" or "trachea" is *hu(r)hurta-* (Harry A. Hoffner, Jr., "An English-Hittite Glossary," *Revue Hittite et Asianique* 25/80 [Paris: Klincksieck, 1967], 99; "From Head to Toe in Hittite: The Language of the Human Body," in *Go to the Land I Will Show You: Studies in Honor of Dwight W. Young*, ed. Joseph E. Coleson and Victor H. Matthews [Winona Lake: Eisenbrauns, 1996], 247-59), not *auli-*.

66. On the disabled in Hatti, see Harry A. Hoffner, Jr., "The Disabled and Infirm in Hittite Society," *ErIsr* 27 (2003): 84*-90*.

67. Erich Neu, *Das hurritische Epos der Freilassung* 1: *Untersuchungen zu einem hurritisch-hethitischen Textensemble aus Hattusa.* StBoT 32 (Wiesbaden: Harrassowitz, 1996); English translation in Hoffner, *Hittite Myths*, 65-80.

position was to explain the destruction of Ebla. In similar manner, the Judean chronicler attributed the destruction and exile of the kingdom of Judah to her failure to observe 70 of Yahweh's Sabbatical Years (2 Chr. 36:17-21; Exod. 23:10-11).[68] The stated beneficiaries of the biblical Sabbatical Year are the poor, the wild animals, and the soil. The principal objection to observing it would be the greed of the land owners. If there is a common thread running through all parts of the Song of Release — parables, feast in the netherworld palace of Allani, demand for debt release, threatened destruction of Ebla — it may be that in refusing to release their slaves the wealthy leaders of Ebla personify the foolish figures described in the fables, who despise their weak and elderly parents and are overweening in their ambition for wealth and advancement. And in the episode where the leaders refuse to obey Teššub's demand to release their slaves, they even defend themselves by pledging their willingness to relieve the god Teššub himself, if he should ever fall into poverty and need. One is reminded here of the scene of the Last Judgment in Matthew 25, where Jesus says to those granted admission to the kingdom of heaven: "I was hungry and you fed me, . . . naked and you clothed me, . . . in prison and you visited me. . . . For as you have done this to the least of my brothers, you have done it to me" (Matt. 25:31-46). The promise of the leaders of Ebla to help Teššub is a hollow one, since his need is for them to release their own slaves, which they refuse to do.

A second important new source published in 1991 is the corpus of letters from the Hittite provincial capital of Tapikka, modern Maşat Höyük.[69] In several of the letters from this site (nos. 58 and 59), and reportedly in an unpublished letter from the Hittite center at Šapinuwa,[70] there is mention of the employment of blinded captives in the mill houses, just as the Philistines employed the blinded Samson to grind at the mill. Furthermore, lists of captives to be used as hostages include the notations "blinded" or "sighted" and specify the proposed ransom price for each captive.[71] In these texts it appears that these blinded captives worked in groups in the mill houses. The incident involving Samson is in a Philistine context. He too has been captured and was blinded in order to make him less dangerous and to prevent his attempting to escape, precisely the same motivations assumed for the Tapikka and

---

68. See my remarks in Hoffner, *Hittite Myths*, 76, introduction to Episode 3.

69. Sedat Alp, *Hethitische Briefe aus Maşat-Höyük*. Türk Tarih Kurumu Yayinlari 6/35 (Ankara: Türk Tarih Kurumu Basimevi, 1991).

70. Aygül Süel, "Ortaköy'ün Hitit çagindaki adi," *Belleten* 59 (1995): 271-83.

71. Harry A. Hoffner, Jr., "The Treatment and Long-term Use of Persons Captured in Battle According to the Maşat Texts," in *Recent Developments in Hittite Archaeology and History*, ed. K. Aslihan Yener and Hoffner (Winona Lake: Eisenbrauns, 2002), 61-71.

Šapinuwa prisoners. And since the Anatolian connections of the Philistines are well known, and Hieroglyphic Luwian seals have been found at Philistine Aphek,[72] there is every reason to regard this detail in the Samson story as reflecting historical reality and to relate it to the information in the Maşat texts.

A final example of the new possibilities is that the term used in the Hebrew Bible to designate pagan priests *(kômer,* plural *kᵉmārîm)* originated in Anatolia, where it is found in both Old Assyrian and Hittite documents. According to my view,[73] the Hittite word *kumra-* — like its Old Assyrian counterpart *kumrum* — alternates with the Sumerogram $GUDU_{12}$ and denotes one of the top two classes of male priestly personnel of the Hittite temple, the other being the SANGA (Akk. *šangû,* Hitt. *šankunniš).* If this Anatolian source for biblical *kᵉmārîm* is correct, it suggests a conduit for Anatolian cult influences observable in Ugaritic and Biblical Hebrew, namely the use in Syro-Palestine of a class of priest originating in Anatolia in the 2nd millennium. Benjamin Mazar argued for years that the Hivites, Hittites, and Jebusites began to settle in the hill country of Palestine as part of the massive migrations from Syria and Anatolia after the collapse of the Hittite Empire at the beginning of the 12th century.[74] And Singer notes that an excellent etymology of "Hivite" *(hiwwî)* derives it from the (Late) Hittite word for Kizzuwatna/Cilicia.[75] If these migrants included priests of the *kumra*-type, it would help to explain the introduction of the name (and the related cultic institutions) into the religious mix of pre-Israelite Canaan.

Even if some of the many proposals are less convincing, there remain far too many points of comparison between Hittite culture and ancient Israel — especially in legal, ritual, and cult matters — for us to dismiss them as coincidental or accidental. Moreover, some cannot be attributed to a late 1st-millennium intermediary. So we must take seriously the possibility of a channel of cultural influence in the late 2nd and early 1st millennium that allowed influences from Anatolia to be felt in Palestine. Singer (under "Conclusions")[76] makes an excellent point:

---

72. Itamar Singer, "A Hittite Hieroglyphic Seal Impression from Tel Aphek," *TA* 4 (1977): 178-90; Moshe Kochavi, "Canaanite Aphek: Its Acropolis and Inscriptions," *Expedition* 20/4 (1978): 12-17; Singer, "Takuḫlinu and Haya: Two Governors in the Ugarit Letter from Tel Aphek," *TA* 10 (1983): 3-25.

73. Harry A. Hoffner, Jr., "Hittite Equivalents of Old Assyrian *kumrum* and *epattum,*" *WZKM* 86 (1996): 151-56.

74. "The Early Israelite Settlement in the Hill Country," in *The Early Biblical Period: Historical Studies* (Jerusalem: Israel Exploration Society, 1986), 35-48.

75. Singer, "The Hittites and the Bible Revisited."

76. Singer, "The Hittites and the Bible Revisited."

Consider the fact that none of the biblical authors arbitrarily includes Egyptians, Babylonians or Assyrians among the nations of Canaan before the Israelite conquest. Since they insist on including Hittites, Hivites, etc., in their description of Canaan, this terminology must have had some historical credibility in the eyes of the biblical authors, unless we reduce their story to a totally nonsensical fairy tale. . . . Should it be found not to fit second millennium circumstances, it should demonstrably fit into some first millennium reality.

For decades now — in the "Albright debunking" generation of Old Testament scholarship — a 1st-millennium setting has been assiduously sought for every parallel adduced for a 2nd-millennium one. But in my judgment, the weight of evidence grows too heavy for the nay-sayers. In the past I have been reluctant to say that this late 2nd-millennium channel of cultural influence was attributable to the "Hittites" and "sons of Heth" mentioned in the narratives of events antedating the reigns of Saul and David. I am still not convinced that this is the case, since I believe that this observable cultural influence could have been mediated by groups who were in contact with Hittite culture, for example in Syria. This seems also to be the preferred opinion of Singer.[77] But in the future scholars in both Anatolian and biblical studies must pay more attention to the developing evidence.

77. Singer, "The Hittites and the Bible Revisited."

Genesis in History and Tradition:
The Syrian Background of
Israel's Ancestors, Reprise[1]

DANIEL E. FLEMING

My current job involves a combination of teaching and research interests that is in some sense out of date, an artifact of another scholarly age. I work with both Mesopotamian cuneiform texts and the Hebrew Bible, along with other writing in Northwest Semitic dialects. My particular Assyriological specialization is 2nd-millennium Syria, and I have worked extensively with the Late Bronze Age ritual texts from Emar, and now the Middle Bronze archives from Mari. At the same time, I have pursued a variety of biblical applications of the new evidence I found in these 2nd-millennium Syrian texts.[2]

In drawing these applications from Bronze Age texts, I am introducing comparative material to the Bible that some today consider so distant from

1. I would like to thank James Hoffmeier for inviting me to participate in the colloquium on The Future of Biblical Archaeology, as well as Harvey Miller for his support of and obvious interest in the proceedings. This article has been considerably expanded from my talk at the colloquium, and it benefited from the comments of Mark Smith, my colleague at New York University. In the end, both the ideas I present here and the errors that accompany them are naturally my own responsibility.

2. For the Syrian work, see esp. Daniel E. Fleming, *The Installation of Baal's High Priestess at Emar.* HSS 42 (Atlanta: Scholars, 1992); *Time at Emar* (Winona Lake: Eisenbrauns, 2000); and *Democracy's Ancient Ancestors: Mari and Early Collective Governance* (Cambridge: Cambridge University Press, 2004). For biblical applications, see e.g., "The Israelite Festival Calendar and Emar's Ritual Archive," *RB* 106 (1999): 8-34; "A Break in the Line: Reconsidering the Bible's Diverse Festival Calendars," *RB* 106 (1999): 161-74; "The Biblical Tradition of Anointing Priests," *JBL* 117 (1998): 401-14; "Mari and the Possibilities of Biblical Memory," in *Les traditions amorrites et la Bible,* ed. Jean-Marie Durand and Bertrand Lafont. *RA* 92 (1998): 41-78; "Mari's Large Public Tent and the Priestly Tent Sanctuary," *VT* 50 (2000): 484-98.

the dates of biblical writing as to have no conceivable relevance to it. Of course, I could take refuge in the idea that early Israel shared a regional cultural background with these Syrian peoples, but even this notion supposes a continuity between north and south, early and late, that may be problematic without some ultimately historical framework to explain any similarities. Short of that, I might consider casting all comparisons from the Bronze Age as purely analogical, as Jack M. Sasson has done with Mari, but these comparisons are less powerful without their historical aspect and thus less interesting.[3] It is no wonder that few younger biblical scholars have even bothered to pursue Mari applications seriously.[4] For those who wish to find a historically controlled cultural context for any part of the Bible, pursuing the potential contribution of cuneiform texts, it is natural to look instead to the advent of the great empires in the land of Israel, beginning with the Assyrian of the late 8th century and continuing with the Babylonian, Persian, and even Hellenistic. Such applications are entirely worthwhile, though they treat a set of influences that were experienced in Israel as foreign.

The Bronze Age texts from Syria, in contrast, would illuminate ancient traditions in the Bible that are native, without any implication of cultural borrowing. No direct contact ever occurred between Israel and the peoples of Emar, Mari, or the like. The question is whether early Israelite culture really stood in some historical continuity with ancient Syria. Oddly, the book of Genesis portrays Israel's ancestors as coming from Syria, and one part of our answer will depend on how we explain the Genesis traditions of ancient northern roots.

In this article, I will sketch a proposal for how Bronze Age cuneiform writing, and especially the documents from Mari, may be of direct use for evaluating the Genesis traditions of Israel's tribal ancestry. To anticipate my conclusions, I will present and try to explain a series of points of contact between Genesis and specific features of the tribal peoples that are displayed in unusual detail in the Mari archives. There are four of these:

3. Jack M. Sasson, "About 'Mari and the Bible,'" *RA* 92 (1998): 98-9. As analogy, the Mari material has the same kind of explanatory power as modern ethnographic evidence from similar types of societies worldwide.

4. The most prominent and thorough exponent of Mari evidence for understanding ancient Israel and the Bible has been Abraham Malamat, whose work on Mari was launched in the 1950s, in a completely different intellectual environment. See esp. *Mari and the Early Israelite Experience* (Oxford: Oxford University Press, 1989); *Mari and the Bible.* SHANE 12 (Leiden: E. J. Brill, 1998).

1. the tribe named Benjamin, in relation to the Syrian tribal coalition called the Binu Yamina;
2. an ancestral homeland associated with the particular city of Harran, in far-northern Syria, a gathering point for the Binu Yamina tribes;
3. the biblical use of the adjective "Hebrew" for identifying Joseph and his family in Egypt, in relation to the Binu Yamina *'ibrum*, the part of the tribal population that remains full-time with the flocks;
4. the division of pasture between Abram and Lot by right and left hands in Gen. 13:9, in light of the broad definition of Syrian tribal peoples into two coalitions, as "sons of the right hand" (Binu Yamina) and "sons of the left hand" (Binu Sim'al).

Both this cluster of Mari applications and my argument from them are essentially new, with all of the pitfalls that accompany the potential of novelty. My work on the Bible depends on my own Mari research, though this follows remarkable advances in Mari studies by the current team of editors.

Many American readers, especially those with more traditional approaches to the Bible, may not understand the extent to which my very effort will seem ill conceived and misplaced to a large body of serious European biblical scholars. There is little secure common ground in contemporary biblical scholarship, especially regarding historical questions, including their very relevance. I write with this diversity in view and with the hope of introducing into the broad debate about the Bible a fresh argument for finding evidence in the Genesis traditions for Israelite identity and even historical background.

Changing Times: After Albright

What has happened? How is my comparative work either out of date or stripped of direct historical significance? A few decades ago, in the heyday of William F. Albright, Ephraim Speiser, and others, and even with the more cautious German company of someone like Martin Noth, it was common to look for light on early Israel and the Bible in the many new discoveries from Syria and beyond.[5] The Amarna archive from Egypt had long been known,

5. Claus Westermann calls the method exemplified by Albright the "archaeological approach," which leapfrogs the problem of literary and tradition history by appealing directly to evidence that is conceived to prove the "historicity" of the biblical setting; *Genesis 12–36* (Minneapolis: Augsburg, 1985), 30-1, 58-9. For mature versions of this approach, see William F. Albright, *Yahweh and the Gods of Canaan* (Garden City: Doubleday, 1968); Ephraim A. Speiser,

but the early 20th century produced finds at Nuzi, Ugarit, Mari, and then Alalakh, along with the generally expanding knowledge of Mesopotamian and Anatolian cuneiform writing.[6] Biblical scholars immediately picked up on the obvious applications, even as archaeologists working in Palestine and Israel were piecing together a picture of Bronze and Iron Age history that was understood to correspond at least roughly to the biblical accounts. The trend was strongest in the United States, with further influence in Israel and Europe. German scholars, with their heritage of literary-historical and tradition-historical study, were most hesitant to relinquish these methods in favor of essentially external solutions to historical problems in the Bible. In its general definition, I must acknowledge that my own application of textual evidence from 2nd-millennium Syria to biblical problems hearkens back to the earlier American work, but such applications must now proceed on entirely different terms. Times have changed.

The late 1960s and 1970s brought a broad new critique of both the archaeological and the textual interpretations that had been thought to provide a 2nd-millennium setting for early Israel and early biblical traditions for Israelite origins. This critique began with the two main biblical stages of Israelite formation, of "patriarchal" ancestry and of establishment in the land as Israel. I am concerned here with the first of these, which occupies most of the book of Genesis. During the earlier generation, the Genesis stories of Abraham and sons had been understood to find a compelling context in both the archaeological and the textual discoveries of the Bronze Age.[7]

Genesis. AB 1 (Garden City: Doubleday, 1964). By the late 1950s, Martin Noth felt that he could not refuse the possibility that such archaeologically-based arguments might even apply to the ancestor stories of Genesis. In spite of the fact that Genesis is more focused on the promises made to the patriarchs than on the people as such, Noth allows, "Nevertheless it might be possible to find in the relatively familiar history of the ancient Orient in the 2nd millennium B.C. a situation in which the patriarchs might have appeared in the vicinity of Palestine as, in accordance with Old Testament tradition, the first heralds of the later Israel"; *The History of Israel,* 2nd ed. (New York: Harper and Row, 1960; from 1958 German), 123.

6. Albright (53, etc.) triumphantly lists these new discoveries, with their dates, as "extraordinary progress in our understanding of the Patriarchal background of Israel": Nuzi (1925); the Egyptian Execration Texts and first study of West Semitic names in early Babylonian tablets (1926); Ugarit (1929); Mari (1933).

7. Influential expressions of this earlier confidence include John Bright, *A History of Israel,* 3rd ed. (Philadelphia: Westminster, 1981), 69-70; Roland de Vaux, *The Early History of Israel* (Philadelphia: Westminster, 1978; from 1971 and 1973 French), 153-57 for approach, 161-287 on this period; Abraham Malamat, vol. 1 of *A History of the Jewish People,* ed. H. H. Ben-Sasson (Cambridge, MA: Harvard University Press, 1976 [Hebrew, 1969]), 31-40. De Vaux was particularly cautious and meticulous, aware of the pitfalls that soon attracted a critique of the whole program.

Two major works from the mid-1970s, however, attempted a systematic dismantling of the accepted context: John Van Seters's *Abraham in History and Tradition* (1975); and Thomas Thompson's *The Historicity of the Patriarchal Narratives: The Quest for the Biblical Abraham* (1974).[8] Although not all scholars accepted the positions staked out by Van Seters and Thompson, their criticisms were received as extremely serious, and these two books mark a subtle sea change in the whole approach to Genesis research.[9] John Bright's enthusiastic reconstruction of a patriarchal world in *A History of Israel* now seems to take far too much for granted, and Gösta Ahlström's careful but more skeptical account offers an attractive alternative for many.[10] In Europe, there is considerable disagreement over both the dating of the pentateuchal writings and of the traditions carried by them. For those who continue to work within the framework of documentary hypotheses, the Yahwistic narrative (J), once dated to the 10th century's united monarchy, is now often dated in or near the Babylonian exile, as Van Seters proposed.[11] With the first ex-

8. The dates are somewhat deceiving, as both volumes were based on several years of ongoing research and appeared almost simultaneously, each author unaware of the other's work.

9. Both volumes were widely reviewed, and even scholars who remained basically unpersuaded acknowledged the force of their challenge. For an idea of the contrasting responses, see the following reviews: unreservedly positive toward Thompson, Matitiahu Tsevat (*JBL* 94 [1975]: 588-89) and Dennis Pardee (*JNES* 36 [1977]: 222-24); respectfully critical, Siegfried Herrmann (*WO* 8 [1975-76]: 343-46). Van Seters's radically new literary criticism inspired more reservations. Anson Rainey (*IEJ* 28 [1978]: 131-32) had less at stake in this domain and was among the most positive. Many were impressed but resisted either Van Seters's literary conclusions, including Sean McEvenue (*Bib* 58 [1977]: 573-77) and George W. Coats (*Int* 31 [1977]: 88, 90), or his late dates, including Aelred Cody (*CBQ* 38 [1976]: 601-3) and Henri Cazelles (*VT* 28 [1978]: 241-55). Albert de Pury reviewed both volumes together at length (*RB* 85 [1978]: 589-618), concluding that their critique of German scholars such as Alt and Noth was less effective than their demolishing of the likes of Albright and Speiser.

10. Compare Bright: "it has become increasingly evident that a new and more sympathetic evaluation of the traditions is called for" (69); "As the Middle Bronze Age (early second millennium) has emerged into the light of day it has become evident that the patriarchal narratives, far from being literary creations of monarchic times, contain authentic reflections of a far earlier day . . ." (70); and Gösta Ahlström, *The History of Ancient Palestine* (Minneapolis: Fortress, 1993): "It is quite clear that the narrator of the Genesis stories did not have accurate knowledge about the prehistory of the Israelites"; and "his purpose was not to write history" (186). Ahlström attempts to say much less than Bright about either Genesis or the ancestors portrayed there, and focuses mainly on what can be learned about Palestine in the Middle Bronze Age from nonbiblical evidence.

11. See for example Christoph Levin, *Der Jahwist.* FRLANT 157 (Göttingen: Vandenhoeck & Ruprecht, 1993), 35, 434-35. Alternatively, a deuteronomistic edition of the Pentateuch plays a similar role at a similar date in the work of Erhard Blum, *Studien zur Komposition des Pentateuch.* BZAW 189 (Berlin: de Gruyter, 1990).

tended literary works now dated to the 7th century and beyond, the earlier material that was revised and incorporated into these works is reduced, and much less early Israelite tradition is likely to be found in it. The "Jacob cycle" that moves the patriarch to Syria and back is more easily understood as originating in early Israel, in part because of the independent rendition of it in Hosea 12.[12] Rainer Albertz, whose history of Israelite religion is far from the skeptical extreme in recent German evaluation of history in the biblical narrative, keeps an older thread in the Genesis traditions by proposing that patriarchal religion is not "a preliminary stage" but a "substratum of Yahweh religion" that the largely late texts still recall and preserve.[13] Many are even less receptive to the possibility of any survival at all of ancient Israelite traditions in Genesis. Harald-Martin Wahl, for example, argues that the earliest Jacob texts in Genesis cannot date from before the 7th century, and oral tradition cannot have retained any genuine historical memory at all across the centuries since the origins of Israel.[14] In this intellectual environment, it is not clear why Mari or other Bronze Age archives should offer any particular help in understanding Genesis.

These days, it is too easy to dismiss the relevance of historical questions for Genesis because the results are in doubt. The search to define the social-historical contexts for this writing is not rendered impossible or uninteresting by the possibility that these could be discovered to have nothing to do with actual Israelite ancestry. If, however, any elements of the Genesis literature do reflect and therefore help explain Israelite origins, these would offer invaluable insight into both the Bible and Israelite history. As such, these elements would be well worth identifying and evaluating. My target is not histo-

---

12. See esp. the extensive argument of Albert de Pury, "Situer le cycle de Jacob: Quelques réflexions, vingt-cinq ans plus tard," in *Studies in the Book of Genesis,* ed. André Wénin. BETL 155 (Leuven: Peeters, 2001), 213-41. The Abraham story, in contrast, has no such attestation in the earlier prophetic literature, and Abraham is mentioned much less often than Jacob outside the book of Genesis. In the same volume edited by Wénin, Thomas Christian Römer ("Recherches actuelles sur le cycle d'Abraham," 193) places the written origins of the Genesis Abraham stories in 8th/7th-century Hebron, and Jean-Louis Ska ("Essai sur la nature et la signification du cycle d'Abraham (Gn 11,27–25,11)," 174) says that the picture of Abraham as the faithful man from Mesopotamia already reflects the mindset of exiles who have just done likewise, in the late 6th century.

13. Rainer Albertz, *A History of Israelite Religion in the Old Testament Period* (Louisville: Westminster John Knox, 1994), 1:29. Albertz does consider the portrayal of this household religion to be based on Israelite tradition that is much older than the actual texts, so that we have "the piety of early Israelite families projected onto the patriarchs" (42).

14. Harald-Martin Wahl, *Die Jakobserzählungen*. BZAW 258 (Berlin: de Gruyter, 1997), 271-73, 287-88, 302. He concludes that "the Jacob narratives have no historical relevance" (310).

ricity but history; not the ancient historiography sought by Van Seters in his second major work, but the interpretation of the past that constitutes the modern discipline.[15]

Genesis in History and Tradition: Van Seters and Thompson

I begin with Van Seters and Thompson, both because of their historical role and out of respect for the substance of their actual challenges to accepted wisdom, which still stand as landmarks. They themselves do not endorse every aspect of their own early work, but I am more interested here in the critique that they helped to launch than in their individual development. My discussion reflects the trajectory of American debate in particular, though this debate has been very much informed by European and Israeli scholarship. So far as historical issues are at stake, the work of Van Seters and Thompson still raises the most pressing problems.[16] It is no accident that the most telling critique of a very North American approach has come from North America. Although I disagree with some of their conclusions, their work has benefitted the field tremendously by refining the analysis of history in Genesis. They have exposed the weaknesses of both individual arguments and certain methods, and by this critique, they raised the bar for identifying any elements in Genesis that might reflect actual Israelite origins. Whether the bar is now impossibly high, the future will decide.

Van Seters

I will address only the first half of this book, which treats the historical problems. Van Seters began by objecting to the idea of an "Age of the Patriarchs," when scholars could not even agree on any particular period of the Bronze Age, ranging from the Middle Bronze I (Albright) to the Late Bronze II (Cyrus Gordon). He then reviewed the idea of patriarchal nomadism, including the various nomadic peoples of the broader region, from the Amorites through the Arabs. His summation (38): "Considering the basic characteristics of nomadism — transhumance, belligerence, and migrations — the sto-

15. John Van Seters, *In Search of History* (New Haven: Yale University Press, 1983).

16. In the recent volume edited by Wénin, Graham I. Davies still treats the books of Van Seters and Thompson as representing the essential argument against finding any historical information about Israelite ancestry in Genesis ("Genesis and the Early History of Israel: A Survey of Research," 118-22).

ries, on the whole, reflect little of the nomadic way of life. . . ." Three more chapters take on evidence that had been considered to demonstrate a 2nd-millennium setting for the biblical patriarchs: personal names, along with those of people and places; social customs, especially relating to family law; and archaeological evidence for the Middle Bronze Age, including a critique of efforts to find any historical roots for the war with named kings in Genesis 14.

As is well known, Van Seters found little of even general historical value in the Genesis stories. Among his conclusions (121-22):

- "There is no real portrayal of a nomadic pre-settlement phase of Israel-ite society, nor any hint of the migratory movements or political reali-ties of the second millennium B.C."
- "The few nomadic details that occur in the stories, such as the refer-ences to camels and tents, the patriarchs' presence and movement pri-marily in the Negeb, and their contact and political agreement with the established 'Philistines' in the border region, all point strongly to the social and political circumstances of the mid-first millennium B.C."
- The archaic designations for the indigenous populations such as the Canaanites, Amorites, and Hittites are idealized and later.
- The reference to Ur of the Chaldeans and Abraham's association with Harran reflect the Neo-Babylonian period.

Thompson

Thompson's work overlapped considerably with Van Seters's, though its style is quite different, providing much more detailed arguments regarding specific historical and archaeological problems, but less sensitivity to and interest in the biblical text itself.[17] He started with the personal names, admitting that they belong to an archaic type, but pointing out similar 1st-millennium ex-amples. They do not provide a date for the characters portrayed.[18] There fol-lows an entire chapter devoted to Mari, with specific attention to the name Benjamin, which is also found in one of the prominent tribal groups of the Mari archives.[19] Thompson then took on the Amorites, from the various lines

---

17. Thompson returned to this problem in later work; see *The Origin Tradition of Ancient Israel, I. The Literary Formation of Genesis and Exodus 1–23* (Sheffield: JSOT, 1987).

18. Chapter 2, especially pp. 36, 43.

19. Chapter 3, "Mari and the Patriarchs."

of textual and archaeological argument. He found nothing to fit the biblical portrayal of Amorites and Canaanites and nothing to indicate a period of southern invasions by Amorite "semi-nomads" (chs. 4-7).

Thompson went on to address a number of individual historical hypotheses and problems. His assault on Albright's theory of Abraham as a donkey caravaneer is effective, and he anticipates Van Seters's critique of various suggested historical backgrounds to Genesis 14 (chs. 8 and 9). In a long chapter (10) on the frequent comparisons of social customs with legal documents from Nuzi, he pointed out that the parallels were not in fact terribly exact, certainly not adequate for dating the Genesis stories. In sum, he found an early-2nd-millennium context for the patriarchal stories impossible, based on "a harmonization of historical hypotheses" drawn from bits and pieces of many fields of ancient Near Eastern and biblical studies (317).

A Brief Review

Van Seters and Thompson made a tremendous contribution to the study of Genesis by forcing interested scholars of every persuasion to tighten considerably their historical method and their biblical interpretation. Many of their points remain telling. Both scholars directed us toward 1st-millennium examples of the same phenomena that had been proclaimed at home in the 2nd millennium, including patriarchal names and social customs. Van Seters articulates well the truly "Israelite" nature of the texts, based on an Iron Age understanding of southern Palestine's social and political landscape. Thompson is particularly persuasive when he objects that free selection of comparative evidence often does not lead to believable controls on dating. Together, they pushed the burden of proof back onto those who would see a 2nd-millennium context for any aspects of the Genesis stories of Abraham and his family, and I see this as a healthy development.

In spite of the effectiveness of their critique, however, I believe that there is still a case to be made for identifying a Bronze Age setting for specific elements of the Genesis ancestor stories. This possibility depends in part on issues in the interpretation of ancient social history, based on which these scholars ruled out any possibility for historical accuracy in the Genesis literature. Both Van Seters and Thompson were wrong to conclude that the Genesis stories of Israel's ancestors cannot fit the Bronze Age as we now know it. Their reconstruction of the Bronze Age appears to me to be incorrect, especially as it relates to pastoralists. We do not need to call Abraham a donkey caravaneer, when we have a trove of evidence in the Mari archives for the varieties of pastoralist life during the Middle Bronze Age. If we are going to find a 2nd-millennium setting for any part of the Genesis stories, it will be Mari pastoralism that supplies it.

Moreover, I will argue that the 1st millennium does not provide an adequate context for explaining all elements of the Genesis stories, and that Iron Age texts need not have lost all memory of earlier realities. In my contribution to the proceedings of the Paris round table on Mari and the Bible, I offered a more extensive argument for specific points of biblical memory of the Bronze Age in the book of Genesis.[20] That article includes a longer interaction with the serious critiques of Van Seters, Thompson, and others, along with an introduction to the state of current research on Syrian society as known in the Mari archives. Here, I do not intend to rehearse all of this material again, but will confine myself to a limited resumé that will allow me to focus on the book of Genesis as the primary bearer of a tradition of ancestral origins for Israel in northern Syria.

Getting Mari Right

The one feature that most distinguishes Abraham, Isaac, and Jacob from the characters of later Israel is their mode of subsistence. For these ancestors, as described in Genesis, keeping herds is more than an adjunct to cultivating grain or fruit. It is their primary basis of survival, and their wealth is measured in animals.[21] Moreover, their freedom of movement and separate identity from the settlements they share have long suggested comparison with a way of life commonly called "nomadic." Naturally, this mobility has remained at the core of most attempts to prove a 2nd-millennium historical setting for the characters portrayed in the Genesis stories. Likewise, any response has had to deal with the whole idea of migrating "Amorites" who managed to upset much of the ancient Near East in the transition from the Early to the Middle Bronze Ages.

Van Seters (9) complained that the whole project of comparing 2nd-millennium cuneiform texts with Genesis fails exactly here. The Germans, he said, are surely correct in their expectation that Israel ultimately had nomadic

20. *RA* 92 (1998): 41-78.
21. Compare Abraham in Gen. 12:16 (starting with flocks and herds, then donkeys, servants, and camels); Isaac in 26:14 (flocks and herds measuring wealth, though one mention of planting crops while living in the town of Gerar in v. 12); Jacob's work for Laban as shepherd (30:29, 43), and his gift of animals to Esau (32:13-16). For the ancestors' primary subsistence from their flocks, see also Gen. 13:5; ch. 31; 34:5; 37:12-17; 46:32; and 47:1-6.

origins, but the largely American effort to find 2nd-millennium parallels depends entirely on writing from cities with an agriculturally-based economy. We cannot have it both ways, however: either the ancestors should be understood in urban terms, or the cuneiform texts do not apply.

Mari belongs at the center of this debate, and any reconstruction of early-2nd-millennium society gains much by a careful reading of its massive diplomatic correspondence. Oddly, both the early enthusiasm for 2nd-millennium parallels to Genesis and the trenchant critique occurred before 1983, when the new Mari publication led by Jean-Marie Durand began to produce reams of fresh textual evidence and interpretation. Since then, the number of published texts has doubled, and deep revisions have been proposed in the interpretation of the archive. Few biblical scholars have followed the recent developments or pursued their implications. The two main exceptions are Abraham Malamat and Jack Sasson, neither of whom has responded with any essentially new interpretive frameworks for applying this knowledge to the Bible. Malamat has maintained and extended the basic approaches that he initiated in the 1960s and 1970s.[22] Sasson always remained cautious about the project of finding proof of a 2nd-millennium setting for the Genesis stories,[23] and in recent years he has shied away from trying to build any explicit framework for explaining the relevance of the Mari archives to biblical problems.[24]

Perhaps the biggest difficulty with the whole framework for understanding the Mari archives before the 1980s was the assumption that the Mari administration functioned as a force foreign to the tribes. Even Mari, then, provided an ultimately urban perspective on its world. This whole analysis was radically altered when king Zimri-Lim, during whose reign most of the

22. For Malamat's early work, see e.g., "Mari and the Bible: Some Patterns of Tribal Organization and Institutions," *JAOS* 82 (1962): 143-50; "Aspects of Tribal Society in Mari and Israel," in *La civilisation de Mari,* ed. Jean-Robert Kupper. CRRAI 15 (Paris: Les Belles Lettres, 1967), 129-38; "UMMATUM in Old Babylonian Texts and Its Ugaritic and Biblical Counterparts," *UF* 11 (1979): 527-36.

23. In a 1982 dictionary article, Sasson declared, "It would be fair to state that attempts to use Mari documentation to confer historicity on the patriarchal narrative have largely failed. Success has been achieved, however, when some Mari institutions were compared with those drawn from the OT"; "Mari," *IDBSup,* 570. Compare Jonas Greenfield's review of Thompson, where he applauds Thompson's assault on the "historicity" of the patriarchal narratives, but maintains that 2nd-millennium texts are still useful for understanding the legal and social aspects of the Genesis texts; *IEJ* 27 (1977): 185-87.

24. In his contribution to the Paris round table on Mari and the Bible, Sasson warns to beware any "homologous" comparisons that look for an "Amorite bridge" between Mari and Israel, an approach that "draws us into expounding on Israel's nebulous origins" (*RA* 92 [1998]: 98-99). He proposes that comparisons remain at the level of ahistorical analogy (see n. 3, above).

letters were written, was discovered to be the tribal king of the Binu Sim'al coalition, newly ensconced at Mari.[25]

Because Zimri-Lim maintained both his identity as a tribal king and active ties with the mobile pastoralist component of his tribal people, the letters from his administration must be treated as a secure source of information regarding both tribal organization and pastoralist subsistence during this period. Zimri-Lim even created a new administration for the Mari kingdom with two entirely separate hierarchies, one for districts defined by their settled populations and ruled by governors called *šāpiṭum*s, and the other for his own Binu Sim'al tribespeople who could be ruled from the back country without registration by towns. Along the way, we discover that the two dominant tribal confederacies of early-2nd-millennium Syria, the Binu Sim'al and the Binu Yamina, had distinct social and political structures. This means that in some cases, specific terms can be identified as having separate Sim'alite and Yaminite usage.[26]

In the end, much of both the early application of Mari texts and the critique by Thompson and Van Seters is simply obsolete. Van Seters said that we cannot have it both ways, wanting to use urban archives to illuminate tribal and mobile pastoralist peoples, but in fact we can. The entire reign of Zimri-Lim gives us both ways, a king who retains his tribal and pastoralist connections at the same time as he embraces the achievements of urban civilization. Mobile pastoralists of the Mari period do not live as desert nomads set against the settled cultivators, because their herding communities are strongly linked to tribal settlements. Moreover, it turns out that the Yaminites and Sim'alites are not local tribes from northern Syria, but rather are a complementary pair, "sons of the right (hand)" and "sons of the left," the two great tribal confederacies of early-2nd-millennium Syria, with populations scattered across the whole region.[27] The Mari archives tell us about the

25. See my discussion in *RA* 92 (1998): 45-56. I develop these ideas much more fully in *Democracy's Ancient Ancestors*, 147-69. For two important expressions of the new interpretations from the Mari team, see Dominique Charpin and Jean-Marie Durand, "'Fils de Sim'al': Les origines tribales des rois de Mari," *RA* 80 (1986): 141-83; and Durand, "Unité et diversités au Proche-Orient à l'époque amorrite," in *La circulation des biens, des personnes et des idées dans le Proche-Orient ancien*, ed. Dominique Charpin and Francis Joannès. CRRAI 38 (Paris: Editions Recherche sur les Civilisations, 1992), 97-128.

26. See Daniel E. Fleming, "The Sim'alite *gayum* and the Yaminite *li'mum* in the Mari Archives," in the proceedings of the 46th Rencontre Assyriologique Internationale (2000), *Nomades et sédentaires dans le Proche-Orient Ancien*, forthcoming; and *Democracy's Ancient Ancestors*, 43-63.

27. I discuss this interpretation of the Binu Sim'al and the Binu Yamina in *RA* 92 (1998): 60-62. The most revealing text has not yet been published by Jean-Marie Durand, who very gen-

goings-on of regions from Babylon and Elam in the east to Aleppo, Qatna, and Hazor in the west.

Earlier attempts to associate the Genesis ancestors with the Amorite "Westerners" who contributed to the overturn of the last great dynasty of Ur were unnecessary. The setting for the Genesis stories, with the ancestors moving freely among thriving Canaanite populations, fits naturally into the Middle Bronze Age itself, including the time of the 2nd-millennium Mari texts. Genesis does not call for a setting marked by turmoil or widespread social disruption, but at most, the possibility of long-distance migration, hardly a rarity in any period. In fact, the Mari archives belong to a period of intense movement and cultural interplay across all of Syria and Mesopotamia. According to Durand:

> So far as the Amorite world is documented for us by the 20 years that constitute the end of Yasmaḫ-Addu's reign and the entirety of Zimri-Lim's, it does not show itself to us as compartmentalized. We observe on the contrary that there was a constant and extensive circulation of ideas, of people, and of goods.[28]

This free movement of people and their cultural accoutrements seems to have spilled over into Palestine during the Middle Bronze II Age, judging by the arrival of building forms such as the single-axis long-room temple and massive earthen ramparts for city defenses.[29]

This quick sketch provides little detail, but it is intended to show that we must abandon the assumptions that have so far guided the application of Mari evidence to Genesis interpretation. Reformulation of the grounds for a comparison between the world of the Genesis ancestors and the Bronze Age by no means establishes any relationship between the two, which I will address in the next section.

---

erously allowed me to cite the crucial lines (61 and n. 91): "While the land of Yamḫad, the land of Qatna, and the land of Amurru are the range (?) of the Yaminites — and in each of those lands the Yaminites have their fill of barley and pasture their flocks — from the start (?), the range (?) of the (Sim'alite) Ḫana has been Ida-Maraṣ" (*ki-ma ma-at Ia-am-ḫa-ad*[ki] *ma-at Qa-ṭá-nim*[ki] *ù ma-at A-mu-ri-im*[ki] *ni-iK-ḫu-um ša* DUMU[meš] *Ia-mi-na ù i-na ma-tim še-ti* DUMU[meš] *Ia-mi-na še-em i-ša-bi ù na-wa-šu-nu i-re-i-em ù iš-tu da-ar-ka-tim ni-iK-ḫu-um ša* Ḫa-na[meš] *I-da-Ma-ra-aṣ*).

28. Durand, "Unité et diversités au Proche-Orient à l'époque amorrite," 97 (my translation). Notice that Durand uses "Amorite" for this period of strong influence by West Semitic speakers across all of Syria-Mesopotamia, esp. during the early Old Babylonian period. He does not refer to the great disruption that initiated it.

29. See Ahlström, 197-200; Amihai Mazar, *Archaeology of the Land of the Bible, 10,000-586 B.C.E.* (New York: Doubleday, 1990), 201-2.

Genesis in History and Tradition: An Alternative Analysis

At this point, I am overwhelmed with the scope of Genesis scholarship and the number of issues that must be addressed in order to provide any convincing account of the ancestor stories. Two large categories present themselves, the same two recognized by Van Seters. So far as we are concerned with Israelite history and want to know whether Genesis can make any contribution, we are faced with a host of historical concerns. At the same time, however, we must grapple with Genesis as a book with a complex literary history. Without this, our historical analysis will be founded on naive assumptions about the grounds for comparison with the outside evidence that must guide our historical conclusions. I will begin with this second problem.

Genesis Tradition: The Book

In order to understand both the capacity for and the nature of any historical memory in the book of Genesis, we must recognize its literary depth. By this, I simply mean to accept the basic project of modern critical biblical scholarship, as it has probed the process by which Genesis came into being. For our historical analysis, it is not necessary to adopt any one interpretive system, though I have some opinions. In fact, I am leery of leaning too heavily on the idiosyncrasies of a single system, if doubt over a debatable position can undermine a particular historical conclusion. Ideally, a proposed analysis of history, religion, or society should be capable of persuasive argument that succeeds within multiple literary-critical systems.

The Character of the Genesis Traditions

First of all, some oral background to the written text is extremely likely, though I acknowledge the difficulty of discerning specific oral lore with certainty.[30] We are severely hampered by simple lack of evidence, both for Israelite-period manuscripts of biblical writing and for ancient Hebrew writing generally before the 8th century. In this silence, it is impossible to recon-

---

30. Few scholars doubt the reality of a base in oral traditions, though the extent and historical value of these receive widely diverse evaluations. For instance, even Van Seters, who emphasizes the primarily written development of the biblical traditions, defends Julius Wellhausen's awareness of the folklore "derived from oral tradition" underlying the J source in Genesis; John Van Seters, *Prologue to History: The Yahwist as Historian in Genesis* (Louisville: Westminster John Knox, 1992), 20.

struct the real interaction between written and oral narrative in ancient Israel. Hosea's fascinating citation of the Jacob story seems to require a familiarity with the tale that would have been oral, while the numerous points of direct reference to Jacob's life that correspond to elements of our Genesis text make it likely that a written version of some such form must have existed at the same time.[31] We should not assume that such conditions were possible only for the late 8th century and later, because we know too little about the use of writing in Israel before that time. A Genesis-like text could have come into being as one fixed form of a tale that existed in parallel and mutually influential oral and written renditions. Methodologically, it is probably a mistake to imagine that we can explain the history of tradition for a given text by dating the earliest core of that text and then defining a pristine period of orality for all that came before.

Accepting the probability of an elusive background in underlying oral and written renditions of the Genesis tales, I then recognize two secure types of literary material. One type is strongly identified with the structure of Genesis as part of the Pentateuch, with the genealogy and chronology of the book, its "generations," its eternal covenants, and more. This is the material that is most often called "priestly." Beyond this, we have a large body of diverse traditions, some linked together and some not, in different combinations.[32] For this material, whose individual literary strands are vigorously debated, I prefer to evaluate the nature and historical foundations of each text case by case. This choice may seem to European eyes to smack of what is often called the "archaeological" approach of Albright and his American peers. Even for scholars such as Erhard Blum and Albert de Pury, however, who take the possibility of

---

31. See the discussion by de Pury, in *Wénin*, 231-34. De Pury dates the Hosea passage to the early 7th century, just after the fall of the northern kingdom.

32. Note that I am avoiding definite use of either the traditional documentary hypothesis or the system of fragmented units suggested by Rolf Rendtorff, developed by Blum, and adopted by Albertz and David M. Carr. (For these, see Rolf Rendtorff, *The Problem of the Process of Transmission in the Pentateuch*. JSOTSup 89 [Sheffield: JSOT, 1990]; Erhard Blum, *Die Komposition der Vätergeschichte*. WMANT 57 [Neukirchen-Vluyn: Neukirchener, 1984]; *Studien zur Komposition des Pentateuch*; Albertz; David M. Carr, *Reading the Fractures of Genesis: Historical and Literary Approaches* [Louisville: Westminster John Knox, 1996]). I see strong links between some elements of nonpriestly writing in the ancestors, esp. in the promised blessings and children, and in the genealogical scheme of Abraham, Isaac, and Jacob with their relationships to the Transjordanian peoples of Edom, Moab, and Ammon. These continuities would fit a unified composition of the sort usually attributed to the "Yahwist" (J), without any need for the organizing influence of either the priestly writing or of a redaction that joined this to prior material. I do not, however, see persuasive links between the nonpriestly material in Genesis 1-11 and the ancestor stories.

early tradition very seriously, it is necessary to face the historical abyss that lies behind what they identify as the earliest written text.[33] In the end, each biblical text must be evaluated in light of the independent evidence from Israel and the ancient Near East that offers our strongest basis for external control. Controlling evidence from the earliest possible periods portrayed through all possible stages of development in the tradition and the written text needs to be brought to bear. Archaeology will not by itself solve the historical riddles of our biblical texts, but it has enriched tremendously our historical perspective on the periods and texts in question, and we would be foolish to neglect its application. The above sketch may be unbearably rough, but I need to make clear that I am working under the methodological umbrella of literary-historical and tradition-historical investigation, even as I wish to avoid limiting my historical analysis by unnecessarily narrow conclusions.[34]

The book of Genesis has three main sections, all of which include material of both literary types. This means that the pentateuchal "priestly" writers did not create any of these anew, though I believe that they contributed to combining them. The prehistory in chapters 1–11, with its genealogical frame and stories of all humanity, is beyond the scope of our historical evaluation. A second section may be defined by the family line that culminates in the 12 tribes of Israel, built around Abraham, Isaac, and Jacob. The coherent sequence of three patriarchs is found in both types of materials. Although the Joseph story has been incorporated into the life of Jacob, it nevertheless constitutes a separate component of Genesis in that it offers a long, coherent literary piece that serves at one key level to explain how Israel got into Egypt.[35] This story forms the strongest narrative link between the book of Genesis and the Moses story in Exodus, in both the priestly and nonpriestly materials of both books.[36]

33. E.g., de Pury speculates that the Jacob story may go back to migrations from Aramean Syria at the end of the 2nd millennium, based on attempts to connect details from Genesis with the political geography of that period; see de Pury in *Studies in the Book of Genesis*, 237, 240; and "La tradition patriarcale en Genèse 12–35," in *Le Pentateuque en question*, ed. de Pury (Geneva: Labor et Fides, 1989), 268-70.

34. In this regard, I find the recent work of David M. Carr particularly refreshing, as he both grapples with literary-historical problems and warns against forcing a too-severe certainty on our reconstructions; see "Genesis 28,10-22 and Transmission-Historical Method: A Reply to John Van Seters," *ZAW* 111 (1999): 399-403.

35. Note that Carr understands an early Jacob-Joseph story, already combined, to be one of the two primary reconstructable literary precursors to the full "proto-Genesis" story that was built around the promises to the ancestors. (The other is the preexilic, nonpriestly material in the primeval history of Genesis 1–11.) See Carr, *Reading the Fractures of Genesis*, 177, 233.

36. In fact, the link between the books of Genesis and Exodus does not run tremendously

Genesis offers the first biblical account of Israel's origins, and the book locates them in northern Syria and eventually southeastern Mesopotamia, through the specific cities of Harran and Ur. This ancient family origin contrasts with Israel's later departure from Egypt and entry into the land through Moab in the Transjordan. We thus have three separate geographical associations for Israelite roots. The Syrian tradition in Genesis is the one that is most directly related to the social framework of mobile pastoralism that is associated with West Semitic speakers in various sources and is displayed in great detail in the Mari archives. This northern connection appears only in the central section of Genesis, the section devoted to Abraham, Isaac, and Jacob.

I have just said that I hesitate to attach my analysis of Genesis to a fixed set of literary- and tradition-historical conclusions that could unnecessarily restrict its range of application. At the same time, however, I am particularly interested in clues regarding the specific constituencies in Israel that would have provided a home for certain Genesis stories. This interest follows two central elements of my approach to the Genesis ancestor texts. First, it seems clear to me that all of the Genesis stories, as found in the Bible, are narrated in an Israelite setting, no earlier than the Iron Age. Only one God is acknowledged, and this is Yahweh, the God of Israel. The geography reflects the world of Iron Age Israel, a perspective that is clearest in the references to the Philistines in the southwest (21:32; 26:1, 8, etc.) and to Syria as "Aram" (24:10; 25:20; 28:2; 31:18, 20, etc.). Both of these names came to identify these regions only with the rise of the first Philistine and Aramean states in the Iron Age, in the 12th and 11th-10th centuries, respectively. Moreover, the entire goal of the ancestor stories is to account for Israel and its neighbors in terms that make sense only after the people were established in the land. Jacob's 12 sons are Israel's tribes, Esau represents the people of Edom, Lot's sons are Moab and Ben-Ammi, and so on. Most of the towns are significant to Israel, regardless of their status in the Bronze Age: Bethel, Shechem, Jerusalem (Salem), Beer-

---

deep. Along with the location in Egypt, we find the family of Israel called "Hebrews" (Gen. 39:14, 17; 41:12; etc.; Exod. 1:15, 19; 2:11; etc.). Joseph's family are identified as shepherds in Genesis (37:12-16; 46:31-34; 47:1-6), and this is the logic behind the assignment of their home in Goshen. It seems that this work as shepherds still underlies Israel's identity in its departure, as seen by the fact that Moses flees to the land of herdsmen and then works as a shepherd (Exod. 3:1). At the moment of their departure, the one possession the Pharaoh tells the Israelites to bring with them is their flocks and herds, perhaps continuing the same assumption (Exod. 12:32). Ronald S. Hendel has observed the narrative parallels between Jacob's flight and return and those of Moses, including the episodes at shepherds' watering places, where each man helps young women who then lead him to their fathers, who allow the men to marry into the family; *The Epic of the Patriarch*. HSM 42 (Atlanta: Scholars, 1987), 137-65.

sheba, and Hebron, for example. The whole idea that Jacob's family enters Egypt because of Joseph anticipates the Bible's scenario for Israel's establishment as a people in their promised land in the famous exodus. All of this may seem obvious, but any notion that the ancestor stories came from the Bronze Age must confront the overwhelmingly Israelite presentation.

If all of the stories of Genesis are in fact composed in Israelite terms, to serve Israelite interests, we should then ask whether it is ever possible to narrow the clientele in terms other than the purely source-critical ones. In particular, I have looked for clues to regional interests. One obvious example has always been Joseph, whose centrality would surely have been the heirloom of Ephraim and Manasseh.[37] Reading the Jacob story as a whole, we must then wonder who would have guarded a portrayal of Jacob's family in which his preferred wife Rachel was the mother of Joseph and Benjamin. The central hill country of Israel was thus presented as Rachel's.[38] Overall, the presentations of Jacob's Israelite family in Genesis do not seem to reflect or advance the interests of Judah, though Judah dominates the eventual history of the two kingdoms in the books of Samuel and Kings.[39] Rachel's centrality to the Israelite tribal family contrasts with the tradition of key ancestral bases at Hebron and Beer-sheba, which do serve the interests of a Judahite regional memory. One might add the Transjordan as a third location for regional tradition, as found in the story of Jacob's flight from Laban and meeting with Esau (Genesis 31–33). Regardless of the exact literary route by which the Genesis ancestor lore arrived at its final form, these geographical points of reference may provide useful evidence for the earliest Israelite settings in which they may have lodged.

The Family of Abraham

The ancestor stories of Genesis have as their goal to explain Israel's origins in terms of kinship and descent, not simply for Israel itself but as part of a net-

---

37. Carr offers a helpful review of the reasoning, including the affinities between the Joseph and the Jacob stories; *Reading the Fractures of Genesis,* 277-80.

38. For recent advocacy of a northern formulation of the Jacob story, see Carr, *Reading the Fractures of Genesis,* 264-66; and Blum, *Die Komposition der Vätergeschichte,* 125-26, 184-86. This northern setting would apply to the older core of the Jacob story, which Carr defines as quite extensive: Jacob and Esau (25:1-34; 27:1-45); Bethel (28:10-12, 17-22*), Jacob and Laban (chs. 29-31); return (32:2-9; 32:14–33:20); closure (35:1-8, 16-20).

39. Judah's importance seems to lie behind the prominent role he plays in the Joseph story, even as he must accept Jacob's preference for Joseph and Benjamin (37:26-28; 43:3-5, 8-10; 44:14-34). The exact period of this northern view of Judah is not clear.

work of family in an otherwise foreign territory. In an important recent dissertation, the archaeologist Anne Porter observes that the notion of territory tends to be different in cultivation- and in husbandry-based societies, though both may have tribal organizations built around kinship and descent. Where the people are tied to appropriated relations of land, as with fixed-plot cultivation, time is the primary focus. Their genealogies need temporal depth, and the ancestors are often individually recognized and named.[40] This is the style of Israel's genealogy through Abraham, Isaac, and Jacob, as well as of the foundational genealogies in Genesis 5 and 11, in the material from the final (priestly) Pentateuch structure. Where appropriation of land is weak, however, and territorial associations are fluid, as with people who rely more heavily on mobile flocks, space is the primary focus. Their ancestors tend to be treated more as a generalized group. In Genesis, we have an account of descent that serves a settled people in a cultivation-based economy who nevertheless think of their ancestors as having a different geographical origin and a different economy, based mainly on animal husbandry and involving frequent movement.

The book of Genesis contains a number of lists that can be viewed as genealogical texts in the strict sense.[41] The more important genealogical aspect of the book, however, is built into the whole notion of explaining Israelite origins in terms of ancestors. As soon as we find Israel presented as a family, we must expect a genealogical aspect to the definition of Israelite identity. In both the priestly and the remaining material, the ancestors are organized into the same coherent family tree, from Abraham to Isaac, from Isaac to Jacob and Esau, and from Jacob to the sons who become the tribes of Israel. This genealogy also appears in Yahweh's first encounter with Moses at Mount Horeb, as "the God of your father, the God of Abraham, the God of Isaac, and the God of Jacob" (Exod. 3:6; cf. vv. 15, 16; 4:5). Unless one insists on removing Abraham and Isaac from Jacob's confrontation with Laban (Gen. 31:42, 53) and on attributing their inclusion to editors simply because the genealogical line must not already be part of an early Jacob cycle, the same family tree seems deeply imbedded in this material as well.[42]

40. Anne Porter, *Mortality, Monuments and Mobility: Ancestor Traditions and the Transcendence of Space* (diss., University of Chicago, 2000), 49, 436-37.

41. Contrast the linear lists in Genesis 5 and 11, with their temporal focus, with Genesis 10, which explains the world population geography by descent from the sons of Noah. Genesis 36 explains the clans of the Edomites as descendants of Esau (vv. 1-30) and also provides a linear list of consecutive rulers (vv. 31-39).

42. See the discussion of Horst Seebass, *Genesis 2: Vätergeschichte II (23:1–36:43)* (Neukirchen-Vluyn: Neukirchener, 1999), 367-68. In Gen. 31:29, Laban says that "the God of

In religious terms, Genesis presents us with a genealogical chain from Abraham to Isaac to Jacob, and this chain provides the backdrop for the special identity of Israel as the chosen possession of its God. At the same time, however, Genesis establishes the identity of Israel in regional political terms, using Abraham's family tree as the framework. Here, Jacob and Abraham have different ideological and genealogical roles, and it is difficult to tell how far back in time these roles were integrated. Both ancestors define Israelite identity in relation to others outside of Israel. The Jacob story takes its structure from his flight to and return from Harran, an exile from the fury of his twin brother Esau, who represents Edom. It is Abraham, however, who takes most of the genealogical burden of explaining Israel's regional identity. All of the remaining descent-based relationships described in Genesis are constructed from Abraham, and through him *all* of these peoples share the north Syrian origins claimed for Israel. This geographically distant ancestry seems to be a treasured part of the biblical account of Israel's roots, always so frankly foreign, refusing to admit identity as a transformation of the local Canaanite population. At some level, the whole extended family is to be judged in relation to its Syrian purity.

Israel itself is entirely Syrian by ancestry, though of course Jacob himself was born in Canaan. The patriarch acquired not only his wives Leah and Rachel in the north, but also their servants Zilpah and Bilhah, who become the mothers of tribes who are accepted as equally Israelite. In their origins, Israel and Edom are equally pure in their Syrian mother Rebekah, though Esau then weakens this heritage by marrying local women, only one of whom has any claim to a family connection through Ishmael (Gen. 36:2-3). Even so, Jacob and Esau are twins, so that Edom stands uniquely close to Israel among the neighboring peoples. Moab and Ammon are less closely related to Israel but share the same full northern Syrian background, odd though may be the details. Lot's wife dies in unflattering circumstances during their flight from Sodom, when she disobeys the command to look away from the destruction (Gen. 19:26). Lot had married off daughters to local men, though he ends up with two who join him in flight (19:16), whether or not these are the same daughters who are mentioned in v. 14. In the end, Moab and Ammon are born of wholly Syrian parentage through the incest initiated by Lot's daughters. The Arabian peoples are understood to share the family connection with Abraham, but all of them are conceived through marriages outside the north Syrian family circle. Ishmael's mother Hagar is Egyptian (Gen. 16:1, 3), and

---

your (plural) father" spoke to him, where the plural already assumes the inclusion of at least one of the ancestors who will be invoked later.

Abraham's last wife, Keturah, is presented as a local woman of unnamed origin (25:1-4).

All of these regional relatives live inland, in the pastoralist back country, where tribal social organization was prevalent. It is no wonder that Israel also had a tradition of entering the land from the east, from the midst of its natural kin. According to the book of Joshua, Israel's actual invasion of the promised land begins east of the Jordan River, at the north end of the Dead Sea. Genesis identifies Israel with a specific set of inland neighbors at the same time as it expresses a deep sense of alienation from the people remembered to have been the prior inhabitants of the land, most often called Canaanites. These Canaanites come from lowland cities that tend to be oriented toward the coast, cities with agricultural economic bases and strong ties to neighboring urban powers.

Genesis History: The Possibilities

The ancestor stories of Genesis appear to have been written in the Iron Age, probably in the 1st millennium (Iron II). How is it possible, then, to identify any of their contents with the Bronze Age? Of course, it is not hard to imagine that certain broad social or religious features of 1st-millennium Israel had roots that went back centuries earlier.[43] It is much more difficult to establish that any elements of the Genesis stories can be understood to reflect an actual Israelite heritage that goes back to the Bronze Age in the heart of the 2nd millennium.

Any persuasive redefinition of a Bronze Age background for the ancestor stories of Genesis must go beyond two inadequate arguments. We cannot simply say that the stories depict a world that could fit a 2nd-millennium setting, if all of their details could belong equally well to the 1st millennium. The Bible is largely a 1st-millennium book, and it is not hard to date the whole content of Genesis to the same period, without compelling evidence to the contrary.[44] Also, any argument based only on paddling back and forth the burden of proof and disproof is ultimately futile. It is not enough to say that the skeptics have failed to disprove outright the early setting and to await further critique.

43. This is how Albertz (1:29) views the religion of the ancestors in Genesis.

44. By this dating of the Bible, I simply take the texts at face value. Only the Pentateuch, Joshua, Judges, and Ruth tell about events before the united monarchy. Ruth openly anticipates David. I am acknowledging here the broad logic of the widespread inclination to level the dates of all biblical writing toward the later periods.

In the last part of my article entitled "Mari and the Possibilities of Biblical Memory," I offer a first attempt at producing positive arguments for elements of the Genesis traditions that can be explained only by origin in the Bronze Age and no later. My approach to the problem includes Israel with a larger group of new Iron Age states in Syria-Palestine that display signs of tribal roots, and whose peoples speak Northwest Semitic dialects. These include the Arameans and the Transjordan states of Edom, Moab, and Ammon. Any historical relation to Mari's tribal peoples will not be the special property of Israel, but rather all of these Iron Age groups beg to be explained against the earlier situation.

The Building-Blocks of Memory in Genesis

The raw material for my reevaluation of the historical problem in Genesis comes from a series of points of contact with specific features of the tribal populations known from the Mari archives. These include the tribe named Benjamin, Harran as the ancestral home in northern Syria, the biblical use of the adjective "Hebrew" for identifying Joseph and his family in Egypt, and the division of pasture by right and left hands in Gen. 13:9.

Benjamin and Harran I begin with two prominent details of the biblical ancestor tradition that are difficult to explain in the context of the 1st millennium: the specific identification of Harran as the north Syrian home of Abraham's kin; and the existence of a tribe of Benjamin. It is Harran that immediately dislodges us from the familiar geography of Israel and Judah, demanding some explanation in broader geo-political and historical terms. Harran has no direct interest for the biblical writers outside of the book of Genesis, where it defines Abraham's point of departure for the promised land (12:4-5; cf. 11:31), and it is Jacob's destination when he flees to his mother's family (27:43; 28:10; 29:4).[45] Judging by the degree to which Harran is imbedded in the core narrative, the primary associations of this Syrian location seem to belong to the Jacob cycle.[46] There, Harran is difficult to remove from the essential geography of Jacob's journey, though the combination of its dis-

45. Outside of Genesis, Harran is only mentioned with Assyria's other conquests in the Rab-Shaqeh's harangue (2 Kgs. 19:12; Isa. 37:12), and in Ezekiel's long list of Tyre's trading partners (Ezek. 27:23).

46. Gen. 12:4-5 is linked to the statement of Abram's age, in priestly material, and the reference in 11:31 belongs to the bridge from Abram's family tree to his first calling to leave Syria. The only episode in the Abraham tale that takes place in Syria is the mission of his servant, which ends up in "the town of Nahor" in Aram Naharayim (24:10).

tance and its lack of obvious interest to Israel provokes a variety of literary interpretations.[47] Far from suggesting an awkward editorial addition, the geography of the Jacob-Laban sequence in chapters 29-31 gives the impression that the narrator had little sense of Harran's actual distance. When Jacob arrives in Laban's neighborhood, it is identified with the Qedemites ("sons of the east," 29:1), and Laban only has to chase Jacob for the stereotypical interval of seven days in order to catch up with him in Gilead (31:22-23).[48]

Because the Bible indicates no interest in Harran for either Israel or Judah, recent studies have generally concluded that this name could have entered the biblical tradition only in the age of the Mesopotamian empires, which brought defeat, destruction, and exile.[49] When would Israel's ancestors have been imagined to come to this promised land from distant Mesopotamian Harran and Ur? According to J. Alberto Soggin, these cities represent an itinerary for Judahite exiles on their way home.[50] The obvious

47. In the past, all three Jacob texts were understood as part of the core narrative of the Yahwistic source (J). Recent scholars who date this core material to the exilic period or nearby still tend to maintain the centrality of Harran to the original narrative; see Van Seters, *Prologue to History*, 288-95. Wahl (271) argues that Gen. 28:10 is essential to launch the Bethel story, even so far as that story stood originally on its own, and observes that only v. 10 names Jacob as the protagonist, so that v. 11 has no subject without it. Blum wants to recognize a much older Jacob tradition but cannot explain how the people of the early northern kingdom would have maintained any interest in this far-northern town, so he proposes a Harran redaction from the exilic period; *Die Komposition der Vätergeschichte*, 164-66. After Van Seters reminded Carr of Blum's view, Carr emended his previous interpretation of Gen. 28:10 to match Blum's; see Van Seters, "Divine Encounter at Bethel (Gen 28,10-22) in Recent Literary-Critical Study of Genesis," *ZAW* 110 (1998): 505; Carr, *ZAW* 111 (1999): 400. Edward Lipiński has recently suggested that fast camels could cover the true distance to Harran in seven days, though this over-literal interpretation would require Jacob's entire party to cover the same ground in 10 days; *The Aramaeans: Their Ancient History, Culture, Religion*. OLA 100 (Leuven: Peeters, 2000), 65, 68.

48. With Blum, I prefer not to divide Gen. 29:1 and 4 across two literary strands (*Die Komposition der Vätergeschichte*, 166). For the seven-day journey, compare Keret's march to the city of Udm in KTU 1.14 iii 2-20 (cf. iv 44–v 15); see my general discussion in "The Seven-Day Siege of Jericho in Holy War," in *Ki Baruch Hu: Ancient Near Eastern, Biblical, and Judaic Studies in Honor of Baruch A. Levine*, ed. Robert Chazan, William W. Hallo, and Lawrence H. Schiffman (Winona Lake: Eisenbrauns, 1999), 211-28. Note that Laban is linked repeatedly to Aram, even to the point of naming the witness cairn in Aramaic (31:47), while the Qedemites are never associated with Aram.

49. One exception is Lipiński, who argues (73-74) that Harran can be explained by the possibility that the 10th-century scribe came from there. This explanation is far too narrowly grounded to explain such a prominent tradition for Israel's Syrian origins. The writers of such texts must also relate to their audiences.

50. J. Alberto Soggin, *A History of Ancient Israel* (Philadelphia: Westminster, 1985), 92. See also Ska's idea (174) that Abraham is cast in Genesis as a father to the generation of returning exiles.

difficulty is the focus of the Jacob tradition: not Babylonia but Harran, which has no biblical connection with either the exile or the return.[51] Van Seters's attribution of the biblical tradition to the period and religious preoccupations of Nabonidus remains equally unconvincing.[52] Both Ur and Harran had a long-standing connection with worship of the moon-god, an association that may indeed underlie their combination in Genesis. The religious environment that produced biblical writings during the exilic period, however, with the arrival of a polemical monotheism, does not provide persuasive roots for an identification of Israelite origins with places sacred to the moon-god. If anything, such an association would make better sense in earlier periods, before the encroachment of the Mesopotamian empires. It is really no further help, therefore, to locate the origin of the Harran tradition in the time of Assyrian rule.[53] Without a compelling political or population link to Harran, for which we have no evidence, an ideology of ethnic identification with this far-northern town makes no sense.

When the periods of Israelite and early Jewish history offer no good explanation for the north Syrian origins of Abraham and his family, and the point of Genesis is to locate these in a time long before, it is surely worth considering an older alternative. This alternative carries its full weight only after we examine a second feature in Genesis, the name of Jacob's youngest son, Benjamin. Bin-yamin always represented the one most obvious possibility for a direct link between the tribal peoples of Israel and Mari, because the Israelite tribal name matches exactly the form and meaning of the earlier Binu Yamina.[54] Thompson objected that the designation of "Yaminites" at Mari could not be understood as a proper name, but only as a geographical reference to "southerners." Furthermore, the eventual use of such directional terms for proper geographical names is so common that one can expect more than one group of "Sons of the South," without any genetic relationship. As

51. For a similar opinion, see de Vaux, 188.

52. *Abraham in History and Tradition*, 23-5; followed by Ahlström, 183 and n. 5.

53. This slightly earlier period is the solution of de Pury, in Wénin, 238.

54. See first of all Georges Dossin, "Benjaminites dans les textes de Mari," in *Mélanges syriens offerts à M. René Dussaud* (Paris: Paul Geuthner, 1939), 983; and André Parrot, *RHPR* 30 (1950): 6. Thompson (*The Historicity of the Patriarchal Narratives*, 66) objected that the necessary reading of the cuneiform DUMU^meš *Ia-mi-na* as *mārū yamina* reduced the direct verbal similarity; see for the idea that the logogram cannot represent West Semitic *binu(m)*, Hayim Tadmor, "Historical Implications of the Correct Rendering of Akkadian *dâku*," *JNES* 17 (1958): 130 n. 12. However the professional scribes read this spelling, we now have at least one personal name that shows the western form, *Bi-ni-ia-mi-na* (ARM XXII 328 iii:16), suggesting that native West Semitic speakers would have used the expected noun *bin-*; see Jean-Marie Durand, "Les Bédouins," *Les documents épistolaires du palais de Mari*. LAPO 17 (Paris: Cerf, 1998), 418.

examples of the latter phenomenon, he cites Yemen in southern Arabia, a Transjordanian Arabic tribe of Benjamin, Teman of Edom, and, for a "northern" alternative, the Aramean city of Sam'al (Zinjirli).[55]

Countless texts show the impossibility of treating Mari's Binu Yamina as anything other than a proper name.[56] The Binu Sim'al and the Binu Yamina formed a complementary pair of tribal coalitions among a tribal population who represented their larger identity in terms of this left/right division. As a dual terminology, the "left" was meaningless without the corresponding "right," and this grand split was understood to reflect not a narrow concentration of settlement but an ancient allotment of pastoral grazing ranges. The crucial text describes the long-accepted pasturage of the Sim'alite "sons of the left (hand)" as the upper Ḫabur River basin, while that of the Yaminite "sons of the right (hand)" encompassed the territories of Yamḥad (Aleppo), Qatna, and Amurru.[57] Yamḥad and Qatna represent the major western kingdoms of the Old Babylonian Mari period, and the latter governed territories that reached south into what is now southern Syria and Lebanon. The name Amurru, already derived from the Mesopotamians' word for "westerners" (Amorites), appears to identify some part of the region along the Mediterranean coast, as reflected in the Late Bronze kingdom by that name south of Ugarit.[58]

It is evident that the "right hand" *(yamina)* was associated with the south, as in Biblical Hebrew, so that the Mari coalitions are indeed divided as "Northerners" (Binu Sim'al) and "Southerners" (Binu Yamina), in broad terms that span modern Syria. Can Israel's Ben-yamin, the "son of the right hand," share this designation without any historical relationship to the earlier group? This solution succeeds only if the right/left hand tribal designation is in some sense generic and standard, but we do not have evidence to demonstrate this standard use. Moreover, the terminology found in the Mari archives offers a framework for understanding it that is lacking in Israel's solitary "son of the right hand." The combination of both right and left hands in the Mari usage displays a built-in symmetry, based on the metaphor of the human body. The names of the two Amorite tribal coalitions are evidently self-assigned, self-referential, ideologically symmetrical, and therefore neutral. There is no junior partner, one defined from the centrality of the other.[59]

---

55. *The Historicity of the Patriarchal Narratives,* 66.

56. See the discussion of tribal categories in Charpin and Durand; and Durand, "Les Bédouins," 417-511.

57. See n. 27, above, for the text and translation.

58. See the literature cited in my "Mari and the Possibilities of Biblical Memory," 62.

59. From Thompson's list, only the Arabic Benjamin would offer an exact match, and the

Biblical scholars have long explained Israel's tribe of Benjamin as "southern" with reference to Ephraim, the dominant region and tribe in the northern hill country.[60] If Benjamin is really "southern" in local terms, however, it is from an Ephraimite point of view, not that of Benjamin itself. Our two "Benjamins" would be based on two wholly different conceptions. This interpretation of Israel's Benjamin in purely local terms was more viable when the earlier Binu Yamina could also be understood as a local northern phenomenon of modest scale.[61] Now that we know the Binu Yamina as a far-flung coalition whose pastures were oriented toward southwestern Syria, Israel's tribe is surely easier to explain as a secondary application of the old name. So far as the name Benjamin was actually understood to originate by reference to Ephraim, this would have been an effort to interpret an existing term against local geography.

The presence of the Middle Bronze Binu Yamina in southwestern Syria constitutes a key part of the evidence that compels reevaluation of the Bible's Benjamin. When the Binu Yamina are recognized to be the primary tribal people from the Mari evidence who move through the back country of southwestern Syria in this period, and we can be fairly sure that a tribe named Benjamin played a leading role in Israel at the end of the 2nd millennium, the insistence on treating these tribal names as totally unrelated becomes artificial.[62] At the same time, however, Israel's Benjamin is not to be imagined as a simple extension of the ancient Yaminite coalition. Even in the Mari archives, individual Yaminites did not identify themselves as Binu Yamina but by tribe: Yariḫû, Amnanû, Rabbû, Yaḫrurû, or Uprapû. In Israel, the tables were turned, and Benjamin was a tribe within a larger coalition. I am proposing, however, that Israel would not have included a

name may derive directly from the biblical tradition, or even (less likely) from the same older Syrian tribal split.

60. Benjamin would be the southernmost tribe derived from Rachel, with the Joseph tribes of Ephraim and Manasseh ranging to the north and east. This widespread explanation seems to have originated with Otto Eissfeldt. More recently, see Klaus-Dietrich Schunck, *Benjamin: Untersuchungen zur Entstehung und Geschichte eines Israelitischen Stammes.* BZAW 86 (Berlin: A. Töpelmann, 1963); Hans-Jürgen Zobel, *Stammespruch und Geschichte.* BZAW 95 (Berlin: A. Töpelmann, 1965), 111-12; A. D. H. Mayes, *Israel in the Period of the Judges.* SBT N.S. 29 (Naperville: Allenson, 1974), 82; Thompson, *The Historicity of the Patriarchal Narratives,* 59-60; de Vaux, 640-41; and Ahlström, 178.

61. See Manfred Weippert, *The Settlement of the Israelite Tribes in Palestine.* SBT N.S. 21 (Naperville: Allenson, 1971), 112; Schunck, 7; Thompson, *The Historicity of the Patriarchal Narratives,* 64.

62. Consider Benjamin in the Song of Deborah (Judg. 5:14) and the fact that king Saul belonged to Benjamin (1 Sam. 9:1, 4, 16, 21; 10:21).

tribe named Benjamin if this population had no background in the Syrian tribal division.

By emphasizing the connection between these names, I am also not saying that Benjamin was the one Yaminite tribe in Israel. Rather, the name is a clue that there were ancient Binu Yamina somewhere in Israel's ancestry, probably not limited to the tribe of Benjamin. Any relation of the local Israelite tribe to the larger Syrian entity is entirely forgotten. This in itself reflects the Iron Age setting for the Genesis stories as written.

This brings us back to Harran. During the Mari period, Harran was a sacred center for the Binu Yamina coalition. One text records an alliance oath sworn in the moon-god temple of Harran by all of the Yaminite rulers, along with the kings of Zalmaqum, an alliance of four towns in the Baliḫ River basin.[63] It appears, then, that both the existence of a tribe named Benjamin and the attachment of Israel's ancestors to Harran are not simply ancient or Amorite, but are specifically features of the Yaminite tribal people who are known from the early-2nd-millennium texts from Mari.

It is this identification of Harran with the Yaminites, who offer the most plausible ancestry for Benjamin, that suggests a previously unrecognized historical link between Genesis and the players known from Mari.[64] Many aspects of the patriarchal stories are ageless within the broad confines of Israelite history, impossible to date precisely, and important details of the narratives display the later setting of their writing. The core idea, however, of tribal beginnings among pastoralists centered in the Baliḫ River basin may make sense only as the specific heritage of tribes descended from the Syrian Binu Yamina coalition. By placing Abraham, Jacob, and their family in Harran, the ancestor tradition shows an unconscious link to the Bronze Age Yaminites.

---

63. ARM XXVI 24:10-12; "Asdi-takim and the kings of Zalmaqum, with the chiefs and elders of the Yaminites, have slain the ass together in the Sîn temple of Harran" (ᵐ*Às-di-ta-ki-im ù* LUGAL^meš *ša Za-al-ma-qí-im*^ki *ù* ^lú*su-ga-gu*^meš *ù* ^lúŠU.GI^meš [*š*]*a* DUMU^meš *Ia-mi-na*^[i]*-na* É ^dSU'EN *ša Ḫa-ar-ra-nim*^ki ^anše*ḫa-a-ri iq-ṭú-ú-lu-*[*n*]*im*.

64. Jack Sasson, who always sets a standard for caution and rigor that I would like to imitate, warns against inappropriate definition of Mari-Bible comparisons in "homologous" terms, as having a "generic or genealogical lineage" between the objects in question; *RA* 92 (1998): 98-9. I realize that I am attempting to demonstrate a basis for the possibility of this very homology, and my entire point is that no such basis has been adequately shown and requires a new foundation. At the same time, my exploration of the names Harran and Bin-yamin is not perhaps comparative in the sense that Sasson has in mind. Harran, at least, is unquestionably the same town in both sources, and the issue is simply how and when Israel conceived a connection with it. Benjamin and the Binu Yamina are slightly different, in that the derivation of one from the other must be argued for or against, but the question is still not comparative.

Hebrew/ʿibrî If it is possible to accept the link argued above, other connections may be proposed. One striking example may be the word "Hebrew," which has often been compared to the Bronze Age ḫabiru or ʿapiru. While the consonantal root for ʿapiru can be associated plausibly with the Hebrew root ʿbr in the adjective ʿibrî,[65] there remain problems of both form and meaning. In purely formal terms, the two substantives are of different type, regardless of the vowel lengths of the -a- and the -i- in ʿapiru. Then, the Hebrews of the Bible are not easily derived from the outcasts of the Late Bronze ʿapiru class. In the Egypt stories of Genesis and Exodus, the family of Jacob become foreign guest workers of separate but respectable standing. Both coming in as Jacob's family and leaving as Yahweh's people, these Hebrews are portrayed as having a coherent social identity that is defined in terms of kinship.

In Mari evidence from the periods of both Samsi-Addu and Zimri-Lim, the ʿibrum (written ḫibrum) is the component of the Binu Yamina population that is based in the back country, travelling with the flocks.[66] The Sim'alites do not seem to have applied this term to their own social structure. All of the published examples of the word ʿibrum are spelled with the ḪI-sign, which may render the consonant ʿayin in West Semitic words found in the Mari archives.[67] The ʿibrum is not known to us from anything like the number and range of documents that attest the ʿapiru, but this surely reflects its use for the mobile pastoralists among a tribal confederacy that left us no urban archive of the sort represented by the remarkable collection preserved at Mari. In spite of its relative obscurity, the ʿibrum was no minor local phenomenon. It

65. Weippert accounts for the variation of b/p as "*oscillation* of the labial plosive before the following voiceless consonant"; see his detailed discussion, 74-82. The ʿayin is explicit at Ugarit.

66. ARM XXVI 168:16-24 divides the whole Yaminite people between "the contingent of the towns" and "the ʿibrum of the back country." For other occurrences of the word, see also ARM I 119:9-10; VIII 11:9-11, 21-22; A.981:36 (Durand, "Unité et diversités au Proche-Orient à l'époque amorrite," 118); A.2801:13-16 (Georges Dossin, RA 66 [1972]: 118-20; = Durand, Les documents épistolaires du palais de Mari. LAPO 16 [Paris: Cerf, 1997], no. 268, 418-19); A.2796:16-17 (Durand, MARI 6 [1990]: 288); M.5172, in Charpin and Durand, 154 n. 67. I discuss these together in Democracy's Ancient Ancestors, 97-100.

67. There is no difficulty with reading ḫibrum as ʿibrum in West Semitic words from the texts stored at Mari, though Akkadian had lost the ʿayin. One prominent example of a West Semitic substantive in which the laryngeal consonant ʿayin is written consistently with signs in -Ḫ- is the noun merʿûm, the "chief of pasture," derived from the root rʿy, "to pasture, graze." This word also belongs to the native vocabulary for pastoralist social categories. The merʿûm occurs repeatedly in spellings with the ḪU and the ḪI signs, never to my knowledge with any alternative. See e.g., ARM XIV 53:7, 18; 80:12; 81:9, 11, 16; 86:18; 121:45; XXVI 86:11; 114:5, 7; 388:19; 389:10, 12; 394:10', 12'; ARM XXVII 48:7'; 61:11; 70:22; 93:8, 12; 113:7; FM II 63:14. This list is far from exhaustive, even among the published texts.

was the dominant social category for the mobile pastoralist communities that ranged across southwestern Syria during the Mari period, usually dated to the mid-18th century.

An etymology of Hebrew *'ibrî* that is focused on the ancient *'ibrum* retains many of the advantages of the *'apiru* etymology. The word *'ibrum* comes from the same root as *'apiru,* in documentation that attests both nouns, along with the verb from which they are derived.[68] Like the *'apiru,* the *'ibrum* consists of people who have left their settled residence, but in the latter case without cutting ties with their settled communities. These ties are preserved by the ideology of tribal identity. The *qitl* noun form of *'ibrum* offers a better match to *'ibrî.* Moreover, the *'ibrum* offers a better social fit with the biblical traditions for "Hebrew" identity. The Hebrews of Joseph's family finally move into Egypt en masse as a coherent clan of shepherds, a class that is "repugnant" to the Egyptians (Gen. 46:34). The identification of Jacob's sons as belonging to a herdsmen type is indirectly linked to the word "Hebrew" itself when we recall the one other "repugnance" *(tô'ēbâ)* of the Egyptians in the Joseph story: eating with "Hebrews" (Gen. 43:32).[69]

Pastureland by Right Hand and Left Hand (Gen 13:9) One more specific connection between the Mari tribal systems and Genesis has been observed by Durand, who with laudable caution declines to imagine any historical relationship. When the shepherds of Abram and Lot can no longer live together peaceably, Abram offers his nephew a proposal (Gen. 13:9): "Is not the whole

---

68. For the verb in active use, see the following sampling of published texts. The verb seems to refer to a move not from one building to another in the same town but to removal from one political domain for another. The implication may be "refuge" in some cases, but this nuance is not essential to the verbal action. Individual "emigration" is generally in view, not group action, though it is not clear whether such change of residence is viewed as permanent. In all cases, the laryngeal consonant is rendered in -Ḫ-, either with the sign AḪ/IḪ/UḪ or with ḪA, and the BU/PU sign does not distinguish between the two labials. ARM XIV 50:14, "I left for the land of (geographical name)," *aḫ-bu-ur;* 72:18, "the one who takes refuge with you (plural)," *ḫa-bi-ru-ku-nu;* ARM XXVI 510:25, "(personal name), who came to take refuge here from Mari (was put in prison)," *iḫ-bu-ra-am;* ARM XXVII 70:17, a man was wanted for questioning, but "this man has left for (emigrated to) Kurdâ," *iḫ-bu-úr;* ARM XXVII 116:322, identifying two men by residence, one still in the Mari kingdom settled at Saggaratum (verb *wašābum*), the other "left for Kurdâ," *iḫ-bu-ra-am;* ARM XXVIII 46:6', the king of Urgiš says he has had to leave his residence in that city for neighboring Šinaḫ, "I have departed in exile," *a-na ḫa-bi-ru-tim at-ta-ṣi.*

69. The discussion of the "Hebrew" etymology here is still extremely limited and omits any systematic treatment of the biblical usage. I presented a somewhat more extensive argument under the title, "Refining the Etymology for 'Hebrew': Mari's *ḫibrum*," at the 2001 Annual Meeting of the SBL.

land before you? Suppose you split off from me. If (you choose) the left *(haśśĕmō'l)*, I will go to the right, and if (you choose) the right *(hayyāmîn)*, I will go to the left." The terms here for "left" and "right" in this text do not refer to north and south and are directly cognate with the Amorite Sim'al and Yamina in the Mari archives. Durand proposes that Genesis 13 describes the same ideology of tribal division that lies behind the left/right duality of the Sim'alites and the Yaminites, though independently conceived.[70]

In fact, the Genesis tribal split and the Amorite tribal pair share a remarkably similar set of assumptions. Both traditions use the language of right and left hands, a pair defined by the human body, for tribal pastoralists who are allotting pasturelands. In both, the original corporal sense is preserved, not dependent on the application of these to south and north. It is significant that in both cases it is grazing land that is in dispute and that is distributed by this kind of division. We are not dealing with political domains or even with settlement. Finally, both uses of the left/right ideology are large-scale, defining regions that reach beyond local terrain. In effect, Abram takes the hill country of the promised land, and Lot takes the rift valley of the Jordan River. For both the Genesis and the Amorite pastoralists, the division of pasture does not imply political control. Abram does not rule the Canaanite highland towns any more than Lot rules Sodom and Gomorrah. The same is true for the Binu Yamina pasturage in the lands of Yamḫad, Qatna, and Amurru.

Indeed, none of the Genesis language is specifically Amorite, as Durand emphasizes. Nevertheless, one might ask the same question that I asked of Benjamin. Would we find this whole way of conceiving the division of grazing land among people *not* of Amorite background, when we know that this idea was deeply ingrained among the Yaminites and the Sim'alites as the framework for their entire identity as two confederacies? It is perhaps easier to explain the similarities as reflecting, at considerable distance, the Middle Bronze II Yaminite/Sim'alite way of explaining the division of pasture between large kin groups.

---

70. This discussion comes from Durand's advanced seminar at the École Pratique des Hautes Études in April 1998, based on a draft of an eventual monograph on the peoples and society of the Mari archives. I have tried to represent Durand's ideas as precisely as possible, but the reader should realize that this is my rendition of material communicated orally, and that M. Durand has not yet to my knowledge committed himself to a specific formulation of them in print.

The Rachel Tribes in the Ancestral Traditions

Documentary analysis has long attributed the J and E literary sources to the southern and northern kingdoms respectively, regardless of the particular dates.[71] In Genesis, however, the geographical interests imbedded in the text run deeper than such source divisions. The biblical texts represented in the above list of possible points of contact between Genesis and the tribal peoples of Middle Bronze Age Syria show a striking pattern. Rather than being distributed unevenly across a variety of northern- and southern-oriented material, all four of these features display particular affinity with the Rachel tribes of Joseph and Benjamin.

First, Benjamin himself is the second son of Rachel, bound to the Joseph tribes of Ephraim and Manasseh by their common mother. The tribal territory of Benjamin indeed lay to the south of Joseph, in land that came to be disputed between the kingdoms of Israel and Judah, but the idea that Joseph and Benjamin both came from Rachel belongs to a tradition that orients Benjamin toward the north.[72] In the Song of Deborah, perhaps the one text in the Bible that is most widely acknowledged to reflect premonarchic traditions, Benjamin follows Ephraim as the first two tribes to join in the fight against Sisera of Hazor (Judg. 5:14).[73]

Harran is most strongly rooted in the story of Jacob's flight from Esau (Gen. 27:43; 28:10; 29:4), as discussed previously, and it is the location of narrative action only in the last of the Jacob texts (29:4), where it represents the home of the first shepherds that Jacob meets upon his arrival in the land of his Syrian kinsmen. Interestingly, the particular purpose of this story is to introduce Jacob to Rachel, who becomes his passion (29:1-12). By contrast, the first Laban story, when Abraham's servant acquires Rebekah as a wife for Isaac, never mentions Harran and locates Laban instead in "Aram Naharayim," in "the town of Nahor" (24:10).[74] In Genesis 24, the focus of their

71. See, e.g., Norman K. Gottwald, *The Hebrew Bible: A Socio-Literary Introduction* (Philadelphia: Fortress, 1985), 137-38. Countless others could be cited.

72. The account in 1 Kings 12 of the initial split between Jeroboam and Rehoboam, which led to separate northern and southern kingdoms, states that Benjamin followed Rehoboam and Judah (vv. 21, 23); cf. C. H. J. de Geus, *The Tribes of Israel* (Assen: van Gorcum, 1976), 94.

73. For recent discussion of the Song of Deborah and its early date, see Kenton L. Sparks, *Ethnicity and Identity in Ancient Israel* (Winona Lake: Eisenbrauns, 1999), 109-21. Sparks concludes that even if the final poem may be as late as the 9th century, it "probably reflects an earlier and perhaps premonarchical tradition" (113).

74. In the generation of Albright and Speiser, it was common to look for parallels between the names of Abraham's immediate family in Syria and places from that northern region. Speiser (80) himself cites both Naḥur from the Mari archives (with Nahor) and a town named

return is not Abraham but Isaac, who is living in the Negev, far south of the territory eventually identified with Joseph and Benjamin (see v. 62). Even in the itinerary of Gen. 12:5-6, Harran is the point of departure for a journey that ends in Shechem, in what becomes the land of Ephraim, Joseph's heir. Harran thus seems to be imbedded in the same block that recounts Jacob's Syrian sojourn in terms that give Rachel priority and that launched Jacob's new life and relationship with God from the sacred place of Bethel, again in Ephraim (28:10-22).

In Genesis, the word "Hebrew" is used in Egypt by Egyptians, just as in the story of the exodus that follows, but the main character from the outset is Joseph, Rachel's firstborn, who becomes the deliverer and leader of his family. As currently placed, the tale of Moses and the exodus from Egypt is linked to the Joseph story to form the bookends of Israel's stay in Egypt, so that the combination would then share the same northern Israelite orientation. The other notable use of the word "Hebrew" in biblical narrative is associated with the reign of Saul, during which the Philistines identify the Israelites as Hebrews from the inland back country (1 Sam. 13:7, 19; 14:11; 29:3). Saul is from the tribe of Benjamin. I am not trying to demonstrate that the word Hebrew was the exclusive possession of northern traditions, but in this case also, the biblical feature has strong links to the peoples of Rachel.

Finally, Genesis 13 presents an odd combination of geographical interests that continues the same pattern. According to the framework of the chapter, Abram is already based in the south, which becomes his primary home in Canaan. Having left Egypt after his encounter there with Pharaoh, Abram goes to the Negev (13:1-3), and the end of the chapter recounts his initial settlement at Hebron (v. 18). Between these southern poles, the action of chapter 13 is associated with Bethel in what became southern Ephraim (vv. 3-4). The definition of the promised land as all that Abram can see to the north,

---

Sarugu in the region of Harran (with Serug). While the name *Naḥôr* does indeed fit the form of Naḥur, the nature of the comparison is quite different. According to the Mari archives, the town of Naḥur was part of Ida-Maraṣ, a coalition of towns in the upper Ḫabur River basin that kept strong ties with the Binu Sim'al of Mari's king Zimri-Lim. This town had no close relationship to Harran, which was part of the rival coalition of Zalmaqum in the Baliḫ River basin to the west, and which maintained a bond with the Binu Yamina. Another of the four towns that made up Zalmaqum was called Niḫriya, from the same root as Naḥur, but the biblical name allows a direct match only with the Sim'alite location. So far as Nahor in Genesis may derive from this name, though not necessarily the same place, the relationship is both more loose and more distant. For the exact location of Sarugu between Harran and Carchemish, as part of the Neo-Assyrian Empire, see Simo Parpola and Michael Porter, eds., *The Helsinki Atlas of the Near East in the Neo-Assyrian Period* (Finland: Casco Bay Assyriological Institute and the Neo-Assyrian Text Corpus Project, 2001), 325.

south, east, and west is thus linked to Bethel, as is the entire account of Lot's separation from Abram. After this, through the account of his death in Gen. 25:8-11, Abraham never again appears in the land of the northern tribes, outside the sphere of Judah.

It appears, then, that the book of Genesis preserves a small set of features that display a heritage in the tribal peoples known from the Mari archives. I argue from the combination of Benjamin and Harran that these features are not best explained by cultural analogy, but they can only reflect a background among the Binu Yamina tribal coalition, whose grazing lands spanned southwestern Syria, across the lands of Yamḫad, Qatna, and Amurru. This southern range, which was not previously known, explains how a tribal tradition known from the Mari archives in far eastern Syria could have echoes in the biblical lore regarding Israelite origins. In the connections that I draw between Genesis and the Mari texts, the tribal aspect is central to all of the Middle Bronze Age evidence. The Binu Yamina name itself is the tie with the tribe of Benjamin (Bin-yamin) and with the right/left division of grazing land in Gen. 13:9. Harran was a prominent city in the northern center of Yaminite settlement in the Baliḫ River region, and appears to take its place in Genesis as the tribal origin of the whole Abrahamic family by way of this Binu Yamina association. Finally, my proposed etymology of *'ibrî* ("Hebrew") through Mari's *'ibrum* follows the same Yaminite tribal stream.

The book of Genesis presents Israel and its inland neighbors as sharing an ancient ancestry in northern Syria through Abraham. Mari's evidence for Syrian peoples in the Middle Bronze II period indicates a real tribal heritage from the north. The particular Syrian pool from which that heritage derived seems to have been Yaminite, judging by the concentration of related features from this southwestern tribal coalition. In Iron Age Israel, this Yaminite heritage may have been preserved especially in the Rachel tribes that formed the core of the northern kingdom, the tribes identified with Joseph and Benjamin. We should not assume that all of the Israelite tribes came from Binu Yamina ancestry, but perhaps the Joseph tribes of Ephraim and Manasseh offer the most obvious second possibility, after Benjamin itself.

By isolating a particular region and tribal community within Israel as displaying a Yaminite and north Syrian background, we find a vehicle that could explain its preservation in Israelite lore, at the same time as we establish a basis for identifying other Genesis traditions that do not show this background. For example, Isaac has no link to northern Syria. Unlike Abraham and Jacob, he never sets foot there. Also unlike Abraham and Jacob, he never sets foot in the territory that came to belong to the northern kingdom and its tribes.[75] Isaac's primary role in the genealogical scheme of Genesis is to relate Israel and Edom as twin brothers through Jacob and Esau, and this purpose also assumes a southern perspective, with Edom juxtaposed to the very land Isaac traversed in the life portrayed in Genesis.[76] Another example is the story of Lot's capture by and rescue from foreign troops in Genesis 14. This chapter is recounted from the perspective of Abram's permanent camp at Hebron (14:13, 24). Abram's encounter with king Melchizedek of Salem (or Jerusalem) fits the same geography, involving the second leading town in Judah that became a seat of David's power.[77] Whatever we are to make of the named kings and kingdoms who take part in the great battle, they have nothing to do with the tribal traditions suggested by the Mari evidence.[78]

Returning to the association of the Mari links with the Rachel tribes of Israel, I must emphasize that this tribal-territorial coherence is the only evident basis for relating the biblical appearances of the four features. They are not part of a single literary strand, according to any hypothesis of which I am aware, though I have argued that all of them are rooted in core Genesis traditions, not easily explained by later stages of redaction. This occurrence in separate stories from the north-central hill country adds to the sense that they belong to broad-based regional tradition and are not the contribution of a single writer or period.

---

75. Isaac is the cause of Hagar's second expulsion, and she journeys into the wilderness of Beer-sheba (Gen. 21:14). Abraham establishes a base at Beersheba (21:31-33), and the binding of Isaac at Moriah seems to assume a southern location, three days from camp (22:2-4; cf. v. 19). Isaac meets Rebekah in Beer Lahoi Roi of the Negev (24:62). Like Abraham, Isaac passes time in Gerar (26:1), from which his flocks are pastured in the region of Beer-sheba (26:23, 33). By the time Jacob is reconciled with his brother, Esau already lives in Seir, in Edom, and no mention is made of Isaac (33:14, 16). Gen. 35:27-29 records Isaac's death at Mamre, near Hebron.

76. It is interesting that Isaac's firm southern associations are incorporated into the northern-oriented tale of Jacob, in the first segment, which introduces Jacob and Esau together, with the basis for their conflict (see Gen. 25:19-34; 27:1-45).

77. David is said to have ruled Judah alone for seven years from Hebron (2 Sam. 2:1-4; 5:1-5), before he made Jerusalem the royal seat for all of Israel (5:6-10).

78. Durand understands the episode in Genesis 14 to be "pure fiction" (in French as in English!), but he suggests that the activity of an Elamite ruler in lands far west of Elam makes best sense in the early 2nd millennium. In the period of the Mari archives, the king of Elam was considered the superior of all the Syria-Mesopotamian rulers, and one text suggests that the great western Syrian kingdom of Qatna allied itself with Elam, evidently as its inferior (*RA* 92 [1998]: 17).

Prospects for the Genesis Ancestor Traditions

During the years since Thompson and Van Seters published their ground-breaking books, the case for finding in Genesis any reliable information about Israelite ancestry has grown more and more stale. Little new has been proposed, with most of the creative work involving the radical reevaluation of literary-critical hypotheses, mostly toward later dates, especially for any large-scale documents in the Pentateuch. My presentation of Mari comparisons in the preceding section is intended to bring some fresh material to the table, to revitalize the debate about history and tradition in the book of Genesis. It should be clear that I have looked for more than just the illumination of biblical customs by Bronze Age cuneiform texts. The more important historical question has been whether Genesis offers anything to assist our reconstruction of actual Israelite origins. Could the Syrian or Mesopotamian points of departure have any historical basis? Is the migratory aspect even conceivable? Does the portrait of ancestors living in tents, depending mainly on their flocks for subsistence, and only occasionally shifting their base camp reflect any more than speculation based on projection back from much later realities?

My selection of comparative evidence from Mari is limited and depends especially on the presence of Harran and Benjamin in the biblical tradition, joined to the new realization that Mari's Binu Yamina were a huge tribal coalition whose range brought some of them remarkably close to Palestine, even in the early 2nd millennium. I argue that these two names would not appear in the ancestor traditions of Genesis unless some component of the Israelite population had roots among the Yaminite tribal peoples of Syria. Such roots would require neither the formation of Israel itself by group migration nor any particular relationship to people from the time of the Mari archives. They would, however, mean that the idea of sweeping identification with inland tribal peoples from Syria carries historical weight.

Given the tribal ideology associated with both the Binu Yamina and the Genesis portrait of Israel, the proposed relationship would substantiate the biblical notion that early Israel not only identified itself tribally but also emerged at least in part from tribal peoples. As archaeologists and historians struggle to account for the configuration of finds in the transition from the Late Bronze to the Iron Age in Palestine, Genesis suggests that inland tribal peoples, with ultimate links to the Syrian back country, should not be excluded in favor of purely local "Canaanite" populations, shifting between larger urban and smaller rural settlements. The Binu Yamina of the early 2nd millennium represented one component of a complex tribal society that included a large settled population, even in fortified towns, but these people incorporated a permanent pastoralist population as well, the 'ibrum. In Genesis, the picture of primary subsistence by flocks tended at substantial distance from tent settlements contrasts with the Israelite economy in all periods. The points of contact with the Binu Yamina add to the sense that some Israelites did in fact come from such a way of life, though once established in the land as politically distinct peoples, they came to depend increasingly on cultivation.

So far as this is true, the dominant pastoralist mode of subsistence does itself suggest another feature of the Genesis ancestral narrative that is remembered from the time before small-scale agriculture swept across the central hill country in the early Iron I period. The remarkable absence of hill-country settlement during the Late Bronze Age (ca. 1550-1200) does suggest a significant pastoralist use of land during that time, and it is clear that the scores of new settlements at the start of the Iron I mark a strong shift toward farming.[79] There is a certain amount of uncertainty about the exact chronology of the economic shift because the material evidence for mobile pastoralist subsistence is more difficult to find than the villages of farmers. Israel Finkelstein suspects that the Iron I period was characterized by a substantial population of mobile pastoralists that had been largely displaced by the time of the Iron II.[80] Regardless of the precise timing of the transition, the trend toward farming the hill country was certainly well under way during the first century of the Iron I.

In Genesis, the pastoralist assumptions of the ancestor tales are woven deeply into the narrative fabric and reflect a confident separation of this mode of subsistence from practices current at the time of writing. The point is not that such pastoralism ceased to exist in later periods, and even during the Iron II period herding groups from the eastern interior would have offered a constant reference point for how Israel's ancestral practice was conceived. The point is rather that Genesis presents Israel's ancestors as living according to an old custom that no longer characterized Israel as a group, and that the Iron I marks the archaeological definition of the transition.

Here, it is necessary to return to the question of dates. In drawing these

---

79. For specific information on settlement patterns through time, see Israel Finkelstein, *The Archaeology of the Israelite Settlement* (Jerusalem: Israel Exploration Society, 1988), esp. 185-87. On the shift toward small-scale farming on plots adjacent to village settlements, see Elizabeth Bloch-Smith and Beth Alpert Nakhai, "A Landscape Come to Life: The Iron Age I," *NEA* 62 (1999): 74-5. Lawrence E. Stager links the new phase of hill-country agriculture to the first use of terracing in this region; "The Archaeology of the Family in Ancient Israel," *BASOR* 260 (1985): 5.

80. Finkelstein, 193.

specific links between Genesis and the tribespeople attested at Mari, what am I saying about the ancestral stories? Why not date both the pastoralist way of living and the Syrian ancestry to the early Iron I period, when the first transition occurs? After all, Genesis has always offered an alternative to the distant Bronze Age that is also geographically ready at hand: the Arameans of Iron Age Syria. The travels of both Abraham's servant and then Jacob are defined in terms of "Aram," the name for Syria during the later Iron Age.[81] Deuteronomy 26:5 says, "my father was a perishing Aramean," so why should we not take this in literal ethnic terms?[82] Or, if the component of Israel with a Syrian heritage did not consist of actual Aramean tribes, could we not imagine Iron I peoples of similar character?

At one level, the second possibility is exactly what I am suggesting: that Israelites who settled the north-central hill country during the Iron I period carried with them the tradition of Syrian origins. Whatever the basis for this Syrian connection, a solution to the Genesis tradition that regards these as actual Aramean tribespeople is awkward on its own terms. It is difficult to locate any significant movements of Arameans into southern Syria, and supposedly into Palestine, before the 12th century. We do not have adequate evidence for the early stages of these migrations, but inscriptions from the Aramaic kingdoms established by the start of the 1st millennium indicate that the language of the Arameans generally survived the moves. For example, the southernmost Aramean kingdom was Damascus, which left us Aramaic texts for this period. This linguistic pattern does not fit Israel, whose Hebrew is more like the dialects of the Transjordan, regardless of how it may have been related to late-2nd-millennium Canaanite. Moreover, the biblical use of the regional term "Aram" seems to derive from its specific identification with the Damascus state, the only Aramean state to be identified regularly by the broad tribal name.[83] The Damascus usage would be at home especially in the

81. Aram Naharayim (Gen. 24:10); Paddan Aram (25:20; 28:2, 5, 6, 7; 31:18; 33:18; 35:9, 26; 46:15); Aramean (25:20; 28:5; 31:20, 24). This is the solution of de Pury in *Le Pentateuque en question*, 269-70. André Lemaire has suggested that the Aramean movements that contributed to the Israelite tribal population were launched in the 13th century, after the breakup of Mitanni; "La Haute Mésopotamie et l'origine des Benê Jacob," *VT* 34 (1984): 95-101.

82. In fact, recent scholars have identified this phrase as a loose definition of Israel's ancestors as poor foreigners from the interior. See esp. J. Gerald Janzen, "The 'Wandering Aramean' Reconsidered," *VT* 44 (1994): 359-75. Most recently, note Felice Israel, "L'Arameo errante e le origini di Israele," in *The World of the Aramaeans* 1, ed. P. M. Michèle Daviau et al. (Sheffield: Sheffield Academic, 2001), 275-87.

83. P.-E. Dion, *Les araméens à l'âge du Fer: histoire politique et structures sociales*. EBib N.S. 34 (Paris: Lecoffre, 1997), 171, based on the use of "Aram" in the Zakkur inscription and in the biblical books of Kings. The Assyrian annals use the general term "Aramean" from the 11th

9th-8th centuries, also quite distant in time from the peoples who settled the Israelite hill country in the early Iron I period. In the end, the mere use of the name "Aram" in Genesis cannot be regarded as any more likely to express a specific tribal memory than any other details from the book, and it must be evaluated on its merits. If Aram itself is the defining category, rather than the names of earlier tribes from this stock, its use is not attested until the middle of the Iron I, too late to explain the wave of hill-country settlers in Israel.[84] The contrasting linguistic families of Hebrew and Aramaic represent a stubborn barrier to any hypothesis of kinship from this period. In any case, a Syrian element to Israelite origins must go back farther in time, Aramean or not. The Mari archives show us specific connections between traditions preserved in the Genesis ancestor stories and details from the life of tribal peoples from pre-Aramean Syria. This evidence leads us even further away from identifying the Genesis ancestors with the Aramean tribes.

None of this logic indicates exactly how far back the Syrian heritage might go. In the book of Genesis itself, the full picture is ambiguous. With the exception of one direct reference to 400 years in Egypt (Gen. 15:13-16), most of the stories of Abraham, Isaac, and Jacob unfold without reference to a sojourn away from the land of Canaan. Nothing reveals how long it will take for these ancestral families to grow into the tribes of Israel and their neighbors. Some distance in time is indicated by the portrayal of Jacob's sons as a single household, living and working together, not distributed to their eventual tribal territories. Jacob's story incorporates into it the story of Joseph, which does anticipate the long stay in Egypt.

The Mari connections presented in this article offer some concrete controls for evaluating the chronology of the tradition of Syrian origins. A tribal people in Iron Age Palestine who include a tribe named Benjamin, and whose ancestor lore includes special association with Harran, betray an ultimate affiliation with tribal groups from centuries earlier. This evidence does not date either the first arrival of such Syrian ancestors in Palestine or the biblical stories about them to the Bronze Age. Rather, it suggests that the tribal *background* of those who carried the Syrian tradition reaches back even to the Middle Bronze II period. The historical anchor provided by the Mari evidence helps resolve the tribal identity of the Syrian ancestors, not the date of their arrival. Whether these groups first encountered the south in the heart of

---

through the mid-9th centuries, when they switch to naming the Aramean kingdoms by the phrase "house of X" (226-27). This early Assyrian usage is not likely to have affected biblical terminology.

84. The first definite occurrence of the name is found in the annals of the Assyrian king Tiglath-pileser I, at the very end of the 12th century (Dion, 16).

the Bronze Age, as the Joseph story seems to require, or they entered the land only in the early Iron I, the Mari connections move their ancient origins back in time before the Aramean migrations. According to the genealogical schema of Genesis, these roots are shared by the Transjordan peoples of Edom, Moab, and Ammon, so that Israel's Syrian ancestry becomes the basis for defining a strong identification with the eastern interior, a region characterized by the abiding predominance of pastoralist subsistence.

How could the Bible have preserved any memory of this ancient past, if the texts as we have them were composed in the Iron Age, probably in the early 1st millennium? Our Mari evidence suggests that certain tribal traits could be carried across time imbedded in ongoing social or political institutions that kept a place for them. The name Benjamin survived through attachment to an individual group of tribespeople with Yaminite origin, even after the larger category was forgotten. It seems that the idea of a north Syrian homeland could not be shaken from this tribal tradition of foreign roots, and for the Israelites of Binu Yamina background, the homeland was identified with Harran. Scattered tribal peoples may have maintained an association with distant urban centers when they represented points of assembly. These were particularly important when they were associated with ancestral burial monuments that helped maintain the ideologies of tribal identity.[85] During the reign of Zimri-Lim, the great annual festival of Eshtar may reflect a similar capacity to remember a distant tribal gathering point. The Mari king celebrated this feast by gathering all of his vassals and tribespeople to a local town called Der, which had been named after a city far to the north and west, near the Balikh River. The original Der may have been an ancient meeting place for the Sim'alite tribespeople, perhaps associated with their ancestors.[86] We know that Harran was a point of Yaminite assembly, though we do not know enough about its larger tribal associations.[87]

It is no bad thing that the Mari comparisons suggested in this article perhaps raise as many questions as they answer. Their importance should lie in the directions they indicate for future research. It should not be surprising that Israel's background included both tribal and pastoralist aspects, but we

---

85. See Porter, 431-37, on the role of the "White Monument" in the urban center of Tell Banat, a 3rd-millennium city on the Euphrates River in northern Syria.

86. Jean-Marie Durand, "Les rituels de Marin," in Durand and Guichard, *FM* III (1997): 33-39. The feast of Eshtar included the participation of the ancestors, and one wonders whether the distant city of Der was associated with a collective burial site of the sort represented by the White Monument at Tell Banat.

87. Zimri-Lim's Eshtar festival at Der required the presence of all his vassals, so that they could reiterate their loyalty to the king; Durand and Guichard, *FM* III, 39.

should reach farther back in time than the moment of change that arrived with the wave of new settlement in Israel's Iron I Age. We need to understand better the interactions between the lowlands and the interior, northern and southern Syria-Palestine, cultivation and pastoralism through the whole Middle and Late Bronze Ages. If Israel's intimate connection with Canaan was once underestimated, current interpretive trends now underestimate Israel's relationship to the interior. The Mesopotamian word "Amorite" is terribly inadequate to describe the variety of West Semitic speakers, pastoralist or not, migrating or not, who inhabited ancient Syria during this period. As for the book of Genesis, it has been too quickly removed from the body of evidence that could throw light on Israel's particular heritage in this early social environment. The work of past generations has been rightly criticized, but it is time to return with new questions and fresh external comparisons. For this effort, expertise in the texts of Bronze Age Syria, as well as in the archaeology of this period, will be very much in need.

Multiple-Month Ritual Calendars in the West Semitic World: Emar 446 and Leviticus 23

RICHARD S. HESS

Biblical Cultic Calendars

From the time of Julius Wellhausen, the fixing of the priestly material as postexilic has been axiomatic in biblical scholarship. Yehezkel Kaufmann challenged this proposition, and scholars who followed him have attacked the foundations of an exilic or postexilic date with particular attention to the vocabulary used in the texts.[1] Similar analysis has led to further questioning of the long-accepted assumption that the priestly editor was responsible for in-

---

[1]. Yehezkel Kaufmann, *The Religion of Israel: From Its Beginnings to the Babylonian Exile*, trans. and abridged by Moshe Greenberg (Chicago: University of Chicago Press, 1960); Avi Hurvitz, *A Linguistic Study of the Relationship between the Priestly Source and the Book of Ezekiel* (Paris: Gabalda, 1982); "Dating the Priestly Source in Light of the History Study of Biblical Hebrew a Century after Wellhausen," *ZAW* 100 (Supplement): 88-100; Menahem Haran, *Temples and Temple-Service in Ancient Israel* (1978; repr. Winona Lake: Eisenbrauns, 1995); Jacob Milgrom, *Leviticus 1–16*. AB 3 (New York: Doubleday, 1991), 3-35. A challenge to this tendency came from Joseph Blenkinsopp, "An Assessment of the Alleged Pre-Exilic Date of the Priestly Material in the Pentateuch," *ZAW* 108 (1996): 495-518. This has been addressed in terms of the priestly narratives and the priestly law. For the former, see Gordon J. Wenham, "The Priority of P," *VT* 49 (1999): 240-58, who contends that the priestly material in Genesis can stand on its own, while the J material, which normally envelops it, cannot. For the latter, see Milgrom, "The Antiquity of the Priestly Source: A Reply to Joseph Blenkinsopp," *ZAW* 111 (1999): 10-22; *Leviticus 17–22*. AB 3A (New York: Doubleday, 2000), 1327-64; Hurvitz, "Once Again: The Linguistic Profile of the Priestly Material in the Pentateuch and Its Historical Age: A Response to J. Blenkinsopp," *ZAW* 112 (2000): 180-91. These cite multiple sanctuaries and the absence of a ban on intermarriage, as well as linguistic arguments, for dating the priestly source to the time of Classical Hebrew, i.e., before the exile.

corporating the bulk of the material in the Holiness legal collection of Leviticus 17–26. In particular, Israel Knohl's linguistic study challenged this assumption.[2] The Holiness editor is thought to have followed the priestly figures and to have edited the commonly called Holiness Code into the present collection.

A focal point for this discussion has been the cultic calendars, due to their obvious similarity of content with each other and yet at the same time clear evidence of development and change. Examples of these are preserved in Exodus 23 and 34; Leviticus 23; Numbers 28–29; and Deuteronomy 16. Those of Leviticus and Numbers, thought to have derived from the priestly sources, have been analyzed in terms of vocabulary and style. Recent works of Knohl and Jacob Milgrom have turned around the presumed sequence in which the Holiness source of Leviticus 23 was thought to precede the fuller and more complete priestly description of the festivals in Numbers 28–29. More than any other argument, Milgrom in particular has maintained that the calendar from Numbers must be logically prior because it explicitly details the contents of the sacrifices for the special events, whereas Leviticus 23 presumes them; that is, for Yom Kippur and for the Feast of Booths there is no information as to what the *'iššeh* "food gifts" should consist of in Leviticus 23 (vv. 27 and 36), but the text in Numbers (29:7-38) is explicit.[3] Thus, unless Leviticus 23 allowed for personal preference in what constituted the offerings for these days, it must have presumed another text, such as the priestly calendar of Numbers.

While there has been a growing sense that the legal material of the Holiness Code preserves earlier material of great antiquity, comparative analogies have been lacking and the question of where original legal sources end and editorial redaction begins has continued to be debated. The absence of comparative materials has been ameliorated by study of the Hittite rituals and the comparative legal collections from Anatolia as well as Mesopotamia.[4] Unfortunately, the dominant role of the king and royal family, at times to the exclusion of the populace, compromises the similarities to the biblical priestly traditions.

---

2. Israel Knohl, *The Sanctuary of Silence: The Priestly Torah and the Holiness School* (Minneapolis: Fortress, 1995). An important part of the linguistic evidence for his conclusions is available only in the first chapter of the earlier Hebrew volume by the same name (Jerusalem: Magnes, 1992). I thank Dr. Jeffrey Tigay for directing me to this earlier source.

3. See Milgrom, *ZAW* 111 (1999): 10-22; *Leviticus 17–22*, 1350. His translation of *'iššeh* as "food gifts" is followed here.

4. David P. Wright, *The Disposal of Impurity: Elimination Rites in the Bible and in Hittite and Mesopotamian Literature.* SBLDS 101 (Atlanta: Scholars, 1987); David T. Stewart, "A Brief Comparison of the Israelite and Hittite Festival Calendars," in Jacob Milgrom, *Leviticus 23–27.* AB 3B (New York: Doubleday, 2001), 2076-80.

Closer to the discussion are the cultic texts recovered from the 13th-century B.C.E. West Semitic city of Emar in northern Syria. In particular, Daniel E. Fleming's studies of the relationship between these texts and the priestly literature of Israel have provided many fruitful insights into the ancient West Semitic cultic world.[5] Unlike the Hittite literature, the king and royal family have no dominant roles in many of the Emar cultic texts. This provides a similarity with the biblical material.

This essay will consider a text discovered and published from the city of Emar. It will identify and examine the form and contents of this text as a cultic calendar that describes six months of rituals relative to Emar. The results will be compared with biblical calendars, especially Leviticus 23. The purpose of this study is to consider the nature of some of the similarities between multimonth West Semitic calendars, particularly those that may address assumptions about priestly editors and their insertions and revisions. These similarities of form and content will not demonstrate an early date for the biblical text, nor will they disprove later editorial work. Instead, they will add evidence to an alternative understanding of Leviticus 23; one in which the origins of the text and the development of its constituent elements may be described in ways other than those customarily suggested.

Emar 446

Physical Description

The tablet on which the ritual text of Emar 446 appears suffers from damage that renders one of the four columns unreadable and much of the rest of it difficult to interpret at best. The writing of the text itself appears to be older than many of the other tablets.[6] Indeed, this text and another (text A of the annual *zukru* festival) exhibit archaic features that justifiably date their composition into the 14th century, before the imperial political and cultural pene-

---

5. Gerald A. Klingbeil, *A Comparative Study of the Ritual of Ordination as Found in Leviticus 8 and Emar 369: Ritual Times, Space, Objects and Action* (Lewiston: Edwin Mellen, 1998); "The Anointing of Aaron: A Study of Leviticus 8:12 in Its OT and ANE Context," *AUSS* 38 (2000): 231-43; Daniel E. Fleming, *The Installation of Baal's High Priestess at Emar: A Window on Ancient Syrian Religion.* HSS 42 (Atlanta: Scholars, 1992); "More Help from Syria: Introducing Emar to Biblical Study," *BA* 58 (1995): 139-47; "The Biblical Tradition of Anointing Priests," *JBL* 117 (1998): 401-14.

6. Daniel E. Fleming, *Time at Emar: The Cultic Calendar and the Rituals from the Diviner's Archive* (Winona Lake: Eisenbrauns, 2000), 45 n. 115, 109-13.

tration of the Emar region by the Hittites. Thus Emar 446 preserves ancient forms and practices of a West Semitic people (not unlike Israel) without the cultural coloring of the later Anatolian incursions.

Although Daniel Arnaud's study provided an important first step in the initial publication of the text along with transliteration and translation, Fleming's new edition, as well as his discussion of it, form the basis for the following description.[7] The text is unique in the cuneiform world insofar as it presents a collection of rituals that occur over a period of more than one month — indeed, a period of more than one season.

Contents and Purpose

Emar 446 has rites for six months of the year, most likely beginning in the autumn and ending in the spring. The contents of festivals, described in greater detail in other texts, are compressed here. This leads to the supposition that Emar 446 is a collection of administrative notes.[8] The structure is fluid and unpredictable. There is no line division between the first two months, but it occurs with all the other months. The second month begins in the midst of column III, and the remaining four months are all found on column IV. This is a key contribution of Fleming's study, as it overturns earlier interpretations that placed several months into the breaks in column II of the text.

At Emar, both the shorter *zukru* text and Emar 446 position the key ritual events during the full moon of the month SAG.MU/Zarati,[9] the first month in the autumn.[10] Emar 446 is not exhaustive in its description of rituals at Emar, nor does it preclude the celebration of other rites associated with the

---

7. Fleming, *Time at Emar,* 143-73 (analysis), 264-76 (edition, translation, and notes), 297-300 (collations). The primary text is Meskene 74280a with the additional fragment, 74291. The original publication may be found in Daniel Arnaud, *Recherches au pays d'Aštata Emar 6/2: Textes Sumériens et Accadiens.* Synthèse 18 (Paris: Éditions Recherche sur les Civilisations, 1985), 588-90 (copy); *Recherches au pays d'Aštata Emar 6/3: Textes Sumériens et Accadiens.* Synthèse 18 (Paris: Éditions Recherche sur les Civilisations, 1986), 420-25 (transliteration and translation). I express gratitude for the kindness of Daniel E. Fleming in allowing me to view his manuscript before its publication and for opportunities to discuss this study with him.

8. Fleming, *Time at Emar,* 145.

9. The tablets from Emar are written syllabically in Akkadian with several word-signs that are represented by their Sumerian readings in small capitals.

10. Fleming, *Time at Emar,* 160, refers to the full moon of this month as "the crown of Emar's ritual calendar in the diviner's archive." He also notes that "Similar clustering of rituals at one time and in close proximity must have occurred at Ḫattuša during the spring and autumn axes of the cult year."

months named. Although the first month contains by far the most detailed description of rituals, the second month and the sixth month on the list have an equal length of about 24 lines each for the next most detailed discussions of rites. The third, fourth, and fifth months are all briefer, at six, three, and ten lines respectively. Thus the rites of the autumn and spring months are the most detailed and provide the two most important times for ritual activity on this calendar. As in the rites of the Hittites, the spring and autumn "axes" form poles around which many rituals cluster.

In light of the writing on the tablet, it may be assumed that the scribe did not run out of room and let this control its organization. Even though it may have originated as a set of notes kept by the ritual specialist for the occasions, the text indicates something of the intended emphasis on rituals and their focus and detail in specific months.

Form and Structure

There is a single line at the beginning that is broken. However, it appears to provide a heading that indicates the purpose of the tablet and associates the rituals with the city (URU.KI).

Although only in column IV are the months divided by lines, each of the six major sections begins with the name of the month. With one exception, this is immediately followed by the first day of that month in which a ritual is recorded. Only the third month, at the beginning of column IV, omits the number of the day on which the first ritual should be performed. In fact, there are no days specified or any temporal referents in the sacrifices of this month, unlike every other month listed. Elsewhere, the text always provides the preposition, *i-na*, followed by the word or logogram for day, u_4-*mi* or U_4, and the number of the day (see lines 1, 58, 83, 86, and 96).[11] Because the day listed is never the first day (8, 17, 7, 14, 2), it may be that the third month does not begin like the others because the ritual concerned is assumed to take place on the first day of that month. Fleming, however, suggests that this absence of noting specific days means that the rites could have taken place at various times during the month.[12]

For each of the months (other than the third month already noted), there is more than one day mentioned during which rituals take place. The

---

11. For the last month, [d]*Ḫalma*, in line 96, the number of the day precedes the preposition plus "day" sequence.

12. Fleming, *Time at Emar*, 162.

days are listed in temporal sequence. In a number of cases multiple rites take place, and this is noted by the expression *i-na* U$_4$ *šu-wa-tu-ma* (lines 18, 22, 106). Sometimes, as in the case of the first month, further divisions within a day are noted, whether evening (lines 47 and 54) or morning (line 98).

Within this temporal and apparently sequential framework there are a variety of ritual activities. These include details about the procession of deities, offerings given to them, people who give and others who receive the offerings, and other ritual activities. The details about offerings include what is given, how it is prepared, and the deities to whom it is given.

In Emar 446, some 13 individual deities or clusters of deities are described as having a feast day(s) during the six months and as processing in some way. In the first month the god Shaggar, the god of the *zukru* full moon, helps to prepare draft animals for their work. This figure, especially when compared with other lunar deities, may be associated with both the cattle (their horns reflecting the crescent of the moon) and the moon itself.[13]

The first god to receive offerings is Dagan. He is called *be-el* NUMEN.MEŠ, "Lord of the Seed" (line 50). As part of the rite, the officiant, the diviner, NUMEN.MEŠ *i-na ki na-di*, "throws down seed onto the ground" (line 51). Thus Dagan has an association with grain. This is the only ritual calendar at Emar that contains clear agricultural allusions and that specifically deals with the grain. In this sense it contrasts with the important ritual text from Ugarit that describes rituals regarding the grape harvest.[14]

Among the deities mentioned in Emar 446, the storm-god of Canaan is the last (lines 107-117). This would place the ritual for the storm-god of Canaan in the spring. The offering includes an ox and six sheep. Afterwards, it seems that at least the hides, intestines, and fat belong to the diviner and the king receives the kidneys. The sacrifice and the distribution are identical to those given to the storm-god during the ritual installing the NIN.DINGIR priestess.[15]

Leviticus 23

In the pre-Hellenistic West Semitic world the only other known attestations of ritual calendars that cover multiple months are found in the legal and

---

13. *Time at Emar*, 155-57.

14. Fleming, *Time at Emar*, 228. Baruch A. Levine and Jean-Michel de Tarragon, "The King Proclaims the Day: Ugaritic Rites for the Vintage (KTU 1.41//1.87)," *RB* 100 (1993): 76-115; Fleming, *Time at Emar*, 160 n. 87.

15. Fleming, *The Installation of Baal's High Priestess at Emar*, 108.

cultic texts of the Pentateuch and in Ezekiel.[16] Various forms of the calendar appear in Exod. 23:14-19; 34:18-26; Leviticus 23; Numbers 28–29; and Deut. 16:1-17. All of these mention three major periods of festivals: the spring rites associated with Passover in the month of Abib, also designated as Nisan; the Feast of Weeks, the wheat harvest, about two months later; and the autumn rituals associated with Yom Kippur and the Feast of Booths. All five of these biblical calendars mention these three periods. However, only one specifically dates the three, either by a month name, or by their relationship to an earlier month. The following omit a means of dating the second ritual period, the feast of the wheat harvest: Exod. 23:14-19; 34:18-26; and Numbers 28–29. Deut. 16:1-17 omits a time reference to the autumn rituals. Leviticus 23 includes some means of dating all three ritual periods, either according to the name of the month on which it falls, or by reference to a specific period of time from an earlier ritual. It provides a suitable example of a biblical ritual calendar for comparison with the ritual calendar found in Emar 446.[17] Further, its listing of offerings throughout the holy year, in this sense similar to Numbers 28–29,[18] parallels the concern of Emar 446 with the specific offerings prescribed for each festival. Indeed, Numbers 28–29 provides much more detail as to the sacrifices for each day. However, it omits other rituals, such as the need to live in huts during the Feast of Tabernacles. Further, it does not specify the date for the Feast of Weeks. As will be seen, there are a number of similarities between Leviticus 23 and the Emar text.

The rituals mentioned in Ezek. 45:18-25 also deserve note. Rites in the first and seventh months occur so that only two periods appear. The text is

16. There is a possibility that two cultic calendars from Ugarit continue events into a second month. KTU 1.41 appears to recapitulate the same month in lines 33-49 with new rituals on different days. Line 49, listing a sacrifice on a "new moon," may be an "afterthought" that returns again to the month already discussed. See Levine and de Tarragon, 88. KTU 1.119 has a clear discussion of the rituals of one month on the recto of the tablet. The beginning of the verso is missing but picks up with the numbering of days at the beginning of a month. Nicolas Wyatt, *Religious Texts from Ugarit: The Words of Ilimilku and His Colleagues*. Biblical Seminar 53 (Sheffield: Sheffield Academic, 1998), 420, identifies the verso as beginning with a month other than that on the recto. Dennis Pardee, "2. Prayers: Ugaritic Prayer for a City under Siege (1.88) (RS 24.266)," in *COS* 1:283-85, is not so sure and leaves the matter undecided.

17. Important comparisons may also be drawn between the feasts described in Leviticus 23 and other Emar ritual texts, esp. the description of the *zukru* festival. See Daniel E. Fleming, "The Israelite Festival Calendar and Emar's Ritual Archive," *RB* 106 (1999): 8-34. The parallels suggested there should complement the ones identified in the comparison with Emar 446.

18. Baruch A. Levine, *Leviticus*. JPS Torah Commentary (Philadelphia: Jewish Publication Society, 1989), 153. The greater detail on offerings in Numbers 28-29 leads Gordon J. Wenham to suggest that Leviticus is written for the laity while the Numbers calendar focuses on the priests; *The Book of Leviticus*. NICOT (Grand Rapids: Wm. B. Eerdmans, 1979), 300.

derivative from pentateuchal materials.[19] The focus is almost entirely on the Passover of the first month, with a brief note added in v. 25 that mentions the autumn feasts as another set during which the prince must present specific offerings. This focus on the prince, found in half of the calendar (vv. 22-25), is opposite to that of the Emar text where there is no emphasis whatsoever on the king or the royalty. Again, Leviticus 23 appears to be closer to the Emar ritual text.

After examining the cultic calendar of Leviticus 23 in comparison with the other cultic calendars in the Hebrew Bible, the immediate literary context of the annual festival calendar should also be considered. It is preceded and followed by festival matters. The titular aspect of Lev. 23:4 makes it clear that the annual calendar preserves a distinct identity within the larger cultic context.[20] While it is possible, as Milgrom contends,[21] that parts of vv. 1-3 on the Sabbath and vv. 39-43 on the Feast of Booths may constitute an exilic addition enveloping the whole calendar with celebrations that do not require a sanctuary, it is also arguable that these texts have their own literary function. Verses 1-3 introduce the Sabbath, occurring weekly. Verses 4-44 discuss the annual festivals. Leviticus 25 turns to consider the Sabbatical and Jubilee Years, that appear every seven and 49 years. Thus there is a literary reason for the inclusion of the Sabbath at the beginning of the cultic calendar. It introduces all the special festivals over two chapters, beginning with the most frequent and proceeding to those that occur less often.

Emar 446 and Leviticus 23

There are, of course, many differences between these two texts. As noted, Emar 446 represents a Late Bronze Age document from a polytheistic urban culture. The text itself has no larger literary context and stands alone. It forms

19. Walther Zimmerli, *Ezekiel 2*. Herm (Philadelphia: Fortress, 1983), 480-86.

20. It is perhaps not surprising that both Emar 446 and Lev. 23:4 begin with a title that forms a summary statement of the text. Thus Emar 446: 1, *[tup-pu/i pár-ṣ]i ša* URU.KI "Tablet of the rites of the city" (see Fleming, *Time at Emar*, 267); and Lev. 23:4 (RSV), "These are the appointed feasts of the LORD, the holy convocations, which you shall proclaim at the time appointed for them." The significant point is that the levitical introduction occurs at v. 4, subsequent to the Sabbath command. Thus within the larger concern for weekly, annual, and events every seven years that are to be remembered, the listing of annual feasts receives its own introduction. This sets it apart from the others with an integrity that allows for the text to be compared with Emar 446 apart from the rest of chs. 23 and 25 of Leviticus. For other comparative structural features, see below comparison 4, Division by Months.

21. Milgrom, *Leviticus 23–27*, 2050-52, 2055-56.

what has been described as a set of administrative notes by the diviner, who was an important actor in many of the rituals described.[22] Leviticus 23 is an edited calendar that appears in an Israelite document whose origins and development have been the source of controversy. Nevertheless, both provide an insight into their respective worlds. In the scholarly debate regarding the origins and development of a text such as Leviticus 23, the unique opportunity to examine a similar ritual text from a related West Semitic cultural milieu, however distinct in other background features, may provide insights into the meaning and significance of the form and structure of this biblical text. A comparison between Emar 446 and Leviticus 23 reveals a number of points of similarity that can be divided into three groups: general formal matters, editorial issues, and parallel points of specific content.

General Formal Matters

Third Person Narrative Elements

It is clear that the calendar information found in Leviticus 23 has been presented in its current form as direct speech.[23] This is different from the Emar text as well as other cultic ritual texts from Emar and Ugarit. There the third person dominates in the presentation. However, it may be noted that Leviticus 23 preserves the third person in some of its own narrative. It may be found in at least 17 of the 41 verses that constitute the calendar of Lev. 23:4-44.[24] If Leviticus 23 is addressed to the people of Israel, while Emar 446 has as its purpose a record for an official concerned with performing or supplying the sacrifices, then it is no surprise that there is a difference in person. Nevertheless, the strong presence of third person forms in Leviticus 23 demonstrates the importance of this means of recording West Semitic ritual calendars.[25]

---

22. Fleming, *Time at Emar*, 145.

23. Donn F. Morgan, *The So-Called Cultic Calendars in the Pentateuch: A Morphological and Typological Study* (diss., Claremont Graduate School, 1974), 169, identifies the speech of Yahweh notations as the first and major structuring principle.

24. Vv. 4a, 5, 8b, 9, 11, 13, 14b, 17b, 20, 21b, 23, 26, 27a, 29-30, 33-35a, 37b, 43-44. The remaining cultic calendars in the Pentateuch contain only nine third person references altogether: Exod. 23:15, 17; 34:20; Num. 28:14-15, 17, 28; 29:6; Deut. 16:16.

25. This view contrasts with that of John E. Hartley: "Only a few verses remain completely in the archaic impersonal style (vv. 5, 13, 20, 29, 34)"; *Leviticus*. WBC 4 (Waco: Word, 1992), 372.

Half-Year Survey with Emphasis on Spring and Autumn

Emar 446 appears to include a discussion of rituals that cover a sequence of six months through the year. Although there are seven months inclusive from Nisan until Tishri, the Israelite ritual calendar also reflects this interest in one half of the year. Of course, Emar begins in the autumn and concludes with the spring months, whereas the Israelite calendar begins in the spring and concludes in the autumn. Leaving aside the much debated question as to when the new year in Israel began,[26] the important point for comparison is that the spring and autumn provide the beginning and ending points for both Emar and Israel.

Emphasis on Agriculture and Grain

Both the ritual calendars of Emar and of Leviticus 23 focus on feasts that emphasize grains, whether the planting of them, as at Emar, or their harvest, as found in Israel. At Emar this is clear with respect to Dagan, the first deity to receive offerings in the first month. He is "Lord of the Seed." As the chief deity in the region, his concern for the grain harvest is sought by Emar. In Israel both the Feast of Unleavened Bread in the first month and the Feast of Weeks seven weeks later describe concern for the grains of barley and wheat that form staples of the ancient Israelite's diet. Thus Emar's ritual to prepare for the sowing of the fields in the autumn corresponds to the spring time of Israel with its harvest festivals and focus on the grain in the form of unleavened bread and grain offerings.[27] While Emar's focus on the period of sowing and planting may suggest concern for divine support in guaranteeing the crop of that particular season, Israel's focus on the period of harvesting points in a different direction. It would suggest that Israel recognized the harvest as given by God and emphasized divine ownership of it.

Division by Months

Major structural features invite comparison between these cultic calendars of Emar and Israel. The key junctures are highlighted by the designation of

26. David J. A. Clines, "The Evidence for an Autumnal New Year in Pre-Exilic Israel Reconsidered," *On the Way to the Postmodern: Old Testament Essays, 1967-1998* 1. JSOTSup 292 (Sheffield: Sheffield Academic, 1998), 371-94.

27. Fleming, *Time at Emar*, 158: "Dagan Lord of the Seed represents the fertility needs of the grain fields, the foundation for sustenance." At 159 n. 79 he compares the Gezer calendar in which months 3 and 4 are related to the season of sowing. This would be the autumn.

a new month. In Leviticus 23, this occurs three times, at vv. 5, 15-16, and 24.[28] Verse 5 designates the month as the first month and v. 24 names it as the seventh month. In between, vv. 15-16 include reference to a feast some seven weeks after the previous one. Thus while the first and third major feasts are designated by their relationship to the lunar calendar and the months in which they take place, the second Israelite ritual period is determined by the earlier cultic time. There is no comparable month designation known from Emar 446. Nevertheless, both calendars prefer a designation of the month as the primary means of identifying periods of time within the annual cycle.[29]

28. Of the other pentateuchal cultic calendars, the short forms in Exodus 23 and 34 do not mention the dates of the celebrations. Deuteronomy 16 describes the month, but not the day of the month, for the celebration of Passover (vv. 1-8). It does not name any other month or day of the month for the Feast of Weeks or the Feast of Tabernacles. In Numbers 28-29 there is a consistent formula for the name or number of the month and the day of the month on which the Feasts of Passover and Tabernacles are celebrated. However, neither of these is stipulated for the intervening Feast of Weeks (Num. 28:26). This is unlike Leviticus 23 and Emar 446, but see the discussion on "Diverse Ritual Formulae" below. Further, for the seventh month, every time a new feast is introduced and the first day is defined, the phrase "of the seventh month" is repeated. See Num. 29:1, 7, 12. This parallels Leviticus 23.

29. Within each month, most festivals are designated as beginning on specific days. However, in Emar 446 there are occasions when the particular date within the month is unspecified. For example, in the first month, a festival is described, beginning on line 47, with a time specification that does not give the day of the month, but merely states: *i-na* ITI *šu-wa-tu-ma nu-ba-te* "On an evening during that month. . . ." This nonspecific date may be compared with the famous reference in Lev. 23:11 (also vv. 15 and 16): *mimmāḥărat haššabbāt* (RSV) "On the day after the Sabbath. . . ." Much discussion has arisen as to whether the context suggests that this is the first Saturday after the Feast of Unleavened Bread, or the first day of that Feast, and other possibilities regarding the specific date of the event. For a summary of the four major positions concerning this text, which "gave rise to arguably the most long-lasting schism in the history of the Jewish people," see Milgrom, *Leviticus 23–27*, 2056-63. See also David Hoffmann, *Das Buch Leviticus* (Berlin: M. Poppelauer, 1906), 2:159-215; Klaus Grünwaldt, *Das Heiligkeitsgesetz Leviticus 17–26*. BZAW 271 (Berlin: de Gruyter, 1999), 81-82. Perhaps the waving of the sheaf is intentionally ambiguous to allow for a date as close as possible to the harvest. If so, this would parallel the ambiguity of the Emar text where, despite the custom of specific dating procedures for most feasts, at least one remains open. In support of this last option for Leviticus 23, see Martin Noth, *Leviticus*, rev. ed. OTL (Philadelphia: Westminster, 1977), 170-71; and Erhard S. Gerstenberger, *Leviticus*. OTL (Louisville: Westminster John Knox, 1996), 343, who mentions this as an option but goes on to conclude that the articular use of Sabbath requires one of the other options already mentioned. He opts for the first day of the feast (344).

RICHARD S. HESS

Editorial Issues

Diverse Ritual Formulae

For the first and last months, Leviticus 23 identifies the ritual actions that occur by introducing each one with a phrase that includes the ב preposition, the number of the day, and a reference to the word for month (vv. 5, 6, 24, 27, 34, and 39). This parallels most of the rituals on the Emar calendar, as it does other Akkadian and Ugaritic ritual calendars.[30] In Emar 446 many cultic actions are defined by their position in a given month. The biblical Feast of Weeks that occurs in the middle of the calendar resembles the description of the Emar festivals during the month of Anna. In both cases, these are intermediate, occurring between the major festivals at the beginning and the end of the calendar. In both cases, specifics as to the particular month and day of the month (for Leviticus) and the day of the month (for Emar 446) are missing. It is not clear whether these omissions reflect lesser importance placed upon the intermediate ritual actions or some other reason. However, the phenomenon occurs in the cultic calendars of both Emar and Israel.

Therefore, it seems unlikely that a single standard formula can be identified for introducing calendar festivals. Certainly, suggestions that each of the biblical calendar's lead sentences originally began with the date, the feast's name, the expression "for Yahweh," and additional items do not find support in existing calendars, whether from the Bible or from Emar.[31] In all cases, the structure of leading sentences appears to vary within each calendar, although that for the first and last months appears consistent and dominant. The Emar calendar demonstrates that such variation by itself does not prove a later editorial innovation.

---

30. Morgan, 186. However, it is unlike other pentateuchal ritual calendars, except Numbers 28–29. See the note at the above discussion of "Division by Months."

31. Cf. for Leviticus 23, Henning Graf Reventlow, *Das Heiligkeitsgesetz, formgeschichtlich-untersucht*. WMANT 6 (Neukirchen-Vluyn: Neukirchener, 1961), 105; Alfred Cholewiński, *Heiligkeitsgesetz und Deuteronomium*. AnBib 66 (Rome: Biblical Institute, 1976), 82-83. For the latter author, Lev. 23:4-8, 23-25, and 33-38 form the original layer, while vv. 9-22 and 39-43 are a second layer. For vv. 9-22, of course, this assumption is based upon the idea of a uniform pattern introducing each festival. However, since the Emar calendar does not preserve a regular pattern, it cannot be assumed that this variation forms an adequate basis for distinguishing editorial layers.

Simultaneous, Multiple Rituals during the Autumn Axis Month

In the first month of the Emar calendar, there are numerous rituals. Several of these occur on the 15th day of the month. Lines 8 and 45 identify this day as the one for the rituals that follow and concern first Dagan and then Shaggar. In both cases, images of the deities are brought forth and there are processions. In both cases, sheep are slaughtered (lines 9-10 and 46). Although the deities are different and different details of the rituals appear, their two festivals are related. The first ritual, that of Dagan, is identified with the *zukru* festival of the shorter text, as one in which (1) the gates of the city play an important role, (2) both Dagan and NIN.URTA are involved, (3) the populace participates, and (4) the roles of the king and even the diviner recede into the background.[32] Shaggar is the only lunar deity associated with the *zukru* month, and the 15th day as the day of the full moon is of special importance. In fact, both of the rituals of Dagan and Shaggar may be associated with one another, occurring at the same time and with similar processions, and both having an association or identification with the *zukru* festival of this autumn month.[33]

This repetition of special events on the same day may be compared with the Feast of Booths as described in Leviticus 23. It appears twice, in vv. 34-36 and 39-43. Both descriptions begin by noting the same date, the 15th day of the seventh month. Both levitical descriptions outline a festival with some similarities. There is the common designation, "festival" (Heb. חַג), and both emphasize the first and eighth days as times of rest. However, all the other details are different. The term, "feast of booths" (Heb. חַג הַסֻּכּוֹת), occurs only in v. 34. In v. 39 it is called the "feast of Yahweh" (Heb. חַג־יְהוָה). The first text describes two elements of observance, abstinence from work and the presentation of *'iššeh* or "food gifts" to Yahweh. The second description mentions resting, the gathering of branches, living in booths, and the remembering of Yahweh's deliverance from Egypt. Were it not for other texts, it could be argued that these are two different feasts that occur simultaneously.

Now the practice of recapitulating a particular month is known from Ugaritic text KTU 1.41, where the month includes rituals on the 13th and 14th days (lines 3-45a) followed by ones on the sixth day (lines 45b-48a).[34] Thus it is not true that a ritual text that returns to the same month and reviews additional festivals must reflect an editorial addition. The Emar text goes a step

---

32. Fleming, *Time at Emar*, 153-54.
33. Fleming, *Time at Emar*, 103-4, 155-57.
34. Levine and de Tarragon, 87-93.

farther in its comparison with Leviticus 23. In both of these ritual calendars, the differences in various details are matched by parallel periods of time when the feasts are celebrated, by similar general actions during the holy days, and by an association or even identification of the festivals with one another. What the Emar text suggests is that a second description of a ritual occurring on the same day or days as the first, and positioned soon after the first description in a text, does not by itself necessitate an editorial addition.[35] Instead, this practice is now known and attested in more than one West Semitic ritual calendar.

In light of this, it is worth revisiting Lev. 23:37-38, which is often assumed to be a concluding summary after the discussion of the seventh Israelite month's rituals in vv. 33-36. To this, the additional material on the seventh month is appended in vv. 39-44. It may be that this is an editorial addition as suggested by nearly all commentators.[36] However, there are no definitive reasons for such to be the case, especially in the light of the Emar parallel.[37]

In summary, the Emar and Ugaritic parallels establish precedent for the appearance of an apparently duplicate text side by side with one that goes back over festivals on the same month and even describes the same festival or at least one occurring on the same day.

Diverse Lengths for Ritual Descriptions

Emar 446 describes a number of feasts in its calendar. Some of these are mentioned very briefly, in a single line. For example, the two ceremonies during the month of Adamma each appear on a single line (lines 84-85). Other rituals are longer, such as that on the first month that concerns the deity

---

35. This observation contradicts the view that Lev. 23:39-43 constitutes an addition to vv. 34-36 and that the duplication of various details (such as the same specific days for the celebration) provides the primary evidence for this editorial supplement. See Hartley, 372-73. Levine (Leviticus, 163-64) observes that the biblical text provides two different emphases in terms of content. Vv. 33-38 focus on the public celebration and resemble earlier regulations in Leviticus 23. Vv. 39-44 focus on the family's responsibilities.

36. So Hartley, 372; cf. Noth, 166; Gerstenberger, 348; Milgrom, Leviticus 23–27, 2036. Milgrom follows Hartley in arguing that the similar dating of vv. 35 and 39 demonstrates two independent sources. Yet exactly the same similarity appears in the Emar text. See, however, Mark F. Rooker, Leviticus. NAC 3A (Nashville: Broadman & Holman, 2000), 290.

37. Further, Lev. 23:22 provides evidence of an unexpected note placed at the end of the discussion of the Feast of Weeks (vv. 15-21) and the whole spring/early summer festival cycle (vv. 9-21). Perhaps a similar note is placed after vv. 33-36, this time dealing with sacrifices and offerings for God just as v. 22 dealt with the offerings that would be left for the poor among the people in the ungleaned corners of the harvested fields.

NIN.URTA, occupying at least 19 lines (22-40) and perhaps more, since the text breaks off before it is clear that the rite has ended. The same is true of the rituals described in Leviticus 23. The Feast of Trumpets is described in 19 Hebrew words (vv. 24b-25). However, the Feast of Weeks occupies vv. 10-22 and contains 197 words.[38] Again, the size of a ritual description in such a calendar cannot be used to determine its origin as an editorial addition.[39] Also, like the Feast of Booths, this text contains a duplicate description of the ritual, in vv. 9-14 and again in vv. 15-22.

Parallel Points of Specific Content

The Storm God of Canaan and Yahweh

In the Emar 446 text the ritual for the storm-god of Canaan seems to occur in the early spring (lines 107-110), just as the ritual for the Passover takes place in

---

38. This difference of 178 words between the shortest feast and the longest one has no close parallel in the other four cultic calendars in the Pentateuch. Exodus and Deuteronomy all divide their presentations into the three major festivals. In Exodus 23, the shortest description concerns the Feast of Harvest (Weeks) in v. 16a, with 7 words, while the longest is the Feast of Passover and Unleavened Bread in v. 15, with 17 words. In Exodus 34, most of the calendar (vv. 19-21 and 23-26) is composed of notes that apply to all the festivals or at least to other times of the year. The shortest description concerns the Feast of Ingathering (Tabernacles) in v. 22b, with 4 words, while the longest is the Feast of Unleavened Bread in v. 18, with 18 words. In Deuteronomy 16, the longest is the Feast of Passover and Unleavened Bread in vv. 1-8, with 129 words, while the shortest is the Feast of Tabernacles in vv. 13-15, with 43 words. The Feast of Weeks in vv. 9-12, has 60 words. Numbers 28–29 adds two additional feasts, the Feast of Trumpets in 29:1-6 and the Day of Atonement in 29:7-11. The lengths are shorter than, but not unlike those of the Feast of Passover and Unleavened Bread in 28:16-25 and the Feast of Weeks in 28:26-31. The shortest of these, the Day of Atonement, includes 61 words. This is followed closely by the Feast of Weeks with 63 words and the Feast of Trumpets with 68 words. The Feast of Passover and Unleavened Bread has 112 words. At first glance, the description of the Feast of Tabernacles in Num. 29:12-39 appears to be the longest, with some 280 words. However, vv. 17-38, which detail the offerings from the second to the eighth day, involve a repetition of three verses for each of those days, with the only differences being the number of the day and the number of bulls to be sacrificed on each day. Since this has no parallel in Leviticus 23, Emar 446, or any other cultic calendar in the Bible, it seems that a proper comparison of length would be better served by counting the 28 words that are repeated seven times as 28 words, rather than 196 words. If this is done, the length of the description of the Feast of Tabernacles in Numbers 29 becomes 112 words, far fewer than the 197 words that describe the Feast of Weeks in Lev. 23:10-22. In any case, the structure and style of Numbers 28–29 betray a greater uniformity and regularity than either Emar 446 or Leviticus 23.

39. Hartley, 373.

the spring in Israel (e.g., Lev. 23:5-8). Although little is known about the storm-god of Canaan at Emar, it is clear that this deity has associations at Ugarit and in the Bible with Baal in his roles as warrior and as one who provides for the fertility of the land and the bringing forth of a rich harvest. The biblical Passover's position in the spring also associates the roles of Israel's God with a warrior who fights against Egypt and delivers Israel from there and with the one who has given the harvest and blessings of the land to Israel. The historical element does not occur in the Emar calendar, but the emphasis upon agricultural concerns does.

Dates Determined by the Seasonal Cycle

In light of the farming emphasis in both calendars, it is important to note that this is integrated with specific dates for various festivals. In particular, the 15th day of the first month, in the autumn, includes a festival to Shaggar, who prepares the draft animals for a season of work in the fields:[40]

> 45. *i-na* U$_4$.15 ^{d}ḪAR [*a*]-*na* É GUD.MEŠ *ú-še-ra-du-u*
> 46. *i-ṭa-<ba*(?)*>-ḫu* 1 UDU *a-na* É ANŠE.KUR.RA *i-ṭa-*
> 47. : *ba-ḫu*
> "On the 15th day, they bring Shaggar down to the cattle barn and (perform) sacrifice. They slaughter one sheep at the horse stables."

Shaggar visits both the cattle barn and the horse stables, and sacrifices are performed in both places. Draft work could be performed by both types of animals. This ritual prepares the animals for the plowing and sowing to be done in the coming season. Note, however, that the date is specifically set according to the full moon of the first month. The Emar calendar thereby contradicts the view, expressed regarding Leviticus 23, that such fixation of dates renders the calendar independent from an original connection to an agricultural cycle and thus betrays a late development in the evolution of the cultic calendar.[41] To the contrary, both at Emar and in Israel the specific dates correlated, not only with the days during the month, but also with seasonal events.

---

40. For the text and translation, see Fleming, *Time at Emar*, 270-71, and 155, for a similar analysis of the text as that presented here.

41. Gerstenberger, 338.

Passover Origins among Settled Peoples

There are many critical issues surrounding the biblical Passover and its associated Feast of Unleavened Bread, described in Lev. 23:5-8. Since Wellhausen, many scholars have argued that the Passover and the Feast of Unleavened Bread were originally separate rites, the former pastoral and the latter a settled agricultural festival, that were joined during the time of Josiah.[42] Not all have agreed with this reconstruction. Various criticisms have been made regarding aspects of this theory, especially its speculative nature and the consistent connection of the two rites in the Bible, so that the hypothesis is not required.[43] Nevertheless, the transhumant pastoral origins of the Passover has been argued, in no small measure, because the biblical festival uses a lamb roasted with fire and lacks mention of an altar or a priest. A third element, the Maṣṣôt festival of Unleavened Bread, was incorporated by this nomadic people when they settled permanently in Canaan.[44]

Emar 446 describes festivals in which lambs are burnt (line 92; a bird is burnt at line 99),[45] breads of various types are used (lines 21, 51, 78, 105), and there is the absence of an altar or priest. In fact, an altar is never mentioned and a "diviner"[46] appears to function in place of a priest. This is not uncommon for ritual texts at Emar and is a phenomenon that has led some scholars to find in these ritual texts practices that derive from pastoral origins, as well.[47] However, the combination of these elements in a festival celebrated by

---

42. See Julius Wellhausen, *Prolegomena to the History of Ancient Israel* (1885; repr. Gloucester: Peter Smith, 1973), 100-8; Martin Noth, *A History of Pentateuchal Traditions* (1972; repr. Chico: Scholars, 1989), 67-68; Roland de Vaux, *Ancient Israel: Its Life and Institutions* (1961; repr. Grand Rapids: Wm. B. Eerdmans, 1997), 488-92; Brevard S. Childs, *The Book of Exodus*. OTL (Philadelphia: Westminster, 1974), 186-94; Hartley, 378; Bernard M. Levinson, *Deuteronomy and the Hermeneutics of Legal Innovation* (Oxford: Oxford University Press, 1997).

43. B. N. Wambacq, "Les origines de la *Pesaḥ* israélite," *Bib* 57 (1976): 206-24; "Les origines de la *Pesaḥ* israélite (suite et fin)," *Bib* 57 (1976): 301-26; John Van Seters, "The Place of the Yahwist in the History of Passover and Massot," *ZAW* 95 (1983): 167-82; T. Desmond Alexander, "The Passover Sacrifice," in *Sacrifice in the Bible,* ed. Roger T. Beckwith and Martin J. Selman (Grand Rapids: Baker, 1995), 1-24; J. Gordon McConville, "Deuteronomy's Unification of Passover and Maṣṣôt: A Response to Bernard M. Levinson," *JBL* 119 (2000): 47-58. See now Levinson's response to the latter, "The Hermeneutics of Tradition in Deuteronomy: A Reply to J. G. McConville," *JBL* 119 (2000): 269-86.

44. See the review of this view in Milgrom, *Leviticus 23–27*, 1972.

45. Similar to the offerings of fire in Leviticus 23, there is no precise statement as to how these offerings are burnt. See Levine, *Leviticus,* 157.

46. LÚ MÁŠ.ŠU.GÍD.GÍD.

47. Cf. esp. the *zukru* festival as discussed by Fleming, *The Installation of Baal's High Priestess at Emar,* 229-55; *BA* 58 (1995): 139-47 (esp. 144-45).

a settled West Semitic people in the Late Bronze Age raises additional questions about the degree of certainty that can be ascribed to the posited evolutionary development of the biblical festival.[48]

The Major Grain Festivals and the Attendant Ritual

The Feast of the Firstfruits appears in Lev. 23:9-22. As already noted, it is described twice. The first description, in vv. 9-14, is of special interest and may be quoted in full (RSV):

9 And the LORD said to Moses,

10 "Say to the people of Israel, When you come into the land which I give you and reap its harvest, you shall bring the sheaf of the first fruits of your harvest to the **priest**;

11 and he shall **wave the sheaf before the LORD**, that you may find acceptance; on the morrow after the sabbath the priest shall wave it.

12 And on the day when you wave the sheaf, you shall offer a male **lamb** a year old without blemish as a burnt offering to the LORD.

13 And the cereal offering with it shall be two tenths of an ephah of fine **flour** mixed with oil, to be offered by fire to the LORD, a pleasing odor; and the drink offering with it shall be of **wine**, a fourth of a hin.

14 And you shall **eat neither bread nor grain parched or fresh** until this same day, **until you have brought the offering of your God**: it is a statute for ever throughout your generations in all your dwellings."

The actions and components described in this festival include: (1) the priest waves a sheaf of grain before the Lord; (2) a lamb, grain (= flour), and wine are offered to the Lord; and (3) the warning that the harvest must not be consumed until the offering is made.

Compare this with the concluding lines for one of the key festivals described on the first month in Emar 446 lines 50-57. The offerings are for Dagan, chief deity in the region and here described as "Lord of the Seed" (*be-el* NUMEN.MEŠ). They take place before the planting of the seed and concern its success, just as the Feast of the Firstfruits takes place before consuming the

---

48. Milgrom (*Leviticus 23–27*, 1972) already observed, in light of the one-day preparatory rites before both the Emar *zukru* festival of seven days and the seven-day installation of the high priest, that the *pesaḥ* and *maṣṣôt* festivals "could always have been conjoined." The evidence presented here add to this conclusion.

grain harvest. Like the waving of the sheaf in Israel, in Emar there is also an initial rite involving the cult leader and grain. In this case the diviner throws seed onto the ground (line 51, LÚ MÁŠ ŠU.GÍD.GÍD. *i-na* KI *i-na-di*). Mutton, bread, and drink are involved in the rite (lines 51b-52, NINDA *x iš-tu* É DINGIR (?) *ka₄-sà-tu₄* UZU ZAG GAB). Some of this is offered to Dagan, though the text is broken here. Finally, the ritual concludes with a warning that the planting of grain must not begin until these sacrifices are performed (lines 56b-57, *a-di ku-ba-di₄ ú-ga-ma-ru ma-am-ma e-ri-ši ú-ul u-si*).

Although these festivals concern two different seasons, they both focus on grain. They both begin with a ritual involving that grain, whether throwing it on the ground, a rite clearly associated with sowing,[49] or waving a sheaf of the harvest — unusual, if not unique, ritual actions. They both involve mutton, drink, and bread. They both conclude with a warning not to proceed to the next stage, whether planting the seed or eating the harvest, until the ritual is completed.

It seems unlikely that the similarities are merely coincidental. Rather, this event betrays a common heritage related to the planting and harvesting of the basic food that formed the staple for the diet of West Semitic peoples. The chief deity, also the deity responsible for the food, was called upon to acknowledge it and to bless it, whether at the planting in the beginning of the season or at the final harvest, after the barley and wheat were gathered in.

The key importance of this rite may provide the reason for its central position in the descriptions of the grain festivals of Unleavened Bread and Feast of Weeks in Leviticus 23. The Feast of Unleavened Bread is described in vv. 5-8 and the Feast of Weeks is described in great detail in vv. 15-22. Both of these feasts begin with a clear statement of the time of the year when they are to take place. In between, in vv. 9-14, there appears the ritual for the harvest just described. Due to the emphasis upon the first and eighth days in both accounts, its specific dating that ties together the preceding and the following feasts (vv. 11, 15) leaves open the possibility that this feast had a more general significance that applied to both harvests.

In any case, the similarity of the ritual performances in both calendars, the association with the chief deity, the correlation with one of the key events of the production of the major food source (whether planting or harvesting),

---

49. Fleming, *Time at Emar,* 158: "These offerings are also the occasion for a unique sowing rite that is probably mentioned only because it was performed by the diviner. He scatters seed, a procedure that could hardly portray the act of planting more directly. Although such a rite seems entirely natural in association with the planting season, it is not widely attested." See Lucian Turkowski, "Peasant Agriculture in the Judaean Hills," *PEQ* 101 (1969): 32-33, for this as one of two means of sowing seed in the ground.

and the tie with the first month of festivals described in each calendar all emphasize both the critical role of this event and a form of ritual that persisted in Israelite and West Semitic cultic performance for centuries.

Conclusion

It is important to recognize that the cultic calendars of Leviticus 23 and Emar 446 reflect many differences that describe and define the distinct cultural contexts in which they were produced. However, these two ritual texts also share important features in terms of the period of time they cover, the nature of some of their rites, various structures, and specific rituals. Although the Emar text can be securely dated, the traditions behind the cultic calendar of Leviticus have been the source of much discussion. Attempts to place the development of this calendar late in the sequence of biblical cultic calendars need to be reconsidered in the light of similarities between Leviticus 23 and the Late Bronze Age text.[50] In particular, many assumptions about editorial additions and various exilic and later redactions can no longer be advanced solely on the basis of that which appears odd or repetitive to the modern reader.

In light of the Emar parallels, some of the distinctive developments of Leviticus 23 may have sources outside those of the earlier biblical calendars, sources that preserve ancient traditions and structures.[51] The discovery of Emar 446 and its initial comparison with a similar literary form in the Hebrew Bible provide a new context for multiple-month cultic calendars of the West Semitic world.

Given the similarities between Emar 446 and Leviticus 23, the differences in structure and style with the other cultic calendars of the Pentateuch, and the fact that multimonth cultic calendars remain a rare occurrence, little separates the Emar and Leviticus calendars from one another. They remain similar in many features of form, structure, and content, despite the distinct

---

50. For the traditional scholarly assignment of a later exilic/postexilic date for the distinctive features of Leviticus 23 (and the similar Numbers 28–29), cf. e.g., Levine, 263-68.

51. On the basis of parallels with the Emar texts, Daniel E. Fleming, "A Break in the Line: Reconsidering the Bible's Diverse Festival Calendars," *RB* 106 (1999): 161-74, argues that the rituals of Leviticus 23 are not developments from earlier biblical calendars but preserve authentic early practices (Syrian, not 1st-millennium Babylonian; *RB* 106 [1999]: 33-34). He suggests that the differences between Leviticus 23 and other biblical ritual calendars are best understood in terms of regional Israelite centers and competing groups of religious professionals advocating and practicing distinct aspects of the various festivals.

religious worldviews that each embodies. The anomalies that have traditionally been used to justify later redactions now appear to preserve authentic forms that reach back to the Late Bronze Age of West Semitic agrarian and pastoral societies.

Thus these multimonth ritual calendars yield new insights as to the possible origins of many elements of Leviticus 23 that do not necessarily occur in other biblical calendars. The evidence for the antiquity of these elements, as attested in Emar 446, pulls the dating of aspects of the original structure of Leviticus 23 as well as various rituals described in it into an earlier preexilic context. This evidence accords with the conclusions of other recent studies of the priestly material.

The Repopulation of Samaria
(2 Kings 17:24, 27-31) in Light
of Recent Study

K. LAWSON YOUNGER, JR.

The passage in 2 Kings 17 which relates the repopulation of Samaria with Assyrian deportees has presented interpreters with a number of difficulties. Two of the major questions are: Are these deportations the work of one Assyrian king or the work of several? What are the identifications of these people and who are the gods associated with them?[1] While to a certain extent these questions are interrelated, the new publication of two cuneiform contracts from Tel Hadid,[2] as well as some other recent publications, add new information to the discussion.

This is all the more important since the archaeological evidence for the identification of these peoples and their deities is rather meager. In fact, apart from the usual Assyrian clay vessels uncovered in the 7th-century strata, the pottery assemblage displays remarkable continuity with local traditions.[3] Adam Zertal suggests that the so-called wedge-shaped decorated bowl — which may have been influenced by Mesopotamian prototypes and which has

---

1. Not knowing the identities of these deities, the Babylonian Talmud turned to creative etymologies so that all the deities were likened to animals: Succoth-benoth to a chicken, Nergal to a cock, Ashima to a bald buck, Nibhaz and Tartak to a dog and an ass, Adrammelech and Anammelech to a mule and a horse (*Sanh.* 63b). See *The Talmud of Babylonia: An American Translation* 23B: *Tractate Sanhedrin Chapters 4-8*, trans. Jacob Neusner. BJS 84 (Chico: Scholars, 1984), 194-95.

2. Nadav Na'aman and Ran Zadok, "Assyrian Deportations to the Province of Samerina in the Light of Two Cuneiform Tablets from Tel Hadid," *TA* 27 (2000): 159-88.

3. Ephraim Stern, *Archaeology of the Land of the Bible*, 2: *The Assyrian, Babylonian, and Persian Periods, 732-332 BCE.* ABRL (New York: Doubleday, 2001), 51.

been found at 34 hill-country sites located to the north and east of the city of Samaria — was brought by deportees from southern Mesopotamia and should be dated to the 7th century.[4] However, the origin and date of the pottery have not yet been satisfactorily established.[5] Summing up the archaeological evidence Ephraim Stern puts it this way:

> Almost nothing has been uncovered that can be attributed to the countries of the different groups of deportees, who are said to come from the Iranian plateau or Elam. Even in the capital cities of the two Assyrian provinces, only a handful of finds can be attributed to them. This is difficult to understand. In any case, in the present stage of the research, the evidence provided by the written sources is superior to that of the archaeological record concerning the identification of the new ethnic elements that settled in Samaria.[6]

Thus this essay will attempt to synthesize the recent insights gained from the textual evidence in order to suggest a more comprehensive view of the repopulation of Samaria.

The deportations to Samaria (or the province of Samerina, as it was called in the Assyrian sources) follow the usual Assyrian bidirectional pattern. This is in contrast to the Assyrian unidirectional deportations of the other areas of the northern kingdom of Israel at the time of Tiglath-pileser III (ca. 734-732 B.C.E.).[7] Archaeological evidence seems to confirm these different deportation policies. Zvi Gal's survey conducted in Lower Galilee demonstrates a marked decline in the settlement of Lower Galilee at the end of the 8th century that continued through the 6th century.[8] This seems to confirm

---

4. Adam Zertal, "The Wedge-shaped Decorated Bowl and the Origin of the Samaritans," *BASOR* 276 (1989): 77-84; "The Pahwah of Samaria (Northern Israel) during the Persian Period: Types of Settlement, Economy, History and New Discoveries," *Transeuphratène* 3 (1990): 9-30, esp. 11-14.

5. Gloria London, "Reply to A. Zertal's 'The Wedge-shaped Decorated Bowl and the Origin of the Samaritans,'" *BASOR* 286 (1992): 89-90.

6. Stern, 45.

7. K. Lawson Younger, Jr., "The Deportations of the Israelites," *JBL* 117 (1998): 201-27. The deportation of the Shephelah of Judah in the days of Sennacherib (701) was also a unidirectional deportation.

8. Zvi Gal, *Lower Galilee During the Iron Age* (Winona Lake: Eisenbrauns, 1992), 109; "Lower Galilee in the Iron Age II: Analysis of Survey Material and Its Historical Interpretation," *TA* 15-16 (1988-89): 56-64. Gal concludes: "It appears as if Lower Galilee was significantly deserted and its inhabitants exiled to Assur. Moreover, . . . no new settlers were brought into the region, as was done later in Samaria. The events of 733/732 B.C.E. provide a tragic landmark in the history of Israelite settlement in Galilee, particularly Lower Galilee. This was an extremely

the unidirectional deportations made by Tiglath-pileser III. On the other hand, surveys of the area that was the Assyrian province of Samerina indicate a two-stage rebuilding process.[9] In the first stage, the capital city of Samaria was restored and a network of unfortified secondary centers (such as Dothan, Shechem, Tell el-Far'ah [North], Gezer, and Hadid) was established. In the second stage, many small villages and agricultural estates were (re)established. Since some of these were newly established in previously unpopulated areas, this may attest to a period of growth and prosperity.[10]

Sargon II was the first Assyrian monarch involved in deportations to Samaria. He vividly describes some of these deportations in his Nimrud Prisms.

> I repopulated Samerina more than before. I brought into it people from countries conquered by my hands. I appointed my eunuch as governor over them. And I counted them as Assyrians.[11]

While Sargon does not specify these countries, 2 Kings 17:24 + 27-31 explain that the deportees came from Babylon *(bābel),* Cuthah *(kûtāh),* Avva *('awwā'),* Hamath *(ḥᵃmāt)* and Sepharvaim *(sᵉparwayim),* and brought the worship of their deities with them.

> The king of Assyria brought people from Babylon *(bābel),* Cuthah *(kûtāh),* Avva *('awwā'),* Hamath *(ḥᵃmāt)* and Sepharvaim *(sᵉparwayim)* and settled them in the towns of Samaria in the place of the Israelites; they took possession of Samaria, and settled in its cities. . . .
> Then the king of Assyria commanded: "Send there one of the priests whom you (pl.) deported from there; let him go back and live there, and teach them the rule *(mšpt)* of the god of the land." So one of the priests whom they had deported from Samaria came; and lived in *Bethel* (emphasis mine); and taught them how they should worship *(yr')* Yahweh. But each nation made its own gods and put them in the shrines of the high places that the people of Samaria had made, each nation in the cities

violent and almost total destruction. Whatever had not been destroyed by the wars was removed or laid waste by the exiles, and the region was not occupied during the seventh and sixth centuries B.C.E." (*Lower Galilee During the Iron Age,* 108).

9. Israel Finkelstein, "Israelite and Hellenistic Farms in the Foothills and in the Yarkon Basin," *ErIsr* 15 (1981): 331-41 (Hebrew), 402 (English summary); Adam Zertal, *The Manasseh Hill Country Survey* (Haifa: University of Haifa, 1992) (Hebrew).

10. Stern, 50-51.

11. 2.118D, *COS* 2:295-96; C. J. Gadd, "Inscribed Prisms of Sargon II from Nimrud," *Iraq* 16 (1954): 179-80, lines 37-41.

in which they lived. The men of Babylon *(ʾanšê-bābel)* made Succoth-benoth *(sukkôt bᵉnôt)*, the men of Cuthah *(ʾanšê-kût)* made Nergal *(nērgal)*, and the men of Hamath *(ʾanšê-ḥᵃmāt)* made Ashima *(ʾăšîmāʾ)*; the Avvites *(hāʿawwîm)* made Nibhaz *(nibḥaz)* and Tartak *(tartāq)*, and the Sepharvites *(hasᵉparwîm)* burned their children in the fire to Adrammelech *(ʾadrammelek)* and Anammelech *(ʿănammelek)*, the gods of Sepharvaim.

These verses are part of the narrative unit of chapter 17 comprised of verses 24-33 which explain that the non-Israelite worship in Samaria is a syncretism of the worship of Yahweh with other deities. As Marc Zvi Brettler, Mordechai Cogan, and others have noted, there is no reason to posit extensive postexilic redaction here.[12]

Initially, it might appear that the order of the entities in the lists might be helpful in the identification process. In fact, many scholars have appealed to the additional listings found in 2 Kgs. 18:34 and 19:13 (Isa. 36:19 and 37:13). However, a comparison of the lists demonstrates that the entities are not arranged according to any discernable geographic pattern:

2 Kgs. 17:24	Babylon, Cuthah, Avva, Hamath, Sepharvaim
2 Kgs. 17:30-31	Babylon, Cuth(a), Hamath, Avva, Sepharvaim
2 Kgs. 18:34//	Hamath and Arpad, Sepharvaim, Hena, Ivvah, + Samaria[13]
Isa. 36:19	Hamath and Arpad, Sepharvaim + Samaria
2 Kgs. 19:13//	Hamath, Arpad, Lair, Sepharvaim, Hena, Ivvah
Isa. 37:13	Hamath, Arpad, Lair, Sepharvaim, Hena, Ivvah

---

12. Marc Zvi Brettler, *The Creation of History in Ancient Israel* (London: Routledge, 1995), 215-16, n. 114: "In general, the fact that Kings ends with the release of Jehoiachin from prison rather than the Cyrus proclamation, like Chronicles, argues against extensive post-exilic editing of Kings. This point speaks against those who see extensive sections of 2 Kings 17 as post-exilic, such as Shermaryahu Talmon, 'Polemics and Apology in Biblical Historiography: 2 Kings 17:24-41,' *The Creation of Sacred Literature: Composition and Redaction of the Biblical Text* [ed. Richard E. Friedman; Berkeley: University of California Press, 1981], 57-68 (reprinted in Talmon's *Literary Studies in the Hebrew Bible: Form and Content* [Jerusalem: Magnes, 1993], 134-59)." See also Mordechai Cogan, "Israel in Exile — The View of a Josianic Historian," *JBL* 97 (1978): 40-44; "For We, Like You, Worship Your God: Three Biblical Portrayals of Samaritan Origins," *VT* 38 (1988): 289-90. Interestingly, Talmon declares that "the 'factual annals-nucleus' in the text unit 17:24-31 can be identified as consisting of vv. 24, 29-31" (62).

13. For the variant, see Moshe Anbar, "Καὶ ποῦ εἰσὶν οἱ θεοὶ τῆς χώρας Σαμαρείας: 'et où sont les dieux du pays de Samarie?,'" *BN* 51 (1990): 7-8.

Moreover, the listings in 2 Kings 17 are found in a very different type of passage[14] and are serving a very different purpose than the other listings that are dominated by Assyrian propagandistic purposes. In addition, there is some question whether the Hamath of 2 Kings 17 is the same place as the Hamath mentioned in 2 Kings 18–19/Isaiah 36–37 (see further below).

The recent discovery and publication of two cuneiform tablets from Tel Hadid by Nadav Na'aman and Ran Zadok provide additional knowledge about the deportations to Samaria and confirm the Mesopotamian disposition of Samaria's repopulation.[15] Since, in the 1st millennium, cuneiform writing on tablets appeared in Palestine only after the Assyrian annexations and deportations, there can be little doubt that these tablets are the product of some of the Mesopotamian deportees to the region.

The first tablet appears to be a real estate transaction and is dated by eponym to 698 B.C.E. (only three years after Sennacherib's invasion of the Levant in 701). With the exception of one name, all of the personal names are Akkadian and most likely individuals who were part of the deportations to Samaria or their descendants.

The second tablet is a debt note with a pledge (the debtor pledges his wife and sister) and is dated by eponym to 664 (during the earlier years of Assurbanipal). The debtor appears to be indigenous (he has a West Semitic personal name), while the creditor probably belonged to the deportees or their descendants.

These tablets add to the small number of other documents that belonged to the deportees to Samaria.[16] These include two cuneiform tablets from Gezer (Gezer 1; Gezer 2) and a court order from Samaria (Samaria 1825/Fi 16).[17] Na'aman and Zadok conclude: "On the whole, it is noteworthy that so far there is hardly any difference between the tiny group of neo-Assyrian deeds from Palestine and those from the Assyrian heartland: both display the same formulary and scribal conventions."[18] Thus as we investigate the identities of the deportees and their deities, it is important that we keep this Mesopotamian connection in mind.

---

14. See the discussion of Pauline A. Viviano, "2 Kings 17: A Rhetorical and Form-Critical Analysis," *CBQ* 49 (1987): 548-59, esp. 554.

15. Na'aman and Zadok, *TA* 27 (2000): 159-88. For translations, see *COS* 3:262-63.

16. Na'aman and Zadok, *TA* 27 (2000): 176-77.

17. See *COS* 3:263-265; 270-271.

18. Na'aman and Zadok, *TA* 27 (2000): 177.

Babylon/Succoth-benoth

The first place mentioned, Babylon, appears at first to be straighforward. Yet, on the one hand, this could be a reference to a deportation resulting from Sargon's campaigns against Merodach-baladan in 710-709.[19] Sargon reports that he deported 90,580 people from the cities of Bīt Yakin and adjacent areas in the region. On the other hand, this could be a reference to Sennacherib's well-known destruction of the city in 689.[20] But it could also be a reference to deportees from the region of Babylonia in the days of Assurbanipal.[21] Finally, the biblical text may be telescoping the deportations of several Assyrian kings together.

Unfortunately the identification of the deity Succoth-benoth *(sukkôt bᵉnôt)* is more complex. The individual name components as well as the double name are unknown in cuneiform sources, at least as they are preserved in the Hebrew text. Moreover, the first component may not be a name at all, but a common noun.

One solution has been to emend the MT, reconstructing the Babylonian divine pair *mrdk wzrbnyt* "Marduk and Zarpānītu."[22] Marduk was Babylon's chief deity and the goddess Zarpānītu *(Ṣarpānītu)* was his consort.[23] But such emendation is unnecessary since the consonantal text yields some reasonable alternatives.

Today there seems to be a general consensus that *bnwt* is to be identified with the goddess Bānītu (ᵈBānītu), literally, "the creatress."[24] Interestingly, she is the only goddess in the list of deities worshiped by the deportees.

---

19. See e.g., N. Na'aman and R. Zadok, "Sargon II's Deportations to Israel and Philistia (716-708 B.C.)," *JCS* 40 (1988): 36-46, esp. 44-46; *TA* 27 (2000): 178.

20. See e.g., Mordechai Cogan and Hayim Tadmor, *II Kings.* AB 11 (Garden City: Doubleday, 1988), 209; for the text, see *COS* 2:301. See also Esarhaddon Babylon Texts, Episode 37 (*Asarh.* 25, lines 12-24; Riekele Borger, *Die Inschriften Asarhaddons, Königs von Assyrien.* AfO Beiheft 9 [1956; repr, Osnabruck: Biblio-Verlag, 1967]).

21. *ARAB* 2 §§791-798. See Riekele Borger, *Beiträge zum Inschriftenwerk Assurbanipals: Die Prismenklassen A, B, C = K, D, E, F, G, H, J, und T sowie andere Inschriften* (Wiesbaden: Harrassowitz, 1996), 58-75. Cf. Ezra 4:9-10.

22. Bernhard Stade, *The Books of Kings.* The Sacred Books of the Old Testament 9 (Baltimore: Johns Hopkins University Press, 1904), 267; Paul Dhorme, "Les pays bibliques et l'Assyrie," *RB* 10 (1910): 368-90, esp. 375; James A. Montgomery and Henry Snyder Gehman, *The Books of Kings.* ICC (Edinburgh: T. & T. Clark, 1951), 474. *BH*² (Kittel) and *BHS* suggest this emendation.

23. See e.g., John Gray, *I & II Kings,* 2nd ed. OTL (Philadelphia: Westminster, 1970), 653-54.

24. See most recently Mordechai Cogan, "Sukkoth-Benoth," in *DDD,* 821-22.

The divine name Bānītu is attested in both Neo-Assyrian[25] and Neo-Babylonian personal names.[26] There was a shrine to the goddess in Nineveh.[27] As an epithet, Bānītu is applied to Ištar of Nineveh,[28] and the name of the goddess Ṣarpānītu was popularly etymologized as Zēr-bānītu, "seed producing."[29] The cult of the goddess Bānītu appears to have spread westward so that later certain Arameans residing in Egypt during the Persian period worshipped her at a temple in Syene.[30] Furthermore, at Syene and Elephantine, she is attested as a theophoric element in a number of masculine personal names, e.g., Banit (*TAD* D20.1),[31] Banitsar (*TAD* A2.2:5, 2.6:8), Banitsarel (*TAD* 2.3:2), Baniteresh (*TAD* B2.1:19),[32] and Makkibanit (*TAD* A2.1:8, etc.).

The evidence for the worship of this goddess comes primarily from the 1st millennium, although the term *bānītu* appears earlier as an epithet of several goddesses. Interestingly, this is attested even in a mid-2nd millennium Transjordanian context. For example, the personal name *Amat-ᵈBānītu* is found on a cylinder seal.[33] Thus what was originally a popular epithet for the mother goddess may have been hypostasized.[34]

There is also a growing consensus that the first component *skwt* should

---

25. Both masculine and feminine Neo-Assyrian personal names contain Bānītu as an element. E.g., see the names listed in *PNA* (1999): 1/2:265-67. One of the more important individuals bearing this name was Bānītu, the queen of Assyria, wife of Shalmaneser V. See A. Kamil, "Inscriptions on Objects from Yaba's Tomb in Nimrud," in *Gräber assyrischer Königinnen aus Nimrud*, ed. M. S. B. Damerji. Jahrbuch des Römisch-Germanischen Zentralmuseums 45 (Mainz: Verlag des Römisch-Germanischen Zentralmuseums, 1999), 13-18. In a masculine personal name, Bānītu may be attested in a Neo-Assyrian contract, though the reading is not certain. See J. N. Postgate, *Fifty Neo-Assyrian Legal Documents* (Warminster: Aris & Phillips, 1976), 102-3 (no. 13:34 = ADD 307 r. 16).

26. See Knut L. Tallqvist, *Neubabylonisches Namenbuch: zu den Geschäftsurkunden aus der Zeit des Šamaššumukîn bis Xerxes* (Helsinki: Helsingforsiae, 1905), 232a/b; cf. *CAD* B 95a.

27. *STT* 88, III 6; cf. R. Frankena, "New Materials for the Takultu Ritual: Additions and Corrections," *BiOr* 18 (1961): 199-201.

28. *AkkGE* 70-71.

29. *AHw* 1520a s.v. Zēr-bānītu, "Samenschaffende."

30. See *TAD* A2.2:1, 12, 2.3:7, 2.4:1. For further discussion, see Karel van der Toorn, "Anat-Yahu, Some Other Deities, and the Jews of Elephantine," *Numen* 39 (1992): 80-101, esp. 86. Cf. also E. Bresciani and M. Kamil, *Le lettere aramaiche di Hermopoli* (Rome: Accademia nazionale dei Lincei, 1966), no. 1:1. nos. 2:1, 12; 3:1; cf. 1:7).

31. See Bezalel Porten, "Offering Table from the Memphis Serapeum," *COS* 2.60.

32. See Bezalel Porten, "Grant of a Built Wall," *COS* 3.59.

33. Raymond J. Tournay, "Un cylindre babylonien découvert en Transjordanie," *RB* 74 (1967): 248-54, esp. 248. See also the evidence in Alfred Haldar, *BiOr* 31 (1974): 34-35.

34. K. Deller, "STT 366: Deutungsversuch 1982," *Assur* 3/4 (1983): 139-53, esp. 142.

be understood as a common noun meaning "aspect, image," an interpretation suggested in particular by Edward Lipiński.[35] Thus the phrase *skwt bnwt* in the MT should be translated as "image of Bānītu."

While this understanding of *skwt* as "image" may, in fact, be the best option, there remains the possibility that this term should be understood as a divine name, Sakkut (^{d}SAG.KUD). Some scholars have related this first component *skwt* (MT *sukkôt*) in 2 Kgs. 17:30 with *skwt* (MT *sikkût*) in Amos 5:26 and hence to this deity known in cuneiform sources. While the meaning of *skwt* (*sikkût*) in Amos 5:26 is much disputed — a study in itself,[36] this does not necessarily affect the occurrence of the deity in 2 Kgs. 17:30.

Sakkut is identified with Ninurta (CT 25,11:34) and is known as an official (*asakku* "demon") of Anu (CT 24,3:18).[37] He was a "cupbearer" of the gods and was associated with the city of Dēr,[38] bordering on Elam. Riekele Borger has assembled many of the occurrences of this divine name with appropriate citations.[39] Moreover, Borger has invalidated the alleged association of this Sakkut with Saturn in *Šurpu* II 180, since the originals do not read SAG.UŠ ("Saturn") but UŠ (= Nita).[40] Both Sakkut and Nita were identified with Ninurta. *Šurpu* II 180-81 now has the sequence AN.TI.BAL (Tibal[41]) — Sakkut — Nita — Immeriya (Wēr). Apparently, during the Old Babylonian period, Sakkut (^{d}SAK.KUD) was a personal deity of individuals from Uruk and Sippar.[42]

---

35. Edward Lipiński, "*Skn* et *sgn* dans le sémitique occidental du nord," *UF* 5 (1973): 202-4. See also William W. Hallo, "New Moons and Sabbaths," *HUCA* 48 (1977): 1-18, esp. 15. Hallo understands both *skwt* (*sikkût*) of Amos 5:26 and *skwt* (*sukkôt*) of 2 Kgs. 17:30 as "image."

36. Marten Stol argues that the parallelism in Amos 5:26 between Sakkut (*sikkût*) and Kaiwan (*kiyyûn*) suggests that, since Kaiwan goes back to Babylonian *Kayyamānu* (the planet Saturn), then Sakkut must be a divine name; "Sakkuth," *DDD*, 722-23.. For the most thorough discussion of this problem, see Shalom M. Paul, *Amos.* Herm (Minneapolis: Fortress, 1991), 194-98.

37. A. Livingstone, *Mystical and Mythological Explanatory Works of Assyrian and Babylonian Scholars* (Oxford: Clarendon, 1986), 180, 186.

38. . . . ^{d}*Sag-kud šá* URU *bu-bé-e* DINGIR.MEŠ *a-ši-bu-ut* URU.BÀD.DINGIR.KI ". . . Sakkud of the city of Bubê, the gods who dwell in Dēr." See *RIMA* 3:190, iii.46′-48′; Ernest Weidner, "Die Feldzüge Šamši-Adads V. gegen Babylonien," *AfO* 9 (1933-34): 89-104, esp. 92. ^{d}*Sag-kud šá Bu-bé-e* "Sakkud of Bubê." See Borger, *Asarh.* 84, 42.

39. Riekele Borger, "Amos 5,26, Apostelgeschichte 7,43 und Šurpu II, 180," *ZAW* 100 (1988): 70-81, esp. 73-74. The name Sakkut could be Elamite rather than Sumerian; cf. the Elamite god *Šimut* (Borger, 73). This fits the final -*t* in the Hebrew text (Stol, 723).

40. Borger, *ZAW* 100 (1988): 74-76.

41. An astral god as elsewhere identified with the position of Venus.

42. Karel van der Toorn, "Migration and the Spread of Local Cults," in *Immigration and Emigration Within the Ancient Near East: Festschrift E. Lipiński,* ed. Karel van Lerberghe and

If the deity Sakkut is the correct understanding of the MT's *skwt*, then two deities are mentioned in association with the deportees from Babylon: Sakkut (and) Bānītu.

Cutha/Nergal

The identifications of Cutha and the god Nergal are the most straightforward and certain of all the places and deities mentioned in 2 Kings 17. Cutha (Tall Ibrāhīm) was located ca. 25 km. north of Kish.[43] Unfortunately, the site has not been extensively excavated.[44]

The city is not specifically mentioned in Sargon's royal inscriptions. Nevertheless, it might be inferred from Sargon's inscriptions that people from this city were deported as a result of his 710-709 campaigns.[45] Furthermore, it might also be inferred from a letter of Sargon to Aššur-šarru-uṣur[46] that mentions citizens of Babylon, Borsippa, Kish, Nippur, Dēr, and at least one other city (lost in the break) who apparently were residing in Que. J. N. Postgate[47] considers these people to be deportees.[48] Unfortunately, however, these are only inferences and not direct evidence of a deportation of Sargon from Cutha.

On the other hand, the city of Cutha joined Merodach-baladan in his rebellion against Sennacherib; and it was punished by Sennacherib with a deportation in 703.[49] Consequently, since Cutha is specifically mentioned in

A. Schoors. OLA 65 (Leuven: Peeters, 1995), 365-77, esp. 370. See J. J. Finkelstein, *Late Old Babylonian Documents and Letters*. YOS 13 (New Haven: Yale University Press, 1972), 12, 93a, pl. 521 seal a. Perhaps the god is to be identified with Ishtaran at Der. See Dominique Charpin, *Archives familiales et propriété privée en Babylonie ancienne: étude des documents de 'Tell Sifr'*. Hautes Études Orientales 12 (Geneva: Librairie Droz, 1980), 291; W. G. Lambert, "The Reading of the God Name ᵈKA.DI," *ZA* 59 (1969): 100-3.

43. See D. O. Edzard and M. Gallery, "Kutha," *RLA* 6 (1980-83): 384-87.

44. Some artifacts from an early excavation of the tell by Hormuzd Rassam are in the British Museum.

45. See Nadav Na'aman, "Population Changes in Palestine Following the Assyrian Deportations," *TA* 20 (1993): 104-24, esp. 110-11.

46. See Simo Parpola, *The Correspondence of Sargon II, 1: Letters from Assyria and the West*. SAA 1 (Helsinki: Helsinki University Press, 1987), 4-7 (no. 1, lines 66-71).

47. J. N. Postgate, "Assyrian Texts and Fragments," *Iraq* 35 (1973): 13-36, esp. 29.

48. See also Na'aman and Zadok, *TA* 27 (2000): 178. S. W. Cole offers the option that these "citizens" may have been merchants residing in the region; *Nippur in Late Assyrian Times, c. 755-612 BC.* SAAS 4 (Helsinki: Neo-Assyrian Text Corpus Project, 1996), 56, n. 2. His suggestion, however, is based on the assumption that Sargon or his predecessors never made deportations from any of these cities, except Dēr.

49. See Mordechai Cogan, *COS* 2:301.

Sennacherib's annals as a place from which he made a deportation, the probability is greater that this is the deportation referred to in 2 Kgs. 17:24, 30.

In the case of Nergal *(nērgal)*, Cutha was one of the cities holy to this deity.[50] The city was "the cult center par excellence for deities connected with the netherworld."[51] Nergal was the god of "inflicted death," whether human or animal.[52] Thus from the Old Akkadian period onwards, he was a god of war, supporting the king, and sharing the title with Ninurta of "strong warrior, son of Enlil."[53] In addition, from the Old Babylonian period onwards, Nergal is explicitly associated with plague *(mūtānū)*. Because of his role in inflicting death through war and/or plague, he was the "lord of the underworld" (EN.ERI$_{11}$.GAL).

The worship of Nergal was an important part of the official Assyrian cult in Neo-Assyrian times.[54] In the form of standards *(urigallu)*,[55] Adad and Nergal accompanied the Assyrian army on campaigns and received cultic attention in the camp. The month of Kislim was Nergal's month, when he came out of the netherworld. The 14th and 28th days of the month, evil days, were the days of Nergal.

That Nergal was a deity venerated by some of the deportees to Samaria is seen in some of the personal names found in the cuneiform texts discovered in this region. For example, a small tablet (Samaria 1825/Fi 16) discovered in excavations at Samaria at the beginning of the 20th century (i.e., 1908-10)[56] contains a court order, a "*šumma* text,"[57] not a grain loan (as previously read).[58] The first personal name, Nergal-šallim, is Akkadian, hardly indigenous. Another example can be seen in the tablet known as Gezer 2[59] which re-

---

50. Nergal's other cult centers were: Apiak, Ḫubšal, Marad, Maškan-šapir, Me-Turna/Sirara, Tarbiṣu, suburban Umma, and Uṣarpara. See F. A. M. Wiggermann, "Nergal A & B," *RLA* 9 (1999): 215-26, esp. 222.

51. Edzard and Gallery, 387.

52. Wiggermann, 221.

53. Wiggermann, 221.

54. Alasdair Livingstone, "Nergal," *DDD*, 621-22.

55. For a discussion of these standards, see Wiggermann, 226.

56. See G. A. Reisner et al., *Harvard Excavations at Samaria, 1908-1910*, 2 vols. (Cambridge, MA: Harvard University Press, 1924), 1:247 and photo, 2: pl. 56.

57. Remko Jas, *Neo-Assyrian Judicial Procedures*. SAAS 5 (Helsinki: Neo-Assyrian Text Corpus Project, 1996), 76-81.

58. Veysel Donbaz, "Once Again Fi. 16 (= Samaria 1825)," *NABU* (1998): no. 22. See *COS* 3:270-71.

59. C. H. W. Johns, "The New Cuneiform Tablet from Gezer," *PEFQS* 37 (1905): 206-10; Kurt Galling, "Assyrische und Persische Präfekten in Geser," *PJ* 31 (1935): 81-86; Bob Becking, "The Two Neo-Assyrian Documents from Gezer in Their Historical Context," *JEOL* 27 (1981-82): 76-89, esp. 86-88.

cords a land sale by an Israelite named Natan-Yau. One of the witnesses is named Nergal-šar-uṣur. Finally, it is worth noting that the term *kutîm* stuck as the later Jewish pejorative term for the Samaritans.[60]

Avva/Nibhaz and Tartak

The place name is vocalized Avva (*ʿawwā*ʾ) in 2 Kgs. 17:24; but it is vocalized Ivvah (*ʿiwwâ*) in 2 Kgs. 18:34; 19:13 and Isa. 37:13. The form of the gentilic in 2 Kgs. 17:31 is *hāʿawwîm*. The place name is Semitic, and two different locations have been proposed. Some scholars have proposed a location for the city in Syria.[61] While Sargon's conquest of some of the Syrian states would, at first, appear to be the context, there is no mention of a Syrian city with this name.[62] Other scholars have suggested locating the city on the Babylonian-Elamite border near the Uqnu River, in the district of Gambulu, equating Avva with the city of Amâ (uruA-ma-a).[63] Amâ is mentioned in Sargon's annals during the 710 campaign against Merodach-baladan (Marduk-apla-iddina) and Šutruk-Nahhunte II (the Elamite king),[64] although no deportation of the city is mentioned.[65]

60. Cf. talmudic tractate *Massecheth Kuthim*.

61. See Montgomery and Gehman, 472; and Gray, *I & II Kings*, 651.

62. The Arabic place name Kafr ʿAya on the Orontes (SW of Homs) has been proposed based on the LXX spelling Αια. See F. M. Abel, *Géographie de la Palestine* (Paris: J. Gabalda, 1933-38), 2:256; and D. J. Wiseman, *1 and 2 Kings*. TOTC 9 (Downers Grove: Inter-Varsity, 1993), 268. However, this site is not mentioned in any ancient source. Simo Parpola does not list a single reference; *Neo-Assyrian Toponyms*. AOAT 6 (Kevelaer: Butzon & Bercker, 1970).

63. Ran Zadok, "Geographical and Onomastic Notes," *JANES* 8 (1976): 114-26, esp. 120-21; and Naʾaman and Zadok, *JCS* 40 (1988): 45; Bob Becking, *The Fall of Samaria: An Historical and Archaeological Study*. SHANE 2 (Leiden: E. J. Brill, 1992), 98.

64. Assuming that Elamite *šutur-* and *šutruk-* are different forms of the same name component. See M. W. Waters, *A Survey of Neo-Elamite History*. SAAS 12 (Helsinki: Neo-Assyrian Text Corpus Project, 2000), 81-82 and esp. 111-16. This king's name is spelled Šutur-Nahundi (mšu-túr-dna-ḫu-un-di) in Sargon's Annals (see next note). For the campaign, see 19-21.

65. The context reads: "The rest of the hostile Arameans who dwelt in their district, and who had put their trust in Marduk-apla-iddina (Merodach-baladan) and Šutur-Nahundi (Šutruk-Nahhunte), and had occupied the Uqnû River, a distant abode, their dwellings like the deluge I overthrew, and the date palms, their sustenance and the gardens, the abundance of their province, I cut down, and (the contents of) their granaries I let my army eat. To the Uqnû River, the place of their concealment I sent my warriors, and they inflicted a defeat upon them, . . . and the people together with their property they carried off.

The cities of Zamê, Aburê, Iaptiru, Maḫiṣu, Ḫilipanu, Dandan, Pattianu, Ḫaimanu, Gadiati, Amate (uruA-ma-te), Nuânu, Amâ (uruA-ma-a), Ḫiuru and Saʾilu, 14 strong cities, to-

This same city is also mentioned in Sennacherib's annals, spelled [uru]*Ha-ú-a-e*, which is closer to the Aramaic and Hebrew spellings than the spelling in Sargon's annals. In a later document from Nippur, it is spelled [uru]*A-ú-a*.[66] Although neither Sargon nor Sennacherib specifies a deportation from this city, the fact that the city is mentioned in connection with "Amate"[67] may strengthen the tie to Sargon. But this is far from conclusive evidence.

The identification of the deities significantly strengthens or weakens the arguments for the suggested locations of Avva. Since some scholars have assumed a Syrian location for Avva, they have naturally sought a Syrian origin for Nibhaz *(nibḥaz)* and Tartak *(tartāq)*. But there is no clear-cut evidence for a Syrian origin for either of these two deities.

In the case of Nibhaz, there is no good possible Syrian divine candidate. A rather strained attempt has been made to derive Nibhaz from *mizbēaḥ* "altar" by a series of phonological shifts.[68] This suggestion is very doubtful on rather obvious linguistic grounds.

In the case of the second deity, it has been suggested that Tartak should be identified with Atargatis,[69] a Syrian fertility-goddess known from Aramaic and Greek texts. Thus the Hebrew term *trtq* would derive from a dissimilated and metathesized form of an Aramaic original.[70] Montgomery and Gehman state: "The present form is reduction of original *'trqth*, with proper ancient Aramaic *q* for *ġayin*."[71]

As Lowell K. Handy points out,[72] this interpretation should now be abandoned. The goddess's name is a compound of Ashtarte and 'Anat. In Aramaic her name is spelled: *'tr'th*, *'tr't'*, *'tr'th*, *'tr't'*, *tr't*; in Greek: Ἀταργτῖς,

---

gether with towns in their environs along the Uqnû River that had feared the advance of my mighty weapons and had devastated their province, came out of the midst of the Uqnû River, a distant place, and seized my feet. That province more than before I caused to rest in safety, and I entrusted it into the hands of my governor of Gambulu." (A. Fuchs, *Die Inschriften Sargons II. aus Khorsabad* [Göttingen: Cuvillier, 1994], 148-50, lines 288b-95a).

66. See Zadok, *JANES* 8 (1976): 120.

67. See n. 65, as well as discussion below. Note the order in Sargon's text: Amate . . . Amâ; cf. 2 Kgs 17:30-31; reversed order in v. 24.

68. See Montgomery and Gehman, 474: "But the word is thus to be explained: *nbḥz* < *mbḥz* (by common dissimilation) < *mzbḥ*, 'altar,' i.e., the deified altar"; J. T. Milik, "Les papyrus araméens d'Hermoupolis et les cultes syro-phéniciens en Égypte perse," *Bib* 48 (1967): 578, 606.

69. A sanctuary of this goddess, called an Atargateion, near Qarnaim is mentioned in 2 Macc. 12:26.

70. Albert Šanda, *Die Bücher der Könige*. EHAT 9 (Münster: Aschendoff, 1912), 2:230-31; Gray, *I & II Kings*, 654.

71. Montgomery and Gehman, 474.

72. Lowell K. Handy, "Tartak," *ABD* 6:334-35.

Ἀτάργατις, Ἀτταγάθη, Ἀταράτη, and Ἀταργάγτη.[73] Note that Montgomery and Gehman's supposed original form *'trqth* is unattested. Thus it seems that on linguistic grounds[74] an identification of *trtq* in 2 Kgs 17:31 with this Syrian goddess is out of the question.[75]

Accepting the southern Mesopotamian location for Avva, Lipiński has recently suggested that Nibhaz *(nbḥz)* corresponds exactly to the Akkadian *nabû āḫiz* "Nabu master of . . .," the first word of a series of Neo-Babylonian *épiclèses* that exalt the deity Nabu, patron deity of the scribes, and a major deity worshiped by the Arameans of southern Babylonia.[76] Some of the epithets that Lipiński cites are: *nabû āḫiz šukāmi* "Nabu, the master of scribal art," *nabû āḫiz ṭuppi šīmāti ilāni* "Nabu, the master of the tablet of destinies of the gods," and *nabû āḫiz ṭēmi u milki* "Nabu, the master of understanding and counsel."[77] While the consonants *nbḥz* match the deity's name in 2 Kgs. 17:31, this is hardly convincing. First, the verb *aḫāzu* is not the only verb used in these epithets.[78] Therefore, the chance of combination with the divine name, as Lipiński has suggested, is greatly diminished. Second, since Nabu is a deity known in the Hebrew Bible spelled *nbw*,[79] it is doubtful that the *waw* would have been dropped in the spelling[80] or that the first word of an epithet would join with this divine name in this manner.

Therefore, it may be more likely that Nibhaz and Tartak should be identified with two Elamite deities. Fritz Hommel was the first to propose these identifications.[81] He identified Nibhaz *(nbḥz)* with the deity [d]*Ibnaḫaza* (asso-

---

73. H. J. W. Drijvers, "Atargatis," *DDD*, 114-16, esp. 114.

74. Even permitting the apheresis of the *ayin/aleph*, there is no evidence of a metathesis of the final *ayin* and *taw*. The *ayin* to *qoph* is certainly a possibility in Aramaic, though the Aramaic spellings listed above do not support it.

75. Mordechai Cogan, "Tartak," in *DDD*, 836-37. Edward Lipiński's suggestion that the name is derived from the transcription of *šarrat ēqi* seems very doubtful; *Dictionnaire encyclopédique de la Bible*, ed. P.-M. Bogaert et al. (Brussels: Brepols, 1987), 1241-42, *s.v.* "Tartaq"; 169, *s.v.* "Avva, Ivva."

76. See *Dictionnaire encyclopédique de la Bible*, 898-99, *s.v.* "Nibhaz"; and 169, *s.v.* "Avva, Ivva."

77. Lipiński cites these epithets from Francesco Pomponio, *Nabû: Il culto e la figura di un dio del Pantheon babilonese ed assiro*. Studi semitici 51 (Rome: Università di Roma, 1978), 181-88.

78. Thus, e.g., in the case of the second epithet, *āḫiz ṭuppi šīmāti ilāni*, the more common verb used in this epithet is *našû*. See Pomponio, 182, n. 29.

79. Alan R. Millard, "Nabû," *DDD*, 607-10.

80. Nabû is most frequently spelled in West Semitic texts *nb'* or *nbw*.

81. See Fritz Hommel, "Die Götter Nibḥaz und Tartak: 2 Kön. 17,31," *OLZ* 15 (1912): 118; "Die Elamitische Götter-Siebenheit in CT 25,24," in *Oriental Studies*. Festschrift Paul Haupt (Baltimore: Johns Hopkins University, 1926), 159-68; *Ethnologie und Geographie des Alten Ori-*

ciated with Ea [Aya], the god of fresh water and wisdom) in a list of Elamite gods.[82] The text is preserved in three exemplars: YBC 2401; K 8219 and K 7620 (the last two published in CT 25, 24). It reads: ^{d}Ib.na.ḫa.za | ^{d}É-[a]. Unfortunately, nothing else is known about this deity.

Likewise, Hommel identified Tartak *(trtq)* with a deity ^{d}*Dakdadra* who is supposedly listed in the line immediately following ^{d}*Ibnaḫaza* in the same list of Elamite deities.[83] He read the line as ^{d}Dag/k.da.ad.ra | ^{d}EN-[zu]. This is the reading of CT 25, 24 (K 8219 and K 7620). However, the same line in YBC 2401 reads ^{d}AN.KAL.da.ra.kar | ^{d}Sin (EŠ). On this basis, Richard L. Litke suggested that the line in K 8219 should read: ^{d}AN.KAL.da.ad.ra.[84] Litke also notes a reading in CT 25, 32:10, ^{d}AN.KAL.da.kar.ra (who is also identified with ^{d}EŠ). Thus while the reading ^{d}*Dakdadra* is accurate for CT 25, 24 (i.e., K 8219 and K 7620), it is not free of difficulties.

Hommel also suggested that a transposed form of the name ^{d}*Dakdadra* appears in the Naram-Sin treaty as ^{d}*Dirtak* (dir.tak).[85] But more recently, Walther Hinz has suggested that the reading of the cuneiform should be ^{d}*Siašum* (dir = si + a; tak = šum).[86] Hence, this text does not contain an attestation of the deity as Hommel proposed. In any event, like ^{d}*Ibnaḫaza*, nothing more is known about ^{d}*Dakdadra*, if this is the correct reading of the name in CT 25, 24.

In sum, it can be asserted that there is no evidence that links this pair of deities to Syria. While not as conclusive as one might hope, the evidence is stronger in favor of the pair of deities being identified with Elamite gods. Thus a location of Avva in the Babylonian-Elamite border region is more likely. In addition, there may be further evidence of Elamite cultural and political influence on the West Semites who lived in this region.[87] Furthermore,

---

ents (Munich: C. H. Beck, 1926), 987; Cogan and Tadmor, 212; William J. Fulco, "Nibhaz," *ABD* 4:1104; Alan R. Millard, "Nibhaz," *DDD*, 623.

82. For this text, see L. W. King, *Cuneiform Texts from Babylonian Tablets in the British Museum* 25 (London: British Museum, 1909), pl. 24 (K 8219 and K 7620) (henceforth CT 25,24). Richard L. Litke, *A Reconstruction of the Assyro-Babylonian God-Lists An:* ^{d}*A-nu-um and* AN : *An ša ameli.* Texts from the Babylonian Collection 3 (Potomac, MD: Yale Babylonian Collection, 1998), 214 (YBC 2401: Tablet VI, line 188), pl. XXXVII; *A Reconstruction of the Assyro-Babylonian God-Lists,* AN : ^{d}*A-NU-UM and* AN : *ANU ŠÁ* AMĒli (diss., Yale University, 1958), 233-34.

83. Hommel, *OLZ* 15 (1912): 118.

84. Litke, *A Reconstruction of the Assyro-Babylonian God-Lists* (1998), 214 (YBC 2401: Tablet VI, line 189).

85. Hommel, *OLZ* 15 (1912): 118. He stated: *"Dir-tak* (geschrieben *Si-a* und *tak* oder *šum)."*

86. Walther Hinz, "Elams Vertrag mit Narām-Sin von Akade," *ZA* 58 (1967): 66-96, esp. 74; See Mordechai Cogan, "Tartak," *DDD*, 836-37.

87. Zadok, *JANES* 8 (1976): 121-23; "Elamites and Other Peoples from Iran and the Persian

the Tell Jemmeh ostraca contain a number of non-Semitic names that may possibly be linked to these deportees.[88] But this cannot be proved.

Hamath/Ashima

While at first glance Hamath might seem to refer to the well-known Syrian city on the Orontes River conquered by Sargon in 720, there are three significant problems with this identification. First, Sargon's inscriptions specifically state that the Hamatheans were deported to Assyria. In particular, the Aššur "Charter" states that the inhabitants were "brought to my city, the city of Aššur."[89] Some of the defeated Hamathean troops from this campaign were incorporated into the Assyrian army.[90] While it is not impossible that the Hamatheans were deported to multiple locations (as with Israel), there is no evidence presently to support this.

Second, it is also questionable whether the Assyrians would have put Samarians and Hamatheans together in Samaria, since they had just been al-

---

Gulf Region," *Iran* 32 (1994): 31-51. Na'aman and Zadok (*JCS* 40 [1988]: 45) argue that the name of the town Avva in Josh. 18:23 in the list of Benjamite towns comes from the inhabitants of Avva whom Sargon resettled in the region in the late 8th century. While this may well be the case, unfortunately the evidence is not so clear-cut. In Josh. 18:23, the gentilic *(hā'awwîm)* is used for the place name, while in 13:3, the same gentilic *(hā'awwîm)* is used in connection with other gentilics describing the Philistines (or more precisely the territory occupied by the Philistines). According to Deut. 2:23, the Avvites *(hā'awwîm)* dwelt in villages in the vicinity of Gaza; and the Caphtorim (Philistines), who came from Crete, wiped them out and settled in their place. Zechariah Kallai suggests that the gentilic in Josh. 18:23 may be connected with the inhabitants of Ai or Aiatha; *Historical Geography of the Bible: The Tribal Territories of Israel* (Leiden: Brill, 1986), 400-1. Obviously, homonyms may be involved, which complicates the matter. Thus it is impossible to know with certainty whether Avva in Josh. 18:23 is named for the deportees to Samaria or an earlier people in the land.

88. Na'aman and Zadok, *JCS* 40 (1988): 36-46. For Tell Jemmeh ostraca, see Johannes Renz and Wolfgang Röllig, *Handbuch der Althebräischen Epigraphik*, 1: *Die Althebräischen Inschriften* (Darmstadt: Wissenschaftliche Buchgesellschaft, 1995), 253-56 (Gem[7]:3-4); Joseph Naveh, "Writing and Scripts in Seventh-Century B.C.E. Philistia: The New Evidence from Tel Jemmeh," *IEJ* 35 (1985): 11-15.

89. H. W. F. Saggs, "Historical Texts and Fragments of Sargon II of Assyria. I: The 'Aššur Charter,'" *Iraq* 37 (1975): 11-20, lines 25b-28; *COS* 2:295. In addition, see the Great Summary Inscription (Fuchs, 200-1, lines 33-36, *COS* 2:296); the Iran Stela (Louis D. Levine, *Two Neo-Assyrian Stelae from Iran* [Toronto: Royal Ontario Museum, 1972], 34: 2:11).

90. See Barbara Parker, "Administrative Tablets from the North-West Palace of Nimrud," *Iraq* 22 (1961): 15-67, esp. 15 and 40-41 (ND 2646). In addition, the Cyprus Stela states: "300 charioteers and 600 cavalry of Hamath" were enrolled in the Assyrian army (VS I, 71, right side, 51ff.). See also Becking, *The Fall of Samaria*, 99, n. 23.

lies against Sargon in the battle of Qarqar in 720.[91] Aware of this difficulty, Karel van der Toorn suggests that some of the Arameans of Hamath and vicinity looked upon Israel as a haven and fled to the south.[92] However, 2 Kgs. 17:24-31 is not suggesting this, but rather is attributing this people's movement to the deportation process, not a migration before the 720 debacle at Qarqar and certainly not after it. It is possible that there was a much later deportation from Hamath that sent some of them to Samaria, but there is no indication of this in the Assyrian records. The only other possibility is that the Assyrians deported Hamatheans to Assyria proper in the days of Sargon, and then later during the reign of another Assyrian king moved some of these people to Samaria. But again this is speculative, having no evidence whatsoever.

Third, the deity Ashima is not attested in any of the inscriptions from Hamath on the Orontes, whether Aramaic, Hieroglyphic Luwian, or cuneiform.[93] While this may simply be the product of chance in discovery, it is presently problematic and may point to another solution.

Therefore, it seems likely that the Hebrew word *(hᵃmāt)* refers to Amate on the Uqnu River, taken in 710.[94] Sargon's text does not specifically mention a deportation from the city of Amate — only a submission of the city. However, since serious doubt can be raised for the reference being to the Syrian city of Hamath, and since Amate is mentioned in conjunction with Amâ (Avva) in Sargon's annals, it seems more likely to be the correct identification.[95]

Additionally, the southern Mesopotamian city's name seems to be derived from the Aramaic tribe called "Amatu." In the Suhu and Mari area, this tribe was one of the tribes that made up the Hatallu confederacy.[96] The tribe is also mentioned in the texts of Tiglath-pileser III. Thus, as pointed out by Zadok,[97] "Amatu" is an example of a toponym in eastern and western Babylonia that was named after the same Aramean tribe.

---

91. Becking, *The Fall of Samaria*, 99.

92. Van der Toorn, *Numen* 39 (1992): 94.

93. André Lemaire, "Les inscriptions araméennes anciennes de Teima," in *Présence arabe dans le Croissant fertile avant l'Hégire*, ed. Hélène Lozachmeur (Paris: Éditions Recherche sur les Civilisations, 1995), 59-72, esp. 70.

94. Fuchs, 148-50, lines 288b-95a (see n. 65 above).

95. See Na'aman and Zadok, *JCS* 40 (1988): 44. If the biblical writer were utilizing a cuneiform source, the confusion would be more understandable since Hamath is sometimes spelled without indication of the ḫ/h. For examples, see Parpola, *Neo-Assyrian Toponyms*, 14-15.

96. Written: ᶫᵘ*a-mat-a-a*; "Suhu Annals," text 2, I:17. See A. Cavigneaux and B. Kh. Ismail, "Die Statthalter von Suu und Mari im 8. Jh. v. Chr.," *BaM* 21 (1990): 321-456, esp. 343; *COS* 2:279.

97. Zadok, *JANES* 8 (1976): 117-22.

Interestingly, the people from this Hamath/Amate are attributed with the worship of Ashima *('šym')*, a West Semitic, and especially Aramaic, deity, rather than the worship of Elamite deities like their counterparts from Avva/Amâ (discussed above). Early on, Ashima *('ašîmā')* was identified by biblical scholars with Eshmun, a Phoenician god of healing whose name is written as ᵈ*Ia-su-mu-nu* in the treaty of Esarhaddon with Baal of Tyre.[98] However, in light of the growing number of attestations for the Aramaic deity Ashima, it is doubtful that there was any confusion with Eshmun.[99]

Very important in the identification of this deity was the discovery of an Aramaic dedicatory inscription from Teima.[100] The text, written in Imperial Aramaic and dating to around 400, records the dedication of a temple of the god Ṣalm *(ṣlm)* of Rabb along with its pedestal/postement[101] "to the gods Sengallā *(šngl')* and Ashima *('šym')*, the gods of Teima" (lines 6-7).[102] This

98. Simo Parpola and Kazuko Watanabe, *Neo-Assyrian Treaties and Loyalty Oaths*. SAA 2 (Helsinki: Helsinki University Press, 1988), 27, line iv.14.

99. Mordechai Cogan, "Ashima," *DDD*, 105-6. The resemblance of the divine names Ashima and Eshmun may be merely morphological, having no bearing upon their characters, powers or functions; Zadok, *JANES* 8 (1976): 118-19. It seems very likely that Ashima ≠ Eshmun. See Sergio Ribichini, "Eshmun," *DDD*, 306-9; and Matthias Delcor, "La divinité Ashima de Samarie en 2 R. 17,30 et ses survivances: Du paganisme au Judaïsme samaritain," in *Proceedings of the First International Congress of the Société d'Études samaritaines. Tel Aviv, 11-13 April 1988*, ed. Abraham Tal and Moshe Florentin (Tel Aviv: Tel Aviv University, 1991), 33-48, esp. 38. For some early reflections on the deity, see Edward König, "Die Gottheit Aschima," *ZAW* 34 (1914): 16-30.

100. A. Livingstone, B. Spaie, M. Ibrahim, M. Kamel, and S. Taimani, "Taima: Recent Sounding and New Inscribed Material," *Atlal* 7 (1983): 102-16 and pls. 87-97, esp. 108-11, pl. 96; and Klaus Beyer and Livingstone, "Die neuesten aramäischen Inschriften aus Taima," *ZDMG* 137 (1987): 285-96, esp. 286-88; and "Eine neue reicharamäische Inschrift aus Taima," *ZDMG* 140 (1990): 1-2.

101. Livingstone (in *Studia Aramaica: New Sources and New Approaches*, ed. Markham J. Geller, Jonas C. Greenfield, and Michael P. Weitzman. JSSSup 4 [Oxford: Oxford University Press, 1995], 140) translates "as a postement." See *DNWSI*, 697, s.v. *mšb₁*.

102. Understanding Hamath in 2 Kgs. 17:30 to be a reference to Hamath on the Orontes, Basile Aggoula attempts to explain the presence of Hamatheans in Teima (since the deity Ashima is now clearly attested there) by positing a military campaign against Hamath by Nabonidus in his second year followed by a campaign against Adammu in Arabia in his third year. Thus he ingeniously theorizes a deportation of Hamatheans to Teima to account for the presence of the deity there. He bases this on the Nabonidus Chronicle. See B. Aggoula, "Studia Aramaica II," *Syria* 62 (1985): 61-76, esp. 70. The problem with Aggoula's proposal is the Nabonidus Chronicle (Grayson, *ABC*, Chronicle 7, 104-11, esp. 105) does not record a military campaign against Hamath in year 2. The text states "[The second year . . .] in the month of Tebet, it was cold in Hamath *(ina* ᵐᵃᵗ*Ha-ma-a-tú* SID; note not *ana* ᵐᵃᵗ*Ha-ma-a-tú)*. For further discussion, see Paul-Alain Beaulieu, *The Reign of Nabonidus, King of Babylon, 556-539 B.C.* YNER 10 (New Haven: Yale University Press, 1989), 127, 144.

text now confirms the reading of the deity's name as Ashima *('šym')* in the Louvre stela from Teima (lines 3 and 16).[103] Teima[104] is mentioned in the recently published Suḫu Annals and linked with the Arameans; and these are the same inscriptions that mention the Aramaic "Amatu" tribe.[105]

The deity may also be attested at Elephantine in the form Ashem-Bethel *('šmbyt'l)*.[106] Some Aramaic personal names contain the deity as a theophoric element (e.g., 'Ašimkudurri, 'Ašimrām, 'Ašimšēzib, 'Ašimzabad).[107] A Greek inscription from Kafr Nebo near Aleppo mentions Συμβέτυλος (= Ashem-Bethel).[108]

Finally, Ashima is very likely attested at Syene in an Aramaic text written in Demotic script known today as Papyrus Amherst 63.[109] The text contains three occurrences of the name:

103. For the text of the Louvre Stela, see *KAI* 1, no. 228; *SSI* 2, no. 30. *KAI* reads line 3: [*w'š*]*yr'* and line 16 *w'šyr'*; *SSI* reads line 3: [*w'š*]*yŕ'* and line 16 *ŵ'šyŕ'*. However, the fact that the sequence in both instances is *šlm* → *šngl'* → DN, "the gods of Teima" (same as in the new dedicatory inscription from Teima) seems to prove that the reading of the DN should be read *'šym'*, and not *'šyŕ'*. See Lemaire, "Les inscriptions araméennes anciennes de Teima," 70.

104. Delcor (42) notes the problem posed by the presence of the cult of Ashima at the oasis of Teima for connections of the deity with Hamath on the Orontes, although he maintains this connection in his article.

105. See *COS* 2:279-82, lines i.7b-16a and iv.26b'-38'; and Paul-Eugène Dion, "Les Araméens du moyen-euphrate au VIIIe siècle à la lumière des inscriptions des maîtres de Suhu et Mari," *Congress Volume, Paris 1992*, ed. J. A. Emerton. VTS 61 (Leiden: E. J. Brill, 1995), 53-73.

106. *TAD* (1993), 234, 127; van der Toorn, *Numen* 39 (1992): 80-101. The deity's name may be a theophoric element in over a half-dozen Aramaic personal names. Edward Lipiński suggests that the theophoric element is attested in a 7th-century personal name from Calaḥ (CTN II no. 247, lines 5' and 11'); *The Arameans: Their Ancient History, Culture, Religion*. OLA 100 (Leuven: Peeters, 2000), 573, nn. 101 and 607. However, this theophoric element in the name is not clearly preserved. See *PNA* 1/1:232, *s.v.* Atara[. . .].

107. See Pierre Grelot, *Documents araméens d'Égypte*. LAPO 5 (Paris: Éditions du Cerf, 1972), 464.

108. Mark Lidzbarski, *Ephemeris für semitische Epigraphik* (Giessen: J. Ricker, 1915), 2:323-24.

109. See Richard C. Steiner, "The Aramaic Text in Demotic Script," *COS* 1:309-27; "The Aramaic Text in Demotic Script: The Liturgy of a New Year's Festival Imported from Bethel to Syene by Exiles from Rash," *JAOS* 111 (1991): 362-63; "Papyrus Amherst 63: A New Source for the Language, Literature, Religion, and History of the Arameans," in Geller, Greenfield, and Weitzman, 199-207; Steiner and Charles F. Nimms, "You Can't Offer Your Sacrifice and Eat It Too: A Polemical Poem from the Aramaic Text in Demotic Script," *JNES* 43 (1984): 89-114; "Ashurbanipal and Shamash-shum-ukin: A Tale of Two Brothers from the Aramaic Text in Demotic Script," *RB* 92 (1985): 60-81; Ingo Kottsieper, "Anmerkungen zu Pap. Amherst 63 Teil II-V," *UF* 29 (1997): 385-434.

Passage	Writing in Demotic	Aramaic transliteration	Translation
XV.1	*šbytr*[ᵍ]	*'š(m)-bytl*	Ashim-Bethel
XV.14	*š.bytr*[ᵍ]	*'š(m)-byt-(')l*	Ashim-Bethel
XV.15	*šbytl*[ᵍ]	*'š(m)-byt-(')l*	Ashim-Bethel

Two of these occurrences are in a mostly complete prayer to the deity (lines XV.13-17).[110] Furthermore the text may also refer to the deity with the epithet "Resident of Hamath" (*t.r̄ ḥ.m.t*ᵐ — *d(')r ḥmt*) (lines VIII.6, 10).[111] If this is correct, this could be construed as evidence for the deportees coming from Hamath on the Orontes. But this is far from certain since Richard C. Steiner notes that the original homeland of these Arameans at Syene is called *rš* and *'rš* in the papyrus — a land between Babylonia and Elam[112] (see also the three problems with this geographic identification with Hamath on the Orontes discussed above).[113]

While some scholars have suggested that the text of Amos 8:14 should be emended from *bᵉ'ašmat šōmrôn* "by the guilt of Samaria" to either *bᵉ'ašimat šōmrôn* "by Ashima of Samaria"[114] or *bᵉ'ašērat šōmrôn* "by the Asherah of Samaria," Judith M. Hadley rightly comments:

> since the text as preserved has a perfectly good Hebrew word (*'ašmāh*) which admirably fits the context, there is no need whatsoever for emendation. One can only speculate upon the real meaning behind the "guilt of Samaria," but if the asherah was still standing there, it is easy to believe that the phrase might bring it to mind.[115]

---

110. Steiner, *COS* 1:321.

111. Steiner, *Studia Aramaica*, 205.

112. The internal textual evidence for this is discussed by Steiner, *JAOS* 111 (1991): 362-63.

113. Lemaire gives the further suggestion: "En fait, ce rapprochement entre la deuxième divinité de Teima (*'šym'*) et un culte étranger pratiqué à Samarie à l'époque néo-assyrienne s'éclaire surtout à la lumière des annales de Sargon II qui rapportent la défaite des tribus arabes (Tamud, Ibadid, Marsimani et Ephah) et leur déportation à Samarie vers 716/715 av. J.-C."; "Les inscriptions araméennes anciennes de Teima," 70.

114. Alasdair Livingstone, "New Light on the Ancient Town of Taimā'," in Geller, Greenfield, and Weitzman, 133-43, esp. 142; Stephanie M. Dalley, "Yahweh in Hamath in the 8th Century B.C.: Cuneiform Material, and Historical Deductions," *VT* 40 (1990): 21-32, esp. 30; Delcor, 39-40.

115. Judith M. Hadley, *The Cult of Asherah in Ancient Israel and Judah: Evidence for a Hebrew Goddess* (University of Cambridge Oriental Publications 57; Cambridge: Cambridge University Press, 2000), 77. Delcor's argument (39-40) that the word *'šmh* is late is based on circular lexical reasoning.

Sepharvaim/Adrammelech and Anammelech

Sepharvaim (*s^eparwayim*) has been the most difficult entity to identify. One suggestion has been to locate it in Phoenicia.[116] This identification has been based on two points: the identifications of the deities Adrammelech and Anammelech with Phoenician deities, and the geography implied by the serial order in 2 Kgs. 17:24. The latter point is not a very strong argument, since the serial order is so varied and used for different purposes (see the discussion above). The identifications of these deities will be discussed below. Although the Assyrian kings Sennacherib and Esarhaddon did deport Phoenicians, there is no evidence of any deportation of Phoenicians to Samaria, but rather to other locations.

Another suggestion is to locate Sepharvaim in Syria.[117] This understanding equates Sepharvaim with Sibraim (Ezek. 47:16).[118] But Sibraim was located on the border between the lands of Hamath and Damascus, and it is thus likely to have belonged to one or the other's territory.[119]

A third suggestion is to equate Sepharvaim with the Babylonian city of Sippar.[120] But G. R. Driver's proposal that Sepharvaim is a dual form reflecting the two parts that formed the city of Sippar is untenable.[121]

Finally, it has been argued that "Sepharvaim was probably a settlement in the Chaldean territory of Bīt Awukāni."[122] Bīt Awukāni is mentioned in the texts of Sargon. Zadok has pointed to the city of Sipraʿani ([uru]*Si-pí-ra-i-ni*), a Chaldean toponym in the Murašû archive from Nippur.[123] This city is appar-

---

116. See Stephen A. Kaufman, "The Enigmatic Adad-Milki," *JNES* 37 (1978): 101-9, esp. 102, n. 9; cf. Becking, *The Fall of Samaria*, 101-3.

117. John Day, *Molech: A God of Human Sacrifice in the Old Testament.* University of Cambridge Oriental Publications 41 (Cambridge: Cambridge University Press, 1989), 46.

118. Montgomery and Gehman, 472; van der Toorn, *Numen* 39 (1992): 92. It is quite erroneous to cite the Babylonian Chronicle as evidence of this city mentioned in Ezekiel and equate it with 2 Kgs. 17:24ff. See e.g., Gray, *I & II Kings*, 652; T. R. Hobbs, *2 Kings.* WBC 13 (Waco: Word, 1985), 237. This interpretation was first popularized by Hugo Winckler, *Die Keilschriften und das Alte Testament,* ed. Eberhard Schrader (Berlin: Reuther & Reichard, 1903), 62. But the Babylonian Chronicle reads *Samara'in* (Samaria), not *Sabara'in* (Chronicle I, col. i, lines 27-32). See *ABC,* 73. For further discussion, see Stefan Timm, "Die Eroberung Samarias aus assyrisch-babylonischer Sicht," *WO* 20-21 (1989-90): 62-82, esp. 65-66; and K. Lawson Younger, Jr., "The Fall of Samaria in Light of Recent Research," *CBQ* 61 (1999): 461-82.

119. Zadok, *JANES* 8 (1976): 115-16.

120. G. R. Driver, "Geographical Problems," *ErIsr* 5 (1958): 16*-20*, esp. 18*-19*.

121. Zadok, *JANES* 8 (1976): 155, n. 15. Michael C. Astour's attempt to locate Sepharvaim in Media seems strained; "Sepharvaim," *IDBSup* 807.

122. Na'aman and Zadok, *JCS* 40 (1988): 44; Zadok, *JANES* 8 (1976): 115-17.

123. Zadok, *JANES* 8 (1976): 115-16.

ently mentioned in Sennacherib's annals, where it is spelled [uru]*Šá-par-ri-e*.[124] Thus this city of Saparrê/Sipra'ani would be located south of Nippur. This identification appears to be the most likely.

The first deity mentioned in connection with the people of Sepharvaim is Adrammelech (*'adrammelek*).[125] Some scholars suggest emending Adram to Adad (*'dd*) and linking the name Adrammelech to Adad-milki (an Assyro-Babylonian deity[126] supposedly known from personal names in the archive of Tell Halaf from the region of Harran and Gozan).[127] Some serious doubts about this identification have been voiced.[128] Olof Pedersén has argued that the signs read Adad-milki (i.e., U.U) are simply to be read Dada or Dadda, caritative forms of Adad.[129] Alan R. Millard comments:

> If the Sepharvites were of Aramean or Phoenician origin, it is very un-likely that the name of their god would have lost its initial *h*, unless the Hebrew authors of Kings copied the information from a cuneiform text in Babylonian, which would not express it.[130]

The preferred interpretation of *'adrammelek* is to see it as an adjective + noun: *'dr* + *mlk* "the glorious one is king."[131] This explanation would link the deity to a Phoenician origin, since the root *'dr* is absent in Aramaic.[132] None-

124. D. D. Luckenbill, *The Annals of Sennacherib*. OIP 2 (Chicago: University of Chicago Press, 1924), 53, line 45.

125. Alan R. Millard, "Adrammelech," *DDD*, 10-11. While one of Sennacherib's sons is called Adrammelech according to 2 Kgs. 19:37, this should not be confused with the deity.

126. First suggested by P. Jensen, "Review of H. V. Hilprecht (ed.), *The Babylonian Expedition of the University of Pennsylvania*," *ZA* 13 (1898): 333 n. 1; and then later by A. Ungnad, in *Die Inschriften vom Tell Halaf*, ed. Johannes Friedrich, G. Rudolf Meyer, Ungnad, and Ernst F. Weidner. AfO Beiheft 6 (Berlin: Ernst F. Weidner, 1940), 58; and accepted by many, e.g., William F. Albright, *Archaeology and the Religion of Israel*, 5th ed. (Garden City: Doubleday, 1968), 157-58; Montgomery and Gehman, 476; Cogan and Tadmor, 212.

127. K. Deller, "Review of R. de Vaux, Les sacrifices de l'Ancien Testament," *Or* 34 (1965): 382-83.

128. Kaufman, 101-9.

129. Olof Pedersén, "The Reading of the Neo-Assyrian Logogram U.U," *OrSuec* 33-35 (1984-86): 313-16. See now the "Adad-milki-X" names in *PNA* 1:28-29; and the "Dādî," "Dādi-X" names in *PNA* 1:360-65.

130. Millard, "Adrammelech," 10.

131. Millard, "Adrammelech," 10.

132. Kaufman, 102-3, n. 9. Adarmilk (*'drmlk*) occurs as the name of a king of Byblos in the 4th century. See Charles R. Krahmalkov, *Phoenician-Punic Dictionary*. OLA 90. Studia Phoenicia 15 (Leuven: Peeters, 2000), 37; Edward Lipiński et al., eds., *Dictionnaire de la Civilisation Phénicienne et Punique* (Paris: Brepols, 1992), 5; George Francis Hill, *Catalogue of the Greek Coins of Phoenicia* (London: British Museum, 1910), 96, no. 10 + pl. XII.3 (but photo is unclear);

theless, the movement of peoples and cults by natural processes of migration and trade, as well as Assyrian deportations, could account for the movement of a group of Phoenicians who worshiped *'adrammelek* to a Babylonian context, only to see their descendents transplanted to Samaria (this is perhaps not dissimilar to the Aramaic tribe of "Amatu" who worshipped Ashima discussed above). The worship of the deity (by burning of children) may indicate a link to Molech.

The second deity, Anammelech (*'ănammelek*) has been understood as a composite of the Babylonian divine name *Anu(m)* + the West Semitic noun *melek* "king."[133] More specifically, John Gray suggested a "syncretism between the cult of Mesopotamian Anu and West Semitic Melek, the Venus-star Atar, to whom human sacrifice was made"[134] and hence a Hebrew version of Atar-Melek.[135] But the divine name Anu is written with an *aleph* in West Semitic transcription, never with an *ayin*.[136] Thus there is no evidence in this name (*'ănammelek*) for syncretism of Babylonian Anu with West Semitic Melek (Attar).[137] Preferably, the name should be understood as a composite of *'n* + *mlk*. The first element is the West Semitic male counterpart to the goddess 'Anat (*'nt*). The second element would create the sentence name "'An is king."

Personal names from the early 2nd millennium may incorporate the form.[138] Herbert B. Huffmon lists two names from Mari that contain the divine name 'An (written: ḫn; ḫan-): *Ba-lí-ḫa-an* and *Bi-na-ḫa-an*.[139] The theophoric *'n* is found in a number of personal names from Ugarit: *'bd'n*, *Ml'n*, *Šm'n*, *'nil* and *Bin*(DUMU)-*a-nu*, *Nûr*(NE)-*dA-na*.[140] The divine name

Maurice Dunand, *Fouilles de Byblos.* Bibliothèque archéologique et historique 24 (Paris: Paul Geuthner, 1939), 1:407.

133. Gray, *I & II Kings*, 655; Montgomery and Gehman, 476; Cogan and Tadmor, 212.

134. Gray, *I & II Kings*, 655.

135. John Gray, "The Desert God 'Attar in the Literature and Religion of Canaan," *JNES* 8 (1949): 78-80.

136. Alan R. Millard, "Anammelech," *DDD*, 34-35; For examples of Anu as a theophoric element spelled with an *aleph*, see Joseph A. Fitzmyer and Stephen A. Kaufman, *An Aramaic Bibliography, Part I: Old, Official and Biblical Aramaic* (Baltimore: Johns Hopkins University Press, 1992), 170, seal no. 24 (*'n'h'tn*); 52, Uruk Bricks (*'n'blt*). See Wolfgang Röllig, "Griechische Eigennamen in Texten der babylonischen Spätzeit," *Or* 29 (1960): 376-91.

137. Karel van der Toorn has suggested that the name *'nmlk* in 2 Kgs. 17:31 be emended to read *'gmlk* (Og-melech). But in light of a clear alternative that does not require emendation, it seems preferable to retain the reading *'nmlk*.

138. Herbert B. Huffmon, *Amorite Personal Names in the Mari Texts* (Baltimore: Johns Hopkins University Press, 1965), 199; Ran Zadok, *On West Semites in Babylonia during the Chaldean and Achaemenian Periods* (Jerusalem: H. J. and Z. Wanaarta, 1977), 39.

139. Huffmon, 199.

140. Frauke Gröndahl, *Die Personennamen der Texte aus Ugarit.* Studia Pohl 1 (Rome:

occurs in a personal name found in an Amarna letter: *Bin*(DUMU)-*a-na* (EA 170:37).[141] This might be the same *An(n)a* found in the Old Assyrian texts from Cappadocia[142] and in the Execration text in Posener, E.8: *'prw'nw*.[143] Unfortunately, the deity remains obscure,[144] known primarily through personal names.[145]

Interestingly, at the site of Emar, a god called Anna (*Anna*) is attested. Not only does this deity receive offerings at Emar (the temple of ᵈ*An-na* [AN/ DINGIR.AN.NA] is included among recipients of sacrifice on the 7th of the month of Zerati in Emar 447:13), but even a month is named after the deity (Emar 446:77-82).[146] A form of the same deity is written without the repeated

---

Päpstliches Bibelinstitut, 1967), 110. '*bd'n* (KTU² 4.75:v.23); *bn.'n* (RS 163.355; *PRU* 2.46.47; KTU² 4.232:47); '*n'il* (RS 15.064; *PRU* 2.66:3; KTU² 4.159:3); *Nûr*(SI)-ᵈ*A-na* (de Langhe, II, 265); *Bin*(DUMU)-*a-nu* (RS 17:38 rev. 3'; Ug. 5 8); *Bin*(DUMU)-ˡ*a-ni* (RS 17:86 + 441 + 208:17).

141. For this name, see Richard S. Hess, *Amarna Personal Names*. ASORDS 9 (Winona Lake: Eisenbrauns, 1993), 58, 235; "Divine Names in the Amarna Texts," *UF* 18 (1986): 149-68, esp. 150; D. O. Edzard, "An," in *Götter und Mythen im vorderen Orient*, ed. Hans Wilhelm Haussig, 2nd ed. Wörterbuch der Mythologie, 1: *Die alten Kulturvölker 1* (Stuttgart: E. Klett, 1983), 40-41.

142. Julius Lewy, "Amurritica," *HUCA* 32 (1961): 31-74, esp. 36-38. Note the names: *Ma-nu-um-ba-lu-um-A-na*, *En-um-A-na*, *A-na-lí* (var. *An-na-ili*), *Puzur-A-na*, ˥*Ša-at-A-na*. Also a number of seal inscriptions from the Old Babylonian period define the god Amurrum as the son of the god *An-na*. Lewy sums up by stating: "To be sure, L. Delaporte and other savants who saw in AN.NA a Sumerogram of Akkadian Anum rendered these legends by 'Amurrum, the son of Anum.' But while it is obvious that the ancients came to identify Anna with Anum just as they identified Amurrum with Adad, it cannot well be assumed that this identification was readily accepted by the people of West Semitic extraction. In fact, the Kültepe texts make it virtually certain that, in the period here under discussion, people still distinguished between Amurrum's father Anna and Anum. For the defective spelling *A-na* which alternates with *En-na* and *E-na* but never with AN.NA shows that the idea of regarding AN.NA as a Sumerogram for Anum did not occur to the Old Assyrian scribes of the twentieth and nineteenth century (sic)" (37-38).

143. Georges Posener, *Cinq figurines d'envoûtement*. Bibliothèque d'étude 101 (Cairo: Institut français d'archéologie orientale du Caire, 1987), 16; Kurt Sethe, *Die Ächtung feindlicher Fürsten, Volker und Dinge auf altägyptischen Tongefässscherben des Mittleren Reiches* (Berlin: Akademie der Wissenschaften, 1926); Posener, *Princes et pays d'Asie et de Nubie* (Brussels, 1940); Robert Kriech Ritner, *The Mechanics of Ancient Egyptian Magical Practice*. SAOC 54 (Chicago: Oriental Institute, 1993), 136-90.

144. See also Walter C. Kaiser, Jr., *The Ugaritic Pantheon* (diss., Brandeis, 1973), 151. According to Kaiser, this deity occurs in RS 24.244 (*KTU²* 1.100). However, on closer inspection the word '*n* should be translated "spring." See Dennis Pardee, "Ugaritic Liturgy against Venomous Reptiles (RS 24.244)," *COS* 1.94 (295).

145. Sergio Ribichini and Paolo Xella, "Problem di onomastica ugaritica il caso dei Teofori," *SEL* 8 (1991): 149-70, esp. 166. They list the following Ugaritic names: *abd'n*, *ml'n*(?), '*bd'n*, *bn'n*, '*nil*(?), *šm'n*.

146. Daniel E. Fleming, *Time at Emar: The Cultic Calendar and the Rituals from the Diviner's Archive* (Winona Lake: Eisenbrauns, 2000), 162, 272-73.

AN/DINGIR sign: *a-na An-na ša kib-ri* "Anna of the River-bank" (Emar 373:99).[147] According to Daniel E. Fleming,[148] the divine name may be attested in personal names from Mari (written AN/DINGIR.AN.NA), although Jean-Marie Durand reads the AN.NA as *Ilu-na*.[149]

Fleming notes that the identity of Anna at Emar is uncertain, though the name resembles closely the name of the Old Mesopotamian sky-god Anu. Furthermore, there is a precedent for the incorporation of a Mesopotamian deity in the long-established local cult in the rites for the month following the month of ᵈAnna where the writing *Il-li-la* appears to represent Enlil.[150] If this is the case, then the writing of *'ănammelek* (with the *ayin*) removes any connections of the Emar deity with the deity mentioned in 2 Kgs. 17:31. However, the writing of the name with and without the doubled AN/DINGIR sign (i.e., AN/DINGIR.AN.NA or AN.NA) may indicate that the deity in view at Emar is the West Semitic deity 'An. Further investigation into the deity's use in 2nd-millennium personal names may bear this out.

In the 1st millennium the deity is attested in a Phoenician name *bn'n* incised on an 11th/10th-century arrowhead from the Beqa'.[151] Like Adrammelech above, this deity was worshipped by the burning of children, which may suggest a relationship with Molech.[152]

Synthesis

Unfortunately, the king responsible for the repopulation of Samaria is not identified in the text of 2 Kings 17. The only Assyrian monarch mentioned by name in the chapter is Shalmaneser V (v. 3), who can hardly be the king in view in v. 24.

Some scholars believe that these deportations were primarily the work of Sargon II that occurred approximately from 716 to 708.[153] Certainly if these

147. Fleming, 242.

148. Fleming, 162, n. 97.

149. See Jean-Marie Durand, *Les documents épistolaires du palais de Mari*. LAPO 16 (Paris: Cerf, 1997), 1:338: *Ilu.na*-Addu.

150. Fleming, *Time at Emar*, 163.

151. J. T. Milik, "An Unpublished Arrow-head with Phoenician Inscription of the 11th-10th Century B.C.," *BASOR* 143 (1956): 3-6; F. L. Benz, *Personal Names in the Phoenician and Punic Inscriptions*. Studia Pohl 8 (Rome: Pontifical Biblical Institute, 1972), 89, 380.

152. Benz, col. 59. Kaufman, 102-3.

153. Na'aman and Zadok, *JCS* 40 (1988): 36-46: "All these areas were conquered by Sargon II during his campaigns against Merodach-baladan in the years 710-709 BCE" (44). See also Na'aman, *TA* 20 (1993): 110-12; Na'aman and Zadok, *TA* 27 (2000): 177-79.

deportations were the work of only one Assyrian monarch, Sargon is the best candidate in light of the discussion of the identifications above. Of course, even if 2 Kings 17 refers only to deportations made by Sargon, this does not exclude any later waves of deportations to Samaria made by later Assyrian kings. But the fact is 2 Kings 17 does not even record all of the deportations to Samaria made by Sargon. Sargon claims to have defeated and deported some Arabs to Samaria (Samerina):[154]

> The Tamudi, Ibadidi, Marsima[ni] and Hayappâ, the land of distant Arabia, inhabitants of the desert, who knew[155] neither overseer nor commander, who never brought their tribute to any king — with the help of Aššur, my lord, I defeated them. I deported the rest of them. I settled (them) in Samaria/Samerina.

Not much is known about these nomadic Arabian tribes.[156] However, all of them, except for the Tamudi, can be regarded as Midianite tribes.[157] The fact that the Hayappâ[158] (who may be equated with the Old Testament *'ph*) had to pay tribute to Tiglath-Pileser III[159] exposes Sargon's claim to have conquered a people "who never brought tribute to any king" to be a stereotyped expression used for ideological purposes.

Not only does 2 Kings 17 not include all of the deportations to Samaria made by Sargon, but it may not include all other deportations to the province

154. Annals, lines 120b-23a. Fuchs, 110; *COS* 2:293. The same event is reported in Sargon II's Cylinder inscription: ". . . who conquered the Tamudi, the Ibadidi, the Marsimani and the Hayappâ, of whom the remainder I removed and settled in the land of Bīt-Ḫumria (Israel)"; Fuchs, 34, lines 19-20; *COS* 2:298. For the date of this deportation, see the discussion of Na'aman and Zadok, *JCS* 40 (1988): 43.

155. The Arab tribes are the subject and not the object of *idūma*; see Cogan and Tadmor, 337; Becking, *The Fall of Samaria*, 103.

156. According to Israel Eph'al, it is doubtful whether there were ever any military engagements between the Assyrians and these Arab tribes. He feels that the text reflects a spontaneous settlement of some Arab tribes in the territory of the Assyrian province Samerina that was simply tolerated by the Assyrians; *The Ancient Arabs* (Leiden: E. J. Brill, 1982), 105-11. However, there is some evidence for some type of military engagement between the Assyrians and the Arab tribes. See K. Lawson Younger, Jr., "Recent Study on Sargon II, King of Assyria: Implications for Biblical Studies," in *Mesopotamia and the Bible: Comparative Explorations,* ed. Mark W. Chavalas and Younger. JSOTSup 341 (Sheffield: Sheffield Academic, 2002), 288-329, esp. 310-11; and Becking, *The Fall of Samaria*, 102-4.

157. Ernst Axel Knauf, *Midian: Untersuchungen zur Geschichte Palästinas und Nordarabiens am Ende des 2. Jahrtausends v. Chr.* (Wiesbaden: Harrassowitz, 1988).

158. It is often thought that they controlled the caravan routes on the Arabian peninsula.

159. Hayim Tadmor, *The Inscriptions of Tiglath-Pileser III, King of Assyria* (Jerusalem: Israel Academy of Sciences and Humanities, 1994), 200-1, line 9'.

made by other Assyrian kings. The biblical material mentions some of these later deportations.[160] For example, in Ezra 4:2, the deportees to Samaria implore Zerubbabel:

> Let us build (the temple) with you, because like you we seek your God, and we have been sacrificing to him ever since the days of Esarhaddon, king of Assyria, who brought us here.[161]

One more witness is found in Ezra 4:9-10 which mentions:

> ... the Persians, the people of Erech, the Babylonians, the people of Susa, that is, the Elamites, and the rest of the nations whom the great and honorable Osnappar (Assurbanipal) deported and settled in the city (var. cities) of Samaria and in the rest of (the province of) Beyond the River (Trans-Euphrates). ...

Papyrus Amherst 63, the Aramaic text in Demotic script mentioned above, contains an interesting New Year's festival liturgy of some exiles imported to Upper Egypt, probably Syene, from Bethel. These exiles came originally from places called *rš* and *'rš* in the papyrus. These place names should most likely be identified with land between Babylonia and Elam known as Rāši and Arāšu in the Assyrian sources. Steiner suggests that the people of these two areas were captured by Assurbanipal during his campaign against Elam, and deported to the Assyrian province of Samaria. According to Steiner, there is reason to believe that most if not all of them wound up in Bethel (cf. 2 Kgs. 17:28 above), joining the foreign colonists settled there by earlier Assyrian kings.[162] Their subsequent migration to Egypt may be recorded in the text's account of the arrival of soldiers from Judah and Samaria.[163]

While Steiner's reconstruction may remain the best explanation for all

---

160. The personal names attested in the Wadi Daliyeh papyri witness to the ethnicity of these deportees, although the date of the inscriptions makes them more indirect witnesses than primary evidence. See Douglas M. Gropp, *The Samaria Papyri from Wâdi ed-Dâliyeh: The Slave Sales* (diss., Harvard, 1986); M. J. W. Leith, ed., *Wadi Daliyeh I: The Wadi Daliyeh Seal Impressions.* DJD 24 (Oxford: Clarendon, 1997); Gropp, James C. Vanderkam, and Monica Brady, eds., *Wadi Daliyeh II: The Samaria Papyri from Wadi Daliyeh.* DJD 28 (Oxford: Clarendon, 2001).

161. The tradition preserved in Isa. 7:8 ("Within sixty-five years [i.e., ca. 669-667] Ephraim will be too shattered to be a people . . .") should probably be linked to this passage. Whether it is a gloss or not is not the issue here. Rather, it is a witness to an additional tradition concerning the repopulation of Samaria.

162. Steiner, *COS* 1:310.

163. See Steiner, *COS* 1:321, lines XVI.1-6.

of the sources, it is important to note, as Na'aman correctly points out, that Sargon II attacked Rāši[164] and may have deported some of the inhabitants from this area to Bethel.

Conclusion

In conclusion, it is very evident from the biblical texts, as well as from the Mesopotamian texts, that 2 Kings 17 does not give a complete account of all the deportations to Samaria. The text was, no doubt, written at least three generations after the first deportations (2 Kgs. 17:41). Thus it telescopes many years into its presentation,[165] perhaps covering the entire period from Shalmaneser V to Assurbanipal.[166] But thankfully due to the ancient Near Eastern textual evidence, there is a much better knowledge of the identifications of the peoples and their deities who inhabited Samaria after its fall.

---

164. See Fuchs, 152, line 302.

165. See Younger, *CBQ* 61 (1999): 461-82; *JBL* 117 (1998): 201-27.

166. Cogan and Tadmor, 208-13; Bustenay Oded, *Mass Deportations and Deportees in the Neo-Assyrian Empire* (Wiesbaden: Reichert, 1979), 66. An analogy can be drawn from the Aramaic Assur ostracon, which contains a list of various ethnic groups deported to the region of Uruk in four successive reigns. See *KAI* 233 (lines 15-16): "Tiglath-pileser deported captives from Bit-Amukani; and Ululai (Shalmaneser V) deported [captives] from Bit-Adini; and Sargon deported captives from Dur-Sin; and [Sen]nacherib [deported cap]tives from Kish. . . ." The Israelites themselves were deported by Tiglath-pileser III and Sargon II over a minimum period of 734-716. See Younger, *JBL* 117 (1998): 201-27.

Methodological Issues in Reconstructing Language Systems from Epigraphic Fragments[1]

CYNTHIA L. MILLER

Introduction

Artifacts of language pose unique challenges for reconstruction and interpretation. Like other material artifacts, epigraphic remains are often physically fragmentary, but the task of reconstruction does not end when all of the pieces of the ostracon or tablet have been joined.[2] Nor does it end when the script has been deciphered and a relatively coherent text can be read. Rather, as we decipher, read, and interpret texts, one of our important goals as Semitists must be to reconstruct the language systems, the relevant structural features of those languages that are represented in the texts.

The reconstruction of a *language system* should not be construed as the reconstruction of a *language*.[3] Linguistic expression as found in any language

1. I am grateful to Michael Patrick O'Connor for discussions relating to the paper, to Dennis Pardee and Pierre Bordreuil for allowing me to cite a sentence from a Ugaritic text they are publishing (RS 96.2039), and to Dennis Pardee, John A. Cook, and Robert D. Holmstedt for reading a previous draft. This research was supported in part by Ettinger Foundation research funds donated to the Department of Hebrew and Semitic Studies, University of Wisconsin-Madison.

2. In using the term "epigraphic," I refer to all West Semitic texts that are outside of the manuscript traditions, regardless of whether they are written on durable materials (i.e., epigraphic in the strict sense) or not. At various points in the discussion, reference will be made to linguistic analyses involving the Hebrew Bible, even though the Bible is within a manuscript tradition and falls outside of the rubric of "epigraphic" and even though linguistic research on scribally redacted texts involves additional difficulties not considered here.

3. The distinction originated with Ferdinand de Saussure, the founder of modern lin-

is infinite — anything, literally, can be said, and it can be said in an infinite number of ways. Reconstruction of an ancient language is thus impossible. By contrast, a language system — the formal, abstract structure underlying linguistic expression — is finite. The language system is thus amenable to description.

The distinction between linguistic expression and the language system can be illustrated by considering the sound stream of language. An acoustic analysis of speech reveals that no two speakers ever pronounce the same word with precisely the same acoustic features; instead, there are minor variations in pitch, duration, and frequency of the sound wave. By contrast, within the language system, a particular word has a distinctive phonological shape — a shape that is an abstraction or idealization, rather than a transcription of the acoustic realization of that word as it is pronounced by any speaker.[4] The reality of the structural shape of the word lies rather in the fact that a speaker must pronounce the word within the boundaries of its phonological structure, if s/he is to be understood.[5] Language structure, as opposed to linguistic expression, is thus necessarily an abstraction, but an abstraction that is central to the shaping (and perception) of linguistic expressions.[6]

Although our goal must be the description of the language system, we have no direct access to it. Instead, we have only instantiations of the language system as found in linguistic expression. That is, it is only by analyzing specific texts (instantiations of language) that we are able to discern the language system (the abstract structures of language).

Among the basic components of language structure that must be accounted for in any linguistic description are phonology, morphology, and syntax. Phonology, the sound system, is the most highly constrained, comprising a discrete set of relevant members or phonemes, numbering in the dozens.[7] The syntactic component is much larger and allows for greater vari-

---

guistics, who differentiated *langue* (the language system) from *parole* (instantiations of language); *Course in General Linguistics*, ed. Charles Bally and Albert Sechehaye, trans. Wade Baskin (New York: McGraw-Hill, 1966), 9-15.

4. See Andrew Spencer, *Phonology: Theory and Description*. Introductory Linguistics 1 (Oxford: Blackwell, 1996), 1-42.

5. For a description of the acoustic features of speech that are relevant to speech perception, see J. M. Pickett, *The Sounds of Speech Communication: A Primer of Acoustic Phonetics and Speech Perception*. Perspectives in Audiology (Baltimore: University Park, 1980), 169-87.

6. One of the important goals of linguistic theory involves determining the universal grammar of language, i.e., those features of language structure that are innate, thus allowing children to learn any language.

7. A phonemic analysis of a language should include the following components: the phonemic inventory (the list of distinctive sounds), allophonic rules (conditioned variations of the

ation and alternate grammatical strategies, although its structures are also finite. In between these two extremes lies morphology, the part of the system involving the smallest grammatically relevant building blocks of language. Of these components of language structure, phonology is substantially different, in that it is the only part that is not essentially meaning-bearing.[8] The inventory of phonemes does not, after all, affect our interpretation of any text. Even our understanding of the Shibboleth incident in Judg. 12:6 does not depend upon knowing precisely the two dialectal pronunciations of the word.[9]

Reconstructions of ancient language systems, then, are derived from, but not isomorphic with, the remnants of linguistic expression that are recorded in the epigraphic fragments. The possibility of accomplishing this task — the linguistic analysis of epigraphic remains — meets with considerable pessimism within our field. It is perhaps best summarized by the Lambdinian dictum that we are "working with no data."[10] Although his comment is framed as hyperbole, Lambdin correctly observes that our language data are indeed very limited. Furthermore, acquisition of additional data is sporadic and serendipitous, utterly dependent upon the excavation of sites or — more controversially — the "excavation" of private collections.[11] Additional sources of pessimism are the related refrains that our only linguistic sources

---

distinctive sounds), and phonotactics (statements concerning permissible strings of phonemes); Roger Lass, *Phonology: An Introduction to Basic Concepts.* Cambridge Textbooks in Linguistics (Cambridge: Cambridge University Press, 1984), 21.

8. Saussure (66-70) described this feature of language by saying that the relationship between the shape of a word (the "signifier") and its meaning (the "signified") is arbitrary. As Saussure noted, however, there is a small subset of exceptions — words whose phonological shape is iconic of their meaning (e.g., onomatopoetic words).

9. For one attempt at determining the phonetic values of the sibilants, see Ronald S. Hendel, "Sibilants and *šibbōlet* (Judges 12:6)," *BASOR* 301 (1996): 69-75. Note esp. p. 72: "This solution to the phonetic situation of Judg 12:6 does not require that we know how the sibilants of the various dialects were actually pronounced, it merely involves a recovery of some details of phonetic correspondences as represented in writing."

10. The dictum has been immortalized in Lambdin's Festschrift: David M. Golomb, ed., *"Working with No Data": Semitic and Egyptian Studies Presented to Thomas O. Lambdin* (Winona Lake: Eisenbrauns, 1987).

11. Two important Hebrew ostraca from a private collection were published by Pierre Bordreuil, Felice Israel, and Dennis Pardee, "Deux ostraca paléo-hébreux de la collection Sh. Moussaïeff," *Sem* 46 (1996): 49-76. The authenticity of the inscriptions has been questioned; see Angelika Berlejung and Andres Schüle, "Erwägungen zu den neuen Ostraka aus der Sammlung Moussaïeff," *ZAH* 11 (1998): 68-73; and Israel Eph'al and Joseph Naveh, "Remarks on the Recently Published Moussaieff Ostraca," *IEJ* 48 (1998): 269-73.

are written language as opposed to spoken language, and that there are no native speakers of any of the languages represented in these texts.

In this essay, I reconsider the task of linguistically analyzing epigraphic fragments, focusing upon West Semitic texts. I begin by re-examining three difficulties associated with the task — a limited corpus, a written corpus, and lack of native speakers — in light of linguistic analysis involving modern, spoken languages. Then I suggest that the difficulties we face as Semitists should be reformulated as difficulties involving the assessment of productivity, grammaticalization, and variation. Finally, I consider the use of language typology as an important complement to comparative philology in reconstructing ancient language systems.

The Corpus, Written Texts, and the Native Speaker

The Corpus

The limited nature of the epigraphic corpus is sometimes considered a nearly insuperable obstacle to linguistic analysis. In this regard, the ancient textual remains are unfavorably compared with the language data that are available for analysis of a modern, spoken language.[12] However, because linguistic expression in a modern language is infinite, the problem that Semitists face of too little data is replaced by a different but equally vexing problem — the vastness of the data. As a result, a linguist analyzing a modern language must exercise selectivity in one of two ways. Either the linguist elicits from a native speaker only those linguistic expressions that suit the purposes of analysis; or the linguist must select for analysis a representative number of texts, an approach known as corpus linguistics. Because only the latter approach is available to Semitists, it is worthwhile considering how corpus linguists identify and select a corpus of modern language data for linguistic analysis.

There are three essential design criteria which a linguistic corpus must satisfy. First, the corpus must be *extensive* so that the relevant linguistic features are present within the texts to be analyzed. Second, the corpus must be *representative*, both with respect to the varieties of language contained in it and with respect to the kinds of texts that are included. Third, the corpus

12. D. A. Cruse's remarks are representative: "Probably the most disadvantaged researchers . . . are those who study 'dead' languages. Often virtually the only direct evidence available to them is a corpus of written utterances, of somewhat fortuitous make-up, and now probably fixed for eternity"; *Lexical Semantics*. Cambridge Textbooks in Linguistics (Cambridge: Cambridge University Press, 1986), 8-9.

must be *varied* — an extensive, monolithic corpus is not as valuable as a smaller, diverse one.[13]

What constitutes an extensive, representative, and diverse corpus depends upon the kind of linguistic analysis that one wishes to accomplish. In linguistic studies of modern language corpora, a 1000-word sample has been determined to reflect common grammatical features reliably.[14] Lexicographical research, however, requires a much larger corpus (a million words or more) in order to represent adequately the range of lexical items within the language and the various collocations of those items within different contexts.[15]

In terms of an analysis of epigraphic language data, the discipline of corpus linguistics highlights important issues. Our texts are most limited for lexicographic analysis — no West Semitic language is adequately attested.[16] It is understandable, then, that lexicographers attempt to extend the corpus in one of two ways. One approach groups texts from diverse geographical and temporal contexts together. This approach is exemplified by Charles R. Krahmalkov's *Phoenician-Punic Dictionary*, in which he drew together "material from all sources, irrespective of provenience . . . , period . . . , dialect . . . ,

13. Douglas Biber, Susan Conrad, and Randi Reppen, *Corpus Linguistics: Investigating Language Structure and Use*. Cambridge Approaches to Linguistics (Cambridge: Cambridge University Press, 1998), 246-50. Similarly, see the discussion in Elena Tognini-Bonelli, *Corpus Linguistics at Work*. Studies in Corpus Linguistics 6 (Amsterdam: Benjamins, 2001), 47-64.

14. Douglas Biber, "Methodological Issues Regarding Corpus-based Analyses of Linguistic Variation," *Literary and Linguistic Computing* 5 (1990): 257-69. Biber examined the following grammatical features: first person pronouns, third person pronouns, contractions, past tense verbs, present tense verbs, prepositions, relative clauses, passive constructions, and conditional subordinate clauses.

15. Beyond questions of size, the selection of a corpus also varies with respect to the kinds of questions one seeks to answer. The corpus linguist who investigates differences in the grammatical constructions of men as opposed to women, for example, will need to construct a corpus that includes extensive, representative texts from both categories of speakers.

16. The addition of many Hebrew names to the corpus from seals and bullae has enlarged the range of lexical items; see the collections by Nahman Avigad and Benjamin Sass, *Corpus of West Semitic Stamp Seals* (Jerusalem: Israel Academy of Sciences and Humanities, 1997); Graham I. Davies, *Ancient Hebrew Inscriptions: Corpus and Concordance* (Cambridge: Cambridge University Press, 1991); Robert Deutsch, *Messages from the Past: Hebrew Bullae from the Time of Isaiah through the Destruction of the First Temple* (Tel Aviv: Archaeological Center, 1999); and Deutsch and André Lemaire, *Biblical Period Personal Seals in the Shlomo Moussaïeff Collection* (Tel Aviv: Archaeological Center, 2000). Another source of additional data involves improved readings based on computer imaging. See Bruce Zuckerman, "Working with a Little More Data: New Finds in the Twentieth Century: The Semitic Languages of the Ancient World," in *Semitic Linguistics: The State of the Art at the Turn of the Twenty-first Century*, ed. Shlomo Izre'el. Israel Oriental Studies 20 (Winona Lake: Eisenbrauns, 2002), 481-97.

and sub-dialect."[17] Krahmalkov acknowledges the problems presented by this approach: "I openly acknowledge the highly problematic nature of this methodology. . . . Unfortunately, the lexicographer of Phoenician-Punic has at his/ her disposal a very meager body of written materials and, for this reason, must to some extent abandon rigor for the sake of completeness, even if this may lead to misrepresentation of aspects of Phoenician-Punic lexicon and usage."[18] A second approach groups related languages together, as exemplified by the *Dictionary of the North-West Semitic Inscriptions*.[19]

At the same time, it is important not to overstate the difficulties of lexicographic analysis of ancient texts, nor the poverty of the lexicographical remains. Edward Ullendorff's important and thought-provoking article "Is Biblical Hebrew a Language?" examined the 300,000-word corpus of the Hebrew Bible, which represents about 8000 separate lexical items.[20] After examining primarily the semantic range of the lexicon, he concluded that the Hebrew of the Bible is "no more than a linguistic fragment . . . , scarcely a fully integrated language which in this form . . . could ever have been spoken and have satisfied the needs of its speakers."[21]

Although Ullendorff is correct that the lexical inventory of the Bible is incomplete, a very different assessment of its lexical resources has been made by computational linguists at the University of Maryland. These linguists, headed by Philip Resnik, have produced artificial intelligence computer programs for processing multilingual parallel texts, that is, identical texts in different languages.[22] In their search for multilingual parallel texts, they settled

17. Charles R. Krahmalkov, *Phoenician-Punic Dictionary*. OLA 90 (Leuven: Peeters, 2000), 14.

18. Krahmalkov, 14.

19. J. Hoftijzer and and K. Jongeling, *Dictionary of the North-West Semitic Inscriptions*. Handbook of Oriental Studies. The Near and Middle East 1, 2 vols. (Leiden: E. J. Brill, 1995) [DNWSI]. This dictionary combines both approaches in that it draws together material from related languages as well as material from diverse geographical and temporal contexts; importantly, these diverse materials are clearly indicated within each lexical entry. On the heterogeneous nature of the language data, see the editors' preface, ix-xvii.

20. Edward Ullendorff, "Is Biblical Hebrew a Language?" in *Is Biblical Hebrew a Language? Studies in Semitic Languages and Civilizations* (Wiesbaden: Harrassowitz, 1977), 3-17 (originally published in *Bulletin of the School of Oriental and African Studies* 34 [1971]: 241-55).

21. Ullendorff, 16-17. Note that Ullendorff's assessment relates to Biblical Hebrew as a language (i.e., the attested range of linguistic expression) and not to what we know of Biblical Hebrew as a linguistic system.

22. Philip Resnik, "Exploiting Parallelism: Some Recent Computational Investigations." Similarity and Translation Conference, American Bible Society, New York, 31 May 2001; and Resnik, Mari Broman Olsen, and Mona Diab, "The Bible as a Parallel Corpus: Annotating the 'Book of 2000 Tongues,'" *Computers and the Humanities* 33 (1999): 129-53.

upon the use of the Bible in French and English translations. They argue that the Bible (in this case the 66 books of the Old and New Testaments) is adequate as a computer corpus, both in terms of size and of vocabulary coverage. In contrast to Ullendorff's investigation of the margins of biblical vocabulary, Resnik et al. compared the lexical inventory of the Bible to Longman's *Contemporary Dictionary of the English Language* (1984). They found that the Bible, in spite of its subject matter and ancient cultural context, covers between 78 and 85 percent of the vocabulary of contemporary English.[23] They decided, therefore, to use the Bible in English and French as representative parallel texts for their research, rather than the Canadian parliamentary proceedings, which comprise a far more extensive and ever-expanding corpus, but one that is less lexically diverse. This astounding decision by computational linguists who have many other texts available for analysis might cause us to ask: Should we consider the limited language data from our ancient texts to be a glass that is half empty or half full?

In contrast to lexicographical research, which requires a very large corpus, phonological and morphological research can proceed with a more modest corpus, perhaps as small as 1000 words. In these areas, then, language data from the better-attested West Semitic languages should be largely adequate, though there are some surprising gaps.[24] For example, the first person plural independent pronoun is not attested in Ugaritic, although it is attested in the much smaller Hebrew epigraphic corpus.[25] Both Ugaritic and Hebrew,

---

23. The missing vocabulary items involved modern artifacts and concepts, political and religious groups, names of measurements and units of time; Resnik, Olsen, and Diab, 147. They also note that the size of the Bible (800,000 words) is comparable to the size of the commonly-used Brown Corpus of American English (130). Comparison of the vocabulary of the New International Version to the Brown Corpus revealed a range of 91 percent coverage of the top 500 vocabulary items to 63 percent coverage of the top 4000 vocabulary items (148-50).

24. Ullendorff (14) argues that there are "grammatical gaps" in the Bible. He mentions as examples the fact that the second person feminine verbal forms are often unattested. But this is not a paradigmatic grammatical gap; i.e., we know what the form would be and the fact that it is attested with only a few verbs is not detrimental to our understanding of the language system of ancient Hebrew. He also notes that many verbs are unattested in the Hophal. This fact also does not affect our knowledge of the system of *binyanim* in ancient Hebrew; furthermore, the gap may be related to semantic restrictions of the verbs. Ullendorff's observations relate to the question of productivity, which is discussed below.

25. The Hebrew example is: *wyd' ky 'l mš't lkš nḥnw šmrn* "And he will know that we are watching the Lachish (fire-)signals" (Lachish 4:10-11). Epigraphic Hebrew, however, lacks the following pronominal forms: third person masculine plural, second person masculine plural, and all feminine forms; see Sandra Landis Gogel, *A Grammar of Epigraphic Hebrew*. SBLRBS 23 (Atlanta: Scholars, 1998), 152.

however, have two alternate forms of the first person singular independent pronoun.[26]

The discipline of corpus linguistics also raises the question of the degree to which the epigraphic remains are representative and varied. In these respects, each corpus must be examined independently. In the Phoenician corpus, for example, dedicatory texts are disproportionately represented, especially in the remains from Carthage. As Wolfgang Röllig noted: "The size of the corpus, numerically so impressive, gives a misleading impression of plenty, since the inscriptions are hallmarked by a monotony of contents and a formulaic and laconic style."[27] Analysis of the linguistic structures of Phoenician, then, must take into account the skewing of the data as a result of this distributional fact.

Because the epigraphic remains are limited, analysis of some features of language use may require corpora that cut across language boundaries. M. O'Connor has argued that all West Semitic inscriptions should be grouped together according to their interpretive (or dictional) contexts into three categories: literary texts, transactional texts (that is, letters, contracts, deeds), and material texts (such as seals, weights, coins).[28] Designing a supercorpus in this way allows for generalizations of language use within the broader cultural context.

Conversely, some kinds of linguistic analysis may require that a subset of the available data be selected as the corpus for analysis. For example, an analysis of the discourse-pragmatic features of language requires a corpus that is free from the interference of diachronic or dialectal factors; exhaustive analysis of all of the language data would skew the results.[29]

The epigraphic textual remains, then, pose challenges with respect to how the available data are selected and organized into corpora for linguistic

26. Epigraphic Hebrew ordinarily uses *'ny* as the first person singular pronoun. The long form *'nk[y]* has been restored in Lachish 6:8, but the word appears in a broken context; see Dennis Pardee, *Handbook of Ancient Hebrew Letters: A Study Edition.* SBLSBS 15 (Chico: Scholars, 1982), 100.

27. Wolfgang Röllig, "The Phoenician Language: Remarks on the Present State of Research," *Atti del i Congresso Internazionale di Studi Fenici e Punici, Roma, 5-10 Novembre 1979.* Collezione di Studi Fenici 16 (Rome: Consiglio Nazionale delle Ricerche, 1983), 2:375-85, esp. 375.

28. M. O'Connor, "Diction and the Ancient Northwest Semitic Inscriptions," *West Asia and North Africa,* vol. 1 of *Contacts Between Cultures,* ed. Amir Harrak (Lewiston: Edwin Mellen, 1992), 108-14.

29. As an example of this principle, see the discussion concerning the distribution of Biblical Hebrew *'ănî* and *'ānōkî* in Judges, Samuel, and Kings, in the section entitled "Linguistic Variation" below. Analysis of the discourse-pragmatic distribution of the forms requires that diachronic factors influencing their distribution be eliminated first (see n. 68).

analysis. Different arrangements of corpora are appropriate to different re-search goals. Conversely, the nature and scope of corpora deeply affect the re-sults of linguistic analysis. In these respects, linguistic work on ancient lan-guages mirrors that of modern corpus linguistics.

Written Language

The second concern regarding the epigraphic data is that we have only writ-ten language data. We have already described the work of corpus linguists, many of whom choose to use written texts for analysis, even though they could use native speakers and even though often they themselves are native speakers of the languages they study. So in spite of the theoretical predilection for the analysis of spoken language within modern linguistics, the use of writ-ten language is perfectly acceptable and, for some purposes, preferable. But granted that only written records are available for the ancient West Semitic languages, what can be extrapolated about how those languages might have been spoken? Or, put differently, how do written and spoken varieties of a language differ?

The question of the interrelationship between spoken and written mo-dalities of language has been studied extensively for English as well as some other languages.[30] Cross-linguistic studies of variation between spoken and written registers (or oral and literate registers) suggest that written language tends to have more complex linguistic structures, both syntactically and lexi-cally. In addition, written varieties of language change much slower than their oral counterparts.[31] These differences reflect the different communicational burdens of spoken and written language. Spoken language ordinarily takes place with both speaker and hearer present — it is thus focused on fast, effi-cient, interactive communication, with "on-line" (real-time) language pro-cessing. Written language, by contrast, ordinarily takes place apart from an interactive communicational context. This greater communicative burden is compensated for by the fact that language processing can be nonlinear, thus allowing for denser, more explicit language structures.[32] Cross-linguistic

---

30. See, e.g., Jack Goody, *The Interface between the Written and the Oral* (Cambridge: Cambridge University Press, 1987); and Deborah Tannen, ed., *Spoken and Written Language: Exploring Orality and Literacy.* Advances in Discourse Processes 9 (Norwood, NJ: Ablex, 1982).

31. M. O'Connor, "Writing Systems and Native-Speaker Analyses," in *Linguistics and Biblical Hebrew,* ed. Walter R. Bodine (Winona Lake: Eisenbrauns, 1992), 231-54.

32. Douglas Biber, *Dimensions of Register Variation: A Cross-Linguistic Comparison* (Cambridge: Cambridge University Press, 1995), 238-39.

studies of diachronic patterns of variation between spoken and written language suggest that in the early periods of literacy, the written register develops linguistically in ways that more sharply distinguish it from oral language.[33]

For our purposes, it is important to note that spoken and written registers are not absolutely distinguished in any language. Rather, varieties of spoken and written language vary along a spectrum from oral to literary. Written varieties of language may thus exhibit more features of oral language or more features of literary language. In looking at epigraphic texts, then, it may be helpful to consider those kinds of texts whose situational context is closer to that of oral language and those whose situational context is closer to that of literary language.

An example of the ways in which these cross-linguistic generalizations about oral and literary language can be applied to written texts can be seen in the work of Frank H. Polak on biblical prose narrative.[34] He concludes that some portions of biblical narrative exhibit more complex linguistic structures — greater frequency of subordinate clauses, more explicit syntactic constituents in the clause, and more complex noun phrases. These dense syntactic features he considers to be indications of literate, scribally-produced narrative.[35] Other portions of biblical narrative exhibit greater frequency of pronominal reference and deictics; Polak considers these features to be indicative of orally-produced narrative.[36]

Cross-linguistic studies that compare spoken and written language, then, provide two promising avenues of research with respect to syntax. On the one hand, they suggest ways in which the epigraphic texts may differ in register — some may have more literate features, others may have more oral features. On the other hand, they suggest ways in which literary texts that reflect complex syntax may have differed from spoken varieties of the language to which we do not have access.

33. Biber, *Dimensions of Register Variation*, 311-12. In later periods of literacy, written registers sometimes split between formal registers (which maintain greater structural density) and informal registers (which become more like oral language).

34. Frank H. Polak, "The Oral and the Written: Syntax, Stylistics and the Development of Biblical Prose Narrative," *JANES* 26 (1998): 59-105.

35. Polak includes Persian era texts (prose narratives of Jeremiah) and 7th-century texts (e.g., the Deuteronomistic history of the Judean kings in 2 Kings 11–22).

36. He includes in this category most texts belonging to the tales of the patriarchs, the rise of the monarchy (Samuel, Saul, David), the Omride dynasty and the northern prophets, and parts of the Exodus narrative. Similar linguistic features were observed in the speeches of 1 Samuel; see J. Macdonald, "Some Distinctive Characteristics of Israelite Spoken Hebrew," *BiOr* 32 (1975): 162-75, esp. 166-69, 172-73.

With respect to other areas of language structure, especially morphology and phonology, these cross-linguistic studies are much less helpful. Morphological features are more consistent in spoken and written varieties of the language, so little is learned about morphology from a comparison of oral and written language. It is in the area of phonology that our ancient written texts are most deficient in telling us what we would like to know about the spoken varieties of these languages.

Native Speaker

A final concern involves the lack of native speakers for the languages represented in the epigraphic texts.[37] Historically, linguists working on modern languages have used native speakers in three ways: for eliciting specific linguistic expressions for analysis, for judgments about the grammaticality of linguistic expressions, and to provide metalinguistic intuitions about the structure or function of the language.

The use of native speakers for each of these tasks is not unproblematic.[38] By asking a native speaker to produce specific linguistic expressions, the linguist receives uncontextualized sentences, which may be only marginally acceptable. It is this problem that has led some linguists away from the use of native speakers as a source of data to the methodology of corpus linguistics. By requesting judgments about the grammaticality of sentences, linguists often discover that native speakers do not agree. And finally, it is very difficult, if not impossible, for a native speaker to provide metalinguistic judgments about language structure. It is somewhat easier for a native speaker to provide metalinguistic information concerning the pragmatic implications of an utterance (e.g., "We say it like that when we are insulting someone").[39]

---

37. There are modern, spoken languages that are the descendants of some of the ancient West Semitic languages discussed in this essay. Native speakers of those modern languages provide only limited assistance in this endeavor because of their temporal and cultural distance from the ancient texts. The value of native speakers may also be restricted by extensive interference from other languages. Analysis of those modern languages, however, assists us in filling out the trajectory of language change from ancient to modern counterparts.

38. On both the theoretical difficulties in the concept of a "native speaker" and the practical difficulties in linguistic analysis using native speakers, see Florian Coulmas, "Introduction: The Concept of Native Speaker," in *A Festschrift for Native Speaker*. Janua Linguarum, Series Maior 97 (The Hague: Mouton, 1981), 1-25.

39. On the limited abilities of native speakers to reflect on the pragmatics of their utterances, see Michael Silverstein, "The Limits of Awareness." Sociolinguistic Working Paper 84 (Austin: Southwest Educational Development Laboratory, 1981), 1-30.

In analyzing epigraphic texts without recourse to native speakers, what kinds of information do we lack?[40] We lack specific linguistic expressions that would allow us to fill in the gaps in our understanding of language structure, such as the first person plural pronoun in Ugaritic. We lack judgments concerning the grammaticality of seemingly anomalous constructions as opposed to the probability that the reading involves a scribal error. We lack judgments concerning dialectal variants or the use of utterances for specific pragmatic purposes. In addition, native speakers could be used to help us know how to interpret the orthography of our texts.[41] For example, a native speaker could confirm that the orthographic symbol ʿayin (ע) was used to represent two sounds in ancient Hebrew — the pharyngeal /ʕ/ as well as the postvelar fricative /ɣ/.[42] But perhaps our greatest lack in examining epigraphic texts is knowing to what degree our limited corpus is representative of the language. It is in this respect that a community of native speakers would be most valuable.

So although resurrected native speakers for the ancient languages of the Near East would assist us in linguistic analysis by providing additional data or in interpreting and assessing the data, it is important to remember that native speakers would not and could not tell us all we wish to know. Native speakers never provide direct access to language structure; native speakers do not provide invariant or uncontroversial language data; and the judgments and intuitions of native speakers are not necessarily accurate or helpful to the linguistic enterprise.

---

40. As Konrad Ehlich notes, the work of a philologist of a "dead" language must approximate that of a linguist working with a native speaker; "Native Speaker's Heritage: On Philology of 'Dead' Languages," in Coulmas, A Festschrift for Native Speaker, 153-65.

41. As M. O'Connor notes, the West Semitic alphabetic orthographies reflect a native speaker analysis both in the ways in which the writing systems are developed and in the ways in which they are adapted; "Writing Systems, Native Speaker Analyses, and the Earliest Stages of Northwest Semitic Orthography," in The Word of the Lord Shall Go Forth: Essays in Honor of David Noel Freedman in Celebration of His Sixtieth Birthday, ed. Carol L. Meyers and O'Connor. ASOR Special Volume Series 1 (Winona Lake: Eisenbrauns, 1983), 439-65.

42. Without a native speaker, philologists must rely on the ways in which Hebrew proper names were transcribed into Greek and Egyptian; see Joshua Blau, On Polyphony in Biblical Hebrew. PIASH 6/2 (Jerusalem: Israel Academy of the Sciences and Humanities, 1982), 5-40; and Edward Lipiński, Semitic Languages: Outline of a Comparative Grammar, 2nd ed. OLA 80 (Leuven: Peeters, 2001), 152.

Productivity, Grammaticalization, Linguistic Variation

In the preceding section we examined the difficulties inherent in the linguistic analysis of epigraphic texts with respect to the facts that the corpus is limited, the texts are written, and there are no native speakers. When framed in this way, the difficulties of our task are characterized with respect to the ways in which the data are limited.

In this section, I suggest that it is more insightful to reformulate the difficulties of the task with respect to the ways in which limited data affect our ability to accomplish the task — the description of the linguistic systems of ancient languages. The central problems involve three interrelated issues: productivity, grammaticalization, and variation.

Productivity

Productivity refers to the property of language which allows the speaker/user of a language to generate an infinitely large number of utterances (or, linguistic expressions) on the basis of the language system. We can illustrate productivity by considering two kinds of morphological productivity — inflection and derivation.[43]

Both kinds of morphological productivity were a concern of some of the Medieval Hebrew grammarians. Saadia Gaon, for example, was interested in calculating the number of possible verbal forms that could be produced using the 1565 verbal roots attested in the Bible;[44] that is, he was concerned with the *productivity of inflectional morphology*.[45] Like Saadia, we can assume that inflectional verbal morphology was fully productive — the fact that we have few attested feminine verbal forms in the Bible, for example, does not diminish our understanding of the language system of Biblical Hebrew, so long as we know what shape the feminine form would have taken.[46]

---

43. On the distinction between inflection and derivation, see George Yule, *The Study of Language,* 2nd ed. (Cambridge: Cambridge University Press, 1996), 76-78.

44. The figure is given in Bruce K. Waltke and M. O'Connor, *An Introduction to Biblical Hebrew Syntax* (Winona Lake: Eisenbrauns, 1990), 361 n. 37. They give the number of attested verbal forms (not the number of possible verbal inflections) as 71,510.

45. Saadia determined the number of possible verbal forms to be 19,169, but Dunash protested that Saadia had neglected to include Piel forms and thus the number should be much higher. See Solomon L. Skoss, *Saadia Gaon: The Earliest Hebrew Grammarian* (Philadelphia: Dropsie College Press, 1955), 17.

46. See above, n. 24.

Saadia was also intrigued by the question of the *productivity of derivational morphology*, specifically the morphology for deriving a noun from a verb. Since Hebrew has multiple strategies for forming nouns, it is impossible to predict the shape that an unattested noun would take. But Saadia suggested that nominal derivation should be considered to operate systematically on the basis of analogy — verbal forms with similar inflections should produce similar nominal forms.[47] His logic concerning the productivity of derivational morphology is faulty at this point, but his concern with the question is quite interesting.

A related question concerning derivational morphology was not addressed by Saadia: the productivity of verbs with respect to the various stems (or, *binyanim*).[48] In the Hebrew Bible, only a very few lexical roots (e.g., *pqd* "to attend to, visit") appear in every verbal stem; in the much smaller epigraphic Hebrew corpus, no lexical root appears in every verbal stem. As a result, the productivity of a particular verb with respect to the system of stems is difficult to assess. For example, the verb *šwb* "to return" occurs infrequently in the epigraphic Hebrew corpus and only in the causative active stem (Hiphil) meaning "to cause to return, return (transitive)."[49] In the Bible, the verb occurs frequently (1056 times) and appears in the basic stem (Qal), factitive active (Polel) and passive (Pulal), and causative active (Hiphil) and passive (Hophal) stems. The question is: was the verb fully productive within the system of stems? That is, could a native speaker have produced and understood the forms in the two stems (Niphal and Hithpael/Hithpolel) that are unattested? If so, then the fact that forms in those stems are not attested in either the epigraphic corpus or the Bible is simply an accident.

A consideration of the productivity of the verb in Modern Hebrew assists us in approximating an answer. In Modern Hebrew, *šwb* appears in all of the stems attested in the Bible. In addition, it may appear in the reflexive-reciprocal stem (Hithpolel) (meaning "to seduce, lead astray"), but not in the Niphal.[50] The absence of a Niphal (passive-reflexive) form of *šwb* in Hebrew from all eras

---

47. For example, Saadia noted that the verb *pṣḥ* "to burst forth," which has no nominal form in the Bible, appears in the imperatival forms *piṣḥî* (Isa. 54:1) and *piṣḥû* (Isa. 44:23). Saadia then compared these forms of *pṣḥ* with the verb *šmʿ* "to hear," which appears in the imperatival forms *šimʿî* and *šimʿû*. Because *šmʿ* has the nominal form *šēmaʿ* (Gen. 29:13), Saadia determined that the nominal form of *pṣḥ* must be *pᵉṣaḥ*. See Skoss, 17-18.

48. For a discussion of this question in Modern Hebrew, see Shmuel Bolozky, "Semantic Productivity and Word Frequency in Modern Hebrew Verb Formation," *Hebrew Studies* 27 (1986): 38-46.

49. See the entry in *DNWSI*, 114-15.

50. Reuben Alcalay, *The Complete Hebrew-English Dictionary* (Tel Aviv: Massada, 1963-1965), 2555-56.

probably relates to a semantic constraint: grammatical productivity may be curtailed when the semantics of a verb are not compatible with the semantics of the stem. In this case, *šwb* is semantically a verb of motion and most intransitive verbs of motion (e.g., *bwʾ* "to come," *rwṣ* "to run," *yrd* "to go down," *yṣʾ* "to go out," *swr* "to turn aside," *brḥ* "to flee") do not occur in the Niphal.[51] However, neither the productivity of the system of stems nor the semantic limits of productivity is fully predictable. Lacking both native speakers and an extensive written corpus, the limits of productivity can only be approximated.

In an examination of epigraphic data, assessing the productivity of grammatical processes is often particularly difficult. For example, in West Semitic the dual is clearly productive in Ugaritic.[52] In Hebrew, Phoenician, and Old Aramaic the dual is attested primarily with paired body parts and secondarily with numerals and a few geographical names; the dual appears to be only semiproductive.[53] Although this conclusion is probably correct, the limited data in Hebrew, Phoenician, and Old Aramaic coupled with the fact that the dual and plural are often indistinguishable in consonantal writing systems make the assessment of productivity less certain.[54]

---

51. There are exceptional instances of intransitive motion verbs in the Niphal. For example, *hlk* "to walk" occurs once in the Niphal (Ps. 109:23) meaning "to be gone, to vanish"; *nḥt* "to descend" occurs once in the Niphal (Ps. 38:3) meaning "to penetrate." A few intransitive verbs of motion use the Niphal in a passive causative sense, e.g., *ʿlh* "to go up" in the Niphal means "to be brought up" (e.g., Ezra 1:11), and *tʿh* "to err" may be used in the Niphal to mean "to be led astray" (Isa. 19:14; Job 15:31). The exceptions demonstrate that although the system of *binyanim* is productive, the semantics are not fully predictable.

52. Josef Tropper, *Ugaritische Grammatik.* AOAT 273 (Münster: Ugarit-Verlag, 2000), 239; and Stanislav Segert, *A Basic Grammar of the Ugaritic Language* (Berkeley: University of California Press, 1984), 50. Juan-Pablo Vita has assembled the data using strict methodological controls; "Bemerkungen zum ugaritischen Dual," *Orientalia Lovaniensia Periodica* 28 (1997): 33-41.

53. Gogel, 192-93, 200; Stanislav Segert, *A Grammar of Phoenician and Punic* (Munich: C. H. Beck, 1976), 111; Rainer Degen, *Altaramäische Grammatik der Inschriften des 10-8 Jh. v. Chr.* Abhandlungen für die Kunde des Morgenlandes 38/3 (Wiesbaden: Deutsche Morganländische Gesellschaft, 1969), 53. Sabatino Moscati notes: "The dual is used for the linguistic expression of natural pairs, but it also serves, in some of the Semitic languages, to indicate duality outside these narrow limits. Its extensive use in Old Akkadian, Ugaritic, and Arabic suggests that the restricted employment in other languages is secondary"; Moscati et al., *An Introduction to the Comparative Grammar of the Semitic Languages: Phonology and Morphology.* Porta Linguarum Orientalium N.S. 6 (Wiesbaden: Harrassowitz, 1980), 93. For a discussion of degrees of productivity, see Laurie Bauer, *Morphological Productivity.* Cambridge Studies in Linguistics 95 (Cambridge: Cambridge University Press, 2001), 15-20.

54. For a survey of the dual in West Semitic and a description of the problems of identifying dual forms, see Charles Fontinoy, *Le duel dans les langues sémitiques.* Bibliothèque de la Faculté de Philosophie et Lettres de l'Université de Liège 179 (Paris: Société d'Edition "Les Belles Lettres," 1969), 47-77, esp. 63-70. The loss of the dual as a productive morphological category

CYNTHIA L. MILLER

An important component in the description of a language system involves knowing the extent to which grammatical processes are productive. In
the analysis of a modern language, the linguist determines the limits of productivity in one of two ways: through examination of the relevant linguistic
expressions in a large corpus, or through elicitation of a sampling of relevant
expressions by a native speaker.[55] The limited nature of the epigraphic data
means that assessment of productivity must be approximated on the basis of
comparative data or typological data.

Grammaticalization

Grammaticalization, in some respects, produces effects that are the opposite
of productivity. Grammaticalization is the historical process by which a lexical item acquires a specialized grammatical function.[56] Grammaticalization is
often accompanied by a generalization of the original meaning of the word, a
process known as "semantic bleaching." There may also be a generalization of
the grammatical meaning of the word, or the word may shift to a different
grammatical category. As a result, there may be a reduction in morphological
or syntactic productivity of the word.

Within a limited corpus, a word may exhibit limited productivity acci-
dentally as a result of the limitations of the data. Or a word may have limited
productivity because it has been — or is in the process of becoming —
grammaticalized.

We can illustrate this problem by examining an example of grammaticalization in ancient Hebrew as it is attested in the biblical and epigraphic Hebrew
data. The grammaticalization of *lēʾmōr* is clearly indicated in Biblical Hebrew.[57]

---

can be more clearly traced in East Semitic, where as early as Old Babylonian the dual is semantically restricted, in that it is usually used for natural pairs; see Wolfram von Soden, *Grundriss der
Akkadischen Grammatik,* 2nd ed. AnOr 33 (Rome: Pontifical Biblical Institute, 1969), 76;
Lipiński, 242-44; and John Huehnergard, *A Grammar of Akkadian.* HSS 45 (Atlanta: Scholars,
1997), 8-9.

55. Measuring productivity has been the source of much debate in linguistics. One approach that is relevant for West Semitic epigraphy involves comparing the ratio of the actual
words produced by a grammatical process to the potential words produced by the process. See
Bauer, 143-62.

56. Paul J. Hopper and Elizabeth Closs Traugott, *Grammaticalization.* Cambridge Textbooks in Linguistics (Cambridge: Cambridge University Press, 1993), 2-7. See also the discussion
of grammaticalization as a theory: Lyle Campbell and Richard Janda, "Introduction: Conceptions of Grammaticalization and Their Problems," *Language Sciences* 23 (2001): 93-112.

57. See the more detailed argumentation in Cynthia L. Miller, *The Representation of*

The word was originally composed of two morphemes: the preposition *l-* ("to") used as a complementizer to introduce the infinitival complement of the verb *'āmar* ("to say"). However, the form as a whole was reanalyzed as a complementizer to introduce direct speech quotations.[58] Syntactically, there was a loss of productivity — the infinitive construct no longer could govern objects or prepositional phrases like ordinary infinitives construct. Semantically, there was a bleaching of the meaning of the verb "say" so that *lē'mōr* could be used with nonspeech verbs such as *šāmaʿ* "hear," even though *šāmaʿ lē'mōr* ("he heard by saying") is nonsensical in a literal sense — it is impossible to hear by saying.[59] Phonologically, the unusual form of *lē'mōr* also suggests that grammaticalization has taken place. On the basis of the usual form of the infinitive construct with a prefixed preposition (*beʾemōr* "in saying"), the productive form would be *leʾemōr*, which never occurs.

The Biblical Hebrew data are quite clear concerning the grammaticalization of *lē'mōr*. The epigraphic Hebrew data support these conclusions, but they do not give as clear a picture. It is much harder to determine the extent of syntactic productivity because constructions with *lē'mōr* are much less frequent. Furthermore, *lē'mōr* is attested only with the verbs *higgîd* ("to inform")[60] and *kātab* ("to write")[61] and (perhaps) the noun *sēper* ("letter").[62] The epigraphic data demonstrate that *lē'mōr* has undergone some semantic bleaching, since it can be used with verbs and nouns in which the mode of communication is not speech. But the epigraphic data do not provide evidence for the same degree of semantic bleaching as is evident in Biblical Hebrew, where *lē'mōr* may be used after psychological verbs and nonspeech verbs;[63] without the additional biblical data it is impossible to assess the extent of grammaticalization.

Identifying grammaticalization within a limited epigraphic corpus involves the same difficulties that we encountered in assessing productivity.

Speech in Biblical Hebrew Narrative: A Linguistic Analysis. HSM 55 (Atlanta: Scholars, 1996), 163-212.

58. The grammaticalization of a verb of speaking as a complementizer is well-attested cross-linguistically. See Bernd Heine, Ulrike Claudi, and Frederike Hünnemeyer, *Grammaticalization: A Conceptual Framework* (Chicago: University of Chicago Press, 1991), 158-59.

59. See Gen. 24:30; 31:1.

60. Lachish 3:13-18.

61. Lachish 6:8-10.

62. Lachish 3:19-21.

63. See the discussion and lists of attested verbs in Miller, 185-95. Note in particular that *lē'mōr* can be used after verbs that refer to the absence of communication, e.g., *ḥrš* "to be silent" (Judg. 16:2).

Without the assistance of a native speaker who can be asked to produce additional examples, it is very difficult to assess whether productivity has been systematically curtailed for grammatical reasons.

Linguistic Variation

A third difficulty in analyzing epigraphic texts involves linguistic variation. All languages (or rather linguistic communities) exhibit variation.[64] There are many sources of linguistic variation, but they can be subsumed under two main categories: dialectal variation and superposed variation.[65] Dialectal variation involves subgroups of speakers whose speech is distinguished by geographical, social, or demographic factors (e.g., location, class, gender, age). Superposed variation involves varieties of language that are connected with a specific communicational activity. Variation of this sort is a result of the context of use (e.g., speech to superiors/inferiors, ritual language, letter, legal document), register (e.g., oral/literate, formal/informal), or linguistic environment (e.g., discourse-pragmatics). The central insight is that language varies "both according to who is speaking it and what they are doing as they speak."[66]

One problem as Semitists is that in our concern to understand the language systems reflected in our texts, we have tended to assume that linguistic expression as represented in the texts is uniform and systematic. We forget that linguistic variation is not an alien element to the language system. Variation should not be relegated immediately to scribal error; nor should a text that exhibits variation from language structure as previously described be classified necessarily as a forgery. Scribal errors and forgeries do exist. But at the same time, all languages exhibit linguistic variation because all speakers exhibit variation. Our goal, then, must be to attempt to discover the nature and source of the variation.[67]

---

64. Synchronic variation is a critical component for diachronic change; see James Milroy, "On the Social Origins of Language Change," in *Historical Linguistics: Problems and Perspectives,* ed. Charles Jones. Longman Linguistics Library (London: Longman, 1993), 215-36.

65. William F. Hanks, *Language and Communicative Practices.* Critical Essays in Anthropology (Boulder: Westview, 1996), 219-20.

66. Hanks, 220.

67. On the methodological difficulties in this enterprise, see Susan C. Herring, Pieter van Reenen, and Lene Schøsler, "On Textual Parameters and Older Languages," in *Textual Parameters in Older Languages.* Amsterdam Studies in the Theory and History of Linguistic Science 195 (Amsterdam: Benjamins, 2000), 1-31.

Within West Semitic philology, we have made important strides in under-standing the geographical sources of dialectal variation.[68] The isolation of re-gional dialects is possible to the extent that the provenience and approximate date of epigraphic materials can be determined. Other sources of dialectal vari-ation are less well understood, in part because of the nature of the sources.[69] So-cial and demographic information concerning the individuals that produced individual texts is usually not known, except when there are internal references in the texts. One group of texts, the Aramaic legal documents from Elephan-tine, provides a wealth of social information: the name(s) of the individual(s) executing the contract, as well as his/her patronymic and often ethnic identifi-cation, city of origin, and profession. Furthermore, most documents indicate the name(s) of the individual(s) receiving the letter or contract; many docu-ments include the name of the scribe, along with his patronymic, and many in-clude the individuals serving as witnesses to the legal transaction. These social features of the individuals who are connected with the texts can often be corre-lated with the variable features present in the texts.[70]

Superposed variation is also evident within epigraphic texts, although the factors involved in the variation have not always been recognized. An ex-ample involves the various contexts within which we find alternation of the long form (*ʾank*) and short form (*ʾan*) of the first person singular pronoun in Ugaritic.[71] Although Daniel Sivan states that "from the standpoint of usage there is no difference in Ugaritic between *ʾan* and *ʾank*,"[72] he makes two sug-gestive observations concerning the distribution of the forms. His first obser-vation is: "As for distribution, it would appear that *ʾan* is more typical of liter-ary texts while *ʾank* is characteristic of all kinds of texts."[73] That is, there is superposed variation relating to literary register. The second observation is:

---

68. W. Randall Garr, *Dialect Geography of Syria-Palestine, 1000-586 B.C.E.* (Philadelphia: University of Pennsylvania Press, 1985).

69. On the difficulties of determining the sociolinguistics of ancient texts, see Werner Winter, "Sociolinguistics and Dead Languages," in *Language Change: Advances in Historical Sociolinguistics,* ed. Ernst Håkon Jahr. Trends in Linguistics Studies and Monographs 114 (Berlin: Mouton de Gruyter, 1999), 67-84.

70. See M. L. Folmer, *The Aramaic Language in the Achaemenid Period: A Study in Lin-guistic Variation.* OLA 68 (Leuven: Peeters, 1995); and Cynthia L. Miller, "Variation of Direct Speech Complementizers in Achaemenid Aramaic Documents from Fifth Century B.C.E. Egypt," in *Variation and Reconstruction,* ed. Thomas D. Cravens. Current Issues in Linguistic Theory (Amsterdam: Benjamins, forthcoming).

71. Tropper, 208.

72. Daniel Sivan, *A Grammar of the Ugaritic Language.* HO. Der Nahe und Mittelere Osten 28 (Leiden: Brill, 1997), 50.

73. Sivan, 50. As Tropper notes (208), *ʾan* appears only in poetic texts.

"In some texts both pronouns are used together, especially in literary passages."[74] This second observation suggests that there is another factor at work in addition to register.

The work of E. J. Revell in examining the cognate first person singular pronouns in the Bible provides a useful comparison. In Biblical Hebrew, *'ănî* and *'ānōkî* are free variants syntactically, but Revell demonstrates that in biblical narrative the use of the two forms relates to social and pragmatic factors.[75] In speech among humans, the choice of pronoun is connected to differences in social status, emotional intensity, and personal concern of the speaker — factors that Revell subsumes under the heading of "immediacy." *'ănî* is the form that marks immediacy; *'ānōkî* does not.[76] Although the Ugaritic data do not immediately suggest the same rationale for the distribution of the forms, Revell's study demonstrates that lexical variation in first person pronouns could be exploited within a literary text for discourse-pragmatic effect.

Variation is perhaps the most difficult problem facing linguists who are analyzing epigraphic data. Because dialectal variation is tied to the demographics of the speaker, analysis of this kind of variation is particularly problematic unless there are indicators concerning the speaker (writer) within the text or associated with the text. Because superposed variation is tied to communicational activity, identifying this type of variation within written texts requires representative numbers of texts for each communicational context.

Language Typology

We have seen that reconstructing the linguistic structures of ancient languages is complicated by language variation and limited data for assessing productivity and grammaticalization. Traditionally, Semitists have solved the problem of limited data primarily through comparative philology.[77] That is, one compares

---

74. Sivan, 50.

75. Revell's analysis examines only the variation present in Judges, Samuel, and Kings; see E. J. Revell, *The Designation of the Individual: Expressive Usage in Biblical Narrative.* CBET 14 (Kampen: Kok Pharos, 1996), 341-49. There is also a diachronic factor in the variation between the two forms; in late Biblical Hebrew, *'ănî* is displacing *'ānōkî*. See Robert Polzin, *Late Biblical Hebrew: Toward an Historical Typology of Biblical Hebrew Prose.* HSM 12 (Missoula: Scholars, 1976), 126-27.

76. Revell, 341-49.

77. For a recent survey of the contributions of the comparative historical method, see Jo Ann Hackett, "The Study of Partially Documented Languages," in Izre'el, 57-75.

the linguistic structures and lexical resources of genetically-related languages. Secondarily, philologists have considered the characteristics of genetically-unrelated languages that were geographically proximate; language contact may result in shared features in unrelated languages. To these two ways of grouping languages, we can add another linguistic tool — language typology.

Language typology classifies languages (or individual structural components of languages) based upon shared formal characteristics.[78] With this methodology, languages that are genetically unrelated and that have no geographical proximity can be grouped together by structural features. As a result, typologists can make relatively broad claims concerning the types of language structures represented among the world's languages, as well as observations concerning the diachronic development of linguistic features.

Language typology has a great deal to offer Semitists in our reconstructions of the linguistic structures of ancient languages.[79] As an example, let us consider two proposals concerning the development of the definite article in Ugaritic. Ugaritic, as opposed to Aramaic, Hebrew, and the other West Semitic languages, has no definite article.[80] Is there any evidence for the incipient emergence of a definite article in Ugaritic? Two suggestions have been advanced, one by David D. Testen and one by Josef Tropper.

As part of a larger discussion concerning the development of the definite article in Semitic, Testen briefly speculates that the asseverative particle *l-* in Ugaritic may be "an early forerunner of the *l* of definiteness."[81] Testen suggests that the asseverative particle serves to convey "the speaker's commitment to the veracity of his utterance";[82] the particle essentially marks the topic of the sentence, which becomes grammaticalized as a marker of definiteness. The use of *l*, he suggests, as a topic marker "was a midway point on the road to the full definite article."[83]

---

78. Lindsay J. Whaley, *Introduction to Typology: The Unity and Diversity of Language* (Thousand Oaks, CA: Sage, 1997), 7.

79. See Roman Jakobson, "Typological Studies and Their Contribution to Historical Comparative Linguistics," in *A Reader in Historical and Comparative Linguistics*, ed. Allan R. Keiler (New York: Holt, Rinehart and Winston, 1972), 299-305; and Anthony Fox, "Language Typology and Linguistic Reconstruction," *Linguistic Reconstruction: An Introduction to Theory and Method.* Oxford Textbooks in Linguistics (Oxford: Oxford University Press, 1995), 247-74.

80. Akkadian is another Semitic language (albeit East Semitic rather than West Semitic) that has no definite article. On the forms and distribution of the definite article within Semitic, see Moscati, 96-102; and Lipiński, 274-85.

81. David D. Testen, *Parallels in Semitic Linguistics: The Development of Arabic* la- *and Related Semitic Particles.* Studies in Semitic Languages and Linguistics 26 (Leiden: Brill, 1998), 166.

82. Testen, 155-56.

83. Testen, 167.

A different hypothesis concerning the emergence of the definite article is advanced by Tropper. Tropper believes that the deictic element *hn* may be developing into the definite article.[84] He understands the element **han(n)* as having the basic meaning of "hier, da" and especially "siehe da!" and argues that it functions as the presentative particle and not as a demonstrative pronoun,[85] even though the element forms a part of the demonstrative pronouns in Ugaritic.[86] He cites three kinds of evidence for his hypothesis concerning the grammaticalization of *hn* as a definite article: (1) examples of *hn* preceding a noun that has appeared previously in the text so that *hn* could be understood as functioning anaphorically like a definite article;[87] (2) texts where *hn* is used in conjunction with another demonstrative element in a construction that mirrors the Hebrew construction in which the definite article precedes the noun and a demonstrative element follows;[88] and (3) a text where he interprets a prefixed *h* as the demonstrative element *hn* with the final *n* assimilated to the following word.[89]

What light can language typology shed on these alternative hypotheses? In lacking a definite article, Ugaritic is typologically aligned with a number of

84. Tropper, 32-34, 737-38. Tropper does not specifically use the term "grammaticalization," nor does he describe the historical linguistic process(es) by which *hn* becomes grammaticalized as a definite article.

85. Josef Tropper, "Die Herausbildung des bestimmten Artikels im Semitischen," *JSS* 46 (2001): 1-31, esp. 17-18.

86. Tropper understands the element *hn to be the underlying element of the demonstrative pronouns, deictic adverbs, and the presentative particle (*Ugaritische Grammatik*, 229; *JSS* 46 (2001): 17). Additionally, there is the problem of distinguishing *hn* as the "Frühartikel" from the homonymous proximal demonstrative adverb *hn* "here" and the presentative particle *hn* "behold." This is a difficulty which Tropper himself acknowledges (*Ugaritische Grammatik*, 232).

87. As an example, Tropper cites RS 1.1002 (= KTU 1.40) where he understands *hn š* (lines 17, 25) as "(nämlich) der Widder da!" Although it is also possible to understand *hn* as the deictic presentative and to translate "here is (the) ram," Tropper rejects this possibility (*Ugaritische Grammatik*, 232-34).

88. As an example, Tropper cites RS 16.402:31-32 (= KTU 2.33), where he understands *tngyy hn ʾalpm ššwm hnd* as "Diese 2000 Pferde da sollen herkommen." In that *hn* is preposed and the demonstrative *hnd* is postposed, he considers the noun phrase to be formally equivalent to Hebrew *ham-mélek haz-zeh* "this king" (*Ugaritische Grammatik*, 233). Dennis Pardee (personal communication) points out a similar example in a recently-discovered text, RS 96.2039: *w yʾuḥd hn bnš hw w štnnh bd mlʾakty* "and let that servant be seized and send him (to me) with the messenger party." (I am grateful to Pardee and Pierre Bordreuil for permission to cite the text.)

89. As an example, Tropper cites RS 29.093:16 (= KTU 2.70), where *hbt* has been understood as the demonstrative element *hn* with *nun* assimilated to the following word as an article ("the house") (*Ugaritische Grammatik*, 233-34).

modern languages, such as Finnish and Serbo-Croatian, which do not have a definite article.[90] Cross-linguistically, all languages have demonstrative pronouns, which may be considered to be inherently definite, but the grammatical encoding of (in)definiteness "is far from universal; indeed, languages marking it are in a distinct minority."[91]

Languages that historically develop a definite article often do so from a demonstrative pronoun,[92] either the near demonstrative or more commonly the far demonstrative.[93] Syntactically, the article appears in the same position relative to the noun as the demonstrative pronoun did. That is, in a language in which the demonstrative pronoun follows the noun, when the demonstrative pronoun is grammaticalized as an article, the article also follows the noun. Semantically, the grammaticalization of a demonstrative into the definite article involves the semantic weakening or generalization of the notion of deixis inherent in demonstratives. One way to think about the grammaticalization of a demonstrative into a definite article is metaphorically, as the transference of a spatial demonstrative to a textual deictic.[94] It is therefore common for the demonstrative initially to be reanalyzed as a definite article in contexts involving anaphoric (and cataphoric) reference, a function that may be fulfilled either by demonstratives or definite articles.[95]

A less frequent pattern for the development of the definite article involves verbs of seeing. The development of the definite article begins with the verb "see" used in the ostensive sense of French *voici/voilà* (which are etymologically related to the French verb *voire* "to see"), Latin *ecce*, and archaic English *behold*. One language that has developed a definite article in this way is Sissala (a Niger-Congo language). In Sissala the word *ná* "see" has shifted from a finite verbal form to a semireferential deictic particle (similar to

---

90. Ritva Laury, *Demonstratives in Interaction: The Emergence of a Definite Article in Finnish.* Studies in Discourse and Grammar 7 (Amsterdam: Benjamins, 1997); and Ljiljana Progovac, "Determiner Phrase in a Language without Determiners," *Journal of Linguistics* 34 (1998): 165-79.

91. Christopher Lyons, *Definiteness.* Cambridge Textbooks in Linguistics (Cambridge: Cambridge University Press, 1999), 48.

92. For a cross-linguistic survey of the grammaticalization of demonstratives as definite articles, see Bernd Heine and Tania Kuteva, *World Lexicon of Grammaticalization* (Cambridge: Cambridge University Press, 2002), 109-11.

93. Joseph H. Greenberg, "Some Iconic Relationships among Place, Time, and Discourse Deixis," in *Iconicity in Syntax*, ed. John Haiman. Typological Studies in Language 6 (Amsterdam: Benjamins, 1985), 271-87. It is also possible for the definite article to derive from the "fourth person" or unmarked demonstrative.

94. Heine, Claudi, and Hünnemeyer, 179.

95. Lyons, 332.

French *voici*), then to an inferential particle (similar to French *voilà*) before becoming a definiteness marker.[96]

Tropper's hypothesis, then, is feasible in that he understands *hn* to be functioning anaphorically, a typical function for emerging articles. His hypothesis is also typologically possible in that he suggests that a deictic presentative element is becoming grammaticalized as the definite article. However, if Tropper is correct, what is interesting is that, in contrast to the emergence of the definite article in many other languages, it is not a demonstrative pronoun *per se* that is becoming grammaticalized in Ugaritic. This claim can be further buttressed by the fact that the emerging article *hn* appears before the noun it modifies (rather than after the noun in the position of attributive demonstrative pronoun).[97]

Testen's hypothesis, although plausible on comparative Semitic grounds, has less typological support. Although the overlap between topic-comment (or, given-new information) and definiteness has been noted, there is little evidence for the grammaticalization of an asseverative particle (or topic-marking particle) into a definite article. Instead, languages that grammatically mark the topic do not usually have grammatical markers of definiteness.[98] Although it is possible for a language to develop historically in ways that are less well-attested cross-linguistically, a hypothetical reconstruction that is typologically unusual should be considered carefully.

Language typology, then, assists us by providing a broader framework within which to examine language structure. Typology helps us to know what kinds of features are relevant in analyzing language structure. After an analysis has been made, typology helps us to evaluate the analysis in one of two ways. Typology may provide additional confirmation for the analysis through comparison with similar structures in attested languages. Typology can also be used to question a reconstruction that is potentially problematic and requires further validation.[99]

96. Regina Blass, *Relevance Relations in Discourse: A Study with Special Reference to Sissala.* Cambridge Studies in Linguistics 55 (Cambridge: Cambridge University Press, 1990), 199; see also 133, 184-85, 191-201. See also Christopher Lyons, *Definiteness,* 331. For a discussion of the ways in which deictics, demonstratives, the definite article, and anaphora are semantically related, see John Lyons, *Semantics,* 2 vols. (Cambridge: Cambridge University Press, 1977), §15.2-3.

97. As Tropper notes, the word order of the definite article in Ugaritic conforms to the pattern in Canaanite (and Arabic) as opposed to Aramaic and Old South Arabic (*Ugaritische Grammatik,* 234).

98. Christopher Lyons, *Definiteness,* 227-36.

99. In conjunction with these two uses of typology for reconstruction, Bernard Comrie notes that the validity of an objection to a reconstruction on typological grounds depends upon

Conclusions

Reconstructing the linguistic systems of ancient texts is difficult in many ways. The texts available for analysis are limited, the language data are written, and there are no native speakers. These factors should not be minimized, but they do not render the task of linguistic analysis impossible, nor are they the most crucial problems that we face.

Instead, reconstruction of language systems is difficult because linguistic expression is infinite and language structure is abstract. Analyzing fragments of linguistic expression means that we are not always sure whether we can posit productivity of language structures with respect to lexical items; gaps in attested expressions may be a result of grammaticalization or systematic language constraints. And a limited, written corpus means that we often have linguistic expressions that cannot be connected to a sociolinguistic context; it is thus much more difficult to evaluate language variation with respect to language structure. When we are faced with these difficulties, one of the most important linguistic tools involves language typology. Whether analyzing a modern language or an ancient language, it is important to consider whether the language system as described conforms to typological expectations.

---

the level of development of the typology: ". . . typological generalizations may also turn out, as the result of a broader or deeper understanding of language, to be incorrect"; "Typology and Reconstruction," in *Historical Linguistics*, ed. Jones, 74-97, esp. 95.

Hermeneutics and Theology

The Role of Context and the Promise
of Archaeology in Biblical Interpretation
from Early Judaism to Post Modernity

JOHN M. MONSON

Introduction

In 1838 the biblical scholar Edward Robinson left his home in Tennessee to explore the land of the Bible. Despite the enormous challenges of 19th-century travel, he felt compelled to encounter firsthand the geographical, cultural, and linguistic context of the Hebrew Bible and New Testament before assuming a prestigious post at Union Theological Seminary in New York. The physical and intellectual journey to the land of the Bible revolutionized his understanding of the ancient world and of Scripture.[1]

Since Robinson's day, discoveries in archaeology, linguistics, and geography have come to light at an accelerated pace. These discoveries breathed new life into the historical critical scholarship of the late 19th and mid-20th centuries. In light of widespread excavation and scientific advances during the past two decades, today one can argue that the biblical world is better understood and more easily accessible than at any other time since the biblical period itself.

What, then, is the proper role of context and archaeology in biblical interpretation, and to what degree can it or should it influence our exegesis? Of what concern was original context to the interpreters of early Judaism, the early church, the Reformation, and the Enlightenment?[2] And what is the

---

1. Edward Robinson, *Biblical Researches in Palestine and the Adjacent Regions,* 3 vols. (1856; repr. Jerusalem: Universitas, 1970).

2. For an overview of biblical interpretation, see Bernard L. Ramm, *Protestant Biblical Interpretation,* 3rd ed. (Grand Rapids: Baker, 1970), 23-92; and Mark S. Burrows and Paul Rorem, eds., *Biblical Hermeneutics in Historical Perspective* (Grand Rapids: Wm. B. Eerdmans, 1991).

proper role of archaeology in biblical interpretation? I will address these questions by first considering briefly the role of historical and cultural context in the history of biblical interpretation. Next, I will describe the unique role of archaeology in biblical interpretation and suggest that we are entering an era of new promise in this field. Finally, I will illustrate the value of geographical, cultural, and historical context through several case studies and conclude by advocating a more aggressive and widespread use of the contextual approach.

Before turning to the first point, however, it seems appropriate to clarify further what is meant by context. According to William W. Hallo, the contextual approach enables one to "silhouette the Biblical text against its wider literary and cultural environment and thus to arrive at a proper assessment of the extent to which the Biblical evidence reflects that environment or, on the contrary, is distinctive and innovative over against it."[3]

In addition to these comparative and contrastive methods of literary study I would like to stress the importance of geography and material culture as tools for ascertaining context. The former is a significant factor in the flow of ancient history and society, while the latter testifies to the cultural matrix from which the text arose. Language and *realia* are, after all, both products of culture, and hence are best studied in tandem. While written texts are the preeminent sources, we should not forget that art, architecture, and even mundane items are each a language of sorts. In my view, therefore, text, material culture, and geography form an inseparable triad, which together define the context of Scripture. This is the definition that I will use below.

The Role of Context in Historical Perspective

Until the 1800s context, as we have described it above, was for the most part unavailable, which meant that the choice of exegetical tools was relatively limited. Since the late 1800s, however, the use of original context in biblical interpretation has gone in and out of fashion, even with the increase in comparative material. As in preceding periods, the work of each interpreter reflects the *Zeitgeist* of his or her era, the expectations of the community, and in some cases a personal intellectual journey. The work of Augustine, Calvin, Wellhausen, Albright, Philip Davies is all in some measure reflective of their times.

In the earliest stage we see a continuation of the interpretive process al-

---

3. William W. Hallo, *The Book of the People.* BJS 225 (Atlanta: Scholars, 1991), 23-35.

ready at work within the biblical corpus itself, such as the retelling of Israel's history in the book of Chronicles.[4] Cultural and historical data are included, but these are put in the service of glorifying David and Israel's past. A similar process was at work in the biblical interpretation of early Judaism. Specifically in the Qumran literature, the Torah and prophetic texts are seen through the interpretive lens of sectarian peculiarities and political strife. And so in the Habakkuk pesher the community faces the unrelenting wrath not of Babylon, but of Rome.[5] Seeming contradictions in the text are explained through rambling commentary or allegorical ingenuity.[6] Philo typifies the allegorical method. Abraham's journey represents the "God-given impulse of the soul towards complete salvation."[7] In this period, the Jewish interpreters either took for granted what contextual tools they had or ignored them altogether. Theirs was a quest to be aligned with Torah, prophecy, and tradition, and, in the case of Qumran, to insure that they were on the Lord's winning side. Local geography or cultural traditions contemporary with the Bible were irrelevant as the text and the community defined the author's understanding of the past.

The work of the church fathers followed in the same vein as Philo, but with a Christian twist. In his sermon on the David and Goliath story, Augustine refers to David's five pebbles as the five books of Moses, the chosen stone symbolizing the unity of those who fulfill the law through love.[8] Eventually, however, the translations of Jerome and the literalist approach of the Antioch school began to counter this type of allegorical exegesis. Consider his statement on geography:

> Just as those who have seen Athens understand Greek history better, and just as those who have seen Troy understand the words of the poet Virgil, thus one will comprehend the Holy Scriptures with a clearer understanding who has seen the land of Judah with his own eyes.[9]

---

4. See Sara Japhet, *I and II Chronicles*. OTL (Louisville: Westminster John Knox, 1993).

5. Michael Fishbane, "Jewish Biblical Exegesis: Presuppositions and Principles," in *Scripture in the Jewish and Christian Traditions: Authority, Interpretation, and Relevance,* ed. Frederick Greenspahn (Nashville: Abingdon, 1982), 92-110.

6. For numerous examples and bibliography, see James L. Kugel, *The Bible as It Was* (Cambridge: Belknap, 1997).

7. "On the Migration of Abraham" 1-2, in C. D. Younge, *The Works of Philo, New Updated Edition* (Peabody: Hendricksen, 1993).

8. "Sermon 32: Goliath, David, and Contempt of the World, 1" in *Nicene and Post-Nicene Fathers,* ed. Philip Schaff (repr. Grand Rapids: Wm. B. Eerdmans, 1994).

9. Source unavailable.

It is surprising to me that Jerome's concern for context never took root among the church fathers. Even Eusebius, renowned for his work in history and geography, did not inject more comprehensively his careful geographic work, the *Onomasticon,* into his biblical exegesis.

During the Middle Ages literal exegesis moved into the mainstream in Jewish and Christian circles.[10] For example, following a discussion of the Hebrew imperfect form of *šyr* ("to sing") in Exod. 15:1, Rashi writes of the passage, "This explanation settles the literal meaning of the text."[11] Historical and grammatical meaning was the basis for all interpretation of the Bible. And so Greek and Hebrew were invoked with increasing frequency. Meanwhile, Aquinas was instrumental in the separating the strands of exegesis and theology into a type of two-step hermeneutic. The first sense of the text was the literal and historical meaning from which a spiritual and theological application could then be sought.[12] Turning to the Reformation, Luther's emphasis on original languages and the setting of the authors is noteworthy. He sought to understand the life situation of the Israelites, even though there was at the time no vehicle for reconstructing life in Israel and the ancient Near East. John Calvin's work, influenced as it was by Luther on the one hand and the humanist tradition on the other, was a precursor to the historical-critical method. Although he worked within a theological rubric, Calvin employed in his rigorous exegesis every resource available in his day, including especially primary languages.[13] I have no doubt that the exegetes of this period would have exploited *realia* and comparative literature to their fullest potential had they been available at the time. It is intriguing to speculate how the exegesis of the Reformers — and perhaps in some ways their theology — might have been influenced had they at their disposal the vast contextual resources we take for granted today.

The ascendancy of reason in the following centuries subjected the Bible to intellectual scrutiny without the perceived constraints of religion. From the 18th through 20th centuries, modern scientific examination became the primary means of interpreting Scripture. Biblical exegesis, infused with the rigorous methods of the Reformation, gradually drifted towards the skepticism of modern secular criticism. These developments culminated in the

10. Ramm, r44-45.

11. Commentary on Exod. 15:1 in *Pentateuch with Targum Onkelos, Haphtaroth and Prayers for Sabbath and Rashi's Commentary,* trans. M. Rosenbaum and A. M. Silberman (London: Shapiro, Vallentine, 1929-1934).

12. Beryl Smalley, *The Study of the Bible in the Middle Ages,* 3rd ed. (Oxford: Blackwell, 1983), 10-42.

13. Paul Traugolt Fuhrman, "Calvin, the Expositor of Scripture," *Int* 6 (1952): 188-209.

work of Julius Wellhausen and Adolf von Harnack.[14] This hermeneutic was already reflected in the words of Spinoza in the 17th century:

> Lastly, such a history should relate the environment of all the prophetic books extant; that is, the life, the conduct, and the studies of the author of each book, who he was, what was the occasion, and the epoch of his writing, whom did he write for, and in what language. Further it should inquire into the fate of each book; how it was first received, into whose hands it fell, how many different versions there were of it, by whose advice was it received into the Bible, and lastly, how all the books now universally accepted as sacred were united into a single whole.[15]

The increasing sophistication in the 1700s and 1800s was met with an explosive sequence of discoveries beginning with Napoleon's scientific exploration of Egypt in 1799.[16] The 19th century was the golden age of exploration in the Near East. It brought with it a veritable gold rush for artifacts and the discovery and translation of Akkadian, Egyptian, and Northwest Semitic texts.[17] Explorations by individuals such as Edward Robinson and Charles Clermont Ganneau paved the way for the establishment of European schools of biblical research.[18] Foremost among them was the Ecole Biblique, established by Marie-Joseph Lagrange in 1882. He sought to harness the new discoveries in the service of biblical studies, and to this end assembled a team of stellar scholars including the brilliant archaeologist Louis Hugues Vincent. The Ecole's second generation produced the Jerusalem Bible, a nuanced and fresh translation that drew many insights from comparative languages, material culture, and the geography of the Levant.[19]

By the late 1800s, one could describe in some detail the historical and cultural contexts of many biblical authors and passages. Archaeological dis-

---

14. Julius Wellhausen, *Prolegomena to the History of Ancient Israel* (Atlanta: Scholars, 1994); Adolf von Harnack, *The Origin of the New Testament and the Most Important Consequences of the New Creation* (New York: Macmillan, 1925).

15. "A Theologico-Political Treatise, Chapter VII, Of the Interpretation of Scripture," in *Benedictus Spinoza: Chief Works*, trans. R. H. M. Elwes (New York: Dover, 1955), 103.

16. John Baines and Jaromír Málek, *Atlas of Ancient Egypt* (New York: Facts on File, 1980), 24-27.

17. P. R. S. Moorey, *A Century of Biblical Archaeology* (Louisville: Westminster John Knox, 1991), 1-24; Thomas W. Davis, *A History of Biblical Archaeology* (diss., Arizona, 1987), 8-42.

18. The British established the Palestine Exploration Society in 1870, and the Germans introduced the Deutscher Palästina-Verein in 1877.

19. Benedict T. Viviano, "Ecole Biblique et Archéologique Française de Jérusalem," *BA* 54 (1991): 160-67; Jean-Luc Vesco, ed., *L'Ancien Testament: cent ans d'exégèse à l'Ecole Biblique.* CahRB 28 (Paris: Gabalda, 1990).

coveries in the Near East and the decipherment of Akkadian, hieroglyphics, and Semitic inscriptions made concrete the physical and cultural world so often disregarded by the source critics. This progress coincided with the ascendancy of higher criticism. Archaeologist Archibald H. Sayce complained that biblical critics too often projected their own ideas onto the text, and predicted that eventually the proponents of these two approaches would collide:

> It is indeed strange how seldom we think of even trying to understand what a passage of Scripture must have originally signified to the author and his readers, or to realize its precise meaning.[20]

During the same decade, W. M. Flinders Petrie's introduction of scientific archaeology to the Holy Land provided the most dramatic tool for ascertaining original context.[21] Then William F. Albright brought the discipline to new levels of sophistication in the early 1900s. He employed Petrie's methods in tandem with philology as a tool against the growing tide of the Wellhausen school. Albright's mastery of ancient sources and artifacts embodied the full flowering of the contextual resources that continues unabated today.[22]

It is a supreme irony that the more radical trends in literary criticism have recently brought about a retreat back to study of the biblical text devoid of context. In part this is a natural reaction to the overly confident, positivist approach of the Albright school. But it also reflects the prevailing philosophical winds of our times. In the wake of D. F. Strauss, Hans Frei, and others, many literary critics have little regard for context.[23] In previous decades biblical scholars sought to interpret the Bible and harmonize it with extrabiblical data. But in our day many scholars would argue that the biblical text — including the individuals and events that it describes — must be decontextualized and deconstructed to suit the presuppositions of the reader. The original intent of the author, along with the original setting of the text, is often overshadowed by other concerns.[24] Today scholars such as John Van Seters,

20. A. H. Sayce, The "Higher Criticism" and the Verdict of the Monuments (London: SPCK, 1894), 27.

21. Davis, 54-79.

22. Peter Machinist, "William Foxwell Albright: The Man and His Work," in The Study of the Ancient Near East in the Twenty-First Century: The William Foxwell Albright Centennial Conference, ed. Jerrold S. Cooper and Glenn M. Schwartz (Winona Lake: Eisenbrauns, 1996), 385-403.

23. For a summary and evaluation, see V. Philips Long, The Art of Biblical History (Grand Rapids: Zondervan, 1994), 88-119.

24. For a harsh critique of this approach, see William G. Dever, "Archaeology, Ideology, and the Quest for an 'Ancient' or 'Biblical' Israel," NEA 61 (1998): 39-52.

Thomas L. Thompson and Philip Davies sometimes choose to set aside contextual study and its disciplines altogether for various ideological and political reasons.[25] As Scott J. Hafemann has written, "the rising popularity of the 'postmodern' skepticism concerning the 'objectivity' of historical studies, with its suspicion concerning the possibility of ascertaining an author's original intention in any significant way, has now called the 'modern' hermeneutical consensus into question."[26] Today biblical archaeology is facing this same challenge, as we shall note below.

Looking back, the center of gravity in biblical interpretation has shifted multiple times over the course of the past two millennia. The interpreters of each era were trying to resolve seeming inconsistencies in the text. Context as we have defined it here has been available only since the mid-1800s and is one resource employed with various results since then. It is unfortunate, to say the least, that the study of context has recently gone out of fashion in many circles of biblical scholarship after it provided such illumination during the past century and a half. As the schematic indicates, these latest trends bring us full circle back to a type of allegorical approach, only this time without its religious framework. We are left with subjective humanism devoid of historical contextual constraints.

The Unique Role of Archaeology

Today as never before, the cultural setting of the biblical text is accessible through discoveries in archaeology and related disciplines. As Thomas Davis and Roger Moorey have shown, biblical archaeology has matured from a romantic quest for treasures to an established discipline that draws upon social science and textual study alike.[27] During the past three decades, competing trends in biblical interpretation and the growing influence of the social and natural sciences softened the positivist obsession with re-creating the past. One benefit of William G. Dever's foray into anthropology and the "new archaeology" is that it introduced up-to-date methods and brought a much-needed dose of humility to those who used archaeology to create forced reconstructions of biblical events.

Today biblical archaeolgy is facing many of the same challenges encountered in biblical studies during the past 15 years. It is ironic that a wealth

---

25. See, for example, Thomas L. Thompson, *The Mythic Past: Biblical Archaeology and the Myth of Israel* (New York: Basic, 1999), 200-28.

26. "The Use of the Bible in Daily Life: The Question of Hermeneutics," paper presented to Wheaton College Faith and Learning Program, 1999, 28.

27. Davis, 285-302; Moorey, 146-73.

of archaeological and epigraphic finds has become available just as the prevailing intellectual trends of our time tend to discount the concepts of history and purposeful text. According to this late modern view, little of the Bible's historical record can be trusted, regardless of "objective" evidence. Paradoxically, the "battle for the Bible" has migrated to the realm of history, language, and archaeology at precisely the moment when corroborative evidence, which abounds as never before, is intentionally swept aside.

The "maximalist-minimalist" debate also demanded a healthy reassessment of the methods and presuppositions of the discipline.[28] And yet it is disturbing that the "minimalists" do not accept critiques of their own presuppositions. Not only the biblical accounts but also archaeological and epigraphic finds are all too often re-created in the reader's image or dismissed.[29] Moveover, a good number of the so-called minimalists have limited linguistic training and no field experience, as Dever has noted.[30] They engage in a type of guerilla warfare against any position that contradicts their assertions, regardless of how grounded their opponent's view may be in the classical disciplines of philology and archaeology. This leads to pointless controversy over the legitimacy of the Tel Dan inscription, the Siloam Tunnel inscription, and more recently the nature of 10th-century Jerusalem.[31]

The recent book *Life in Biblical Israel* by Lawrence E. Stager and Philip J. King represents a new approach in biblical archaeology that offers a way out of the current impasse.[32] Rather than reconstruct history or simply illuminate the Bible, this method places the material culture of ancient Israel within a long-term geographic, historical, and social dynamic. Through the combined use of texts, artifacts, sociology, and ethnography it seeks to enter into the world of the ancients in order to acquire a fuller understanding of Israelite society and its literary record. Stager initiated this approach in 1985 with his article "The Archaeology of the Family."[33] More recently J. David Schloen

28. Israel Finkelstein and Neil Asher Silberman, *The Bible Unearthed: Archaeology's New Vision of Ancient Israel and the Origin of Its Sacred Texts* (New York: Free Press, 2001).

29. See e.g., Philip R. Davies, "'House of David' Built on Sand: The Sins of the Biblical Maximizers," *BAR* 20/4 (1994): 54-55.

30. *What Did the Biblical Writers Know and When Did They Know It?* (Grand Rapids: Wm. B. Eerdmans, 2001), chs. 2 and 3.

31. For a representative comparison of tone, scholarship, and presuppositions, note the following two articles: John Rogerson and Philip R. Davies, "Was the Siloam Tunnel Built by Hezekiah?" *BA* 59 (1996): 138-49; Jo Ann Hackett, Frank Moore Cross, P. Kyle McCarter, Jr., Adam Yardeni, André Lemaire, Esther Eshel, and Avi Hurvitz, "Defusing Pseudo-Scholarship: The Siloam Inscription Ain't Hasmonean," *BAR* 23/2 (1997): 41-50, 68.

32. (Louisville: Westminster John Knox, 2001).

33. *BASOR* 260 (1985): 1-35.

has moved this paradigm further in his robust study on the economic and so-cial organization of Ugarit.[34] The hermeneutics of Paul Ricoeur and the ideal types of Max Weber are tested through a dialectic between text and artifact focused on the patrimonial household at Ugarit. Instead of following the functionalist approach of Emile Durkheim or the positivist tendency of Albright, Stager and Schloen "bring textual and archaeological data into his-torical discourse by selecting and interpreting them through the problematics of social history."[35] In his recent book Stager writes:

> Agrarian life, kinship relations, domestic objects, the routines of the day and the year, and other such details of the mundane world play a far greater role on the pages of the Hebrew Bible than we might initially real-ize. They figure into stories, laws, historical accounts, songs, prophetic critiques, and wisdom sayings — sometimes as prominent features, but just as often as background minutiae.[36]

New paradigms aside, discoveries in the ancient Near East during the past century have reached a "critical mass" of biblically relevant material that ought to figure prominently into every scholar's interpretation of the biblical text. With each new discovery, the fascinating nexus between *realia* and text brings to life the context of Scripture.

For those who have the specific purpose of engaging the biblical text, archaeology's primary role *vis-à-vis* the Bible should be illumination and probability, not proof. We must learn to enter the biblical world and harmo-nize it with the text without the burden of "proving" historical reliability, much less theological truth. And yet, with presuppositions aside, the weight of evidence leads us to more historical probability than the "minimalists" al-low. For example, in my study of the Jerusalem temple I first treated the bibli-cal and archaeological material separately, gleaning all that I could from se-mantics, etymology, and a temple typology.[37] Next I sought correlations between the biblical account and comparable temples in the northern Levant. The Jerusalem temple clearly fell within the north Syrian style and chrono-

34. J. David Schloen, *The House of the Father as Fact and Symbol: Patrimonialism in Ugarit and the Ancient Near East.* Studies in the Archaeology and History of the Levant 2 (Winona Lake: Eisenbrauns, 2001).

35. *BASOR* 260 (1985): 3.

36. *Life in Biblical Israel*, 9.

37. John M. Monson, *The Jerusalem Temple: A Case Study in the Integration of Text and Artifact* (diss., Harvard, 1999). For a summary, see Monson, "The Temple of Solomon: Heart of Jerusalem," in *Zion, City of Our God*, ed. Richard S. Hess and Gordon J. Wenham (Grand Rapids: Wm. B. Eerdmans, 1999), 1-22.

logically belonged in the early 1st millennium B.C.E. While this does not prove the existence of the Israelite temple or the veracity of the Bible, it does lend qualified support to the existence of the Solomonic kingdom centered in Jerusalem.

Today there are plentiful examples of archaeological discovery that illuminate the biblical text and may even increase the probability that its cultural and historical record is reliable. Examples include Area G of Jerusalem and the Ketef Hinnom amulet from the time of Jeremiah inscribed with the Priestly Benediction of Numbers 6,[38] statues of Canaanite deities in metal and stone,[39] the dramatic high place of Jeroboam at ancient Dan,[40] the great wall and water tunnel protecting Jerusalem during the days of Isaiah,[41] and inscriptions naming the officials of the Judean monarchy.[42] These are but a few examples of the fascinating nexus between *realia* and text that brings the context of Scripture to life.

In light of the quantum advances in method, together with a massive amount of excavated material and the innovative approaches of scholars like Stager, I have no doubt that biblical archaeology has a bright future.[43] As an integrative discipline it lies at the junction of literature, history, and science. It is the primary instrument for grasping the "context" of Scripture, the first principle of biblical exegesis and hermeneutics.[44]

---

38. Philip J. King, *Jeremiah: An Archaeological Companion* (Louisville: Westminster John Knox, 1992), 65-78, 100-102; See also Gabriel Barkay, "The Priestly Benediction on Silver Plaques from Ketef Hinnom in Jerusalem," *TA* 19 (1992): 139-92.

39. Note esp. Isa. 2:8; Hos. 13:2. See the discussion by Ziony Zevit, *The Religions of Israel* (New York: Continuum, 2000), 267-349, and the analysis in Othmar Keel and Christoph Uehlinger, *Gods, Goddesses, and Images of God in Ancient Israel* (Minneapolis: Fortress, 1996), 209-82.

40. E.g., 1 Kings 12; Avraham Biran, *Biblical Dan* (Jerusalem: Israel Exploration Society, 1994), 168-91.

41. Recorded only in 2 Chr. 32:3-4. See Steven P. Lancaster and G. A. Long, "Where They Met: Separations in the Rock Mass near the Siloam Tunnel's Meeting Point," *BASOR* 315 (1999): 15-26.

42. Isa. 22:15-18; Jer. 36, 43. See, e.g., David Ussishkin, *The Village of Silwan* (Jerusalem: Israel Exploration Society, 1993), 241-56; and Stager and King, 300-18.

43. Those who would disagree need only look at the steep rise in academic positions filled during the past five years.

44. A brief summation of the goals in hermeneutics and exegesis is offered in the introductory book by Gordon D. Fee and Douglas Stuart, *How to Read the Bible for All Its Worth* (Grand Rapids: Zondervan, 1983), 19-27.

Case Studies: The Value of Context in Biblical Interpretation

Context comprises text, geography, and material culture (or *realia*), as we have noted above. Few would disagree with the assertion that the cognate literature is the most significant part of the biblical context. The exciting prospects for this avenue of research are clearly evident in the recent *Context of Scripture* volumes[45] and many of the papers in the current volume. And yet it is extraordinary that even today with ease of travel and the achievements of archaeology most research is narrowly planted in either text or artifact. It is even less common to find in biblical literature a meaningful dialectic that includes geography in more than a cursory way. Ideally, all three components of context should be used in harmony whenever this is possible.

If the combined approach we are advocating allows us to view biblical texts in new ways, it also has the potential to reassess the exegetical work of previous eras. Only several brief examples can be offered here. In each case we will comment on earlier exegetical tradition and demonstrate the value of the contextual approach advocated here.

Archaeology

The vision of Ezekiel in the opening chapter of the book depicts a heavenly scene replete with lions, fire, coals, and cherubim astride wheels.[46] As would be expected, early interpreters found creative ways to exegete this passage. Original context was not a concern. The *Songs of Sabbath Sacrifice* at Qumran paraphrase Ezekiel 1 and clearly interpret the Lord's platform as a chariot.[47] Origen and Chrysostom emphasized the fact that Ezekiel, like believers before and after him, did not actually see God but rather the glory and splendors

---

45. William W. Hallo and K. Lawson Younger, Jr., eds., *The Context of Scripture*, 3 vols. (Leiden: E. J. Brill, 1997-2002).

46. The scene is described in Ezek. 1:5-11: "In the middle of it was something like four living creatures. This was their appearance: they were of human form. Each had four faces, and each of them had four wings. Their legs were straight, and the soles of their feet were like the sole of a calf's foot; and they sparkled like burnished bronze. Under their wings on their four sides they had human hands . . . the four had the face of a human being, the face of a lion on the right side, the face of an ox on the left side, and the face of an eagle; such were their faces. Their wings were spread out above; each creature had two wings, each of which touched the wing of another, while two covered their bodies" (NRSV).

47. Note esp. 4Q403 1 ii:15: "The chariots of his innermost sanctum shall offer praise as one, and their cherubim and wheel-beings shall marvelously bless [. . .]." See also 4Q403 1 ii:16: "the chiefs of the divine building. They shall praise him in his holy innermost sanctum."

that accompany him.[48] Irenaeus emphasized the same point, adding that the four faces of the cherubim reflect the perfection of the four Gospels.[49] Likewise, Augustine and Jerome sought to find associations between the faces of each creature and the nature of the individual Gospels.[50]

Calvin, although he pursued the grammar and context with more rigor, was inclined to interpret the four creatures as evidence that "God wished to teach us that his influence is diffused through all regions of the world." The turning of the four wheels represented the changing world according to God's divine plan.[51] An analysis of the text yielded theological truth but was restricted from access to the culture and life setting from which this passage emerged.

The discovery of ancient Near Eastern temples and iconography over the past 100 years has facilitated a much richer representation of Ezekiel's first chapter. Moshe Greenberg writes, "Virtually every component of Ezekiel's vision can thus be derived from Israelite tradition supplemented by neighboring iconography."[52] Many would interpret the cherubim and wheels as comprising the chariot of God based upon verses 22-28 and passages such as 1 Chr. 28:18, which mentions the "chariot of the cherubim" whose wings cover the ark of the covenant.[53] And yet, even with ancient Near Eastern parallels Greenberg is adamant that "there is no ground for asserting that he saw an earthly equivalent anywhere, or that he followed a Babylonian prototype."[54]

An archaeologically informed reading of Ezekiel 1 causes us to think otherwise. Ezekiel is describing the inner sanctum of the Jerusalem temple. Several observations lead to this conclusion. Cherub and genii figures from religious and royal iconography in Egypt, Mesopotamia, and the Levant correspond nicely to this passage.[55] The Ain Dara temple, closest parallel to the Jerusalem temple, contains relief, especially of cherubim, that is reminiscent

48. St. Chrysostom Homilies: Homily XIII.

49. *Against Heresies* iii.11.8.

50. Augustine, *De consensu evangelistarum* 1.6.9.

51. *Commentary on Ezekiel,* Chapter 1 (Grand Rapids: Christian Classics Ethereal Library, Online: http://ccel.org.1999), 11-24.

52. *Ezekiel 1–20.* AB 22 (Garden City: Doubleday, 1983), 58.

53. See the commentary by Leslie C. Allen, which makes excellent use of Near Eastern iconography; *Ezekiel 1–19.* WBC 28 (Waco: Word, 1994).

54. Greenberg, 58.

55. Othmar Keel, *The Symbolism of the Biblical World* (1978; repr. Winona Lake: Eisenbrauns, 1996), 167-76. See more appropriately Keel's work that includes four-faced creatures from Mesopotamia: *Jahweh-Visionen und Siegelkunst: Eine neue Deutung der Majestäts-schilderungen in Jes 6, Ez 1 und 10 und Sach 4.* Stuttgarter Bibelstudien 84/85 (Stuttgart: Katholisches Bibelwerk, 1977), 125-273.

of this passage.[56] In the case of the Jerusalem temple, the Israelites appropriated elements from surrounding cultures and put them in the service of Yahweh. More significantly, the image of wheels and cherubim conforms perfectly to the stands described in 1 Kgs. 7:36 as "borders [on which] he carved cherubim, lions, and palm trees, where each had space, with wreaths all around."[57] Stager is, in my view, correct to associate the temple stands with Ezekiel 1 rather than chariots as described in later traditions.[58] The glory of God is reflected in the accoutrements of the Jerusalem shrine. Ezekiel had no doubt been in the temple in Jerusalem, and hence the vision reflects so precisely what we now know about that artifact through the parallels in ancient Near Eastern culture. The cultural matrix of the ancient Near East situates Ezekiel's words not in a surreal vision but literally in the early-6th-century temple of Jerusalem.[59]

There are plentiful examples of the way archaeology can contribute to our understanding of a biblical text or concept. Israelite religion has been all but redefined as a result of archaeological data. The paradigms of Yehezkel Kaufmann and Wellhausen have been replaced by syntheses that are far more nuanced.[60] Today there is broad consensus that, for all its innovation, Israel's religion was inextricably linked to its West Semitic context.[61] The nature and use of religious artifacts such as the tabernacle and the altar are placed securely within the traditions of the ancient Near East.[62]

56. Elizabeth Bloch-Smith, " 'Who Is the King of Glory?' Solomon's Temple and Its Symbolism," in *Scripture and Other Artifacts,* ed. Michael D. Coogan, J. Cheryl Exum, and Lawrence E. Stager (Louisville: Westminster John Knox, 1994), 18-31. See also Monson, "The Temple of Solomon," 19.

57. For a detailed description of cultic stands, see Pirhiya Beck, "The Cult-Stands from Taanach: Aspects of the Iconographic Tradition of Early Iron Age Cult Objects in Palestine," in *From Nomadism to Monarchy: Archaeological and Historical Aspects of Early Israel,* eds. Israel Finkelstein and Nadav Na'aman (Washington: Biblical Archaeology Society, 1994), 352-81. 1 Kgs. 7:28-36 records the construction of the stands. Each had borders, frames, images of lions, oxen, and cherubim, with basins in the middle. The frames included palm and wreath motifs, hearkening back to the garden of Eden.

58. Stager and King, 341-44; See also Helga Weippert, "Die Kessel-wagen Salomos, *ZDPV* 108 (1992): 8-41.

59. Other biblical texts support this conclusion. The scene in Ezekiel 1 conforms with temple interior as described in 1 Kings 6–7; Isaiah 6; Psalms 89, 97, etc.

60. Note e.g., Zevit; and William G. Dever, "The Contribution of Archaeology to the Study of Canaanite and Early Israelite Religion," in *Ancient Israelite Religion,* ed. Patrick D. Miller, Jr., Paul D. Hanson, and S. Dean McBride (Philadelphia: Fortress, 1987), 209-48.

61. Frank Moore Cross, *From Epic to Canon* (Baltimore: Johns Hopkins University Press, 1998), 241.

62. Note esp. the promising approach used by Michael M. Homan, *To Your Tents, O Is-*

As with ancient religion, our evaluation of the social world of biblical Israel has been transformed. The vast accumulation of archaeological data has reached such a size that it can be used to test hypotheses old and new. As noted above, Schloen's work on the "house of the father" applies Weber's "ideal types" to arrive at a patrimonial model that is scalable from the family up to the patron deity.[63] In a recent essay that utilizes similar methods, Daniel M. Master argues forcefully against the evolutionary model of state formation in the kingdom of ancient Israel. He shows that archaeology and text better suit a patrimonial paradigm that allows for an ebb and flow to and from the configurations of tribe and state.[64]

Finally, we should not forget the contribution of archaeology to historical reconstruction. The classic convergence of text, geography, and archaeology is evidenced in the Assyrian assault on Lachish in 701. Here the geography of the Shephelah, the detail of the Assyrian annals, the dramatic evidence of siege, and the theological commentary of Isaiah converge around one archaeological site.[65] In this classic case the combined evidence fits together so tightly that there is no room for the type of rancorous debate we witness over the 10th century. The discovery of new archives such as Emar continues to invite a reassessment of biblical periods from the patriarchs through the exile.[66]

The preceding examples, though brief, attest to the fact that that material culture, like texts, represents a language of sorts. Architecture, iconography, small finds, etc., and not text alone must be considered as they too are the social, intellectual, and religious reflexes of ancient culture. This field of study did not exist until the advent of biblical archaeology in the later part of the 19th century.

---

rael! The Terminology, Function, Form, and Symbolism of Tents in the Hebrew Bible and the Ancient Near East (Leiden: E, J. Brill, 2002). For the tabernacle, see K. A. Kitchen, "The Tabernacle: A Bronze Age Artifact," ErIsr 24 (1993): 119-29; and Cross, Epic to Canon, 84-98.

63. Schloen, 29-54.

64. Daniel M. Master, "State Formation Theory and the Kingdom of Ancient Israel," JNES 60 (2001): 117-31. For a study of similar quality, see Øystein S. LaBianca, "Salient Features of Iron Age Tribal Kingdoms," in Ancient Ammon, ed. Burton MacDonald and Randall W. Younker. SHANE 17 (Leiden: E. J. Brill, 1999), 19-29.

65. See David Ussishkin, "The Excavations at Tel Lachish — 1978-83: Second Preliminary Report," TA 10 (1983): 97-185; Andrew G. Vaughn, Theology, History, and Archaeology in the Chronicler's Account of Hezekiah. SBLABS 4 (Atlanta: Scholars, 1999); Richard S. Hess, "Hezekiah and Sennacherib in 2 Kings 18-20," in Hess and Wenham, 23-41.

66. Daniel E. Fleming, "Emar: On the Road from Harran to Hebron," in Mesopotamia and the Bible: Comparative Explorations, ed. Mark W. Chavalas and K. Lawson Younger, Jr. JSOTSup 341 (Sheffield: Sheffield Academic, 2002), 222-50; See also Fleming, "More Help from Syria: Introducing Emar to Biblical Study," BA 58 (1995): 139-47.

Geography

Geography as a tool for establishing context is made use of far less often than archaeology. Yet the geographical "dynamic" of the land has much to offer as Robinson, Lagrange, F.-M. Abel, and others recognized long ago.[67] Through the work of Fernand Braudel, archaeologists have gained a deeper appreciation for the geographical realities that animate ancient culture and history.[68] The same is needed for the geographical data embedded in the biblical text. Routes, agriculture, building materials, settlement patterns, and trade all factor into the flow of events described in the Hebrew Bible and New Testament. When events are overlaid upon geographical regions, a previously unnoticed pattern emerges and locations become what Walter Brueggemann would describe as a "storied place."[69] An appreciation for these regional dynamics and "code words" can facilitate a fresh reading of many passages in the Hebrew Bible and New Testament.

We may take as an example the territory of Benjamin. Located at the convergence of two anticlines, it is comprised of a relatively flat plateau along the "Way of the Patriarchs," the ridge route that runs along the crest of the Judean range. The plateau is slightly lower and much less rugged than the hills that flank it on the north and the south. By virtue of easier and shorter ascents from the Aijalon Valley in the west and the plain of Jericho in the east, this territory serves as the most convenient link between Transjordan, the Jordan Valley, and the Mediterranean coast.[70] Since the early 2nd millennium this region has held strategic importance, as attested by the routes that run

---

67. Robinson, *Biblical Researches in Palestine and the Adjacent Regions;* F-M. Abel, *Géographie de la Palestine* 1, 3rd ed. (Paris: Gabalda, 1933). See modern works such as Yohanan Aharoni, *The Land of the Bible,* 2nd ed. (Philadelphia: Westminster, 1979). For the Second Temple period, see Michael Avi-Yonah, *The Holy Land, From the Persian Period to the Arab Conquests, 536 B.C. to A.D. 640: A Historical Geography* (Grand Rapids: Baker, 1966).

68. In his work *On History* (Chicago: University of Chicago Press, 1980), Fernand Braudel wrote of the influence that geography and environment have upon long-term human history and society. The *Annales* school continues to have a profound influence upon archaeology. See also Braudel's seminal book of 1949, *The Mediterranean and the Mediterranean World in the Age of Philip II* (Berkeley: University of California Press, 1995). The benefits of geographical study are also clearly evident in the preliminary surveys conducted by the Tell el-Borg Expedition led by James Hoffmeier (see above, pp. 53-66).

69. Walter Brueggemann, *The Land.* OBT (Philadelphia: Fortress, 1977), 185.

70. Other approaches in the north and south exist, but this is much easier than other approaches such as from the Elah Valley to Bethlehem, etc. See David A. Dorsey, *The Roads and Highways of Ancient Israel* (Baltimore: Johns Hopkins University Press, 1991), 181-207.

through it and by the large number of ancient cities on and adjacent to it, such as Gibeon, Mizpah, and Bethel.[71]

The number of military campaigns and geopolitical maneuvers that transpired in this small region is so large that the mere mention of it in biblical and historical sources should cause one to take special notice.[72] This was the location of Joshua's ascent via Ai and victory at Gibeon. As the tribal settlement expanded southward from the territory of Ephraim, the region fell to the tribe of Benjamin, which became a buffer between the powerful houses of Ephraim and Judah.[73] The Benjaminite civil war almost destroyed the tribal alliance altogether but was resolved in part to stave off an even greater confrontation between Judah and Ephraim.[74] Samuel's circuit centered on this plateau and Saul's home was on its periphery.[75] The Philistines ascended into this region for the purpose of driving a wedge between the northern and southern tribes, and it was here that Jonathan and Samuel won great victories against them.[76] David's move to Jerusalem made the Benjamin district a part of the religious and geopolitical hub of the united monarchy by which David expanded to the east and to the west. This created a bridge between north and south and brought hegemony to the whole region for the first time. In contrast, Pharaoh Shishak exploited the strategic value of the plateau to threaten Jerusalem and launch a campaign against its rival, the nascent kingdom of Israel in the north.[77] During the Hellenistic and Roman periods the plateau and its ascents were used in similar fashion to unite, divide, or conquer the

71. For an archaeological description of the cities in this region (but with limited geographical commentary), see Patrick M. Arnold, *Gibeah: The Search for a Biblical City.* JSOTSup 79 (Sheffield: Sheffield Academic, 1990). Note also Shlomo Bunimowitz's attempt to apply Braudel's approach to the socio-political transformations in the region of Benjamin: "Socio-Political Transformations in the Central Hill Country in the Late Bronze-Iron I Transition," in Finkelstein and Na'aman, 179-202.

72. For an overview of the region's geography and history, see James M. Monson, *Regions on the Run* (Mountain Home, Ark.: Biblical Backgrounds, 1988), 26-27; and S. Lancaster and James M. Monson, *Regional Study Guide* (Rockford, Ill.: Biblical Backgrounds, 2000), 62-95.

73. Archaeological surveys by Israel Finkelstein and others contribute significantly to our understanding of this region's history. See Israel Finkelstein and Itzhak Magen, eds., *Archaeological Survey of the Hill Country of Benjamin* (Jerusalem: Israel Antiquities Authority, 1993) (Hebrew). See also Zechariah Kallai-Kleinman, "Notes on the Topography of Benjamin," *IEJ* 6 (1956): 180-87.

74. Judges 19–21.

75. 1 Samuel 7–25.

76. 1 Samuel 13–15.

77. 2 Chronicles 12; Benjamin Mazar, "Pharaoh Shishak's Campaign to the Land of Israel," in *The Early Biblical Period: Historical Studies* (Jerusalem: Israel Exploration Society, 1986), 139-50.

highland of Judah.[78] And the same patterns are evident from the Crusader period through the present.[79]

Given its location and the events that have transpired on it, the territory of Benjamin as a geographical region takes on a significance of its own. This can be read back into the biblical and historical passages where this region plays a role. It is the epitome of a "storied place."[80]

Such combinations of geographical features and historical layering can be applied to a myriad of regions in the Levant. The geographical openness and vulnerability of Naphtali and Zebulun illuminate the darkness and oppression described in Isaiah 9. The priorities and challenges of the Philistines are brought into focus through an appreciation that their homeland comprised a homogeneous region bordering the international coastal highway and the Shephelah, or western flank of Judah.[81]

In sum, the geography of the Holy Land, with its full set of subdisciplines, represents a vast, untapped resource for the study of the Hebrew Bible through regional realities that still exist today. Indeed, rather than comprising a simple list of sites isolated from their setting, the land is a complex but well-ordered matrix that gave birth to the biblical text. Like the stage in a drama, it serves to enliven the history and culture of the Bible and to clarify its message.

Conclusion: Archaeology and the Contribution of Context

My purpose in this paper has been to contrast the varied roles that context has played over the past two millennia of biblical interpretation. We have found that until the Reformation historical and cultural context played an insignificant role in biblical interpretation. Clearly, one reason for this was a lack of access to the land and the absence of *realia* that became available only later through archaeological excavation. Jewish exegesis attempted to resolve

---

78. See the vivid description of the ascent of Beth Horon offered by Josephus (*Jewish Wars* 2.19) in his account of the First Revolt against Rome in A.D. 70.

79. George Adam Smith, *The Historical Geography of the Holy Land*, 25th ed. (1932; repr. Jerusalem: Ariel, 1974), 195-215, offers a most eloquent review.

80. Brueggemann, 185. Could it be that Paul has in mind the troubled history of this region when he refers to himself as a Benjaminite who has received God's grace (Rom. 10:21–11:1)? James M. Monson suggests this idea in *The Land Between* (Mountain Home, Ark.: Biblical Backgrounds, 1982), 121.

81. James M. Monson names this the "Philistine alluvial plain"; *The Land Between*, 124-28. A good description of the region's dynamic can be found in William M. Schniedewind, "The Geopolitical History of Philistine Gath," *BASOR* 309 (1998): 69-77.

seeming contradictions in the text through creative and sometimes fanciful explanations. Early Christian interpreters did the same in the service of the gospel message. The Reformers pioneered the historical-critical approach, which by the mid-1900s was fixated upon source-critical issues. During the past decade the new criticism and the minimalists hijacked and eclipsed this legitimate avenue of study.

What, then, should the place of context be today, now that the geographical, historical, and cultural realities of the biblical world are so accessible? A profound one, no doubt! The biblical authors *assumed* that their readers were familiar with the world as it was in their day. The assessments of Jerome and Sayce were correct. We should follow their lead and exploit fully the vast resources that have become available in recent years. One question that might be addressed is whether or not context as we understand it today has the potential to change fundamentally the meaning of certain biblical texts rather than simply illuminating them. In the end, we are likely to find that even the exponential advances in understanding biblical context described above cannot remove the uncomfortable paradoxes at times found in the text.

We have also sought to advocate the increased use of geography and *realia* alongside textual study. In many ways we need the spirit of Lagrange and Albrecht Alt to stem the continuing "balkanization" of our field.[82] The first challenge is to find ways to "translate" and make available the archaeological data and geographical realities so that all scholars in the field of biblical studies have equal access to them. Hopefully, this will lead to further use of these disciplines in exegesis that ultimately will impact our religious communities as well.

In conclusion, biblical archaeology in the interdisciplinary sense includes geography, material culture, and text.[83] Defined in this way, it is the centerpiece of the biblical context. It is currently experiencing a renaissance that revisits the innovation and syntheses of the 19th century. But now it has acquired up-to-date sociological and anthropological models while incorporating scientific advances and shedding the positivist emphasis of the past 100

---

82. The classic work of Albrecht Alt incorporates this approach; *Kleine Schriften zur Geschichte des Volkes Israel*, 3 vols. (Munich: C. H. Beck, 1953-1959).

83. Unlike most excavations to date, some recent archaeological expeditions follow an approach that is intentional in its use of regional surveys and specialists from the hard sciences. The Tell el-Borg Expedition is a fine example (see report in *JEA* 89 [2003]), as is the Madaba Plains Project (*The 1984 Season at Tell el-'Umeiri and Vicinity and Subsequent Studies*, ed. Lawrence T. Geraty, Larry G. Herr, Øystein S. LaBianca, Randall W. Younker [Berrien Springs: Andrews University Press, 1989]).

years. One hundred and fifty years of discovery can now yield a bountiful harvest of nonpartisan investigations. Conceived and applied in this manner, biblical archaeology has the potential to revolutionize biblical interpretation and to marginalize those who allow their personal presuppositions to eclipse empirical evidence. Far from being moribund, it is a field whose greatest contribution has only just begun.[84]

84. I would like to express my gratitude to James K. Hoffmeier and Harvey Miller for hosting a conference on the Future of Biblical Archaeology. Meetings such as this and expeditions like Tell el-Borg demonstrate the innovation and promise of biblical archaeology.

Ancient Near Eastern Mythography as It Relates to Historiography in the Hebrew Bible: Genesis 3 and the Cosmic Battle

RICHARD E. AVERBECK

One of the most fascinating dimensions of the study of the Bible in its ancient Near Eastern context is the appearance of mythological allusions and themes in the Bible for which we have clearly recognizable data from the world of the ancient Near East. The goal of this paper is to investigate the relationship of theology, history, and ancient Near Eastern mythology in the Hebrew Bible. It is unfortunate that so much of the discussion on this topic has been clouded by serious problems of perspective, definition, and method. One scholar's mythology may be another one's history or theology, and both could be mixed up or confused with historiography. It seems to me that the discussion too often ends up going around in circles without getting to the heart of the problem of the relationship between biblical and ancient Near Eastern history and myth. We too easily end up in a tangle of unclear or unhelpful definitions, confused or misguided perspectives, and/or inadequate or even misleading methodologies.

I will make every effort to avoid such confusion in the following discussion. In order to do so, as we proceed it will be very important to clearly distinguish between the verifiable data from the Bible and from the ancient Near East and the various scholarly theories about those data. In this area of study scholars sometimes confuse their own or someone else's theory with the actually verifiable data that are available, and end up treating a theory as if it were confirmed data and/or ignoring data that do not fit the specific theory. Precisely because this is such a difficult topic to manage, it requires intellectual honesty and openness to the available data, whether biblical or extrabiblical, but we must be sure to distinguish between data and theories about the data.

Historiography

The confusion in the realms of definition and perspective mentioned above is not just a matter of interference from creedal convictions, or degrees of conservatism (of one sort or another) versus revisionism. John Van Seters, for example, is willing to call Genesis through Kings "*history* writing," whereas Thomas L. Thompson considers virtually the entire narrative to be an account of Israel's "*mythic* past."[1] Neither of these men holds his view based on confessional considerations, and both are committed revisionists. So how can *one* call this section of the Hebrew Bible "history writing" and *the other* call it "myth"?[2]

One element of special importance in this discussion is the definition and nature of "historiography" — the study of the theoretical principles, methods, techniques, usefulness, and even the very history of history writing itself. As those who are familiar with the discussion will know, by using the term "history writing" Van Seters does not mean to suggest that the bulk of Genesis through Kings is historically accurate. In fact, he is not really all that concerned about "historicity." He works from Johan Huizinga's well-worn definition of history as "the intellectual form in which a civilization renders account to itself of its past."[3] A civilization's own account of its past, according to Van Seters, may well be largely fictitious, but, nevertheless, it is still "history writing." He even argues that Genesis 1–11 is "history writing" in the sense that it is presented as an integral part of Israel's history, although he would call it a case of the "historisization of mythology."[4]

In my opinion, Huizinga's definition is a good one, perhaps the best,

---

1. John Van Seters, *Prologue to History: The Yahwist as Historian in Genesis* (Louisville: Westminster John Knox, 1992), 24-42 and passim; Thomas L. Thompson, *The Mythic Past: Biblical Archaeology and the Myth of Israel* (New York: Basic Books, 1999), 7 and passim.

2. I have sought to untangle this confusing web of competing presuppositions, definitions, and arguments in another article: Richard E. Averbeck, "Sumer, the Bible, and Comparative Method: Historiography and Temple Building," in *Mesopotamia and the Bible,* ed. Mark W. Chavalas and K. Lawson Younger, Jr. (Sheffield: Sheffield Academic, 2002), 88-125. I will not review that discussion in full detail here, but will focus on specific points of special significance for the present essay.

3. Johan Huizinga, "A Definition of the Concept of History," in *Philosophy and History: Essays Presented to Ernst Cassirer,* ed. Raymond Klibansky and H. J. Paton (1936; repr. New York: Harper & Row Publishers, 1963), 9. This is, in fact, the same definition with which Van Seters begins his discussion; *In Search of History: Historiography in the Ancient World and the Origins of Biblical History* (New Haven: Yale University Press, 1983), 1-2. See also review of Van Seters by K. Lawson Younger, Jr., *JSOT* 40 (1988): 110-17.

4. Van Seters, *Prologue to History,* 26-27, 188-93, 330-31.

but those who use it do not always use it fairly. On the one hand, following Huizinga, and over against Thompson, Van Seters properly resists the scholarly temptation to impose modern standards and criteria for history writing on the ancients. We need to allow them their own way of rendering account to themselves of their past. This is essential. On the other hand, Huizinga is also concerned that there be a substantial correspondence between what actually happened in the historical past of a civilization and their history writing:

> Every civilization and every sectional civilization must hold *its own* history to be the true one, and is entitled to do so, provided that it constructs this history in accordance with the critical requirements imposed by its conscience as a civilization, and not according to the cravings for power in the interests of which it imposes silence upon this conscience.[5]

This is where Thompson has made a good point. The degree to which Genesis through Kings accurately recount what actually happened in the past, even if the writers did put a certain interpretation on it, to that degree those books constitute legitimate "history writing." If Genesis through Kings consist largely of fictitious misrepresentations of historical fact for purposes of political propaganda or even theological tendenz, or if these biblical books are outright fictional fabrications that have no basis in the real past, then they should not be called "history writing." By definition, legitimate history writing cannot be substantially fictional, whether in ancient or modern times. The problem with Thompson, of course, is his radical historical skepticism and associated nihilism regarding the use of the Bible in writing the history of ancient Israel today.

Mythography

This brings us to the relationship between history and myth, or better historiography and mythography, in the study of history writing. "Mythography" may be defined as the critical study of the nature, principles, significance, and history of myths and mythical literature. It also includes the study of mythical elements in various other kinds of literature.[6] The very fact that we conceive

5. Huizinga, 9 (emphasis his).
6. William G. Doty, *Mythography: The Study of Myths and Rituals* (University, Ala.: University of Alabama Press, 1986), 1-40, esp. 8. See also the remarks on myth, legend, and history in the Bible in Richard E. Averbeck, "The Sumerian Historiographic Tradition and Its Implica-

of "the presence of either myth or legend in a historical work" as that which "requires some explanation"[7] is, in my opinion, the real underlying problem. We have tended to identify myth and legend with fiction, and as I have just argued, fiction is by nature not "history writing," even if, as the saying goes, the truth (of history) *can* be stranger than fiction.

It is most certainly true that the Israelites were ancient Near Easterners themselves. They were not a cultural *tabula rasa*. Certain common cultural foundations were well known across that world, and Israel was no exception. Moreover, people in the ancient Near East were given to speculating about and articulating their understanding of the world through stories about power and relations among the gods — mythology.[8] Basically, myths are creative and imaginative stories about important things. They often carry significant weight in the cultural context in which they develop and into which they speak. We are not talking here about a limited kind of "primitive mentality" that treats the ancients as ignorant prescientific people. They did not lack the ability to think in empirical and sophisticated ways. However, ancient Near Easterners did indeed make it their practice to express their speculations about world forces and their situation amid them by means of very sophisticated compilations of mythological motifs and patterns.

It is not my intent here to play semantic games with "different kinds of truth." What I am concerned about is different ways of understanding and describing what really *is* or *was* true in history, nature, culture, society, and so on. Myth is much more than fiction, even if it has fictional elements in it.[9] The term fiction, on the one hand, refers to imaginative stories that have no actual basis in historical fact. Myth, on the other hand, consists of imaginative stories that do have a basis in reality and/or history. In fact, myth reflects foundational understandings of the world that are important to the culture of the composer and those who read his compositions or hear them read. There is a natural correspondence linking fiction, myth, and history because all three manifest themselves primarily in story form, but they are different kinds of stories.

A rather large body of scholarly literature about mythology has arisen in the fields of cultural anthropology, philosophy, and literary studies in the last half of the 20th century. The most convenient summary of this scholar-

tions for Genesis 1–11," in *Faith, Tradition, and History: Old Testament Historiography in Its Near Eastern Context*, ed. Alan R. Millard, James K. Hoffmeier, and David W. Baker (Winona Lake: Eisenbrauns, 1994), 92-93, 95-96.

7. Van Seters, *Prologue to History*, 25.

8. See Doty, esp. 61-65, for his remarks on "mythmaking" and "mythopoeic" thought.

9. Doty, 7-8.

ship is found in Mary Douglas's book on reading Leviticus as literature. She spends 50 pages explaining and illustrating the difference between what she calls "analogical" and "rational-instrumental" ways of thinking and writing.[10] The remainder of her book illustrates her understanding of how essential this distinction is for understanding the ritual descriptions and prescriptions in Leviticus. For our purposes here it is important to know that she actually begins her discussion with myth as analogical thinking, and moves from there to ritual.[11]

Treating myth and ritual together is common, and there is good reason for it.[12] In general, the kind of "myth" we are concerned about here might be labeled "historical myth." It consists largely of analogical *thinking* about what is perceived by the writer(s) as reality, specifically historical, natural, geographical, cultural, economic, or social reality.[13] By way of contrast, sacred "ritual" is analogical *action,* by means of which the performer engages actively with that which is perceived as reality in the world of the gods or other supernatural beings. The kind of myth referred to here reflects upon the human world by describing or imaging creative analogies between the circumstances and experiences of human beings in the world and beliefs about the world of the gods and other supernatural beings. In the process, therefore, this kind of myth naturally contemplates and describes the perception and understanding that the writer has of her or his world.[14]

Yes, there are fictional elements here to one degree or another, but myth is not just fiction. There are two main points here. First, a myth was not nec-

10. Mary Douglas, *Leviticus as Literature* (Oxford: Oxford University Press, 1999), 15-65.

11. Douglas, 15-33.

12. See even Doty's subtitle, *The Study of Myths and Rituals.*

13. See the helpful distinctions made between four different modes of mythic composition in Kenton L. Sparks, "The Problem of Myth in Ancient Historiography," in *Rethinking the Foundations: Historiography in the Ancient World and in the Bible: Essays in Honour of John Van Seters,* ed. Steven L. McKenzie and Thomas Römer. BZAW 294 (Berlin: Walter de Gruyter, 2000), 271-77. Of the four types (psychological, metaphorical, historical, and pleasure myths), our focus here is on "historical myths," and among those the "analogical" type (275-76), which "produces a text that the author views to be referentially accurate and true. . . ."

14. It seems to me that the same principle applies *mutatis mutandis* to other kinds of literature as well. Again, myth is not just about the gods. Nevertheless, it often refers to gods or supernatural creatures of some sort, and the kind of myth we are talking about here creates and makes effective use of analogies between the world of the gods and the world of people. Similarly, "legend" or "epic," like myth, is also analogical to the real world, but in this instance significant people rather than gods or other supernatural beings are the source of the analogical elements in the story. Likewise, "fable" is analogical to the real world of people with animals and/or plants as the analogical center of attention, etc.

essarily fictional at all to the ancient writers and readers.[15] This is not just a matter of whether or not they believed in the gods or the events about which they wrote. Many of them surely did, although some probably did not, and some may have believed in an alternate mythology. In either case, one side of the analogy was associated with the author's knowledge and experience of the historical, natural, geographical, cultural, economic, or social reality in which he or she lived. They were not writing out of pure imagination, even though their religious and/or literary imagination could be fully exercised in their myths.

Second, since their myths were not just pure imagination but were analogical reflections of their view of the real world, therefore, they are not just fiction to us either when we read them today. They have something to say about the world the ancients lived in, so they are often useful in understanding that ancient world and the way at least some people experienced it. Moreover, and this is of great significance to us here, there are often some important correspondences between their world and ours, both in terms of the nature of the world and the way we experience it today. The mythical analogical character of the story does not eliminate the fact that the realities upon which the story is based did exist and were important to the ancient people and, in fact, may correspond at least in some instances to things that are important to us today. Yes, there is fiction here, but not *just* fiction.

In our modern day we sometimes pride ourselves on the scientific method as an objective means of investigation that makes exclusive use of what Douglas refers to as rational-instrumental thinking. There have even been attempts to use the so-called scientific method in the soft sciences, such fields as sociology, psychology, and history, thereby supposedly limiting our investigation to completely naturalistic causes and effects of one kind or another. In recent decades, however, we have been made more aware of what has always been true even in the hard sciences such as mathematics, physics, and chemistry. The fact is that mathematical and scientific inquiry is based on the construction of models — that is, paradigms or analogies. In reality, analogical thinking provides the larger framework of the model within which rational-instrumental thinking can do its legitimate work. Rational-instrumental thinking is not imaginative and creative enough to develop the models themselves.[16]

---

15. Sparks, e.g., makes the point that a "historical myth" consists of ". . . a creative narrative that is for the author anything but fictive. . . . While we might readily associate the trait of manifest impossibility with the mythic genre for heuristic purposes, we ought to restrain ourselves from presuming too quickly that a myth was, for its author, referentially fictive" (275-76).

16. See esp. Douglas, 21, 27-28, 32. Compare Thomas S. Kuhn, *The Structure of Scientific*

In the ancient and the modern world we find analogical as well as rational-instrumental thinking. In the ancient Near East mythology served the need for analogical thinking, and rational-instrumental thinking was necessary to accomplish feats such as the irrigation agriculture of ancient Sumer. In our modern world we need models to give direction to scientific inquiry, whether in the hard or soft sciences. In physics, for example, it might be the wave or particle model of light, or in psychology it might be the medical model of mental "illness." We should not be so foolish as to think that we have left "mythology" behind either. The only real difference is that we tend to do mythology scientifically, so we have a lot of what we call today "*science* fiction," which is really scientifically articulated mythology. Furthermore, this mythology has captured the imagination of our culture to such a degree that it even motivates actual scientific inquiry into such things as the quest for life in other solar systems. Recently, with the development of what some have been calling "postmodernism," there has been a reaction to the dehumanizing effect of "modernism." This has brought with it a reintroduction of spiritual concerns and spiritual beings into our modern mythologies and even some of the sciences.[17]

Ancient Near Eastern Mythology

The point is that this is not really a matter of ancient versus modern thinking at all.[18] Who knows how much their myths captured the imagination of the ancient Near Eastern peoples, or at least some of them, as ours do for some of us? One of the clearest examples of such mythological analogical thinking in the ancient Near Eastern world that I am aware of is the Sumerian myth known as Enki and the World Order.[19] It is a long and relatively well-

---

Revolutions, 2nd ed. (Chicago: University of Chicago Press, 1970); and the most helpful recent summary of Kuhn's analysis with a review and critique of its use in the social sciences and biblical studies by Robert F. Shedinger, "Kuhnian Paradigms and Biblical Scholarship: Is Biblical Studies a Science?" *JBL* 119 (2000): 453-71.

17. So we now have, e.g., "transpersonal psychology" as a legitimate branch of modern counseling psychology, which concerns itself with "the study of humanity's highest potential, and with the recognition, understanding, and realization of unitive, spiritual, and transcendent states of consciousness." Quoted in James E. Strohl, "Transpersonalism: Ego Meets Soul," *Journal of Counseling and Development* 76 (1998): 397 from a study by Lajoie and Shapiro.

18. See John W. Rogerson, *Myth in Old Testament Interpretation.* BZAW 134 (Berlin: Walter de Gruyter, 1974), esp. 180-89, for a summary and critique of the whole problem of myth in biblical studies, in which we have been hindered for too long by socio-evolutionary schemes that misrepresent not only the ancients but also ourselves.

19. I have recently had occasion to examine this text with some care. The observations

preserved composition having many extant copies, although there are some tantalizing lacunae in the story. The myth begins with the author's opening praise of Enki, the god of Eridu, the god of fertility and productivity, whom Enlil, the chief god of Nippur and Sumer overall, commissioned to make rulers and common people alike happy, prosperous, and secure in Sumer.[20]

In the following section Enki speaks in praise of himself twice. In his first self-praise, Enki speaks initially of how his brother, Enlil, had given him control of the *me*'s; literally, "the *me* to my hand he set" (*me šu-ĝu₁₀-šè mu-un-ĝuₐᵣ,* line 65). These are the offices, arts, and crafts with their associated functional powers that, according to the Sumerian view, shaped and tooled their culture and society so that it worked for both gods and people. Then Enki turns to the fact that Enlil had likewise granted him control of the decreeing of destinies/fates, literally, "decreeing destiny/fate . . . in my hand he placed" (*nam-tar-ra . . . šu-ĝuₐ ₘᵤ₋ᵤₙ₋ĝuₐₗ,* line 76), which makes him the one who determines what happens in heaven and earth, whether good or bad.[21]

At a certain point in the composition, Enki turns his attention to the proper development of the Sumerian homeland. This is a very lengthy third person narrative (lines 250-386), and of special interest to our considerations in this essay. The passage takes us through 12 cycles, each of which recounts how Enki himself first initiated a particular set of forces of nature and/or cultural phenomena that would make Sumer a prosperous place (or perhaps revived or restored them, depending on how one interprets the composition as a whole), and then put one of the gods in charge of each. This cyclical pattern creates a set of analogical relationships between these gods and the realities of man's world, which is one of Douglas's points about the analogical nature of mythical thinking and ritual action. Texts of this sort create their own inter-

---

here are based on Richard E. Averbeck, "Daily Life and Culture in Enki and the World Order and Other Sumerian Literary Compositions," in *Life and Culture in the Ancient Near East,* ed. Averbeck, Mark W. Chavalas, and David B. Weisberg (Bethesda: CDL, 2003), 23-61. See also Samuel Noah Kramer and John Maier, eds., *Myths of Enki, the Crafty God* (Oxford: Oxford University Press, 1989), 38-56, which refers to this composition as "Enki and Inanna: The Organization of the Earth and Its Cultural Processes."

20. For a brief sketch of the competing but relatively compatible theologies of Nippur, Lagash, and Eridu in ancient Sumer, see the review of Kramer and Maier in William W. Hallo, "Enki and the Theology of Eridu," *JAOS* 116 (1996): 231-34.

21. For more on the *me*'s and decreeing of destiny, see Richard E. Averbeck, "Ritual Formula, Textual Frame, and Thematic Echo in the Cylinders of Gudea," in *Crossing Boundaries and Linking Horizons: Studies in Honor of Michael C. Astour on His 80th Birthday,* ed. Gordon D. Young, Mark W. Chavalas, and Averbeck (Bethesda: CDL, 1997), 82-83, n. 98; see also Averbeck, "The Cylinders of Gudea," in *COS* 2:418, nn. 1-2, and the primary and secondary literature cited in those places.

nal sets of analogies that organize the view of the world presented in the composition and carry the story along.

First Enki ejaculates to fill the Tigris and Euphrates with the flow of life-giving water, and predicts that this will cause there to be sweet wine and abundant barley. He puts "Enbilulu, the inspector of rivers" in charge of this. The second cycle is fragmentary, but it refers to the marsh regions and the abundance of reeds, fish, and fowl supplied there. Third, he puts the goddess Nanše in charge of the area near the awesome sea in the south (the Persian Gulf) and the high flood of the subterranean waters. The first three cycles, therefore, appear to move from north to south through the land in terms of the supply of waters and the abundance that naturally comes with that. There is no lack of correspondence to the real geography of the land here, although it is certainly fictional on another level. The same is true for the rest of the composition.

The next three cycles focus on the natural and socio-cultural resources for irrigation agriculture including rain, the making of canals, agricultural implements such as the plow, and the crops barley, lentils, and chickpeas. The seventh and eight cycles relate to the construction of houses and other buildings, which involved the fabrication of bricks with hoe and brick mold, laying the bricks to make foundations, and the various levels of design work that go into such construction work. In cycles nine and ten Enki moves from the river basin and canal regions to the plain (Sum. *edin*) where ecology, vocations, and lifestyle are of a different kind altogether. The upland plains were a place where wild animals such as the ibex and wild goats grazed on grass and herbs. The inland plains were also a place of grass and herbs, but here the focus is on domesticated sheep and cattle, sheepfolds and cow pens, fat and cream. The eleventh cycle tells us how Enki organized Sumer by establishing boundaries between the various cities, provided dwellings for the Anunna gods in them, divided the agricultural land among them, and put Utu, the sun-god and divine judge, in charge of maintaining this order. Finally, the twelfth cycle tells us that Enki also established the textile industry as the task of women and placed the goddess "Uttu, the dependable woman, the silent one" in charge of it.

We have extensive archaeological and geographical surveys as well as a wealth of administrative and economic documents that fill out our understanding of much of the *realia* lying behind this Sumerian mythological literary composition and others that coordinate with it in one way or another, to one degree or another.[22] The conceptual analogies between the world of the

---

22. See the references and summary discussion in Averbeck, "Daily Life and Culture," and esp. the very helpful data collections, analyses, and summaries in Robert McCormick Ad-

gods and humans are manifestly evident here. This should survive even the careful scrutiny of some interpreters of Sumerian myths, who characteristically, and sometimes rightly, question virtually any proposed substantial correspondence between the real world of the ancient Sumerians and their literary compositions.[23]

Ancient Near Eastern Myth in Biblical History and Theology

Moving closer to home as far as the Hebrew Bible and ancient Israel are concerned, we turn now to the Ugaritic Baal myth. Unlike the Sumerian myth Enki and the World Order discussed above, there has been a great deal of legitimate scholarly debate about the proper analogical understanding of the Baal myth. I will not belabor that problem here, since it is not essential to the concerns of this essay.[24] The purpose for discussing the Baal myth here is to show that when an ancient Near Eastern mythological analogy suited the historical and/or theological purpose of the biblical writers, they did not hesitate to use it for their own purposes.

Leviathan at Ugarit and in the Bible

In general, the main story line involves four major deities: El, the chief god of the pantheon; Baal, the main weather-god; Yam, the sea *serpent* and god of the sea; and Mot, the god of death. The most commonly accepted sequential arrangement and understanding of this six-tablet composition suggests that

---

ams, *Heartland of Cities: Surveys of Ancient Settlement and Land Use on the Central Floodplain of the Euphrates* (Chicago: University of Chicago Press, 1981); P. R. S. Moorey, *Ancient Mesopotamian Materials and Industries: The Archaeological Evidence* (Oxford: Clarendon, 1994); and Daniel C. Snell, *Life in the Ancient Near East, 3100-332 B.C.E.* (New Haven: Yale University Press, 1996).

23. See, e.g., the very careful remarks on these kinds of issues in Jerrold S. Cooper, "Literature and History: The Historical and Political Referents of Sumerian Literary Texts," in *Historiography in the Cuneiform World*, ed. Tzvi Abusch, Paul-Alain Beaulieu, John Huehnergard, Peter Machinist, and Piotr Steinkeller. Proceedings of the XLVe Rencontre Assyriologique Internationale 1 (Bethesda: CDL, 2001), 131-47.

24. For a full review of the major interpretations of the Baal cycle at Ugarit see Mark S. Smith, *The Ugaritic Baal Cycle*, 1: *Introduction with Text, Translation and Commentary of KTU 1.1–1.2*. VTSup 55 (Leiden: E. J. Brill, 1994), 58-114. Other briefer reviews are Simon B. Parker, ed., *Ugaritic Narrative Poetry*. SBLWAW 9 (Atlanta: Scholars, 1997), 83-85; Dennis Pardee, "The Ba'lu Myth (1.86)," in *COS* 1:241-42.

there were three main parts to the story. First, with the permission of El, Baal challenged Yam's kingship and won the ensuing battle. Second, since he was the victor, Baal obtained permission from El to have a palace built for himself as was fit for one with dominion among the gods. Third, Mot challenged Baal to a battle, which he won by defeating and killing Baal. In due course, however, Baal returned from the underworld, resumed his throne, and subdued Mot.[25]

At the beginning of the third part of the story, when Mot voices his challenge to Baal's supremacy, he refers back to Leviathan's defeat at the hands of Baal and predicts that he himself will not suffer the same fate. He introduces the subject of Baal's defeat of Leviathan as follows (KTU[2] 1.5 col. i lines 1-3; cf. also lines 27-30):[26]

k tmḫṣ . ltn . bṯn . brḥ	When you smote *Lotan* (or Litan), the *fleeing* serpent,
tkly . bṯn . ʿqltn . [[š]][27]	finished off the *twisted* serpent,
šlyt . d . šbʾt . rʾašm	the tyrant with seven *heads*[28]

The correspondence with Isa. 27:1 is indisputable:

בַּיּוֹם הַהוּא יִפְקֹד יְהוָה בְּחַרְבּוֹ הַקָּשָׁה וְהַגְּדוֹלָה וְהַחֲזָקָה
עַל לִוְיָתָן נָחָשׁ בָּרִחַ וְעַל לִוְיָתָן נָחָשׁ עֲקַלָּתוֹן
וְהָרַג אֶת־הַתַּנִּין אֲשֶׁר בַּיָּם:

---

25. See the summary of scholarship and translation with substantial notes by Pardee, 241-74. For the transliterated text, see KTU[2] = Manfried Dietrich, Oswald Loretz, and Joaquín Sanmartín, *The Cuneiform Alphabetic Texts from Ugarit, Ras Ibn Hani, and Other Places*, 2nd ed. ALASP 8 (Münster: Ugarit-Verlag, 1995), 1-28, texts 1.1-6. Introductions with side-by-side transliteration and translation along with a few textual and interpretive notes can be found in J. C. L. Gibson, *Canaanite Myths and Legends* (Edinburgh: T.&T. Clark, 1978), 2-19, 37-81; and Mark S. Smith, "The Baal Cycle," in Parker, 87-180. We eagerly await the future vol. 2 of Smith, *The Ugaritic Baal Cycle*, for a more extensive commentary on KTU[2] 1.3-6.

26. See KTU[2] 22 for the transliteration (although I have transliterated more strictly *rʾašm* rather than KTU[2] *rašm* in line 30 to match more closely its Hebrew cognate in Psalm 74 below). Cf. the translation and remarks in Smith, "The Baal Cycle," 141-42, and Pardee, 265. The translation offered here is mine.

27. The [[š]] transcription with the double brackets means that a *š* was written and then erased on the tablet. Perhaps the scribe began writing the next word *(šlyt)* and then decided to move to the next line instead.

28. For the important parallel passage in the Anat section of the Baal myth, see the discussion of Wayne Pitard's recent contribution to this subject, below n. 33. The reference to plural (i.e., seven) "heads" compares with Ps. 74:13-14 (see below). The other highlighted words correspond to Isa. 27:1 cited and discussed presently.

In that day the Lord will punish *Leviathan* (Heb. *lwytn* = Ugar. *ltn*)
the *fleeing* (Heb. *brh* = Ugar. *brh*) serpent with his harsh
and great and mighty sword,
even Leviathan the *twisted* (Heb. *'qltwn* = Ugar. *'qltn*) serpent;
and he will kill the *dragon* (Heb. *tnnyn*) who is in the *sea*
(Heb. *ym;* cf. the Ugaritic god Yam).

Take special note of the close parallels between these two passages, which I
have highlighted in some of the parenthetical insertions in the rendering of
Isa. 27:1 above. "Leviathan" is obvious even in the English translations, but
consider also the adjectives "fleeing"[29] and "twisted." The term rendered
"twisted" occurs only here in the Hebrew Scripture, which makes it difficult
to avoid the conclusion that this is a free quotation of the myth of Baal's battle with the sea monster or perhaps a stock phrase.[30] The term for "serpent"
here is Hebrew נָחָשׁ, not the same as Ugaritic *btn* in the parallel passage, but it

---

29. Aside from Isa. 27:1, the adjective בָּרִחַ occurs only two or perhaps three other times in
the Hebrew Bible. For other possible meanings of the term, see *HAL,* 1:156 (e.g., "flashing" as in
"fast," or "hairless, slippery" as serpents are). Whatever the correct meaning might be, it is obviously the same in Ugaritic and in Hebrew. It occurs once or twice meaning "fugitives" (Isa. 15:5
and perhaps also 43:14, but the latter is problematic), and once in a passage that has significant
parallels to Isa. 27:1, including the exact expression "fleeing serpent" in Job 26:12-13:

> "He quieted the *sea* (Heb. *ym*) with his power,
> And by his understanding he shattered *Rahab.*
> By his breath the heavens are cleared;
> His hand has pierced the *fleeing serpent* (נָחָשׁ בָּרִיחַ)."

Aside from the reference to the "sea" (cf. the last word in Isa. 27:1b), the term "Rahab"
(רַהַב) occurs several times in the Hebrew Bible in reference to the monster of the sea who sym-
bolizes the violent storminess and crashing of the waves (the related verb means "to storm, act
arrogantly"; *HAL,* 3:1192-93). See e.g., Isa. 51:9-10:

> "Awake, awake, put on strength, O arm of the Lord!
> Awake, as in days of old, the generations of long ago!
> Was it not you who cut *Rahab* in pieces, who pierced the *dragon?* (תַּנִּין; cf. Isa. 27:1)
> Was it not you who dried up the *sea* (Heb. *ym*), the waters of *the great deep* (תְּהוֹם,
> another word for the "sea");
> who made the depths of the *sea* (Heb. *ym* again) a way for the redeemed to cross
> over?" (NRSV)

Compare also "Rahab" in Job 9:13; Ps. 89:10-11(9-10), and perhaps also its use in reference to
Egypt as a useless support in Isa. 30:7 (cf. Ps. 87:4). Pay special attention to the mixture of the
primordial motifs and historical allusions here, especially the reference to drying up the sea so
the people could cross over (cf. Exodus 14–15).

30. The related pual participle occurs in Hab. 1:4, "The wicked surround the righteous —
therefore judgment comes forth *perverted*)" (NRSV). The intensive adjective appears in two

is the same word used in Gen. 3:14 (see more below). The significance of *tnnyn* and *ym* in this verse will become apparent later in this essay.

Isaiah 27 belongs to the so-called "little apocalypse" of Isaiah 24–27, which looks forward to the day when the Lord will set all things right.[31] In that day it will be the Lord, *not* Baal, who will defeat the great enemy of God and his people. One can hear the polemic against Baal in favor of the Lord resounding, even as Isaiah baldly alludes to the "twisted serpent" Leviathan.

Unlike Isaiah 27, Psalm 74 puts the battle(s) in Israel's past, "from of old," and refers to God's victory or victories in the past in order to call upon him to intervene once again on behalf of his people Israel. The Psalmist writes in verse 11, "Why do you hold back your hand; why do you keep your hand in your bosom?" He then goes on to say:

12 וֵאלֹהִים מַלְכִּי מִקֶּדֶם פֹּעֵל יְשׁוּעוֹת בְּקֶרֶב הָאָרֶץ:

13 אַתָּה פוֹרַרְתָּ בְעָזְּךָ יָם שִׁבַּרְתָּ רָאשֵׁי תַנִּינִים עַל־הַמָּיִם:

14 אַתָּה רִצַּצְתָּ רָאשֵׁי לִוְיָתָן תִּתְּנֶנּוּ מַאֲכָל לְעָם לְצִיִּים

12 Still, God is my King from of old, performing salvation in the earth.
13 You divided the sea by your might; you broke the heads of the *dragons* (Heb. *tnnynym*; cf. sg. *tnnyn* in Isa. 27:1) in the waters.
14 You *crushed* the *heads* (Heb. *rā'šê*) of *Leviathan (lwytn);* you gave him as food for the creatures of the wilderness.

Compare the plural "heads" of Leviathan here with the "seven heads" of Lôtan in the passage from the Baal epic cited above (see more below).

At this point we need to briefly turn our attention to a longstanding problem in the interpretation of the Ugaritic mythology of Yam and Leviathan. In the past, some scholars have argued that the god Yam in the Ugaritic texts was not to be identified with Leviathan and Tunnan (cf. the references to *tnnyn* and *tnnynym* in Isa. 27:1 and Ps. 74:13, respectively). Baal's battles with Yam and Leviathan in the Baal text were thought to derive from two different myths.[32] The identification of the two was considered a biblical innovation. Wayne T. Pitard has laid this problem to rest in his analysis of KTU² 1.83 (RS

---

places: (1) Judg. 5:6, "In the days of Shamgar son of Anath, in the days of Jael, the roads were abandoned; travelers took to winding (עֲקַלְקַלּוֹת) paths" (NIV); and (2) Ps. 125:5, "But those who turn aside to their own crooked ways (עֲקַלְקַלּוֹתָם) the Lord will lead away with evildoers. Peace be upon Israel!" (NRSV).

31. See the helpful discussion in Bernhard W. Anderson, "The Slaying of the Fleeing, Twisting Serpent: Isaiah 27:1 in Context," in *Uncovering Ancient Stones: Essays in Memory of H. Neil Richardson*, ed. Lewis M. Hopfe (Winona Lake: Eisenbrauns, 1994), 3-15.

32. See the remarks on this in Pardee, 252 n. 92.

16.266).[33] Lines 8-12 of this mythological or incantational text identify Yam with Tunnan through poetic parallelism. The subject of the verbal action is not completely clear from the context, but there is little doubt that it refers either to Baal or Anat. The t- prefix of the verbal form could be either third person feminine singular or second person masculine singular in Ugaritic, as is the case also in Hebrew. This is reflected in the parenthetical variant readings inserted into the translation here:

8 *tan.lšbm* 9 *tšt.*	She (Anat; or "you" Baal) set(s) a muzzle on Tunnan.
trks 10 *lmrym. lbnn*	She (you) bind(s) him on the heights of Lebanon.
11 *pl.tbtn.yymm*	Dried up you shall be scattered, O Yamm!
12 *ḥmlt.ht.ynhr*	In a tumult of panic, O Nahar (river)!

In this text Yam and Tunnan are clearly identified as the same. Tunnan is muzzled and then addressed in the vocative as Yamm/Nahar.

The reason for suggesting that the subject of the action in this text could be either Baal or Anat is that the Baal myth also refers to a time when Anat defeated Leviathan on behalf of Baal. There is no actual record of the battle itself, but Anat refers to it when she speaks (KTU² 1.3 col. iii lines 38-42):

lmḫšt.mdd il ym.	Surely I smote Yam, the beloved of El;
lklt.nhr.il.rbm	surely I finished off Nahar, the great god;
lištbm.tnn.ištmdh	surely I bound Tunnan and destroyed him.
mḫḫšt.btn.ʿqltn	I smote the twisted serpent,
šlyṭ.d.šb ʿt.rašm	the tyrant with seven heads.

The combination of passages cited above demonstrates that Leviathan, Yam, Tunnan (Heb. *tannîn*), and Nahar all refer to one and the same enemy of Baal in the Ugaritic material. This was not a biblical innovation. Leviathan is the twisted serpent in Mot's challenge to Baal, and Tunnan is the same as Yam in KTU² 1.83, so the twisted serpent in the Anat section of the Baal myth is the same as Yam, Tunnan, and Leviathan. The association of Leviathan with "the dragon" (Heb. *tnnyn*) who is in the "sea" (Heb. *ym*; cf. the Ugaritic god Yam) in Isa. 27:1 makes perfectly good sense against the backdrop of the world of the Ugaritic Baal myth. The point of all this is that in the biblical text we have clear allusions to an ancient Near Eastern myth about an evil serpent with whom Yahweh does battle.

---

33. Wayne T. Pitard, "The Binding of Yamm: A New Edition of the Ugaritic Text *KTU* 1.83," *JNES* 57 (1998): 261-80.

Returning now to the main argument, we have moved from the future in Isaiah 27 to the past in Psalm 74, but how far into the past? Some have taken this passage in Psalm 74 as a reference way back to primordial times, exclusively, while others see it as a complex mixture of primordial and historical allusions.[34] The next few lines seem to suggest a primordial focus:

15 You cut openings for springs and torrents; you dried up
      ever-flowing streams.
16 Yours is the day, yours also the night; *you established* the
      luminaries and the sun.
17 *You have fixed* all the bounds of the earth; *you made* summer
      and winter. (NRSV)

So do not the complex of Leviathan motifs in the previous verses also refer to primeval time? In fact, Jon D. Levenson sees Ps. 74:12-17b as "the *locus classicus* of the idea that the God of Israel not only defeated the Sea and its monsters, but also dismembered Leviathan altogether and then created the familiar world," reflecting not only on the battle between Baal and Leviathan in the Ugaritic Baal myth but also Marduk and Tiamat in the Babylonian Epic of Creation (on this Babylonian background see below).[35]

If the allusions in Ps. 74:12-17 are more than just primordial,[36] then the lines cited above consist of a complex mixture of the same mythical cosmic battle motifs employed in Isaiah 27 with historical allusions to God's past victories on behalf of Israel. One of those was when God "divided the sea" to deliver them from the chariots of Egypt (v. 13; cf. Exodus 14–15). Some scholars today would argue that the story of deliverance from Egypt itself is mythical, but at least to the ancient Israelites it was historical and the mythological references used to depict it here in Psalm 74 highlight it as a historical event of cosmic proportions — that is, if this interpretation of Psalm 74 is correct. The

34. Marvin E. Tate, e.g., limits the application to primeval activities of God, but Hans-Joachim Kraus sees a mixing in of the metaphors for his work in primeval as well as historical events. Compare Tate, *Psalms 51–100*. WBC (Waco: Word, 1990), 250-51, with Kraus, *Psalms 60–150* (Minneapolis: Augsburg, 1989), 99-100.

35. Jon D. Levenson, *Creation and the Persistence of Evil: The Jewish Drama of Divine Omnipotence*, 2nd ed. (Princeton: Princeton University Press, 1994), 18; cf. 7-13, 18-19.

36. See, e.g., Nicolas Wyatt's analysis, in which he suggests that in the process of its formation into what we now have, this passage constitutes a mixture of the historical with what was originally a purely primordial recollection, in the sense that there is a link between God's original creation and his redemptive work on behalf of Israel; *Myths of Power: A Study of Royal Myth and Ideology in Ugaritic and Biblical Tradition* (Münster: Ugarit-Verlag, 1996), 163-69, esp. 165 and the reference there to Isa. 51:9-10 (cf. n. 29 above).

fact that in v. 12 the author refers to God as "my King from of old, performing salvation in the earth," suggests that historical acts of salvation are indeed in view from the start. Moreover, in the current situation, Israel stood in need of deliverance and the psalmist called upon God as the deliverer, whether primordial or historical. The point in Psalm 74 is open to question, but the fact is that, from their own point of view, Israel's history does include the primeval days. The historical story becomes mythologized, but not fictionalized.

It has been argued that "through its myth every civilization finds its own historical dimension, connecting it with the events of mythical time, which give it a permanent sacred guarantee."[37] As Van Seters has observed, this is especially true in the Hebrew Bible in a way that is unprecedented in ancient Near Eastern history writing. Genesis 1–11 presents itself to us as "history," not "myth" or "fiction," although he would see it as historicized myth.[38] The early chapters of Genesis are bound to the rest of Genesis through Kings by means of the genealogical framework that runs through the entire book and beyond. The *tôlĕdōt* "generations" formula that shapes and unifies the whole book of Genesis (Gen. 2:4; 5:1; 6:9; 10:1; 11:10, 27; 25:12, 19; 36:1, 9; 37:2) is continued, for example, in Ruth 4:18-22 ("generations" formula and all) with links back to Judah and Perez in Genesis 38 and forward to the books of Samuel and Kings in terms of the ancestry of David.

This does not mean that the Israelites would have seen no distinction between the primeval history in Genesis 1–11 and the patriarchal and national history beginning in Genesis 12. Surely they would have recognized the difference between, on the one hand, the origins of mankind and all the nations from creation to the tower of Babel and, on the other, their own national history. The main point here, however, is that their "history writing" presents Yahweh as the one true God who stands above and outside of both the world and history. He created the world from outside of it and still stands in that transcendent position even within history. He is neither bound by nature nor determined or undermined by history. Nevertheless, Genesis 12 through 2 Kings proceeds to tell us why and how this God has committed himself by covenant bond to a particular people, Israel, who stand in a particular kind of relationship to the world. It is through *them* (lit., Abraham their father) that "all the families of earth shall be blessed" (Gen. 12:3b). The whole earth belongs to the Lord, but Israel is his "treasured possession," his "kingdom of

---

37. Anna Maria G. Capomacchia, "Heroic Dimension and Historical Perspective in the Ancient Near East," in Abusch et al., 91 and passim.

38. Van Seters, *Prologue to History,* 25-27, 188-93. See also my previous remarks on this in Averbeck, "The Sumerian Historiographic Tradition," 92-93, 98-100, and the literature cited there.

priests," his "holy nation" (Exod. 19:5-6). The comprehensiveness of Israel's history derives from the comprehensive sovereignty of Israel's God.

The Cosmic Battle in Genesis 1–3

The sovereignty of Yahweh over Leviathan in the Bible is part of its comprehensive presentation of the history of Israel and the world. There are actually two groups of Leviathan passages in the Hebrew Bible. One group reflects a knowledge of the ancient Near Eastern mythological analogues, but does not partake of the cosmic battle motif in any direct sense. They either ignore or react against any notion of a challenge to God's/Yahweh's sovereignty in the creation or the maintenance of the cosmos (e.g., Ps. 104:26; Job 41).[39] The other group of passages uses the ancient Near Eastern repertoire of cosmic battle motifs, including Leviathan the twisted serpent, in a more engaging and interactive manner. Some of these, the major ones, have been treated above (e.g., Ps. 74:12-17; Isa. 27:1). The remainder of this essay focuses on the latter set of passages and their importance in reading Genesis 3.

History of Scholarship

A survey of the most recent scholarly literature reveals two major problems in the discussion of the cosmic battle motif. On the one hand, there has been a tendency to override the basic principle of comparative method in which it is important to give intrabiblical parallels priority over extrabiblical parallels. On the other hand, Genesis 3 has been generally taken too lightly in the scholarly treatment of the ancient Near Eastern "cosmic battle" motif.

First, one of the most basic methodological rules for comparing extrabiblical ancient Near Eastern texts with the Bible is that careful analysis of the biblical passages and their intrabiblical parallels should always take precedence over comparisons with external texts. There are times in this discussion of cosmic battle passages in the Bible where this principle has been violated. For example, Bernard Batto's interpretational rendition of the Genesis 2–3 account is creatively dependent on reading the ancient Near East and especially Babylonian mythological tradition into the story. There is a ten-

---

39. Job 3:8 reflects the same basic point, but with the emphasis upon the fact that no regular human who values life would dare to rouse Leviathan. Such a person would need to be especially brave and mighty: "Let the cursers of the day (or 'the sea') curse it (i.e., the day of Job's birth), those who stand ready to rouse Leviathan."

dency, sometimes blatant, to allow the data from the ancient Near East to overwhelm the biblical basis of the discussion or push it aside in favor of the worldviews reflected in texts outside the Bible.[40] It is important to resist this temptation and, instead, allow the Hebrew Bible to carry its own weight within the conceptual world of its ancient west Asian environment.

Indeed, Batto makes an important distinction between "mythopoeic" and "mythopoetic" literature.[41] The former term comes from *mythos* "story" and *poiein* "making," and refers to the making of new myths or extending old ones to include new elements. This is what Batto thinks the biblical writers are doing. The term "mythopoetic," on the other hand, refers to literature in which mythological images are used but the stories themselves have lost their power. Neither of these terms, however, captures what is truly happening in the biblical references to the ancient Near Eastern myths of cosmic battle. The writers of the Hebrew Bible used the repertoire of ancient Near Eastern cosmic battle motifs and patterns to articulate certain aspects of faith and commitment to God/Yahweh in ancient Israel. They used them precisely because these stories were powerful in the conceptual world of the ancient Israelites and, therefore, provided a set of motifs that could be used to speak powerfully about Yahweh.[42] In doing so, however, they were not just reusing the myths but tailored them to the distinctiveness of their belief in One God who is the creator of all and to whom Israel was to show loyalty at all cost.

Second, Genesis 3 has not always been given due attention in treatments of the "cosmic battle" motif in the Bible. In fact, some of the most important works either completely ignore this chapter or underplay the relationship between Genesis 3 and the complex of cosmic battle references in the ancient Near East and the Hebrew Bible.[43] Others follow and continue to develop the

---

40. Bernard F. Batto, *Slaying the Dragon: Mythmaking in the Biblical Tradition* (Louisville: Westminster John Knox, 1992), 44-62. E.g., because it is supposedly so in Atrahasis, the Yahwist's (Genesis 2–3) is not a story of a fall from an originally perfect creation, but of a continual improvement from the time of creation forward (45-46). In specific, e.g., as in Atrahasis, the garden of Eden was not created for the benefit of mankind, but man was created "to relieve the deity of the burden of cultivating his own plantation" (51). Examples could easily be multiplied. Now and then, Batto's readings are truly interesting and properly suggestive, but, by and large, his arguments depend on imposing the ancient Near Eastern materials from Atrahasis, Gilgamesh, Adapa, and other compositions on the biblical text in a way that overrules it.

41. Batto, 12-13.

42. See Wyatt, *Myths of Power*.

43. See Mary K. Wakeman, *God's Battle with the Monster* (Leiden: E. J. Brill, 1973), 84-86, 136-38, according to whom the myth is obscured in Genesis 3; cf. also Tremper Longman III and Daniel G. Reid, *God Is a Warrior* (Grand Rapids: Zondervan, 1995), 72-74.

Susan Niditch (*Chaos to Cosmos: Studies in Biblical Patterns of Creation* [Chico: Scholars,

groundbreaking work of Hermann Gunkel.[44] In this scholarly tradition, on one level the serpent story in Genesis 3 is largely an etiological fable that explains the snake's mode of transport and the natural enmity between people and snakes,[45] or the serpent is a magical source of life and wisdom as, for example, in the cult of the serpent in Numbers 21 and 2 Kgs. 18:4. In that case, the Genesis 3 curses have the heathen practice of deriving higher knowledge through magic and divination as their object of concern.[46]

On another level, however, Gunkel also argued that behind the etiological fable in Genesis 3 lurks another tradition. There was an original mythological serpent that had demonic characteristics, but this one in Genesis 3 derives from an ancient Near Eastern tradition different from that of Tiamat in the Babylonian tradition reflected in Genesis 1. They are "separate figures" altogether.[47] Moreover, the mythical foundation of the more ancient story in Genesis 3 has receded further into the background, so here we have an actual serpent rather than a serpent-demon.[48] With help from the Ugaritic texts not available in Gunkel's day, other scholars have carried this interpretation forward. Brevard S. Childs, for example, argues that:

1985], 35-36) sees the serpent as "a betwixt and between creature, one appropriate for linking paradise and reality," a wise creature who introduces mankind to wisdom, the ability to distinguish between good and evil; cf. also *Oral World and Written World: Ancient Israelite Literature* (Louisville: Westminster John Knox, 1996), 28-38. Batto (59-62, 96) argues, on the one hand, that the serpent was an enemy of God but not of people, since he enabled the latter to obtain a divine level of knowledge and, on the other hand, "the serpent embodied the illegitimate human aspiration to divine wisdom" (60), so by enticing mankind to overstep the boundary of knowledge that distinguished man from God, the serpent brought a curse upon all animals and humankind as well.

Levenson; John Day, *God's Conflict with the Dragon and the Sea* (Cambridge: Cambridge University Press, 1985); and Hugh Rowland Page, Jr., *The Myth of Cosmic Rebellion: A Study of Its Reflexes in Ugaritic and Biblical Literature.* VTSup 65 (Leiden: E. J. Brill, 1996) completely ignore Genesis 3.

44. See Hermann Gunkel, *Schöpfung und Chaos in Urzeit und Endzeit: Eine religionsgeschichtliche Untersuchung über Gen 1 und Ap Joh 12* (Göttingen: Vandenhoeck & Ruprecht, 1895), 3-120; and the abridged English translation by Charles A. Muenchow, "The Influence of Babylonian Mythology upon the Biblical Creation Story," in *Creation in the Old Testament,* ed. Bernard W. Anderson. IRT 6 (Philadelphia: Fortress, 1984), 25-52.

45. Hermann Gunkel, *Genesis* (Macon: Mercer University Press, 1997), 21; Claus Westermann, *Genesis 1–11* (Minneapolis: Augsburg, 1984), 260-61. Gerhard Von Rad, *Genesis,* rev. ed. OTL (Philadelphia: Westminster, 1972), 92-93, argues that the narrative is not just etiological but also sets forth the basic struggles that humankind has with evil.

46. See the summary of this view and the literature cited in Westermann, 237-38.

47. Gunkel, *Genesis,* 16.

48. Gunkel, *Genesis,* 15 and 39.

Demonic elements of a Canaanite myth were associated with the serpent who epitomized that which is sinister and strange among the animals. The Yahwist retained the demonic character of the snake arising out of the myth, but affirmed that it was a mere creature under God's power.[49]

The question is whether or not the serpent in Genesis 3 would have naturally called the image of Leviathan and the cosmic battle to mind for the ancient author and his readers.

Genesis 1 and Creation

The Ugaritic exemplars, or the traditions that underlie them, are by far the most fully developed of the West Semitic world, and are the most likely to have been readily available to the ancient Israelites, at least in oral form. Of course, there are also many other cosmic battle traditions that we know of from elsewhere in the ancient Near East, especially Mesopotamia. The cosmic battle motif shows amazing depth of perspective and breadth of distribution in the Fertile Crescent and in the Bible.[50] There is debate over whether or not, or the degree to which, these traditions have influenced certain biblical passages. In a groundbreaking work written over 30 years before the Ugaritic texts were recovered, Gunkel argued for the incorporation of the ancient Near Eastern cosmic battle myth into the Bible from the story about Marduk versus Tiamat in the Babylonian Creation Epic *(Enuma Elish)*. Since then much of the scholarly debate has revolved around a supposed cosmic battle in Genesis 1. Genesis 3 has seldom entered into the discussion in a significant way.[51]

49. Brevard S. Childs, *Myth and Reality in the Old Testament*, 2nd ed. SBT 27 (London: SCM, 1962), 49.

50. See now the helpful collection of data and discussion in Nicolas Wyatt, "Arms and the King: The Earliest Allusions to the *Chaoskampf* Motif and Their Implications for the Interpretation of the Ugaritic and Biblical Traditions," in *"Und Mose schrieb dieses Lied auf": Studien zum Alten Testament und zum Alten Orient*, ed. Manfried Dietrich and Ingo Kottsieper. AOAT 250 (Münster: Ugarit-Verlag, 1998), 833-82. See also F. A. M. Wiggermann, "Transtigridian Snake Gods," in *Sumerian Gods and Their Representations*, ed. I. L. Finkel and M. J. Geller. Cuneiform Monographs 7 (Groningen: STYX, 1997), 33-55.

The cosmic battle motif is found in literature and iconography from the 3rd to the 1st millennium B.C.E., and in virtually every corner of the ancient Near Eastern world, to one degree or another. On the iconography, see now Martin Klingbeil, *Yahweh Fighting from Heaven: God as Warrior and as God of Heaven in the Hebrew Psalter and Ancient Near Eastern Iconography*. OBO 169 (Freiburg: University-Verlag, 1999).

51. See Gunkel, *Schöpfung und Chaos in Urzeit und Endzeit* and the abridged English translation by Muenchow.

Gunkel himself argued that "a fragment of a cosmogonic myth is preserved in Genesis 1," that "Genesis 1 is *not* the free composition of an author but is rather the deposit of a tradition" (emphasis his), and that "this tradition must stretch back to high antiquity."[52] He concluded that, in light of the background of all the other allusions to the cosmic battle in scripture (e.g., Rahab, Leviathan, Behemoth, the Dragon in the Sea, and Tannin), "ultimately, Genesis 1 is also of Babylonian origin."[53] There are those who still follow this basic line of argument. Batto, for example, is fully committed to it, with refinements and expansions from Atrahasis, the Baal myth, and other ancient Near Eastern texts discovered since Gunkel. He argues that Genesis 1 retains reminiscences of the belief that God created us and our world through defeating the great sea monster known elsewhere in the Bible and the ancient Near East as Leviathan, Yam, Tannun, and Tiamat (cf. *těhôm* in Gen. 1:2).[54]

Others hold to an alternate form of this view. For example, even some scholars who reject the notion of myth in Genesis 1 because of their conservative view of Scripture, nevertheless argue that Gen. 1:2 refers to a chaotic state that is unformed and unfilled because of the ravages of the fall of Satan. According to this view, Genesis 1:3 begins an account of God's *re*-creation of the world, which was his first redemptive act.[55] Still others reject the cosmic battle interpretation of Genesis 1 altogether, including the notion that there are such traditions lying behind the current text. Claus Westermann, for example, reviews Gunkel's hypothesis and more recent elaborations of it in some detail. He concludes that, "for the most part it is quite clear that the victory over the monster of Chaos has nothing to do with creation" in Genesis 1.[56] Even in regard to the parade example of *těhôm* (cf. "Tiamat" in *Enuma Elish*) and other terms in Gen. 1:2, he argues:

> We can be certain then that Gen 1:2 belongs to a history of creation narratives in which the motif of the primeval deep, with or without darkness, very often represents the situation before creation, but that the link between creation and the struggle of the gods is *not part of its pre-history*.[57]

52. Gunkel, "The Influence of Babylonian Mythology," 26 and 31.

53. Gunkel, "The Influence of Babylonian Mythology," 47 (cf. 35-37).

54. Batto, 73-84.

55. See, e.g., Allen P. Ross, *Creation and Blessing: A Guide to the Study and Exposition of the Book of Genesis* (Grand Rapids: Baker, 1988), 106-7.

56. Westermann, 33.

57. Westermann, 106 (italics mine). He argues that it is not just a matter of the current text not holding to or reacting against the ancient Near Eastern cosmic battle motif, but this does not even lie behind the text in its prehistory. This flies directly in the face of Gunkel's argument that the prehistory of the text of Genesis 1 is found primarily in the Babylonian myth. See

The fact of the matter is that there is no serpentine sea monster in Genesis 1, no hint of cosmic battle either, nor the supposed devastations of Satan. The great sea creatures known as *tnnynm* (see Ugar. *tunnan* in some of the texts cited above) are created on day five along with all the other water animals (1:21). They raise no challenge to God. The term *těhôm* "deep" in v. 2 is cognate to the goddess Tiamat who did battle with Marduk in the Babylonian Creation Epic, but this *těhôm* is not personal and expresses no resistance to God's creative activity. Even if this is a shrouded allusion to Tiamat or a reflection on ancient Near Eastern traditions that lie behind the Tiamat motif in *Enuma Elish*,[58] nevertheless, this has the same effect as the reference to the *tnnynm* in Gen. 1:21. *Těhôm*/Tiamat raises no challenge to God or his creative work.

Similarly, *tōhû* and *bōhû* "formless and empty" yield no resistance, but are treated simply as the conditions into which God spoke his creative word. The term *bōhû* occurs only two other times in the Hebrew Bible, both with *tōhû*. Jeremiah 4:23 describes the earth as "formless and empty" and the heavens as having no light in the day when the Lord judges Judah and Jerusalem. Similarly, Isa. 34:11 refers to God's day of vengeance on Edom when he will "stretch out over Edom the measuring line of chaos *(tōhû)* and the plumb line of desolation *(bōhû)*" (NIV).

Tōhû is used in other contexts of this sort as well (see esp. Deut. 32:10; Job 6:18; 12:24; 26:7; Ps. 107:40; Isa. 24:10; 45:18-19). The most interesting one is Isa. 45:18-19:

> 18 For thus says the LORD, who created the heavens
> (he is God!),
>   who formed the earth and made it
>   (he established it; he did not create it a chaos [*tōhû;* i.e.,
>   waste land],
>   he formed it to be inhabited!):
>   I am the Lord, and there is no other.
> 19 I did not speak in secret, in a land of *darkness;*

---

also the very helpful review of the history of scholarship and helpful discussion in Gordon J. Wenham, *Genesis 1–15*. WBC 1 (Waco: Word, 1987), 8-17, and secondary literature cited there.

58. Gunkel was right, there is no article on *těhôm* in Gen. 1:2, suggesting that perhaps this is more than simply a term for the deep; "The Influence of Babylonian Mythology," 26. But see the careful analysis of *těhôm* in the Old Testament in Westermann, 104-5, where he argues that there is no personification of *těhôm* in the Hebrew Bible even though it has no article in all but two of its 35 occurrences. See also W. G. Lambert, "A New Look at the Babylonian Background of Genesis," *JTS* 16 (1965): 287-300.

I did not say to the offspring of Jacob,
"Seek me in chaos (*tōhû*; i.e., waste land)."
I the LORD speak the truth, I declare what is right. (NRSV)

Here the Lord is talking about delivering Israel eternally so that they will not be ashamed any longer (v. 17). In the end they will be justified and glorified (v. 25). God did not create the world to be a place of uninhabitable chaos *(tōhû)* and neither did he call Israel to seek him in such a place. There will be a restoration of Israel, a recovery from the *tōhû* and darkness of judgment and exile.[59]

As noted above, some have argued that these references should be taken as evidence that the condition of the world in Gen. 1:2 was not just formless, empty, and dark in the sense that God had not yet finished his creative activity. Instead, it refers to the devastation caused by a previous battle between God and the great evil serpent, or it bears a dim reflection of the ancient Near Eastern myth about the cosmic battle creation motif that underlies the account. After all, the biblical passages just cited above certainly see this *tōhû wābōhû* condition as something brought about by rebellion against God and God's response to that rebellion in the present creation.

It is indeed true that, according to Genesis 1, God progressively through the six creation days eliminated the totally dark and watery unformed and unfilled conditions of v. 2. Moreover, darkness, as opposed to light, is often used as a metaphor for evil or catastrophe in Scripture, including some of the passages cited above. However, in Genesis 1 God progressively pronounces that what he has made is "good," and then final "very good" (v. 31). To argue that the darkness here stands for a state of destruction caused by evil is, in my opinion, an instance of "illegitimate totality transfer."[60] Westermann is correct. The point of v. 2 is to provide a starting point for God's creative activity that the ancient Israelites could understand. In their ancient Near Eastern world numerous creation accounts from Mesopotamia and Egypt began with a deep dark watery abyss. In these texts this condition is seen as uncreated but *not* evil.

For example, at the beginning of *Enuma Elish* (= "when on high," a

---

59. See the discussion of *tōhû wabōhû* in David Toshio Tsumura, *The Earth and the Waters in Genesis 1 and 2*. JSOTSup 83 (Sheffield: JSOT, 1989), 17-43.

60. "Illegitimate totality transfer" occurs when meanings and/or implications of terms and expressions from various other contexts are illegitimately piled together and forced upon a context where the argument does not call for it. See James Barr, *The Semantics of Biblical Language* (Oxford: Oxford University Press, 1961), 218, and all the books written since then on the hermeneutics and especially biblical word usage and definition.

temporal beginning similar to *bĕrēʾšît* "In the beginning" or "When (God) began," Gen. 1:1) this point of departure carries no evil meaning or implication, even though Tiamat is on the scene. Instead, the watery abyss conditions provide the starting matrix for creation:

> When on high no name was given to heaven,
> Nor below was the netherworld called by name,
> Primeval Apsu was their progenitor,
> And matrix-Tiamat was she who bore them all,
> They were mingling their waters together. . . .[61]

A theogony follows. The battle between the forces of evil and good associated with creation does not come into play until later in *Enuma Elish,* when Marduk defeats the enraged Tiamat and creates heaven and earth out of her corpse (Tablets IV-V). The original conditions are treated neither as inherently evil nor reflective of cosmic battle imagery. Moreover, even in the Ugaritic Baal myth one would be hard pressed to show that Baal's battle with Leviathan had anything at all to do with the creation of the world.

The same is true in Genesis 1–3. Genesis 1, of course, does not include a theogony, and this is part of the underlying polemic against the ancient Near Eastern environment of the Israelites. This polemic, it seems to me, also includes a reaction against the notion that God created the world by defeating the evil forces of chaos. Instead, the evil forces of chaos appear in the Bible as an attack on God's holiness and authority in an already created world. The closest link to the Leviathan motif in early Genesis is the account in chapter 3 of the serpent-led temptation and corruption of mankind in the garden of Eden.

Genesis 3 and the Cosmic Battle

The fact of the matter is that there is more to the serpent in Genesis 3 than has generally been recognized. As the discussion above on the parallels between poetic texts in the Hebrew Bible and the mythological ideas and motifs expressed in the Ugaritic Baal myth demonstrates, the theme of a cosmic battle between God and a serpentine monster bent on evil and destruction was alive and well in ancient Israel. The narrative in Genesis 3 is relatively subtle as compared to some of the poetic texts, but to the Israelites the message was anything but subtle precisely because of their awareness of the theme and its

---

61. Benjamin Foster, "Epic of Creation (1.111)," in *COS* 1:391, Tablet I lines 1-5, the very beginning of the composition, as in Gen. 1:1-2.

significance for their understanding of their God, Yahweh, and his involvement in their lives and their national history. There is a shift in genre here, and it is natural that the allusions to the cosmic battle in biblical poetic texts would be closer in kind to those found in the Ugaritic poetry than those of the prose narrative account in Genesis 3. Nevertheless, the prose narrative account in Genesis 3 makes full use of this mythological background in the sense that the writer depends on the readers' (or hearers') awareness of it as it is expressed in biblical and/or extrabiblical intertextual parallels.[62]

The "heads" of Leviathan referred to in Ps. 74:14 (cf. also v. 13) are of particular interest here. Genesis 3:15 refers to the seed of the woman crushing the "head" of the serpent. The same word for "serpent" (Heb. *nāḥāš*; Gen. 3:14) is used as as in Isa. 27:1. More than that, Ps. 74:14 has God crushing (*rṣṣ*, admittedly not *šwp* as in Gen. 3:15) "the *heads* of Leviathan." The "crushing" of the serpent's head in Gen. 3:15 is conspicuous in light of these parallels.[63] Also, once again Hebrew *tnnyn* "dragon," which is the same as Ugaritic *tunnan*, occurs in poetic parallel with Leviathan, and Ps. 74:13 refers to God as the king who "divided the sea (Heb. *ym*; cf. Ugar. *Yam*) by his might" and "broke the heads of the *dragons* (Heb. *tnnynym*; cf. sg. *tnnyn* in Isa. 27:1) in the waters."

In Psalm 74, all of this is in the context of God "performing deliverances (Heb. *yᵉšûʿôt*) in the midst of the earth" (v. 12). The vitality of the serpent motif in Genesis 3 for the ancient Israelites arose from the very fact that they would have identified this particular primeval scene with the origin of the real battle, the cosmic one. They would have seen it as more than a simple etiological fable about snakes or a polemic against divination, or whatever. It was not just a snake story to them. The fact of the matter is that this is the first appearance of a serpent in the canonical Hebrew Bible. We must not lose track of this point amid all the historical critical debate surrounding the composition of the book of Genesis. Moreover, this serpent issued a direct challenge to the Lord's truthfulness and authority (Gen. 3:1-5), and the Lord responded with a curse that involved crushing the serpent's "head."[64]

In light of all this, it seems eminently reasonable to assume that the Is-

---

62. For a helpful discussion of intertextuality as it relates to the Leviathan serpent motif, see Elaine A. Phillips, "Serpent Intertexts: Tantalizing Twists in the Tales," *BBR* 10 (2000): 233-45.

63. On the verb rendered here "crush," see the remarks in Wenham, 79-81; and Westermann, 259-60.

64. Johannes C. de Moor's rendition and interpretation of two Ugaritic incantation texts against snakebite suggests even more interesting parallels between the snake tradition in Genesis 3 and the whole of the Genesis 2–3 Eden narrative; "East of Eden," *ZAW* 100 (1988): 105-11. In light of the extreme difficulty of these texts, however, one wonders how reliable some of his interpretations and comparative applications are.

raelites would have seen a great deal more in Genesis 3 than a simple tale about snakes and mankind. This was the great serpent, the archenemy of Yahweh and the people of God. From their point of view, this would have been the very beginning of a cosmic battle that they were feeling the effects of in their own personal experience (see the curses that follow) and their national history. Psalm 89 comes at the same point in a different way, as a praise to God for his faithfulness. Verse 8 says:

> 8 O Lord God Almighty, who is like you?
>   You are mighty, O Lord, and your faithfulness surrounds you.

The Psalm continues (vv. 9-13):

> 9 You rule over the surging sea;
>   when its waves mount up, you still them.
> 10 You crushed Rahab like one of the slain;
>   with your strong arm you scattered your enemies.
> 11 The heavens are yours, and yours also the earth;
>   you founded the world and all that is in it.
> 12 You created the north and the south;
>   Tabor and Hermon sing for joy at your name.
> 13 Your arm is endued with power;
>   your hand is strong, your right hand exalted. (NIV)

Rahab here probably refers to Egypt. Consider, for example, Isa. 30:7, "Egypt's help is worthless and empty, therefore I have called her, 'Rahab who sits still'" (NRSV).

Psalm 104, on the other hand, refers to Leviathan in an altogether different light. Verses 24-26 say:

> 24 O Lord, how manifold are your works!
>   In wisdom you have made them all;
>   the earth is full of your creatures.
> 25 Yonder is the sea, great and wide,
>   creeping things innumerable are there,
>   living things both small and great.
> 26 There go the ships,
>   and Leviathan that you formed to sport in it. (NRSV)

Here Leviathan is treated as a sea monster that challenges the Lord *not at all*. He is like the great *tnnynym* of Genesis 1:21.

The point is that biblical writers could use these motifs in various ways, depending on the point being made in the context. In Psalm 104 the creation without opposition perspective of Genesis 1 comes through forcefully. In Psalm 74 the Baal myth battle motif is used to call upon God to be the divine warrior for Israel in their current dilemma. The key in Psalm 74 seems to be that God is "King" (v. 12) and needs to exert his kingship in the world on behalf of Israel. The fact of the matter is that the Baal myth seems to have nothing to do with creation of the world. The concern there, as in Psalm 74, is with kingship.[65] This helps to make sense of the historical and perhaps also primeval perspectives on Yahweh's kingship. If the Leviathan motif in Psalm 74 is taken as an allusion to creation, it should be understood as an elaborate mythological way of talking about the whole narrative in Genesis 1–3. Genesis 3, in fact, is included in the time of creation by its readily apparent connection back to Genesis 2. There are *not* two views of creation in Genesis 1 and 2–3 — just two different ways of articulating it. Both see God as the sovereign king, but only the latter expresses it in terms of cosmic battle.

From the point of view of the canonical shape of the text, the serpent was the first to raise an explicit challenge to God in the Bible, and this happened in Genesis 3. The challenge, and so also the battle between God and the serpent, is actually over mankind. *People are the battleground — the "territory" under dispute* — and the central concern of this battle of the ages has as much to do with people as with the great serpent. Both mankind and serpent "fell" out of favor with God here, so the battle rages between all three. We stand right in the middle of a ferocious cosmic fray. Ancient Israel's preservation — and ours, believe it or not — depends on Yahweh's willingness to redeem us in the midst of this brawl. The apocalyptic vision is that there will come a day when God will bring all this to final resolution by making an end of the "twisted serpent" of old. One could, of course, follow the main theme of this essay through the intertestamental period and into the New Testament (e.g., Revelation 12), but that is a story for another time and another place.

Conclusion

Those who know the texts will be aware that I have only scratched the surface of the evil serpent myths that could be referred to. We have considered some of the most important ones but, for example, we have said nothing of the ser-

---

65. See the special emphasis on this point as it is developed in Smith, *The Ugaritic Baal Cycle*, 59-60, 96-114.

pent that stole the plant that rejuvenates life from Gilgamesh at the end of the flood story in the Gilgamesh Epic tablet 11. From Anatolia we have Iluyanka, the evil serpent in Hittite myth, and from Egypt the story of the repulsing of the dragon, in which Seth binds the serpent "who goes on his belly" and then runs off with his strength. Nevertheless, what we *have* considered has some important implications that need consideration.

Modern biblical scholars have often voiced complaints about the exegesis of the church that imposes elaborate theories about Satan on the text in Genesis 3. This is understandable. In my opinion, however, they have overreacted in two ways. First, with Terence E. Fretheim and others,[66] I maintain that, as it stands in the canonical text, Genesis 3 is indeed a "fall" narrative, a "falling out" with God on the part of the serpent and humankind. Second, many have failed to take seriously the ancient Near Eastern Israelite awareness of cosmic battle mythology as the conceptual world for the reading or hearing of Genesis 3 in that day.

In any case, different scholars will have different views of the truth-value these passages in the Bible have for history, theology, and for their own faith or worldview. This is to be expected. One of the points I have labored to make here is that, no matter what one believes about the historicity of the Bible and its claims to truth, the way forward in the study of the relationship among history, theology, and ancient Near Eastern myth in the Bible is through reading myth as analogical thinking about history and reality. We are not talking about some kind of alternative truth system, but a different way of talking about what *was* and *is* in fact *true*, historically and experientially.

Moreover, the use of ancient Near Eastern mythological stories or motifs in the Hebrew Bible cannot be treated in a monolithic way. The writers used them in different ways for manifold purposes in numerous places without any sense of inconsistency. No doubt various (groups of) readers would have had different views regarding the truth of the original myths and even the truth of biblical faith and history. In any case, the problem of evil associated with the use of the Leviathan mythological complex in the Bible cannot be ignored.

Some of us may want to distance ourselves in one way or another, to one degree or another, from the presentation of these biblical stories as historical. But we still have analogies for them today, whether they are more historical than fictional, such as Hitler, or more fictional than historical, such as the evil emperor of Star Wars fame. Even the fictional characterization of the latter is based on cultural historical perceptions of the embodiment of evil

---

66. See, e.g., Terence E. Fretheim, "Is Genesis 3 a Fall Story?" *WW* 14 (1994): 144-53.

that rise to prominence, for example, in the wicked witch of the Wizard of Oz and her human counterpart in the nasty old neighbor lady, right down to the evil laugh.

As it turns out, then, the ancients were on to something important with their mythology, and the biblical writers took advantage of it. The more we realize this, the more likely we are to understand what was going on for them in life, its correspondence to important issues in our own experience of life, and how we should handle this kind of material as scholars. Yes, sometimes the truth really is stranger than fiction.

"Splendid Truths" or "Prodigious Commotion"?
Ancient Near Eastern Texts and the Study of the Bible[1]

DAVID B. WEISBERG

The title of our paper was borrowed from two phrases relating to the research of Friedrich Delitzsch, the 100th anniversary of whose Babel und Bibel lectures occurred in January 2002.

The first phrase, "Splendid Truths," was used in a compliment to Delitzsch by an admirer from South Africa, who, when he praised Delitzsch, intended the phrase "Splendid Truths" to refer to Delitzsch's courage for "telling it as it is."[2] Implied was the fact that the truths of the ancient Near East were more impressive than those of the Bible and that biblical Israel had taken its most important institutions and cherished ideas from its neighbor in Mesopotamia.

The second phrase, "Prodigious Commotion," was used by Delitzsch himself in his Notes to Lecture II in the series.[3] The words were intended as praise for the interest that Delitzsch's lectures stirred up among the scholars and the members of the general public.

We shall use the same phrases, but in a different manner. For us, the

---

1. I wish to express my thanks to James Hoffmeier, Alan Millard, Bill T. Arnold, and Edwin Yamauchi for their help.

2. Letter of Edgar H. Rex Evans to Friedrich Delitzsch from Cape Colony, South Africa, 2 May 1903, cited in Reinhard G. Lehmann, *Friedrich Delitzsch und der Babel-Bibel-Streit*. OBO 133 (Freiburg: Universitätsverlag, 1994), 340.

3. "The prodigious commotion . . . excited by my second Lecture serves to show convincingly enough that in quarters from which Church and school are governed an essentially different view from that of my highly-esteemed critic prevails." Cited in C. H. W. Johns, ed., *Babel and Bible: Two Lectures by Friedrich Delitzsch* (New York: Putnam, 1903), 217-18.

phrase Splendid Truths refers to the fact that the truths of the biblical text stand in place. Seeing Scripture more distinctly today in its ancient Near Eastern context, it is clear that some things *were* borrowed; but it is also clear that in many cases the uniqueness of biblical values and institutions has been highlighted even more vividly than before. They can be augmented by the other Splendid Truths, namely those from the ancient Near East. For Delitzsch, "Prodigious Commotion" (= publicity) was a good thing. We shall argue that "commotion" is — if anything — detrimental to the cause of science, and prodigious commotion even more so. Of what scientific value is the oft-repeated fact that Delitzsch's lectures took place before the Kaiser? One might ask oneself: Is some of today's "commotion" — lacking as it is in scientific evidence or even aesthetic value — of the same ilk?

We should like to bring three major points in our presentation:

1. The value and importance of text-archaeology;
2. Proof by examining not only individual ancient Near Eastern Texts, but by mass of evidence;
3. The informed theological approach.

The Value and Importance of Text-Archaeology

Zipora Talshir offers a sound methodology in her article, "Textual and Literary Criticism of the Bible in Post-Modern Times. . . ."[4] Talshir critiques postmodernism:[5]

1. An "immense amount of information [is available] but with no lasting value."
2. "There is no one meaning of a text."
3. "Scientific scepticism has evolved into total chaos."

Talshir describes the foundation of modern biblical scholarship as "undermined" by a recent school whom some have called "deconstructionists." She herself uses the term "destructionists."[6] "The 'deconstructionists' claim that all of biblical literature is the product of the 6th-3rd centuries B.C.E. and that ancient Israel is merely the invention of the Persian/Hellenistic Jewish society."

4. *Henoch* 21/3 (1999).
5. Talshir, 235.
6. Talshir, 236.

She continues: "Post-modern approaches seem to defy the major achievements of centuries of specialized research and revert to over-all [= overarching] theories. They have thus forfeited the scientific methods which have long been used to reconstruct lost contexts of ancient literatures."[7]

Here we do not want to rehearse the series of arguments that review the state of the field, since these are well-known — we are thinking of such debates as those surrounding the reading of the critical passage in the Tell Dan inscription — "Beth dod . . ." which, as is known, "Lemche . . . [labeled] a forgery."[8] Rather, let us move on to the points raised by Avi Hurvitz[9] in his careful critique of Philip Davies.[10] Hurvitz finds Davies's approach to be "methodologically unsound,"[11] and he brings logical arguments to support this observation. First is Davies's failure to "review earlier studies relevant to the issue at hand,"[12] and second is Davies's nonappreciation of extrabiblical sources from the First Temple period.[13]

Hurvitz asks the fundamental question: "Does or does not Biblical Hebrew exhibit diachronic changes indicative of continuous historical developments?"[14] In answer, Hurvitz observes ". . . a comparative analysis of all this material . . . conclusively demonstrates that . . . there is a far-reaching uniformity underlying both the pre-exilic inscriptions and the literary biblical texts written in classical Hebrew" (e.g., Classical Hebrew *seper* is replaced in late Biblical Hebrew by *'iggeret*).[15] These observations make it unimaginable that Biblical Hebrew is a "scholarly construct" or "fabrication" from a later time, as Davies claims.

Continuing now within the rubric of "text-archaeology," we would like to shift the focus from the textual material in Biblical Hebrew to that in Akkadian, written in cuneiform characters on clay.

Working in reading clay tablets through a period of years brings with it a feeling of closeness to the ancient writers and personalities mentioned therein and also a kind of intuitive sense — sometimes subtle and sometimes

---

7. Talshir, 237.

8. Talshir, 240.

9. Avi Hurvitz, "The Historical Quest for 'Ancient Israel' and the Linguistic Evidence of the Hebrew Bible: Some Methodological Observations," *VT* 47 (1997): 301-15.

10. Philip R. Davies, *In Search of "Ancient Israel."* JSOTSup 148 (Sheffield: JSOT, 1992).

11. Hurvitz, 303.

12. Hurvitz, 305.

13. Hurvitz, 307.

14. Hurvitz, cited in Talshir, 241.

15. Hurvitz, cited in Talshir, 241.

more obvious — of the differences and contrasts between the writings of one period and those of another. True, the clear differences in types and shapes of characters, of grammatical features, lexemes and syntactic variances, not to mention the external appearance of the clay tablet itself, are characteristics that can easily be identified and taught. But in addition, there is a more subtle — today one might say "nuanced" — appreciation of the unique and special presentation of this text and language that is shared by no other place and no other period. Many scholars can undoubtedly identify with this experience. Our point is that no one would claim that all texts, genres, and types were written much later than the texts themselves claim — and all at the same time.

Though we do not yet have the biblical manuscripts themselves — the exception being a partial text of the "Priestly Benediction" found by Gabriel Barkay at Ketef Hinnom[16] — to reduce everything between the boards of *BHS* to one smoke-filled room in the Hellenistic period simply is out of accord with the realities of ancient texts.

In his chapter "Historical Sources or Literature?" in *Ancient Mesopotamia*, A. Leo Oppenheim makes a related, and we believe powerful, supporting point about the appreciation for the varied sources and periods of a living and vibrant literary tradition, by no means to be viewed as frozen and monolithic.

> He [Nabonidus] quotes in scholarly fashion the texts of the documents his workmen had excavated from the ruins of temples he was in process of rebuilding. He even gives us on one such occasion the text of an inscription of a Kassite king that would otherwise have been lost . . . [finally] let me point out Assurbanipal's repeated descriptions of his training and his achievements as a scholar and a soldier which — one-and-a-half millennia later — include a *topos* from the Sumerian royal hymns. This illustrates the continuity and tenacity of a living literary tradition other than that literary tradition frozen and preserved in the royal library of Nineveh. Anyone who intends to write a history of Mesopotamian literature that is more than an inventory of extant fragments will have to consult these living, changing royal inscriptions.[17]

Were the "minimalists" to treat these Assyriological texts as they treat the biblical material, would they be inclined to view Nabonidus and

---

16. See P. Kyle McCarter, Jr., "The Ketef Hinnom Amulets," in *COS* 2:221.

17. A. Leo Oppenheim, *Ancient Mesopotamia: Portrait of a Dead Civilization* (Chicago: University of Chicago Press, 1964), 150.

Assurbanipal as "forgers" whose interest was in deceiving the public? Or would they be willing to concede that the Kassite and Sumerian inscriptions were not counterfeits from a later period but authentic texts preserved by a "living, changing" culture? While this is no proof for our argument, it does furnish a convincing parallel for how ancient texts were viewed in antiquity.[18]

Oppenheim speaks of other practices that preserved links from the past with a more distant past.

> We have a number of copies (from the Middle Babylonian through the Neo-Babylonian period) of older inscriptions, often imitating their script. To this interest we owe much of what we know today of the Old Akkadian period and the rule of the kings of Ur III. . . .[19]

Thus, instead of contrasting the situation in biblical manuscript study with that in Mesopotamia, we might use the insights garnered from our study of the transmission of written records to compare the two.

To summarize: the sensitive text-archaeological study of the Hebrew language of the biblical period, as well as the richness of cuneiform sources, make it likely that we can discover a multidimensionality and profundity in-compatible with the views of those who see composition, editing, and canon-ization as a one-time act of a later period. This is not, as some would contend, an "old-fashioned" idea but rather an elegant, modern methodology suitable for appreciation of our texts.

Proof by Examining Not Only Individual Ancient Near Eastern Texts, but by Mass of Evidence

Our second point is that proof for the antiquity of materials including the Hebrew Bible can be obtained not only by examination of *individual* ancient Near Eastern texts, but by presentation of a *mass* of evidence, whose existence and relevance make it unlikely, if not virtually impossible, that we can seat the major parts of the Hebrew Bible in the last centuries before the foundation of Christianity. In fact, one can point to a program of advancing scholarship

18. In her recent dissertation, "The Lure of the Past: Ancient Man's Interest in His History: With Translations of the Neo-Babylonian Texts from the Carlos Museum" (Cincinnati, 2000), Sara Fudge examines the antiquarian interests of ancient man, showing how nations, in-cluding biblical Israel, had a healthy interest in their past. They sought to collect materials from it, establish museums, and preserve authentic records.

19. Oppenheim, 150.

that does not involve answering points or accusations, but instead quietly continues to contribute to our knowledge.

William W. Hallo and K. Lawson Younger, Jr.'s *Context of Scripture* is by its nature an answer to the minimalists — insofar as the enterprise situates the Bible in its ancient Near Eastern setting, thus demonstrating conclusively that the Hebrew Bible was not a product of the Hellenistic, Persian, or (perhaps) even 8th-century periods. The parallels demonstrate beyond doubt that the Bible is the product of the earlier age that it purports to be.

We would like to quote from Hallo's "Introduction" to *Context 2*:

> The combination of an intertextual and a contextual approach to biblical literature holds out the promise that this millennial corpus will continue to yield new meanings on all levels: the meaning that it holds for ourselves in our own contemporary context, the meanings it has held for readers, worshipers, artists and others in the two millennia and more since the close of the canon; the meaning that it held for its own authors and the audiences of their times; and finally the meanings that it held when it was part of an earlier literary corpus. It is to the clarification of that oldest level of meaning that the *Context of Scripture* is dedicated.[20]

Another point in this section pertains to the *attitude* of those who hold for a Hellenistic date. The argument has been raised in another context in an article by Hallo entitled "The Limits of Skepticism," his Presidential Address to the American Oriental Society of March 1989.[21] Here Hallo is opening the door, or inviting one, to place a limit upon skepticism as one places a limit upon credulity. One who holds this approach has recently, and humorously, been referred to as a "golden meanie" (neither a maximalist nor a minimalist).

The Informed Theological Approach

Our third point is the importance of the informed theological approach. To us it is of interest that in all of the *contemporary* "commotion" about the minimalist-maximalist viewpoints, something very important has fallen out — that is, an appreciation of the uniqueness of biblical prophecy. Abraham Heschel stated:

20. W. W. Hallo, "Introduction," *COS* 1:xxviii.
21. W. W. Hallo, "The Limits of Skepticism," *JAOS* 110 (1990): 187-99.

The history of the Western world may be written . . . by the way the various generations understood or misunderstood, revered or repudiated, the spirit of the prophets.[22]

It was an interesting exercise to reread H. H. Rowley's "Trends in Old Testament Study" published as the *Introduction* to his edited volume, *The Old Testament and Modern Study: A Generation of Discovery and Research*.[23] There one can get an idea about the state of the field 50 years ago as contrasted with the state of the field today.

The essays of Albright, Baumgartner, Robinson, Snaith, Eissfeldt, Winton Thomas and others, when taken in and of themselves, were — and in numerous parts, still are — of great value in our understanding of archaeology, pentateuchal criticism, historical books, prophetic literature, Psalms, and others.

Otto Eissfeldt's "The Prophetic Literature," included in *The Old Testament and Modern Study*, had many insights that are still relevant to us today, and that moreover can play a role in our evaluation of the failure to appreciate the uniqueness of prophetic literature in some of today's scholarship. Eissfeldt notes that ". . . many observations by earlier generations of scholars still retain their value."[24]

Eissfeldt mentions the names of scholars who have contributed to our understanding of "The Prophets of Israel" going as far back as 1882. He notes that these scholars

> have still much to contribute to anyone concerned with a real understanding of Israelite prophetism. . . . To neglect the insight into the nature of Israelite prophetism gained by the preceding generation would inevitably wreck our whole understanding of that phenomenon. In this field, no less than in that of Pentateuchal criticism, we must be careful to safeguard continuity of research with the work of earlier scholars.[25]

In a passage that might be interpreted as a rejoinder to the minimalist position as cited above by Talshir, Eissfeldt describes a process of transmission that is the last stage of a complex process that had occurred through many centuries of transmission: "In fact, this writing down gives us simply the mechanical preservation of an already completed structure."[26]

---

22. Abraham J. Heschel, *The Prophets* (New York: Harper and Row, 1962), 305.
23. (Oxford: Clarendon, 1951).
24. Otto Eissfeldt, "The Prophetic Literature," in Rowley, 115.
25. Eissfeldt, 115.
26. Eissfeldt, 117.

Why have today's "minimalists" downplayed to such a degree the greatness of the Israelite prophets? Can literature like this be "manufactured" so readily by people intent on patching together a history allegedly so desperately needed?

> No one who has really and truly sought to comprehend the personality and message of the great prophets of the Old Testament can avoid the impression that here we have men not only speaking a word to their own generation, but having something of value for us today also.[27]

Now as two persuasive contemporary examples of an "informed theological approach," we should like to cite the works of Alan Millard and John Bright.

In Part I of his essay, "Story, History and Theology,"[28] Alan Millard unpacks James Barr's approach on how the narrative material of the Old Testament, which Barr feels could be suitably described as "story," differs from "history." Characteristics of Old Testament narrative, according to Barr as understood by Millard, are four:

Barr's first point is that myth and legend are present in Old Testament material. In his section on "Legend, Folklore and History,"[29] Millard argues that "the sources can be treated soberly as the basis for satisfactory historical reconstructions."[30]

Barr's second point is that the narratives of the Hebrew Bible contain a mixing of human and divine elements. In his section "Divine Intervention and History," Millard contends that

> The presence of a report of a divine communication does not invalidate the accompanying episodes in biblical or other ancient texts any more than it does in the story of Joan of Arc. Whether scholars today share the belief that these figures were in communication with a supernatural power, or not, has no effect on the fact that these people possessed such beliefs. . . .[31]

Barr's third point is that aetiological motives appear in Old Testament reports. Under "Etiology and History," Millard asserts that

---

27. Eissfeldt, 136.

28. In *Faith, Tradition, and History: Old Testament Historiography in Its Near Eastern Context*, ed. Alan R. Millard, James K. Hoffmeier, and David W. Baker (Winona Lake: Eisenbrauns, 1994).

29. Millard (43-47) analyzes Barr's units in *reverse* order from Barr's presentation. We have reverted to the original order.

30. Millard, 47.

31. Millard, 43.

There is . . . reason to contest the claim that the paradigmatic form of reporting events is "not really historical in original basis and motivation." Ancient writers deliberately set out the reports of military campaigns in paradigmatic form, demonstrating sequences of events, actions, and their consequences, which they saw repeated and accepted as conforming to certain patterns. Rebellion against the suzerain brought his forces to the vassal's territory in punishment, just as Israel's apostasy brought her enemies to humiliate her.[32]

Barr's fourth and final point is that in Hebrew Scripture, one notices the "absence of critical evaluation of sources." In his investigation of "The Authors as Critics," Millard writes:

> . . . it is surely possible that a critical attitude did lie behind the selection the compilers of Kings made from more extensive records. The Israelite presentation of history did involve critical judgment, inasmuch as it claims to be true. . . . Moabite or Assyrian viewpoints were denied. . . .[33]

In order to evaluate narratives for their role in re-creating the history of Israel, Millard proposes we establish certain criteria such as an appreciation of the function of anachronism, a differentiation of fantasy from (e.g.) claims of hearing divine voices, and that biblical texts not find themselves in contradiction with other texts.[34]

In Part II, "Theology and History," Millard rejects "paths of assumption and speculation that lead to increasingly subjective hypotheses."[35]

Bringing attention to Assyrian royal inscriptions ("Ancient Records and Religious Beliefs"), Millard notes that "Overt theological intent . . . [has] not brought rejection [by modern scholars] of the 'historical' narratives, nor cast much doubt on them."[36]

Evaluating modern editorial assessments of Assyrian and Babylonian records ("Bias and Historicity"), Millard observes that "Undoubted bias . . . need not carry a totally adverse attitude to a document or give rise to allegations that the accounts are untrue or imaginary."[37]

In the section "Opposing Biased Views," Millard notes that there is no reason to doubt the essential truth of the Hebrew accounts of Sennacherib's

32. Millard, 41.
33. Millard, 40.
34. See Millard, 50.
35. Millard, 51.
36. Millard, 54.
37. Millard, 55.

invasion of Judah when compared and contrasted with the Assyrian records.[38]

Is the fact that a period of time — say 20 years — has elapsed between the time events were reported in biblical texts and the time they were written down enough of a reason to reject those texts as "historical," as some modern scholars have done ("'Narrative Theology' versus 'Historical Narrative Proper'")? Citing the biblical texts "in the ancient Near Eastern context," we find that the question "loses its force."[39]

Both Israelite writers and other writers "saw divine intervention as a historical reality. . . . The continuity of that [Israelite] belief through the Exile and other adversities, a continuity that contrasts with the extinction of all the contemporary religions, is a noteworthy testimony to faith firmly founded in history" ("Divine Intervention in Human Affairs").[40]

In the *Prelude to Israel's Past,* Niels Peter Lemche identified the writers who hold that the biblical "narratives are authentic reflections of antiquity."[41]

> Among these scholars belong the circle of William F. Albright. . . . The most important description of the time of the patriarchs from this circle is, however, John Bright, *A History of Israel.* . . .[42]

In 2000, the fourth edition of John Bright's *A History of Israel* appeared posthumously. It had an "Introduction" and "Appendix" by William P. Brown that helped update the approach originally taken by Bright in the first edition of 1959.[43]

In describing "the center of Bright's *History,*" Brown wrote:

> All in all, Bright's textbook is more than a work of historical reconstruction. It is a robustly theological investigation. And for that Bright has been severely criticized. Martin Noth's review of Bright's first edition sums it up well: 'It is certainly a serious question whether a presentation of Israel's history could and should present a "Theology of the Old Testament," at the same time. The question is not easily answered and cannot be solved by interpolating references to the history of religion into a His-

---

38. Millard, 57ff.

39. Millard, 60ff. and 63.

40. Millard, 64.

41. Niels Peter Lemche, *Prelude to Israel's Past: Background and Beginnings of Israelite History and Identity* (Peabody: Hendrickson, 1998), 27.

42. Lemche, 27.

43. Earlier editions of Bright's *History* are: 2nd ed. 1972; 3rd ed. 1981; 4th ed. 2000. Bright died in 1995, in Richmond, Virginia.

tory of Israel.' Bright, however, cannot be criticized for indiscriminately interjecting his own 'interpolations.' Considering himself primarily a historian, Bright intended all along to convey his theological insights, subjected to external controls, 'at the right time and in the right way,' so as not to violate the integrity of historical inquiry.[44]

Brown pointed to the reality of biblical material for Bright by underlining that an authentic understanding of the Deity is not possible without an authentic understanding of Israel's history and vice versa.

> On the one hand, Israel's story is no imaginative construct severed from the harsh realities of historical experience. The Bible is about a particular people who embodied a peculiar history.[45]

We think that the remarks of a Hebrew Union College graduate student, Christopher Morgan, offered privately to the present writer, summarize very well the thinking involved here, as we try to argue for the informed theological approach:

> Modern scholarship in general fails adequately to address what is perhaps the central reason for the existence of the biblical materials — the religious impulse and religious experience. Why is the reality of the religious impulse and experience less "scientific" than, say, power politics? When historians a priori reject one facet of human experience (which humans seem to have experienced in all ages and all geographic locales), how can we hope to achieve anything approaching an accurate understanding of a historical reality which undeniably includes the very element they have ruled out of court?[46]

---

44. Brown, "Introduction," 21. Brown cites Bright's *Early Israel in Recent History Writing: A Study in Method*. SBT 19 (London: SCM, 1956), 29.

45. Brown, "Introduction," 21.

46. Christopher Morgan, communication of 7 December 1999.

Can We Write a History of Israel Today?

ANDREW G. VAUGHN

In a sense it is foolish to question the value of writing biblical history. Of course we can write a history, and many people are writing them. Publishers recognize the appeal of these types of books, and they encourage scholars to write them because they will sell. However, the situation in our field calls us to question whether this is a legitimate enterprise. We acknowledge that all histories are biased or give privilege to certain ways of thinking, so in our postmodern context we question whether a positive history of Israel is even something that should be desired ("positive" in the sense of making statements about ancient Israel's history that provide a background for reading and engaging with the biblical narratives, as opposed to a "negative" history that concentrates on "yes/no" questions).

It is worth emphasizing my definitions of "negative" and "positive" (or background) history. For the purposes of this essay, negative history is understood as the scientific endeavor to ask "yes/no" questions — whether an event happened or not. It should go without saying that positive conclusions arise from a determination of "yes" (the event actually happened) or "no" (the event did not happen the way it was described). The term "negative" merely refers to the goal of determining "yes/no" about a description or event in the Bible. On the other hand, I define positive history as an investigation that concentrates rather on providing the background for understanding and experiencing the text as narrative. For example, information about how people lived during the 10th century B.C.E. is crucial for understanding the narratives that describe the united monarchy, but such data need not address "yes/no" questions of whether descriptions of the united monarchy found in the Bible actually happened. Unfortunately, scholarly debates between liberals and conservatives have tended to limit the discussion of history to the "yes/no" questions when the exploration of how history and archaeology can provide a constructive background is the more interesting question. My goal here is to make a case for incorporating both types of investigations as necessary for doing biblical theology.

My approach is to argue for the inclusion of history in the theological inquiry rather than to enter into the debate with the so-called minimalists of what some have labeled as the Copenhagen school.[1] The debate with the minimalists is an easy route for historians, and we must move beyond it. The claim that the Bible is completely or almost completely nonhistorical is easy to refute.[2] The problem for our task of discussing how history can be included in biblical theology is that our common refutation of the minimalists leads us into a greater quandary where biblical theologians ignore historical work. My position is thus that we must strive to write a history that is theologically useful in order to move beyond this impasse.

The refutations of the Copenhagen school have for the most part focused on showing how the biblical narratives contain much historical information even if they are ideologically biased. Yet, the problem arises with the way we as biblical historians argue that the Bible is historically valuable. By concluding that there are factual inaccuracies and that the narratives are ideological, we run the risk of confusing the difference between a narrative that is factual and a narrative that is "true."

It has been three decades since Hans Frei published his seminal work on the *Eclipse of Biblical Narrative*,[3] in which he convincingly showed that the

---

1. In this regard, it is not a mistake that my title is very similar to titles of essays by Thomas L. Thompson and Niels Peter Lemche.

2. It is obvious from a close reading of the Pentateuch as well as the Deuteronomistic History that the texts contain information from different time periods. In other words, the text is diachronic and not synchronic. Any attempt to reconstruct a history from the text must recognize this complex character. The Copenhagen school attempts to simplify the narrative by imposing a unified structure based on the postulation of a late date for the entire narrative or narratives.

In my opinion, the Copenhagen school does not hold a monopoly on this type of presuppositional mistake. Recent attempts by Israel Finkelstein and other scholars at Tel Aviv University simplify the complexities found in the historical narratives of the Bible by classifying them all as Josianic. Even if the texts underwent a major redaction during Josiah's reign, we must recognize that the narratives also contain material that is much earlier and much later. Stated another way, both archaeologists and biblical historians must tackle and deal with the diachronic nature of the narratives in order to avoid these simplifying pitfalls.

3. Hans Frei, *Eclipse of the Biblical Narrative: A Study in Eighteenth and Nineteenth Century Hermeneutics* (New Haven: Yale University Press, 1974).

historical question of the factualness of the text has become the primary question in our critical method of investigating the Bible. Thus, the text as a living, dynamic narrative has been eclipsed. He showed that since the 18th century (1) a biblical text was either true because it was factual or (2) the text was true apart from the question of its factuality, and that truth of the text was found in its meaning. The latter method has become the common way for most mainstream theologians to read the Bible as valid even if it contains factual inconstancies.[4] The problem that Frei so aptly highlights is that by assigning the "truth" of a text to the location of meaning, we necessitate that the narrative be demythologized and interpreted in order to be "true." In this way, the narrative itself becomes static.

The problem for the task of writing a biblical history is that, while most biblical historians acknowledge that the Bible is not completely factual, they remain focused on the 18th-century questions concerning whether the text can be verified or not. The recent book *What Did the Biblical Writers Know and When Did they Know It?* by William G. Dever[5] is a prime example in this regard. Dever's book presents an excellent rebuttal of the simplistic views set forward by the minimalists, but in doing so he limits the parts of the Bible that are most relevant to history to the books of the Deuteronomistic History.[6] Is one supposed to assume that history is not relevant for the rest of the Hebrew Bible, including all of the Prophets, Chronicles, and the Pentateuch? Moreover, the way in which Dever has framed the question places him right back into Frei's eclipse. If one were to use Dever's method for doing Old Testament theology, the texts would either be valuable because there is some degree of historicity in them[7] or because they were true apart from the question of factuality. In either case, the historical question comes first and the meaning of the text second. The dynamic character of the narrative through contemporary interaction comes third, and so it is essentially lost.

4. See e.g., William C. Placher, "Is the Bible True?" *Christian Century* 112 (11 October 1995): 924-28.

5. William G. Dever, *What Did the Biblical Writers Know and When Did They Know It? — What Archaeology Can Tell Us about the Reality of Ancient Israel* (Grand Rapids: Wm. B. Eerdmans, 2001).

6. Dever, 97-101.

7. It is interesting that Dever argues for the importance and validity of some parts of the historical books because he finds a certain degree of essential continuity between the historical narratives and the verifiable historical "facts." Yet one notes that this very approach of locating an essential continuity between the biblical narratives and the historical "facts" is one of Dever's chief criticisms of G. Ernest Wright (see among many publications, William G. Dever, *Recent Archaeological Discoveries and Biblical Research* [Seattle: University of Washington Press, 1990], esp. 17-22, 50).

Returning to the definitions of "negative" and "background" history presented above, one notices that an investigation such as Dever's focuses on the "yes/no" questions (negative history). It should be emphasized that important positive conclusions can be drawn from this negative mode of inquiry. It is certainly significant and positive to conclude that the claims of the minimalists are without merit. However, if the investigations do not move beyond this negative mode of inquiry, the studies will remain stuck in Frei's eclipse and biblical theologians will find it difficult to use them. We as historians and archaeologists must do more.

This failure of historical investigations to allow for dynamic and changing interpretations has led to the situation where more and more biblical theologians choose to jettison historical investigations. Scholars who make this choice include not only those who undertake a canonical approach, but also a growing number of scholars who focus on literary and rhetorical readings as the primary means to uncover the theological meat of the Bible. Walter Brueggemann's system presented in his *Theology of the Old Testament* falls into this latter group.[8] In what follows, my main goal is to show how history is necessary, not merely permissible, in a theological interpretation such as the one presented by Brueggemann.

An Old Testament Theology without History — Review of Brueggemann's *Theology*

Brueggemann's *Theology* is perhaps strongest in its ability to embrace the plurality of testimonies to and of God in the Hebrew Bible. Another major strength of Brueggemann's work is his ability to present the relevance of his readings and observations to contemporary settings in a postmodern world. Thus, Brueggemann has written an important volume that encompasses David Tracy's three different kinds of theology.[9] There is a fundamental theology that converses with the academy, a systematic theology that explains how the Old Testament functions for the church (or for Brueggemann, churches), and a practical theology that explores the relevance of the Old Testament for the larger society. In this sense, Brueggemann's *Theology* represents a coming

8. Walter Brueggemann, *Theology of the Old Testament: Testimony, Dispute, Advocacy* (Minneapolis: Fortress, 1997).

9. See David Tracy, *The Analogical Imagination — Christian Theology and the Culture of Pluralism* (New York: Crossroad, 1981), esp. ch. 1: "The Social Portrait of the Theologians — The Three Publics of Theology: Society, Academy, Church" (3-28); and ch. 2: "A Theological Portrait of the Theologian — Fundamental, Systematic, and Practical Theologies" (29-98).

of age for the task of Old Testament theology. His *Theology* is a leader, if not the first, to take into account the postmodern age while at the same time presenting a biblical theology that is comprehensive.

Brueggemann's work is clearly very important for making the Bible available to different contexts. Through close readings of rhetorical narratives, and through the study of the varied testimonies of Yahweh, Brueggemann presents a multifaceted interpretation of Yahweh. In fact, the identity of Yahweh includes competing claims. God can be seen as a warrior and at the same time a loving mother. For Brueggemann these competing images or metaphors should not be reconciled, but rather held up next to each other as one uses the process of imagination[10] to understand Yahweh. His presentation is thus attractive for a postmodern setting because he resists a static, dominant, or colonizing definition of Yahweh. Moreover, the process of defining Yahweh does not end in the past. As Brueggemann states, "God in the Old Testament is not a mere rhetorical construct, but is endlessly in the process of being rhetorically reconstructed."[11]

Brueggemann tackles this theological task without incorporating history into his method. He insists that historical criticism and historical inquiries have collapsed and are not useful in Old Testament theology. Brueggemann's *Theology* thus presents biblical historians with a challenge and a quandary. On the one hand, this volume presents a helpful way for churches and contemporary society to understand and benefit from the theological messages found in the Bible, but on the other hand, there is little need for historical investigations. One is left to wonder if the biblical narratives could be just as valuable today if they had occurred in a vacuum.

Brueggemann's arguments about history are a development of what Leo Perdue refers to as "the collapse of history" for the task of doing biblical theology.[12] Brueggemann goes further than Perdue and develops the phrase "the collapse of history" to move beyond a changing of methods for reading the Bible. For Brueggeman, the phrase refers to a collapse of "the cultural assumptions and political supports that made interpretive work of a certain

---

10. See below for a definition of "imagination." For now it should be noted that "imagination" does *not* mean make-believe.

11. Brueggeman, 65, no. 11. It should be emphasized that Brueggemann consciously tries to avoid defining God as a rhetorical construct. He specifically states that textual utterances must be read as making assumptions about being. Yet, as will be seen below, since Brueggemann insists the external reality of God can be seen only through the narratives, he is making a move similar to Schleiermacher and is at risk for falling into the very trap he tries to avoid.

12. Leo Perdue, *The Collapse of History: Reconstructing Old Testament Theology,* OBT (Minneapolis: Fortress, 1994).

kind tenable through the twentieth century."[13] He concludes, "Thus our current, postmodern situation of interpretation cannot easily appeal to any essentialist tradition in an attempt to articulate the faith of Israel. Rather the interpreter must be an at-risk participant in a rhetorical process."[14] For Brueggemann, this means that rhetoric and speech constitute reality and not history. He says, "Speech constitutes reality, and who God turns out to be in Israel depends on the utterance of the Israelites or, derivatively, the utterance of the text."[15] Yet, at this point we must ask if the move to define the reality of Israel's God solely and completely by the utterance of the text puts Brueggemann at risk of creating a God that is a mere rhetorical concept.

One of the problems that I face with Brueggemann's *Theology* is that I, as a biblical historian who also considers himself a biblical theologian, am left at the side of the road as other biblical scholars talk about God. It is not enough for scholars like myself to profess an affinity and love for historical-critical investigations and for archaeology. Brueggemann, and others, are certainly correct in their assessment that to date archaeology has only been most successful in undertaking what I have defined above as "negative" investigations (those investigations and conclusions that focus on "yes/no" questions). Archaeology has been able to show that certain interpretations of biblical narratives are at odds with the archaeological facts (however one might define "fact"), and in other places archaeology has been able to show that certain descriptions in the Bible are consistent with the archaeological facts. Yet, archaeology has failed to substantiate or prove the biblical narratives in a comprehensive manner. Even in an investigation such as Dever's as discussed above, the "yes/no" conclusions lead the theologian into Frei's eclipse.

All of these observations show that Brueggemann is also correct in citing Perdue's study highlighting a collapse of history in the task of reading the Bible theologically. Yet, Brueggemann fails to emphasize that Perdue also provides suggestions for how to move beyond the state of collapse and reconstruct a theology of the Old Testament that includes a place for history and historical reconstructions. We as biblical historians and biblical archaeologists should join Perdue in articulating the role of history in doing theology. In what follows, I develop my definition of background (or positive history) as a way that will allow us to move forward.

---

13. Brueggemann, 61.
14. Brueggemann, 65.
15. Brueggemann, 65.

Problems with Brueggemann's System

The first step in this conversation is to show how and why history is needed in a theological interpretation such as the one presented by Brueggemann. A major drawback can be found in the way Brueggemann argues that humans can know God. He makes the rhetorical interaction with the text almost sacramental with his claim that "*I shall insist, as consistently as I can, that the God of the Old Testament theology as such lives in, with and under the rhetorical enterprise of this text, and nowhere else and in no other way.*"[16] One notes clearly the parallel with Luther's theology that the presence of God is found "in, with, and under" the elements of the Eucharist. Brueggemann seems to be saying that God is seen through rhetorical readings in almost the same manner. By maximalizing the rhetorical enterprise and minimalizing the historical enterprise, Brueggemann overly restricts the ways in which God can be known. If Yahweh exists solely through the rhetorical interaction with the text, Brueggemann is at the very least being too narrow in his articulation about how humans can know God.

This extreme importance placed on knowing God solely through the rhetorical interaction of the text leads to another drawback. Brueggemann claims that God is not a mere rhetorical construct under his system, but he admits that "this is an exceedingly important and dense issue, one I am not able to resolve clearly."[17] He attempts to resolve the issue by stating that the rhetorical narratives assume a reality of God outside of the text, but for Brueggemann the only way we can know God is through the rhetorical narratives. In this sense, his argument about how we can know God is very similar to Friedrich Schleiermacher's argument about how we can know God as the object of the feeling (or awareness) of absolute dependence.

Schleiermacher concludes that God must be taken to be the "whence" or the object of the feeling (or awareness) of absolute dependence. In this way, Schleiermacher is able to show how the existence of God can be assumed or postulated based on the feeling of absolute dependence.[18] This is a much

16. Brueggemann, 66 (emphasis his). I am grateful to my colleague Garrett Paul for calling my attention to the parallel with Luther's theology of the Eucharist.

17. Brueggemann, 65, n. 11.

18. Friedrich Schleiermacher, *The Christian Faith* (Edinburgh: T. & T. Clark, 1928), ¶4.4 (p. 16): "As regards the identification of the absolute dependence with 'relation to God' in our proposition: this is to be understood in the sense that the *Whence* of our receptive and active existence, as implied in this self-consciousness, is to be designated by the word 'God,' and that this is for us the really original signification of that word." It is important to note here that for Schleiermacher the idea of "feeling" is not an emotion. It includes the idea of "awareness" or "self-consciousness"; ¶3.2 (p. 6).

needed development of Immanuel Kant's conclusions that rationally a person must postulate the existence of God. Schleiermacher points out that Kant is incorrect in asserting that such a proof for God can be understood rationally. There are aspects of thinking that are neither rational nor irrational, and these ways of thinking are central for understanding the concept of God. For Schleiermacher an intuitive awareness or feeling is more important for faith and a comprehension of God than is rational thinking. Schleiermacher does not mean that God does not exist outside of our psychological minds; however, that is the only way we as humans can have access to God. The problem occurs with the skeptical humanism of Ludwig Feuerbach, who takes arguments like these further and concludes that God is merely a human construct.[19]

The problem for both Schleiermacher and Brueggemann is that such a philosophical move runs the risk of reducing God to a psychological or rhetorical concept. Whereas Kant's proof of God ran the risk of reducing God to an essentialist concept and thus a human construct, Schleiermacher runs the risk of superdogmaticism. Both Brueggemann and Schleiermacher run the risk of letting their dogma (which is not necessarily either rational or irrational) dictate and construct their definition of God. Both systems run the risk of sliding into the fiery brook of Feuerbach. Feuerbach concludes that God was a concept created by the collective mind of humanity, and Brueggemann's system could lead to a similar philosophical argument that the identity of Yahweh is a rhetorical concept. Whereas Feuerbach's arguments might have held some degree of hope that humanity could improve itself in the middle of the 19th century, the numerous events of evil that resulted from human inventions during the 20th century have made such a psychological or rhetorical move very dangerous indeed. To summarize, if Brueggemann were correct, what would limit a truly evil rhetorical appropriation of Yahweh as defined by the reading of the narratives by a fascist, racist, or sexist community? Whether his system leads to Feuerbach or not, it is much too restrictive in how we can know and experience God through the narratives, and it is open to a huge postmodern minefield.

Imagination as a Means for History to Correct the Problems in Brueggemann

In what follows, I suggest that Leo Perdue's concept of "imagination" is a helpful means to include history as a necessary component in the theological enter-

---

19. The term "skeptical humanism" is that of David Tracy, *Plurality and Ambiguity: Hermeneutics, Religion, Hope* (San Francisco: Harper & Row, 1987), 83.

prise. It is important to distinguish the concept of "imagination" from the idea of "make-believe" or "fiction." The term describes how humans are able to create and understand basic images from disparate and varied pieces of information that cannot be understood or comprehended on one plane or in a single "snapshot." The term describes something that humans do instinctively to make sense of the world around us. For example, in his response to David Hume's work that showed that we could not prove the relationship of cause and effect, Kant used something similar to the idea of imagination to show that we must postulate the relationship of cause and effect. Hume did not deny the fact that humans choose to see a relationship between cause and effect, but he argued that this relationship could not be proven. For Kant, a concept such as "imagination" allowed him to describe the ability to integrate the varied perceptions of the physical world into reality. Such integration does not take place because we as humans can see the world operating on one plane at one point in time, but rather the integration takes place because we can synthesize varied experiences from different points in time. By using imagination, Kant was able to show that this is not only a possible way to make sense of the physical world, but that this type of correlation is necessary. Thus, imagination allows us to be certain that in a rational world there is a necessity for cause and effect. Imagination is what allows us to "take" all of these different experiences and impulses and understand them "as" if they all took place at once and on the same plane. The key words for the philosophy of imagination are "take" and "as."

As mentioned above, Perdue uses this concept of imagination to enable history to be useful theologically. Perdue defines imagination as "the capacity within the human mind to create basic images. It is the power of the human psyche (conscious and unconscious) to form mental images, either immediately or indirectly derived from perception or sensation, that lead to the attainment of meaning."[20] Perdue continues to explain that common imagination (together with our previous experience) is what allows us to recognize that when we see the front of a large house from the highway, there is a whole house present. Thus, we take our viewing of the front of the house as representing the reality of a whole house. Once again, the important words in the philosophy of imagination are "take" and "as." As Perdue states, "common or ordinary imagination completes the fragmentary data of the senses, since we cannot perceive the whole of an object at once."[21] In other words, we *take* the fragmentary parts *as* the whole.[22]

---

20. Perdue, 263-64.

21. Perdue, 265.

22. It is important to emphasize that the fragmentary parts can be "known" and can be

Other types of imagination are also important for our task of putting history in conversation with rhetorical and literary readings of the Bible. Creative imagination is at work when an artist uses the raw materials of paint and canvas and creates with them so that they might be taken as reality. Again, the operative words are "take" and "as." It is this type of imagination that is important for narrative interpreters such as Robert Alter and Hans Frei who hold that the biblical narratives are "historylike" or taken as history.[23]

Another type of imagination that is important to our task is religious imagination. Here images of God are created that are not associated with perceptions of the past or present. An example is that God can be taken as abstractly all-powerful or ever-present or portrayed as images that are common to our perceptions but are clearly metaphorical: father, king, mother, warrior, and so forth.

In summarizing the importance of imagination for the task before us, we note that imagination allows us to organize varied perceptions, experiences, and even feelings into a coherent whole. By using the philosophical concept of imagination, we do not have to see or observe everything at once in order to have differing perceptions affect our task of putting everything together into a coherent whole. This realization will be especially important for us as we attempt to integrate history into narrative and rhetorical close readings of the biblical narratives.

The Inclusion of Historical Imagination in Narrative Readings

Imagination allows us to organize varied perceptions, experiences, and even feelings into a coherent whole, but the danger of this system is similar to the danger in Brueggemann's system — there are no limits or boundaries. We run the risk of entering into an "anything goes" type of mentality for interpretations of biblical texts. If one does not recognize that all types of imagination are based upon a reality that already exists or events that are already known,

---

considered "facts." Again, imagination is not make-believe or necessarily hypothetical. Rather, imagination allows a person to consider all the pieces of information that are known and look at them and evaluate them at the same time. Such a distinction will be important for us to keep in mind so that we realize that the different types of imagination described below presuppose an external reality that is already known. Therefore, in every instance, the study of history and what is known is important even when using "imagination" to interpret texts.

23. Once again, the reality that is "created" is based upon what the artist (or historian) knows or what is known. Thus, historical data are important for understanding the creative enterprise of the artist or the writer.

one runs the risk of running into the problem of superdogmatism. If imagination is purely subjective, then a person's theological and philosophical presuppositions will dictate what conclusions he or she may draw. Therefore, the problem with Brueggemann's method is not his exclusion of imagination (he is a pioneer in the use of imagination); rather, the problem occurs in using a method that *de facto* excludes history and external realities.

The inclusion of history into this equation allows us to set necessary limits or boundaries around our possible interpretations. History defined in this way is what I call negative or critical history. Critical history asks "yes/no" questions and has a corrective function that helps us avoid misunderstandings in the text.[24] Yet, when history is included in our imaginary world, history can also play a role apart from asking critical (yes/no) questions. History can serve to enlighten and illuminate the narratives and the narrative world. This latter use of history is what I call positive history or background history. I am defining historical imagination in such a way as to include both background history and critical history.

Turning first to the critical use of history (asking yes/no questions), we see that Perdue has already pointed out how part of what I define as historical imagination can be used as a corrective. He shows that narrative readers such as Frei and Alter argue that it is through creative imagination that narrative worlds are constructed that are "taken as" reality or "taken as" history. However, Perdue adds that "one should insist at this point that the distance between text and reader, largely due to historical separation and culture shock, does and should continue. . . . Historical criticism makes readers in the contemporary world aware of the tremendous gulf that separates them from the narrative world constructed by biblical texts."[25]

Building on Perdue's observations, we see that the concept of historical imagination can prevent contemporary readers of the narratives from drawing inappropriate conclusions from the narrative that are "taken as" reality. In this way, critical history is one means among several that prevent contemporary readers from making the message contained in the narratives arbitrary. At this point in our discussion, it is important to realize that history is not a magic medicine pill that can prevent inappropriate interpretations. Our imaginary worlds must also integrate ethical, moral, and rational thinking into the equation. There is even a sense where one must include conclusions based on intu-

---

24. Once again, it should be emphasized that critical history can produce positive results. The terms "negative" and "critical" are used because the goal is to ask questions that can have a "yes/no" answer.

25. Perdue, 259.

itions or feelings that are neither rational nor irrational. Critical (or negative) history is but one means of a corrective, but a vital means nevertheless.

An example of this type of critical (negative) use of history in our imaginary world is instructive. An archaeological and historical-critical investigation of Hezekiah's kingdom reveals that Judah was a prosperous kingdom with a well-developed infrastructure during the late 8th century.[26] This conclusion in and of itself is what I have defined as background history — the reader has a better understanding of what Hezekiah's kingdom looked like as she or he interacts with the narratives in 2 Kings or 2 Chronicles. Yet, critical or negative history comes into play when "yes/no" questions are asked and answered based on these data. In response to "yes/no" questions of whether the Chronicler's account of Hezekiah was pure fiction because many parts of it are not found in Kings, Jonathan Rosenbaum used historical arguments to show why the Deuteronomistic Historian would have had an incentive to omit some details that were not omitted in Chronicles. Rosenbaum follows his teacher Frank M. Cross and begins with the assumption that at least a major redaction of the Deuteronomistic History took place during Josiah's reign. Rosenbaum is then able to posit that this historical setting would have given historians during Josiah's day an incentive to exclude material about Josiah's great-grandfather (Hezekiah) that was not central to the history of Judah and detracted from the picture painted of Josiah.[27] Rosenbaum thus argues that, yes, the material in Chronicles is factual and authentic.

If Rosenbaum is correct, several positive conclusions can be drawn from this critical (negative) mode of inquiry. First, one can learn more about the intentions and motivations of the writers of Kings and Chronicles.[28] Building on this first conclusion, one can learn that the Chronicler may not be a writer of fiction as he undertakes the process of rewriting Judean history in the postexilic period. This conclusion is especially important because it places boundaries around the possible ways a modern reader might interact with the history presented in Chronicles — that history should not be taken to be pure fiction.

---

26. See chapters 2 and 3 in Andrew G. Vaughn, *Theology, History, and Archaeology in the Chronicler's Account of Hezekiah*. SBLABS 4 (Atlanta: Scholars, 1999) for a summary of extensive archaeological data that support this conclusion.

27. Jonathan Rosenbaum, "Hezekiah's Reform and the Deuteronomistic Tradition," *HTR* 72 (1979): 24-43.

28. It is common among biblical scholars to conclude that an author's intent is impossible to understand. In a sense this is true — the full intent of the author will never be comprehended. However, this conclusion does not mean that glimpses of the author's purpose or intent cannot be understood. It is naïve to avoid the question just because it cannot be completely answered.

In a separate study, the present author utilized archaeological data to develop and extend Rosenbaum's arguments. In that study,[29] I showed that (1) Hezekiah was indeed more prosperous that Josiah, and (2) an extensive study of the *lmlk* jar phenomenon revealed that Hezekiah had an extensive infrastructure that was similar to the description found in 2 Chronicles 32. These conclusions were answers to "yes/no" questions about the biblical narratives. I found that, yes, Rosenbaum's hypothesis could be supported because Hezekiah undertook similar reforms to Josiah and yet overshadowed his great-grandson by being more prosperous. This conclusion supported Rosenbaum's theory for understanding one of the purposes of the Deuteronomistic Historian. Similarly, the archaeological data that supported the facts found in 2 Chronicles 32 revealed that, no, the Chronicler did not merely make up events in order to write his history. Again, this negative conclusion places boundaries around possible modern interpretations as well as helps us understand the Chronicler's intent.

In response to the question of whether the Chronicler's account was completely factual, I found evidence to the contrary. A literary study of 2 Chronicles 29–32 showed that many *lexemes* that were used of Solomon were used in 2 Chronicles 32 to refer to Hezekiah. Further, the very descriptions of Hezekiah's prosperity that were found to be accurate used to substantiate the application of these *lexemes* to Hezekiah. I thus concluded that, no, these *lexemes* were not originally attributed to Hezekiah and that the Chronicler took some liberty with his history in making these ascriptions in order to make a particular theological or ideological point. For the purposes of our study in this essay, this negative conclusion allows us to see that the Chronicler was a "selective" historian who used historical remembrances to substantiate his ideological position. Like pre-Socratic historians in Greece, his history was true because it interpreted the past for the present and the future. Once again, this negative conclusion allows the modern interpreter to better understand the Chronicler, and this conclusion also places boundaries around our contemporary interactions with the text.

This negative use of archaeology and history is consistent with what is probably a consensus view among scholars. Roland de Vaux presented a classic articulation of this negative use about 30 years ago. In his essay, "On Right and Wrong Uses of Archaeology," he rightly affirmed that archaeology could not prove the Bible.[30] The Scriptures are "true" apart from historical data.

29. Vaughn.

30. In *Near Eastern Archaeology in the Twentieth Century,* ed. James A. Sanders (Garden City: Doubleday, 1970), 70-76.

Even if an account is found not to be factual, the account is still true in that it explains a religious truth. Thus, de Vaux holds that the "right" way to use archaeology is to disprove or to support previously constructed interpretations of the biblical texts. These interpretations can be supported (but not proven) or disproved, but the actual narrative is "true," regardless of what archaeology might turn up.

We need to move beyond Perdue's proposal, because history as he defines it does not adequately allow for positive statements (that do not seek to ask "yes/no" questions) that enlighten our interactions with the narratives that are "taken as" reality whether the narratives happened or not. Background history and archaeology can also make positive statements about the past without attempting to ask if an event happened or not, and these positive statements serve to increase our imaginative capacity as we enter into these narrative worlds. These positive observations or claims about a biblical narrative need not be radical in order to be significant. For example, my involvement in the narrative of David and Goliath is enlightened and brought alive by my past experience of standing on top of Tel Azekah and studying the geography of the area. I was able to see how the narrative world of the text is described in such a way as to allow a later reader of the narrative to physically place the encampments in real places in the valley below Azekah. Moreover, I could see the importance of a battle that took place at the border between two peoples at a junction that was of immense strategic importance. Although the meaning of the narrative that I experience does not dramatically change, somehow my conversation with that narrative as one of my classic texts is deeper. My imaginary world increased and I am able to understand better the importance of a battle that takes place on the border between peoples. It should be emphasized that my increased imaginary world for reading this narrative does not mean that a real battle actually took place. Rather, the geographical data in this case inform and enlighten my imaginary world, and subsequently my reading and involvement with this classic text.

In a similar manner, my reading of a prophet like Isaiah, the Deuteronomistic History, or Chronicles is informed because my imaginary world is increased by an idea of the extent and power of Hezekiah's kingdom at the end of the 8th century.[31] Likewise, a sociological study of kinship structures in developing societies enlightens my interactions with the biblical narratives of 1 and 2 Samuel. This sociological study does not attempt to answer the factual question or suggest that the narratives are factual or not; rather, this type of study enlightens the narratives that are "taken as" reality. The historical or so-

---

31. Vaughn.

ciological study is vital for my engagement with the narratives as they are written.

Archaeology and background historical investigations can add many other details to our imaginary worlds that are crucial for us to understand any of these narratives. Many issues are critical to our imaginary world: issues such as the nature of kingship, the role of the Assyrian monarch Sennacherib, the success or lack of success of Hezekiah, the status of Jerusalem, the status of the common people, the infrastructure of the Judean kingdom, and the role of prophets in the late 8th century. All of these types of historical investigation serve both a negative and positive function. Negatively, they ask "yes/no" questions and serve to correct our imaginary worlds. Positively, they provide background history that enlightens and illuminates the narratives that are set in the 8th century, regardless of whether or not the events described in the narratives actually happened.

The Inclusion of Historical Imagination in Brueggemann's Method

Historical imagination is not only helpful for narrative readings such as those described above. It should also play a role in close rhetorical readings such as those undertaken by Brueggemann. In fact, even though Brueggemann says that history plays little role, his exposition of the varied testimonies of Yahweh takes into account historical-critical studies of Yahweh and the texts. He thus implicitly increases his imaginary world within which he enters into a rhetorical dialogue with previous readers of the narratives. In fact, I think that Brueggemann's actual interpretations accomplish much of what I am advocating. Brueggemann may want to limit his conclusions to the rhetorical narratives apart from a historical-critical investigation, but in reality he does much more than this. He actually includes historical-critical studies into the background of his imaginary world whenever possible. Brueggemann himself is anything but naïve in his use of history.

The way that historical imagination can interact with Brueggemann's system is very similar to the way in which historical imagination interacts with narrative readings. Historical investigations should play a negative and positive role. On the negative side, history can provide one means among several that limit or provide parameters around the competing testimonies found in the rhetorical narratives. Just as was the case with narrative readings, our imaginary world includes much more than history. It also includes the ability to draw moral and ethical conclusions and to think rationally. However, history remains one of the primary means to place some parameters around the whole subjective process.[32]

Just as was the case with the use of historical imagination for narrative readings, there is a positive use of history for close rhetorical readings. If the conversation between theology and history can take place through a concept such as imagination, then our histories should surely not be limited to "yes/no" questions (what I have defined as "negative" or "critical" history). However, we as biblical historians tend to stick to these "yes/no" questions — we tend to rehearse the various archaeological and historical theories and conclude with what can or cannot be known. Most of the time, we tend to focus on what cannot be known. The reverse is also true; we as historians are normally afraid to move beyond empirical conclusions and explore the background of the texts and how historical and archaeological data might be helpful for understanding the texts as narrative. My argument is that if we limit our histories to asking "yes/no" questions, they will be of little use to biblical theologians, and the gap between historians and biblical theologians will continue to grow wider.

Conclusion — The Interaction of Historical Imagination with a Classic Text

As a means of conclusion, I would like to use Tracy's definition of a classic text as a way to further clarify how positive (or background) and negative (or critical) history and the idea of historical imagination can play a role in enlightening the competing testimonies that result from Brueggemann's system. Tracy defines a classic as a truly exemplary text. He says, "On historical grounds, classics are simply those texts that have helped found or form a particular culture. On more explicitly hermeneutical grounds, classics are those texts that bear an excess and permanence of meaning, yet always resist definitive interpretation."[33] The texts that are considered "classic" are always in flux, but the Bible has been one of the constant classics that has defined Western society for at least the past five centuries. My colleagues in classics often remind me that the founding fathers of the United States saw themselves as being defined by and interacting with the characters in Greek classic texts in ad-

---

32. This does not mean that I am so naïve as to consider history itself as completely objective. Even though our historical investigations are in the end subjective endeavors, they do give us one of the best means at our disposal to think about how our noumenal conclusions interact with the phenomenal world as best we can understand it.

33. Tracy, 12.

dition to individuals in the Bible. Thomas Jefferson, when faced with a vexing problem, might have asked himself how Pericles would have responded in order to save Athens. Just as Jefferson looked at classical architecture to frame his design of the University of Virginia, he looked to Greek classic texts to define how he acted in society.

Tracy goes further to say that contemporary citizens must not only be involved with their classic texts, but they must be in conversation with those texts and that conversation necessarily includes arguments. Building on Tracy's model, I would suggest that Tracy's concept of "conversation" is similar to Brueggemann's concept of being rhetorically engaged with the narratives. Further, historical imagination can assist modern interpreters with negative and positive conclusions as we seek to carry on conversations and arguments with our classic text, the Bible.

Just as explained above, there is a negative and positive role for historical imagination in this conversation. Critical (negative) history can provide limits on our interpretations and provide a corrective lens for misinterpretations. In this sense, this is one way to have boundaries placed on reinterpretations of previous promises (to use Gerhard von Rad's terminology) or on new rhetorical engagements with the narrative (to use Brueggemann's terminology). Historical imagination understood in this way might also allow us to put a traditionizing method in conversation with Brueggemann's rhetorical method. Historical imagination contributes to the argument that we include in our imaginary world when we engage our classic text, the Bible. Critical history (the asking of "yes/no" questions) is a necessary component to prevent us from creating our own God out of the rhetorical narratives of our classic text.

Just as discussed above, historical imagination should not, however, be limited to critical history in this conversation with classic texts. Background history can be used as a basis for us to construct and develop our imaginary world in order to enrich and enliven the ways in which we engage in and with the classic text of the Bible. In this way we should ask ourselves how we would be involved with the rhetorical dialogue of Brueggemann or the narrative history that Frei and Alter describe.

The type of involvement that I am advocating should be considered a modification of what von Rad calls *Vergegenwärtigung* ("actualization"). Von Rad showed that Israel reenvisioned the significance of its faith anew in different times and different places. This reactualization allowed Yahwism to be dynamic and not static. Von Rad recognized that the significance of Yahwism changed in different places and in different times. Thus, the biblical witness itself points towards a faith that fits varying contexts differently. On the other hand, the weakness of von Rad's system is that his method could be reduced to a theology of history, and this method is especially problematic if one is not able to adequately reconstruct the tradition history of the text. The use of historical imagination avoids this weakness, however. The concept of imagination allows us to enter into two modes of inquiry at the same time, so we are able to take the best parts of von Rad's method and use them to correct the weaknesses found in Brueggemann's rhetorical method.

Such a proposal is also attractive for our postmodern world where readers in different social locations will necessarily experience different texts in differing ways. I am proposing that instead of trying to reconstruct a history of Israelite region, the task of Old Testament theology should be to incorporate this type of "traditionizing" program with narrative readings (such as those presented by Frei and Alter) or rhetorical readings (such as those presented by Brueggemann). If we as archaeologists and historians do not undertake such a task, it may not be impossible to write a history of Israel today, but the resulting history will be ignored by the larger audience that desires a theological payoff.